MARKS
of
DISTINCTION

MARKS of DISTINCTION

Christian Perceptions of Jews in
the High Middle Ages

IRVEN M. RESNICK

The Catholic University of America Press
Washington, D.C.

Copyright © 2012
The Catholic University of America Press
All rights reserved

Library of Congress Cataloging-in-Publication Data
Resnick, Irven Michael.
Marks of distinction : Christian perceptions of Jews in the
high Middle Ages / Irven M. Resnick.
   p. cm.
Includes bibliographical references (p.   ) and index.
ISBN 978-0-8132-3569-1 (pbk)   1. Judaism—Relations—
Christianity.   2. Christianity and other religions—Judaism.
3. Physiognomy—Religious aspects—Christianity.
4. Human body—Social aspects—Europe.
5. Human body—Religious aspects—Christianity.   6. Church
history—Middle Ages, 600–1500.   I. Title.
BM535 .R+
305.892′4040902—dc23
2011050255

CONTENTS

List of Illustrations	vii
Acknowledgments	ix
List of Abbreviations	xi
Introduction	1
1. Introduction to Medieval Physiognomy	13
2. Physical Deformities and Circumcision	53
3. The Jews and Leprosy	93
4. The Dietary Laws, Food, and Illicit Sexuality	144
5. The Jews and Melancholy	175
6. Planetary Influences; or, the Jews and Saturn	215
7. Case Studies Revealing a Jewish Physiognomy	268
Conclusion	320
Bibliography	325
Index	3/9

LIST OF ILLUSTRATIONS

following page 178

FIGURE 1. A friar preaching a (conversionary) sermon to *Synagoga* and a synagogue elder, from a fourteenth-century French Franciscan missal. MS Douce 313, fol. 139r. Used by permission of The Bodleian Library, University of Oxford.

FIGURE 2. The circumcision of Isaac, replaced by baptism, from the thirteenth-century *Bible moralisée*. MS Bodl. 270b, fol. 14v, roundels A1 and A2. Used by permission of The Bodleian Library, University of Oxford.

FIGURE 3. Historiated initial depicting a hook-nosed Jew circumcising boys, from "The Bible of Robert De Bello." Burney fol. 90r. Used by permission. ©The British Library Board. All Rights Reserved.

FIGURE 4. Jesus healing a leper (cf. Matt. 8:2), from the *Vita gloriossime virginis Mariae atque venerabilis matris filii dei vivi veri et unici*. MS. Canon. Misc. 476, fol. 66r. Used by permission of The Bodleian Library, University of Oxford.

FIGURE 5. The leprous Constantine comforts the women. Santi Quattro Coronati, Rome, interior: Chapel of Saint Sylvester (c. 1246). Used by permission of Art Resource.

FIGURE 6. A crippled leper, seated, with a bell, c. 1400. Lansdowne 451, fol. 127. Used by permission. ©The British Library Board. All Rights Reserved.

FIGURE 7. The Third Crusade of the Pastoureaux: Jews throwing their children from a tower, from the *Chroniques de France ou de St. Denis*. Royal 20 C. VII, fol. 55v. Used by permission. ©The British Library Board. All Rights Reserved.

FIGURE 8. Initial E(t), depicting a soldier of Antiochus slaying a Jew who refused to eat unclean meat, from a thirteenth-century French bible. MS. Canon. Bibl. Lat. 41, fol. 359v. Used by permission of The Bodleian Library, University of Oxford.

FIGURE 9. Saturn eating his children, from a fifteenth-century English manuscript. MS Rawl. B 214, fol. 197v. Used by permission of The Bodleian Library, University of Oxford.

FIGURE 10. Initial showing the Jew Samuel's wife and son, who convert to Christianity (10a); and image of the Jew Samuel ritually murdering the child martyr Adam of Bristol (10b), from the "Passion of Adam of Bristol." Harleian MS 957, no. 7, fol. 22r (a fourteenth-century codex). © The British Library Board. All Rights Reserved.

FIGURE 11. A hook-nosed Jew menacing Christ, from William of Nottingham's *Commentary on the Gospels* (fourteenth century). MS Laud Misc.165, fol. 280r. Used by permission of The Bodleian Library, University of Oxford.

ACKNOWLEDGMENTS

In the course of my research, I have benefitted from the assistance of countless librarians and scholars. Much of this work was completed during my many research visits to the Oxford Centre for Hebrew and Jewish Studies, for whose hospitality I remain grateful. Thanks are also due to the National Endowment for the Humanities, which enabled me to direct a summer institute for university faculty, "Representations of the 'Other': Jews in Medieval Christendom," in 2003, 2006, and 2010 at the Oxford Centre for Hebrew and Jewish Studies. Its faculty participants prodded me to rethink many of the notions I had considered well established. Special thanks are due to the visiting scholars who contributed to the institutes: Anna Sapir Abulafia, Anthony Bale, Robert Chazan, Jeremy Cohen, Denise Despres, Chaim Hames, Daniel Lasker, Sara Lipton, Miri Rubin, and Robert Stacey. In addition, in 2006 I made good use of the wonderful library resources in London, while a Distinguished Visiting Fellow at Queen Mary, University of London. Finally, I must thank Luke Demaitre, who carefully read the chapter on leprosy and the Jews and offered very helpful criticism. Any errors that remain are, of course, my own.

LIST OF ABBREVIATIONS

GENERAL

art.	article
b.	born
c.	*circa*
cap.	*capitula(e)*
chap.	chapter(s)
col.	column
d.	died
dist.	distinction(s) [Latin, *distinctio*]
ed., eds.	editor(s); edition; edited by
Epist.	Epistula(e)
esp.	especially
fasc.	fascicle(s)
fl.	flourished, when birth and death dates are not available
fol.	folio(s)
lit.	literally
ll.	lines
MS, MSS	manuscript(s)
n.	note
q.	*quaestio*
r.	recto
repr.	reprint
tit.	*titulus*
tr.	tractate
trans.	translated by
v.	verso
vol., vols.	volume(s)

AUTHORS, SERIES, OR TEXTS

B.T.	Babylonian Talmud
CCCM	*Corpus Christianorum: Continuatio mediaevalis*
CCSL	*Corpus Christianorum: Series latina*
CSEL	*Corpus scriptorum ecclesiasticorum latinorum*
Ed. Colon.	*Sancti doctoris ecclesiae Alberti Magni Ordinis Fratrum Praedicatorum episcopi* Opera omnia, *ad fidem codicum manuscriptorum edenda apparatu critico notis prolegomenis indicibus instruenda curavit Institutum Alberti Magni Coloniense.* Edited by Bernhard Geyer (after vol. 37.2 [1978]: ed. Wilhelm Kübel). Monasterii Westfalorum: Aschendorff, 1951–
Ed. Borgnet	*B. Alberti Magni Ratisbonensis episcopi ordinis Praedicatorum Opera omnia.* 38 vols. Edited by Auguste Borgnet. Paris: L. Vivès, 1890–99.
MGH	*Monumenta Germaniae Historica*
Epp.	Epistolae
Epp.	KaiserzeitDie Briefe der deutschen Kaiserzeit
Gesta Pontif. Rom.	Gesta pontificum Romanorum
Ldl	Libelli de lite imperatorum et pontificum saeculis
LL	Leges
QQ Geistesgesch.	Quellen zur Geistesgeschichte des Mittelalters
SS	Scriptores
SS rer. Merov.	Scriptores rerum Merovingicarum
SS rer. Germ.	Scriptores rerum Germanicarum in usum scholarum separatim editi.
SS rer. Germ. n.s.	Scriptores rerum Germanicarum in usum scholarum separatim editi: Nova series.

PL *Patrologiae cursus completus*: Series latina. 217 vols. Edited by J.-P. Migne. Paris, 1844–64.

QDA Albert the Great, *Quaestiones super de animalibus* 1.21–22. Edited by Ephrem Filthaut. *Opera omnia* 12. Monasterii Westfalorum: Aschendorff, 1955.

SC Sources chrétiennes

SZ *Albertus Magnus* On Animals: *A Medieval Summa Zoologica*. 2 vols. Translated by Kenneth F. Kitchell Jr. and Irven Michael Resnick. Baltimore: Johns Hopkins University Press, 1999.

INTRODUCTION

The term anti-Semitism was coined at the end of the nineteenth century to designate a seemingly modern phenomenon—a rational, secular theory of Jewish inferiority and Jewish evil said to be distinct from an older and much discredited religious hostility. It is very likely that this new term was coined in the second half of the nineteenth century by the German publicist and propagandist Wilhelm Marr, the founder of the Anti-Semitic League and author of *The Victory of Judaism over Germanism, Considered from a non-Religious Point of View*.[1] For Enlightenment and post-Enlightenment thinkers, religious hostility increasingly had been dismissed as a sign of ignorance and obscurantism unworthy of a modern, rational, and scientific mentality. By contrast, advocates promoted anti-Semitism as a rational viewpoint supported by the findings of modern science.

Modern anti-Semites eschewed religious hated of Jews and attempted to replace it with a scientific account of Jewish racial differences said to endanger the purity of European blood and civilization. They also sought to explain older, anti-Jewish religious stereotypes as the product of racial characteristics that have consistently manifested themselves in Judaism as a religious culture.[2] For example, it was the Jews' *racial* incapacity

---

1. Wilhelm Marr, *Der Sieg des Judenthums über das Germanenthum vom nicht confessionellen Standpunkt aus betrachtet* (Bern: Rudolph Costenoble, 1879). For Marr and his role in the development of a theory of anti-Semitism, see Moshe Zimmermann, *Wilhelm Marr, the Patriarch of Antisemitism* (Oxford: Oxford University Press, 1986). For discussion of *The Victory of Judaism over Germanism*, see 69–95.

2. Thus F. Roderich-Stoltheim (a pseudonym adopted by Theodor Fritsch) insisted that the Talmud, responsible for so much Christian religious hatred directed against Jews, reflects the racial character of the Jew: his materialism, his sensuality, and lack of spirituality. As a result, "it is doubtful if a Jew can ever

1

for aesthetic experience that explained the Jews' religious prohibitions against artistic representations of God or the human form in the synagogue.³ Because modern anti-Semitism sought evidence of the Jews' racial character in their religious texts and customs, many Jewish intellectuals have dismissed the claim that anti-Semitism represented anything new at all: the religiously based anti-Judaism of the past and the racial anti-Semitism of modern theorists were simply two forms of a single historical phenomenon. For these intellectuals, the term anti-Semitism may be applied to all earlier forms of Judeophobia, obscuring the distinction between modern and ancient or modern and medieval hatred of Jews.⁴

On the surface, however, modern anti-Semitism, which claims to be grounded in the *realia* of racial difference, does depart in one important respect from religious anti-Judaism. The latter at least promised the possibility of transformation through religious conversion. Once a Jew converted to Christianity, for example, he ceased to be a Jew and eliminated the basis for anti-Jewish hostility. Anti-Semitism, on the other hand, held out no such hope. So long as Jewish identity is based on notions of blood or race, no escape from such race hatred is possible, even should religious conversion occur. A clear example will be found in Nazi Germany's First Regulation to the Reich Citizenship Law (November 14, 1935), which not only deprived Jews of German citizenship but also established their racial identification: "a Jew is a person descended from at least three grandparents who are full Jews by race."⁵ This definition caught under its umbrella also Jewish converts to Christianity or the children of such converts; as a result, the German Christian movement under the Nazi regime excluded baptized Jews from the Christian community. This racial principle is explicit in an article that appeared in the German *Arische*

---

completely free himself of the views, derived from his racial peculiarity, which were being prepared and established from the time of Moses to that of Esra and Nehemiah, and which, later on, under the influence of Talmudic Rabbinism, were extended and expanded until they became a gross exaggeration." *The Riddle of the Jew's Success,* trans. Capel Pownall (Leipzig: Hammer-Verlag, 1927), 202.

3. See Elliott Horowitz, "Le Peuple de l'image: les juifs et l'art," *Annales: Histoire, Sciences Sociales* 3 (2001): 665–84.

4. This basic taxonomy is followed in the bibliographic guide by Jack R. Fischell and Susan M. Ortmann, *The Holocaust and its Religious Impact: A Critical Assessment and Annotated Bibliography* (Westport, Conn.: Praeger, 2004).

5. See Yitzhak Arad, Yisrael Gutman, and Abraham Margaliot, eds., *Documents on the Holocaust,* 4th ed. (Jerusalem: Yad Vashem, 1990), 80.

Rundschau in 1933 that proclaimed that "just as a pig remains a pig . . . so a Jew remains a Jew, even if he is baptized."[6] Escape from such racial determinism proved impossible in theory (if not in practice), resulting in legal, economic, and social disabilities under the pre-war Nazi regime, and leading to horrific consequences for Jewish communities during the Holocaust.

Medieval historians have not been absent from the debate over the emergence of anti-Semitism as a distinct historical phenomenon. Generally they have not argued that medieval anti-Jewish sentiment was based on theories of racial difference. Nonetheless, despite the fact that the term itself is a nineteenth-century neologism, approximately two decades ago Gavin Langmuir, a historian of the Middle Ages, propounded an influential albeit controversial definition of anti-Semitism that focused not on the specific content of beliefs commonly dismissed as anti-Semitic, but instead on their psychological origin. Langmuir defined anti-Semitism as the *pathological* or *irrational* hatred of Jews, and consciously subverted claims that anti-Semitism is a modern development; rather, he argued, anti-Semitism appeared first not in the nineteenth but in the twelfth century.

One virtue of Langmuir's analysis is that it recognizes that important changes in Christian perceptions of Jews appeared in the twelfth century, ushering in a dramatically altered relationship between Jewish and Christian communities. A second is that it preserves the distinction between anti-Judaism and anti-Semitism. Langmuir acknowledges that from its origin Christianity was engaged in a religious competition with Judaism that paved the way for medieval hatred of Jews, but insists that anti-Judaism did not become widespread in popular culture until the eleventh century, when it took root among a larger population buffeted by rapid social and economic change.[7] In the twelfth century popular anti-Judaism brought forth more support for legal disabilities against Jews that previously had been unenforced or unenforceable. Thus, a group long assumed to be inferior in religious terms was forced into roles that provided further confirmation of their inferiority. Popular anti-Jewish violence—for

---

6. Quoted in Susannah Heschel, *The Aryan Jesus: Christian Theologians and the Bible in Nazi Germany* (Princeton, N.J.: Princeton University Press, 2008), 55; for the German Christian movement and its racialized theology, passim.

7. Gavin I. Langmuir, *Toward a Definition of Anti-Semitism* (Berkeley: University of California Press, 1990), 59.

example, violence accompanying the First and Second Crusade—forced Jews into urban centers, where they became an even more visible "other" in a Christian world. Following the Fourth Lateran Council's requirement that Jews be marked out by special clothing, Jews became an institutionalized inferior minority easily manipulated to serve the needs of ecclesiastical and secular rulers. These changes opened the door to the development of "a false irrational conception of the Jew" promoted by novel charges of ritual murder, host desecration, well poisoning, and other behaviors that threatened the Christian polity.[8]

For Langmuir it is this "false irrational conception of the Jew" that differentiates anti-Semitism. Older anti-Jewish charges—for example, deicide—seemed to earlier generations of Christians to enjoy some empirical support, at least from the tendentious evidence drawn from the Gospels themselves. In a similar way, empirical evidence could support the contention that Jews had been rejected by God for this crime, for it was abundantly clear to Christians that because after the Crucifixion the Jews had lost their Temple, their land, and their independence, these events had to be causally linked. For Langmuir, then, anti-Judaism is characterized at least by the availability of some empirical or rational support. Although we may reject the interpretation of this evidence, such empirical evidence was used effectively by medieval (and even modern) Christianity in its struggle against Judaism. By contrast, Langmuir views twelfth- and thirteenth-century charges of ritual murder, well poisoning, desecration of the host and of the Cross, as irrational fantasies for which empirical or rational support was altogether lacking. The spread of these irrational fantasies about Jews, he insists, produced for the first time the novel phenomenon of anti-Semitism.

Since these new charges are alleged to lack empirical or rational support and therefore could not have been generated from observed behaviors, one must find another explanation for their appearance. Although they were not universally received, still they spread widely in medieval society. For Langmuir, they spread especially among "all those individuals whose personal need to displace and project guilt and hatred sought a socially ac-

---

8. Langmuir, *Toward a Definition of Anti-Semitism*, 61. R. I. Moore largely accepts this view in "Anti-Semitism and the Birth of Modern Europe," in *Christianity and Judaism. Papers Read at the 1991 Summer Meeting and the 1992 Winter Meeting of the Ecclesiastical History Society*, ed. Diana Wood (Cambridge, Mass.: Ecclesiastical History Society, 1992), 33–58.

ceptable outlet."[9] As a result, he would trace the roots of anti-Semitism to sociological and psychological forces rather than religious conflict.

Langmuir's analysis has been criticized by several prominent medieval historians, including Robert Stacey,[10] Robert Chazan,[11] and Anna Sapir Abulafia.[12] Common to these critiques has been the contention that Langmuir failed adequately to defend his thesis that anti-Semitic beliefs are *irrational* beliefs. Moreover, Langmuir's definition of an irrational belief is flawed, says Chazan: "Langmuir is ultimately distorting our everyday use of the word 'irrational.' In ordinary parlance, we do not reserve the term for perceptions of beings or behaviors that have never been observed or that can be empirically proven false. Much of what constitutes the domain of the irrational involves exaggerated perceptions of the realities of everyday life."[13]

Similarly, Stacey ultimately rejects Langmuir's contention that anti-Semitism is a form of irrationality that contradicts knowable, empirically verifiable facts. For Langmuir, ritual murder charges contradicted what one could otherwise have reasonably established. By contrast, he had defined as anti-Judaic those beliefs that have some empirical basis, no matter how distorted they become. The outcome may be the same: anti-Judaism led to the murder of Jews for a belief that has some basis in reality—for being Jews who had in reality rejected core tenets of Christianity—whereas anti-Semitism led to the murder of Jews for characteristics never observed in any Jew. But Stacey criticizes Langmuir for having judged medieval culture by modern standards of evidence. Thus, Langmuir convicts as anti-Semitic those who received the charge of ritual murder on the assumption that any rational person in the twelfth or thirteenth century could have known and established that Jews were not guilty of such crimes. But, asks Stacey, by the standards of the thir-

---

9. Langmuir, *Toward a Definition of Anti-Semitism*, 61.

10. Robert Stacey, "History, Religion, and Medieval Antisemitism: A Response to Gavin Langmuir," *Religious Studies Review* 20, no. 2 (1994): 95–101.

11. Robert Chazan, *Medieval Stereotypes and Modern Antisemitism* (Berkeley: University of California Press, 1997), 125–34.

12. Anna Sapir Abulafia, *Christians and Jews in the Twelfth-Century Renaissance* (London: Routledge, 1995), 5–7. See also her remarks in "Twelfth-Century Renaissance Theology and the Jews," in *From Witness to Witchcraft: Jews and Judaism in Medieval Christian Thought*, ed. Jeremy Cohen, Wolfenbütteler Mittelalter-Studien 11 (Wiesbaden: Harrassowitz Verlag, 1996), 125–39.

13. Chazan, *Medieval Stereotypes and Modern Antisemitism*, 132.

teenth century was it irrational to believe in the Jews' guilt? By the time of the ritual murder charge in Lincoln in 1255, Jews had been charged with this crime repeatedly. Moreover, the murder occurred at the time that a large group of Jews had gathered in Lincoln, supplying circumstantial evidence for their participation. Furthermore, the miracles that occurred subsequently at Hugh of Lincoln's grave seemed to confirm the judgment against the alleged Jewish perpetrators. Equally important, one of the accused Jews even confessed—admittedly, under torture—but he confessed nevertheless. In fact, concludes Stacey, the conviction and execution of the Jewish perpetrators in 1255 "was fully in keeping with the best rational empirical knowledge of the day."[14] Was it then irrational to believe that Jews *were* guilty of ritual murder, in the context of thirteenth-century jurisprudence?

Although the judicial process in Lincoln may have been "in keeping with the best rational empirical knowledge of the day," at other times allegations of heretofore unknown Jewish crimes were rejected by the highest secular and spiritual authorities, following extensive investigation. For example, in 1235 in Fulda thirty-four Jews were slain following the deaths of five Christian boys, whose blood they were alleged to have drawn off for purposes not made clear in the sources.[15] The next year, in response to growing unrest, Emperor Frederick II convened an assembly of scholars that included Jewish converts to Christianity that declared that both the Bible and the Talmud make it very clear that Jews reject the consumption not only of human blood but all blood whatsoever as a source of pollution. Nor would Jews, the assembly added, who are everywhere confronted by Christian power, endanger themselves so by such conduct. Frederick II, then, rejected the accusation as utterly false. Similarly, in March 1247 in Valreás Jews were accused of crucifying a Christian child and taking its blood. On May 28, 1247 Pope Innocent IV condemned their persecution and declared the accusation false, and on July 9 he reissued a bull of protection for Jews, *Sicut Judaeis*, and forbade future accusations of this sort.[16] While the judicial process in

14. Stacey, "History, Religion, and Medieval Antisemitism," 99.

15. *Annales Erphordenses fratrum Praedicatorum*, ed. Oswald Holder-Egger, MGH, SS rer. Germ. 42 (Hannover: Hahn, 1899), 92.

16. For the texts of these papal letters, see Solomon Grayzel, *The Church and the Jews in the XIIIth Century*, docs. 114, 116, and 118 (New York: Hermon Press, 1966), 264–66, 269–70, and 274.

Lincoln leading to conviction and execution may have been "in keeping with the best rational empirical knowledge of the day," other investigations exonerated the Jews following exculpatory determinations of highest authority. Was it irrational for Christians to embrace the perception of Jews as dangerous, homicidal, vengeful and blasphemous, inclined to ritual murder and other crimes, when medieval authorities themselves disagreed on the plausibility, not to mention veracity, of the accusations?

For Stacey, it seems not, in part because of different standards of evidence at work in the medieval world. For medieval culture (and not only popular culture) the belief that Jews were allies of the devil, for example, was alleged to have empirical support. In numerous sources we find a "proof" of such an alliance based on dreams, visions, and other encounters. For the medieval world, such empirical evidence was credible. In sum, then, what appears to us today to be lacking empirical or rational support may have appeared well established under medieval canons of evidence. And thus the belief that Jews were guilty of ritual murder, which spread so rapidly and so widely in the thirteenth century, could appeal to "empirical evidence" even though, by modern standards, this same evidence would be rejected as tainted, fantastic, or highly circumstantial.

But with equal force Langmuir draws attention instead to an emerging, ideal standard of rationality in twelfth-century Christian culture, a culture that suffered growing anxiety concerning new or expanded dogmatic claims that seemed to violate the principles of philosophical reason. This intellectual conflict is perhaps most clearly evident in the debate over Eucharistic change going back to Berengar of Tours in the second half of the eleventh century. Some have argued that Berengar of Tours held an empiricist concept of substance, which argued for the impossibility of a real conversion of the elements of the Eucharist.[17] It is precisely because Christian philosophers were unable to reconcile their rational principles with the demands of faith that, Langmuir suggests, they sought support for dogmatic theology by projecting onto the Jews convictions that they themselves found problematic. Consequently, accusations that Jews regularly desecrated the Eucharistic host rendered much needed support for the contention that the host was indeed, af-

17. K. M. Purday, "Berengar and the Use of the Word *Substantia*," *Downside Review* 91 (1973): 101–10.

ter its consecration, the real body of Jesus Christ.[18] Why else would the Jews, who were believed guilty of having crucified Jesus and who remained perpetually his enemy, attack the host unless they believed that which some educated Christians found so exceedingly problematic: that the host was in reality the body and blood of Jesus? In this way Langmuir's medieval anti-Semitism is rooted in a psychological or cognitive dissonance. On the one hand some Christians recognized that the dogma of real change in the Eucharist violated standards of reason and natural possibility; on the other hand, they were compelled to accept the dogma by ecclesiastical authority. To resolve this internal psychological conflict, they sought in the Jews' alleged crimes implied "proof" for the new dogma. By projecting onto the Jews a conviction their own reason found difficult to justify, they hoped to suppress the contradiction. But by suppressing a manifest contradiction, they are guilty of an irrational belief regarding the Jews, engendering anti-Semitism for the first time, in Langmuir's assessment.

It seems quite plausible that some Christian intellectuals sought to mitigate the internal conflict they may have experienced as a result of their own religious doubt by attributing to Jews a behavior that seemed to support a dogma that was otherwise difficult to accept, at least from a philosophical point of view. It seems at least plausible as well that medieval Christians may sometimes have attributed to Jews the practice of host desecration, for example, to resolve certain cognitive tensions arising from their own debate over substantial change in the Eucharist. The irrational nature of the host desecration charge depends too upon the assumption that medieval Jews, guided by a rational sense of self-preservation, would never have intentionally abused a Christian symbol—indeed, the central sacrament of Christian life—when doing so would place them in very grave danger. This assumption was voiced by the investigative assembly convened by Frederick II and contributed to its finding on behalf of Jews. Moreover, only if one assumes that Christ is really present in the host does host desecration signify an act of vengeance against the Christian God. But since Jews clearly rejected

---

18. As Miri Rubin notes, the first fully documented case of a host desecration accusation appeared in Paris in 1290, but the elements of the abusive relationship between Jews and the Eucharist can be traced back to an earlier period. See her *Gentile Tales: The Narrative Assault on Later Medieval Jews* (New Haven: Yale University Press, 1999), 40.

this religious belief in the real presence and rejected the dogma of transubstantiation formally articulated at the Fourth Lateran Council, host desecration could not function among Jews as an act of religious dissent or revenge. Langmuir's assumption is that in the absence of *reliable* empirical evidence, and in the presence of an informed understanding that Jews rejected the doctrine of the real presence in the Eucharist, a reasonable Christian must reject the attribution of such behavior among Jews or be identified a medieval anti-Semite.

The debate among medieval historians, however, has been complicated more recently by other findings. Elliott Horowitz, for example, has shown from the evidence of medieval Jewish sources that behaviors that modern historians suspect Jews scrupulously would have avoided in order not to inflame public opinion against them—for example, spitting or urinating upon the Cross—in fact were not unknown.[19] Similarly, Horowitz makes the same argument for host desecration: that, despite its inflammatory nature, medieval sources lend credible support to the claim that on occasion Jews did attack the host as an outlet for religious aggression.[20] This challenges the prevailing interpretation, which views anti-Jewish host desecration narratives as merely a literary *topos* engendered by growing Eucharistic (and Marian) devotion in Christian communities.[21] More recently still, historian Ariel Toaff achieved unwanted notoriety for the suggestion, based on confessions extracted under torture from Jews at Trent in 1475, that some medieval Ashkenazi Jews *may* have used Christian blood in religious rituals.[22] While I do not endorse his suggestion, historians continue to search for an empirical reality behind these charges, indicating dissatisfaction with Langmuir's thesis. If some modern Jewish historians are unwilling to reject categorically that

---

19. See Elliott Horowitz, "The Jews and the Cross in the Middle Ages," in *Philosemitism, Antisemitism and 'the Jews': Perspectives from the Middle Ages to the Twentieth Century,* ed. Tony Kushner and Nadia Valman, Studies in European Cultural Transition 24 (Aldershot: Ashgate, 2004), 114–31.

20. For Horowitz's argument, see his *Reckless Rites: Amalek, Purim, and the Legacy of Jewish Violence* (Princeton, N.J.: Princeton University Press, 2006), 172–74.

21. For example, Miri Rubin, "Desecration of the Host: The Birth of an Accusation," in Wood, *Christianity and Judaism,* 169–85. This is reproduced in *Medieval Religion: New Approaches,* ed. Constance Hoffman Berman (New York: Routledge, 2005), 363–76. Also see her *Gentile Tales,* passim.

22. See Toaff's *Pasque di sangue, Ebrei d'Europa e omicidi rituali* (Bologna: Il Mulino, 2008).

an empirical reality lies behind these charges, should medieval contemporaries be regarded as irrational for having received them?

Regardless of the empirical reality medieval Christian authors, based on their theological constructions of Jewish identity, also sought to attribute rational *motives* to Jews for such crimes. Not only did they receive, then, testimonies and accounts of Jewish crimes as part of a judicial process, but the behaviors themselves conformed to what they already believed to be the essential character of the Jew. No better example, perhaps, can be found than the *Historiae Memorabiles*, a collection of fifty-six crudely realistic tales (of which twenty treat the behavior of Jews), by the late thirteenth-century Dominican Rudolph of Schlettstadt.[23] For Rudolph, prior of the Dominican convent of Schlettstadt in Alsace (after 1294–after 1303), these tales of host desecration served to reinforce existing anti-Jewish stereotypes. Rudolph reveals that Jews routinely procured the host either to avenge themselves upon it in an act of religious hatred, or to obtain material gain. Their behavior also provided empirical evidence supporting the doctrine of the real presence that Jews inexplicably (or unreasonably) rejected.

Rudolph had witnessed the bloody Rintfleisch massacres of Jews that took place in Franconia in 1298.[24] Anti-Jewish violence in Würzburg alone, according to Rudolph, resulted in the murder of 30,000 Jews, although Grabmayer argues that between April and November 1298 the number of Jews slain was probably closer to 5,000.[25] From a political standpoint, however, Rudolph's host desecration tales also sought to justify the violence as an appropriate response to Jewish blasphemies, while at the same time correcting nobles and prelates who, in his view, had for too long tolerated Jewish crimes.

Significantly, in this source it is often Jewish converts to Christianity that provided the most persuasive evidence to support the accusations. For example, tale no. 16 introduces a Jewish woman that had fled Würz-

---

23. See Miri Rubin, "Rudolph of Schlettstadt, O.P.: Reporter of Violence, Writer on Jews," in *Christ among the Medieval Dominicans: Representations of Christ in the Texts and Images of the Order of Preachers*, ed. Kent Emery and Joseph Wawrykow (Notre Dame: University of Notre Dame Press, 1998), 283–92.

24. On the Rintfleish massacres, see also Rubin, *Gentile Tales*, 50–55.

25. Johannes Grabmayer, "Rudolf von Schlettstadt und das aschkenasische Judentum um 1300," *Aschkenas: Zeitschrift für Geschichte und Kultur der Juden* 4, no.2 (1994): 302. See also 302, n. 6, for his criticism of Poliakov's estimate of 100,000 dead.

burg and embraced Christianity. When she arrived in the city of Colmar in Alsace during the reign of Adolf of Nassau (1291–98), she sought the hospitality of a Christian widow, to whom she revealed the reason for her conversion: she had observed Jewish crimes against the Eucharistic host in Würzburg that caused her estrangement from the Jewish community. The woman remarked that, "When I had seen this [attack on the host] I was so frightened that I dared not stay among them any longer. I left their faith and, upon the advice of Christ's faithful, I was baptized. When later I revealed to Christians these deeds and the others they had done, they struggled with all their strength to kill me."[26] With this, Christians could explain the Jews' hostility toward converts to Christianity, as well as alleged attempts among Jews to suppress the evidence of the crimes. At the same time, such testimony, which we might regard as tainted by personal motives as converts sought to establish their *bona fides* (lit., their good faith, but here meaning their credentials as good Christians), a medieval audience came to view it as all the more persuasive because it was supported by one that had previously been a member of the Jewish community.

For medieval culture, then, empirical evidence—eye-witness testimony, hearsay, confessions, reports of converts, and the witness of dreams, visions, or miraculous events—was offered to support charges that Langmuir dismissed as irrational. In the same way, authoritative texts were invoked to support accusations that may seem fantastic to us. These brought to bear not only the influence of the Bible or of the Fathers of the Church, but also the authority of scientific traditions. It is especially these scientific traditions that will be investigated here, traditions that were held to predispose Jews to certain types of offensive behavior or even to communicate certain types of illness and disease. By arguing for a Jewish "nature" dictated by a specific humoral complexion, medieval scientific authorities rendered all the more plausible the emerging allegations of ritualized murder and desecration that characterized the growing fear of a Jewish threat. In so doing, it will become clearer that medieval culture

---

26. "Hec cum vidissem, nimirum perterrita manere cum eis amplius non audebam. Dereliqui fidem eorum et consilio Christi fidelium sum baptisata. Cum autem hec et alia eorum facta postea Cristianis referebans manifestavi, me occidere pro viribus laborabant." Rudolf von Schlettstadt, *Historiae Memorabiles zur Dominikanerliteratur und Kulturgeschichte des 13. Jahrhunderts* 16, ed. Erich Kleinschmidt (Cologne: Böhlau, 1974), 66–67.

could appeal to its scientific theories to support anti-Jewish sentiment in much the same way that modern anti-Semitism will appeal to a scientific culture to support its theories.

This brings us back to the question with which we began: Is medieval anti-Jewish sentiment so different from modern anti-Semitism? Although the medieval world had not yet developed fully the concept of race that modern anti-Semites employed, nonetheless there did appear a medieval sense of Jewish difference that was not rooted only in religious belief and practices, but in the physical nature or biology of Jews themselves. These differences were sometimes evidenced by marks that distinguished them physically from their Christian neighbors. In addition, these biological differences were sometimes viewed as ineradicable, even following religious conversion; or, at best, they might be erased with only the greatest difficulty over several generations. As a result, the one feature of modern anti-Semitism sometimes thought to distinguish it so clearly from older religious anti-Judaism—namely, the impossibility of escaping one's identity as a Jew even through religious conversion—had also begun to appear by the end of the Middle Ages in certain locales of Christian Europe when physical, somatic distinguishing marks were attributed to Jews.

1

INTRODUCTION TO MEDIEVAL PHYSIOGNOMY

It is a medieval commonplace that the soul directly moves or acts upon the body, but the body only indirectly influences or acts upon the soul. Consequently, although bodily deformities or illness need not imply a corresponding corrupt state in the soul, one expects to see defects in the soul revealed in the body. Because the body follows the soul when the soul is disturbed, and the soul follows the body in its accidents, the two—the healing of body and soul—cannot be completely separated, leading to a coincidence of interests for medieval theology, medicine, and the natural sciences.[1] This coincidence of interests is especially evident in discussions of physiognomy which, by the twelfth century, had emerged as a practical discipline useful for discerning in the outward, physical appearance of a human (or other animal) the secrets of the soul. The twelfth-century biographer of Archbishop Aldabero of Trier (d. 1152), Balderich, provides evidence of the archbishop's interest in this new, practical study, and describes him as one who "was exceedingly skilled in physiognomy, to such a degree that he would discern the secrets of character and behavior from different facial ap-

---

1. See *Religion and Medicine in the Middle Ages*, ed. Peter Biller and Joseph Ziegler (York: York Medieval Press, 2001), introduction. Several contributions to this volume remind us of medieval physicians who were also theologians or who obtained advanced degrees in theology. See Michael R. McVaugh, "Moments of Inflection: The Careers of Arnau of Villanova," 47–67; and William Courtenay, "Curers of Body and Soul: Medical Doctors as Theologians," in *Religion and Medicine in the Middle Ages*, 69–75.

pearances."[2] Such "profiling" would prove very useful to a ruler or administrator. The assumption that the "secrets of character" were mapped onto the body, and especially onto the face, led John of Salisbury (d. 1180) to warn in his *Policraticus,* a book on political science or government that "the physiognomers report that those that have flecked eyes are more prone to wickedness."[3] In other words, external appearances, when properly interpreted in physiognomy's semiotic system, became a mirror of the soul's character.[4]

The development of such a medieval discipline depended first on the introduction of ancient Greek medical texts and treatises on physiognomy. Although a few pre-Scholastic authors reveal some acquaintance with physiognomy, a genuine interest in and systematic account of physiognomy is entirely absent among them.[5] For the Scholastics, the most influential treatises on physiognomy were those attributed erroneously to Plato, Aristotle, or other ancient worthies.[6] The Aristotelian, or rather pseudo-Aristotelian materials, include the *Secret of Secrets (Secretum*

---

2. "Phisionimiam admodum sciebat, adeo ut diversorum aspectu vultuum secreta discerneret mentium et morum." Balderich Scholasticus, *Gesta Alberonis archiepisopi,* ed. G. Waitz, MGH SS 8 (Hannover: Hahn, 1847), 257, ln. 15; Balderich [of Florennes], *A Warrior Bishop of the Twelfth Century: The Deeds of Albero of Trier,* trans. Brian A. Pavlac (Toronto: Pontifical Institute of Mediaeval Studies, 2008), 70.

3. "Tradunt etiam phisiognomi eos, qui habent oculos maculosos, ad nequitiam proniores." John of Salisbury, *Policraticus* 5.15, ed. K. S. B. Keats-Rohan, CCCM 118 (Turnholt: Brepols, 1993), 345. This is available in translation as *Policraticus,* ed. and trans. Cary J. Nederman (Cambridge: Cambridge University Press, 1996). Nederman also studies John's thought and career in *John of Salisbury,* Medieval and Renaissance Texts and Studies 288 (Tempe, Az.: Arizona Center for Medieval and Renaissance Studies, 2005).

4. For this theme, see especially Jole Agrimi, "Fisiognomica: nature allo specchio ovvero luce e ombre," in *Il Teatro della natura,* vol. 4 of *Micrologus. Natura, scienze e società medievali* (Turnholt: Brepols, 1996), 129–78.

5. Boethius briefly discusses physiognomy. See his *Interpretatio priorum analyticorum Aristotelis* 2.28 (PL 64: 712A–B). Nevertheless, physiognomy was popular among Roman authors and its principles were certainly known to some early Christian writers. For discussion, see Elizabeth C. Evans, "The Study of Physiognomy in the Second Century A.D.," *Transactions and Proceedings of the American Philological Association* 72 (1941): 96–108.

6. For a collection of such treatises, see especially *Scriptores physiognomonici Graeci et Latini,* 2 vols., ed. Richard Foerster (Leipzig: 1893, repr. Stuttgart: Teubner, 1994). For the very popular anonymous Latin treatise *De physiognomonia liber* with a French translation, see *Anonyme Latin Traité de physiognomie,* trans. Jacques André (Paris: Les Belles Lettres, 1981); for a more recent Latin-English text and translation, see Ian Repath, "Anonymous Latinus, *Book of Physiognomy,*" in *Seeing the Face, Seeing the Soul: Polemon's* Physiognomy *from Classical Antiquity to Medieval Islam,* ed. Simon Swain (Oxford: Oxford University Press, 2007), 549–636.

secretorum)—introduced to the court of Frederick II in the long form translated by Philip of Tripoli[7]—and Ps.-Aristotle's *Physiognomy*, translated by Bartholomew of Messina sometime before 1262, although a draft or outline of the work seems to have been available earlier.[8] These works, as well as Arabic sources that transmitted their doctrines and emphasized their medical applications, presented to the Latin world the physiognomy of the ancients.[9]

In the first half of the thirteenth century Michael Scot, the translator of Aristotle's *History of Animals* (*Historia animalium*), produced a *Book on Physiognomy* (*liber phisionomiae*), better known in the Renaissance under the title *On the Secrets of Nature* (*De secretis nature*) that has been described as the first true work on physiognomy composed in the medieval West.[10] Dedicated to Frederick II, Michael Scot composed the work to enable the emperor to distinguish, from outward appearances, trust-

---

7. For a brief summary, see William Eamon's *Science and the Secrets of Nature: Books of Secrets in Medieval and Early Modern Culture* (Princeton, N.J.: Princeton University Press, 1994), 45–49. For the claim that Michael Scot used Philip of Tripoli's translation at Frederick II's court, see Steven J. Williams, "The Early Circulation of the Pseudo-Aristotelian *Secret of Secrets* in the West: The Papal and Imperial Courts," in *Le scienze alla corte di Federico II*, vol. 2 of *Micrologus. Natura, scienze e società medievali* (Turnholt: Brepols, 1994), 127–44, esp. 136.

8. Danielle Jacquart suggests that, based on similarities found between Michael Scot's *Liber phisionomiae* and Ps.-Aristotle's *Physiognomy*, perhaps an outline of the latter was introduced at the court of Frederick II. See Danielle Jacquart, "La Physiognomonie à l'époque de Frédéric II: Le traité de Michel Scot," in *Le scienze alla corte di Federico II*, vol. 2 of *Micrologus. Natura, scienze e società medievali*, 25. Ps.-Aristotle's text on physiognomy was frequently commented on. For a discussion of John Buridan's fourteenth-century commentary, see Lynn Thorndike, "Buridan's Questions on the Physiognomy Ascribed to Aristotle," *Speculum* 18, no.1 (1943): 99–103. For a translation of Ps.-Aristotle's *Physiognomonics*, see vol. 1 of *The Complete Works of Aristotle: The Revised Oxford Translation*, 2 vols., ed. Jonathan Barnes (Princeton, N.J.: Princeton University Press, 1984), 1237–50. For some discussion of Ps. Aristotelian texts on physiognomy in the Latin medieval world, see Charles Schmitt, "Pseudo-Aristotle in the Latin Middle Ages," in *Pseudo-Aristotle in the Middle Ages*, ed. Jill Kraye, W. F. Ryan, and C. B. Schmitt (London: The Warburg Institute, 1986), 6–7.

9. For medieval Arabic texts and physiognomy, see Anna Akasoy, "Arabic Physiognomy as a Link between Astrology and Medicine," in *Astro-Medicine: Astrology and Medicine East and West*, ed. Anna Akasoy, Charles Burnett, and Ronit Yoeli-Tlalim, Micrologus' Library 25, (Florence: SISMEL, 2008), 119–41.

10. See Jacquart, "La Physiognomonie à l'époque de Frédéric II," 20. Michael's *Liber phisionomiae* is the third book of his tripartite *Liber introductorius*, following after the *Liber quattuor distinctionum* and *Liber particularis*, and relies heavily on al-Rāzī's *Book to al-Mansūr*, either in the Arabic or Latin translation. His authorship of the *Liber phisionomiae* or, in general, of the *Liber introductorius*, seems well established but Charles Burnett, noting the extensive use Bartholomew of Parma made of Michael's work, has suggested that

worthy and wise counselors from their opposite numbers. Such a science is so useful to a ruler that Michael Scot does not hesitate to describe it as a "doctrine of salvation" that enables its practitioners to identify those inclined to virtue or vice.[11] Physiognomic doctrine was useful not only to emperors but also to popes and ecclesiastics. About the middle of the thirteenth century Albert of Behaim (d. c. 1260), a papal delegate and enemy of Frederick II, included within his personal collection of letters a copy of Philip of Tripoli's Latin translation of the *Secret of Secrets* made for him in Lyon c. 1246 that likewise described physiognomy as a "great science" (*scientia magna*).[12] The eminent natural philosopher and theologian Albert the Great (d. 1280) devoted two questions to a defense of physiognomy in his *Questions Concerning Aristotle's On Animals* (*Quaestiones super de animalibus*),[13] and gave so large a section of the first book of his *On Animals* (*De animalibus*) over to the study of physiognomy that it sometimes circulated independently under the title *De physiognomia*.[14] By the second half of the thirteenth century, then, physiognomy was well

---

Bartholomew edited Michael's *Liber particularis* and *Liber quattuor distinctionum*. Therefore, he warns, "great caution must be exercised in accrediting anything in the *Liber introductorius* to Michael." See Charles Burnett, "Michael Scot and the Transmission of Scientific Culture from Toledo to Bologna via the Court of Frederick II Hohenstaufen," in *Le scienze alla corte di Federico II*, vol. 2 of *Micrologus. Natura, scienze e società medievali*, 117.

11. "Phisionomia est doctrina salutis: electio boni et vitatio mali, comprehensio virtutis et praetermissio vitiorum. Hoc autem inducit verus amor dei." Michael Scot, *Liber phisionomiae*, proemium. I have used the Venice edition (1477). At least eighteen editions appeared subsequently, indicating the popularity of the work.

12. Albert of Behaim, *Das Brief- und Memorialbuch* 73, ed. Thomas Frenz and Peter Herde, MGH, Briefe des späteren Mittelalters 1 (Munich: MGH, 2000), 334.

13. Albert the Great, *Quaestiones super de animalibus* 1.21–22, ed. Ephrem Filthaut, Ed. Colon. 12 (Monasterii Westfalorum: Aschendorff, 1955), 94–96 (QDA, 48–51). This text has appeared in translation as *Albert the Great's Questions Concerning Aristotle's* On Animals, trans. Irven M. Resnick and Kenneth F. Kitchell Jr., Fathers of the Church, Mediaeval Continuation 9 (Washington, D.C.: The Catholic University of America Press, 2008). I will provide corresponding page numbers to the translated text in parenthesis, as above, using the abbreviation QDA.

14. See P. G. Meersseman, *Introductio in opera omnia B. Alberti Magni O.P.* (Bruges: Beyaert, 1931), 139. Note, too, that in *On Animals* Albert alludes to a work of his own with the title *Physonomya*. See Albert the Great, *De animalibus* 23.1.1.46, ed. Hermann Stadler, Beiträge zur Geschichte der Philosophie des Mittelalters 15 and 16 (Münster: Aschendorff, 1916–20), 16:1454. These volumes have been translated as *Albertus Magnus On Animals. A Medieval Summa Zoologica*, 2 vols., trans. Kenneth F. Kitchell Jr. and Irven Michael Resnick (Baltimore: Johns Hopkins University Press, 1999). Typically, I will provide in parenthesis a reference to this translation, abbreviated hereafter as *SZ*. Thus, the passage above will be found at (*SZ* 2:1573).

integrated into the study of science and natural philosophy in medieval Europe.[15] By the fourteenth century, physiognomy was taught at a number of medieval universities.[16]

The reasons for its appeal are not difficult to locate. In his *On Animals* Albert the Great explains how "physiognomy . . . teaches one to make predictions about human dispositions using the physical shapes of their members."[17] The physiognomist can read out certain predictable forms of behavior, then, from our physical appearance, while physical appearance is dictated in part by humoral complexion and the form or arrangement of our members.[18] This is not to say that we are predetermined to act in a certain way at birth but only that since the soul is united to the body, our body—and bodies in general, to include the influence of celestial bodies on those below—can affect the soul *per accidens*, even though the rational soul ought to regulate the appetites and inclinations of the body. The soul's freedom and the freedom of the will remain, but the body's complexion inclines the soul to act in a certain way, unless the will develops a habit contrary to the inclination created by the body. As a result of the body's composition or complexion, says Albert the Great, "some are naturally disposed to courage and some to liberality and some to chastity, who nevertheless can be changed or inclined to the opposite by habitual action. And similarly certain ones are naturally disposed to vice, like melancholiacs are to envy and cholerics to wrath, who yet can

15. For a review of the route by which physiognomy entered into medieval science and philosophy, see Jole Agrimi, "Fisiognomica e 'Scolastica," in *I Discorsi dei corpi*, vol. 1 of *Micrologus. Natura, scienze e società medievali* (Turnholt: Brepols, 1993), 235–71.

16. For the study of Ps. Aristotle's *Physiognomy* as part of the university curriculum at Bologna, see "The Curriculum in Arts and Medicine at Bologna (early fifteenth century)," trans. M. Michèle Mulcahey, in *Medieval Italy: Texts in Translation*, ed. Katherine L. Jansen, Joanna Drell, and Frances Andrews (Philadelphia: University of Pennsylvania Press, 2009), 328.

17. "Physonomia . . . divinare docet de affectibus hominum per physicas formas membrorum." *De animalibus* 1.2.2.126, vol. 15, 46 (*SZ* 1:93). No good general studies of Albert's treatment of physiognomy exist, although two articles appeared before WWII comparing some of Albert's views with the racial science of pre-war Germany. See Hans Scharold's "Die Physiognomie des Albertus Magnus und die moderne Wissenschaft," *Bayerische Blätter fur das Gymnasial-Schulwesen* 68, no.5 (1932): 289–301; and F. M. Barbado, "La physionomie, le tempérament et le caractère, d'après Albert le Grand et la science moderne," *Revue Thomiste* 36 (1931): 314–51.

18. For the notion of complexion (and its endurance) see Valentin Groebner, "*Complexio*/Complexion: Categorizing Individual Natures, 1250–1600," in *The Moral Authority of Nature*, ed. Lorraine Daston and Fernando Vidal (Chicago: University of Chicago Press, 2004), 361–83.

be habituated to the contraries by the discretion of the intellect."[19] To the extent that our behavior can be molded by the rational will, Albert will discuss it in his commentary on Aristotle's *Nicomachean Ethics*; to the extent that it is affected and revealed by the body, he will discuss it under the science of physiognomy.

In a very real sense, then, physiognomy was linked to several disciplines: to zoology, for its discussion of animals and their characteristics and temperaments; to medicine and anatomy, for its discussion of the human body and its organs and operations; and to ethnology or anthropology for a discussion of the generally recognized characteristics and temperaments of groups. From external appearances and from the face in particular, the physiognomist may infer a great deal about moral character, mental abilities, or the passional nature and affections of the soul, in the same way that the physician may discover something about interior states from the body's pulse rate or heartbeat. According to the late fifteenth-century *Malleus Maleficarum* (*Hammer of Sorceresses*) "a human's secret will is read in his facial expression and the emotions of the soul are recognized by physicians from the movement of the heart and from the quality of the pulse."[20] One's passional nature and psychology will largely be dictated by the body's humoral complexion, and while the body's humoral complexion does not act upon the soul with a necessary causation, the soul is inclined to imitate the body's complexion, creating in it a sort of predisposition to act in certain ways.[21]

By the fourteenth century the claims of physiognomists must also have achieved a wide popular acceptance, as evidenced by Chaucer's physiognomic sketches of the pilgrims in the *Canterbury Tales*.[22] From the physical descriptions of the Pardoner, the Reeve, or the Summoner, Chaucer's readers would certainly have deduced the most important features of their character.[23] Physiognomic science was equally useful to slave traders, purchasers of thoroughbred horses, and merchants. The

---

19. Albert the Great, *Quaestiones super de animalibus* 1.22, 95, 19–25 (QDA, 49).

20. Henricus Institoris and Jacobus Sprenger, *Malleus Maleficiarum* 2, q. 4, col. 107D, 2 vols., ed. and trans. Christopher S. Mackay (Cambridge: Cambridge University Press, 2004), 1: 415 (trans. 2: 286).

21. Ibid. 1, q. 6, col. 31D, 1: 265.

22. See especially Walter Clyde Curry, *Chaucer and the Medieval Sciences* (New York: Barnes and Noble, 1960), chaps. 3–4.

23. For discussion of the Summoner, see chap. 3, n. 145.

fifteenth-century Swiss-born Dominican pilgrim to the Holy Land, Felix Fabri (d. 1502), remarks that he met slavers so knowledgeable in physiognomy that they "were exceedingly sharp-eyed and skilled [in selecting a slave], and there is no physician or natural philosopher who can compare to them when it comes to recognizing human complexions and conditions."[24] They would strip slaves offered for sale in the public market and from an inspection of the shape and formation of the body and its members determine almost immediately the slave's character, health, and breeding potential.

THE THEORY OF THE BODY'S COMPLEXION

Physiognomy and a theory of bodily complexion went hand in hand, since the former provided visible markers to complexion, while complexion helped to determine physiognomic signs. Complexional theory is simple in its basic principles, and complex in its application. A brief summary here will have to serve as an introduction. According to Avicenna's (d. 1037) influential *Canon of Medicine*, "complexion is that quality which results from the mutual interaction ... of the four primary qualities residing within the elements."[25] The four elements—air, fire, earth, and water—combine in material bodies and are associated with the four primary qualities—the moist, the hot, the dry and the cold. Complexion, then, results from the interaction of these qualities, to produce composite bodies that are hot and dry (choleric), hot and moist (sanguineous), cold and moist (phlegmatic), cold and dry (melancholic), or, when the four qualities are equal, temperate or balanced. Since the primary elements in bodies are never found in a pure state, in isolation from all the others, these primary qualities are typically paired with the elements in a primary and secondary association. Thus, earth is dry and cold; water is cold and moist; air is moist and warm; and fire is warm and dry.

From antiquity Galen's disciples, if not the physician Galen (d. c. 200)

---

24. "sunt oculatissimi et expertissimi, non enim est medicus aut physicus, qui valeat eis comparari in cognoscendis complexionibus et conditionibus hominum." Felix Fabri, *Evagatorum in Terrae Sanctae, Arabiae et Egyptii peregrinationem* fol. 131a, 3 vols., ed. Konrad Dietrich Hassler (Stuttgart: Stuttgart Literary Society, 1843–49); 3:165.

25. *Canon* 1.1.3.1. I have used here the translation found in *A Source Book in Medieval Science*, ed. Edward Grant (Cambridge, Mass.: Harvard University Press, 1974), 717. This selection reprints portions from *A Treatise on the Canon of Medicine of Avicenna*, trans. O. Cameron Gruner (London: Luzac and Co., 1930), although Michael McVaugh modified the translation for Grant's volume.

himself, sought in addition to relate the four elements and their qualities to the four bodily fluids or humors: namely, blood, yellow or red bile, black bile or melancholy, and phlegm. Thus, Isidore of Seville reports that "Just as there are four elements, however, there are also four humors. Each of the humors imitates its element: blood [imitates] air, bile [imitates] fire, melancholy [imitates] earth, and phlegm [imitates] water. And these are the four humors, just as there are four elements that preserve our bodies."[26] Similarly, the humors and the elements also evince a comparison to the seasons: like earth, autumn is dry and cold; like water, winter is cold and moist; like air, spring is moist and warm; and like fire, summer is warm and dry.[27] Especially in the human, who is a microcosm or *minor mundus,* the four humors—blood, bile (red or yellow), black bile or melancholy, and phlegm—mirror the nature of the seasons as well. Like spring, blood is warm and moist; like summer, bile is warm and dry; like autumn, black bile is cold and dry; and like winter, phlegm is cold and moist.

Homeostasis or humoral stability and perfect balance only existed, for Christian medical savants, before the fall in Paradise. Our present state is necessarily more volatile and subject to imbalance or *discrasia.* Even seasonal variations occur in the body, so that bile increases somewhat in summer, for example, because summer is, like bile, warm and dry.[28] In the same way, the humors and their qualities vary according to the ages of man, that is, to the four divisions of human life: childhood, adolescence, adulthood, and old age. Typically in these periods the humor corresponding to that age will prevail. For Bede (d. 735), in children, blood will be dominant; in adolescents, (red) bile; in adults,

26. "Sicut autem quatuor elementa, sic et quatuor humores, et unusquisque humor suum elementum imitatur: sanguis aerem, cholera ignem, melancholia terram, phlegma aquam. Et sunt quatuor humores, sicut quatuor elementa, quae conservant corpora nostra." Isidore of Seville, *Etymologiae* 4.5.3 (PL 82: 184C-D).

27. Bede notes: "Terra namque sicca et frigida, aqua frigida et humida, aer humidus et calidus, ignis est calidus et siccus; ideoque haec autumno, illa hiemi, iste ueri, ille comparatur aestati." *De temporum ratione liber* 35, ed. Ch. W. Jones and Th. Mommsen, CCSL 123B (Turnholt: Brepols, 1977), 391, 10-15.

28. Bede adds: "Sed et homo ipse, qui a sapientibus microcosmos, id est minor mundus, appelatur, hisdem per omnia qualitatibus habet temperatum corpus, imitantibus nimirum singulis eius quibus constat humoribus, modum temporum quibus maxime pollet. Sanguis siquidem, qui uere crescit, humidus et calidus; cholera rubea, quae aestate, calida et sicca; cholera nigra, quae autumno, sicca et frigida; phlegmata, quae hieme, frigida sunt et humida." *De temporum ratione liber* 35, 392-93.

black bile; and in the elderly, phlegm dominates for the "winter" of our life.[29] Although William of St. Thierry and Albert the Great transpose the humoral quality of the last two ages, the basic metaphor remains unchanged.[30]

This quadripartite structure became a root metaphor and organizational principle for medieval medical discourse.[31] The four qualities of warm, moist, cold and dry are variously paired and then linked with the four elements, the four seasons, the four winds, and even the four compass points, since the East will be associated with spring and blood, the South with summer and yellow bile, the West with autumn and melancholy, and the North with winter and phlegm. Those living in these different regions, then, cannot help but be influenced by the qualities of their geography and climate. Such external influences on complexion

---

29. "Et quidem sanguis in infantibus maxime uiget, in adolescentibus cholera rubea, melancholia in transgressoribus, id est fel cum faece nigri sanguinis admixtum, phlegmata dominantur in senibus." Bede, *De temporum ratione liber* 35, 393. Although one sometimes finds a human lifespan divided into more than four periods—cf. Thomas of Cantimpré's seven stages in his *Liber de natura rerum* 1.78-84, 80-82—the quadripartite scheme was fairly consistent, although various authors assigned slightly different durations to the four ages.

30. In William of St. Thierry's *The Nature of the Body and Soul* the first stage, adolescence, continues until the twenty-fifth or thirtieth year, during which the quality of blood prevails; young manhood, a period of relative stasis, is akin to red bile because of its dryness and heat, and ends about age thirty-five or forty; old age, cold and dry, corresponds to black bile, ending about age fifty-five or sixty; and then last is debility, naturally the driest and coldest age, although accidentally humid because of indigestion and the abundance of phlegm. William of St. Thierry's treatise is translated in its entirety in *Three Treatises on Man: A Cistercian Anthropology*, ed. Bernard McGinn (Kalamazoo, Mich.: Cistercian Publications, 1977). See esp. 122. (The Latin text of the *Liber de natura corporis et animae* is found in CCCM 86-88, part 3, ed. Stanislas Ceglar and Paul Verdeyen [Turnholt: Brepols, 1988].) The inclination to identify the last age as the coldest and driest, deprived then of the two natural qualities most necessary to life (heat and moisture), is also evident in Albert the Great's *Quaestiones super de animalibus* 7.29, 184 (QDA, 259) where Albert remarks: "age follows upon the complexion, because in the first age the complexion is warm and moist, as it is in children, and in the second age it is warm and dry, as it is in youths, and in the third it is cold and moist, and in the fourth age cold and dry." Although old age is naturally cold and dry, it is often characterized by "unnatural" phlegmatic discharges, e.g., watery eyes and runny nose, while at the same time the desiccated cold of old age impedes fertility or sexual potency. See Carol A. Everest, "Pears and Pregnancy in Chaucer's 'Merchant's Tale,'" in *Food in the Middle Ages: A Book of Essays*, ed. Melitta Weiss Adamson (New York: Garland, 1995), 161-75.

31. For a good discussion, see Jean-Marie Fritz, "La théorie humorale comme moyen de penser le monde. Limites et contradictions du système," in *Ecriture et modes de pensée au Moyen Age (VIIIe-XVe siècles)*, ed. Dominique Boutet and Laurence Harf-Lancner (Paris: Presses de l'ecole normale superieure, 1993), 13-26.

belong to the category known as the six "non-naturals," which includes also the influence of diet, sleep, exercise, sexual intercourse, and mental affections like fear or joy.[32]

In another way, the humors intersected: thus heat is common to both blood and yellow bile; dryness is common to yellow bile and melancholy; coldness is common to melancholy and phlegm; and moistness is common to blood and phlegm. In this pairing, blood (moist and hot) and melancholy (cold and dry) become opposites, as do yellow bile (hot and dry) and phlegm (cold and moist). As a result, as Constantine the African notes, there are nine possible complexions: one that is balanced or temperate, and eight that display imbalance. Of the latter, four are imbalanced in a simple way (because of the excess of an elemental quality) and four are imbalanced in a composite way (because of the excess of a bodily humor).[33]

Although the human was created with a naturally temperate, balanced complexion out of the primary elements in a creative act sometimes compared to a sort of divine alchemy, since Adam's fall this ideal complexion will be more or less temperate in humans according to degrees.[34] Some will naturally be hotter or colder, drier or moister. In addition, quantitative or qualitative variations in individuals, that is, incidental alterations in the balance of the elements, the qualities, and the corresponding humors, will produce change. Growth, aging, psychological disposition—all have their root in changes to the balance of the humors.

Similarly, planetary bodies, which possess their own complexions, may influence the complexional balance found in an animal body. Because the moon is intemperately cold and moist, Saturn intemperately

---

32. A basic medical text for the Middle Ages, Johannitius's *Isagoge*, divided the influences upon complexion into three categories: naturals (which include the elements, qualities, and humors), the nonnaturals (including the seasons, diet, and exercise) and contranaturals (influences stemming from illnesses and disease). For a translation of this text, see E. T. Withington, *Medical History from the Earliest Times: A Popular History of the Healing Art* (London: The Scientific Press, 1894), 387–96.

33. Constantine the African. *L'Arte universale della medicina (Pantegni), Part 1—book 1* 1.6, trans. Marco T. Malato and Umberto de Martini (Rome: Istituto di storia della medicina dell'università di Roma, 1961), 50–51.

34. See, for example, the description in William of Conches's *De philosophia mundi* 23 (written between 1125–35, but published in error under the name of Honorius of Autun; PL 172: 55B–56D), with a nearly identical description in his *Glosae super Platonem in Timaeum* 30A, cap. 52, in Guillaume de Conches, *Glosae super Platonem*, ed. Édouard Jeauneau (Paris: Librairie Philosophique J. Vrin, 1965), 121.

cold and dry, Mars intemperately hot and dry, Venus temperately cold and moist, and Jupiter temperately hot and moist, these planetary bodies (as well as the Sun and Mercury) may affect the humoral balance in animal bodies.[35] This is especially evident in the perceived influence of the moon on a female's menstrual cycle, for example, since in general the watery humors in the body increase and move to the body's surface when the moon waxes.[36] This influence explains why the good physician must understand astronomy as well as anatomy and the other medical disciplines.

Despite all of these factors that can affect a body's humoral complexion, in general the best complexion in present circumstances is understood to be hot and moist, that is, sanguineous. The reason for this stems from the Aristotelian conviction that a complete or perfected nature is one that can successfully reproduce itself. Nature herself demonstrates that, in the plant world for example, nothing will grow where there is not sufficient moisture or warmth from the sun. Yet according to medieval physicians and natural philosophers, because women have a weaker complexional heat, they are unable fully to decoct the body's nutriment, resulting in the accumulation of impurities and superfluities that must be purged on a regular basis. This provides the principal physiological (as opposed to theological) explanation for menstruation: women must purge their bodies monthly of these superfluities which, if they remain in the body, will cause illness or permanent disability. Indeed, the menstrual flow evacuates the body's poisons or toxins, such that if a woman retains menstrual blood the body must find another outlet, which comes to explain the notion of the "evil eye":[37] the body's poisons will be emitted through the eyes, just as the gaze of a menstruating woman, it was

---

35. See Albert the Great, *De generatione et corruptione* 2.3.5, 206, 38ff.; and Albert the Great, *De causis proprietatum elementorum* 1.2.9, ed. Paul Hossfeld, Ed. Colon. 5.2 (Münster: Aschendorff, 1980), 78; for English translation, see *On the Causes of the Properties of the Elements*, trans. Irven M. Resnick, Mediaeval Philosophical Texts in Translation 46 (Milwaukee, Wisc.: Marquette University Press, 2010).

36. See Albert the Great, *De causis proprietatum elementorum* 1.2.7, 73–74; Albert of Behaim, *Das Brief- und Memorialbuch* 73, 309 (citing Pliny).

37. Ps. Albert the Great, *Women's Secrets: A Translation of Pseudo-Albertus Magnus's* De Secretis Mulierum *with Commentaries*, trans. Helen Rodnite Lemay (Albany: SUNY Press, 1992), 129–31; for a historical introduction to the "evil eye," see Leonard W. Moss and Stephen C. Cappannari, "*Mal'occhio, Ayin ha ra, Oculus fascinus, Judenblick*: The Evil Eye Hovers Above," in *The Evil Eye*, ed. Clarence Maloney (New York: Columbia University Press, 1976), 1–15.

thought, would infect or stain a newly polished mirror.[38] Equally important, however, the woman's weaker complexional heat implies her insufficiency for the purpose of generation or reproduction. Unlike the male, whose heat is perfected, she cannot fully complete the body's fourth digestion which, in males, produces semen or sperm. Consequently, although her menstrual blood provides the material principle for reproduction, she is unable to contribute the active, formal power for procreation.[39] It is the male seed that contributes the formative principle for the fetus, acting on the blood like a coagulant added to milk.[40] Since Aristotle viewed the power of generation as a sign of a creature's perfection, this defect in the woman signified that she is always imperfect and incomplete. Indeed, she can be completed only through the active power of the male. Therefore, although the human is the noblest being in nature, the male represents the nobler sex.[41] The female is necessary for the perpetuation of the human nature, but she remains apart from or separate from nature's primary intention, since nature intends only the best. As Thomas

38. See Alexander Neckam, *De naturis rerum libri duo* 2.156, ed. Thomas Wright (London: Longman, Green, Longman, Roberts, and Green, 1863), 252; Robert Grosseteste, *Expositio in epistulam sancti Pauli ad Galatas* 3.3, CCCM 130, ed. J. McEvoy and L. Rizzerio (Turnholt: Brepols, 1995); Ps. Albert the Great, *Women's Secrets*, 131; Albert the Great, *De animalibus* 7.2.5.133, vol. 15, 553 (SZ 1:647); Albert the Great, *Quaestiones de animalibus* 9.9, 207, 38 (QDA, 312) ; Albert the Great, *Summa de creaturis* 2.1, q. 45, art. 4, in Ed. Borgnet 34, 418; Pseudo-Aristotle, *Problemata varia anatomica after University of Bologna MS 1165 (2327)*, ed. L. R. Lind, University of Kansas Publications Humanistic Studies 38 (Lawrence: University of Kansas Publications, 1968), 20; Henricus Institoris, *Malleus Malificarum* 1, q. 2, col. 17C, 1:236. This tradition, however, can be traced back to Pliny, *Historia Naturalis* 7.13.63f. It was repeated by Jewish authorities as well, like Nachmanides. See Sharon Faye Koren, "Kabbalistic Physiology: Isaac the Blind, Nahmanides, and Moses de Leon on Menstruation," *AJS Review* 28, no.2 (2004): 325.

39. See Albert the Great, *De vegetabilibus libri VII* 1.1.12.91–92, ed. Ernst Meyer and Charles Jessen (Berlin: Georgius Reimeris, 1867), 47. On the female's material, passive contribution in generation, see Maaike Van der Lugt, *Le Ver, le Démon et la Vierge: Les théories médiévales de la génération extraordinaire* (Paris: Les Belles Lettres, 2004), 70–79.

40. David of Dinant, *Davidis de Dinanto Quaternulorum Fragmenta*, ed. Marianus Kurdzialek, Studia Mediewistyczne 3 (Warsaw: Panstwowe Wydawnictwo Naukowe, 1963), 23–24; 32–33.

41. Albert the Great, *Quaestiones super de animalibus* 6, 24–26, 168, 25 (QDA, 223). See also the influential text of the *Secreta secretorum*, which notes that "Man is the noblest of all animals in construction, and the preponderating element in him is fire." Roger Bacon, *Secretum secretorum*, ed. Robert Steele, in *Opera hactenus inedita*, fasc. 5 (Oxford: Clarendon, 1920), 229. I have not yet had the opportunity to examine Theodor W. Köhler, *Homo Animal Nobilissimum: Konturen Des Spezifisch Menschlichen in Der Naturphilosophischen Aristoteleskommentie des dreizehnten Jahrhunderts*, Studien und Texte zur Geistesgeschichte des Mittelalters 94 (Leiden: Brill, 2008).

Aquinas remarks, "nature intends that there be perfection. Nonetheless ... when nature cannot lead one to greater perfection, it introduces the lesser, just as when it cannot produce a male it makes a female, which is a flawed male."[42] Females are necessary for the perpetuation of the human species, but in each individual act of generation, explains Albert the Great, nature would produce a male if nothing impeded the father's reproductive power.[43] There is little doubt that in terms of an appropriate taxonomy women are *human*, but in comparison to a male they are defective and consigned to a lower order. The Franciscan Johannes de Fonte (fl. early fourteenth century?) cites Aristotle's *On Animals* to defend the view that an animal body derives from the female, but the soul derives from the male. Since soul is the substance and substantial form of the body, a female is only a flawed male.[44] Similarly, adds Albert the Great, when an angel assumes bodily form it will naturally choose a male rather than female body because of its greater perfection.[45] For Thomas Aquinas, in the Old Testament only male animals were offered to God as burnt offerings, because these alone are a perfect sacrifice, since the female is an imperfect animal (*foemina est animal imperfectum*).[46] At the Incarnation God chose to assume a male's body for the same reason, since it is this body that will be offered as a perfect sacrifice in the Eucharist.[47] This reasoning also implied that priests offering the Eucharist must be male, and provides a basis for the exclusion of women from the priesthood.[48]

Albert the Great explains that because woman has a cold and moist,

42. Thomas Aquinas, *In IV Sent*. dist. 36, q. 1, art. 1, resp. ad arg, 2, ln. 1 [*Scriptum super libros Sententiarum*, 4 vols., ed. P. Mandonnet and M. F. Moos (Paris: Lethielleux, 1929–47)].

43. Albert the Great, *Quaestiones super de animalibus* 15.2, 260 (QDA, 442); Albert the Great, *De fato* art. 4.5, ed. Paul Simon, Ed. Colon. 17.1 (Münster i. West.: Aschendorff, 1975), 74, 18–27; see also Thomas Aquinas, *Summa theologica* 1, q. 92, art. 1, resp. 1; and *Summa theologica* 1, q. 99, art. 2, resp. 1–2.

44. Iohannes de Fonte, *Auctoritates Aristotelis, Senecae, Boethii, Platonis, Apulei, Porphyrii, Gilberti* (Speyer: Johann and Konrad Hist, c. 1490), fol. 32. For his dates, see Jacqueline Hamesse, "Johannes de Fonte, compilateur des *Parvi flores*. Le témoignage de plusieurs manuscrits de la Bibliothèque Vaticane," *Archivum franciscanum historicum* 88 (1995): 515–531.

45. A view that Dyan Elliott attributes to William of Auvergne. See her "The Physiology of Rapture and Female Spirituality," *Medieval Theology and the Natural Body*, ed. Peter Biller and A.J. Minnis, York Studies in Medieval Theology 1 (Woodbridge, Suffolk: York Medieval Press, 1997), 157.

46. Thomas Aquinas, *Summa theologica* 1.2, q. 102, art. 3, resp. 9.

47. Albert the Great, *De incarnatione* tr. 3, q. 2, art 4, ed. Ignatius Backes, Ed. Colon. 26 (Monasterii Westfalorum: Aschendorff, 1958), 198, 81–85.

48. See chap. 3, n. 95.

phlegmatic humoral complexion her sensory powers are weaker than a male's and, consequently, she will also have a weaker intellect, since understanding begins with sensory input. This intellectual weakness results in inaccurate moral judgments, unless she is properly guided by a man and subordinate to him; otherwise she is led into diabolical wickedness, for which she displays greater cleverness or cunning than the male. But it is especially her sexuality that elicits from Albert his greatest misogyny.

> For generally, proverbially, and commonly it is affirmed that women are more mendacious and fragile, more diffident, more shameless, more deceptively eloquent and, in brief, a woman is nothing but a devil fashioned into a human appearance. Thus I saw one like this at Cologne, who seemed to be a saint and yet, in brief, ensnared everyone with her love. . . . A female is less suited for proper behavior than is a male. For a female's complexion is moister than a male's, but it belongs to a moist complexion to receive [impressions] easily but to retain them poorly. For moisture is easily mobile and this is why women are inconstant and always seeking after new things. Therefore, when she is engaged in the [sex] act under one man, at that very moment she would wish, were it possible, to lie under another. Therefore there is no faithfulness in a woman . . . wise men almost never disclose their plans and their doings to their wives. For a woman is a flawed male and, in comparison to the male, has the nature of defect and privation, and this is why naturally she mistrusts herself. And this is why whatever she cannot acquire on her own she strives to acquire through mendacity and diabolical deceptions. Therefore, to speak briefly, one must be as mistrustful of every woman as of a venomous serpent and a horned devil, and if it were allowed to say what I know about women, it would stupefy the entire world.[49]

Albert's remarks offer a fascinating gaze upon gender relations in the thirteenth century. As he says, if he were to tell all that he knows about women, it would stupefy the world. This is a rather astounding claim coming from a man who spent his adult life among the Dominicans, a religious order that demanded chastity and narrowly limited contact with women. His reference to his experience in Cologne hardly helps us to discover or specify the source or nature of his alleged knowledge, since Albert spent much of his career there. About 1229 Albert was likely

---

49. Albert the Great, *Quaestiones super de animalibus* 15.11, 265, 62–266, 6 (QDA, 454). Elsewhere, Albert makes clear that the cold and the moist are qualities specific to the female: "Proprietates autem feminini sunt frigidum et humidum; et humidum est figure et specie receptivum, frigidum vero per coagulationem humidi aquosi eorundem est retentivum." Albert the Great, *De homine* 3.2.8, resp., ed. Henryk Anzulewicz and Joachim R. Söder, Ed. Colon. 27.2 (Monasterii Westfalorum: Aschendorff, 2008), 129, 78–81.

received into the Dominican order in Cologne; he studied in Cologne, a city of approximately 40,000, and later organized and taught there at the Dominican study center (*studium generale*). In his sixties or seventies, Albert served as vicar general for the archdiocese of Cologne. Finally, Albert spent his last decade in Cologne at the Dominican cloister of the Holy Cross (*Heiliges Kreuz*) as *lector emeritus*, where he would remain until his death in 1280. Nonetheless, Albert insists that his knowledge of women is grounded in personal experience and common knowledge. His personal experience may stem from information he acquired from hearing confession, since in his *Questions Concerning Aristotle's "On Animals"* he discusses those amorous activities that most arouse a woman, which he "heard in confessions in Cologne."[50] This personal experience is informed, however, by Aristotelian biology and humoral theory. Thus, a woman's sexual habits stem from the nature of her complexion: because she has a moist complexion that poorly retains impressions (just as an imprint in wet clay is only made permanent when it is "fired" or dried), she is constantly seeking new sexual encounters. Just as matter naturally desires form, so the female naturally desires the male. Her sexual desire, unlike most animals, is not confined to a specific time of the month or year. Following Aristotle, many medieval philosophers held that it is only the woman and, among the animals, only the female horse or mare, that desires intercourse even when she is already pregnant, and at all times of the month or year.[51] On the basis of this analogy, Albert the Great explains that people are accustomed to call women "mares" on account of their wantonness, and lascivious women are said to "whinny."[52]

While for Albert the Great a woman's moist complexion explains her constant desire for new sexual partners, it may appear somewhat paradoxical that women—who have not only a moist but also a *cold* complexion—should "burn" with desire, particularly since elsewhere Albert acknowledges that desire results from heat.[53] One often repeated explanation is found in the work of William of Conches (d. 1154). According

---

50. Albert the Great, *Quaestiones super de animalibus* 13.18, 248, 19 (QDA, 411).

51. Aristotle, *Generation of Animals* 4.5 (773b25ff.), trans. A. L. Peck, Loeb Classical Library (Cambridge, Mass.: Harvard University Press, 1953), 448–49.

52. Albert the Great, *De animalibus* 6.3.1.99, vol. 15, 483 (SZ 1: 572). For the whinny as a sign of the horse's lustful or libidinous nature, see Albert the Great, *Commentarii in Iob*, 39.19, ed. Melchior Weiss (Freiburg: Herder, 1904), 464–65.

53. Albert the Great, *Quaestiones super de animalibus* 5.7. 157 (QDA, 194–95).

to William, although woman is colder than the male by nature her desire is such that, like firewood that is cold and damp, she burns longer and more ardently once she begins to burn.[54] A question remains, however: what causes her to begin to burn at all? Tension appeared, then, as medieval natural philosophers sought to explain how a colder nature could ignite and burn more hotly with desire. Albert the Great attempts to resolve the tension by allowing that "two things come into consideration with respect to desire, namely a judgment about what is desirable and pleasure. If we speak of desire in terms of pleasure, this is naturally greater in the male than in the female. If we speak in terms of the judgment ... [then] desire ... is greater in women."[55] Albert, then, relies on his contention that a cold, moist complexion enfeebles the intellect; the weakness of a woman's intellect leads to poor judgment, which causes her to desire first one man, then another, and then another, and so on. In this way, he sought to explain why women seemingly have stronger sexual appetites than men. In an apparently unnatural way, during pregnancy—when the fetus's heat warms the woman's natural coldness—she is particularly lustful and intent upon renewed sexual pleasure[56] and monastic moralists like Peter Damian (d. 1072) forcefully sought to persuade men to avoid intercourse with pregnant women whose insatiable desire for coition so endangers the health of the fetus that the women will even perform abortions "so that they can satisfy their lust."[57] More ardent in their sexual desire, women, the seductive daughters of Eve, represented an embodied sexual peril to Christian men that was hardly overcome by the few examples of idealized female models of chastity, like the Virgin Mary. Although men also succumbed to sexual desire, gener-

54. William of Conches, *Dragmaticon* 6.8.3, ed. Italo Ronca, CCCM 152 (Turnholt: Brepols, 1997); a translation appeared as *A Dialogue on Natural Philosophy (Dragmaticon Philosophiae)*, trans. Italo Ronca and Matthew Curr (Notre Dame, Ind.: University of Notre Dame Press, 1997). See 135, Ronca trans. See also William's *De philosophia mundi* 23 (PL 172: 55D), incorrectly attributed to Honorius of Autun; and Vincent of Beauvais, *Speculum naturale* 31.5 (= vol. 1 of the *Speculum quadruplex, sive, Speculum maius: naturale, doctrinale, morale, historiale*) (Graz, Austria: Duaci: Akademische Druck-u. Verlagsanstalt; ex officina typographica Baltazaris Belleri, 1964–65), 2294.

55. Albert the Great, *Quaestiones super de animalibus* 5.6, 157 (QDA, 194).

56. William of Conches, *Dragmaticon* 6.9.2 (138–39, Ronca trans.).

57. "ut vota suae libidinis expleant." Peter Damian, Epist. 96.18, in *Die Briefe des Petrus Damiani*, 4 vols., ed. Kurt Reindel, MGH, Epp. Kaiserzeit (Munich: MGH, 1983–93); 3:58; cf. *The Letters of Peter Damian, 91–120*, trans. Owen J. Blum, Fathers of the Church, Mediaeval Continuation 5 (Washington, D.C.: The Catholic University of America Press, 1998), 62.

ally they were viewed as passive rather than active agents of sexual encounters. Even the Bible seemed to confirm such prejudices concerning female carnality and desire: Proverbs 30:16 (Vulg.) identifies the vagina (*os vulvae*) as insatiable and never satisfied.[58]

While bodies, then, reveal the defects of their complexion, and display or signify these defects through physiognomic conventions, popular familiarity with the conventions of physiognomy likely did not stem from widespread acquaintance with Scholastic works of natural science but from their application in pastoral or ordinary religious contexts. For physiognomy to acquire a foothold in common religious discourse, it had first to prove its value to theologians and preachers.[59] Although some, like Helinand of Froidment (d. between 1223–37), would leave the doctrine of complexion so central to physiognomy to the study of medicine, nevertheless an understanding of its principles had a bearing on both speculative and practical theology.[60]

For practical theology, Richard of St. Victor (d. 1173) remarks that owing to their natural complexion, some individuals are likely to be more compassionate than others.[61] Contrariwise, Alan of Lille (d. 1202/3) suggests that individuals may be more inclined to specific sins because of their humoral complexion. Among confessors, then, "the sinner's complexion must be considered, insofar as it can be examined from external signs, because a person is more inclined to one sin than another according to various complexions. If he is a choleric he is more inclined to wrath, but if a melancholic he is more inclined to enmity."[62] For this

---

58. Albert the Great, *In Evang. Lucae* 8:43, Ed. Borgnet 22, 582; Henricus Institoris, *Malleus Maleficiarum* 2, q. 5, 45A, 122.

59. For the influence of physiognomy upon Christian homiletic literature, see Joseph Ziegler, "Text and Context: On the Rise of Physiognomic Thought," in *De Sion exibit lex et verbum domini de Hierusalem: Essays on Medieval Law, Liturgy, and Literature in Honour of Amnon Linder*, ed. Yitzhak Hen (Turnholt: Brepols, 2001), 159–82 but especially 164ff.

60. Helinand of Froidment, *De cognitione sui* 8: "Corporis humani cognitio in duobus est, in materia scilicet et forma. Complexionem autem medicis relinquo." (PL 212: 729B).

61. Richard of St. Victor, *Adnotationes mysticae in Psalmos* 2 (PL 196: 270A).

62. "Complexio etiam peccatoris consideranda est, secundum quod ex signis exterioribus perpendi potest; quia secundum diversas complexiones, unus magis impellitur ad unum peccatum, quam alius. Quia si cholericus magis impellitur ad iram, sed melancholicus magis ad odium." Alain de Lille, *Liber poenitentialis* 1.17, 2 vols., ed. Jean Longère, Analecta mediaevalia Namurcensia 18 (Louvain: Éditions Nauwelaerts, 1965), 2:31. Note that the edition in Migne's *Patrologia* (PL 210: 287D) adds, following this passage, "si sanguineus, vel phlegmaticus, ad luxuriam."

reason, it seems, Bishop Robert Grosseteste (d. 1253) recommends that clerics should impose penance only after having given due consideration to complexion, since complexion has a bearing on an individual's ability to withstand the inclination to sin.[63]

Speculative theology turned to physiognomy and the doctrine of complexion in an altogether different way. Rather than arguing from the complexion of the body to the condition of the soul, some argued from the soul's condition to the complexion of the body. William of Conches (d. c. 1154), for example, gives expression to a tradition that held that when still in Paradise, Adam's complexion "was perfectly temperate, as he had equal shares of the four qualities." As a result of his sin and disobedience, however, Adam's descendants have departed from that perfectly balanced temperate complexion and the human body subsequently suffered corruption. After Adam was driven out of Eden, "his body began to dry out ... [and] his natural heat to fade away.... His descendants, therefore, born as they were from a corrupt ancestor, have all been corrupted, and never afterward has perfect health been found in humans."[64] Alexander Neckam (d. 1217) likewise remarks that had Adam not sinned, there would be no illness, suffering or sorrow now, but instead every creature would enjoy a temperate complexion.[65] Similarly, had Eve not sinned she would have remained hale in Paradise, Hildegard of Bingen (d. 1179/80) affirms, and avoided the woman's "curse" or punishment—the monthly flux of blood, menstruation—which now is necessary to purge a woman's body of impurities stemming from its corruption.[66] Original sin, then, corrupted both the soul and the body.

In contrast, initially God gave to humans the most noble, balanced complexion, and, in general terms, the ideal human complexion—given our seminal position between angelic and animal natures—should ap-

---

63. "Haec sunt diligenter consideranda in penitencia iniungenda.... Complexio: si colericus, vel sanguineus, vel melancolicus." Robert Grosseteste, *Templum Dei* 19.9, ed. Joseph Goering and F. A. C. Mantello (Toronto: Pontifical Institute of Mediaeval Studies, 1984), 64.

64. "Primus enim homo inter quatuor qualitates fuit temperatus. Sed postquam amoenitate paradisi expulsus ... cepit desiccari atque naturalis calor extingui ... Omnes igitur ex eo nati, utpote ex corrupto, sunt corrupti, neque postea perfecta sanitas in homine fuit inventa." William of Conches, *Dragmaticon* 6.13.2–3, 227 (147, Ronca translation). See also his *De philosophia mundi* 1.23, printed under the name of Honorius of Autun (PL 172: 55D).

65. Alexander Neckam, *De naturis rerum libri duo* 2.156, 251.

66. Hildegard of Bingen, *Causae et Curae* 3, ed. Paul Kaiser (Leipzig: Teubner, 1903), 103.

proach that of the celestial bodies.⁶⁷ Consequently, remarks Albert the Great, "man, among all creatures, more closely resembles a heavenly body owing to a balanced complexion participating less in contrary qualities—from which celestial bodies are altogether free."⁶⁸ Yet since Adam's fall is responsible not only for the corruption of the soul but also for bodily corruption among his descendants, it follows too that an ideal human complexion and the standard for physical perfection will be rediscovered only in those uncorrupted by original sin: namely, Mary and Jesus, for they alone, in this life, were "absolutely perfect."⁶⁹ The logic of this position rooted in physiognomy must have been reasonably compelling, and Thomas Aquinas (d. 1274) reflects this view, remarking that "Christ had the best complexion, which clearly is owing to the fact that he had the most noble soul, to which a balanced complexion corresponds in the body." Soul and body then are correlatives: a noble soul should possess a body with a perfectly balanced humoral complexion, and a temperate complexion indicates the noble quality of the soul. Although original sin disturbed the relationship between the soul's character and the body's complexion, Thomas adds that in Jesus the two can be viewed in pristine purity, since, "with respect to the body he had the best complexion because his body was fashioned miraculously by the operation of the Holy Spirit."⁷⁰ Similarly Albert the Great, following Plato, affirms

67. See Albert the Great, *Quaestiones super de animalibus* 6, 24–26, 168, 25 (QDA, 223), where Albert attributes this view to Avicenna (see the *Canon* 1.1.6.3).
68. "homo inter omnia plus accedit ad similitudinem corporis caelestis, propter aequalitatem complexionis minus participans qualitates contrarias, a quibus corpora caelestia sunt omnino libera." *Super Dionysium de ecclesiastica hierarchia* 5, ed. Maria Burger, Ed. Colon 36.2 (Monasterii Westfalorum: Aschendorff, 1999), 123, 2–7; see also *De animalibus* 12.1.4.5, vol. 15, 819 (SZ 2: 914).
69. So, notes Albert, "nullus in hac vita perfectus fuit simpliciter nisi Iesus Christus et mater eius." *Super Dionysium de ecclesiastica hierarchia* 1, 13, 10–11. For discussion of the physiognomy Mary and Jesus in particular, see my "Ps. Albert the Great on the Physiognomy of Jesus and Mary," *Medieval Studies* 64 (2002): 217–40.
70. "Christus fuit optime complexionatus, quod patet ex eo quod habuit nobilissimam animam, cui respondet aequalitas complexionis in corpore." Thomas Aquinas, In *III Sent.* d. 15, q. 2, a. 3. [*Scriptum super libros Sententiarum,* 4 vols., ed. P. Mandonnet and M. F. Moos, (Paris: Lethielleux, 1929–47), 3:495]. See also *Summa theologica* 3.46.6, c.: "nam et secundum corpus erat optime complexionatus, cum corpus ejus fuerit formatum miraculose operatione Spiritus Sancti." Albert the Great also indicates that because of Adam's sin, his semen was corrupted and therefore among those who descend materially from his seed the operative or formative power of the semen fails to fashion a human in the condition Adam had known previously. See his *Super Argumentum Hieronymi*, in *Super Matthaeum,*

that "the most noble soul is owed to the most balanced complexion" because each complexion receives a form proper to it,[71] while the mind's best disposition will be found in a more noble complexion.[72] St. Bonaventure (d. 1274), too, confirms that Jesus' body displayed the best possible complexion.[73] Peter D'Ailly (d. 1420) concluded as well that the favorable disposition of the stars at the time of Jesus' birth will have produced in him the best complexion.[74] As such, according to other Scholastics, Jesus' complexion tolerated no superfluous humors, and he completely utilized or digested all nutriment.[75] [Pseudo?] Albert the Great adds that because the human body possessed the most balanced or temperate complexion, it rightly received the most noble—that is, rational—soul; so too, "among men Christ has had the best and most worthy [soul]. And because among the other creatures man has the most balanced complexion, and on account of this receives the most noble soul, he is rightly said to be the end of all creatures . . . [so] Christ is, moreover, the end of all humans."[76] Perhaps it is a new awareness of Jesus' exemplary complexion and physiognomy that stands behind Jesus' exhortation in the medieval old French version of the apocryphal *Gospel of Nicodemus,* in which Jesus does not

---

ed. Bernhard Schmidt, Ed. Colon. 21.1 (Monasterii Westfalorum: Aschendorff, 1987), 8, 43–47. Jesus' miraculous birth places him outside this material chain of descent.

71. "Et quia secundum merita materiae dantur formae, sicut Plato dixit, et unicuique complexioni propria respondet forma, ideo aequaliori complexioni debetur anima nobilissima." See *De anima* 2.3.23, ed. Clemens Stroick, Ed. Colon. 7.1 (Monasterii Westfalorum: Aschendorff, 1968), 133, 22.

72. Albert the Great, *De homine,* 255, 21–22.

73. Bonaventure, *Sermones dominicales* 14.12, ed. J. G. Bougerol (Grottaferrata: Collegio S. Bonaventura, Padri Editori di Quaracchi, 1977), 231. As such, his body was also the most sensitive, and therefore suffered more intensely the pain of the Crucifixion.

74. Peter D'Ailly, *De legibus et sectis* cap. 7, fol. [F5r]: "Verbi gratia Christus legislator noster a sua nativitate valde bonam complexionem naturalem dicitur habuisse. Non est ergo fidei dissonum et est rationi naturale consonum quod sub bona celi dispositione seu constellatione natus fuerit a quae complectionis bonitas naturaleter [naturaliter] in eo dependere potuit." Cited in Laura Ackerman Smoller, *History, Prophecy, and the Stars: The Christian Astrology of Pierre d'Ailly 1350–1420* (Princeton, N.J.: Princeton University Press, 1994), 38.

75. For advocates for this view, see *Le Ver, le Démon et la Vierge,* 468–69.

76. "inter homines Christus meliorem habuit et digniorem. Quia igitur homines inter alias creaturas summam temperantiam tenet, et ob hoc recipit animam nobiliorem, recte finis dicitur omnium creaturarum . . . Omnium hominum autem finis est Christus." *Philosophia Pauperum 5: Isagoge in libros meteorum* cap. 1, Ed. Borgnet 5, 479. For a review of the debate over the author of this text, see Fernand van Steenberghen, "Travaux récents sur la pensée du XIIIe siècle," *Revue néo-scolastique de philosophie* 42 (1939): 469–85, but especially, 472–74.

call upon those in hell to come to him who *believe* in him, but rather "Come to me, all my sons, who possess *my image and my form.*"⁷⁷

At the same time, this emphasis upon Jesus' exemplary complexion distanced him from the Jews. Although he was born of a Jewish mother, was raised among the Jews, and observed the Law of the Jews, his bodily nature and complexion worked to dejudaize Jesus. If medieval theologians assumed a relationship, then, between the condition of the soul and body—such that a more noble soul demands a more noble body and a temperate bodily complexion—then contrariwise those souls consistently linked to vice and sin may be expected to display a body or bodily complexion that reflects their inner condition. Thus, the Franciscan John Pecham (d. 1292), who was Archbishop of Canterbury from 1279 until his death, remarks that "a defect of the body is caused by a defect of the soul."⁷⁸ The historian should not be surprised to find, then, such principles utilized in medieval Christian anti-Jewish polemics. As the principles of physiognomy become systematized and more broadly accepted in medieval culture, Jews will be consistently depicted with physical deformities and associated with disease and illnesses that somehow reflect a persistent sinful state, seeing that they remain throughout their lives subject to original sin and its consequences, which Christians overcome through the sacrament of baptism. The medieval "hermeneutical Jew," to adopt Jeremy Cohen's expression, is produced not merely from Christian interpretations of sacred texts to establish a Jewish "Other" for the purposes of Christian self-definition: the hermeneutical Jew also arises from the medieval interpretation and transmission of philosophical and scientific texts focused on the physical world or the world of nature and, especially, human nature. Although Joseph Ziegler cautions that learned (that is, Latin) medieval physiognomic texts offer up little for the modern debate concerning the marginalization of non-Christian minority groups in medieval Europe, nonetheless the basic tenets of medieval physiognomy did not remain long only within learned circles; they

---

77. "Venez a mei, toz mes fiz, qui avez ma ymage et ma figure." *L'Évangile de Nicodème: Les versions courtes en ancien francais et en prose,* lns. 723–26, ed. Alvin E. Ford (Geneva: Librarie Droz, 1973), 56. The old French text (Tradition A) is from the twelfth or thirteenth century. Italics are mine.

78. "ex defectu enim animae causatur defectus corporis." In *Quodlibeta quatuor,* quod. 1, q. 15.6, ed. Girard J. Etzkorn and Ferdinand Delorme (Grottaferrata: Collegio S. Bonaventura, 1989), 38.

quickly spread to other disciplines and to popular culture.[79] Thus, Jewish bodies will reveal the corruption of their souls, souls whose very rationality will become subject to doubt in light of their general unwillingness, over many centuries, to acknowledge the truths of Christian faith. As a result, Christian savants not only condemned Jews for their different beliefs but also mapped real or fictive differences onto the Jews' body. Precisely because sin had weakened the Jews' rationality—if reason was not thought absent from them altogether—they would be less successful in developing a rational will to counteract the influence of behavioral inclinations stemming from the body's complexion, as will be shown below. The somatic consequences of sinfulness, then, will serve to point out the Jews for their Christian neighbors.

INTELLECTUAL DEFICIENCIES, GENDER, AND THE IRRATIONALITY OF THE JEWS

From the principles of physiognomy outlined briefly above one may infer that physical or somatic markers that differentiated Jews will also imply internal, psychological differences and differences in mental faculties. This will become apparent in a growing medieval Christian polemical tradition that, by the twelfth century, casts doubt on the presence of a fully rational faculty among Jews. Christians had long insisted that Jews did not believe in Jesus because they were unable or unwilling to do so: unable because they were blinded by God; unwilling because they had blinded themselves with their own envy and pride. Moreover, they remained incapable of understanding God's truth because they could not move beyond the most superficial or literal interpretation of sacred texts. Mired in carnality, trapped by the contours of the sensible world, and deprived of divine grace, they were unable to ascend to heaven's gate. However damaging this explanation may have been to Jewish-Christian relations, nevertheless it allowed Christian thinkers to dismiss Jewish religious challenges and the doubt these may have engendered in Christians as the product of a carnal, defective will. Christian theologians did

---

79. "Il est donc erroné de mobiliser la physiognomie savant du bas Moyen Âge dans les débats virulent de délégitimisation des minorités non chrétiennes." Joseph Ziegler, "Hérédité et physiognomonie," in *L'hérédité entre Moyen Âge et Époque modern. Perspectives historiques,* ed. Maaike van der Lugt and Charles de Miramon (Florence: SISMEL, 2008), 245–71, citing 265.

try to "correct" the Jews' misreading of the Scriptures, or offer evidence from nature to demonstrate by analogy the Christian mysteries, for example, the mystery of the virgin birth. Yet for most theologians, conclusive proof for the mysteries of faith remained elusive, by definition. But a change appears to have occurred in the early twelfth century, when renewed confidence in logic and dialectic among Christian theologians led in two opposite directions, as some more traditional thinkers condemned this new confidence as prideful arrogance, while others held out the hope that religious doubt could be overcome by philosophical argument.[80] A salient example is found in Anselm's (d. 1109) *Proslogion,* which sought to prove to the "fool" the necessary existence of God. Similarly, in *Why the God-Man (Cur Deus homo)* Anselm proposed to satisfy both pagans and Jews on the necessity of the Incarnation with arguments that proceed *sola ratione.*[81] In his preface, Anselm remarks that in the first book of *Why the God-Man* he will treat the matter leaving Christ to one side, as if nothing were known of him, and "prove by necessary reasons that it is impossible for anyone to be saved without him."[82]

The widespread proliferation of philosophical polemics against Judaism during the twelfth century are a further illustration of the attempt to apply dialectic to prove religious dogmas that previously were seen as lying beyond rational demonstration. Thus, Anselm claims in his *Monologion* and *Proslogion* that what is held by faith can be proved by necessary

---

80. These theologians as a group have often been described, not quite accurately, as anti-humanists or anti-dialecticians. Among the most prominent will be St. Peter Damian. For a reconsideration of these themes, see Toivo J. Holopainen, *Dialectic and Theology in the Eleventh Century* (Leiden: Brill, 1996). See also my "*Scientia liberalis,* Dialectics, and Otloh of St. Emmeram," *Revue Bénédictine* 97, no. 3–4 (1987): 241–52, and "Attitudes toward Philosophy and Dialectic During the Gregorian Reform," *Journal of Religious History* 16, no. 2 (1990): 115–25.

81. See *Cur Deus homo* 2.22, in vol. 2 of *Opera omnia,* 6 vols., ed. F. S. Schmitt (Rome: Thomas Nelson and Sons, 1938–61), 133. For a discussion of Jews (and Muslims) as likely targets for *Cur Deus homo,* see also René Roques, "La méthode de Saint Anselme dans le 'Cur Deus Homo,'" *Aquinas. Ephemerides Thomisticae* 5 (1962): 3–57; and Roques, *Anselme de Cantorbéry. Pourquoi Dieu s'est fait homme,* SC 91 (Paris: Les Éditions du Cerf, 1963), 69–74.

82. "probat rationibus necessariis esse impossibile ullum hominem salvari sine illo." *Cur Deus homo,* pref., in vol. 2 of *Opera omnia,* 42. Again, although Anselm invokes "necessary reasons," G. R. Evans has argued that in this work Anselm seeks no more than to discover suitable, commonsense arguments that will appear convincing to any open-minded listener. See Gillian R. Evans, "The *Cur Deus Homo*: The Nature of St. Anselm's Appeal to Reason," *Studia Theologica* 31, no.1 (1977): 33–50.

reasons, apart from the authority of scripture:[83] for example, the Trinity in the case of the *Monologion*,[84] the existence of God in the *Proslogion*, and the necessity of the Incarnation in *Why the God-Man*. Similarly, in his *Debate with the Jew, Leo, Concerning the advent of Christ, the Son of God*, Anselm's contemporary Odo of Tournai (d. 1113) attempted to prove to his Jewish interlocutor both the truth of the Incarnation and the rational necessity of the virgin birth.

In some cases these polemics were irenic in tone. But as the twelfth century unfolded, some historians contend, the theologians' earlier optimism was clearly frustrated. Most Jews were not convinced by their arguments. Quite the contrary, it seemed that occasions for Jewish-Christian debate sometimes led to the Jews' triumph, placing in jeopardy Christians of "simple faith." The failure of rational philosophical polemics led to a more dangerous strategy that alleged the irrationality of the Jews. At times this allegation was based on the contention that Jews ignored both empirical evidence and the testimony of reason. For example, the Cistercian monk Amédée (Bishop of Lausanne from 1144), complained that the Jews irrationally (*irrationabiliter*) still await the messiah's coming, even though the empirical evidence of the Church's triumph and the Jews' exile and miserable servitude demonstrate clearly that the messiah has *already* come.[85]

This appeal to the experience of exile did not destroy the messianic hopes of Jewish communities, however. But if Jews could not be persuaded by this appeal to experience, some Christian polemicists inferred, neither

---

83. In his *Epistola de Incarnatione Verbi* 6, in vol. 2 of *Opera omnia*, 20, Anselm notes that the existence of the God of the Trinity has been demonstrated to the reader in both his *Proslogion* and *Monologion* by "necessary reasons." For the various senses in which the reader may understand a proof determined according to necessary reasons (which extend from the conclusions of a deductive syllogism to conclusions that are deemed fitting or suitable) see Victor W. Roberts, "The Relation of Faith and Reason in St. Anselm of Canterbury," *American Benedictine Review* 25 (1974): 494–512. On Anselm's undestanding of reason, faith, and truth in the *Proslogion*, see Yves Cattin, "Proslogion et De Veritate, 'Ratio, Fides, Veritas,'" in *Les mutations socio-culturelles au tournant des XIe-XIIe siècles*, Actes du Colloque international du CNRS, Études Anselmiennes (IVe session) (Paris: Editions du Centre national de la recherche scientifique, 1984), 595–610.

84. *Monologion* 64, in vol. 1 of *Opera omnia*, 75. On the sense implied by necessary reasons see also Paul Vignaux, "Nécessité des raisons dans le *Monologion*," *Revue des sciences philosophiques et théologiques* 64, no.1 (1980): 3–25.

85. Amédée de Lausanne, *Huit Homélies Mariales*, Hom. 4.163–165, ed. Jean Deshusses and trans. Antoine Dumas, SC 72, Série des Textes Monastiques d'Occident 5 (Paris: Les Éditions du Cerf, 1960), 122.

were they subject to reasoned arguments. Peter the Venerable (d. 1156) remarked in frustration in his *Against the Inveterate Obduracy of the Jews,*

> Surely I do not know whether a Jew, who does not submit to human reason nor acquiesce to prooftexts that are both divine and his own, is human. I do not know, I say, whether he is a human, from whose flesh a heart of stone (cf. Ezek. 36:26) has not yet been removed, to whom a heart of flesh has not yet been granted, in whose midst (*medio*) the divine spirit has not yet been placed, without which a Jew can never be converted to Christ.[86]

Peter's doubts about the Jews' rationality led him to associate them more with animals than other humans, because "that rational faculty that separates a human from the other animals or wild beasts and gives precedence over them is extinct, or rather buried, in you.... Now why should you not be called a wild animal, why not a beast, why not a beast of burden?"[87] Despite their earlier exalted status as a chosen people, Peter laments, the Jews have become worse than pagans and worse even than demons.[88] Their willful ignorance, their "bovine intellect"[89] and their peculiar form of "insanity,"[90] lead him to characterize Jews as more like devils or beasts than men.[91]

Centuries earlier Isidore of Seville (d. 636) had alluded to the herdlike, bestial nature of Jews by invoking an etymology. He remarks that Christians gather in a church or *ecclesia,* a Greek term that in Latin means "convocation," because the church calls (*convocare*) all together. By contrast, he notes, the term *synagoga,* which the Jews use to identify their religious community, means "congregation." The apostles never called the church a synagogue because there is a difference between a "congregation" and a "convocation." Cattle, properly speaking, gather in "herds" (*grex,* gen. *gregis*) and therefore animals are said to "congregate" (*congregare*). It is more fitting for those who use human reason, however, to be "convoked."[92] Peter the Venerable's emphasis on the Jews' irratio-

---

86. Peter the Venerable, *Adversus Judeorum inveteratam duritiem* 3, ed. Yvonne Friedman, CCCM 58 (Turnholt: Brepols, 1985), 58.
87. Peter the Venerable, *Adversus Judeorum* 5, 125. For a consideration of this text, see Anna Sapir Abulafia's "Twelfth-Century Renaissance Theology and the Jews," 135–37.
88. Peter the Venerable, *Adversus Judeorum* 2, 41, lns. 874–75.
89. Ibid., 3, 43, ln. 47.   90. Ibid., 3, 43, ln. 54.
91. Ibid., 3, 54, ln. 438.
92. Isidore of Seville, *The Etymologies of Isidore of Seville* 8.1.7, ed. and trans. Stephen A. Barney, W. J. Lewis, J. A. Beach, and Oliver Berghof (Cambridge: Cambridge University Press, 2006), 173.

nality reflects this "herd-like" character of Jewish communities. Their immunity to reasoned argument was a characteristic that Peter's Jews shared with heretical Petrobrusians—followers of Peter of Bruis—whom he had equally stigmatized in his *Against the Petrobrusians* (*Contra Petrobrusianos*; revised about 1139–41), for their bestial foolishness (*bestialis insipientia*) and profound stupidity (*profunda stultitia*). His slightly later *Against the Inveterate Obduracy of the Jews*, written from about 1144 to 1146 and likely revised in 1147, was composed in the context of the Second Crusade. In his well-known *Letter 130* to the French King Louis VII, in which Peter excuses himself from accompanying the king on crusade, Peter urged royal authority to punish the Jews in his realm not only for their usury but also for their ceaseless violence against Christ, whom they attack continuously with blasphemous words. The Jews of France had prospered and, by the middle of the twelfth century, had established an important rabbinical school and a large Jewish community in Paris itself.[93] Let their wealth, Peter contends, be taken and put to good use during the Second Crusade in order to prevail over the Saracens.[94] Peter's anti-Jewish polemic, then, was wedded to policy recommendations that this powerful abbot of Cluny delivered to the king.

The Saracens concerned Peter at least as much as the Jews and the heretical Petrobrusians, and were themselves the subject of two additional later polemical compositions: his *Summary of the Complete Heresy and of the Diabolical Sect of the Saracens or Ishmaelites* (*Summa totius haeresis ac diabolicae sectae Sarracenorum sive Hismahelitarum*), which describes Islam for a Christian audience, and his *Against the Saracen Sect or Heresy* (*Contra sectam sive haeresim Saracenorum*), which attempts to refute Islam on its own ground.[95] Nevertheless, Peter's harshest condemnation

93. See Gérard Nahon, "Didascali, Rabbins et Écoles du Paris Médiéval 1130–71," in *Rashi et la culture juive en France du Nord au moyen âge*, ed. Gilbert Dahan, Gérard Nahon, and Elie Nicholas (Paris-Louvain: Peeters, 1997), 15–31. Nahon speculates that the Jewish population in Paris c. 1180 may have reached 1000, or about 20 percent of the total population (17).

94. Peter the Venerable, *Letter 130, Ad Ludovicum Francorum Regem*, in vol. 1 of *The Letters of Peter the Venerable*, 2 vols., ed. Giles Constable (Cambridge, Mass.: Harvard University Press, 1967), 330.

95. For the Latin text, see James Kritzeck, *Peter the Venerable and Islam* (Princeton, N.J.: Princeton University Press, 1964). For criticism and corrections to Kritzeck's Latin text, see Jean-Pierre Torrell, "La notion de prophètie et la méthode apologétique dans le *Contra Saracenos* de Pierre le Vénérable," *Studia Monastica* 17 (1975), Appendix (281–82). For a useful review of Kritzeck's arguments, see also Allan Cutler, "Peter the Venerable and

seems reserved for the Jews, an enemy in the bosom of Christendom. This suggests a hardening attitude toward Jews, since in a letter from 1063 Pope Alexander II clearly distinguished the Jews from the Saracens and their threat. Alexander praised the bishops of Spain for defending the Jews from Christians travelling to Spain to battle the Saracens. Jews and Saracens were not to be treated in the same way, he cautioned. "The situation of the Jews and the Saracens is entirely different. One justly engages in battle against the latter, who persecute Christians and expel them from their cities and their very own sees, whereas the former are everywhere prepared to serve [Christians]."[96] Pope Alexander's distinction notwithstanding, Peter the Venerable had come to view the Jews, it seems, as the greater danger.

Although Peter's *Against the Inveterate Obduracy of the Jews* did not see widespread distribution, nonetheless its content may well have enjoyed a wider audience than the number of manuscript copies might indicate, since Cluny in the mid-twelfth century was at the center of an extensive network of Benedictine monasteries and, as such, it was frequently visited by other abbots, priors or monks, as well as by important laymen from across Europe.[97] Peter's attack on the rationality of the Jews, then, likely influenced a much wider circle. Dominque Iogna-Prat adds, moreover, that "By asking apparently rhetorically whether the Jews were really human, Peter the Venerable unwittingly laid one of the essential stones in the road that led from anti-Judaism to anti-Semitism."[98]

Islam," *Journal of the American Oriental Society* 86 (1966): 184–98. For a discussion of the two texts, see also John Tolan, "Peter the Venerable on the 'Diabolical Heresy of the Saracens,'" in *The Devil, Heresy and Witchcraft in the Middle Ages: Essays in Honor of Jeffrey B. Russell*, ed. Alberto Ferreiro, 345–67 (Leiden: Brill, 1998).

96. "Dispar nimirum est Judaeorum et Sarracenorum causa. In illos enim, qui Christianos persequuntur et ex urbibus et propriis sedibus pellunt, juste pugnatur; hi vero ubique parati sunt servire." *The Apostolic See and the Jews. Documents: 492–1404*, 8 vols., ed. Shlomo Simonsohn (Toronto: Pontifical Institute of Mediaeval Studies, 1988), 1:35. For Anna Sapir Abulafia, that the Jews are to *serve* the interests of Christendom emerges as the principal justification for their tolerated minority status in the Middle Ages, even more important than their role as reluctant witnesses to Christian truth. See her *Christian-Jewish Relations 1000–1300: Jews in the Service of Medieval Christendom* (Harlow, Eng.: Pearson Education, 2011).

97. The editor, Yvonne Friedman, identified only four manuscripts; three were completed within a generation or two of the text's composition. See *Adversus Judeorum inveteratam duritiem*, xxviii.

98. Dominque Iogna-Prat, *Order and Exclusion: Cluny and Christendom Face Heresy, Judaism, and Islam (1000–1500)*, trans. Graham Robert Edwards (Ithaca, N.Y.: Cornell University Press, 2002), 319.

Indeed, although the text was not often cited in the Middle Ages, Peter's *Against the Inveterate Obduracy of the Jews* became something of a favorite among German anti-Semites of the early twentieth century.[99]

Some have argued that Peter's conclusion was anticipated at the beginning of the twelfth century even by Odo of Tournai. The fact that at the end of Odo's *Debate with the Jew, Leo,* Leo remains faithful to his own ancestral tradition, having rejected Odo's reasoned arguments, has been viewed as a sign of Jewish obstinacy and irrationality. Consequently, Jeremy Cohen concludes, "Odo's *Disputatio* begins to stigmatize Judaism as inherently irrational."[100] Similarly Anna Abulafia remarks that

> Odo's message is clear enough: Jews accuse Christians of being irrational because they believe that the Virgin Mary gave birth to Jesus who was God and Man. But the ones who are irrational are the Jews themselves. They willfully refuse to accept Christianity because they prefer their literal interpretation of the Bible to exercising reason. As such they are more like animals who lack reason than men.[101]

Since rationality is a defining feature of humanity, Odo, Abulafia concludes, seems determined to deprive Jews of their humanity.

A tendency to dehumanize the Jews spread in the twelfth century in tandem with efforts to demonstrate, rationally, Christian truths. It spread either among those who despaired of the possibility of rational demonstration, or among those who arrogantly considered that they had accomplished the task, whereas the Jews inexplicably continued in their error nonetheless. Thinkers of the twelfth-century renaissance "thought reason was the hallmark of human beings, separating humans from animals, [therefore] they were led to conclude that those who could not accept their rational conclusions about Christianity were not really human." Therefore, "[Jews and heretics] were not only thought to be excluded from salvation in a religious sense; they were seen to be falling outside the parameters of humanity as well."[102]

---

99. See Theodor Fritsch, *Handbuch der Judenfrage: Die wichtigsten Tatsachen zur Beurteilung des jüdischen Volkes,* 40th ed. (Leipzig: Hammer Verlag, 1937), passim.

100. Jeremy Cohen, *Living Letters of the Law: Ideas of the Jew in Medieval Christianity* (Berkeley: University of California Press, 1999), 191.

101. Anna Sapir Abulafia, "Christian Imagery of Jews in the Twelfth Century: A Look at Odo of Cambrai and Guibert of Nogent," *Theoretische Geschiedenis* (= *Historiography and Theory*) 16, no. 4 (1989): 383–91, citing 386.

102. Anna Sapir Abulafia, *Christians and Jews in the Twelfth Century Renaissance* (London: Routledge, 1995), 6, 124. For intellectual context, see Abulafia, "The Intellectual and

Although elsewhere I have rejected the view that Odo of Tournai provided a foundation for this new development, nonetheless there will emerge a growing perception in Christian circles that rational discourse with Jews is impossible.[103] Certainly philosophical and theological disputation with the Jews contained a threat or danger: namely, that the Jews would succeed in converting Christians, and not vice versa. William of Malmesbury (d. c. 1143) reports with dismay that King William Rufus of England (d. 1100), who had accepted money from converted Jews to allow them to return to Judaism, joked at one such disputation in London that if the Jews should overcome his bishops with argument, he would become a Jew himself.[104] For Jews, the threat also existed that Jews might be persuaded by Christian opponents. Thus the twelfth- to thirteenth-century *Sefer Chasidim* (*The Book of the Pious*), perhaps the most important historical source for the depiction of everyday Jewish life in medieval Germany, warned that an unlearned Jew should not enter into religious debate with a priest, monk, or heretic.[105] In the same spirit, two twelfth-century Christian polemicists, Bartholomew of Exeter (d. 1184) and Peter of Blois (d. c. 1212), cautioned their readers or disciples to eschew public disputations with Jews. In Bartholomew's *Dialogue Directed against the Jews for [the Christian's] Correction and Perfection* (*Dialogus contra Judaeos ad corrigendum et perficiendum destinatus*), the Christian teacher remarks:

None of the faithful, who possesses a zeal for God with understanding, should endure their [that is, Jews'] calumnies or blasphemies without any rebuttal, but neither should he strive with them before unbelievers or those who are untutored in the faith. For just so often as we converse with them for their salvation, so always do they obstruct the undertaking in the common manner

---

Spiritual Quest for Christ and Central Medieval Persecution of Jews," in *Religious Violence between Christians and Jews: Medieval Roots, Modern Perspectives,* ed. Anna Sapir Abulafia (New York: Palgrave, 2002), 61–85.

103. Irven M. Resnick, "Odo of Tournai and the Dehumanization of Medieval Jews: A Reexamination," *Jewish Quarterly Review* 98, no. 4 (2008): 471–84.

104. For the accusation that King William Rufus allowed converted Jews to return to Judaism, for a money payment, see William of Malmesbury, *De gestis pontificum Anglorum* 1.55, ed. N. E. S. A. Hamilton (London: Longman, 1870), 104, n. 1; for the claim that he would become a Jew himself should Jews prevail in a disputation, see William of Malmesbury, *Gesta regum Anglorum atque Historia Novella* 4.317, 2 vols., ed. Thomas Duffus Hardy (London: 1840), 2: 500.

105. Rabbi Yehudah HeChasid, *Sefer Chasidim: The Book of the Pious* 651 (296), trans. Avraham Yaakov Finkel (Northvale, N.J.: Jason Aronson, 1997), 366.

of restless animals, unwilling to understand in order to act or believe as they should. Thus, so far as can be done with love unharmed, we ought to decline not only their meetings but even all conversations [with them].[106]

Peter of Blois, who elsewhere opines that it is a greater sin to *desire* to murder one's father than *actually* to murder a Jew,[107] expresses similar reservations about engaging in disputations with Jews and laments that even when Christians succeed in demonstrating their doctrines through arguments, demonstration cannot turn the Jew's heart.[108] Such reservations directly contradict the justification for the frequent public disputations held in the thirteenth century and later, or the compulsory sermons Jews will be compelled to attend in their synagogues for their conversion. (See figure 1.) If these were more than mere public entertainment, then one would expect Christian disputants and homilists to have assumed some possibility of correcting the Jews in attendance.[109] Instead, Guerric of Saint-Quentin (d. 1245) remarks that the Jews' malicious obstinacy is so well known that there is no point is disputing with them except to make known their errors to others and to strengthen Christian faith.[110] Moreover, in his *Memoirs of Louis IX,* the chronicler John de Joinville (d. 1318) records a revealing anecdote concerning France's King, Saint Louis IX

---

106. "Magister. Nullus fidelium qui zelum dei habeat cum scientia eorum [sc. Iudeorum] calumnias seu blasfemias sine aliqua redarguitione sustinet, sed nec cum ipsis coram infidelibus vel imperitis de fide contendit. Quotiens enim cum eis pro ipsorum etiam salute conferimus, inquietorum animalium more commune negotium semper impediunt, nolentes intelligere ut bene agant vel credunt. Unde quantum salva caritate fieri potest, eorum non solum collationes, sed et colloquia universa declinare debemus." For this text, see Richard William Hunt, "The Disputation of Peter of Cornwall Against Symon the Jew," in *Studies in Medieval History Presented to Frederick Maurice Powicke*, ed. R. W. Hunt, et al. (Oxford: Clarendon Press, 1948), 148.

107. Peter of Blois, *The Later Letters of Peter of Blois* 30A, ed. Elizabeth Revell, Auctores Britannici Medii Aevi 13 (Oxford: Oxford University Press, 1993), 158.

108. Peter of Blois, *Contra perfidiam Judaeorum* 1 (PL 207: 827A).

109. The literature on the public disputations is extensive. However, a useful starting point is Hyman Maccoby's translation of primary source materials in his *Judaism on Trial: Jewish-Christian Disputations in the Middle Ages* (London: Littman Library of Jewish Civilization, 1993). For Latin and Hebrew source documents for the second half of the thirteenth century (the second Parisian disputation), see also Joseph Shatzmiller, *La deuxième controverse de Paris. Un chapitre dans la polémique entre chrétiens et juifs au Moyen Age* (Paris: Peeters, 1994). For the famous Barcelona disputation (1263), see especially Robert Chazan, *Barcelona and Beyond: The Disputation of 1263 and its Aftermath* (Berkeley: University of California Press, 1992).

110. *Quaestiones de quolibet* q. 3.art. 3.63, ed. Walter H. Principe, rev. Jonathan Black, Studies and Texts 143 (Toronto: Pontifical Institute of Mediaeval Studies, 2002), 223.

(d. 1270). Although the saintly king encouraged public disputations with the Jews, he conceded that a disputation at Cluny at which a Jew repudiated the Christian doctrine of the virgin birth could lead Christians astray, causing him to remark that "no one, unless he be a very learned clerk, should dispute with them [the Jews]; but a layman, when he hears the Christian law mis-said, should not defend the Christian law, unless it be with his sword, and with that he should pierce the mis-sayer in the midriff, so far as the sword will enter."[111] When rational discourse fails, it seems, the sword still presents the most effective argument.

It is difficult to know how seriously to treat complaints of Jewish irrationality. One must note that it was not Christian polemicists alone who sought to delegitimize the Jewish "Other" with the criticism that the Jews' doctrines or beliefs violated the standards of reason. Twelfth-century Jewish polemics also depicted Christians as irrational, turning the Christian argument back against them.[112] Nonetheless, Christian polemicists like Peter the Venerable subscribed to an implied syllogism: Man is a rational animal; Jews cannot be convinced by reason; they are, therefore, inhuman. If in the twelfth century some Christian polemicists

---

111. The text appears in Jacob Rader Marcus, *The Jew in the Medieval World: A Sourcebook, 315–1791*, rev. ed., introd. Marc Saperstein (Cincinnati: Hebrew Union College Press, 1999), 46–47. Laura Hollengreen has pointed to "the clear visual cultivation of violence" in the Morgan Picture Bible (produced in Paris during Louis's reign) as a reflection of the king's policy against the Jews. See her "The Politics and Poetics of Possession: Saint Louis, the Jews, and Old Testament Violence," in *Between the Picture and the Word: Manuscript Studies from the Index of Christian Art*, ed. Colum Hourihane (Princeton, N.J.: Index of Christian Art, Dept. of Art and Archaeology, Princeton University, in association with Penn State University Press, 2005), 51–71; 90–115.

112. See Gilbert Dahan's "L'usage de la *ratio* dans la polémique contres les juifs, XIIe-XIVe siècles," in *Diálogo Filosófico-Religioso Entre Christianismo, Judaísmo e Islamismo Durante La Edad Media En La Península Ibérica*, ed. Horacio Santiago-Otero, S.I.E.P.M. 3 (Turnout: Brepols, 1994), 289–91. One such Jewish polemic to dismiss Christians (or their doctrines) as irrational was Jacob ben Reuben's *Milḥamot ha Shem*, written c. 1170. For discussion, see Rolf Schmitz, "Jacob ben Rubén y su obra Milḥamot ha-Šem," in *Polémica Judeo-Cristiana Estudios*, ed. Carlos del Valle Rodriguez (Madrid: Aben Ezra Ediciones, 1992), 45–58. Perhaps this criticism that Christians were irrational was itself a Jewish response to a perceived new Christian emphasis on reason. For discussion, see Daniel Lasker, "Jewish-Christian Polemics at the Turning Point: Jewish Evidence from the Twelfth Century," *Harvard Theological Review* 89, no. 2 (1996): 161–73. But note too Lasker's contention that Jewish philosophical polemics, appealing primarily to reason and not to Scripture or tradition, were more common in Sephardi than in Ashkenazi medieval culture. See Daniel Lasker, "Jewish Philosophical Polemics in Ashkenaz," in *Contra Iudaeos. Ancient and Medieval Polemics Between Christians and Jews*, ed. Ora Limor and Guy G. Stroumsa (Tübingen: Mohr, 1996), 195–213.

had begun to doubt that Jews fully participated in reason, then certainly the door was opened to increasingly animal or bestial depictions of the Jew. In late antiquity, St. Augustine (d. 430) had described the human as existing midway between angels and the beasts, sharing rationality with angels, and mortality with beasts.[113] But if the Jews' rationality is imperfect, then their souls are defective and they will undoubtedly draw closer to the beasts in their physical appearance as well, having fallen a greater distance from the ranks of angels and men.

Perhaps, like the higher animals, they may employ a "shadow" or practical reason that enables them to perform certain functions, even to imitate the arts, but they will fall short of that contemplative or speculative reason that is the hallmark of perfected humanity.[114] Or perhaps theirs will be a "weaker" reason, like that possessed by Eve before the fall, according to Peter Lombard's *Sentences*, and by all women descended from her, according to the twelfth-century *Parisian Sentences* (*Sententie Parisiensis*).[115] Because Eve allowed herself to be persuaded by the serpent, who symbolized the bestial and demonic orders below the human, a change appears too in the manner in which Eve is depicted in twelfth-century art. In a shift from older theriomorphic depictions, in twelfth-century illustrations the serpent in the Garden will increasingly be depicted with the head of a woman—usually an attractive woman, even virginal in appearance—based on the philosophical principle that

---

113. *De civ. Dei* 9.13.3, CCSL 47.1 (Turnholt: Brepols, 1955), 261.

114. For this notion that the more perfect animals participate in a "shadow" of reason that enables the animal to be trained to certain tasks and even to learn from experience, see the discussion of Albert the Great, *De animalibus* 21.1.2.11, vol. 16, 1327–28 (SZ 2: 1416–17). For discussion of the medieval concept of "shadow reason," see also Peter G. Sobol, "The Shadow of Reason: Explanations of Intelligent Animal Behavior in the Thirteenth Century," in *The Medieval World of Nature: A Book of Essays*, ed. Joyce E. Salisbury (New York: Garland, 1993), 109–28.

115. Peter Lombard, *In 2 Sententiarum* dist. 21, 1(122), 2. The serpent approached Eve rather than Adam because her reason was "weaker" than his: "hostis accessit ad mulierem, in qua minorem rationis vigorem esse sciebat." *Sententia Parisienses*, in *Écrits théologiques de l'école d'Abélard. Textes inédits*, ed. Artur Landgraf, Spicilegium sacrum Lovaniense, études et documents fasc. 14 (Louvain: 1934), 111. Cf. this same passage in the *Sententie Anselmi* [of Laon], in *Anselms von Laon systematische Sentenzen*, ed. Franz Pl. Bliemetzrieder, Beiträge zur Geschichte der Philosophie des Mittelalters 18 (Münster i. W.: Aschendorff, 1919), 2–3, fol. 47c, 60. Thomas Aquinas confirms too that the serpent approached Eve rather than Adam because she signifies sensual pleasure that is associated with an inferior rationality: "in ratione inferior, quae signatur per mulierum, delectatio." See *Summa theologica* 2.2, q. 165, art. 2, sed contra.

"like is attracted to like." In other words, because sin had to be attractive to Eve, it had to appear in a tempting guise—almost an image of herself, except for the serpent's scaly lower body. Just as the serpent's maidenly countenance attracted Eve, so too Eve's countenance produced in Adam sensual desire. Yet, like Adam, men who submit to bodily appetite lose the form of men and become womanish in their behavior, because they are estranged from reason's perfection.[116]

Just as women embody a "weaker" reason or represent the lower, sense principle, so too do children who, according to Albert the Great, are rather like intermediaries between brute beasts and humans, both because they have not yet perfected their rationality and because their moist or humid complexion results in disordered sense experience.[117] Similarly, Jews too are more material, more tied to the body, the senses, and the vices. But when humans subordinate reason to carnal and material concerns, avers William of St. Thierry (d. 1148), "[They] have put off the image of the Creator and have put on another image, one that looks at the ground like an animal, one that is beastly."[118] When confronted by Christian arguments and proof texts, remarks Peter of Blois, the protean Jew always shifts and changes his response, and transforms himself into monstrous shapes like his father, the devil.[119] They are, he insists, a stiff-necked people marked by a bestial obstinacy.[120] Their carnality encouraged the comparison between Jews and beasts since, as Peter Abelard's (d. 1142) "Philosopher" concluded, "Surely, it is the Jews alone that are moved to faith only by miraculous, external deeds, because they are animals and sensual and are imbued with no philosophy whereby they are able to discuss reasoned arguments."[121]

116. Nona C. Flores, "'Effigies amicitiae . . . veritas inimicitae': Antifeminism in the Iconography of the Woman-Headed Serpent in Medieval and Renaissance Art and Literature," in *Animals in the Middle Ages: A Book of Essays*, ed. Nona C. Flores (New York: Garland, 1996), 187–88.

117. Albert the Great, *Quaestiones super de animalibus* 7.2, 171, 18–31, 52–60 (QDA, 228–29).

118. William of St. Thierry, *The Nature of the Body and Soul* 2.5, trans. Benjamin Clark, in *Three Treatises on Man*, 133.

119. "Judaeus enim inconstans est semper et varius . . . et in modum patris sui diaboli se in monstruosas species saepius transfigurat." *Contra perfidiam Judaeorum* 28 (PL 207: 870C–D).

120. "populo durae cervicis atque pertinaciae vere bestialis." *Contra perfidiam Judaeorum* 1 (PL 207: 827C).

121. "Judaei quippe tantum, quod animales sunt et sensuales, nulla imbuti philosophia,

Because of their carnality, Jews will not only to be likened to animals but to women as well. Thus Peter Damian (d. 1072) complained that the Jews who lived during the apostolic age lived "in a womanly manner."[122] Lack of faith and carnality both defined Jews as "womanish." As early as the middle of the third century, Origen had remarked that "sex is no distinction in the presence of God, but a person is designated either a man or woman according to the diversity of spirit ... that man must be judged among 'women' who says, 'I am not able to observe those things that are written.'"[123] A man that finds the requirements of religious life too difficult, then, is dismissed as womanly. Conversely, St. Jerome (d. 420) remarked that "so long as a woman serves childbirth and children, she is as different from man as body is from soul. But if she would instead serve Christ rather than the world, she will cease to be a woman and will be called man, because we all want to attain to the perfect man."[124] These authors lend support to Lisa Lampert's contention that the "believing Christian subject is posited as normatively masculine ... [and] a believing woman is figured as transcending her sex as she achieves salvation."[125] This is because spirituality will be viewed as a perfection naturally belonging to the male, while carnality and materiality will characterize females who, we recall, are "flawed males." Thus, Peter Lombard (d. c. 1160) adds that "typically Sacred Scripture signifies the

---

qua rationes discutere queant, solis exteriorum operum miraculis moventur ad fidem." Peter Abelard, *Dialogus inter philosophum, Judaeum et Christianum* (PL 178: 1637D; cf. *Collationes*, 2.69, ed. and trans. John Marenbon and Giovanni Orlandi (Oxford: Clarendon Press, 2001), 86.

122. Peter Damian, Epist. 126.19, in *Die Briefe des Petrus Damiani*, 3: 419; for translation see *The Letters of Peter Damian, 121–150*, trans. Owen Blum and Irven M. Resnick, Fathers of the Church, Mediaeval Continuation 6 (Washington, D.C.; The Catholic University of America Press, 2004), 38. For Damian and the Jews, see David Berger, "St. Peter Damian. His Attitudes toward the Jews and the Old Testament," *Yavneh* 4 (1965): 80–112.

123. Origen, *Homilies on Joshua* 9.8, trans. Barbara J. Bruce, ed. Cynthia White, The Fathers of the Church 105 (Washington, D.C.: The Catholic University of America Press, 2002), 106–7.

124. "Quamdiu mulier partui servit et liberis, hanc habet ad virum differentiam, quam corpus ad animam. Sin autem Christo magis voluerit servire quam saeculo, mulier esse cessabit, et dicetur vir, quia omnes in perfectum virum cupimus occurrere." *Commentariorum in Epistolam ad Ephesios* 3.5.28 (PL 26:533). The commentary was composed in the late 380s. For Origenist sources in the commentary, see Elizabeth A. Clark, "The Place of Jerome's Commentary on Ephesians in the Origenist Controversy: The Apokatastasis and Ascetic Ideals," *Vigiliae Christianae* 41, no. 2 (1987): 154–71.

125. Lisa Lampert, *Gender and Jewish Difference from Paul to Shakespeare* (Philadelphia: University of Pennsylvania Press, 2004), 27.

soul through the male sex and the flesh (*carnis*) through the female."[126] By the twelfth century, one finds a clear link between carnality or promiscuous sexuality and effeminacy. In a description of the court of King William Rufus, William of Malmesbury complains of nobles that had been influenced by the prodigal and liberal spirit of the king's court and, having been released from military discipline, had become unmanned, soft like women, and affected a mincing gait and effeminate gestures.[127] Analogously, like *Synagoga*, a symbol for the Jewish community that was often compared to sinful, fallen women like Delilah and Jezebel and consistently depicted by the thirteenth century as a blindfolded (albeit beautiful) woman,[128] Jews were unmanned by their lack of faith. In like manner, Jacques de Vitry (d. 1240), Bishop of Acre and later Cardinal-Bishop of Tusculum, complains that contemporary Jews "have become unwarlike and as weak as women."[129] Peter Biller has demonstrated that Jacques de Vitry borrowed his description from an anonymous text of

126. "quia sacra Scriptura per masculinum sexum animam, per feminam vero carnem significare consueverit." *In 4 Sententiarum* dist. 4, q. 2, art. 2, sed contra. The Lombard attributes this remark to Hugh of St. Victor, *De sacramentis* 1.12.11. Cf. Thomas Aquinas, *In IV Sententiarum* dist. 1, q. 2, art. 2, qc 2, sed contra.

127. William of Malmesbury, *Gesta regum Anglorum atque Historia Novella* 4.314, 2: 498.

128. *Synagoga* is surely depicted most often as female because "synagoga" is a feminine Latin noun, but this is certainly not the only (or even the most important) reason. For *Synagoga* depicted as a beautiful women, when properly subjected to the guidance and instruction of *Ecclesia*, see Nina Rowe, "Idealization and Subjection at the South Façade of the Strasbourg Cathedral," in *Multicultural Europe and Cultural Exchange in the Middle Ages and Renaissance*, ed. James P. Helfers, Arizona Studies in the Middle Ages and Renaissance 12 (Turnholt: Brepols, 2005), 179–201. In the same volume, cf. Elizabeth Monroe, "'Fair and Friendly, Sweet and Beautiful': Hopes for Jewish Conversion in Synagoga's Song of Songs Imagery," 33–61. For a useful introduction to Synagoga imagery and symbolism, see Wolfgang S. Seiferth, *Synagogue and Church in the Middle Ages: Two Symbols in Art and Literature*, trans. Lee Chadeayne and Paul Gottwald (New York: Ungar, 1970). It seems suggestive too that images from Notre-Dame in Paris and Saint Sernin in Bourdeaux (c. 1300) show *Synagoga's* eyes veiled by the tail of a serpent or dragon, evoking a link to Eve, the serpent's bimorphism, and the Jews. See Sara Lipton, "The Temple is My Body: Gender, Carnality, and Synagoga in the Bible moralisée," in *Imagining the Self, Imagining the Other*, ed. Eva Frojmovic (Leiden: Brill, 2002), 153ff.; Seiferth, *Synagogue and Church in the Middle Ages*, 99.

129. "Judaei. . . . Imbelles enim et imbecilles facti sunt quasi mulieres." *Historia Orientalis* 82, ed. F. Moschus (Douai: B. Belleri, 1597), 159. The author also dismisses contemptuously the first generation Latin Christians (*pullani*) born in the Crusader kingdom as weak and effeminate, more accustomed to baths than battles, given over to lust and uncleanness, and clothed more like women than men: "Pullani . . . molles et effeminati, balneis plusquam preliis assueti, immuniditie et luxurie dediti, more mulierum mollibus induti." See his *Historia Orientalis* 73, 133.

the late twelfth century, the *Treatise on the Places and Condition of the Holy Land of Jerusalem* (*Tractatus de locis et statu sancte terre ierosolimitane*). After noting the diversity of Christians living in the Holy Land, this Crusader text examines non-Christians dwelling there. "The first of these are the Jews. Obstinate men; unwarlike, even more than women; everywhere serfs; suffering a flow of blood every month."[130] Their obstinacy is of course reflected in their failure to submit to reasoned argument or to evidence drawn from Scripture or experience. The additional claim that they are "unwarlike" was hardly complimentary, especially to an age that exalted the status of the holy warrior. There was some basis for this claim: Bishop Ivo of Chartres (r. 1090–1116) explains that Jews have lost all dignity as warriors because they do not have license to bear arms.[131] But the complaint goes far beyond the historical evidence, which indicates that at times of crisis Jews did defend themselves and their communities. In a lengthy Hebrew chronicle of the First Crusade, some members of the Jewish community under the leadership of R. Kalonymous of Mainz confronted the crusader army of Count Emicho and "donned armor and strapped on weapons ... [but] did not have sufficient strength to stand up before the enemy."[132] By way of contrast, Albert of Aachen's (fl. c. 1100) *Jerusalemite History* (*Historia Ierosolimitana*), an account of the First Crusade, provides a notable example of Jewish military defense that was more successful, at least for a time. He reports that when Duke Tancred and his soldiers attacked Haifa "citizens of the Jewish race, who lived in the city by the favour and consent of the king of Egypt in return

130. "Quorum primi sunt Judei. homines obstinati. plus quam mulieres imbelles. ubique servi. singulis lunationibus fluxum sanguinis patientes." "Ein Tractat über das heilige Land und den dritten Kreuzzug," ed. G. M. Thomas, *Sitzungberichte der königlich bayerischen Akademie der Wissenschaften,* Philosophisch-philologische Classe (Munich: 1865), 158; transcribed from appendix A in Peter Biller's "A 'Scientific' View of Jews from Paris Around 1300," in *Gli Ebrei e le Scienze/The Jews and the Sciences, vol. 9 of Micrologus. Natura, scienze e società medievali* (Florence: SISMEL/ Edizioni de Galluzzo, 2001), 158.

131. *Decretum* 13:108; see *The Jews in the Legal Sources of the Early Middle Ages*, ed. Amnon Linder (Detroit: Wayne State University Press, 1997), 668.

132. Robert Chazan, *European Jewry and the First Crusade* (Berkeley: University of California Press, 1996), Appendix, 252. For a summary of the debate over Emicho's role in the violence, see Matthew Gabriele, "Against the Enemies of Christ: The Role of Count Emicho in the Anti-Jewish Violence of the First Crusade," in *Christian Attitudes toward Jews in the Middle Ages: A Casebook*, ed. Michael Frassetto (New York: Routledge, 2007), 61–82. For Millenarian enthusiasm as a motive factor in the anti-Jewish violence, see also Robert Chazan, "'Let Not a Remnant or a Residue Escape': Millenarian Enthusiasm in the First Crusade," *Speculum* 84, no. 2 (2009): 289–313.

for payment of tribute, got on the walls bearing arms and put up a very stubborn defence, until the Christians, weighed down by various blows over the period of two weeks, absolutely despaired and held back their hands from any attack."[133] He adds, without indicating surprise, that in response to the Christian assault "the Jewish citizens, mixed with Saracen troops, at once fought back manfully, ... and counter-attacked."[134]

Despite evidence that Jews could take up arms in self-defense and even fight back "manfully" (*viriliter*), as Albert of Aachen concedes, a stereotype of Jewish weakness and passivity spread. Christians disdained the Jews' suspect rationality and pacific nature as womanly; Jews, by contrast, sometimes attempted to transform this latter image into a badge of honor. In a Hebrew chronicle from France that has sometimes been identified as from the tenth century, the Jews of Le Mans rebuffed the count's demand that they select a champion for a trial by combat, to defend them against charges that included having fashioned a wax image of the count in order to destroy him. They proclaimed "Our lord, do not do this to your servants. For the custom of the Jews is not to do battle, as is the custom of the Gentiles."[135] These Jews saw the personal combat of the ordeal as a "Gentile" custom, and therefore implied that it was less than honorable. Christians took a very different view, and perceived the Jews' reluctance to do battle as a sign of a fainthearted, effeminate, emasculated nature—a depiction that passed into modern literature in Cervantes's (d. 1616) description of the Jews as a *gente afeminada*.[136]

---

133. "cives ex genere Iudaeorum, qui hanc inhabitabant dono et consensus Regis Babylonie in redditione tributorum, in armis et minibus exurgentes, multum in defensione obstiterunt, quousque Christiani variis plagis gravitati per dies quindecim prorsus diffisi ab omni assultu manus suas continuerunt." Albert of Aachen, *Historia Ierosolimitana* 7.23, ed. and trans. Susan B. Edgington (Oxford: Clarendon Press, 2007), 516.

134. "Quibus Iudei cives, commixtis Sarracenorum turmis, sine dilatione viriliter resistentes ... opposuerunt." Albert of Aachen, *Historia Ierosolimitana* 7.24, 521.

135. For the document, see *Church, State, and Jew in the Middle Ages*, ed. Robert Chazan (West Orange, N.J.: Behrman House, 1980), 299. On the use of wax images for magical purposes, see also Joshua Trachtenberg, *Jewish Magic and Superstition: A Study in Folk Religion* (Cleveland: World Publishing Company, 1961), 6–7. Trachtenberg also points out that medieval Jews did, on occasion, participate in the trial by combat (or hire Christians to defend them in such a process). See *Jewish Magic and Superstition*, 228–29.

136. See *Los Baños de Argel* (*The Baths of Algiers*), part 4. For discussion, see the useful article by Elliott Horowitz, "A 'Dangerous Encounter': Thomas Coryate and the Swaggering Jews of Venice." *Journal of Jewish Studies* 52, no. 2 (2001): 341–53. For masculinity in medieval texts, see also Vern L. Bullough and Gwen Whitehead Brewer, "Medieval Masculinities and Modern Interpretations: the Problem of the Pardoner," in *Conflicted Identities and*

Although other groups within Christian society, namely monks or members of the clergy in general, were not supposed to bear arms on the field of battle, their masculinity remained unchallenged.[137] They substituted spiritual battle and the weapons of the spirit for the soldier's instruments, and manfully engaged the forces of evil and sin in victorious combat.[138] Jews, however, bore neither the weapons of the spirit nor the weapons of the medieval knight. They shrink from all combat, in this cultural construction, and appear more like women than men, that is timid, unstable, and deceitful. Both their customs and their religious error unman the Jew. Guillaume le Clerc's (d. c. 1226) *Bestiaire* moralizes the sex-changing and corpse-eating hyena as a figure of the unclean Jews, remarking that "This beast [the hyena] . . . denotes the children of Israel, who at first firmly believed in the true father omnipotent, and held to him loyally, but afterward became as females."[139] In the Aberdeen bestiary (c. 1200), the hyena was also an animal said to imitate human speech—and therefore possessing a "shadow" reason—making it seem nearly human itself.[140] Just as the hyena could imitate the human voice and change from male to female, so too it seemed that Jews merely feigned humanity. Like the hyena, almost universally regarded as a sym-

---

Multiple Masculinities: Men in the Medieval West, ed. Jacqueline Murray (New York: Garland, 1999), 93–110.

137. Thus, Thomas of Chobham allows and remarks that "clerici non possunt arma ferre nisi sit eis transitus per locum insidiosum et in tempore discordie ad absterrendam et ad repellandam violentiam." Thomas de Chobham, *Summa Confessorum* art. 7, dist. 4, q. 6a, cap. 6, fol. 49vb, ed. F. Broomfield, Analecta mediaevalia Namurcensia 25 (Louvain: Éditions Nauwelaerts, 1968), 426–27.

138. For a useful discussion of masculinity and this spiritual combat, see Katherine Allen Smith, "Saints in Shining Armor: Martial Asceticism and Masculine Models of Sanctity, ca. 1050–1250," *Speculum* 83, no. 3 (2008): 572–602; and Barbara H. Rosenwein, "Feudal War and Monastic Peace: Cluniac Liturgy as Ritual Aggression," *Viator* 2 (1972): 129–57.

139. "Ceste beste [the hyena] . . . les fiz Israel signefie,/ Qui ben crurent premerement/ El verai pere omnipotent/E lealment a lui se tendrent,/mes apres femeles devindrent." Guillaume le Clerc, *Le Bestiaire,* intro. and glossary by Robert Reinsch, Altfranzösische Bibliothek 14 (Leipzig: O. R. Reisland, 1892), 292, lns. 1607–12. Guillaume le Clerc composed his long, versified Norman French bestiary c. 1211. This tradition is much older, however. Not only can it be located in the *Physiologus* 38, trans. Michael J. Curley (Austin: University of Texas Press, 1979), 53, but also in the second- or third-century *Epistle of Barnabas* (10.7), in which the author attributes to Moses a commandment not to become like nor to eat the hyena because it changes its nature from male to female. See Mary Pendergraft, "'Thou Shalt Not Eat the Hyena': A Note on 'Barnabas' Epistle 10.7," *Vigiliae Christianae* 46 (1992): 75–79.

140. See *The Aberdeen Bestiary,* fol. 11v, Aberdeen University Library MS 24, available at http://www.abdn.ac.uk/bestiary/translat/11v.hti.

bol of sexual aberration, Jews changed from male to female, and became a feminine symbol for medieval society.[141]

In spite of the intellectual accomplishments of some very remarkable twelfth-century women—for example, the abbess Hildegard of Bingen (d. 1179/80)[142] and Peter Abelard's lover and quondam student, Heloise (d. 1164)[143]—Jews were perceived to share with women carnality, unbridled sensual appetite, and a defective nature. Women in general remained descendents of Eve, whose "weaker" reason was more susceptible to the serpent's wiles in the Garden. As a result, one expects that all women descended from Eve will suffer from a similar defect. Scholastic theologians sometimes argued that while Adam was made in the image of God, Eve, having been fashioned from Adam's rib, only imperfectly reflected that image because hers was a mediated creation. Since God's image is located especially in the human intellect and reason, a woman's intellect is consequently weaker than a man's.[144] Although children too were viewed as not having the full use of reason, at length male children could perfect their rational faculty.[145] Especially as Aristotelian biology spread in the

141. John Boswell, *Christianity, Social Tolerance, and Homosexuality: Gay People in Western Europe from the Beginning of the Christian Era to the Fourteenth Century* (Chicago: University of Chicago Press, 1980), 305.

142. Hildegard became abbess of Disibodenberg until, in 1147, she and other nuns migrated to a new convent on the Rupertsberg, linked by a bridge to the medieval town of Bingen. Her scientific, encyclopedic interests are usefully outlined in Charles Singer, "The Scientific Views and Visions of Saint Hildegard of Bingen," in *Studies on the History and Method of Science*, 2nd ed (London: William Dawson and Sons, 1955), 1–55; Gertrude Engbring, "Saint Hildegard, Twelfth-Century Physician," *Bulletin of the History of Medicine* 8 (1940): 770–84; Laurence Moulinier, "Une encyclopédiste sans précédent? Le cas de Hildegarde de Bingen," in *L'enciclopedismo medievale: Atti del convegno 'L'enciclopedismo medievale', San Gimignano 8-10 Ottobre 1992*, ed. Michelangelo Picone (Ravenna: Longo, 1994), 119–34; and in a collection of essays found in *Hildegard of Bingen: A Book of Essays*, ed. Maud Burnett McInerny (New York: Garland, 1998).

143. Heloise was distinguished not only because of her remarkable liaison with Peter Abelard, but also by her devotion to learning and her knowledge of languages, which included Hebrew and Greek. For her knowledge of Hebrew, see Constant J. Mews, "Abelard and Heloise on Jews and *Hebraica Veritas*," in *Christian Attitudes toward Jews in the Middle Ages: A Casebook*, ed. Michael Frassetto (New York: Routledge, 2007), 97; and Peter Abelard, *Collationes*, xlvii.

144. William of Auxerre, *Summa Aurea* 2, tr. 9, cap. 1, q. 3, 6 vols., ed. Jean Ribailler, Spicilegium Bonaventurianum 16–20 (Grottaferrata : Collegii S. Bonaventurae ad Claras Aquas, 1980–87), 2: 232.

145. St. Antoninus of Florence cites the absence of a complete rational faculty in children to condemn the practice of baptizing Jewish children without their parents' consent. See *Summa theologica* 2, tit. 12, cap. 2, §4, 4 vols. (Verona: 1740; repr. Graz: Akademische Druck- u. Verlagsanstalt, 1959), 2:1149C–D.

thirteenth century, however, some Dominican and Franciscan masters in Paris, a city described by Caesarius of Heisterbach as "the fountain of all knowledge and the well of the Holy Scriptures," came to view women as inferior representatives of the species nature.[146] Indeed, as already noted, they are in actuality only an inferior or flawed nature (*occasio naturalis*)[147] and a "flawed" or "imperfect" male (*mas* or *vir occasionatus* or *imperfectus*).[148] Their defect is not only intellectual but also physiological and stems from a flaw in a woman's humoral complexion. Both Jews and women suffered in their reason and intellect the debilitating influence of a weaker complexion or humoral composition. Their bodies too reveal the effects thought to be revealed by their intellectual shortcomings. Among Jews, the clearest sign of their feminine character was located in the ritual of circumcision, a ritual that best defined them for the Christian community.

146. Caesarius of Heisterbach, *The Dialogue of Miracles* 5.22, 2 vols., trans. H. von E. Schott and C. C. Swinton Bland (London: George Routledge & Sons, 1929), 1: 347.

147. Aristotle, *De animalibus: Michael Scot's Arabic-Latin Translation; Part Three: Books XV-XIX: Generation of Animals*, 775a, ed. Aafke M. I. Van Oppenraaij (Leiden: Brill, 1992), 201.

148. For Aristotle's view on a woman as a flawed male, see Maryanne Cline Horowitz, "Aristotle and Women," *Journal of the History of Biology* 9 (1976): 183-213. For his medieval interpreters, see especially Paul Hossfeld, *Albertus Magnus über die Frau* (Bad Honnef: s.p. 1982); also Hossfeld, in *Trierer Theologische Zeitschrift* 3 (1982): 222-39; and Albert Mitterer, "Mas occasionatus: oder zwei Methoden der Thomasdeutung," *Zeitschrift für katholische Theologie* 72 (1950): 80-103. For medieval examples, see *Davidis de Dinanto Quaternulorum Fragmenta*, 23, lns. 13-14; Albert the Great, *Quaestiones super de animalibus* 3.22, 15.2, 135 and 260 (QDA,143 and 441); Albert the Great, *De animalibus* 3.2.8.158, 16.1.14.73, vol. 15, 347, and 16, 1100 (SZ 1: 421-22 and 2: 1195); Albert the Great, *Politica* 1.3, Ed. Borgnet 8, 28B; Thomas Aquinas, *De veritate* q. 5 a. 9 ad 9, *Super I Tim.* cap. 2 l. 3, *II Sententiarum* dist. 18, q. 1, art.1, sed contra 1, 3, and dist. 20, q. 2, art. 1, *IV Sententiarum* dist. 36, q. 1, art. 1, resp. ad, 2, ln., dist. 44, q. 1, art. 3, q. 3, arg. 3, *Summa theologica* 1a, q. 92 (but cf. Michael Nolan, "The Defective Male: What Aquinas Really Said," *New Blackfriars* 75 (1994): 156-65); see also *Problemata varia anatomica*, 67; Alexander of Hales, *Summa theologica* cap. 3, 573; cap. 3, contra 1, 620; Ps. Albert the Great, *De secretis mulierum* 5, 109; and the late fifteenth-century Henricus Institoris, *Malleus Maleficiarum*, which describes woman as an imperfect animal (*animal imperfectum*) and not merely a flawed man, and adds that in part this is because she is more carnal than a man. See Henricus Institoris, *Malleus Maleficiarum* 1, q. 6, col. 42C, 1: 286.

2

PHYSICAL DEFORMITIES AND CIRCUMCISION

The Jews' womanly nature was visibly represented by the emasculating ritual that best defined Jewish males as Jews: circumcision. Medieval Latin theologians and polemicists understood that scripture knows various forms of circumcision. Principally, they contrasted the carnal circumcision of the flesh demanded of males eight days after birth (Gen. 17:11) with that spiritual circumcision of the heart promised by God (Deut. 10:16; 30:6; Jer. 9:26). Circumcision of the flesh was required of all those who would participate in the covenant made with the patriarch Abraham (see Lev. 19:8; see figure 2), although its spiritual utility was understood to have ceased with the advent of the Christ. After the coming of the messiah, the Christian sacrament of baptism replaced circumcision to remove original sin. Nonetheless, a Christian should observe a *spiritual* circumcision by cutting off sin and vice, which act the old circumcision of the flesh was said to symbolize.[1] As a result, a ninth-century (?) homily proclaims,

1. For typical expositions of the Christian position on circumcision in contrast to Judaism, see the popular *Altercatio Ecclesiae et Synagogae* (fifth century?), ed. J. N. Hillgarth, CCSL 69A (Turnholt: Brepols, 1999), 33–34; Ps. William of Champeaux, *Dialogus inter christianum et judaeum de fide catholica* (PL 163: 1045–48D). William (c.1070–1121), a French scholastic philosopher, studied and taught in Paris; in 1109 he founded the monastic school of St. Victor. From 1113 until his death in 1121 he was bishop of Châlons-en-Champagne. This work was addressed, however, to Alexander, Bishop of Lincoln from 1123–47, and therefore could not have been composed by William. For a discussion, see Anna Sapir Abulafia, *Christians and Jews in the Twelfth Century Renaissance* (London: Routledge, 1995), 74. For other treatments, see Peter Lombard. *Sentences* 4, dist. 1, part 2, chaps. 7–10; and Thomas Aquinas, *Scriptum super Sententiis* 4, dist. 1, q. 2, art. 1, resp.

"We are the true Jews, that is confessors [of Christ], who cut off not a piece of a single member but rather the vices of the entire body."[2]

Three circumcisions were identified in a text attributed to the twelfth-century Anselm of Laon (d. 1117) or his "school": one of the flesh of the male member alone, performed with a stone knife to symbolize the hard-heartedness of the Jews and intended to "cut off" concupiscence; a second circumcision of the soul alone accomplished by baptism for the remission of sins; and a third of flesh and soul together in the eighth age (that is, at the Resurrection), when the flesh will be rendered immune to desire and the soul will be separated from all vice.[3] The thirteenth-century Dominican Raymund Martini (1236–86) noted that the Old Testament identifies four different types of foreskin or prepuce, and therefore four different forms of circumcision as well. These four are the foreskin of the heart (Deut. 10:16), lips (cf. Ex. 6:12), ears (Jer. 6:10), and the foreskin of the male member (Gen. 17:11). It remains profitable even now, he insists, for Christians to "circumcise" the heart, lips and ears—that is, to guard them from all vice and sin.[4] The circumcision of the flesh of the male member alone he condemned as not only useless now but even harmful spiritually (cf. 1 Cor. 7:19; Gal. 5:6; 6:15), since the true circumcision is that of the spirit (Phil. 3:3). Consistent with Robert Grosseteste's claim that the observances of the Law are not merely superfluous but pernicious,[5] the Dominican Thomas Aquinas (d. 1274) and the Franciscan Duns Scotus (d. 1308) agreed that the rite of circumcision of the flesh is a

---

2. "Nos enim sumus ueri Iudei, hoc est confessores, qui non unius membri particulam, sed totius carnis uitia resecamus." *Homiliarium Veronense* 3, ed. Lawrence T. Martin, CCCM 186 (Turnholt: Brepols, 2000), 40.

3. Anselm of Laon, *Anselms von Laon systematische Sentenzen*, 35, 88–89. For some discussion of Anselm of Laon and his "school," see R. W. Southern, *Scholastic Humanism and the Unification of Europe*, 2 vols. (Oxford: Blackwell, 1995–2001), 2: 32–51. Although the "stone knife" seems most often to symbolize the hard-heartedness and carnality of the Jews, other traditions treat a stone or rock sword positively as symbolizing the Word of God by which the Christian is circumcised or cut off from all impurity. See Origen, *Homilies on Joshua* 26.2, pp. 217–18.

4. Raymund Martini, *Pugio Fidei* pars 2 [sic], dist. 3, cap. 11, par. 16, fols. 612–13 (Leipzig: Sumptibus haeredum Friderici Lanckisi, 1687), 784–85; for the significance of this text to Christian anti-Jewish polemics, see Robert Chazan, *Daggers of Faith: Thirteenth Century Christian Missionizing and Jewish Response* (Berkeley: University of California Press, 1989). For a medieval Jewish treatment of this same fourfold requirement—to circumcise the heart, lips, ears, and foreskin—see *Pirkê de Rabbi Eliezer* 19, trans. Gerald Friedlander (New York: Hermon Press, 1916; repr. 1970), 206.

5. "ceremonialium veteris legis observacio nunc tempore gracie sit non solum super-

mortal sin, while the 1442 Council of Florence declared that any Christian who performs the rite of circumcision forfeits eternal salvation.[6]

This enumeration of different forms of circumcision does not, however, explain why *Jews* were commanded to circumcise the flesh. (See figure 3.) What purpose was served by this rite? Did circumcision merely prefigure Christian baptism, or, as the Dominican Albert the Great inquired in his *On the Sacraments* (*De sacramentis*), did it not have some proper significance for the Jews and some function of its own per se, both in the past and the present?[7] Among thirteenth-century Scholastics in particular, the answer to this question entailed multiple distinctions, but with a somewhat different focus. Richard Schenk has correctly noted that "it was the general tendency of the mid-thirteenth century . . . to stress the intrinsic Jewish reasons for the details of all the cultic ceremonies of the older covenant."[8] Although we can find examples of pre-Scholastic figures who addressed the Jewish context or justification for circumcision—for example, the Jewish convert to Christianity, Petrus Alfonsi—it does seem that it was only in the thirteenth century that interest flourished in identifying multiple reasons for the rite of circumcision and, in particular, reasons that did not only prefigure the Christian sacrament. William of Auxerre (d. 1231), for example, pointed to six different reasons behind the commandment to

---

vacua, sed etiam perniciosa." Robert Grosseteste, *De cessatione legalium* 1.4.1, ed. Richard C. Dales and Edward B. King (London: Oxford University Press, 1986), 16–17.

6. See Nancy Turner, "Jewish Witness, Forced Conversion, and Island Living: John Duns Scotus on Jews and Judaism," in *Christian Attitudes toward Jews in the Middle Ages: A Casebook*, ed. Michael Frassetto (New York: Routledge, 2007), 189. The claim that circumcision for Christians is a sin generally had to be reconciled with the fact that Paul had circumcised Timothy after the death of Jesus (Acts 16:3), but this was often treated as a necessary accomodation in order to avoid scandal. See Thomas Aquinas, *In IV Sententiarum* dist. 1 q. 2 a. 5 qc. 3 arg. 2 and dist. 1 q. 2 a. 5 qc. 3 co. Thomas remarks that after the apostolic age circumcision ceased to be useful and became a mortal sin (*mortifera*). The Council of Florence "strictly orders all who glory in the name of Christian, not to practise circumcision either before or after baptism, since whether or not they place their hope in it, it cannot possibly be observed without loss of eternal salvation." (Session 11 [Bull of Union with the Copts], available at http://www.ewtn.com/library/COUNCILS/FLORENCE.HTM.)

7. Albert the Great, *De sacramentis* tr. 2, q. 1, ed. Albert Ohlmeyer, Ed. Colon. 26 (Monasterii Westfalorum: Aschendorff, 1958), 17–18.

8. Richard Schenk, "Convenant initiation: Thomas Aquinas and Robert Kilwardby on the sacrament of circumcision," *Ordo sapientiae et amoris: Image et message de saint Thomas d'Aquin à travers les récentes études historiques, herméneutiques et doctrinales. Hommage au Professeur Jean-Pierre Torell OP à l'occasion de son 65e anniversaire*, ed. Carlos-Josaphat Pinto de Oliveira, Studia Friburgensia n.s. 78 (Fribourg: Editions Universitaires, 1993), 559.

circumcise the male member.⁹ Albert the Great identified five causes in his long treatment of circumcision in *On the Sacraments* (*De sacramentis*),¹⁰ and his confrere and contemporary Vincent of Beauvais (d. 1264) identified at least five as well.¹¹ All agreed, however, that a primary purpose and function for the circumcision of the flesh was to differentiate the Jews from other nations in order to keep them separate.¹²

Earlier Christian authors had hinted at this as well. According to the fifth-century *Debate over the Law between a Jew, Simon, and a Christian, Theophilus* (*Altercatio Legis inter Simonem Judaeum et Theophilum Christianum*), "circumcision is not a sign of salvation but a sign of a [separate] race."¹³ In the seventh century, Isidore of Seville had made much the same point, identifying circumcision as a principal mark that distinguishes Jews from other peoples.¹⁴ At the beginning of the twelfth century, Petrus Alfonsi added that circumcision physically distinguished the Jews because the Jews' separateness was essential to guarantee a pure line of descent from Abraham, thereby insuring later that the circumcised Jesus was in fact from the seed of Abraham and the tribe of Judah. He also explained

---

9. William of Auxerre, *Summa Aurea* 4, tr. 2, cap. 5, q. 1.

10. Albert the Great, *De sacramentis* tr. 2, q. 6, p. 22.

11. Vincent of Beauvais, *Speculum historiale* 1.105 (= vol. 4 of the *Speculum quadruplex, sive, Speculum maius: naturale, doctrinale, morale, historiale*), 4: 38. For a discussion of the development of this enormous medieval encyclopedia, see the very helpful Monique Paulmier-Foucart and Marie-Christine Duchenne, *Vincent de Beauvais et le Grand miroir du monde* (Turnhout: Brepols, 2004). Note that of the three authentic parts to the *Speculum* (i.e., excluding the *Speculum morale*), the most widely distributed was the *Speculum historiale*. For additional background to the *Speculum*, see *Vincent of Beauvais and Alexander the Great*, ed. W. J. Aerts, E. R. Smits, and J. B. Voorbij (Groningen: Egbert Forsten, 1986). Of particular note in this volume, see E. R. Smits, "Vincent of Beauvais: A note on the Background of the *Speculum*," 1–9; and, J. B. Voorbij, "The *Speculum Historiale*: Some aspects of its genesis and manuscript tradition," 11–55.

12. Petrus Alfonsi, *Dialogus contra Judaeum* 12, in *Der Dialog des Petrus Alfonsi: seine Überlieferung im Druck und in den Handschriften Textedition*, ed. Klaus Peter-Mieth (Inaug. diss.: Freien Universität Berlin, 1982), 127–31. All subsequent references to the Latin will be to Peter-Mieth's edition. For translation, see 250–55 of *Petrus Alfonsi's Dialogue against the Jews*, trans. Irven M. Resnick, Fathers of the Church, Mediaeval Continuation 8 (Washington, D.C.: The Catholic University of America Press, 2006). See also Bruno of Segni, *Expositio in Genesim* cap. 4 (PL 164: 174C); Vincent of Beauvais, *Speculum historiale* 1.105, 4: 38; William of Auxerre, *Summa Aurea* 4, tr. 2, cap. 5, q. 1, p. 39; Albert the Great, *De sacramentis* tr. 2, q. 1, p. 17.

13. "Circumcisio enim signum est generis, non salutis." Evagrius, *Altercatio legis inter Simoneum Judaeum et Theophilum Christianum* 5, ed. R. Demeulenaere, CCSL 64 (Turnholt: Brepols, 1985).

14. Isidore of Seville, *Quaestiones in veterum testamentum: In Genesin* 6.17 (PL 83: 226C).

why circumcision is performed eight days after birth. Before the eighth day, he insists, the male infant was not separated from his mother. On the eighth day, however, the new mother was required to undergo ritual purification (see Lev. 12:1–5), which demanded that she leave her child. Before this, the boy must be circumcised lest he be confused with a non-Jewish child in the mother's absence.[15]

Although other medieval Christian commentators even cited Jewish authorities like Maimonides to explain the literal significance of the requirement to circumcise the child on the eighth day, while they themselves added the anagogical, tropological, and allegorical meanings of the rite, it remained that a primary purpose for the circumcision of Jews was to maintain their separateness from other nations in order to guarantee that Jesus was truly descended from Abraham.[16] Following Jesus' birth, that temporary justification itself ceased. Circumcision was replaced and perfected by the sacrament of baptism that was extended to all nations, among whom all distinctions were to cease as they became members in the one body of Christ (1 Cor. 12:13). No longer would a physical sign distinguish the people of God from other nations; now, faith itself became a distinguishing sign. Albert the Great, citing John of Damascus, remarked: "Holy baptism circumcises sin, imparting the cross to us on the forehead as an honorable sign, not distinguishing us from the nations— for all the nations are received in baptism and are signed by the sign of the cross—but distinguishing the faithful from the unfaithful in every nation."[17] Baptism, then, is viewed as a sign that transcends national distinction, uniting peoples, whereas circumcision of the flesh was given to the Jews to insure their physical difference. In the past, before the advent of the Christ, this fulfilled a divine purpose. Now, however, it opposes the

---

15. See Petrus Alfonsi, *Dialogus contra Judaeum* 12, in *Der Dialog des Petrus Alfonsi*, 128, 39–129, 6. Peter Abelard's Jew supplies the sociological argument too: that both the dictary laws and circumcision were imposed on the Jews in order to keep them separate and distinct from other peoples. See his *Dialogus inter philosophum, Judaeum et Christianum* (PL 178: 1623D).

16. Jacobus de Voragine, *The Golden Legend* 13, 2 vols., trans. William Granger Ryan (Princeton, N.J.: Princeton University Press, 1993), 1:74–75; cf. Thomas Aquinas, *Summa theologica* 3, q. 70, art. 3, resp. 1–3; and *In IV Sententiarum* dist. 1 q. 2 a. 3 qc. 1 co.

17. "Peccatum circumcidit sanctum baptisma tribuens nobis signum honorabile crucem in fronte, non a gentibus determinans nos—omnes enim gentes baptismate potitae sunt et signo crucis signatae sunt—, sed in unaquaeque gente fidelem ab infideli distinguens." Albert the Great, *De sacramentis* tr. 2, q. 1, resp. 5, p. 18.

unfolding divine plan: inasmuch as Jews continue to employ the rite of circumcision as an external sign, they only separate themselves forever from the *true* people of Israel, namely, the Christian community.

If medieval Christian theologians understood circumcision to have performed a positive function in the past by keeping the Jews separate from other, idolatrous nations, they could hardly deny that it continued to establish a sign of separation for contemporary Jews as well. For Jews in the medieval world, this sign of the covenant represented a principal mark that separated them from the world of the uncircumcised and the impure, that is, their Christian neighbors. The ninth-century (?) *Pirkê de Rabbi Eliezer*, remarks that whoever eats with an uncircumcised person, it as though "he were eating flesh of abomination. All who bathe with the uncircumcised are as though they bathed with carrion, and all who touch an uncircumcised person are as though they touched the dead."[18] Circumcision separated Jews physically from the surrounding world, while at the same time it symbolized their cultural distance. Rachel of Mainz, a Jewish martyr of the violence of the first Crusade, slew her own children rather than let them be taken by the "uncircumcised."[19] Elisheva Baumgarten remarks that "Rachel's distinction between the uncircumcised and the Jews, whose skin bore the mark of God's covenant, was a central distinction for Northern European Jews in the High Middle Ages."[20] According to a Hebrew source that describes the second public disputation in Paris in the late thirteenth century, Jews, who were forced to attend the spectacle, complained that they were outnumbered by an audience of 20,000 of the *uncircumcised,* including innumerable members of the clergy of Paris.[21] Circumcision and uncircumcision remained powerful signs of difference.

18. *Pirkê de Rabbi Eliezer,* trans. Gerald Friedlander (New York: Hermon Press, 1916; repr. 1970), 208. Friedlander notes on 208 n.5, that following the term "abomination" the first editions read "as though he were eating with a dog. Just as a dog is not circumcised so the uncircumcised person is not circumcised."

19. For the text in translation, Chazan, *European Jewry and the First Crusade,* Appendix 1, 225–42, but esp. 238; for a study of Jewish martyrdom and the first Crusade, see especially Jeremy Cohen, *Sanctifying the Name of God* (Philadelphia: University of Pennsylvania Press, 2004).

20. Elisheva Baumgarten, "Marking the Flesh: Circumcision, Blood, and Inscribing Identity on the Body in Medieval Jewish Culture," in *La pelle umana; The Human Skin,* vol. 13 of *Micrologus. Natura, scienze e società medievali* (Florence: SISMEL, 2005), 314.

21. Joseph Shatzmiller, *La deuxième controverse de Paris. Un chapitre dans la polémique entre chrétiens et juifs au Moyen Âge* (Paris: Peeters, 1994), appendix III, fol. 109b.

Despite their differences, however, there were remarkable similarities between circumcision and baptism. Like Christian baptism, the Jewish rite of circumcision was performed on infants. Associated with both rites was a naming ceremony, whereby the newborn was initiated into the community. But medieval Jewish tradition held that the patriarch Abraham stands at the gates of heaven and hell to examine all Jews at death. Those without a foreskin were sent to heaven; those with it, to Gehenna or hell, emphasizing once again the difference between the circumcised and the uncircumcised, not only in this life, but in the next as well.[22] The significance awarded the rite of circumcision for entry to the world to come (cf. Jer. 9:25) helps explain, too, the rabbinic practice of postmortem circumcision on infants that died before they were eight days old. *Midrash Tanhuma*, a medieval homiletic collection on the Pentateuch, affirms

All of Israel who are circumcised enter the Garden of Eden, for the holy one blessed be He, has placed his name in Israel so that they will enter the Garden of Eden [. . .] It is the name Shaddai (שדי). He placed the *shin* (ש) in the nose, the *dalet* (ד) in the hand and the *yod* (י) on the (place of) circumcision. Therefore when a Jew dies there is an appointed angel in the Garden of Eden who receives every circumcised Jew and brings him into the Garden of Eden.[23]

God's name, Shaddai (Almighty), given to Abraham at the time that he was instructed to circumcise himself and his offspring, was understood by some authorities, then, as inscribed in the flesh to serve as a protective marker or key enabling the Jew to enter the gates of Eden. The thirteenth-century kabbalist Joseph of Hamadan, who lived in Spain, similarly linked the commandment of Gen. 17:1—"Walk before me and be blameless"—with the imprint of the divine name through circumcision. In his *Sefer Ta'ame ha-Miswot,* an explication of the rationale for the divine commandments (*mitzvot*), the author explains:

"Walk before Me and be blameless" (Gen. 17:1). What is [the meaning of] "blameless" (תמים)? In the nose is the form of a *shin* and in the hand the form

---

22. R. Yom Tov Lippmann Mühlhausen, *Disputatio adversus Christianos ad Jeremie, Ezechielis, Psalmorum et Danielis libros institute,* trans. M. Sebaldus Snellius (Altdorf: Typis Viduae Balthasaris Scherffi, 1645), 1262–63; Johannes Buxtorf, *Synagoga Judaica* cap. 4 (Hildesheim: G. Olms, 1989), 87; cf. Baumgarten, "Marking the Flesh," 318–19. For rabbinic tradition that placed Abraham at the entrance to Gehenna, see *Genesis Rabbah* 48.8.

23. *Midrash Tanhuma* Shemini 8 (New York, 1942), cited in Baumgarten, "Marking the Flesh," 322–23.

of a *dalet*, thus there are found [the letters which make up the name] (שד [demon].... When the *yod*, which is the supernal form, is revealed, the name is completed, and that is the name שדי. Thus the verse says, "I am אל שדי; walk before me and be blameless."²⁴

This tradition connects the *dalet* morphologically to the hand and the *shin* to the nose, but the *yod* clearly suggests the circumcised penis. While *Midrash Tanhuma* emphasizes that the *yod* completes the name *Shaddai* (Almighty), Elliot Wolfson has demonstrated that German Pietists of the thirteenth century conveyed to Spanish kabbalists an interpretation that connected the *yod* of circumcision to the first letter of the Tetragrammaton, YHWH (יהוה),whose apoptropaic power seemed undeniable.²⁵ The late fourteenth-century *Mašōbēb Natībōt* (*Restorer of Paths*) of the Spanish kabbalist, Samuel ibn Matut, likewise related the appearance of the uncovered crown of the penis through circumcision to the letter *yod*.²⁶ Circumcision marked Jews in the flesh, then, with the divine name or one of the divine attributes, and distinguished them thereby from their uncircumcised neighbors.

Such traditions were certainly known to Christians as well. The sixteenth-century Johannes Buxtorf (1564–1629) adds that the Jews say that with circumcision the name of God—Shaddai—is perfected in the flesh, since the letter *shin* is represented in the nostrils, the letter *dalet* in the arms, and the letter *yod* in the circumcised flesh. Those who are uncircumcised, like Christians, lack the final letter, yod, and therefore they only have the letters *shin* and *dalet,* yielding "sched" or "devil", indicating that they are the sons of the devil, and not members of a holy people.²⁷

The medieval rite of circumcision required three elements: 1. the cutting of the foreskin; 2. pulling and cutting or scraping the rest of the foreskin (*peri'ah*); 3. and, finally, sucking the blood off the male member (*metzizah b'peh*). Like the Christian Eucharist, the medieval Jewish rite of circumcision recognized blood as a necessary and sanctifying ele-

---

24. Joseph Hamadan, *Sefer Ta'ame ha-Miswot,* ed. M. Meier (Ph.D. diss., Brandeis University, 1974), 242, cited by Elliot R. Wolfson, "Circumcision and the Divine Name: A Study in the Transmission of Esoteric Doctrine," *Jewish Quarterly Review* 78, no. 1–2 (1987): 77 n. 1.

25. Wolfson, "Circumcision and the Divine Name," 88 and 97.

26. Israel Moshe Sandman, *The Mašōbēb Natībōt of Samuel Ibn Matut ("Motot'): Introductory Excursus, Critical Edition, and Annotated Translation,* 2 vols. (Ph.D. diss., University of Chicago, 2006), 2:490.

27. Buxtorf, *Synagoga Judaica* cap. 4, p. 87.

ment. Rabbinic discussion addressed cases in which an infant was born without a foreskin, and most rabbinic authorities concluded that it was still necessary to extract a drop of blood.[28] According to Shaye Cohen, the emphasis on the blood of circumcision did not appear in Jewish texts until about 800 CE, when the blood seems to be accorded a special power to elicit God's compassion for the people of Israel. *Pirkê de Rabbi Eliezer* claims that when the Israelites left Egypt, all the men were circumcised (cf. Joshua 5:5), and they took the blood from the circumcision and put it on the lintels along with the blood of the paschal lamb, so that the plague of the Egyptians would pass them by.[29] Moreover, "the blood of the covenant of circumcision . . . is like the blood of a sacrifice" and even persuades God to forgive Israel her sins.[30] The text likewise emphasizes a connection between circumcision and atonement by asserting that Abraham was circumcised on the Day of Atonement, and the blood of his cir-

---

28. Baumgarten, "Marking the Flesh," 319. In the later medieval period the natural absence of the foreskin (or a portion thereof) among conversos could be very dangerous, bringing them to the unwelcome attention of the Inquisition. For one such instance from fifteenth-century Spain, see the annotated text edition in Josep Hernando I Angels Ibàñez, "El procés contra el convers Nicolau Sanxo, ciutadà de Barcelona acusat d'haver circumcidat el seu fill (1437–1438): Processus inquisitionis facte contra Sanxo, conversum, civem Barchinone, A.D.B. Processos n.762," *Acta historica et archaeologica mediaevalia* 13 (1992): 75–100. Similarly, in the seventeenth century Abraham Miguel Cardoso claims to have been born without a foreskin. See Bruce Rosenstock, "Messianism, Machismo, and 'Marranism': The Case of Abraham Miguel Cardoso," in *Queer Theory and the Jewish Question*, ed. Daniel Boyarin, Daniel Itzkovitz, and Ann Pellegrini (New York: Columbia University Press, 2003), 199–227, citing 216. For a Christian infant born without a foreskin, it became necessary to seek a deposition from medical authorities that the absence of the prepuce was not the result of ritual circumcision. See José Pardo Tomás, "Physicians' and Inquisitors' Stories? Circumcision and Crypto-Judaism in Sixteenth-Eighteenth-Century Spain," in *Bodily Extremities: Preoccupations with the Human Body in Early Modern European Culture*, ed. Florike Egmond and Robert Zwijenberg (Burlington, Vt.: Ashgate, 2003), 178.

29. Shaye J. D. Cohen, *Why Aren't Jewish Women Circumcised? Gender and Covenant in Judaism* (Berkeley: University of California Press, 2005), 29; Cohen, "A Brief History of Jewish Circumcision Blood," in *The Covenant of Circumcision: New Perspectives on an Ancient Jewish Rite*, ed. Elizabeth Wyner Mark (Hanover, N.H.: University Press of New England, 2003), 30–42. But for an argument that seeks to locate the sacrificial nature of the blood of circumcision even in Ex. 4:20–26, when Zipporah circumcised her son, see Jeremy Cohen, *Christ Killers: The Jews and the Passion from the Bible to the Big Screen* (New York: Oxford University Press, 2007), 48–50. On Zipporah and circumcision, see also Bonna Devorah Haberman, "Foreskin Sacrifice: Zipporah's Ritual and the Bloody Bridegroom," in *The Covenant of Circumcision: New Perspectives on an Ancient Jewish Rite*, 18–29.

30. *Pirkê de Rabbi Eliezer* 10, p. 72. For discussion of the blood of circumcision in *Pirkê de Rabbi Eliezer*, see David Biale, *Blood and Belief: The Circulation of a Symbol between Jews and Christians* (Berkeley: University of California Press, 2007), 71–72.

cumcision atones for all Israel, establishing a Jewish counterpoint to the blood symbolism of the Christian Eucharist. Medieval Jewish texts like the Regensburg Pentateuch (c. 1300) illustrated a connection between circumcision and sacrifice, if not of the paschal sacrifice then of the sacrifice of Isaac.[31] Moreover, in at least one medieval Jewish polemic against Christianity, the analogy between the salvific blood of circumcision and the blood of the Eucharist is explicit. Hasdai Crescas (d. 1410) inquires why the blood from Jesus' circumcision was not sufficient to atone for sin; why should his death on the Cross also be required to provide the blood of Atonement?[32]

Medieval Christians show some familiarity with contemporary customs linked to Jewish circumcision, so that we can assert that they were not dependent merely upon biblical texts for an awareness of the rite.[33] Christians also certainly appreciated the salvific importance of Jesus' blood, and recognized his circumcision as "the first time he shed his blood for us."[34] Moreover, they contemplated the relationship between the blood of Jesus' circumcision and the blood he shed during the crucifixion. In his *Sentences* commentary, Thomas Aquinas insists that it was necessary for Jesus to die on the Cross, even though *some* have said that a single drop of Jesus' blood—like the blood of his circumcision—was enough to accomplish our salvation.[35] Nonetheless, the blood of his circumcision and the blood of his Atonement were brought into harmony, as in an altarpiece from the fifteenth-century century Scandinavian church St. Mary in Helsingborg that shows the blood from the circumcision of the infant Jesus flowing onto the altar itself, seemingly in anticipation of the blood of sacrifice that will flow at the Crucifixion.[36]

---

31. For this text, see Eva Frojmovic, "Reframing Gender in Medieval Jewish Images of Circumcision," in *Framing the Family: Narrative and Representation in the Medieval and Early Modern Periods,* ed. Rosalynn Voaden and Diane Wolfthal, MRTS 280 (Tempe, Az.: Arizona Center for Medieval and Renaissance Studies, 2005), 221–43.

32. Hasdai Crescas, *The Refutation of the Christian Principles,* trans. Daniel J. Lasker (Albany: State University of New York, 1992), 34–35.

33. See Daniel J. Lasker, "Transubstantiation, Elijah's Chair, Plato, and the Jewish-Christian Debate," *Revue des etudes juives* 143, no. 1–2 (1984): 31–58.

34. Jacobus de Voragine, *The Golden Legend* 13, trans. William Granger Ryan, 1:74.

35. Thomas Aquinas, *Scriptum super libros Sententiarum* 3, dist. 20, q. 1, art. 3, arg. 4, resp.

36. See Ulla Haastrup, "Representations of Jews in Danish Medieval Art—Can Images Be Used as Source Material on Their Own?" in *History and Images: Toward a New Iconology,* ed. Axel Bolvig and Phillip Lindley (Turnholt: Brepols, 2003), 341–56, esp. 347–48, with illustration.

The blood Jesus shed during the rite of circumcision was certainly revered by Christians. Nonetheless, by the first half of the thirteenth century, Christians were fully informed of Jewish claims made on behalf of the blood of circumcision from the anti-Jewish polemic, the *Wars of the Lord* (*Liber bellorum Domini*), composed by an early thirteenth-century Jewish convert to Christianity who evidently adopted the name of his patron, William, the Archbishop of Bourges (d. 1209). Our William, who survived the archbishop and became a deacon in the church, composed his *Wars of the Lord* about 1235,[37] at the insistence of certain Christians who believed that he had a good understanding of the Hebrew language. In the history of *adversus Iudaeos* literature, the *Wars of the Lord* is distinguished by its assault upon the Talmud—an assault that had also been advanced in the first decade of the twelfth century by another Jewish convert, Petrus Alfonsi. It seems also likely that both William and the midrashic traditions in his polemical text influenced the artistic program at the church of St. Étienne at Bourges.[38]

In the *Wars of the Lord,* reiterating the guilt of contemporary Jewish communities for the Crucifixion by invoking Matthew 27:25 ("His blood be upon us and our children"), William insists that it is the blood of Jesus, moreover, that the prophet Zachariah identified as the blood of the new testament that has freed captive humanity from hell (cf. Zach. 9:11). Anticipating the Jews' appeal to the salvific efficacy of the blood of circumcision, he adds: "You have not been redeemed by the blood of circumcision, neither in this age nor in the age to come."[39] In addition to this attack on a Jewish "theology" of the blood of circumcision, the specific rabbinic practice of *metzizah b'peh,* in which the one circumcising the infant sucked off the blood from the member, met with harsh condemnation. There is evidence from medieval Ashkenazic communities that Jews graphically linked the blood of circumcision and the blood of the Paschal sacrifice daubed on the doorposts in Egypt by drap-

---

37. For this dating, see Guillaume de Bourges, *Livre des Guerres du Seigneur et deux homélies,* intro., ed. and trans. Gilbert Dahan (Paris, Éditions du Cerf, 1981), 12.

38. See Margaret Jennings, "Prophecy in Glass and Stone: Jewish Influences on the Cathedral of Bourges," in *Insights and Interpretations: Studies in Celebration of the Eighty-Fifth Anniversary of the Index of Christian Art,* ed. Colum Hourihane (Princeton: Princeton University Press, 2002), 182–201.

39. *Epistula ad Hebreos,* "de sanguine circumcisionis non estis redempti, neque in hoc seculo neque in futuro." Ibid., 242, 15–16.

ing a cloth on the lintel of the synagogue on which the ritual circumciser (*mohel*) had wiped the blood from his mouth.[40] Similarly, Katrin Kogman-Appel has identified the sacrificial value of the blood of circumcision as a motif in Jewish illustrations from medieval Spain, where they served a polemical purpose.[41] The Dominican Raymund Martini surely rejects circumcision of the flesh. But he also condemns the specific Jewish practice of *metzizah b'peh*, which for contemporary Jews has some special value since they excuse the practice, he claims, by saying that if they fail to do this the infant will die.[42] A fragmentary thirteenth-century Spanish anti-Jewish polemic, the *Disputation between a Christian and a Jew* (*Disputa entre un cristiano y un judío*), condemns the practice of *metzizah b'peh* by vulgarly identifying the rabbi's mouth, which sucks the blood from the wound of circumcision, with a woman's vagina.[43] This ritual practice seems to have aroused horror among medieval Christians,

---

40. For a description of this custom c. 1230 by R. Jacob ha-Gozer, a *mohel*, see Abraham Gross, "The Blood Libel and the Blood of Circumcision: An Ashkenazic Custom That Disappeared in the Middle Ages," *Jewish Quarterly Review* 86 (1995): 171–74. See also Trachtenberg, *Jewish Magic and Superstition*, 170, referencing Ephraim of Bonn.

41. Katrin Kogman-Appel, *Illuminated Haggadot from Medieval Spain: Biblical Imagery and the Passover Holiday* (University Park: The Pennsylvania State University Press, 2006), 179.

42. "susceptum in os veretrum tamdiu sugunt, quamdiu inde sanguis egreditur, praedicto Rabbinorum suorum cupientes obedire mandato. Excusant autem istud dicentes, quod, nisi hoc fieret, omnes eorum parvuli morerentur, quod falsum est." Raymund Martini, *Pugio Fidei* pars 2 [sic], dist. 3, cap. 11, par. 16, fols. 612–13, p. 786. Jerome, and later the Carolingian bishop Agobard of Lyon, similarly condemned Jewish rabbis for tasting the blood of a virgin or the blood of a menstruant to determine whether her blood is clean or unclean, when they were unable to make a determination by sight. See Jerome's Epist. 121.10, ed. Isidore Hilberg, CSEL 56 (Vienna: F. Temsky, 1910–1918), 48, and Agobard's *De judaicis superstitionibus* 10, in *Opera omnia*, ed. L. Van Acker, CCCM 52 (Turnholt: Brepols, 1981), 207.

43. "Ond, quando bjen vos mesuraredes, fonta vos i iaze & muy grand; que la boca de vestro rabi que conpieça vestra oraicíon, feches cono de muier; & de mas sabedes que la barba y las narizes an y mal logar. E de mas veedes qual fonta de sugar sangre de tal logar. Ond si iusticia fuesse de tierra, mas derecho era apedrear tal omne que osso ni leon." (Whereas when you think well upon it [you will see that] you commit a shameful act that lies herein; that the mouth of your rabbi who begins your prayers, you make it into a woman's cunt; and even more you know that the chin and nose don't belong there. And even more you see how shameful it is to suck blood from such a place. Whereas if justice were an earthly [good], it would be more just to stone such a man than to stone a bear or a lion.) See Américo Castro, "Disputa entre un cristiano y un judío," *Revista der filolgía española* 1 (1914), 176, quoted in Harriet Goldberg, "Two Parallel Medieval Commonplaces: Antifeminism and Antisemitism in the *Hispanic Literary Tradition*," in *Aspects of Jewish Culture in the Middle Ages*, ed. Paul E. Szarmach (Albany: SUNY Press Albany, 1979), 102–3. My thanks to Professor Pedro Campa for assistance with this translation.

and knowledge of it may have contributed to later medieval depictions that show Jews circumcising Christian children before murdering them, for example, Simon of Trent (d. 1475), and collecting the blood from the penis. *Metzizah b'peh* also exercised such fascination among Christians that, in the early modern era, both Michel de Montaigne (d. 1592) and the Englishman Thomas Coryat (d. 1617) witnessed a circumcision and were intent upon describing the ritual practice of *metzizah b'peh*,[44] a ritual that later medical authorities sometimes seek to condemn as responsible for communicating sexually transmitted diseases to the infant.[45]

Furthermore, for Christians the practice of circumcision (not to mention *metzizah b'peh*) could not be separated from the sexual function of the organ on which the physical mark was inscribed. Circumcision was often perceived in medieval Christian circles as having been necessitated by the surpassingly carnal nature of the people of Israel (at a time when humankind had sunk to the lowest depths of sin) whose sexual vices had to be truncated by the truncation of the male member.[46] In part, this stemmed from Christian typology, which sought to understand circumcision "spiritually" as a sign that one should cut off from the soul desire and vice, a sign that was evident especially in the circumcision of Jesus, whose divine nature surely required no such restraint.[47] As such, the Feast of the Circumcision was gradually introduced into the medieval Church and observed on January 1. This date, following eight days after the Nativity, not only commemorated the biblical requirement to circumcise a male infant on the eighth day but also—and likely more importantly—enabled the Church to suppress pagan celebrations on the kalends of January that were given over to illicit sex, cross-dressing, and wild public displays.[48] The Feast of the Circumcision, then, sought to

---

44. For discussion of their observations, see Eva Frojmovic, "Christian Travelers to the Circumcision: Early Modern Representations," in *The Covenant of Circumcision: New Perspectives on an Ancient Jewish Rite*, 128–37.

45. Sander Gilman, *The Jew's Body* (London: Routledge, 1991), 93.

46. See Thomas Aquinas, *In IV Sententiarum* dist. 1 q. 2 a. 1 qc. 3 co.

47. Hermannus de Runa, *Sermo* 5, ln. 29, in *Sermones festiuales*, ed. E. Mikkers, I. Theuws, R. Demeulenaere, CCCM 64 (Turnholt: Brepols, 1986); cf. Thomas Aquinas, *Summa theologica* 3, q. 37, resp. 1–3; *In IV Sententiarum* dist. 1 q. 2 a. 2 qc. 3 co.

48. "Queritur: Quare non alio tempore, sed in Kal. Ian. Christi sit facta circumcisio, quo die maximam gentiles sollempnitatem celebrare solebant? 'Propter errorem gentilitatis. Ianus enim | quidam princeps paganorum fuit, a quo mensis Ianuarii nomen' accipit, 'quem inperiti homines uelud deum quolebant, <diem que> ipsum scenis et luxoriae sacrauerunt. Tunc enim miseri homines, sumentes species monstruosas, in ferarum habitum transform-

constrain the community to follow the example of Jesus, "cutting off" sexual vice and excess.

In a similar manner, Jesus' foreskin became a venerated relic in European Christian communities, even into the modern era. It will figure prominently in the visions or revelations of several late medieval female mystics, and it seems also to have had a miraculous power to assist lay women at childbirth.[49] While Jesus' foreskin enjoyed a positive valence, once circumcision was rendered superfluous following Jesus' baptism, circumcision among Jews underscored their continuing enslavement to desire.[50]

Renaissance artists will sometimes depict the infant Jesus as uncircumcised, despite the historical inaccuracy but anticipating his Resurrection, since some medieval theologians assumed that at that time his foreskin was restored to him to render his body whole and perfect once again.[51] The notion that the foreskin is a sign of a perfected Christian

---

abantur. Alii, femineo gestu demutati, uirilem uultum effeminabant." *Homiliarium Ueronense*, 3, p. 40. This ninth-century (?) sermon responds directly to the question, "Why do we observe the circumcision of Jesus on the kalends of January?" The response, beginning with "Propter errorem gentilitatis," quotes Isidore of Seville's *De ecclesiasticis officiis* 1.41.2. See n. 218. For a general condemnation of cross-dressing, understood to have been condemned by Deut. 22:5, and stipulation of the appropriate penance, see Robert of Flamborough, *Liber Poenitentialis* 5.6.3.335, ed. J. J. F. Firth (Toronto: Pontifical Institute of Mediaeval Studies, 1971), 264.

49. For an investigation of traditions concerning Jesus' foreskin and its veneration and uses, see especially Robert P. Palazzo, "The Veneration of the Sacred Foreskin(s) of Baby Jesus—A Documented Analysis," in *Multicultural Europe and Cultural Exchange in the Middle Ages and Renaissance*, ed. James P. Helfers, Arizona Studies in the Middle Ages and Renaissance 12 (Turnholt: Brepols, 2005), 155–76.

50. Peter of Blois remarks that although Jesus willed to be circumcised to demonstrate that he was of the seed of Abraham and from the tribe of Judah, after his baptism circumcision became unnecessary: "Christus in carnem veniens circumcidi voluit, iudicans se natum fuisse de semine Abrahe et de tribu Iuda, et ideo post baptismum eius circumcisio non debebat manere ulterius." See Peter of Blois, *The Later Letters of Peter of Blois* 65.7, pp. 288–89.

51. Jacobus de Voragine reports that "it is said that" an angel had carried Jesus' foreskin to Charlemagne, who enshrined it in a chapel dedicated to the Virgin Mary in Aix-la-Chapelle, but that this relic was later transferred to Charroux and then to Rome. Jacobus expresses as his own opinion, however, that the foreskin must be in heaven with the resurrected body of Jesus. See Jacobus de Voragine, *The Golden Legend* 13, trans. William Granger Ryan, 1:77–78. The possibility that Jesus' foreskin should remain on earth after the Resurrection was debated by a number of theologians, including the thirteenth-century Franciscan Nicholas of Ockham. See his *Quaestiones disputatae de traductione humanae naturae a primo parente* q. 5.8, ed. Caesaris Saco Alarcón, Spicilegium Bonaventurianum 27 (Grottaferrata: Editiones Collegii S. Bonaventurae ad Claras Aquas, 1993), 184–85. See

body and that it can be restored at the resurrection was ridiculed in the early sixteenth-century *Letters of Obscure Men* (*Epistolae obscurorum virorum*). These polemical letters purport to be from zealous and dedicated Christian theologians engaged in a struggle against perfidious Jewish error, although they are written around 1515 by the liberal humanists Crotus Rubeanus and Ulrich von Hutten, for the most part. In one satirical letter the fictional author Lupold Federfuchser (that is, "Lupold the scribbler") reports that in Erfurt he witnessed a quodlibetal disputation that pitted university theologians against natural philosophers. The theologians argued that when a Jew becomes a Christian his foreskin will be restored to him, otherwise the convert might be mistaken for a Jew at the Last Judgment, leading to his eternal condemnation. The natural philosophers replied that if because of the absence of a foreskin converts may be mistaken for Jews at the Last Judgment, then it follows that all those Christians—both clergy and laymen—who have lost a bit of skin from their member when satisfying their lust will be mistaken for Jews as well, which is a most unseemly outcome.[52] This satirical text highlights our conclusion, however, that in medieval texts a circumcised body is an imperfect, flawed body, much as a woman in her embodied nature is a flawed or defective male. The circumcised body is flawed precisely because the practice is treated as a palliative for an overly carnal nature.

The persistent presence of carnal desire among Jews that was underscored by the practice of circumcision was not merely an unspecified longing, however; it was especially inordinate sexual desire, lust, lechery, or sexual excess (*luxuria*) that circumcision sought to contain.[53] Robert

---

also Johan J. Mattelaer, Robert A. Schipper, and Sakti Das, "The Circumcision of Jesus," *Journal of Urology* 178, no. 31-34 (2007): 31-34. Just as some argued that the foreskin had to be restored to the resurrected body, so too Thomas Aquinas asserts that at the Resurrection the blood Jesus' body had lost during the Passion would be fully restored to it, leaving church relics said to contain Jesus' blood to have blood only from abused images of Jesus. *Summa theologica* 3, q. 54, art. 3, resp. ad 3. Cf. Roger Marston, Quod 4, q. 14: "Whether any of his [Jesus'] blood remained on earth after he ascended," in *Quodlibeta quatuor ad fidem codicum nunc primum edita*, ed. Gerard I. Etzkorn and Ignatius C. Brady (Grottaferrata: Collegio S. Bonaventura, 1994), 393-94.

52. *Epistolae obscurorum virorum* 1.37, 2 vols., ed. and trans. Francis Griffin Stokes (London: Chattowindus, 1909), 1: 96.

53. On *luxuria*, see Claire Catalini, "*Luxuria* and Its Branches," in *Sex, Love and Marriage in Medieval Literature and Reality: thematische Beiträge im Rahmen des 31th International Congress on Medieval Studies an der Western Michigan University* (Kalamazoo-USA), 8.–12. Mai 1996 (Kalamazoo, Mich.: International Congress on Medieval Studies, 1996), 13–20.

of Flamborough (d. before 1234) defines a number of forms of *luxuria*, but notes that strictly speaking it describes sexual intercourse.[54] Likewise, Thomas Aquinas defines *luxuria* as a capital vice referring especially to venereal pleasures, whose material cause is gluttony.[55] St. Antoninus of Florence (d. 1459) likewise asserts that in the strict sense *luxuria* refers to an inordinate sexual appetite and desire, which weakens the power of reason.[56] Lust was imagined to be contrary to rationality, and therefore it was more properly a characteristic of beasts than humans. The ideal human is one whose use of intercourse will be completely guided by reason and love for God and the divine commandments, if not avoided altogether. It is not surprising then that Vincent of Beauvais (d. c. 1264) identifies many types or species of *luxuria* that, in general, distance us from our humanity—among them, rape, sodomy, fornication, and bestiality—but it is especially interesting that he regards *luxuria* as a sin so abominable that it sometimes revealed itself through a terrible smell. Some people have perceived the odor of this sin when it has occurred in their house; to others, the smell may be communicated by physical contact. In an anecdote, Vincent explains that the hermit Pachomius was once visited in the desert by the spirit of fornication, in the guise of an Ethiopian, who transferred the smell of this foul sin to Pachomius's hand when the latter touched him.[57] Toward the end of the eleventh century St. Peter Damian identified a sulphurous stench that arises from *luxuria*,[58] a stench (*foetor luxuriae*) that later St. Bonaventure (d. 1274) suggested should be eliminated by the sweet smell of chastity.[59] Moreover, it is precisely because

---

54. "coitus, qui stricto vocabulo dicitur luxuria." Robert of Flamborough, *Liber Poenitentialis* 4.8.223, p. 195.

55. Thomas Aquinas, *Summa theologica* 2.2.153, art. 1, ad 3; *Summa theologica* 2.2.153, art. 4, ad 1. For Thomas's conceeption of *luxuria*, see also Mark D. Jordan, "Homosexuality, Luxuria, and Textual Abuse," in *Constructing Medieval Sexuality*, ed. Karma Lochrie, Peggy McCracken, and James A. Schultz (Minneapolis: University of Minnesota Press, 1997), 24–39.

56. St. Antoninus of Florence, *Summa theologica* 2, tit. 5, cap. 1, 4 vols. (Verona: 1740; repr. Graz: Akademische Druck-u. Verlagsanstalt, 1959), 2: 635A-B.

57. Vincent of Beauvais, *Speculum morale* 3, dist. 3, pars 9, 3: 1374.

58. "de luxuria sulphureus foetor oboritur." Peter Damian, Epist. 49.18, in *Die Briefe des Petrus Damiani*, 2: 71. For this terrible stench of lust or *luxuria*, see also Epist. 108.14, and Epist. 112.16, in *Die Briefe des Petrus Damiani*, 3: 197; 268; Epist. 162.24, and Epist. 165.55, in *Die Briefe des Petrus Damiani*, 4: 159; 206.

59. Bonaventure, *Sermones domincales*, Sermo 9, par. 11–13, ed. J. G. Bougerol, Bibl. Franciscana Scholastica Medii Aevi 27 (Grottaferrata: Collegio S. Bonaventura, Padri Editori di Quaracchi, 1977).

sexual desire is located in the male member that God commanded the Jews to circumcise their flesh as a sign.[60] William of Auxerre (d. 1231), too, adds that "circumcision was applied to that member in which sexual desire flouishes."[61] In a similar way, in his treatise *On Laws* (*De legibus*) written before 1236, William of Auvergne (d. 1249) identified five reasons for ritual circumcision among the Jews. These include the weakening of concupiscence, resulting from the wound caused from circumcision, and a weakening of sexual desire brought about from a diminished sensitivity in the male member:

Because circumcision is included among those things that were imposed on the fathers [of the Jews] before the [giving of the] Law, and it does not seem to have any useful purpose in its own right, except solely for the good of obedience, it is necessary to reveal its literal causes and the useful purposes it has beyond that good. Of these the first [purpose] is to weaken the libidinous desire that flourishes in that virile member, both because of the wound of circumcision and the effusion of blood that occurs in it. The second [purpose] is the exposure of that part—that is, of that member's defect—to cold and to friction from clothes, by all of which it is rendered less sensitive just as delicate hands are rendered less sensitive and less subject to feeling from rough tasks. In that part [of the member] nothing reduces or weakens concupiscence more than the lessening of sensitivity and its ability to feel.[62]

60. Vincent of Beauvais, *Speculum historiale* 1, 105, 4: 38.
61. "fiebat circumcisio in membro in quo viget luxuria." William of Auxerre, *Summa Aurea* 4, tr. 2, cap. 5, q. 1, p. 39. The same rationale would be applied in later medieval and early modern texts to explain female circumcision (or genital mutilation) as a remedy for female hypersensuality, which was presumed to achieve its fullest expression among women in parts of the Islamic world since, by the thirteenth century, Albert the Great had suggested that black women desire sex more than white women. See his *Quaestiones super de animalibus* 15.19, p. 271 (QDA, 468), and discussion by Peter Biller, "Black Women in Medieval Scientific Thought," in *La pelle umana; The Human Skin*, vol. 13 of *Micrologus. Natura, scienze e società medievali* (Florence: SISMEL, 2005), 477–92, esp. 484–86. Thus, to the extent that the clitoris was perceived to be homologous with the penis, clitoridectomy served the same purpose of restraining excessive sexual desire. See Thomas W. Laqueur, "Amor Veneris vel Dulcedo Appeletur," in *Fragments for a History of the Human Body*, ed. Michel Feher, with Ramona Naddaff and Nadia Tazi (New York: Zone Books, 1989), 3: 91–131, but especially 3: 113–15; also Jonathan Berkey, "Women in Medieval Islamic Society," in *Women in Medieval Western European Culture*, ed. Linda E. Mitchell (New York: Garland, 1999), 95–116, but esp. 103–4. Arguments that circumcision desensitizes the sexual organ are sometimes advanced in parts of the Islamic world today to defend female circumcision or female genital mutilation—i.e., that one of its benefits is to reduce sexual desire (and therefore reduce sexual promiscuity) among young women. See S. A. Aldeeb Abu-Sahlieh, "Jehovah, His Cousin Allah, and Sexual Mutilations," in *Sexual Mutilations: A Human Tragedy*, ed. George Denniston and Marilyn Fayre Milos (New York: Plenum Press, 1997), 41–63, esp. 51–52.
62. "Quia vero circumcisio de his est, quae ante legem patribus imposita sunt, et non

Because original sin was understood to be transmitted specifically through the act of intercourse, it was entirely appropriate, according to the *Sententiae divinae paginae* attributed to the "school" of Anselm of Laon, that circumcision be performed on the private parts (*pudenda*), while Peter Abelard treated circumcision as a punishment among males strictly analogous to the pain of childbirth that daughters of Eve experience as a result of original sin.[63] The persistent practice of circumcision as a defining ritual in Jewish communities, however, also implied that Jews—especially Jewish men—were more easily overcome by sexual licentiousness, and that for that reason they (and not the Gentiles) were commanded to observe this rite. Thus, Abramson and Hanson remark that "Jewish men were perceived as excessively libidinous and Christian women were dangerously susceptible to their sexual power.... On the other hand, the mutilation of the [male] genitalia was also a feminizing wound, a form of emasculation. According to this popular interpretation, Jewish men were 'womanized' by circumcision, even menstruating into adulthood."[64] This seems to be the peculiar paradox of Christian perceptions of Jewish circumcision: they implied both an excessively libidinous Jewish male and an enfeebled, feminized nature. This paradox

---

videtur in seipsa habere utilitatem aliquam, excepto solo obedientiae bono, necesse est aperire causas eius literales, et utilitates quas habet, praeter istud bonum. Harum ergo prima est, debilitatio libidinosae concupiscentiae, quae viget in membro illo virili ex vulnere circumcisionis, et effusione sanguinis, quae in ea fit. Secunda expositio partis illius, idest culpae membri illius frigorii, et defricationibus vestium, ex quibus omnibus efficitur minus sensibilis, quemadmodum et manus duris operibus assuetae minus sensibiles minusque passibiles inde redduntur. Nihil in parte illa magis minuit, aut debilitat concupiscentiam, quam diminutio sensibilitatis, et passibilitatis illius." William of Auvergne, *De legibus* 3, in *Opera omnia*, 2 vols. in 1 (Venice: Ex officina Damiani Zenari, 1591), 32.1F. For this text and its treatment of Jews and Muslims, see Lesley Smith, "William of Auvergne and the Law of the Jews and the Muslims," in *Scripture and Pluralism: Reading the Bible in the Religiously Plural Worlds of the Middle Ages and Renaissance*, ed. Thomas Heffernan and Thomas Burman (Leiden: Brill, 2005), 95-122.

63. *Sententie divine pagine* cap. 5, in *Anselms von Laon systematische Sentenzen*, 35. See also Albert the Great, *De sacramentis* tr. 2, q. 6. *Pudenda*—private parts—can also be rendered "shameful parts." Augustine insists that they received this name only after the fall, since, as a result of original sin, they no longer obey our will. See *De civitate Dei* 14.17.11-14, 2 vols., ed. B. Dombart (Leipzig: Teubner, 1877), 2:39. For Peter Abelard see *A Dialogue of a Philosopher with a Jew, and a Christian*, trans. Pierre J. Payer (Toronto: Pontifical Institute of Mediaeval Studies, 1979), 50-51.

64. Henry Abramson and Carrie Hanson, "Depicting the Ambiguous Wound. Circumcision in Medieval Art," in *The Covenant of Circumcision: New Perspectives on an Ancient Rite*, ed. Elizabeth Wyner Mark (Lebanon, N.H.: University Press of New England, 2003), 101.

is in fact only apparent and not real, since medieval theologians generally identified the man that was unable to withstand the demands of passion or lust as effeminate. Thus, like Bishop Ambrose of Milan (d. 397), Peter Damian condemns the "weak man or rather unmanned man" (*vir enervis, immo vir evirate*), whose lust would satisfy itself even by intercourse with a pregnant woman,[65] and, in his *Book of Gomorrah*, an unrestrained assault on homosexuality and sodomy within the Church, he condemns that "unmanned and effeminate man" (*vir evirate . . . homo effeminate*) whose lust compels him to seek feminine "softness" (*mollities*) in another man.[66] Likewise, Albert the Great defines *effeminati* as those who, inclined to feminine "softness" (*mollities*), are unable to resist vice.[67] The early fourteenth-century epitome of Pseudo-Aristotle's *Problemata*, likely the work of the Oxford scholar Walter Burley, adds that "Effeminate men are insatiable and insane in intercourse, like women."[68]

Other sources identify the female animal in general as the most libidinous.[69] This effeminate weakness seems only most pronounced in Jewish men, who are like the effeminate men (*molles*) identified at 1 Cor. 6:10 that will not possess the kingdom of God or, as Albert the Great remarks,

65. Peter Damian, Epist. 96.20, in *Die Briefe des Petrus Damiani*, 3: 59.
66. Peter Damian, Epist. 31.46, in *Die Briefe des Petrus Damiani*, 1: 313.
67. "Effeminati dicuntur ad mollitiem femineam deducti, qui nullo vitio resistunt, sed ut molles cedunt." *Commentarii in Iob* 36.149, p. 420. Albert cites Aristotle's *Nicomachean Ethics* 7.7.3 (1150b) to establish that *mollis* is worse than incontinence. For Scholastic theologians *mollities* suggests diverse crimes against nature, including masturbation and homosexuality. For Thomas Aquinas, *mollities* represents masturbation (see his *Summa theologica* 2.2.154.11 resp.). Likewise, St. Antoninus of Florence identifies *mollities* as a species of the "vice against nature," alongside sodomy and bestiality (*Summa theologica* 2, tit. 5, cap. 4, 2: 667B–C).
68. "Viri effeminati sunt in coeundo insatiabiles et insani sicut mulieres." Quoted in Joan Cadden, "'Nothing Natural Is Shameful': Vestiges of a Debate about Sex and Science in a Group of Late-Medieval Manuscripts," *Speculum* 76 (2001): 66–89, citing p. 81 and n. 54. The passage is from a manuscript at St. John's College (St. John's 113, fol. 14vb).
69. Peter Damian, Epist. 96.20, in *Die Briefe des Petrus Damiani*, 3: 59. Damian is referring especially to Sodomites in this passage. For discussion, see Larry Scanlon, "Unmanned Men and Eunuchs of God: Peter Damian's Liber Gomorrhianus and the Sexual Politics of Papal Reform," *New Medieval Literatures* 1 (1997): 37–64. For Ambrose's condemnation of those who cannot control their passions as effeminate, see *De Cain et Abel* 2.1.4, and *De Noe* 14.49, ed. C. Schenkl, in *Opera*, CSEL 32.1 (Vienna: Temsky, 1897), 380 and 448; and Ambrose, *Explanatio psalmorum xii* 37.6.3, ed. M. Petschenig, in *Opera*, CSEL 64 (Vienna: Temsky, 1919), 141. According to fifteenth-century Dominican Felix Fabri, the female animal is the most avaricious, irascible, faithless, and the most libidinous: "Avarissimum quippe animal est foemina, iracundum et infidele, libidinosum." See *Evagatorum in Terrae Sanctae, Arabiae et Egyptii peregrinationem*, fol. 14b, 2: 367.

are ruled over by effeminate men as a divine punishment (see Isa. 3:4).[70]

Medieval Christians were of course aware that not only Jews were circumcised. In Peter Abelard's *Dialogue between a Philosopher, a Jew, and a Christian* (*Dialogus inter philosophum, Judaeum et Christianum*), the Jew seems to identify the Philosopher as a Muslim when he remarks that "you yourselves even today keep the practice in imitation of Ishmael your father when you receive circumcision at the age of twelve."[71] Petrus Alfonsi, in his *Dialogue against the Jew* (*Dialogus contra Judaeum*), which was written c. 1109 and therefore at least twenty years before Abelard's text mentioned above, notes that both Muslims, signified by Ishmael, and certain Christian heretics perform circumcision.[72] Likewise, in his *Against the Saracen Sect or Heresy*, the Cluniac Abbot Peter the Venerable remarks that Jews and Muslims share the rite of circumcision, because they descend from a common father, Abraham, through Isaac and Ishmael respectively.[73] Similarly Raymund Martini remarks upon the rite of circumcision in Saracen communities, noting one difference vis-à-vis the Jewish rite: Muslims, he avers, at least do not perform the "abominable" ritual of *metzizah b'peh*.[74] Nonetheless, Muslims were said "not to perform the right of circumcision for spiritual effect, but for car-

---

70. Albert the Great, *Commentarii in Iob* 36.149, p. 420.

71. Peter Abelard, *A Dialogue of a Philosopher with a Jew, and a Christian*, 53. The Latin reads: "sicut et vos ipsi usque hodie servatis, qui Ismahelem patrem vestrum imitantes anno duodecimo circumcisionem accipitis." See Peter Abelard, *Collationes* 39, p. 48. Marenbon rejects the effort to identify Abelard's "philosopher" with a specific Muslim intellectual (Abelard, *Collationes*, li). Instead, he remains a general representative for the philosophical traditions of antiquity, given a contemporary appearance. For medieval Muslim circumcision ritual and practice, see James. E. Lindsay, *Daily Life in the Medieval Islamic World* (Westport, Conn.: Greenwood Press, 2005), 188–91.

72. Petrus Alfonsi, *Dialogus contra Judaeum* 12, in *Der Dialog des Petrus Alfonsi*, 128, 21. For the claim that the Jacobites also circumcise their children, see *Dialogus contra Judaeum* 5, p. 65, 25–26, a claim reiterated in the early thirteenth century by Jacques de Vitry, who claims that when he landed at Acre he encountered Jacobites there, who circumcised their children according to the Jewish custom. See his *Lettres de Jacques de Vitry* 2, ed. R. B. C. Huygens (Leiden: Brill, 1960), 83. In his *Historia Orientalis* 76, p. 145, Jacques de Vitry adds that the Jacobites circumcise children of *both* sexes, following the custom of the Saracens. In the late fifteenth century, Felix Fabri remarks too on the Abassini (*sic*) or Indian Christians who err, like the Jews, Saracens, and Jacobites, by circumcizing their children, and even branding their faces with a hot iron. See Felix Fabri, *Evagatorum in Terrae Sanctae, Arabiae et Egyptii peregrinationem*, fol. 135A, 1: 351.

73. See James Kritzeck, *Peter the Venerable and Islam* (Princeton, N.J.: Princeton University Press, 1964), 192.

74. Raymund Martini, *Pugio Fidei* pars 2 [sic], dist. 3, cap. 11, par. 16, fols. 612–13, p. 786.

nal cleanliness, in order to remove the filth that is accustomed to grow under the prepuce."[75]

On the surface, the recognition that Muslims and certain Christian judaizing heretics also performed the rite of circumcision might seem to subvert the claim that circumcision was given to the Jews to distinguish them from all other nations. One Christian response underscored a difference, however, between the circumcision of Isaac and Ishmael, acknowledging that outwardly the "wound of circumcision" appeared to be the same, but internally Isaac's was distinguished by a faith lacking to Ishmael.[76] In another sense, however, both Muslims and judaizing Christians were often perceived to be heterodox Jews. They practice circumcision because they are branches off a Jewish trunk. To a certain extent, Jewish authorities agreed. Maimonides (d. 1204), for example, recognized that a social and religious bond existed between Jews and Muslims because of the shared rite of circumcision, through which both might be included in the Abrahamic community.[77] By contrast, the medieval Jewish mystical text, the *Zohar*, pointed to the flawed nature of the circumcision ritual among Muslims, who failed to perform *peri'ah*.[78] Yet unlike the Jews and despite their shared ritual circumcision, medieval Christians rarely accused the Saracens—whom the Norman poet and chronicler of the Third Crusade (1188–91) Ambroise identified also as the "people of the circumcision"—of being unwarlike.[79] They were only too aware of the military prowess of Saladin (d. 1193), the conqueror of Jeru-

---

75. "[Sarraceni] nec circumcisionem accipiunt propter effectum spiritualem, sed propter munditiam carnalem, ut careant illa foeditate, quae solet sub praeputio crescere." Felix Fabri, *Evagatorum in Terrae Sanctae, Arabiae et Egyptii peregrinationem*, fol. 92a, 3: 51.

76. See Rupert of Deutz, *Anulus seu Dialogus inter Christianum et Judaeum* 1, in M.L. Arduini, *Ruperto di Deutz e la controversia tra Cristiani ed Ebrei nel secolo XII* (Rome: Istituto storico italiano per il Medio Evo, 1979), 192, lns. 271–90.

77. See Hanna Kasher, "Maimonides' View of Circumcision as a Factor Uniting the Jewish and Muslim Communities," *Medieval and Modern Perspectives on Muslim-Jewish Relations*, ed. Ronald L. Nettler, Studies in Muslim-Jewish Relations 2 (Luxembourg: Harwood Academic Publishers, 1995), 103–8.

78. Wolfson, "Circumcision and the Divine Name," 98–99.

79. Ambroise, *The History of the Holy War: Ambroise's Estoire de la Guerre Sainte*, 2 vols., ed. and trans. Marianne Ailes and Malcolm Barber (Woodbridge, 2003), 2:115. But Felix Fabri attributes the success of King Amalric's (d. 1174) Egyptian campaign, prior to the fall of Jerusalem in 1187, to the efffeminate nature of the Egyptians, whom he describes as not inclined to warfare: "Verum tamen dicitur, quod inhabitantes Cairum et Aegyptum sint effoeminati et non bene ad bella dispositi." See *Evagatorum in Terrae Sanctae, Arabiae et Egyptii peregrinationem*, fol. 11a, 3: 105.

salem, and his armies. But Muslims were also widely assumed to be excessively licentious and given to sensual pleasure.[80] Latin chroniclers of the Crusades "depicted the Muslims as addicted to lurid forms of sexual debauchery and described the Saracens as having a special lust for the charms of virtuous Christian women."[81] These vices, then, they shared with Jews.

As already noted, in a letter from 1063 Pope Alexander II had justified warfare against Saracens in Spain because they persecute Christians, while at the same time trying to provide protection to Jewish communities there.[82] During the Crusades the Saracens were enemy combatants and sometimes were viewed as heretics under canon law; therefore they might be treated more harshly than Jews, who remained a tolerated minority in Christendom.[83] Nonetheless, in important respects, Muslims shared more in common with Christian beliefs than did Jews. The Carolingian theologian Amolo noted approvingly that Christians and Saracens venerated many of the same holy places associated with Jesus and Mary.[84] Burchard of Strasburg, an envoy of Emperor Frederick I that

---

80. See Jacques de Vitry, *Historia Orientalis* 6, pp. 30–31, where he remarks that Muslims regard sexual intercourse and *luxuria* as meritorious. His description here of Muslim sexual depravity depends at least in part on the anti-Muslim polemic that is presented in the fifth titulus of Petrus Alfonsi's *Dialogus contra Judaeum*.

81. James Brundage, "Prostitution, Miscegenation and Sexual Purity in the First Crusade," in *Crusade and Settlement*, ed. Peter W. Edbury (Cardiff, U.K.: University College Cardiff Press, 1985), 60.

82. See chap. 1, n. 96.

83. For a positive view of medieval toleration of Jews, see for example Marc Saperstein, "Religious Intolerance and Toleration in the Middle Ages," in *Themes in Jewish-Christian Relations*, ed. Edward Kessler and Melanie J. Wright (Cambridge: Orchard Academic, 2005), 69–88. For the distinction between Jews and Muslims, see the quodlibet by the thirteenth-century Scholastic, Guerric of Saint-Quentin, who asks why Jews are not to be killed in Christian society, like heretics and *pagani*. The *pagani*, however, are clearly Muslims, because he notes that they were once a part of the Church, until they were turned to their error by Mohammad. *Quaestiones de quolibet* q. 3.art. 3.62–65, pp. 222–23. For a brief discussion of this text, see also Gilbert Dahan, "Juifs et judaïsme dans la littérature quodlibétique," in Cohen, *From Witness to Witchcraft: Jews and Judaism in Medieval Christian Thought*, 229–30. In addition, for Saracens as pagans or heretics under canon law, see B. Z. Kedar, "*De Iudeis et Sarracenis*: On the categorization of Muslims in medieval canon law," in *The Franks in the Levant, 11th to 14th Centuries* (Brookfield, Vt.: Variorum, 1993), 207–13. The same question concerning differential treatment was considered by Alexander of Hales or his followers, who concluded that Muslims were subject to death because they held the holy land unjustly and do injury to Christians there. Jews, by contrast, should be treated as a tolerated minority in Christendom. See Alexander of Hales, *Summa theologica* 2, 2, Inq. 3, tr. 8, sect. 1, q. 1, tit. 2, membrum 1, cap. 1 (Quaracchi: Collegii S. Bonaventurae, 1930), 3:730.

84. Amulon, *Epistola seu liber contra Judaeos ad Carolum Regem* 40 (PL 116: 169C).

travelled to Egypt and Syria in 1175, recorded that both Christians and Muslims gathered on the Feasts of the Assumption and the Nativity to venerate a miracle-working icon of the Virgin Mary at the Greek convent of Our Lady of Saydnaya in Syria.[85] Later Christian pilgrims to the Holy Land often remark upon such shared holy spaces, for example, the tomb of the Virgin Mary in the Valley of Josaphat,[86] as well as the Holy Sepulcher itself where not only Christians but Muslims too gathered on Holy Saturday.[87]

Not only did Christians and Muslims share some holy places, but they also shared certain common beliefs. Toward the middle of the twelfth century, Peter the Venerable remarks that as bad as the Saracens are, at least they share with Christians a belief in the Virgin Birth, as well as many beliefs about Jesus.[88] Later, the very popular polemic of the putative Christian convert R. Samuel of Morocco affirms this same doctrinal agreement between Christians and Muslims,[89] a view shared by the exceedingly popular vernacular *Book of John Mandeville* (second half of

---

85. B. Z. Kedar, "Convergences of Oriental Christian, Muslim, and Frankish Worshippers: The Case of Saydnaya," in *De Sion exibit lex et verbum domini de Hierusalem: Essays on Medieval Law, Liturgy and Literature in Honour of Amnon Linder*, ed. Yitzhak Hen (Turnholt: Brepols, 2001), 63–64. For discussion of Burchard's travels, see Volker Scior, "The Mediterranean in the High Middle Ages: Area of Unity or Diversity? Arnold of Lübeck's *Chronica Slavorum*," in *Mobility and Travel in the Mediterranean from Antiquity to the Middle Ages*, ed. Renate Schlesier and Ulriche Zellmann (Münster: LIT, 2004), 112–14.

86. Niccolò da Poggibonsi, *A Voyage Beyond the Seas* (1346–1350) 82, trans. T. Bellorini and E. Hoade (Jerusalem: Franciscan Press, 1945), 44.

87. Niccolò da Poggibonsi, *A Voyage Beyond the Seas* 35, p. 24.

88. Peter the Venerable, Letter 130.2 in *The Letters of Peter the Venerable*, 2 vols., ed. Giles Constable (Cambridge, Mass.: Harvard University Press, 1967), 1:327–30. For a discussion of Peter's views on Jews in this text, also see Yvonne Friedman, "An Anatomy of Anti-Semitism: Peter the Venerable's Letter to Louis VII, King of France (1146)," in *Bar-Ilan Studies in History* 1 (Ramat-Gan, 1978): 87–102; and Robert Chazan, "Twelfth-Century Perceptions of the Jews: A Case Study of Bernard of Clairvaux and Peter the Venerable," in Cohen, *From Witness to Witchcraft: Jews and Judaism in Medieval Christian Thought*, 187–201; Chazan, *Medieval Stereotypes and Modern Antisemitism*, 47–52. For Muslim views on Mary, see the helpful summary in Miri Rubin, *Mother of God: A History of the Virgin Mary* (New Haven: Yale University Press, 2009), 83–88.

89. R. Samuel of Morocco, *Liber de adventu messiae praeterito* 27 (PL 149: 368). The preface to this text claims that the author wrote it about the time of his conversion in 1085, and that it was later discovered and translated into Latin from Arabic in 1339 by the Dominican Alfonso Buenhombre. Most scholars have tended to dismiss the claim that it was first composed in the eleventh century, and treat Alfonso Buenhombre himself as the real author. For discussion, see especially Ora Limor, "The Epistle of Rabbi Samuel of Morocco: A Best-Seller in the World of Polemics," in *Contra Iudaeos. Ancient and Medieval Polemics Between Christians and Jews*, ed. Ora Limor and Guy G. Stroumsa (Tübingen: Mohr, 1996), 177–94.

the fourteenth century), which catalogues the many doctrines common to both Christians and Muslims and remarks that owing to this affinity Saracens are easily converted to the Christian faith.[90] Similarly, Nicholas of Cusa (d. 1464) proclaimed that because the Qur'an contains many statements concerning Jesus that are received by Muslims and acceptable to Christians, though rejected by Jews, it will be easier to bring Muslims to the faith than the Jews.[91] Christians often perceived a nearer doctrinal affinity to Muslims, then, even though they were circumcised like Jews and were thought to display many of the same vices. This special affinity between certain doctrines of Christianity and Islam may help to explain the contention of Crusaders involved in the anti-Jewish violence of the First Crusade, according to the twelfth-century Hebrew chronicle of Solomon bar Simson, that "they [that is, Jews] are lesser in faith than the Muslims,"[92] or the conclusion reached by an inquisitorial handbook of the late Middle Ages, that "A Jew who embraces the sect of the Saracens should not be punished, for the simple reason that . . . the sect of the Jews is worse than that of the Saracens, and one shall not punish someone who abandons the worst of sects for a bad sect."[93]

90. John Mandeville, *The Book of John Mandeville: An Edition of the Pynson Text with Commentary on the Defective Version*, chap. 15, ed. Tamarah Kohanski, Medieval and Renaissance Texts and Studies 231 (Tempe: Arizona Center for Medieval and Renaissance Studies, 2001), 41–42.

91. Nicholas of Cusa, *De pace fidei* 12.41, from *Nicholas of Cusa's De Pace fidei and Cribratio Alkorani: Translation and Analysis*, 2nd ed., trans. Jasper Hopkins (Minneapolis: A. J. Banning Press, 1994), 654. Equally significant, in this passage Cusa adds that although the Jews will be more difficult to bring into the community of faith, in contrast to the Muslims "[the Jews] are few in number and will not be able to trouble the whole world by force of arms."

92. Chazan, *European Jewry and the First Crusade*, Appendix, 296.

93. From *Le dictionionnaire des inquisiteurs* (Valence, 1494), ed. L. Sala-Molins (Paris: Galilée, 1981), 269–76, cited in *The Jews in Western Europe 1400–1600*, ed. and trans. John Edwards (Manchester: Manchester University Press, 1994), 38. Similarly, according to David Nirenberg, the lawyer Oldradus de Ponte (d. 1337) argued that Jewish conversion to Islam did not constitute apostasy, since Islam is less evil than Judaism. See his "Muslim-Jewish Relations in the Fourteenth-Century Crown of Aragon," *Viator* 24, no. 4 (1993): 259, and citing William C. Stalls, "Jewish Conversion to Islam: the Perspective of a *Quaestio*," *Revista española de teología* 43 (1983): 235–51, esp. 246. In other instances, however, Oldradus de Ponte described Judaism and Islam as equally bad. See Norman Zacour, *Jews and Saracens in the Consilia of Oldradus de Ponte* (Toronto: Pontifical Institute for Mediaeval Studies, 1990), 21 and n. 72 (with reference to Cons. 51). This equality between the two minority religions seems evident in a thirteenth-century decree of King James I that forbade a Saracen to become a Jew, and forbade a Jew to become a Saracen ("Item statuimus quod sarracenus vel sarracena non possit fieri judeus vel judea, nec judeus vel judea non possit fieri sarracenus vel sarracena.

Despite the positive purpose, then, served by the circumcision of the flesh before the advent of Jesus, namely, to maintain the people of Israel as a separate community, for medieval Christians this purpose had long been superseded. In the present, it continues to maintain the Jews as a separate people, but one now that is distanced from the true Israel or the Church. Popular Christian perceptions of circumcision tended to view it as an abominable practice of mutilation that even makes Jewish men abhorrent to women. In Peter Abelard's *Dialogue between a Philosopher, a Jew, and a Christian,* the Jew clearly acknowledges that "the sign of circumcision seems so abhorrent to the Gentiles that if we were to seek their women, the women would in no way give their consent, believing that the truncating of this member is the height of foulness, and detesting the divine sign of holiness as an idolatry."[94] Abelard's Jewish spokesman expresses, then, a Christian perception that circumcision is a disgusting practice to women. But it is also a sign of idolatry, perhaps in the sense that circumcision signifies the Jews' persistent carnality and sensuality, through which they had placed love of the flesh and the material world above love of God. Moreover, since circumcision endured as an indelible sign even among Jewish male converts to Christianity, it remained behind as a reminder of their inclination to error and vice. Elukin may be quite correct that "The mark [of circumcision] may have been thus so disfiguring that it made converted Jews seem only half Christian."[95]

By the fourteenth century explanations other than strictly theological interpretations of circumcision appear among Christian medi-

---

Et qui hoc fecerint, amittant personas suas.") See David Romano, "Conversion de Judios al Islam (Corona de Aragon 1280 y 1284)," *Sefarad* 36, no. 2 (1976): 333–37, citing 333.

94. Peter Abelard, *A Dialogue of a Philosopher with a Jew, and a Christian*, 47. For the Latin text, see PL 178: 1623D-24A. In Marenbon's edition—*Collationes* 30 (p. 40)—*gentilibus* (Gentiles) is emended to read *gentibus*, i.e., "pagans."

95. Jonathan M. Elukin,"From Jew to Christian? Conversion and Immutability in Medieval Europe," in *Varieties of Religious Conversion in the Middle Ages,* ed. James Muldoon (Gainesville, Fla.: University Press of Florida, 1997), 185. Although surgical and quasisurgical procedures were employed in antiquity to extend the prepuce for aesthetic reasons or to reverse the effect of circumcision, I am unaware of any cases in the medieval world. For ancient surgical treatments (and for the Greek cultural predilection for a longer prepuce) see Frederick M. Hodges, "The Ideal Prepuce in Ancient Greece and Rome: Male Genital Aesthetics and their Relation to *Lipodermos,* Circumcision, Foreskin Restoration, and the *Kynodesme,*" *Bulletin of the History of Medicine* 75 (2001): 375–405, but esp. 396–99; in the modern era, "decircumcision" can be treated as cosmetic surgery. See Sander Gilman, "Decircumcision: The First Aesthetic Surgery," *Modern Judaism* 17, no. 3 (1997): 201–10.

cal practitioners, who suggest that circumcision also has a therapeutic purpose related to personal hygiene. Guy de Chauliac (c. 1300–68) indicates that this practice is given in the law of the Jews and the Saracens, so that dirt or filth will not accumulate at the base of the glans of the penis (*quod non congregantur sordities in radice balani*).[96] Despite ecclesiastical condemnation of the religious ritual, Christian physicians could even recommend surgical circumcision to Christian patients in order to address certain health problems, just as from late antiquity physicians might recommend castration to address health concerns, including leprosy.[97] For example, in response to advice he received (from physicians?) Bishop Hugh de Orival of London (d. 1085), suffering from leprosy, allowed himself to be castrated; in the end, this drastic remedy brought no relief, however, but only led him into disrepute.[98] But such medical views, which we might be inclined to identify as "modern" because they seem to appeal to a secular rather than religious justification, certainly do not displace the theological traditions that linked circumcision to carnality and sensuality. When Thomas Aquinas avers that circumcision was given to the Jews in part to reduce sexual desire, this does not imply that contemporary Jews are, as a result, more chaste than Christians, but rather that because Jews *require* this protection and Christians do not, by nature Jews are more libidinous than Christians.[99]

Oddly, in arguing that circumcision reduces sexual desire, Aquinas follows Maimonides.[100] Why then was it provided only to Jewish males

---

96. Guy de Chauliac, *Cyrurgia Guidonis de Cauliaco, et Cyrurgia Bruni, Teodorici, Rolandi, Lanfranci, Rogerii, Bertapalie* tr. 6, doc. 2, cap. 6 (Verona: 1530). fol. 68va. Later, Felix Fabri made a similar claim for the Saracens alone (see n. 72).

97. H. F. J. Horstmanshoff, "La castration dans les texts latins médicaux," in *Maladie et maladies dans les texts latins antiques et médiévaux*, ed. Carl Deroux, Collection Latomus 242 (Brussels: Latomus, 1998), 90.

98. William of Malmesbury, *De gestis pontificum Anglorum* 2.73, p. 145. Although self-emasculation, such as that performed by Origen, was a bar to clerical rank, the thirteenth-century Thomas of Chobham notes that when performed for medical reasons, castration is not a sin and does not represent an impediment to holy orders: "si quis amiserit virilia . . . per consilium medicorum, vel per violentiam hostium non propter hoc efficitur irregularis." See his *Summa Confessorum* art.3, dist. 3, q. 6a, fol. 15vb, 72.

99. Thomas Aquinas, *Summa theologica* 1.2.102.5, ad 1. For his view of Jews and Judaism, see especially John Y. B. Hood, *Aquinas and the Jews* (Philadelphia: University of Pennsylvania Press, 1995).

100. Maimonides, *The Guide of the Perplexed* 3.49 (117a–118a), trans. Shlomo Pines (Chicago: University of Chicago Press, 1963), 609. See the following for Maimonides's twin justifications for circumcision (restraint of concupiscence and the establishment of social com-

DEFORMITIES AND CIRCUMCISION

and not to females? This question was raised repeatedly by Christian interpreters, who sought once more to elevate baptism by pointing to its universal character, since baptism removed original sin from male *and* female. In contrast, in the fifth-century Pseudo-Augustinian polemical dialogue between female personfications of the Church and the Synagogue, the Church objects that were circumcision necessary for salvation, then clearly women cannot be saved![101] Albert the Great provides an interesting reply, however, rooted in his understanding of female anatomy. One reason, he insists, that circumcision was demanded only of males stems from its nature as a sign. A sign is only a sign if it is visible. Although a woman also has a "penis," that is, a homologous organ in which inordinate desire dominates, her "penis" is internal to her body.[102] Circumcision in her case, then, would not be visible because her analogue to the male organ is internal rather than external.[103] It is not, then, that circumcision was not required of women because women are less lustful and licentious or any less guilty of sin. To the contrary, medieval naturalists treated women as more lustful and wanton than men. Rather, women are not circumcised because circumcision had to be a visible sign. Consequently, on the one hand, circumcision seems to have been viewed as intended to restrain the Jewish male's excessive sensuality; on the other, when viewed as an emasculating, feminizing wound, circumcision appears to identify the Jewish male with unrestrained female sexuality. As Joan Gregg has remarked:

This encoding of the Jew as sexually licentious—whether as wanton woman or lecherous beast—persisted in various forms throughout the medieval period.... The containment of the perceived Jewish sexual threat through the feminization of the Jewish male was a useful construct in Christian theology. Cross-gendering the Jewish male as lascivious but female defused the threat of his physical aggression while maintaining his image as a peril to a Christian purity.[104]

---

munity), and also Josef Stern, "Maimonides on the Covenant of Circumcision and the Unity of God," in *The Midrashic Imagination: Jewish Exegesis, Thought, and History*, ed. Michael Fishbane (Albany: SUNY Press, 1993), 131–54.

101. *Altercatio Ecclesiae et Synagogae*, ed. J. N. Hillgarth, CCSL 69A (Turnholt: Brepols, 1999), 33.

102. For the female "penis," see Albert the Great, *De animalibus* 15.1.6.30, vol. 16, 1005 (SZ 2: 1098), and his *Quaestiones super de animalibus* 15.4–5, p. 262, 60–64 (QDA, 446).

103. "Alia ratio est ... quod id quo dominatur libido, in mulieribus est intrinsecus, in viro autem extrinsecus, et ideo circumcidi non potuit in muliere sicut in viro." Albert the Great. *De sacramentis* tr.2, q. 1, 3, p. 20.

104. Joan Young Gregg, *Devils, Women, and Jews: Reflections of the Other in Medieval*

THE JEWS' BADGE

The threat of the Jews' impure sexual appetite also lurks behind thirteenth-century ecclesiastical legislation that demanded that Jews wear distinctive garb. Canon sixty-eight from the Fourth Lateran Council (1215) required both Jews and Saracens of both sexes to wear some distinguishing mark on their clothing for the express purpose of preventing prohibited sexual contact between Christians and these groups.[105] Sexual contact when one or both Christian partners were unmarried would normally be condemned under the rubric of fornication or adultery, but in this case it is all the more reprehensible because it involves relations with Jews or Muslims. Although secular rulers did not always enforce this ecclesiastical legislation, or did so inconsistently, gradually the Jews' badge became another visible symbol of Jewish difference.[106] The badge was not only to identify Jews and Muslims more visibly to Christians, but also to protect Christians from the heightened sexual desire of the "Other." Pope Gregory IX, in a letter to the Archbishop of Gran, dated March 3, 1231, laments that he has heard that in Hungary "Christians mingle with Saracen women, and Saracens with Christian women."[107]

Sermon Stories (Albany: SUNY Press, 1997), 186–87. See also Goldberg, "Two Parallel Medieval Commonplaces," 85–120.

105. For Canon 68 of the Fourth Lateran Council, see Solomon Grayzel, *The Church and the Jews*, 308–9. It was not only Jews and Muslims to be so distinguished in the medieval world, but also prostitutes, certain penitents and, it seems, sometimes lepers. For the forms of legislation and various types of mark on the clothing, see the still useful work by Ulysse Robert, *Les signes d'infamie au moyen age. Juifs, Sarrasins, hérétiques, lépreux, cagots et filles publiques* (Paris: Honoré Champion, 1891). For the special designators for lepers, see 146–74.

106. See for example the complaint of Pope Honorius III (January 27, 1217) that the Jews of Burgos do not wear an identifying garment or badge, a complaint reiterated later by Gregory IX for Burgos as well as other parts of Spain, large parts of Germany, the kingdom of Navarre, and others, for which he clearly blames secular authorities for a failure to insist upon the badge. For the text, see Grayzel, *The Church and the Jews*, 142–43, 188–89, 198–99, 204–7, 244–45. Innocent IV reveals a similar preoccupation with the badge. See 258–59, 282–83, 294–95. Nicholas Vincent examines similarly two papal letters from 1221 and 1229 to Archbishops Stephen Langton and Richard of Canterbury, pressing them to ensure that the Jews wear distinctive clothing (*habitus*) or, in the latter letter, a distinctive badge (*signum*) to prevent sexual encounters between Jews and Christian women. Vincent also explains the lack of urgency felt by secular (and some ecclesiastical) authorities that profited from the selling of exemptions to Jews resisting this imposition. See Nicholas Vincent, "Two Papal Letters on the Wearing of the Jewish Badge, 1221 and 1229," *Jewish Historical Studies: Transactions of the Jewish Historical Society of England* 34 (1997): 209–24.

107. Grayzel, *The Church and the Jews*, 184–85

"Mingle" (*commiscentur*) is no more than a euphemism for sexual intercourse. In the same letter, Gregory complains that Saracens feign Christian identity in order to seduce Christian women, leading them into error. Later, Gregory IX complains to the archbishop of Compostella that a failure to insist upon the Jews' badge in Spain has led to Christians and Jews "mingling" with the other's women. Moreover, Gregory IX provides to the king of Navarre details on the appearance of the badge, which is to be a round yellow badge of felt or linen stitched on the garments of men and women, both in front and in back, so that they will be easily recognized.[108]

The possibility that Jews might be mistaken for Christians was a nagging concern for ecclesiastics. Pope Innocent IV complained to the Bishop of Manguellone in a letter of July 7, 1248 that Jews in his diocese wear wide capes that even imitate the garb of Christian clerics![109] The imitation of clerical dress by some Jews may have merely expressed a desire for the more fashionable and expensive silks and fabrics that many Christian clergymen wore, for which clergy were often condemned by ecclesiastical authorities. But it also reflected a conscious effort on the part of some Jews, especially during times of persecution, to conceal their identity to avoid violent treatment.

The badge, then, is intended to distinguish clearly Jews not only from Christian laymen but even from its clergy and members of religious orders identified by a distinctive habit. In a profound sense for medieval culture, the "clothes make the man" and distinctive forms of clothing or signs attached to garments likely communicated a sense of identity more directly than did physiognomy. Yet distinctive garments that served as identifiers paralleled physiognomic signs and can be viewed, as von Moos remarks, as "a second skin," intended to reveal the character of the wearer.[110]

---

108. Grayzel, *The Church and the Jews*, 216–17; for an attempt to identify the various forms of the *rouelle* in France, based on iconographic evidence, see Danièle Sansy, "Signe distinctif et Judéité dans l'image," in *Le corps et sa parure/The Body and Its Adornment*, vol. 15 of *Micrologus. Natura, scienze e società medievali* (Florence: SISMEL, 2007), 87–106; Danièle Sansy, "Marquer la Différence: L'imposition de la rouelle aux XIIe et XIVe siècles," *Médiévales* 41 (2001): 15–36.

109. Grayzel, *The Church and the Jews*, 280–81.

110. Peter von Moos, "Le vêtement identificateur: L'habit fait-il ou ne fait-il pas le moine?" in *Le corps et sa parure/The Body and Its Adornment*, vol. 15 of *Micrologus. Natura, scienze e società medievali* (Florence: SISMEL, 2007), 41–60, citing 51. Von Moos draws

It is possible that the Jews' badge was imported to western Europe from the Islamic world to the East, where Jews were also compelled to adopt different dress in order to distinguish them from both Muslims and Christians. Obadiah, a Christian who converted to Judaism in 1102, about the time of the First Crusade, and who had likely been a monk previously in Norman Italy, reports that on a visit to Baghdad he saw that "every Jew was required to wear a belt around his waist. [The sultan] Abû al-Shujâ' required that the Jewish women were to wear two signs. They were to wear one black and one red sandal; and every woman was to wear a copper bell that rang as she moved in order to distinguish between Jewish and Gentile women."[111] Although special forms of dress, then, were devices common to both the Christian and Islamic worlds to distinguish religious communities, nonetheless in Europe it was especially a fear of sexual interaction that lay beneath the forms of clothing adopted to distinguish Jews and Muslims from Christians. It is true that papal concerns were not merely that male Jews or Muslims might be mistaken for Christians and engage in intercourse with Christian women, but equally with the danger implied when Christians "inadvertently" had sex with Jews or Saracens, in violation of civil and canon law. Sometimes, Christians apparently sought to explain sexual relations with a Jew or Muslim with the justification that this was intended to bring them to conversion, a practice known among more radical political groups of the

---

attention not only to the fact that clothes contributed to a sense of identity, but also to the significance when one is deprived of these marks—e.g., when a priest is "defrocked" or a monk forced to relinquish his habit.

111. Obadiah the Convert, *Epistle,* trans. in *Other Middle Ages. Witnesses at the Margins of Medieval Society,* ed. Michael Goodich (Philadelphia: University of Pennsylvania Press, 1998), 72. The literature on Obadiah, an important chronicler, scribe, and autobiographer, has grown quite large. Very useful will be Joshua Prawer, "The Autobiography of Obadyah the Norman, A Convert to Judaism at the Time of the First Crusade," in *Studies in Medieval Jewish History and Literature,* 2 vols., ed. Isadore Twersky (Cambridge, Mass.: Harvard University Press, 1979),1: 110–34. Norman Golb reviews Obadiah's possible role in bringing together Hebrew prayer and Gregorian chant in "The Music of Obadiah the Proselyte and His Conversion," *Journal of Jewish Studies* 18 (1967): 43–63. Golb further develops Obadiah's biography, drawn from Hebrew fragments, in his *Jewish Proselytism—a Phenomenon in the Religious History of Early Medieval Europe,* Tenth Annual Rabbi Louis Feinberg Memorial Lecture (Cincinnati: University of Cincinnati, 1988), 21–31. With respect to Muslim requirements for distinctive dress, Muslim authorities first demanded that *dhimmis* wear distinguishing clothing to prevent intermarriage several centuries before the promulgation of Canon 68 at the Fourth Lateran Council (1215). See Ilse Lichtenstadter, "The Distinctive Dress of Non-Muslims in Islamic Countries," *Historia Judaica* 5 (1943): 35–52.

1970s as "horizontal recruiting."[112] The justification was clearly rejected however, and medieval penitentials identify sex with a Jewish or Muslim (*gentilis*) woman, or a heretic, as a sin. When a Christian husband has sexual relations with a Jew or Muslim, he must even be excluded from communion.[113]

The fear of sexual commingling of Christian and non-Christian populations also lay behind canons from the Council of Nablus (1120), which forbid sexual intercourse between Christian and Muslims and threatened male transgressors, whether Christian or Saracen, with castration. This fear of sexual encounters may once more be related to concerns that these might lead to religious conversions—but in this instance to the conversion of Christians, which did in fact occur with some frequency in the Frankish Levant.[114] Unlike legislation in Europe, however, these canons from the Crusader kingdom did not prescribe a badge or other identifying symbol, but only prohibited Muslims from wearing Frankish dress. According to Kedar, this may be explained because "Frankish and Muslim dress in the Holy Land were so different that the mere prohibition of dressing 'according to Frankish custom' (*'Francigeno more'*) was deemed sufficient."[115] The situation in twelfth-century Europe was clearly different: Jews and Christians were all too often indistinguishable in terms of their clothing or dress, which concerned both Jewish and Christian religious leaders.[116] This was likely not entirely accidental: at times, Jews consciously adopted Christian dress for their own safety. For example, the *Sefer Hasidim* records the tale of a Jew who often wore a priest's clothing to pass as a Gentile so that he could travel unmolested, although it also denounces the practice, even if adopted to avoid per-

---

112. Albert the Great, *Super IV Sententiarum* 4, d. 15, art.24, 7, Ed. Borgnet 29, 507A.

113. Robert of Flamborough, *Liber Poenitentialis* 4.8.225; 5.3.5.284, pp. 197; 236.

114. Benjamin Z. Kedar, "Multidirectional Conversion in the Frankish Levant," in *Varieties of Religious Conversion in the Middle Ages*, ed. James Muldoon (Gainesville, Fla.: University Press of Florida, 1997), 190–99. The Christian pilgrim Felix Fabri remarks that when Christians were discovered to have had sex with Muslim women, the Saracens gave them only two choices: apostasy and conversion to Islam, or death. The first alternative would seem to have been the one most favored. See *Evagatorum in Terrae Sanctae, Arabiae et Egyptii peregrinationem*, fol. 87A, 1: 224.

115. B. Z. Kedar, "The Subjected Muslims of the Frankish Levant," in *Muslims under Latin Rule*, ed. J. M. Powell (Princeton, N.J.: Princeton University Press, 1990), 166.

116. For Jewish concerns, see for example Moché Catane, "Le vetement en France au XIe siecle d'apres les ecrits de Rashi," in *Rashi et la culture juive en France du Nord au moyen âge*, ed. Gilbert Dahan, Gérard Nahon, and Elie Nicholas (Paris: Peeters, 1997), 123–33.

secution. In part, its prohibition stemmed from a fear that Jewish men that dressed as priests would also wear the symbol of Christian religion, namely, a cross or crucifix. This same concern appears in its condemnation of Jews endangered by Crusaders that might tonsure themselves or affix a cross to their garments in order to pass as Christians. By contrast, the *Sefer Hasidim* allows a Jewish woman who fears rape while on a journey to dress in a nun's habit, and to pretend to be a nun, in order to avoid violation.[117] Even though this text denounced Jewish men who adopted the garments of Christian priests, it did permit Jewish men generally to adopt the dress of lay Christians in order to escape persecution. But such sartorial confusion also facilitated sexual relations between Jews and Christians and raised fears of conversion, as did occur in a famous incident in Oxford: in 1222 the judgment of a provincial church council, convened by Archbishop Stephen Langton of Canterbury, resulted in the execution of an apostate deacon that had converted to Judaism and been circumcised for love of a Jewish woman.[118] This nameless convert is sometimes confused with Robert of Reading and a plaque at Osney Abbey, Oxford commemorates the martyrdom near that site on April 17, 1222, of "Robert of Reading, otherwise known as Haggai of Oxford."[119]

Another incident from Oxford also illuminates Christian fears of

---

117. Rabbi Yehudah HeChasid, *Sefer Chasidim: The Book of the Pious* 410(702), 618(199), 632(703), 644(220), 645(221), trans. Avraham Yaakov Finkel (Northvale, N.J.: Jason Aronson, Inc. 1997), 227, 351, 357, and 364. Finkel used two Hebrew editions of the *Sefer Chasidim* for his translation: the text edited by Reuben Margaliot (Jerusalem: Mossad Harav Kook, 1957) and *Sefer Chasidim* (Jerusalem: Mechon Rishonim). In the citations above, the first number represents the paragraph number in the English translation; the second number, in parentheses, represents the corresponding paragraph in the Margaliot edition.

118. The historical evidence has been thoroughly examined by Frederic William Maitland in "The Deacon and the Jewess," in *Roman Canon Law in the Church of England: Six Essays* (London: Methuen, 1898), 158–79. The story was embellished by the thirteenth-century chronicler Matthew Paris, who adds that when the deacon was brought before the council he urinated on the Cross. See Horowitz, *Reckless Rites: Purim and the Legacy of Jewish Violence*, 167–69. It is impossible to establish with exactitude the number of Christians who converted to Judaism in western Europe. Norman Golb, extrapolating from Hebrew manuscript testimonies in the Cairo Genizah, has speculated that "the total number of proselytes fleeing their European homelands and arriving in Jewish communities of the Islamic world (excluding those of Iran) between 1000 and 1200 CE was approximately 300 x 50, or fifteen thousand men and women over a span of two centuries." *Jewish Proselytism*, 36. How many other converts to Judaism remained in Europe but attempted to hide their Christian origins is unknown.

119. This plaque may be viewed at http://www.oxfordjewishheritage.co.uk/galleries/medieval-image-library/view/5.

conversion—or rather reversion—to Judaism. On April 6, 1245, a royal writ was sent to the sheriff of Oxfordshire ordering him to capture and imprison an Oxford cleric and acolyte who was a convert to Christianity, but who had relapsed and resumed his Jewish identity. The man's name was to be disclosed to the sheriff by the Oxford Dominican Robert Bacon (possibly a cousin of Roger Bacon, the Franciscan), and his fate was to be determined by Robert Grosseteste, Bishop of Lincoln; regrettably, the relapsed convert's name does not appear in the written accounts, nor do we know the outcome of this episode.[120] It is unknown whether the man had romantic motives for returning to the Jewish community, but the blurring of boundaries between Jewish and Christian communities was a real concern. A more celebrated example occurred in 1275 when a London Dominican known as John, Richard, or Robert of Reading converted to Judaism. According to the *Chronicle of Bury St. Edmunds*, Robert was well trained in the Hebrew language, had himself circumcised, married a Jewish woman, and took the name Haggai. He was then handed over to the Archbishop of Canterbury for correction.[121]

If distinctive dress for Jews was intended to prevent sexual encounters across religious communities and to prevent conversion, nonetheless the imposition of distinctive dress for Jews (and Muslims) was not applied consistently across Europe, at least in part because Jews were sometimes willing to pay secular or ecclesiastical authorities for exemption. As late as 1491, a letter from the Burgos city council to the monarchs Ferdinand and Isabella complains that despite laws regulating the dress

120. For an account, see F. D. Logan, "Thirteen London Jews and Conversion to Christianity: Problems of Apostasy in the 1280s," *Bulletin of the Institute of Historical Research* 45 (1972): 214–29, citing 224.

121. "Londoniis quidam de ordine Predicatorum dictus frater Robertus de Redingge predicator optimus linguaque Hebrew eruditissimus apostavit et ad Iudaismum convolavit atque Iudeam ducens uxorem se circumcidi atque Aggeum fecit nominari." *The Chronicle of Bury St. Edmunds 1212–1301*, ed. and trans. Antonia Gransden (London: Thomas Nelson and Sons, 1964), 58. For sources, see Jens Röhrkasten, *The Mendicant Houses of Medieval London 1221–1539* (Münster: Lit Verlag, 2004), 167. For the assumption that romantic involvement led to his conversion, see Sandra Raban, *England under Edward I and Edward II 1259–1327* (Oxford: Blackwell Publishers, 2000), 93; and Robin R. Mundill, *England's Jewish Solution: Experiment and Expulsion 1262–1290* (Cambridge: Cambridge University Press, 1998), 48. More plausibly, Robert Stacey remarks that Robert was seduced not by love of a Jewish woman, but love for the Hebrew language and literature. See his "'Adam of Bristol' and Tales of Ritual Crucifixion in Medieval England," in *Thirteenth-Century England XI, Proceedings of the Gregynog Conference 2005*, ed. Björn Weiler, Janet Burton, Phillipp Schofield, and Karen Stöber (Woodbridge: Boydell Press, 2007), 12.

of Jews and Muslims, many still fail to wear the badge, and wear clothes of silk and gold so fine that it is impossible to tell them apart from Christians. The council appeals to the king that "Jews and Moors should each wear their badge, the Moorish man his green hood covering his clothing, and the Jew or Jewess their round red badge on the right shoulder on the outside of the clothing, and Moorish women a blue patch on the right shoulder."[122] Again, in the background there seems to lie a concern over sexual encounters between Jews, Christians, and Muslims. But the imposition of the badge seems to presume that, if outwardly differentiated from one another, Christians at least will (or should) properly restrain themselves. The reality was often quite different. One complaint directed against King Peter I of Spain (d. 1369) was not only that he was favorably disposed toward Jews but that "having spurned the Christian religion, he had intercourse with a certain Jewess."[123]

The badge even served a purpose for Christian sex workers. Felix Fabri remarks that in Christian lands "Jews wear a visible sign, so that a prostitute will not admit a Jew while thinking him to be a Christian."[124] This serves as a good reminder that medieval Latin Christian society sought not only to regulate sexual relations between married partners, as well as consensual (or forced) premarital sex, but also professional sexual services. In a letter from 1065, Peter Damian praises three Christian prostitutes who became martyrs to the faith in Spain. In response to the complaints of local Muslim men, with whom the Christian women had refused sexual intercourse, a secular tribunal that seemed committed to the principle of equal access condemned the prostitutes to death unless they offered themselves to all. Steadfast in their refusal, the women were cast into prison but when their executioners, over a period of several days, sought to cut off their heads, their blades could not even scratch the

---

122. Edwards, *The Jews in Western Europe 1400–1600*, document 32, 91, with a source in Luis Suárez Fernández, *Documentos acerca de la expulsión de los Judíos* (Valladolid, 1964), 377–79.

123. "[Peter I] spreta religione Christiana, cum quadam se Judaea foemina miscuisset." Thomas Walsingham, *Historia anglicana*, 2 vols., ed. Henry Thomas Riley (London: Longman, 1863–64), 1: 303.

124. "ut Judaei signa manifesta portent, ne meretrix Judaeum admittat putans Christianum." Felix Fabri, *Evagatorum in Terrae Sanctae, Arabiae et Egyptii peregrinationem*, fol. 132b, 3: 169. The author then polemicizes against Christian pimps (*lenones*) who prostitute Christian women in the East, to satisfy the lust of the infidel, while praising Jews and Saracens who refuse to pimp their women to Christians.

skin, until a vision of Christ appeared to the women presenting to them the crown of martyrdom.[125] By refusing to "mingle" with Muslims, these public women joined the ranks of the saints of the church. While prostitution remained a sin throughout the Middle Ages, nonetheless until the fifteenth century medieval society had generally viewed prostitution as necessary for the preservation of good social order, allowing the passions of unmarried men to find release.[126] So long as prostitutes guarded the boundaries between Christian and non-Christian, refusing the tariff of Jews and Muslims, they even performed an important social function, despite the sinfulness of their profession. When they failed, however, then the entire community was endangered and, as David Nirenberg has argued, for this reason in Iberia before 1391 "prostitutes became the focal point for anxiety about sexual frontiers."[127] Prostitution threatened the social order when Christian prostitutes received members of other religious communities, breaking down the barriers between the people of God and the "Other." The imposition of the badge or other distinctive dress sought, no doubt, to insure that other women followed the example of the unnamed holy martyrs Damian praised, guarding the boundaries between Christians, Jews, and Muslims.

Although the appearance of the badge might vary from one region to the next, its purpose did not. The badge was essential in order to safeguard sexual boundaries and to maintain a distance between Christian and non-Christian worlds. The badge also reminded the Christian majority, however, of the sexual threat posed by Jews. As Jeffrey Richards notes, "It was because of their 'notorious sexual promiscuity' that in 1317 King Philip V ordered that the Jews wear the badges that distinguished them from Christians."[128] Similarly, in Renaissance Italy Jewish women were required to wear earrings as an identifying sign, a practice that as-

---

125. Peter Damian, Epist. 123.15–16, in *Die Briefe des Petrus Damiani*, 3: 406 (for translation, see *The Letters of Peter Damian, 121–150*, 19–20).

126. Thomas of Chobham, *Summa Confessorum* art. 7, dist. 2, q. 6a, cap. 2 (*Quare meretrices ecclesia sustineat*), 347–49. See also Fabienne Chaube, "Prostitution," *Encyclopedia of the Middle Ages*, 2 vols., ed. Andre Vauchez, Barrie Dobson, and Michael Lapidge, trans. Adrian Walford (Chicago: Fitzroy Dearborn Publishers, 2000), 2:1193; for detailed treatment, see Ruth Mazo Karras, *Common Women: Prostitution and Sexuality in Medieval England* (New York: Oxford University Press, 1996).

127. David Nirenberg, "Conversion, Sex, and Segregation: Jews and Christians in Medieval Spain," *American Historical Review* 107, no. 4 (2002): 1065–93, citing 1075.

128. Jeffrey Richards, *Sex, Dissidence and Damnation: Minority Groups in the Middle Ages* (New York: Barnes and Noble, 1990), 107.

similated them as a group to prostitutes and evoked images of sexual impurity.[129] The myth of Jewish sensuality and insatiable desire extended to both men and women.

The myth of the Jews' sexual potency had a long life in European anti-Jewish polemics, and was popularized in inter-war Germany by Theodor Fritsch (d. 1933), writing under the pseudonym F. Roderich-Stoltheim, who insists that "in the Old Testament and in the Talmud, the Israelites are described as a voluptuous and lewd people, who were addicted to the grossest sensual excesses. Lust and desire stand written on the faces of the Hebrews."[130] Fritsch also shares the view that the Jewish male's "physiological circumstances, connected with the act of circumcision" result in excessive sexual demands that have a clearly deleterious effect on the female partner's health.[131] Once more, it seems that circumcision had been given to the Jews to restrain wanton sexuality. The medieval Jews' badge will improve upon circumcision as a sign: it will be on the outer garment, in front and behind, marking members of both sexes.

Jewish interpreters shared some of the same assumptions about circumcision, but arrived at a very different conclusion. In a study of the *Sefer Hasidim* Elliot Wolfson has shown that "Hasidei Ashkenaz [German Pietism] understood the act of cutting the foreskin as a symbolic excision of sexual desire ... and as a consequence of this act the Jewish male is transformed into an angelic being."[132] About the same time, Maimonides reached a similar conclusion. In his *Guide of the Perplexed*, he also considered the purpose of circumcision and remarked:

---

129. See Diane Hughes, "Distinguishing Sign: Ear-rings, Jews, and Franciscan Rhetoric in the Italian Renaissance City," *Past and Present* 112 (1986): 3–59. But, medieval Jewish sources make it clear that Jewish women had long elected to wear earrings, as well as other jewelry (presumably merely for the sake of fashion), generating debate about whether this led to a violation of Sabbath laws. See David Malkiel, *Reconstructing Ashkenaz: The Human Face of Franco-German Jewry, 1000–1250*, Stanford Studies in Jewish History and Culture (Stanford: Stanford University Press, 2009), 155–59.

130. Roderich-Stoltheim, *The Riddle of the Jew's Success*, 262.

131. Ibid., 268.

132. Elliot R. Wolfson, "Martyrdom, Eroticism, and Asceticism in Twelfth-Century Ashkenazi Piety," in *Jews and Christians in Twelfth-Century Europe*, ed. Michael A. Signer and John Van Engen, Notre Dame Conferences in Medieval Studies 10 (Notre Dame: University of Notre Dame Press, 2001), 195–96; also see Engen, "Circumcision, Secrecy, and the Veiling of the Veil: Phallomorphic Exposure and Kabbalistic Esotericism," in *The Covenant of Circumcision: New Perspectives on an Ancient Jewish Rite*, 63.

Similarly with regard to circumcision, one of the reasons for it is, in my opinion, the wish to bring about a decrease in sexual intercourse and a weakening of the organ in question.... The fact that circumcision weakens the faculty of sexual excitement and sometimes perhaps diminishes the pleasure is indubitable.... It is hard for a woman with whom an uncircumcised man has had sexual intercourse to separate from him.[133]

A generation later, R. Isaac ben Yedaiah (b. c. 1215), who lived in southern France, agreed that circumcision is intended to restrain the Jews' lust since, once the foreskin has been removed, lust is diminished and with it the desire to lie with foreign women. In contrast, the uncircumcised Gentile's lust or desire is fueled even more by the foods available to Gentiles but forbidden to Jews, foods that increase the complexional heat of his body, with the result that the Gentile will seek frequent intercourse or multiple sexual partners.[134] Marc Saperstein reports that in his commentary on *Midrash Rabbah*, "R. Isaac explains that one who is uncircumcised cannot master his impulses except in the rare and exceptional case of a man born with a naturally cold temperament."[135] R. Isaac adds that women—even Jewish women—will prefer an uncircumcised man, who will bring her to orgasm more quickly because he must thrust into her with passionate energy, since his foreskin is a barrier to ejaculation and completed intercourse. Christian medical practitioners too asserted with growing frequency that the presence of the prepuce increased sexual pleasure, offering an explanation as to why Jewish (and Muslim) women were thought to prefer Christian men rather than their own.[136] For R. Isaac, because of his difficulty in reaching orgasm, the uncircumcised man may have intercourse two or three times each night, finally ejaculating but

133. *Guide* 3:49, Pines trans., 609–11.

134. The reference to differences in their diet here is interesting, and rests upon the assumption of humoral medicine that what one eats affects the body's complexion, which, in turn, can influence behavior.

135. Marc Saperstein, *Decoding the Rabbis: A Thirteenth-Century Commentary on the Aggadah* (Cambridge, Mass.: Harvard University Press, 1980), 97. Let me note here that Christians typically depicted the Jewish male as having a naturally cold and dry—i.e., melancholy—temperament. The ideal Christian male will have an opposite, sanguineous temperament that is hot and moist. But Christian physicians typically viewed sexual desire and lust as a product of a cold nature, and not as one restrained by a cold nature. Thus women, who were phlegmatic (cold and moist) were also thought to be far more lustful than men. On thirteenth-century efforts to "measure" the female pleasure quotient, see Mary Frances Wack, "The Measure of Pleasure: Peter of Spain on Men, Women, and Lovesickness," *Viator* 17 (1986): 173–96.

136. See José Pardo Tomás, "Physicians' and Inquisitors' Stories?" 180–82.

causing his flesh to waste away and to become emaciated. The notion that ejaculation 'empties' and dries out the body is graphically illustrated in a story found in Albert the Great's *Questions Concerning Aristotle's On Animals* (*Quaestiones super de animalibus*). Albert reports that:

> Clement of Bohemia told me there was a certain hoary old monk who approached a certain beautiful mistress and just like a starving man he demanded her sixty-six times before the striking of matins; the next day he fell down and, on the very same day, was dead. And because he was a noble, his body was opened up and his brain was found to be entirely evacuated, so much so that nothing more of it remained than the size of a pomegranate and, similarly, his eyes were destroyed. Nature marvels at this, although it seems to be consonant with reason. This, then, is an indication that intercourse particularly evacuates the brain.[137]

Following Albert's narrative, one can appreciate Shaye Cohen's remark that, "In R. Isaac's eyes, Christian men were sexual supermen, who could pleasure their women to a degree far beyond the capacities of Jewish men, and who could do so far more often."[138] By contrast, a circumcised man will ejaculate and reach orgasm quickly because the crown of the penis is exposed. Thus the circumcised Jew will require sex only once each week, R. Isaac ben Yedaiah suggests. His partner, on the other hand, will remain unsatisfied and frustrated: "she does not have an orgasm except once a year, except on rare occasions."[139] But it appears that her frustration is precisely the point: because she derives little pleasure from sex,

---

137. Albert the Great, *Quaestiones super de animalibus* 15.14, p. 268, 45–55 (QDA, 460). The notion that frequent intercourse dries out the body and leads to an early or untimely death will also be found in Averroes's commentary on Aristotle's, *De causis longitudinis et brevitatis vite*, in *Averrois Cordubensis Compendia Librorum Aristotelis qui Parva Naturalia Vocantur*, ed. Emilia Ledyard Shields and Henry Blumberg, Corpus Commentariorum Averrois in Aristotelem 7 (Cambridge, Mass.: Mediaeval Academy of America, 1949), 138, 29–139, 44. Vincent of Beauvais understands this evacuation of the brain resulting from excessive intercourse to explain as well weak eyesight. See his *Speculum naturale* 31.2, 1: 2295. Finally, according to Ps. Albert the Great's *De secretis mulierum* 13, because ejaculation of sperm deprives the body of its natural humidity, males generally do not live as long as females (p. 147). Females, on the other hand, may actually benefit from frequent intercourse, because through it they lose their superfluous cold and receive heat, while the opposite is true for men. See Ps. Albert the Great, *Women's Secrets*, 70; and, Orlanda S. H. Lie, "Women's Medicine in Middle Dutch," in *Science Translated: Latin and Vernacular Translations of Scientific Treatises in Medieval Europe*, ed. Michèle Goyens, Pieter de Leemans, and An Smets (Leuven: Leuven University Press, 2008), 449–66, esp. 449–50.

138. Cohen, *Why Aren't Jewish Women Circumcised?* 156.

139. Cited in David Biale, *Eros and the Jews: From Biblical Israel to Contemporary America* (New York: Basic Books, 1992), 94.

she will not often demand that her husband satisfy the commandment of *onah* (that is, conjugal relations), leaving him free to pursue higher intellectual and spiritual pursuits.[140] Moreover, because she does not demand intercourse often from her husband, according to R. Isaac ben Yedaiah the circumcised Jewish male "will not empty his brain because of his wife," in sharp contrast to the empty and emptying sexual encounters attributed to a Christian monk by Clement of Bohemia.[141]

From this it becomes clear that while for the Christian interpreter circumcision is an emasculating sign and a punishment instituted to restrain the natural carnality of the Jewish male, for the Jewish interpreters noted above circumcision is divinely instituted to make it possible for the Jew to master the lust that disturbs the Gentile and may cause the latter to waste away, enabling the Jew to transcend the impulses of the flesh and to live the higher, angelic life of quiet philosophical and theological contemplation. Circumcision establishes the basis then for the Jewish male's virility, whereas the absence of circumcision among the Gentiles makes it impossible for them to achieve the intellectual and spiritual heights that define manliness. It is significant that for both communities, however, the principal assumption was the same: circumcision restrains lust and sexual desire.

This premise must have become well established by the early sixteenth century, as seen in the satirical *Letters of Obscure Men* (*Epistolae obscurorum virorum*). In one letter, the fictional Eitelnarrabianus von Pesseneck defends the integrity of the anti-Jewish polemicist and (Jewish) convert to Christianity, Johannes Pfefferkorn, and his wife who, the Jews claim, has made her husband a cuckold. Von Pesseneck insists that Pfefferkorn's wife enjoys the highest Christian reputation and defends her against the allegation that she regularly engages in adulterous sex with university masters and the town burghers. His satirical defense, which ignores earlier reports that the letter recipient, Ortuinus Gratius, had himself slept with Pfefferkorn's wife, rests upon a claim that the audience must have recognized as mistaken: namely, Pfefferkorn's wife's report that, according to her mother, circumcised men give women greater

---

140. For the commandment of *onah*, based on Exod. 21:10, see David Biale, *Eros and the Jews*, 53–56; R. Avraham Peretz Friedman, *Marital Intimacy: A Traditional Jewish Approach* (Linden, N.J.: Compass Books, 2005), 20–25.

141. Cited in Biale, *Eros and the Jews*, 94.

sexual pleasure and therefore, should her convert-husband die, she will not accept another husband unless he too has been circumcised![142] To appreciate the joke, the audience must have understood that this is not an instance in which mother knows best.

The paramount difference among our sources, however, is that for the Jewish sources circumcision restrains sexual desire successfully and emphasizes a rabbinic conception of Jewish intellectual virility but Gentile impotence, Jewish spirituality but Gentile carnality, and Gentile material power but Jewish weakness. Once more, Shaye Cohen points out that evidence from the fourteenth and fifteenth centuries reveals that some European Jews felt that their sexual performance was disadvantaged vis-á-vis the Gentile male's precisely because of circumcision, attesting perhaps to a sense of sexual incompetence that reflected their powerlessness in the Christian social and political world they inhabited.[143] For Christian interpreters, however, circumcision fails among Jews to achieve its purpose of restraining sexual desire and lust, both because circumcision has been superseded by Christian baptism and therefore has lost its effectiveness, and because of assumptions of Jewish hypersexuality that subverted even circumcision's power to control Jewish lust.

142. "Et ego saepe audivi ab ea, quod audivit frequenter a sua matre quod viri praeputiati faciunt feminis maiorem voluptatem, quam non praeputiati: eam ob causam dicit, quando suus maritus moritur, et ipsa alium accipiet, ille debet etiam nullam cutem habere in membro." *Epistolae obscurorum virorum* 1.36, 1: 95. That this defense rests on an erroneous premise seems confirmed too by the use of the form *praeputiati* for "uncircumcised" when, in classical Latin, it means just the opposite. Nonetheless, in this passage it is clear that it can only mean "circumcised," fully revealing von Pesseneck's foolishness. For the comic or satirical nature of the names of the fictional letter writers, see James V. Mehl, "Language, Class, and Mimic Satire in the Characterization of Correspondents in the *Epistolae obscurorum virorum,*" Sixteenth Century Journal 25, no. 2 (1994): 289–305. For the claim that Ortuinus Gratius slept with Pfefferkorn's wife, see *Epistolae obscurorum virorum* 1.13, 1: 39.

143. For other evidence that some Jews *envied* the foreskinned Gentile because he could provide (and receive) more sexual pleasure, see Cohen, *Why Aren't Jewish Women Circumcised?* 156–58.

3

THE JEWS AND LEPROSY

If the Jews' alleged licentiousness and sexual appetite "feminized" them in some sense, it also tended to assimilate them to another marginalized group in the Middle Ages: namely, lepers. Both constituted at times a pariah minority. Although medieval lepers suffered from a number of illnesses that do not satisfy the definition of modern Hansen's disease, nonetheless even as late as the nineteenth century some medical texts identify elephantiasis and certain related illnesses under the rubric *lepra Judaeorum* ("Leprosy of the Jews"), establishing more than a metaphorical connection between Jews and lepers that extended beyond their shared status as social outsiders or outcasts.[1]

Medieval theology had a number of biblical sources for an understanding of leprosy as both a spiritual and physical infirmity. The Suffering Servant of Isaiah 53:4, whom Christian exegetes understood to prefigure Jesus himself, bore for us our own infirmities, and was struck low and humbled by God just like a leper (*quasi leprosum*).[2] To be "just like a leper" signified his humiliation and outcast status and served as an illustration, for Christian interpreters, that Jesus had truly condescended in the Incarnation to assume fully the weakness and frailties of human nature. But it may also have been understood as more than merely a simile. A sense that real leprosy and its physical symptoms should be associated with the messiah even spread to heterodox Jewish communities. Maimonides describes one Jew-

---

1. Erasmus Wilson, *Diseases of the Skin,* 6th ed. (Philadelphia: Lea and Blanchard, 1865), 335–36.
2. Cf. Rupert of Deutz, *De sancta Trinitate* 13, *In Exodum* 4, ed. R. Haacke, CCCM 22 (Turnholt: Brepols, 1971–72), 752.

ish community that, having misunderstood the meaning of this verse, followed a false messiah who, in fulfillment of Isaiah 53:4, allegedly appeared as a leper at night but arose each morning cleansed and hale.[3]

In addition to other passages in the Old Testament (some of which will be discussed below), there are many New Testament texts in which Jesus heals lepers (Matt. 8.3; Mark 1.40ff.; Luke 5:12–16; Luke 17:11–19; see figure 4) or commissions the apostles to heal lepers (Matt. 10:2–5), suggesting a connection to the messianic age: those who believed and had faith in Jesus as messiah could be miraculously cured of this dread disease. In the first decade of the twelfth century, Petrus Alfonsi rejected his Jewish interlocutor's criticism that Jesus had performed such cures by magic;[4] leprosy can only be cured by medicine or by divine power and it is clear, he remarks, that Jesus healed lepers with his touch (see Mark 1:40; Matt. 8:2) through divine power.[5] Even the portrait of Jesus that, according to tradition, was dispatched to King Abgar of Edessa, as well as various holy relics, were credited with curing leprosy.[6] The Carolingian council of Paris (825) describes the Cross as a physician for the sick, and a source of cleansing or purification for lepers.[7] The thirteenth-century Franciscan Erfurt Chronicle claims that Tiberius Caesar (d. 37) was healed of leprosy by Jesus' image imprinted on Veronica's veil,[8] while the anonymous late twelfth-century romance, *La Vengeance de Nostre-Seigneur*, remarks that the Emperor Vespasian (d. 79) was cured of leprosy when he gazed on Jesus' visage imprinted on the veil. In appreciation for the miracle, Vespasian resolves to avenge himself on the Jews, who had put Jesus to death.[9] In the early medieval *Vindicta Sal-*

---

3. See Maimonides's *Epistle to Yemen* in *A Maimonides Reader*, ed. Isidore Twersky (New York: Behrman House, 1972), 458.

4. For Talmudic accusations that Jesus worked magic, see Peter Schäfer, *Jesus in the Talmud* (Princeton, N.J.: Princeton University Press, 2007), 103–6.

5. Petrus Alfonsi, *Dialogus contra Judaeum* 10, in *Der Dialog des Petrus Alfonsi*, 116, 28–117, 19. That Jesus is said in the Gospels to have touched lepers in order to heal them created a certain theological difficulty, since touching the leper would communicate impurity. See Thomas Aquinas, *In IV Sententiarum* dist. 1 q. 2 a. 2 qc. 3 ad 1.

6. See Ewa Kuryluk, *Veronica and Her Cloth: History, Symbolism and Structure of a 'True' Image* (Oxford: Blackwell, 1991), 201; and also *Histoire du roi Abgar et de Jésus*, ed. Alain Desreumaux (Turnholt: Brepols, 1993).

7. "crux aegrotantium medicus, crux emundatio leprosorum," *Libellus Synodalis Parisiensis*, Nov. Conc. 2.2., cap. 74, in *Concilia aevi Karolini*, 2 vols., ed. Albertus Werminghoff, MGH Leges 3, Concilia 2 (Hannover: Hahn, 1906–8), 1: 504.

8. See *Cronica minor Minoritae Erphordensis*, ed. Oswald Holder-Egger, MGH, SS rer. Germ 42, (Hannover: Hahn, 1899), 533.

9. *La Vengeance de Nostre-Seigneur: The Old and Middle French Prose Versions: The*

vatoris, this same desire to take vengeance against the Jews for having slain Jesus heals Vespasian, Titus, and a crowd of lepers that looked upon Veronica's veil.[10]

In a similar way, hagiogaphical tradition maintains that Pope Sylvester I cured the Emperor Constantine (d. 337) of that leprosy with which God had afflicted him for earlier having persecuted Christians. Constantine had been instructed by pagan priests (in some medieval versions, by physicians)[11] that he could be healed by bathing in the blood of infants but, when the innocents were brought before him, he took pity on them, repented of his crimes against the Church, was baptized by Sylvester and miraculously healed.[12] Although there is no contemporary historical account

---

Version of Japheth, ed. Alvin E. Ford, Studies and Texts 63 (Toronto: Pontifical Institute of Mediaeval Studies, 1984), 80 and 85. For a discussion of this text, see Maureen Bolton, "Anti-Jewish Attitudes in Twelfth-Century French Literature," in *Jews and Christians in Twelfth-Century Europe*, 234–54.

10. For a summary of the text and translation, see *The Apocryphal New Testament: A Collection of Apocryphal Christian Literature in an English Translation based on M. R. James*, ed. J. K. Elliott (Oxford: Oxford University Press, 1993), 213–16. For the relationship between the *Vengeance de Nostre-Seigneur* and the *Vindicta Salvatoris*, see also Loyal A. T. Gryting, "The Venjance Nostre Seigneur as a Mediaeval Composite," *Modern Language Journal* 38, no. 1 (1954): 15–17.

11. See Thomas Ebendorfer's fifteenth-century *Chronica regum Romanorum* 3, ed. Harald Zimmermann, MGH, SS rer. Germ. n.s. 18 (Hannover: Hahn, 2003), 191; and *Chronica regum Romanorum*, 7, p. 684.

12. The tradition of Sylvester and Constantine can be found in the *Liber Pontificalis*, Epitome Feliciana, ed. Theodor Mommsen, MGH, SS, Gesta Pontif. Rom. 1 (Berlin: Weidmannos, 1898), 47, 244; *Donation of Constantine*, in *Documents of the Christian Church*, 3rd ed., ed. Henry Bettenson and Chris Maunder (Oxford: Oxford University Press, 1999), 107–8; Rangerius of Lucca, *Liber de anulo et baculo*, ed. E. Sackur, MGH, Ldl 2 (Hannover: Hahn, 1892), 508; Jacobus de Voragine, *The Golden Legend* 68, trans. William Granger Ryan, 1:280; the Erfurt Chronicle, *Cronica minor Minoritae Erphordensis*, ed. Oswald Holder-Egger, SS rer. Germ 42, (Hannover: Hahn, 1899), 562; and even the composite English compilation, *Flores historiarum*, 3 vols., ed. Henry Richard Luard, Rerum britannicarum medii aevi scriptores 95 (London: H. M. Stat. Off., 1890; repr. Kraus, 1965), 1:179–80. For the medieval spread of the legend, see Lydia Miklautsch, "Der Antijudaismus in den mittelalterlichen Legendem am Beispiel der Silvesterlegende in der Fassung des Konrad v. Wurzburg," in *Die Juden in ihrer mittelalterlichen Umwelt*, ed. Alfred Ebenbauer and Klaus Zatloukal (Cologne: Böhlau, 1991), 173–82. The general belief that bathing in the blood of infants may cure leprosy is repeated in Michael Scot's thirteenth-century *Liber phisionomiae*, cap. 14 (Venice: 1477) although without reference to Constantine or Pope Sylvester. In the fifteenth century, Lorenza de Valla casts doubt on the tale—and on the *Donation of Constantine* as a whole—comparing Constantine to King Azariah (2 Kgs. 15:56), who, although he retained his crown, was forced to dwell apart from his people owing to the leprosy with which God afflicted him for allowing the worship of alien gods. See *De falso credita et ementita Constantini donatione* 4, ed. Wolfram Setz, MGH, QQ Geistesgesch. 10 (Weimar: Böhlau, 1976), 138.

to suggest that Constantine ever suffered from leprosy, the hagiographical narrative became well established in the Middle Ages. By the middle of the thirteenth century, this motif was lavishly illustrated in frescoes in the Saint Sylvester chapel in Rome's Basilica of the Santi Quattro Coronati.[13] (See figure 5.) Vincent of Beauvais (d. 1264) epitomizes the tradition when he remarks that "Constantine, who earlier had been advised to be washed in the blood of innocent children, was healed of both corporeal and spiritual leprosy by the blood of the true innocent, namely Jesus Christ."[14]

The notion that the blood of innocents could provide a cure for leprosy was not only a tradition rooted in later Christian polemical claims that pagan physicians had advised Constantine to bathe in the blood of infants. In the first century, the pagan naturalist Pliny the Elder reported that elephantiasis, a form of leprosy, had originated in Egypt where it especially afflicted Egyptian kings, who sought to ameliorate their condition by bathing in human blood.[15] We find an analogous motif in medieval Jewish biblical commentary and numerous Passover haggadot, which hand down a Jewish legend that Pharoah had Israelite infants slaughtered to provide a "blood bath" to cure his own leprosy.[16] While in this tradition Israelite children were Pharoah's victims, more damaging for Christian-Jewish relations may be the appearance of a medieval legend that it was *Jewish* physicians who advised King Richard I of England (d. 1199) to bathe in the blood of newborns as a cure for leprosy, an illness that some said he contracted during the Third Crusade.[17]

---

13. For illustration and description, see Claude Gaignebet and Jean-Dominique Lajoux, *Art profane et religion populaire au Moyen Age* (Paris: Presses universitaires de France, 1985), 106–7.

14. "Constantinus Imperator fuit curatus a lepra corporali et spirituali, virtute sanguinis Christi veraciter innocentis, qui prius habuerat consilium lavari in sanguine innocentium puerorum." *Speculum naturale* 1.19, 1: 659.

15. Pliny the Elder, *The Natural History* 26.1.5.

16. For some Jewish sources of this legend, see Louis Ginzberg, *The Legends of the Jews*, 7 vols. trans. Henrietta Szold (Philadelphia: 1909–28; repr. Hildesheim: Georg Olms Verlag, 2000), 5: 412–13 n. 101. For the medieval iconography, see David Malkiel, "Infanticide in Passover Iconography," *Journal of the Warburg and Courtauld Institutes* 56 (1993): 85–99. Ephraim Shoham-Steiner has traced the transformation of this tradition in medieval Jewish texts in "Pharoah's Bloodbath: Medieval European Jewish Thoughts about leprosy, disease, and blood therapy," in *Jewish Blood: Reality and Metaphor in History, Religion and Culture*, ed. Mitchell Hart (New York: Routledge, 2009), 99–115. My thanks to Dr. Shoham-Steiner for a pre-publication copy of his fine study. And, last, Ariel Toaff explores this legend at length in his *Pasque di sangue*, 157–65.

17. Carole Rawcliffe, *Leprosy in Medieval England* (Rochester, N.Y.: Boydell Press, 2006),

For Christian culture, however, Constantine's miraculous cure, which substitutes the water of baptism for the blood of innocent children, became a familiar device for later Christian authors. Like a new Sylvester, remarked Hincmar of Reims (d. 882), Saint Remigius (d. 533), the apostle to the Merovingian Franks, led King Clovis to the laver of baptism and cleansed him of his old leprosy and the stains of his old sins.[18] Like Vespasian, Constantine, and Clovis, the body of the Church could hope to be cleansed of leprosy's physical signs in holy waters,[19] by baptism and divine grace, if not by the care of physicians.

As original sin corrupted the body and the soul, so baptism healed the body and the soul. But Jews, refusing baptism, remained symbols of the enduring presence of disease. According to the Bishop Epiphanius (fifth or sixth century), Jesus had wanted to heal the Jews of their diseased constitution, seeing that the Jews are afflicted by the *morbus regius*, that is, the "king's evil," or the royal disease. For classical authors, *morbus regius* might indicate a variety of illnesses and especially jaundice, but for patristic and early medieval Christian texts *morbus regius* seems most often to designate leprosy. The affliction is known as *morbus regius* because of traditions that assert the thaumaturgic healing power of medieval kings (especially the Capetians) to cure it by their touch.[20] By the

---

247; Joshua Trachtenberg, *The Devil and the Jews: The Medieval Conception of the Jew and Its Relation to Modern Antisemitism* (New Haven: Yale University Press, 1943), 142.

18. "Procedit novus Constantinus ad lavacrum salutiferum, in quo delendi erant lepre veteris morbi sordentesque antique peccatorum maculae diluendae, divino muneri obsequente beato Remigio, in quo apostolica doctrina et virtutum gratia alter representari videbatur Silvester." Hincmar of Reims, *Vita Remigii episcopi* 15, ed. Bruno Krusch, MGH SS rer. Merov. 3 (Hannover: Hahn, 1896), 297. For a discussion of this text and its aims, see Thomas J. Heffernan, *Sacred Biography: Saints and their Biographers in the Middle Ages* (Oxford: Oxford University Press, 1992), 67–68.

19. The late sixth-century Piacenza Pilgrim attributed to both the Baths of Elijah in Gedara and the pool of Siloam in Jerusalem a miraculous power to cure leprosy. See *Jerusalem Pilgrims before the Crusades*, trans. John Wilkinson (Warminster, England: Aris and Phillips, 2002), 133, 141.

20. See Marc Bloch, *Les rois thaumaturges: étude sur le caractére surnaturel attribué à la puissance royale particuliérement en France et en Angleterre* (Paris: Gallimard, 1983). This work was first published in 1923, and has been translated as *The Royal Touch*, trans. J. E. Anderson (New York: Dorset Press, 1989). Cf. Frank Barlow, "The King's Evil," in his *The Norman Conquest and Beyond* (London: Hambledon Press, 1983), 23–47, reprinted from the *English Historical Review* 95 (1980): 3–27. Barlow examines the evolving definition(s) of *morbus regius* and attempts to correct Bloch. For an effort to explain the changing signification of *morbus regius*, especially from the thirteenth century, see also Jacques Le Goff, "Le mal royal ay moyen âge: du roi malade au roi guerisseur," *Mediaevistik* 1 (1988): 101–9. Maaike van der

thirteenth century, it will become identified too with scrofula (that is, adenite tuberculosis). Because scrofula was linked etymologically to the pig (sow = *scrofa*), it will also be loosely related to leprosy. Yet for Epiphanius, when the Jews rejected Jesus they also rejected all hope of a cure.[21] Expounding upon Matthew 9:11–12, wherein Jesus responds to Pharisaic criticism with the words "It is not those who are healthy who need a physician, but those who are sick," Chromatius of Aquileia (fifth century) likewise insists that the Jews, trusting in their own righteousness, have repudiated both the physician, Jesus, and all cure for sin. Citing Jerome, he concludes that the only medicine to restore health to the Jews will be found in the wood of the Cross.[22]

Although Chromatius may have in mind only a cure for the affliction of the soul, namely, sin, the boundaries between the physical and the spiritual could not be clearly drawn. In the early seventh century, Isidore of Seville explicated passages from Leviticus 22 in which the Lord rejects imperfect or "blemished" animals as sacrifices, not only because they have broken limbs or missing parts, but also because they show symptoms of various skin ailments, including blisters, impetigo, and scabies, an ailment characterized by severe itching (Lev. 22:22, Vulg.). For Isidore such passages may be interpreted allegorically, to symbol-

---

Lugt points out that in a *quodlibet* from c. 1300, either Henry the German or Henry of Brussels also considers the possibility that the king's healing power may be hereditary, and therefore have a natural and not only miraculous cause. See Maaike van der Lugt, "Les maladies héréditaires dans la pensée scolastique (XIIe–XVIe siècle)," in *L'hérédité entre Moyen Âge et Époque modern. Perspectives historiques,* ed. Maaike van der Lugt and Charles de Miramon (Florence: SISMEL, 2008), 273–320, citing 273–74.

21. "Quantis remediis et medicaminibus dominus noster voluit curare miseros et vulneratos Iudaeos, sed noluerunt suscipere sanitatem! Sed quia morbo regio, id est zelo, repleti erant; morbus regius zelus est et omnis, qui zelat proximum sibi, nullam habet veniam apud deum." *Sancti Epiphanii episcopi Interpretatio Evangeliorum* 34, ed. Alvar Erikson (Lund: Harrassowitz, 1939), 67. Certain medieval glosses on 2 Sam. 11:4 extended to King David's touch the power to stop Bathsheba's menstrual flow, so that he could engage in intercourse with her. See Phillipe Buc, "David's Adultery with Bathsheba and the Healing Power of Capetian Kings," *Viator* 24 (1993): 101–20. Buc has also translated Helgaud of Fleury's eleventh-century *vita* of King Robert the Pious (d. 1031) [*Helgaud de Fleury, Vie de Robert le Pieux. Epitoma vitae regis Rotberti pii,* ed. Robert-Henri Bautier and Gilette Labory, Sources d'histoire médiévale 1 (Paris, 1965)], which contains an episode in which the pious King heals lepers by his touch alone. See Helgaud of Fleury, *A Brief Life of King Robert the Pious* 27, trans. Phillipe Buc (2003), available at www.stanford.edu/dept/history/people/buc/HELG-W.DOC (accessed May 15, 2009).

22. *Tractatus in Matthaeum* 45, ed. R. Étaix and J. Lemarié, CCSL 9A (Turnholt: Brepols, 1974).

ize a person who burns with the "itch" of lust and the ardor of concupiscence.[23] Isidore also condemns those men who, like the sacrificial animals rejected because their testicles were bruised or crushed (Lev. 22:24), act like and appear to be women.[24] But is Isidore only suggesting a symbolic interpretation of these texts or does he think that there is some deeper connection between the external symptoms apparent on the surface of the skin and internal, moral shortcomings? The lines of demarcation between inner and outer, physical and moral infirmity, shift and remain elusive. In the thirteenth century St. Bonaventure likewise blurs these lines when he complains that the Jews remain diseased because they have rejected the fragrant, medicinal liquor expressed from Jesus's wounds, which can heal every sickness. Instead the Jews reject the medicine, spurning the antidote by which the human race is saved and, just like frogs that are repulsed by the fragrant odor of vineyards, they flee the true physician sent to heal both flesh and spirit.[25]

The conviction that physical illness can be removed by spiritual intervention stems simply from the notion that one and the same power removes the imperfections of both body and soul. We can find traces of this notion even in modern culture. In a 2008/2009 court case, Wisconsin residents Dale and Leilani Neumann were convicted of second-degree reckless homicide in the death of their eleven-year old daughter, Madeline, for failing to obtain medical help to treat her undiagnosed diabetes. Over a period of several days, the parents prayed over the child but watched her die. In her own defense, her mother Leilani testified that "illnesses are a spiritual disease that can be cured through prayer."[26] Me-

---

23. Isidore of Seville, *Mysticorum expositiones sacramentorum seu Quaestiones in Uetus Testamentum: In Levit.* 16.5 (PL 83: 335).

24. Isidore of Seville, *Mysticorum expositiones sacramentorum seu Quaestiones in Uetus Testamentum: In Levit.* 16.6 (PL 83: 335); and Isidore of Seville, *De ecclesiasticis officiis* 1.41.2, ed. Christopher M. Lawson, CCSL 113 (Turnholt: Brepols, 1989). In *De ecclesiasticis officiis* 1.41.2, Isidore condemns especially certain Christians in Spain who participated in pagan celebrations at the kalends of January, who donned the skins of animals, made themselves up like women, and danced with wild abandon. Caesarius of Arles had similar complaints about "cross dressers" at such celebrations. See Bernadette Filotas, *Pagan Survivals, Superstitions and Popular Cultures* (Toronto: Pontifical Institute of Mediaeval Studies, 2005), 156–58.

25. Bonaventure, *Sermones dominicales, Sermo* 6.6.

26. Jeff Starck, "Faith-Healing Mom Defends Actions," *Wausau Daily Herald*, January 25, 2010 (available at http://www.wausaudailyherald.com/article/0090729/WDH0101/101260008/0/%22/apps/pbcs.dll/gallery?Avis=U0&Dato=20090728&Kategori=WDH01&Lopenr=907280803&Ref=PH%22).

dieval culture would have endorsed this view with great ardor. In general, like leprosy most bodily infirmity results from sin, a wound of the soul, and therefore for medieval theologians in a real sense most (if not all) illness can be described literally as psychosomatic. This was understood to be the reason why Jesus instructed the infirm man he healed to go and "sin no more lest something worse happen to you" (John 5:14). Alain de Lille (d. 1202) identifies his *Pentiential Book* (*Liber poenitentialis*), dedicated to Archbishop Henry Sully of Bourges and composed as a guide for priests and confessors, as "a book called the Corrector and the Physician, which most fully contains corrections for bodies and medicines for souls, and instructs each priest how ... or when priests ought or can invite the people committed to them to penance and provide aid, just like a faithful physician."[27] Throughout the work he reiterates the ancient *topos* of the priest as physician (*medicus*), who is responsible for the health of his charges. Moreover, a canon of the Fourth Lateran Council (1215) under Pope Innocent III instructs that when physicians are called to visit the sick, they should above all warn and instruct the afflicted first to seek aid from the physicians of the soul, that is, the clergy. Once a priest has provided for the health of the soul, then a physician may attend to the body and attempt a medical cure since "when the cause [sin] ceases so too will the effect."[28] About the same time, Thomas of Chobham explained that because many illnesses are borne as a punishment from sin, having nothing to do with the nature of the elements or the body, they can only be cured by the act of confession, and therefore a physician (*medicus*) should be consulted only *after* the patient has confessed to a priest.[29]

Although leprosy was understood to be a physical ailment, biblical texts that discussed the illnesses grouped under the Latin term *lepra* (Hebrew *tsara't*) also gave theologians ample opportunity for allegorical interpretation.[30] Werner of St. Blaise (d. 1126), following the example of

27. "Hic est Liber qui Corrector vocatur et Medicus, qui correctiones corporum et animarum medicinas plenius continet et docet unumquemque sacerdotem, quomodo ... quo tempore presbyteri debeant vel valeant plebem sibi commissam ad poenitentiam invitare et tamquam fidelis medicus auxilium dare." Alain de Lille, *Liber poenitentialis* prol., 2: 15.

28. Cited by Vincent of Beauvais, *Speculum naturale* 31.99, 1: 2371. The source is canon 22 of the Fourth Lateran Council. See *Decrees of the Ecumenical Councils*, 2 vols., ed. Norman P. Tanner (Washington, D.C.: Georgetown University Press, 1990), 1: 245.

29. Thomas of Chobham, *Summa Confessorum* art. 4, dist. 2, q. 2a, fol. 47va, p, 236.

30. For a useful discussion of the ritual impurity contracted by contact with a "leper" in

Isidore of Seville,[31] analyzed at length the six types of leprosy outlined in Leviticus 13:1ff. and concluded that "leprosy is actually false doctrine. Therefore, it is not absurd that heretics who do not possess the unity of the true faith but profess heterodox doctrines and mix true and false are understood to be lepers."[32] One group of heretics is like those said to have leprosy on their head, because they have sinned against the Father's divinity or against Christ, who is man's head. This group includes Jews, Valentinians, and Marcionites.[33] In the same way, Werner catalogues dozens of heresies, and associates each one with a particular form of leprosy. Nor is Werner unusual in associating heresy with bodily illness or disease. Medieval theologians commonly compared the spread of heresy to the contagion or spread of illness. Bruno of Segni (d. 1123) too, in his explication of Deuteronomy 24:9 (cf. Num. 12:9ff.)—where Moses's sister, Miriam, is cursed with leprosy—explains that "leprosy is a sin of the soul, and that soul is leprous that has been wounded by the stains of sin. Those who refuse to believe the priests of God incur this leprosy. Miriam was struck by this because she spoke against Moses. And the Jews are struck by this, since they speak badly of Christ."[34]

Surely, not every case of leprosy could be viewed as a divine punishment for sin. Jesus himself suffered "like a leper," and not because he was thought to be guilty of sin. Similarly, in the deformed or scarred visages of medieval lepers, especially when they bore their infirmity with hu-

the book of Leviticus, see Hyam Maccoby, *Ritual and Morality: The Ritual Purity System and Its Place in Judaism* (Cambridge: Cambridge University Press, 1999), chaps. 10–11. In particular, Maccoby explains the route by which the Hebrew came incorrectly to be rendered as *lepra* in the Vulgate tradition.

31. Isidore of Seville, *Mysticorum expositiones sacramentorum seu Quaestiones in Uetus Testamentum: In Leviticum* 11.4 (PL 83: 328).

32. "Lepra quippe doctrina falsa est. Proinde leprosi non absurde intelliguntur haeretici qui unitatem verae fidei non habentes varias doctrinas profitentur veraque falsis admiscent." Werner of St. Blaise, *Libri deflorationum* (PL 157: 1135C). For the identification of heresy and leprosy in the twelfth century, see also R. I. Moore, "Heresy as Disease," in *The Concept of Heresy in the Middle Ages (11th–13th C.)*, ed. W. Lourdaux and D. Verhelst (Louvain: Louvain University Press, 1976), 1–11.

33. "In capite lepram portant qui in divinitate Patris vel in ipso capite, quod est Christus, peccant. Caput enim viri Christus. Hanc lepram habuerant Judaei, Valentiniani, Marcianitae et Fotiniani." Werner of St. Blaise, *Libri deflorationum* (PL 157: 1135C).

34. "Animae nameque lepra peccatum est; illa anima leprosa, quae peccati maculis est vulnerata. Hanc lepram incurrunt, qui Dei sacerdotibus credere nolunt. Hac et Maria percussa est, quia contra Moysen locuta est. Hac et Judaei percutiuntur, quoniam de Christo male loquuntur." Bruno of Segni, *Expositio in Pentateuchum—in Deuteronomium* 24 (PL 164: 530B).

mility, some were wont to see in them the image of Christ in a rather special way and accorded to the leper a positive religious significance. Thus Robert, although an honorable, devout, and erudite monk of Cluny under Abbot Hugh (d. 1109), was struck with leprosy by God, the divine physician. Similarly, St. Francis of Assisi, who required his brethren to minister to lepers, remarked to one leper that "the illnesses of the body are given to us by God in this world for salvation of the soul, so they have great value, when they are borne patiently."[35] Nonetheless, despite a sometimes positive religious significance, leprosy still generated fear or horror: although Abbot Hugh kept the good monk Robert at Cluny, he was compelled to place him in an isolated cell, away even from the infirmary, in order to avoid scandal in the community.[36]

But more often, and especially for allegorists like Werner of St. Blaise, leprosy represented not only physical infirmity but also, or even principally, an illness that externalized or embodied sin. As such it symbolized all those who stood isolated outside the Church, both heretics and Jews, who remained outside the body of believers and subject to leprosy. As a result, Werner of St. Blaise demands that heretics be cast outside the Church, just as lepers were separated from the holy community of Israel.[37]

Once the incidence of true (rather than merely metaphorical) leprosy in Europe grew at the end of the eleventh century, expanding throughout the twelfth and thirteenth centuries before beginning to decline in the fourteenth century, the illness raised growing alarm and demanded

35. *The Little Flowers of St. Francis* 25, in *Francis of Assisi, Early Documents*, 3 vols., ed. Regis J. Armstrong, J. A. Wayne Hellmann, and William J. Short (New York: New City Press, 1999–2002), 3: 608.

36. See Gilo, *Vita Sancti Hugonis abbatis*, ed. Herbert E. J. Cowdrey, in "Two Studies on Cluniac History, 1049–1109," *Studi Gregoriani* 11 (1978): 89; for the role of the infirmary at Cluny in this period, see especially Riccardo Cristiani, "Integration and Maginalization: Dealing with the Sick in Eleventh-Century Cluny," in *From Dead of Night to End of Day: The Medieval Customs of Cluny*, ed. Susan Boynton and Isabelle Cochelin (Turnholt: Brepols, 2005), 287–95.

37. Werner of St. Blaise, *Libri deflorationum* (PL 157: 1136D–1137A); Bruno of Segni, *Expositio in Pentateuchum—in Leviticum* 14 (PL 164: 434A); and Rupert of Deutz, *De sancta Trinitate* 15, *In Leviticum* 2, ed. R. Haacke, CCCM 22 (Turnholt: Brepols, 1971–72), 883; Rupert of Deutz, *De sancta Trinitate* 16, *In Numeros* 1, pp. 923–24. Also see Geneviévie Pichon, "Essai sur la lèpre du haut moyen âge," *Le moyen âge* 90, no. 3–4 (1984): 331–56. For the biblical requirement to segregate the leper from the community of Israel, see especially Lev. 14. For Mishnaic categorization of leprosy as a communicable uncleanness or impurity, see especially Mishnah *Kelim* 1.1–5.

a pastoral response.³⁸ Leprosy will be represented in medieval art and iconography with more frequency over the same period.³⁹ Leprosy's impact can be judged from the well-known poem of Jean Bodel (d. 1210), who, having contracted leprosy at the beginning of the thirteenth century, takes his leave of the world in his "Les Adieux du Lépreux," lamenting that only his heart remains hale within his decaying and ravaged body.⁴⁰ Bodel ended his life in a *leprosarium* or leper colony—most likely at Grant Val near Beaurains.⁴¹ Leper colonies in Europe began to appear in greater number and often were organized like communities of Augustinian canons. Canon 23 of the Third Lateran Council (1179) gave such communities official status, and permitted them a cemetery, a chapel, and a priest.⁴² The early thirteenth-century Victorine Robert of Flamborough describes lepers living in community rather than wandering from place to place as "religious," in the same context as monks, canons, Templars and Hospitallers.⁴³ The number of leprosaria in Europe seems to

38. Cf. Francoise Bériac, "À propos de la fin de la lèpre: XIIIe–XVe siècles," in *The Regulation of Evil. Social and Cultural Attitudes to Epidemics in the Late Middle Ages*, ed. Agostino Paravicini Bagliani and Francesco Santi (Florence: SISMEL, Edizioni del Galluzzo, 1998), 159–73. Some scholars dispute the claim that the number of cases of leprosy dramatically increased during this period, arguing instead that new attention was given to a disease that had been endemic in Europe for centuries. See for example P. D. Mitchell, "The Myth of the Spread of Leprosy with the Crusades," in *The Past and Present of Leprosy. Archaeological, Historical, Palaeopathological and Clinical Approaches: Proceedings of the International Congress on the Evolution and Palaeoepidemiology of the Infectious Diseases 3 (ICEPID), University of Bradford, 26th–31st July 1999*, ed. C. A. Robertson, et al. (Oxford: Archaeopress, 2002), 171–77.

39. For the iconography of leprosy in medieval Christian art, see especially William B. Ober, "Can the Leper Change His Spots? Part I," *American Journal of Dermatopathology* 5, no. 1 (1983): 43–58. Ober remarks that leprosy's iconography "does not seem to begin until the late 9th century." (p. 49) Ober continues his study with a focus on late medieval and Renaissance depictions of leprosy in Christian art in "Can the Leper Change His Spots? Part II," *American Journal of Dermatopathology* 5, no. 2 (1983): 173–86.

40. I have used the long excerpt of "Les Adieux du Lépreux," in *Anthologie poétique francaise: Moyen Âge*, 2 vols., ed. André Mary (Paris: Garnier Frères, 1967), 1: 302–13, which is taken from G. Raynaud, "*Les Congés* de Jean Bodel," *Romania* 9 (1880): 216–47. Bodel is best known for his miracle play, *Jeu de saint Nicolas*.

41. For biographical information, see Annette Brasseur, "Jean Bodel," in *Key Figures in Medieval Europe*, ed. Richard K. Emmerson (New York: Routledge, 2006), 370–71.

42. See especially J. Avril, "Le IIIe Concile de Latran et les communautés de lépreux," *Revue Mabillon. Archives de la France monastiques* 60, no. 284 (1981): 21–32; 60, no. 285 (1981): 33–64; 60, no. 286 (1981): 65–76. Jacques de Vitry also describes leprosaria in the West as governed by the Augustianian rule. See his *Historia Occidentalis* 29, ed. F. Moschus (Douai: B. Belleri, 1597), 337.

43. "Personas religiosas voco non solum monachos et canonicos, sed etiam templarios,

have peaked between 1150 and 1250. Because the work of caring for lepers was never taken up in a consistent way by established religious orders,[44] and because the new military Order of St. Lazarus, which was founded in 1098 in Jerusalem during the First Crusade to care for lepers, never grew to any significant size, leprosaria were often simply local institutions dependent upon lay patronage.[45] In the early thirteenth century King Louis VIII of France bequeathed money to about 2000 leper shelters in his kingdom.[46] In Spain, leper hospitals proliferated in the twelfth century, perhaps coinciding with the development of the pilgrim route to Santiago, which brought a growing number of lepers seeking miraculous cure. In Britain the number of leprosaria expanded to about 300 by 1300, followed by declining numbers;[47] the vast majority of these were suburban foundations for residents of nearby towns or cities. Although the number of leprosaria indicates a growing concern with the affliction, the leper colonies or leprosaria themselves were not *primarily* places for medical care—although neither was medical care entirely absent—but rather they were almshouses or charitable places of refuge, in which the afflicted observed a quasi religious rule.[48]

---

hospitalarios, leprosos qui sunt de congregationis (de vagis enim non loquor)." Robert of Flamborough, *Liber Poenitentialis* 3.3.148, p. 150.

44. See Angela Montford, *Health, Sickness, Medicine and the Friars in the Thirteenth and Fourteenth Centuries* (Burlington, Vt.: Ashgate, 2004), 8–9.

45. The Order of St. Lazarus became a military order in order to protect their hospices. The order did found some leprosaria in Europe, but these were but a small number of the total. This Saint Lazarus was a conflation of two New Testament figures: Lazarus, the brother of Martha and Mary who had been raised from the dead (John 11:1–44) and the ulcer-covered beggar Lazarus carried to the bosom of Abraham by the angels (Luke 16:20–25). For further discussion see Luke Demaitre, *Leprosy in Premodern Medicine: A Malady of the Whole Body* (Balitmore: Johns Hopkins University Press, 2007), 80–81.

46. For the number of leprosaria in France and the incidence of leprosy, see Francoise Bériac, "À propos de la fin de la lèpre,"159–73. For Spain, see James W. Brodman, "Shelter and Segregation: Lepers in Medieval Catalonia," in *On the Social Origins of Medieval Institutions: Essays in Honor of Joseph F. O'Callaghan*, ed. Donald J. Kagay and Theresa M. Vann (Leiden: Brill, 1998), 35–45.

47. The declining number of leprosaria may be in response to socioeconomic factors as much as to epidemiological ones, Carole Rawcliffe reminds us. Curiously, although the number of confirmed cases of leprosy in the latter Middle Ages was likely lower owing to a narrower definition of leprosy, stemming especially from Arab medical works, fears of leprosy (and its spread) seem to have increased. See *Leprosy in Medieval England*, 344–57.

48. For a good discussion of medical care for lepers in the Crusader kingdoms, see Piers D. Mitchell, *Medicine in the Crusades* (Cambridge: Cambridge University Press, 2005), chap. 1. For leper hospitals or *leprosaria* in England, whose number Carole Rawcliffe identifies as about 300 in the early fourteenth century, see *Leprosy in Medieval England*, 190. For

The growing incidence of actual cases of leprosy expanded appeals for divine aid. Despite a discussion of various preventatives or therapies, medieval physicians were frustrated in all attempts to find a cure, and they acknowledged their failure to cure full-blown or advanced leprosy.[49] Pope Calixtus II's (d. 1124) sermon on St. James the Greater enumerated many diseases that medicine had failed to heal that might instead be healed by the saint's grace, including leprosy.[50] William of Canterbury, a

a discussion of the development of medieval hospitals from charitable institutions to places for medical treatment, see Jole Agrimi and Chiara Crisciani, "Charity and Aid in Medieval Christian Civilization," in *Western Medical Thought from Antiquity to the Middle Ages*, ed. Mirko D. Grmek, trans. Antony Shugaar (Cambridge, Mass.: Harvard University Press, 1998), 170–96.

49. Saint Bonaventure (d. 1274) acknowledges that leprosy is an incurable disease (*lepra sit morbus incurabilis*), at least when it has fully taken root in the body. See his *Commentaria in Quatuor Libros Sententiarum* 4, dub. 6, resp. Bernard of Gordon remarks that once the signs of leprosy appear, it cannot be cured. See his *Lilium medicinae* 1.22 (Lyon: Gulielmus Rouillius, 1551), 97. Nonetheless, any number of "cures" and palliatives were recommended to ease the symptoms or signs of leprosy. In his *De natura rerum*, the thirteenth-century author Thomas of Cantimpré mentions an ointment that, applied externally, is said to be effective against leprosy: "A mole burned to ashes and sprinkled with the white of egg and placed on the face is a remedy against leprosy." Thomas of Cantimpré, *De natura rerum* (*Lib. IV-XII*): *Tacuinum Sanitatis*, 2 vols., codice C-67 (fols. 2v–116r) de la Biblioteca Universitaria de Granada, commentarios a la edición facsimil, ed. Luis García Ballester (Granada: Universidad de Granada, 1974), 1: fol. 29v, 272. His contemporary, Albert the Great, notes too that certain snake venoms, taken internally, can also be effective against leprosy. See his *Quaestiones super de animalibus* 7.31,p. 185, 69 (QDA, 262). Theodorich Borgognoni recommends phlebotomy, rest, and medication, but does not fail to transmit as well some older remedies. Several of these include eating snake meat, or drinking "serpent wine"—wine in which a snake has been allowed to putrefy. Perhaps this represents a sort of sympathetic magic, as the snake is known to slough off its old skin, and leprosy manifested itself also on the skin. See his *The Surgery of Theodoric, ca. AD 1267*, 3.55, 2 vols., ed. B. Locatellus, trans. Eldridge Campbell and James Colton (New York: Appleton-Century-Crofts, 1955–60), 2: 173–76. This treatment is recounted in an early modern English translation of medical texts as well, where the patient is advised: "Drinke the wine wherin the serpent hath been sodden, tyll the leprous person be swollen and puffed up, and beginne throughe anguishe to be in a manner besyde him selfe, then put the patient in a stewe or hote house, and let the hole body of the patient be anointed with the liquor wherin the adder of serpent was sodden, for the hole fleshe and skinne is therby renued." See *The Treasurie of Health containing Many Profitable Medicines, gathered out of Hipocrates, Galen and Avicenna by one Petrus Hyspanus*, 1.63, trans. Humphry Lloyd (London: Thomas Hacker, 1585). For other examples from the later Middle Ages, see especially Luke Demaitre, "The Relevance of Futility: Jordanus de Turre (fl. 1313–35) on the Treatment of Leprosy," *Bulletin of the History of Medicine* 70 (1996): 25–61. Cf. Francoise Bériac, "Connaisances médicales sur la lèpre et protection contre cette maladie au Moyen Age," in *Maladies et société (XIIe–XVIIIe siècles). Actes du Colloque de Bielfeld, novembre 1986*, ed. Neithard Bulst and Robert Delort (Paris: Editions du C.N.R.S., 1989), 145–63.

50. Commenting on Matt. 3:15, Calixtus II remarked: "Non enim aliquibus medica-

monk who composed a biography c. 1173 of St. Thomas Becket, noted that although the medical authority Galen confessed that he had never seen a patient completely cured of leprosy unless he had drunk wine mixed with theriac (*tyria*), we (says William) have seen two people completely cured of this illness when they drank nothing but the water mixed with the blood of the martyr Thomas.[51] Indeed, William of Canterbury and another biographer, Benedict (d. 1193), Abbot of Peterborough, narrate accounts of dozens of lepers who were healed through the intercession of Thomas Becket.[52] Through his holy instrument, God is wont to cure not only leprosy of the body, says William, but even that which is greater, namely leprosy of the soul.[53] Likewise, Anselm of Canterbury's sanctity was such that the water in which he had washed his hands was said to have cured a leper.[54] Skepticism concerning the effectiveness of the physician was balanced by a genuine faith in the healing powers of the the saint or priest. In many ways, the priest and the physician were in competition with one another: one of the obligations of the priest was the visitation of the sick (*visitare languentes*), and a priest's prayers or invocations (or incantations) could be received with the same hopeful

---

mentis vel electuariis, vel confectionibus, vel syrupis, vel diversis emplastis, vel potionibus, vel solutionibus, vel vomitibus, vel caeteris medicorum antidotis, sed sola Dei gratia sibi a Deo impetrata multos languidos, videlicet leprosos, phreneticos, maniosos, scabiosos, paralyticos, arreptitios, phlegmaticos, febricitantes, cephalalgicos, energumenos, podagricos, stranguriosos, calculosos, hepaticos, fistulosos, phthisicos, dysenteriacos, a serpentibus laesos, ictericos, lunaticos, stomaticos, reumosos, amentes, epistrosos, albuginosos, multisque morbis dolentes sanitati integrae clementissimus apostolus restituit." *Sermo 3, De S. Jacobo* (PL 163: 1397B-D).

51. "Nos vero vidimus duos ad unguem mundatos nec signum leprae reservantes, qui non aliud medicamen acceperant quam aquam et sanguinem martyris"; William of Canterbury, *Vita et Passio S. Thomas* 4.20, in *Materials for the History of Thomas Becket*, 7 vols., ed. James Craigie Robertson, Rolls Series (London: Longman, 1875-85), 1: 332-33.

52. See Benedict of Peterborough, *Miracula sancti Thomas Cantuarensis*, 4.3; and 4.72-74, in *Materials for the History of Thomas Becket*, 2: 182; 242-44. Also see William of Canterbury, *Vita et Passio S. Thomas* 2.52-63; 4.18-25; 6.17-19; and 6.55-57, in *Materials for the History of Thomas Becket*, 1: 212-22; 330-40; 428-32; and 458-61. For discussion of miraculous cures of leprosy attributed to Thomas Becket at his shrine, see also Carole Rawcliffe, *Leprosy in Medieval England*, 170-72, 175-78. This stands in contrast to Katherine Park's claim that lepers rarely appear in lists of miraculous cures at shrines, principally because (at least on the Continent) they were rarely admitted to the saints' shrines. See her "Medicine and Society in Medieval Europe, 500-1500," in *Medicine and Society: Historical Essays*, ed. Andrew Wear (Cambridge: Cambridge University Press, 1992), 73.

53. "[Deus] Curat et spiritualem lepram, quod majus est, varietatem scilicet vitiorum sinceritatem animae commaculantium." William of Canterbury, *Vita et Passio S. Thomas* 1: 333.

54. William of Malmesbury, *De gestis pontificum Anglorum* 1.46, p. 76.

enthusiasm that some moderns confer upon faith healers. Perhaps to invest the physician with the same authority as the priest, at the beginning of the fourteenth century the physician Bernard of Gordon admonished his medical student that, when administering medication, he should also invoke Christ with the words "Christ lives, Christ reigns, Christ commands."[55]

Throughout the twelfth and thirteenth centuries, leprosy could be viewed then as a spiritual illness that manifested itself in the body, even though other causes may also be present which, by the fifteenth century, will include demonic agency exercised through witchcraft or sorcery.[56] Once more, canon 22 of the Fourth Lateran Council (1215) acknowledged that because sickness of the body may be the result of sin, before receiving medical treatment patients should attend to their spiritual health; afterward, they may respond better to treatment "for when the cause ceases so does the effect."[57] This does not necessarily imply that every sick person was *ipso facto* a sinner or to be treated as such since, as Angela Montford remarks, "While all illness had sin as its origin, illness was not usually seen as a punishment except in epidemic disease."[58] It is difficult to estimate the number of sufferers from leprosy in medieval Europe; based on calculations that apply a multiplier to the total number of leprosaria, Biraben speculates that there may have been 600,000 lepers by 1300.[59] Nonetheless, regardless of whether leprosy achieved the level of an epidemic disease, still it engendered a special fear and horror; certainly, preachers who addressed lepers in their sermons called upon them to do penance in order to be healed.[60] Thomas Aquinas acknowledged that

55. "Invoca et benedice nomen dei vivi, quando dabis medicinam, et dicens: 'Christus vivit, Christus regnat, Christus imperat.'" Bernard of Gordon, *Modus practicandi*, in Carmen Fernández Tijero, "Ego Peripateticus Sum: Los textos de clase para la enseñanza de la medicina en Montpellier," *Eä* 2, no. 1 (2010): 1–16, citing12.
56. For the claim that sorceresses can afflict people with leprosy, as well as other illnesses, see *Malleus Maleficarum* 2, q. 1, cap.12, col 134A, 1: 461.
57. *Decrees of the Ecumenical Councils* 1: 245
58. Angela Montford, *Health, Sickness, Medicine and the Friars*, 52.
59. Jean Noël Biraben, "Diseases in Europe: Equilibrium and Breakdown of the Pathocenosis," in *Western Medical Thought from Antiquity to the Middle Ages*, 349.
60. See Nicole Beriou, "L'image de l'autre: Le lepreux sous le regard des predicateurs au moyen age," *L'histoire aujourd'hui*, section d'histoire (Liège: Université de Liège, 1988), 1–12. See also Nicole Bériou and François-Olivier Touati, *Voluntate Dei Leprosus: Les Lépreux entre conversion et exclusion aux XIIème et XIIIème siècles* (Spoleto: Centro italiano di studi sull'alto medioevo, 1991), 81–163, for Latin texts of thirteenth-century sermons delivered to lepers. Also useful for a discussion of medieval perceptions of lepers and leprosy, see Peter

leprosy frequently resulted from sin, and that this provided a justification for the leper's isolation from the community in the Old Testament.[61] The horror that contact with lepers aroused in the general public, moreover, also recommended the forced "retirement" of Christian priests. Because of leprosy's "loathsomeness," leprosy will be an impediment to ordination or,[62] if the illness appears after ordination, leprous priests, says Thomas, ought to celebrate the Eucharist only privately and not in public before the community.[63] In addition, it is entirely appropriate for leprous clerics to be relieved of all administrative responsiblities in the Church.[64]

Gradually, however, theologians like William of Auvergne (d. 1249) conceded that the leprosy identified in the Old Testament and the disease sweeping Europe were perhaps not strictly identical.[65] At the same time, as leprosy occurred with greater frequency, and once Latin physicians had access to Arab medical treatises that discussed it, Latin savants diligently sought the medical etiology of leprosy and recommended palliatives, since the worst types of leprosy, certainly, knew no cure. One important conduit for this information was Constantine the African (d. before 1099), a Benedictine monk at Monte Cassino and translator of Arabic medical materials. Constantine translated a brief *Liber de elephantia*,[66] which epitomized chapters on leprosy from his Latin translation

---

Lewis Allen, *The Wages of Sin: Sex and Disease, Past and Present* (Chicago: University of Chicago Press, 2000), chap. 2. For a review of recent historiographical approaches to medieval leprosy, see also Elma Brenner, "Recent Perspectives on Leprosy in Medieval Western Europe," *History Compass* 8, no. 5 (2010): 388–406.

61. *Summa theologica* 1.2, q. 102, art. 5, resp. 7.
62. Robert of Flamborough, *Liber Poenitentialis* 3.3.173, p. 166.
63. *Summa theologica* 3, q. 82, art. 10, resp. 3; Gratian treats epileptics similarly. See *Decreta* pars 2, causa 7, ques. 2, cap. 1, *Corpus iuris canonici* (Graz: Akademische Druck- u. Verlagsanstalt, 1959; Electronic reproduction, vols.1–2. New York: Columbia University Libraries, 2007), 1: 588. Rawcliffe (*Leprosy in Medieval England*, 266) suggests that it was not only the disgust aroused by the appearance of leprosy that led to restrictions to prevent a cleric from celebrating the Eucharist, but also fears that the priest's leprous ulcers might defile the Host with human blood. But the concession that the leprous priest could consecrate the Host privately seems at odds with this conjecture.
64. *Summa theologica* 2.2, q. 108, art. 4, resp. 2.
65. William of Auvergne, *De legibus* 11, p. 41.1D.
66. See Constantine the African's *Tratado médico de Constantino el Africano. Constantini* Liber de elephancia, ed. Ana Isabel Martín Ferreira (Valladolid: Universidad de Valladolid, 1996). Although often identified as a work by Constantine himself, it is perhaps a translation of a work by Ibn al-Jazzār (fl. 1000). This short text examines the various types and causes of leprosy and skin disease, and reviews appropriate therapies. A similar account can be found in a twelfth-century Anglo-Norman translation of the *Chiurgia* (4.19) of

of the tenth-century *Pantegni*, written by 'Ali ibn al-'Abbas al-Majusi.[67] By the thirteenth century, Constantine's material was widely cited by the English Franciscan Bartholomew the Englishman (*Bartholomaeus Anglicus*), and by the Dominicans Vincent of Beauvais and Albert the Great. Bartholomew the Englishman, precisely because he lacks originality, provides a valuable summary of medical knowledge of leprosy about the middle of the thirteenth century in his *On the Properties of Things* (*De rerum proprietatibus*), completed in Magdeburg c. 1245.[68] Whatever the scientific value of Bartholomew's work, it had enormous influence, as evidenced by the number of translations made of *On the Properties of Things* at the end of the thirteenth century in Italy and by the end of the fifteenth century in Spain and the Low Countries. Thus, it was translated into Italian, Provençal, French, Middle English and, later, Dutch and Spanish.[69] Bartholomew the Englishman traces the appearance of lep-

---

Roger Frugard, drawing attention to the link between leprosy and "corrupt humors." See *Anglo-Norman Medicine*, 2 vols., ed. Tony Hunt (Cambridge: Brewer, 1994), 1: 86–87. For a discussion of the diagnoses of later medieval physicians, see Luke Demaitre, "The Description and Diagnosis of Leprosy by Fourteenth-Century Physicians," *Bulletin of the History of Medicine* 59 (1985): 327–44.

67. In the preface to his *Theorice* (Basel: Henri cum Petrum, 1536), Constantine dedicates the work—indeed, the whole of the *Pantegni*—to the Abbot Desiderius. Desiderius reigned subsequently as Pope Victor III (1086–87). The first book of this work has been translated with commentary. See Constantine the African, *L'Arte universale dell medicina (Pantegni)*, Part 1—book 1, trans. Marco T. Malato and Umberto de Martini (Rome: Istituto di storia della medicina dell'università di Roma, 1961). For a brief biography and assessment of Constantine's influence, see Danielle Jacquart, "Medical Scholasticism," in *Western Medical Thought from Antiquity to the Middle Ages*, 203–5. For a discussion of Constantine's role as a translator of Arabic medical and scientific treatises, see Monica H. Green, "Constantinus Africanus and the Conflict between Religion and Science," in *The Human Embryo: Aristotle and the Arabic and European Traditions*, 47–69; and Joan Cadden, *Meanings of Sex Difference in the Middle Ages* (Cambridge: Cambridge University Press, 1993), 54–70. For treatment of Constantine's contributions and especially his work the *Pantegni*, see also the essays found in *The Pantegni and Related Texts*, ed. Charles Burnett and Danielle Jacquart (Leiden: Brill, 1994). For a near contemporary record of Constantine's medical writings and translations, see Peter the Deacon's *De viris illustribus* 23, in *Monte Cassino in the Middle Ages*, 3 vols., ed. Herbert Bloch (Cambridge. Mass.: Harvard University Press, 1986), 1: 127–29, and largely reproduced by Monica Greene in *Medieval Italy: Texts in Translation*, ed. Katherine L. Jansen et al., 312–14.

68. For useful discussions of the text and for Bartholomew's biography, see M. C. Seymour, *Bartholomaeus Anglicus and His Encyclopedia* (Aldershot, Hampshire: Ashgate, 1992); and Juris G. Lidaka, "Bartholomaeus Anglicus in the Thirteenth Century," in *Pre-Modern Encyclopaedic Texts. Proceedings of the Second COMERS Congress, Groningen, 1–4 July 1996*, ed. Peter Binkley (Leiden: Brill, 1997), 393–406.

69. See Michel Salvat, "Le ciel des vulgarisateurs: note sur les traductions de *De propri-*

rosy to corruption of the humors which,[70] Vincent of Beauvais remarks, results from a bad complexion in the liver, as an efficient cause, whose heat and dryness affects the rest of the body.[71] There are four types of leprosy, corresponding to compositions arising from the four humors.[72] The very worst type, known as *elephantia,* arises from pure adust black bile or melancholy. A second type is called *tyria* or serpentine, and arises from both melancholy and phlegm. A third type arises from a melancholic infection of blood and is called *alopecia* or vulpine. The fourth type comes from red bile and melancholy that has been corrupted in the members, and this one, which corrodes and destroys all the members, is called *leonina* or leonine. All of the forms of leprosy, however, owe their origin in part to corrupt melancholy, which is a cold and dry humor. The four types of leprosy have some symptoms in common, while others are specific to one of the four kinds. In general, however, the flesh is corrupted and its appearance is altered. The eyes become rounded, the eyelids wrinkled, and the nostrils narrow. The voice becomes hoarse and raspy—especially in *elephantia*—and sensation disappears from the legs and other extremities. The nails thicken, the finger joints become distorted, and the hands are dried out. The leper's breath and perspiration is fetid, and very often infects healthy people.[73] Spots appear on the skin (white, reddish, or black) and pustules often form on the shins. In addition, the various types may have specific symptoms. Those suffering leonine leprosy will have a more jaundiced or yellowish skin tint, their eyes will bulge or protrude, their skin will be rougher, and often it will be wrinkled or split. Those with *alopecia* will lose their eyebrows completely, their eyes will swell and redden, and they may have red pustules on their faces. Their nose will become enlarged and they lack a sense of smell. Those with *tyria* have soft pustules, and swollen, whitish skin. Those with *elephantia* have a dull, leaden or grayish pallor to their face (*facies plumbea*), they lose their hair, their eyes are rounded, their nos-

---

etatibus rerum," in *Observer, Lire, Écrire le Ciel au Moyen Age. Actes du Colloque d'Orleans 22–23 Avril 1989* (Paris: Klincksieck, 1991), 301–13.

70. See Bartholomaeus Anglicus, *De rerum proprietatibus* 7.64 (Frankfurt, 1601; repr. Frankfurt on Main: Minerva, 1964), 351–54.

71. *Speculum naturale* 14.30, 1: 1301.

72. For the development of the medieval European emphasis on four types of leprosy corresponding to each of the four humors, see Luke Demaitre, *Leprosy in Premodern Medicine,* 177–78.

73. Avicenna, *Liber canonis medicine* 4.3.2.2 (Venice: 1527; repr. Brussels, 1971), fol. 346.

trils constricted, their muscles waste away, and they experience loss of sensation especially in the larger fingers.

Bartholomew claims that although leprosy arises especially from humoral imbalance, it also is a contagious illness that may spread from cohabitation with or frequent contact with lepers. Vincent of Beauvais confirms that leprosy spreads from one person to another, and also that it can be a hereditary condition transmitted through the semen.[74] Vincent adds that it may be spread through personal contact and cohabitation with lepers "from the release of bad vapors from the patient's body, which he then breathes into the surrounding air."[75] Bernard of Gordon's (d. c. 1318) enormously popular *Lily of Medicine* (*Lilium Medicinae*), written at the beginning of the fourteenth century, reiterates that leprosy may be caused by personal contact with a leper and by bad air that spreads it to others. Similarly the influential fourteenth-century text, *Diverse Anatomical Problems* (*Problemata varia anatomica*), a collection of pseudo-Aristotelian questions, sometimes circulated under its incipit, *Omnes homines*, attributes to Avicenna the claim that the breath of a leper may be so befouled from the release of corrupt humors in the body, that it may even infect birds that fly overhead.[76]

For medieval authorities, the medical opinion that leprosy is *contagious*, that is, communicated by foul or bad air, certainly was thought to justify the visible identification and exclusion of lepers. Once diagnosed, they were often removed to leprosaria and, like other classes of medieval society, identified by special garments—perhaps a grey or black cloak and a scarlet hat or hood, although a great deal of variation seems to have been permitted for their clothing, perhaps precisely because they could more easily be identified by outward, physical signs of illness. They also typically had to carry a bell or "clapper" that would announce their movements on public paths or that served, perhaps, to solicit alms, much like streetcorner Salvation Army bellringers today solicit donations at Christmas. (See figure 6.) Medieval physicians were charged with ex-

74. "Praeterea quaedam aegrititudines contagiosae sunt, quae scilicet de uno ad alium transeunt, ut lepra ... Sunt et quaedam quae in semine hereditantur, ut podagra, phthisis et lepra." Vincent of Beauvais, *Speculum naturale* 31.98, 1: 2370.

75. "Hic etiam morbus in cohabitantes transit, propter dissolutionem malorum vaporum a corpore patientis, quos circumstanti aer respirat." *Speculum doctrinale* 14.28, 2: 1300. Cf. 14.30, 2: 1301. (= vol. 2 of the *Speculum quadruplex, sive, Speculum maius: naturale, doctrinale, morale, historiale*).

76. *Problemata varia anatomica*, p. 28.

amining suspected cases of leprosy, and the judgment of a learned panel could lead to expulsion from family and community.[77] This enforced separation did cause difficulties for church authorities, particularly when the individual suspected of leprosy was married. Albert the Great gives us some insight into the difficulties in his *On the Sacraments* (*De sacramentis*) when he asks whether, since leprosy is contagious, a spouse is obligated to cohabit with and render the conjugal debt to the leprous partner. He explains that spouses are not bound to cohabit "continually" with a partner suffering from leprosy, but they are bound to render the conjugal debt, that is, have sexual relations when the partner demands it.[78] Vincent of Beauvais agrees, although he adds significantly that the leprous spouse absolutely should make no such demand.[79] The *Summula Conradi* (c. 1226–29) goes one step further: while it acknowledges that a husband is bound to render the conjugal debt to his leprous wife, and that it is a sign of a higher perfection to do so, nonetheless he may be excused owing to the horror aroused by the sight of the disease.[80] Nevertheless, it does not seem that leprosy was a bar to marriage, even when its symptoms were already evident.[81]

LEPROSY AND SEXUALITY

The notion that leprosy was contagious would seem to undermine the idea that leprosy is a punishment for sin. However, this was not nec-

---

77. See especially Demaitre, *Leprosy in Premodern Medicine*, chap. 2: "*Iudicium leprosorum*: Medical Judgment," 34–74.

78. Albert the Great, *De Sacramentis* tr. 2, q. 2, art. 5, 13; cf. Hugh of St. Victor, *Summa sententiarum* 7.20 (PL 176: 170B). Cf. *Decretal. Greg. IX*, 4.8.9, cap. 2–3, in *Corpus iuris canonici*, 2:691. For the conjugal debt, see Elizabeth M. Makowski, "The Conjugal Debt and Medieval Canon Law," *Journal of Medieval History* 3 (1977): 99–114.

79. "propter fidem matrimonii leprosae reddendum est debitum, non tamen simpliciter petendum." Vincent of Beauvais, *Speculum historiale* 2.36, 4: 59.

80. "Unde, notandum quod sanus tenetur reddere debitum leprose, set propter horrorem excusatur; perfectius tamen esset si redderet debitum." *Summula magistri Conradi* 2.11, in *Trois sommes de pénitence de la première moitié du XIIIe siècle: la "Summula Magistri Conradi," les sommes "Quia non pigris" et "Decime dande sunt,"* 2 vols., ed. Jean-Pierre Renard (Louvain-la-Neuve: Diffusion, Centre Cerfaux-Lefort, 1989), 2: 25, cited in Jacqueline Murray, "Gendered Souls in Sexed Bodies: The Male Construction of Female Sexuality in Some Medieval Confessors' Manuals," in *Handling Sin: Confession in the Middle Ages*, ed. Peter Biller and A. J. Minnis (Woodbridge, Suffolk: York Medieval Press, 1998), 87–88.

81. See the eighth-century *Decretum Dompendiense* capit. 1.19, Pippini capitularia, in *Capitularia regum Francorum*, 2 vols., ed. Alfred Boretius, MGH LL (Hanover: Hahn, 1883–97), 1: 39.

essarily so. One possibility was that it will be contracted through contact or spread by bad air to those whose bodies have already been weakened by sin. In another way, however, leprosy was held to be communicated through sinful sexual behaviors. William of Canterbury records a tale of a certain Odo of Beumont-sur-Sarthe who lay with a prostitute and immediately afterward contracted leprosy as a "punishment."[82] Although it is not clear in William's account that the leprosy was transmitted by the sexual activity itself, and not merely as the appropriate divine punishment, the former seems more likely given that it is specifically linked to sex for hire. Moreover, all of our texts acknowledge that leprosy may be contracted during intercourse with a woman immediately after she has had carnal knowledge of a leper. Since she can only spread the illness to a second partner—either her spouse or some other—it is clear that this transmission will only occur as the result of fornication or adultery. The only exception would appear to be a new widow, whose spouse was leprous, and who has quickly remarried. The surgical writer Theodorich Borgognoni (d. 1298) notes that the woman herself may not display its symptoms but may only be a carrier of the disease, which she will transmit to her partner or even to the fetus when the act results in conception.[83] Vincent of Beauvais explains the manner of transmission, arguing that when a woman has had intercourse with a leper, the "putrid material" of intercourse—the corrupt sperm—remains behind in her womb. Her cold and moist, phlegmatic complexion offers her protection and repulses this material, leaving her unharmed, but when another man enters her, his penis will attract the corrupt material and infect him with leprosy.[84] If intercourse with a woman who does not reveal signs of leprosy is dangerous, than certainly, Bernard of Gordon adds, one should avoid sex with a woman who has its symptoms. To emphasize his point, he provides a personal anecdote. A certain countess suffering from leprosy came to him for medical care. An assistant, a "bachelor"

---

82. "Contigit [...] Odonem nomine, parochianum quidem nostrum, meretrici adhaesisse, statimque post peccatum poenam peccati lepram contraxisse." William of Canterbury, *Vita et Passio S. Thomas* 4.25, in *Materials for the History of Thomas Becket*, 1: 340.

83. Theodorich Borgognoni, *The Surgery of Theodoric, ca. AD 1267*, 3.55, 2: 168. For a good summary of the relationship between sexuality and the transmission of leprosy for medieval medicine, see especially Danielle Jacquart and Claude Thomasset, *Sexuality and Medicine in the Middle Ages*, trans. Matthew Adamson (Oxford: Polity Press, 1988), 183–93.

84. Vincent of Beauvais, *Speculum naturale* 31.5, 1: 2294.

(that is, with a university bachelor's degree in medicine) lay with her, impregnated her, and became leprous himself as a result.[85] Bernard of Gordon offers practical advice to women who have had intercourse with a leper: cleanse the womb in a bath or douche.[86] Likewise, the fourteenth-century English physician John of Gaddesden (d. 1361) cautioned any man having had intercourse with a woman he believed to be leprous to clean the penis carefully with vinegar or even with his own urine at the first opportunity, and then to have a phlebotomist remove any corrupt matter that had already entered the blood. Similarly, a woman who had lain with a man she believed to be leprous should expel the man's semen and douche the genital area.[87]

Not only is sexual intercourse with a leprous woman or one who has had recent intercourse with a leper dangerous, but so too is intercourse with a menstruating woman, regardless of whether she has known a leper or not. Such contact may spread leprosy not only to the male partner, but even transmit it to the fetus conceived during this period. As early as the fourth century, Jerome explained that the prohibition in Ezekiel 18:6 forbids one to "approach" a menstruating woman because "each month the heavy and torpid bodies of women are relieved by an effusion of unclean blood. If a man has sex with a woman then, the fetuses that are conceived are said to contract a defect from the semen, such that from that conception they will be born lepers or suffering from *elephantia*."[88] In fact, according to Vincent of Beauvais, this is the underlying justification for the biblical injunction that calls for the menstruant to separate herself from her community for seven days (Lev. 15:19)—that is, to prevent conception of a fetus which, if conceived during her monthly flux, will suffer from the corruption of leprosy.[89] Some texts simply assert

---

85. "Quaedam comitissa venit leprosa ad Montem pessulanum, et erat in fine in cura mea, et quidam Baccalarius in medicina ministrabat ei, et iacuit cum ea, et impregnavit eam, et perfectissime leprosus factus est." Bernard of Gordon, *Lilium Medicinae* 1.22, p. 89.

86. Bernard of Gordon, *Lilium Medicinae* 1.22, p. 89.

87. John of Gaddesden, *Rosa Anglica*, fols. 61r–61v, cited by Rawcliffe, *Leprosy in Medieval England*, 207.

88. "per singulos menses grauia atque torpentia mulierum corpora immundi sanguinis effusione releuantur, quo tempore si uir coierit cum muliere, dicuntur concepti foetus uitium seminis trahere, ita ut leprosi et elephantiaci ex hac conceptione nascantur." Jerome, *Commentarii in Ezechielem* 6.18, ed. Francois Glorie, CCSL 75 (Turnholt: Brepols, 1964). This passage is cited verbatim by Rupert of Deutz in his *Commentaria in euangelium sancti Iohannis* 9, ed. Rhabanus Haacke, CCCM 9 (Turnholt: Brepols, 1969), 490.

89. Vincent of Beauvais, *Speculum historiale* 2.36, 4: 58.

a connection between menstrual blood and leprosy, seemingly content with the assumption that this is a divine punishment for depraved sexual activity. Sometimes, it is even implied that a woman almost intentionally communicates leprosy to her partner in sex during her menstrual period. Pseudo-Albert the Great remarks that just as some women insert a piece of iron into the vagina prior to sex in order to injure the penis, so too when a woman is menstruating she wounds the male by transmitting leprosy to him. Since the veins descend from the body's individual members to the testicles, so too in reverse order leprosy enters the testicles and then spreads rapidly throughout the body.[90]

Others struggle to explain the mechanism of transmission across generations, that is, why sex with a menstruant should endanger the fetus. Vincent of Beuavais notes that leprosy may pass to the fetus when conception occurs during her menstrual period because the fetus adopts the complexion of the womb,[91] which is filled with impure blood.[92] Since medieval medicine also understood that menstrual blood rises to the breasts to be transformed into milk to nourish the newborn, Bartholomew the Englishman opines that a newborn may contract leprosy even when suckled by a leprous wetnurse.[93] Among magical or astrological texts, the Latin *Picatrix*, translated from a thirteenth-century Spanish translation of Ps. Al-Majrītī's (d. c. 1008) *Ghāyat al-hakīm*, remarks that if menstrual blood is given to a person—presumably in a drink—the person will become leprous.[94] Medical science and theology, however, reached a consensus that sex with a menstruant was fraught with danger. Although in general Christians insisted that they had been freed from

---

90. Pseudo-Albert the Great, *De secretis mulierum* cap. 2 (Amsterdam: 1643), 53; also see *Women's Secrets*, 88–89.

91. Vincent of Beauvais, *Speculum naturale* 14.30, 1: 1301.

92. Cf. Theodorich Borgognoni, *The Surgery of Theodoric* 3.55, 2: 167. On "impure" menstrual blood as fetal nourishment in medieval medicine, see William F. Maclehose, "Nurturing Danger: High Medieval Medicine and the Problem(s) of the Child," in *Medieval Mothering,* ed. John Carmi Parsons and Bonnie Wheeler (New York: Garland, 1996), 3–24.

93. Bartholomaeus Anglicus, *De rerum proprietatibus* 7.64, p. 354. Cf. *Liber de complexionibus,* which adds that, generally, only when the wetnurse has a superior complexion will the infant's complexion be changed and improved. See Werner Seyfert, "Ein Komplexionentext einer Leipziger Inkunabel (angeblich eines Johann von Neuhaus) und seine handschriftliche Herleitung aus der Zeit nach 1300," *Archiv für Geschichte der Medizin* 20 (1928): 272–99, 372–89, but esp. 298.

94. *Picatrix: The Latin Version of the Ghāyat Al-Hakīm* 3.11.89, ed. David Pingree (London: The Warburg Institute, 1986), 163.

the obligation to observe the "ceremonial" laws of ritual purity outlined in the Old Testament, still women were to be veiled, silent in church (cf. 1 Cor 14:34), and prohibited from reading the Epistle or the Gospel at Mass because of the uncleanness of their menses. This same disability resulting from menstruation, imposed upon the descendants of Eve as a special "curse," underscored too women's unsuitability for clerical ordination.[95] Raymund Martini notes that the prohibition against sex with a menstruant is binding not only for Jews but for Christians as well, both because it is a depraved act and because it can transmit leprosy. As a result, it is a *moral* law, he insists, and not merely a ritual requirement.[96]

Consequently, as medieval physicians and philosophers attempted to give precision to the natural causes of leprosy, they also perpetuated a link between leprosy and debauchery, excessive sensuality or aberrant sexuality, even into the early modern period. In a classical description, Aretaeus of Cappadocia (150–200) identified one symptom of leprosy as "the irresistible and shameless impulse *ad coitum* [for intercourse]."[97] Medieval churchmen and pastoral guides instructed clergy to correct lepers who were thought to be much given to drunkenness. The Dominican minister-general Humbert of Romans (d. 1277) warned his brethren, who might sermonize before lepers, that "They stuff themselves with food and great drunk as a result of an excess of food. Putting aside any rein on the fires of their desires, they abandon themselves to lust and filthy behavior."[98] They were said frequently to congregate at bordellos;

---

95. The *Sententie divine pagine* adds: "Et quia [mulier] magis peccavit, debet esse humilior et infirmior in ecclesia capite velato, debet etiam tacere in ecclesia, ut dicit apostolus (1 Cor 14:34). Penam etiam maiorem habet peccati, quam vir, quia in dolore patitur menstrualis." *Anselms von Laon systematische Sentenzen,* fol. 91d–92a, p. 27. On the woman's body and her unsuitability for clerical ordination, see A. J. Minnis, "*De impedimento sexus*: Women's Bodies and Medieval Impediments to Female Ordination," in *Medieval Theology and the Natural Body,* ed. Peter Biller and A. J. Minnis, York Studies in Medieval Theology 1 (Woodbridge, Suffolk: York Medieval Press, 1997), 122; Philip Lyndon Reynolds, "Scholastic Theology and the Case Against Women's Ordination," *Heythrop Journal* 36, no. 3 (1995): 249–85, esp. 269–74.

96. Raymund Martini, *Pugio Fidei* pars 3, dist 3, cap. 11, par. 26, fol. 618, p. 792; for prohibitions on sex with a menstruant, see also Gratian, *Decreta* pars 1, dist. 5, cap. 4, in *Corpus iuris canonici,* 1: 8.

97. See *The Extant Works of Aretaeus the Cappadocian,* ed. and trans. F. Adams (London: Sydenham Society, 1856), 368–73. For discussion, see Johon Cule, "The Stigma of Leprosy: Its Historical Origins and Consequences with Particular Reference to the Laws of Wales," in *The Past and Present of Leprosy,* 149–54.

98. Humbert of Romans, "To the Leprous" [*ad Leprosos*], in *Other Middle Ages. Witnesses at the Margins of Medieval Society,* 147.

at the same time, these texts cautioned pilgrims and penitents against associating with prostitutes because they often have sex with lepers, whose illness they may transmit to others.[99] Scholastic physicians, who attempted to classify the various types of leprosy and investigated its symptoms, highlighted the link between leprosy and sexuality, a link largely absent from Islamic society.[100]

Like Bartholomew the Englishman, Gilbert the Englishman (Gilbertus Anglicus), the author of the very popular *Compendium medicine* (c. 1250s), identified the four types of leprosy and their relation to the bodily humors, following Constantine the African.[101] He also outlines the general symptoms of leprosy that the physician should look for: loss of sensation in the extremities, coldness in or change in skin color, distortion in the joints, fetid breath, hair loss, etc. Yet in addition, Gilbert contended that "lepers search for sexual pleasure more than usual and more than they should; they are ardent in the act, yet find themselves weaker than usual."[102] About the same time St. Bonaventure linked the

99. Avril cites the *Summa pastoralis* 641, which advises: "Provideat etiam archdiaconus, quantum poterit, de leprosies vagis, ebriosis et luxuriosis, qui de loco ad locum, de foro ad forum discurrunt, et in predictis bordellis in sero convenientes vel etiam in aliquibus de leprosiis alios per malum exemplum corrumpunt, et per mulieres ad quas accedunt, multi leper contagionem incurrunt, unde, quantum fieri poterit, secumdum Deum, discursi ipsorum et tanto periculo est occuendum vigilanter." Also, the thirteenth-century synodal of the West, 200, can. 8, which cautions: "De prostantibus penitenti periculum ostendatur . . . et leprosis sepius se supponunt per quod accedentes ad eas incurrunt frequentius morbum lepre." See his "Le IIIe Concile de Latran et les communautés de lépreux," 70, nn. 262–63.

100. See M. W. Dols, "Leprosy in Medieval Arabic Medicine," *Journal of the History of Medicine* 34, no. 3 (1979): 314–33; Dols, "The Leper in Medieval Islamic Society," *Speculum* 58, no. 4 (1983): 916.

101. Details of Gilbert's life and career remain sketchy. Older studies identified Gilbert as a cleric and physician to Archbishop Hubert Walter of Canterbury and then perhaps to King John, whose career would have flourished in the first decade of the thirteenth century. For overview, see Henry A. Handerson, *Gilbertus Anglicus: Medicine of the Thirteenth Century* (Cleveland, Ohio: Cleveland Medical Library Association, 1918). It has also been thought that he travelled to the Latin East with the crusaders (see Mitchell, *Medicine in the Crusades*, 21–23). Michael McVaugh has argued persuasively, however, that the author of the *Compendium medicine* is more plausibly the son of the physician that served the archbishop—based largely on the chronology of the introduction of Aristotelian texts in natural philosophy that he cited—and proposes that Gilbert may have become a university master of medicine at Montpelier. See Michael McVaugh, "Who Was Gilbert the Englishman?" in *The Study of Medieval Manuscripts of England: Festschrift in honor of Richard W. Pfaff*, ed. G. H. Brown, L. E. Voigts (Turnholt: Brepols, 2010), 295–324.

102. His discussion is found in his *Compendium medicine Gilberti Anglici* 7 (Lyons, 1510), fols. 339–40, trans. Michael McVaugh in *A Sourcebook of Medieval Science*, ed. Edward Grant (Cambridge, Mass.: Harvard University Press, 1974), 752–54.

presence of corrupt (especially melancholy) humors to leprosy, and connected these with illicit sexual thoughts or imaginings:

Thus just as when many corrupt and melancholy humors abound in the body they generate scabies, a certain scaly skin disease, and sometimes leprosy, which remove the cleanness of the body, so too when unclean thoughts, disordered desires, and wicked and deceitful images of women abound in the heart, they generate certain corrupt humors and disordered desires in the flesh.[103]

Consequently, even the faculty of imagination may sometimes cause leprosy.[104] According to Albert the Great, Avicenna remarked that one who is especially sad or fearful of leprosy sometimes will contract it,[105] and simply by imagining leprosy one may become a leper himself.[106] Therefore, a reciprocal causality seems to be at work: corrupt humors may generate leprosy, and disordered desires, impure sexual fantasies, or fears can lead to corrupt humors.

For Mishnaic Judaism as well leprosy not only conveyed impurity or uncleanness, but it also assumed the added dimension of aberrant sexual behavior and venereal transmission.[107] So the fourth- to fifth-century *Leviticus Rabbah* 15:5 notes that a newborn will be born leprous if the mother did not observe the required times of separation, or if the male has overabundant sperm (*Leviticus Rabbah* 15:2), or if the woman conceived during the time of her menses (*Tachuma metzora* 39:22b).[108] The extra-rabbinic *Baraita de niddah* also contends that "She who has relations with her husband while a niddah [menstruant] will cause her sons . . . to

---

103. "Unde quemadmodum quando abundant multi corrupti et melancholici humores in corpore generant scabiem quemdam impetiginem et aliquando lepram quae tollunt munditiam corporis sic quando abundant immundae cogitationes inordinatae affectiones et turpes mulierum imagines et illusiones in corde generant quosdam humores corruptos et inordinata desideria in carne." *Sermones dominicales*, Sermo 43.8.134. It bears noting that just as leprosy transmitted impurity, so too *scabies* rendered an animal unfit as a sacrifice on the Temple altar (see Lev. 22:22, Vulg.).

104. *Problemata anatomica*, p. 58; Albert the Great, *De anima* 3.3.4, p. 213, 87–89; *Malleus Maleficiarum* 1, q. 5, col. 35A, 1: 271.

105. Albert the Great, *De animalibus* 22.1.5.9, vol. 16, 1353 (SZ 2: 1445); *De causis et processu universitatis a prima causa* 2.2.21, ed. Borgnet 10, 511b.

106. Albert the Great, *De fato* art 3.5, p. 70, lns. 15–17.

107. See for example Mishnah *Kelim* 1.4, 7. On signs of leprosy and transmission of impurity, see also *Negaim* 1: 3–9:9 in *The Tosefta*, trans. Jacob Neusner (Peabody, Mass.: Hendrickson Publishers, 2002), 1709–45.

108. For a discussion of the etiology of leprosy in *Leviticus Rabbah* 15–16, see Boris S. Ostrer, "Leprosy: Medical Views of Leviticus Rabba," *Early Science and Medicine* 7, no. 2 (2002): 138–54.

be afflicted with leprosy for one hundred generations."[109] Among Christians, the canons of the First Ecumenical Council at Nicaea (325) noted that "for husbands it is not allowed that they approach their wives during menstruation, so that their bodies and their children will not manifest the effects of elephantiasis and leprosy; in fact that type of blood corrupts both the body of the parents as well as that of their children."[110] In late antiquity, then, it was widely held by both Jewish and Christian authorities that an infant conceived during a woman's menstrual cycle would contract leprosy.[111] Although menstrual blood was understood to purge the woman's body of impurities and toxins, it is retained during pregnancy to nourish the flesh of the growing fetus.[112] However, when conception occurs during a woman's menstrual cycle this same blood will afflict the progeny with leprosy and other congenital deficiencies, evidently as a punishment for the sexual transgression. The apocalyptic text of 4 Esdras 5:8 had declared that "menstruating women will give birth to monsters." This fear was acknowledged too by William of Auvergne (d. 1249), Bishop of Paris, who argued that one reason behind the Old Testament prohibition against sex with a menstruant was that the fetus will be corrupted

109. Sharon Faye Koren, "The Menstruant as 'Other' in Medieval Judaism and Christianity," *Nashim: A Journal of Jewish Women's Studies & Gender Issues* 17 (2009): 33–59, cited on 35. This text, Baraita de niddah, is first identified by name by twelfth-century rabbinic authors; Marienberg suggests that it may have originated in the late second half of the first millenium. See Evyatar Marienberg, "Baraita de-Niddah," Jewish Women: A Comprehensive Historical Encyclopedia, March 1, 2009, in Jewish Women's Archive, available at http://jwa.org/encyclopedia/article/baraita-de-niddah (accessed June 9, 2009).

110. *Sacrorum Conciliorum nova et amplissima collectio*, ed. P. Labb and J. D. Mansi (Florence, 1759), 2: 1038, quoted in Ottavia Niccoli, "*Menstruum quasi monstrum*: Monstrous births and Menstrual Taboo in the Sixteenth Century," in *Sex and Gender in Historical Perspective*, ed. Edward Muir and Guido Ruggiero, trans. Margaret Gallucci, Mary M. Gallucci, and Carole C. Galluci (Balitmore: Johns Hopkins University Press, 1990), 10.

111. For links to sexual transgressions, see especially Joseph Zias, "Lust and Leprosy: Confusion or Correlation?" *Bulletin of the American Schools of Oriental Research* 275 (1989): 27–31. For leprosy as punishment for relations with a *niddah*, see Sharon Koren, "Mystical Rationales for the Laws of *Niddah*," in *Women and Water: Menstruation in Jewish Life and Law*, ed. Rahel R. Wasserfall (Hanover, N.H.: University Press of New England, 1999), 102–3.

112. Peter of Abano, *Conciliator seu enucleatus differentiarum philosophicarum et medicarum*, A II, after q. 109, ed. G. Horst (Giessae: 1621), 150–51. Scholastic theologians debated the role of menstrual blood in the virgin birth, precisely because it seemed untoward that the infant Jesus should have been nourished in the womb on something so impure. See the discussion of Nicholas of Ockham, *Quaestiones disputatae de traductione humanae naturae a primo parente* q. 5.15, p. 187, 15–18. See also Charles T. Wood, "The Doctors' Dilemma: Sin, Salvation, and the Menstrual Cycle in Medieval Thought," *Speculum* 56, no. 4 (1981): 710–27.

by poisonous, menstrual blood and come forth as an abomination.[113] A fear of monstrous births, combined with the risk of leprosy, underlined the Church's insistence that Christians should abstain from sexual intercourse during this time. The canonist Ivo of Chartres demands, "Let each one take care not to have intercourse with a menstrual woman; the Law of God calls this an abomination."[114] Failure to abstain at this time required a severe penance,[115] and most medieval theologians regarded intercourse with a menstruating woman as a mortal sin.[116] Intercourse at an inappropriate time, then, could have serious consequences: some early medieval Christian sources add that a woman who conceives on the Christian Sabbath will be struck down with leprosy.[117]

The Carolingian theologian Rabanus Maurus (d. 856), who treats intercourse with a woman during her menstruation as a capital offense,[118] reiterated Jerome's remark that

At each monthly period the gross and sluggish [nature of] bodies of women are revealed by an effusion of unclean blood. If a man has intercourse with a woman at this time, the fetuses that are conceived are said to receive a corruption of the seed, so much so that they are born leprous and subject to elephantiasis [a virulent form of leprosy] on account of this conception.[119]

---

113. William of Auvergne, *De legibus* 5, p. 35.2C.

114. "Observet unusquisque ne menstruatae mulieri misceatur; hoc enim exsecrabile dicit lex Dei." Ivo of Chartres, *Decretum* 119 (PL 161: 688C). Cf. Lev. 18:19, where a man who has intercourse with a menstruating woman is cut off from his people, and Ezek. 18:6, where avoidance of menstruating women is one of the seventeen virtues of a just man. See also Herard, Archbishop of Tours (d. 870), *Capitula* 124, ed. Rudolf Pokorny and Martina Stratmann, MGH, Capitula episcoporum 2 (Hannover: Hahnsche Buchhandlung, 1995), 154.

115. "Quilibet vir, qui cum uxore in consuetudine ejus menstrua rem habuerit, jejunet quadraginta dies." (Any man who takes advantage of his wife at her menstrual period shall fast for forty days.) Egbert of York, *Poenitentiale* 16 (PL 89: 405C); cf. *Fragmenta ex collectoribus canonum* 249 (PL 99: 971C).

116. See Ralph of Flamborough, *Liber Poenitentialis* 4.8.225, p. 197; Albert the Great appears exceptional in treating this as a venial sin. For a discussion, see Bruno Roy, "Un inédit d'Albert le Grand dans *l'Unguentarius* de Guillaume de Werda," in *Comprendre et Maîtriser la Nature au Moyen Ages, Mélanges d'histoire des Sciences offerts à Guy Beujouan* (Geneva: Libr. Droz, 1994), 171–80.

117. See H. L. Leclercq, "Lepre," in *Dictionnaire d'archéologie chrétienne et de liturgie* 8: 2582.

118. Rabanus Maurus, Epist. 56, ed. Ernest Dümmler, MGH, Epp. 5 (Berlin: 1898–99), 511.

119. "Per singulos menses gravia atque torpolentia mulierum corpora immundi sanguinis effusione revelantur. Quo tempore si vir coierit cum muliere, dicuntur concepti fetus vitium seminis trahere; ita ut leprosi, et elephantiaci ex hac conceptione nascantur." Rabanus Maurus, *Commentaria in Ezechielem* 8.18 (PL 110: 706C). Later medieval texts frequent-

Lothar of Segni (c. 1160–1216), later Pope Innocent III, reiterates that infants conceived by a menstruating woman will be born with leprosy. Rupert of Deutz (d. 1129) cautions that those who engage in sex with a menstruating woman are at special risk for leprosy,[120] while Peter of Poitiers (1130–1205) adds that both the woman's partner(s) and the progeny will contract leprosy.[121] This assumed link between intercourse with a menstruating woman and leprosy may have generated widespread anxiety. One late medieval source relates that Arnaud of Verniolle (1323/4) was so terrified of contracting leprosy from a woman that he turned instead to sex with men.[122]

THE JEWS AND LEPROSY IN CHRISTIAN BIBLICAL EXEGESIS

In sum, then, leprosy may have spread more widely throughout Europe as Crusaders returned from the East, even if it was not introduced by the Crusaders.[123] It seems to have spread and expanded rapidly in the twelfth and thirteenth centuries, when the first leprosaria also appear for the purpose of isolating, rather than curing, those afflicted with the disease.[124] It was thought to be spread by contagion, by intercourse with a menstruant,

---

ly repeated this claim, almost verbatim. See Robert of Flamborough, *Liber Poenitentialis* 5.3.6.288, p. 238; Pseudo-Albert the Great, *Women's Secrets*, pp. 88, 129, 131.

120. Rupert of Deutz, *De sancta Trinitate, In Leviticum* 15, p. 892.

121. Lothar of Segni, *De contemptu mundi sive de miseria conditionis humanae* 1.5 (PL 217: 704); Peter of Poitiers, *Summa de confessione: compiliatio praesens* 65.

122. *Other Middle Ages: Witnesses at the Margins of Medieval Society*, 128. As Ruth Mazo Karras points out, Arnaud cannot simply be characterized as a homosexual, since he seems to have been equally inclined to intercourse with male and female. See her *Sexuality in Medieval Europe: Doing unto Others* (New York: Routledge, 2005), 137.

123. For leprosy in the Latin crusader kingdoms, see Piers D. Mitchell, "Leprosy and the Case of King Baldwin IV of Jerusalem: Mycobacterial Disease in the Crusader States of the 12th and 13th Centuries," *International Journal of Leprosy* 61, no. 2 (1993): 283–91.

124. See Keith Manchester, "Leprosy: The Origins and Development of the Disease in Antiquity," *Maladie et Maladies: histoire de conceptualisation. Mélanges en l'honneur de Mirko Grmek*, ed. Danielle Gourevitch (Geneva: Librarie Droz, 1992), 31–49. For attempts to estimate the number of those afflicted with leprosy in the twelfth and thirteenth centuries in Europe, see especially Francoise Bériac, "Connaisances médicales sur la lèpre et protection contre cette maladie au Moyen Age," in *Maladies et société (XIIe–XVIIIe siècles). Actes du Colloque de Bielfeld, novembre 1986*, ed. Neithard Bulst and Robert Delort (Paris: Editions du C.N.R.S., 1989), 145–63; and Bériac, "À propos de la fin de la lèpre," 159–73. In this same volume is found a useful bibiliographical guide to scholarship on leprosy in the Middle Ages: Patrizia Salvadori, "La Peste e la Lebbra in 'medioevo Latino.' Un prospetto biblio-geografico," 177–93.

and by heredity. Although leprosy became a medieval metaphor for sin and heresy, it is equally true that it became a metaphor for Judaism.[125] One need only examine two Scriptural motifs in order to discover the basis. First is the example of the Syrian general Naaman, a leper who sought a cure from the prophet Elisha. After having fulfilled Elisha's instruction to bathe seven times in the Jordan River Naaman was healed (2 Kgs. 5:10ff.). Although medieval Jewish polemics cited this passage positively as evidence that the prophets too could perform miracles,[126] in Luke's Gospel Jesus remarks that Naaman alone was healed of leprosy, whereas others in Israel remained afflicted (Luke 4:27–28). Christian theologians clearly understood Naaman's cure in the cleansing waters of the Jordan to prefigure Christian baptism and the implication of Luke 4:27–28 seemed to be, then, that only those who were baptized could be healed.[127]

Medieval polemicists sometimes treated Naaman's leprosy as a metaphor for the deserved punishment visited upon Jews, or simoniacs and other Christian heretics.[128] In addition, the figure of Elisha's acquisitive servant Gehazi, who sought payment for the miraculous cure after his master had refused Naaman's every gift, for which Gehazi and all of his descendents were cursed with leprosy (2 Kgs. 5:20–27), became a symbol for all the Jews. According to Caesarius of Arles (d. 542), Gehazi represents the whole of the Jewish people that is afflicted with the sin of leprosy, but from which the Gentiles have been freed.[129] Sometimes, Christian

---

125. See especially Saul N. Brody, *The Disease of the Soul: Leprosy in Medieval Literature* (Ithaca, N.Y.: Cornell University Press, 1974). Note Jacques de Vitry's (d. 1240) remark that whereas it was a function of the priests of the Old Testament to distinguish "between leper and leper (Deut. 17:18)," it falls to Christian priests to differentiate and to heal the "the leprosy of sins" in the faithful. *Lettres de Jacques de Vitry* 2, p. 83.

126. See the *Account of the Disputation of the Priest* 11, in *The Polemic of Nestor the Priest*, 2 vols., ed. and trans. Daniel J. Lasker and Sarah Stroumsa (Jerusalem: Ben-Zvi Institute for the Study of Jewish Communities in the East, 1996), 1: 54.

127. Although Vincent of Beauvais remarks that Naaman was cleansed of leprosy by washing seven times in the Jordan, just as the sinner is cleansed of the seven stains of mortal sin by the seven effusions of Christ's blood. See *Speculum morale* 1.19, 3: 659 (= vol. 3 of the *Speculum quadruplex, sive, Speculum maius: naturale, doctrinale, morale, historiale*).

128. Manegold of Lautenbach, *Ad Gebehardum* 21, ed. Kuno Francke, MGH, Ldl 1 (Hannover: Hahn, 1891), 347; Humbertus a Silva Candida, *Adversus simoniacos* 1.16–17; 1.19; 2.21, ed. F. Thaner, MGH, Ldl 1 (Hannover: Hahn, 1891),126–28; 133; 165; Honorius of Autun, *De offendiculo* 44, ed. J. Dietrich, MGH, Ldl 3 (Hannover: Hahn, 1897), 53; Bruno di Segni, *Libellus de symoniacis* 2, ed. E. Sackur, MGH, Ldl 2 (Hannover: Hahn, 1892), 555; See *Decreta* pars 2, causa 1, q. 1, cap. 16, in *Corpus iuris canonici* 1:362.

129. Caesarius of Arles, *Sermo* 129, 3, ed. Gervais Morin, CCSL 103 (Turnholt: Brepols,

thinkers treated Naaman's leprosy as a symbol for that universal spiritual estrangement from God brought down upon us as a consequence of original sin. Peter Damian (d. 1072) asks, "what does the Syrian Naaman signify but the human race? For as formerly Naaman was a leper, as soon as he had washed seven times in the waters of the Jordan, he was cleansed of all the filth of leprosy."[130] And although leprosy is an affliction both physical and spiritual that is found in all humanity, nonetheless it was located principally among pagans and Jews, because while "baptism" removed Naaman's leprosy, in medieval Europe the only tolerated minority that refused baptism was the Jews.[131] Therefore, according to St. Jerome, the Jews will only be restored to health and cured of this leprous condition in the fullness of time, once the period established for the incorporation of the Gentiles into the Church has been completed.[132] Medieval authors continued to attribute to the waters of the Jordan River a special power to heal lepers who bathed in them, especially at the spot where Jesus was baptised.[133] One may infer, then, that Jews who refuse baptism remain cursed with leprosy, even if its appearance remains hidden or dormant—as in the case of a woman who acts as a carrier of the disease. This link between the unbaptized Jew and leprosy seems clearly conveyed in Herman of Cologne's account of his conversion from Judaism to Christianity c. 1128–29. Herman writes:

1953). See also *Decretum magistri Gratiani* 2, cap.1, q. 4.11.1, vol. 1, ed. A. Friedberg (Leipzig: Tauchnitz, 1879–81).

130. Peter Damian, Epist. 49.22, in *Die Briefe des Petrus Damiani*, 2: 74; for the translation, see *The Letters of Peter Damian, 31–60*, trans. Owen J. Blum, The Fathers of the Church, Mediaeval Continuation 2 (Washington, D.C.: The Catholic University of America Press, 1990), 285.

131. "Cum enim sit universalis lepra, qua diligitur plus creatura quam creator magisque ambiuntur temporalia quam aeterna, tamen ita specificatur, ut hec radix omnium malorum in multos ramos pullulet, inter quos tamquam principales duae species eminent paganismus et iudaismus." Gerhoh of Reichenberg, *De quarta vigilia noctis* 6, ed. E. Sackur, MGH, Ldl 3 (Hannover: Hahn, 1897), 505. Note that Ambrose of Milan remarked that while Naaman was cleansed, the Jews remained corrupted by leprosy that afflicted them equally in the body and the mind (*lepra corporis pariter et mentis*). See *Expositio euangelii secundum Lucam* 4, ed. M. Adrien, CCSL 14 (Turnholt: Brepols, 1957).

132. "populus iudaeorum lepra sorde perfunditur nec redit ad tabernaculum et pristinam recipit sanitatem, donec statutum plenitudinis gentium tempus inpleat." Jerome, Epist. 78.16, ed. Isidore Hilberg, CSEL 55 (Vienna: F. Temsky, 1910–18), 65.

133. See Gregory of Tours, *Glory of the Martyrs* 16–17, trans. Raymond Van Dam (Liverpool: Liverpool University Press, 1988), 37; and see n. 126.

Naaman, washed in the waves of the Jordan seven times, was visibly cured of leprosy of the flesh. I, [washed] in baptism by the seven-form grace of the Holy Spirit, was invisibly cured of leprosy of the soul. His flesh, with the stains of leprosy washed off, took on the purity of an infant. The Church, a virgin mother, gave birth to me in a new infancy; through the washing of regeneration, I was stripped of the skin of the old existence. Indeed, just as I changed the order of my former life in this washing, so also I changed the name that belonged to me. I, who was called Judah, now took the name Herman.[134]

The waters of regeneration removed the stain of leprosy from his soul and also stripped from Herman "the skin of the old existence." It does not seem to be mere coincidence that the oaths Jews were compelled to swear in court during the Carolingian age threaten them with leprosy should their word prove false. Thus, when testifying against a Christian, a Jew must place his hand on the Mosaic torah, and proclaim, "So help me God, that God who gave the Law to Moses on Mount Sinai, that the leprosy of Naaman shall not come on me as it came on him, and the earth shall not swallow me as it swallowed Dathan and Abiron, that I have not done you any wrong in this case." Or, "I swear to you in God the living and the true ... and if not [truthfully], the leprosy of Naaman the Syrian shall envelop my body, and if not, the earth shall swallow me alive, as it did Dathan and Abilon."[135] Should they break faith with the court by perjuring themselves, let God curse them with leprosy. But since in every sense they were outside the community of faith that Christians shared, one cannot help but think that these oaths threatened a visible punishment that Jews were thought already to endure in the soul.

A second biblical example is that of King Uzziah, who was struck with leprosy for having usurped sacerdotal functions (2 Chron. 26:19–20). Among Christian exegetes, his affliction prefigures the punishment visited upon the Jews who refuse to recognize Jesus as the new High Priest. With Uzziah and Gehazi as representatives for all Jews, then, it

---

134. Herman of Cologne, *Opusculum de conversione sua* 4, ed. Gerlinde Niemeyer, MGH, QQ Geistesgesch. 4 (Weimar: H. Böhlaus, 1963), 120; for the translation, see *A Short Account of His Own Conversion*, in *Conversion and Text: The Cases of Augustine of Hippo, Herman-Judah, and Constantine Tsatsos*, trans. Karl F. Morrison (Charlottesville: University of Virginia Press, 1992), 108–9.

135. Both oaths are from the *capitula de judaeis* falsely attributed to Charlemagne. Both the Latin texts and the English translation will be found in *The Jews in the Legal Sources of the Early Middle Ages*, ed. and trans. Amnon Linder (Detroit: Wayne State University Press, 1997), 346–47. On the oaths required of Jews generally, see Joseph Ziegler, "Reflections on the Jewry Oath in the Middle Ages," in Wood, *Christianity and Judaism*, 209–20.

is not surprising that among the apologists in the early Church Origen had insisted that *Synagoga* was infected with leprosy.[136] In the twelfth-century window of the abbey church at St. Denis, blindfolded *Synagoga* carries a hyssop branch, which represents one of the offerings required of lepers following their purification (see Lev. 14:4) but which, as shown below, Thomas Aquinas interprets as a symbol of the foul odor of leprosy.[137] Similarly, the thirteenth- or fourteenth-century *Bible historiée toute figurée* shows *Synagoga* collapsed upon the ground, with the accompanying text proclaiming that God has smitten her with *mesele*, that is, leprosy.[138]

Although in Christian culture leprous *Synagoga* represents religious Judaism, nonetheless the link between Jews and leprosy antedates Christianity. Centuries earlier, certain pagan anti-Jewish polemicists—for example, Manetho, Chaeremon, Lysimachus, and Apion[139]—argued that the Jews had originated from a group of leprous Egyptians. This association of Jews with leprosy—whether in a spiritual or physical form—continued throughout the Middle Ages and well into the modern era. The leper Baude Fastoul d'Aras (d. 1272) composed a *congé*, a lyric poem of farewell, in which he refers to leprosy as *l'oevre Israel*, that is, as a disease introduced by Jews to Europe;[140] he died in the Beaurains leper colony.

---

136. *Selecta in Leviticum* (PG 12: 403). For this image of *leprosa synagoga*, see also Rupert of Deutz, *De sancta Trinitate* 10, *In Exodum* 1, p. 917; and *In Deuteronomium* 1.18, CCCM 22, 1051.

137. Seiferth, *Synagogue and Church in the Middle Ages*, 104 and fig. 31. For Thomas Aquinas, see also chap. 6, p. 233.

138. Codex Fr. 9561, Bibliothèque Nationale, Paris, fol. 89, cited by Seiferth, *Synagogue and Church in the Middle Ages*, 134–35. Just as for the *Bible historiée toute figurée*, in the Old French *Bible française du XIIIe siècle* "mésel" signifies a leper. See Wendy Ayres Bennett, *A History of the French Language through Texts* (New York: Routledge, 1996), 74–75; for *mésel* (= afflicted with leprosy) and *mésellerie* (= leprosy), see H. dE Meric, *Dictionnaire des termes de médicine Français-Anglais* (London: Ballière, Tindall and Cox, 1899), 127. In Latin texts, *leprosus* or *leprosa* are sometimes glossed as *misellus* or *misella*. See *Statuts d'hôtels-Dieu et de léproseries; recueil de textes du XIIe au XIVe siècle*, ed. Léon Le Grand (Paris: A. Picard, 1901), 182.

139. See especially Josephus' *Against Apion* 1.229ff. This text may be found in the Loeb Library edition, *Josephus* 1: *The Life; Against Apion*, trans. H. St. J. Thackeray (Cambridge, Mass.: Harvard University Press, 1976), 257ff. For other ancient sources, see Louis H. Feldman, *Jew and Gentile in the Ancient World: Attitudes and Interactions from Alexander to Justinian* (Princeton, N.J.: Princeton University Press, 1993), 240–41, 250–51; and, *Jewish Life and Thought among Greeks and Roman: Primary Readings*, ed. Louis H. Feldman and Meyer Reinhold (Minneapolis, Minn.: Fortress Press, 1996), 350–57.

140. *Fabliaux et contes des poètes Francois des XI, XII, XIII, XIV et XVe siècle . . . publiés par Barbazon*, 4 vols., ed. Dominique Martin Méon (Paris: B. Warée,1808), 1: 121, v. 293; cf. Francisque Michel, *Histoire des Races maudites de la France et de l'Espagne*, 2 vols. (Paris:

In the modern era, John Locke (d. 1704) intimated that the Jews may have been responsible for introducing leprosy to medieval France,[141] and Voltaire (d. 1778) identified leprosy as a distinctively Jewish evil.[142]

Even when physical signs of leprosy were absent, allegations of a shared hypersexuality forged a link between lepers and Jews.[143] The medieval statutes of leper houses contain numerous allegations of sexual promiscuity, and reveal the common belief already noted that leprosy was communicated especially via illicit sexual activity. Vernacular literature reinforced this perception of the leper's untamed wantonness. In Béroul's twelfth-century *Romance of Tristan* a band of lepers persuades King Mark to punish queen Yseut more dreadfully by handing her over to them to satisfy their sexual desires (thereby to be made one of them) than by burning her at the stake. Such punishment will be unequalled, implies Yvain, the leader of the lepers, for "we [lepers] burn with so much lust! There is no lady in the world who could survive our embraces, even for a single day."[144] Similarly, Chaucer's Summoner in the *Canterbury Tales*, often seen as afflicted with leprosy, is marked as well by unbridled lechery.[145] Although modern science finds no correlation between heightened sexual appetite and leprosy, some researchers have

---

A. Franck, 1847), 1: 257. For discussion of Fastoul's *congé* see Michel Zink, "Le ladre, de l'exil au Royaume. Comparaison entre les Congés de Jean Bodel et ceux de Baude Fastoul," in *Exclus et systems d'exclusion dans la literature et la civilization medievales* (Aix-en-Provence: CUERMA, 1978), 71–88.

141. Kenneth DeWhurst, *John Locke (1632–1704): Physician and Philosopher* (London: Wellcome Historical Medical Library, 1963), 72.

142. Voltaire wrote: "La lèpre, ainsi que le fanatisme et l'usure, avait été le caractère distinctif des Juifs." *Oeuvre complètes*, ed. Beuchot (Paris, 1879) 19: 574, quoted in Francois-Olivier Touati, *Maladie et société au moyen âge: La lèpre, les lépreux et les léproseries dans la province ecclésiastique de Sens jusqu'au milieu du XIVe siècle* (Paris: De Boeck, 1998), 33. In a letter to Jean Jacques Paulet from 23 April, 1768, Voltaire more generally described "Jews . . . [as] the most infected people that have ever soiled the face of the earth." For reference and discussion, see Arnold Ages, "Tainted Greatness: The Case of Voltaire's Anti-Semitism," *Neohelicon* 21, no. 2 (1994): 357–67, citing 365.

143. See Anne Marie D'Arcy, "Li anemis meismes: Satan and Synagogue in La Queste del Saint Graal," *Medium Aevum* 66, no. 2 (1997): 218ff.

144. Béroul, *The Romance of Tristan*, ed. N. J. Lacy (New York: Garland, 1989), 56–59, quoted in Rawcliffe, *Leprosy in Medieval England*, 10. Cf. Bédier's translation, which refers to leprosy as a "disease [that] inflames our desires." Joseph Bédier, "The Legend of Tristan and Isolt," *International Quarterly* 9, no. 1 (1904): 121.

145. See the "General Prologue" to the *Canterbury Tales*, ln. 628, ed. A. C. Cawley (London: Dent, 1984), 19; for a discussion of leprosy and the Summoner, see Bryon Lee Grigsby, *Pestilence in Medieval and Early Modern Literature* (New York: Routledge, 2004), 87–90.

suggested an explanation for their medieval linkage. For example, there is a correlation between pregnancy, which acts as a T-cell suppressor, and the development of overt symptoms of leprosy. Consequently, it may be that a woman who conceived and then developed signs of leprosy during her pregnancy would attribute the leprosy to the sex act. Another possible explanation for the link between leprosy and hypersexuality may be that about 10 percent of leprosy patients also have syphilis (compared to .045 percent of the general population) and early manifestations of the two diseases may be quite similar, possibly leading the sufferer to attribute the symptoms of syphilitic lesions to the leprosy.[146]

Regardless of these apparent empirical links between sex, conception, and leprosy, it was especially for their alleged sexual appetite that Jews were associated with leprosy. Although Jews may have been seen as cursed with leprosy as a divine punishment, their allegedly insatiable sexual appetite was an external sign of a disease that failed to manifest itself in Jews in ordinary ways. This appears, on the surface, to be something of a paradox, since some medieval Christian observers remark on the fact that Jews seem virtually immune to leprosy. This alleged immunity is contradicted by the Old Testament evidence, since priests would not have been required to identify and separate lepers from the Jewish community had leprosy in some sense not existed there. In the same way, it is contradicted by the existence of medieval Jewish leprosaria,[147] and by the fact that medieval Jewish physicians did not fail to discuss treatments for leprosy.[148] Shoham-Steiner argues that since the number of Jews in medieval Europe was small, the

---

146. Stephen R. Ell, "Blood and Sexuality in Medieval Leprosy," *Janus: Revue internationale de l'histoire des sciences, de la médicine de la pharmacie et de la technique* 71, no. 1–4 (1984): 153–64.

147. The *Chronicle of the Abbey of Saint-Pierre-le-Vif de Sens* attributed to Louis VII the following acts: "He made new towns; and, driven by the thirst for gold, despite the respect he owed to the faith, he granted certain liberties to the Jews—leproseries, new synagogues, and cemeteries." Geoffroy de Courlon, *Chronique de l'Abbaye de Saint-Pierre-le-Vif de Sens, rédigée vers la fin du XIIIe siècle par Geoffroy de Courlon* (Sens: C. Duchemin, 1876), 476–77, quoted in Gérard Nahon, "From the *Rue aux Juifs* to the *Chemin du Roy*: The Classical Age of French Jewry, 1108–1223," in *Jews and Christians in Twelfth-Century Europe*, 316. For additional evidence concerning Jewish lepers and their treatment, see also Ernest Wickersheimer, "Lèpre et Juifs au Moyen Âge," *Janus* 36 (1932): 43–48, and Ephraim Shoham-Steiner, "An Ultimate Pariah? Jewish Social Attitudes toward Jewish Lepers in Medieval Western Europe," *Social Research* 70, no. 1 (2003): 237–68.

148. See *Sefer Hanisyonot: The Book of Medical Experiences Attributed to Abraham Ibn Ezra*, fols. 140v, 33–141r, 8, ed. and trans. J. O. Leibowitz and S. Marcus (Jerusalem: Magnes Press, 1984), 277–78.

number of Jewish lepers would have been proportional to the population, perhaps accounting for a Christian perception that leprosy was almost unknown among the Jews. The evidence for Jewish leprosaria, he argues, is ambiguous but certainly identifies no more than two European Jewish institutions for lepers.[149] This argument assumes that the alleged immunity to leprosy among Jews stemmed from an empirical observation, namely, the virtual absence of Jewish lepers. Yet Peter of Poitiers (1130–1205) sought a medico-theological explanation and attributes this perceived immunity to the fact that, because of their ritual laws, Jews will not have intercourse with a menstruating woman.[150] Just such sexual transgression, as we have seen, was thought to introduce leprosy. The immunity Peter of Poitiers confers upon Jews seems to be an inference drawn from received science and theology, in disregard of empirical evidence. Nonetheless, it was introduced to the medieval university medical curriculum. In his surgical textbook Henri de Mondeville (d. 1320), surgeon to France's King Philip the Fair—a king who was himself said to have cursed his family with leprosy as a divine punishment for his violent treatment of both lepers and Templars[151]—echoes Peter of Poitiers when he remarks that "because Jews rarely have intercourse during the menstrual period, few Jews are leprous."[152] The perceived salutary effect of ritual purity legislation in Torah upon the health of Jews did not, however, result in a more positive image of Jews or of Jewish law, as we will see. There seems to be no parallel medieval counter narrative, as does emerge in the early modern era, to challenge the depiction of Jews as the source of disease and corruption.[153]

Many Christian authorities, as we have seen, insisted that menstrual

149. Shoham-Steiner, "An Ultimate Pariah?" 11.

150. Peter of Poitiers, *Summa de confessione: compiliatio praesens* 12.51, ed. Jean Longère, CCCM 51 (Turnholt: Brepols, 1980). David Biale cites the detailed penances assigned in the thirteenth-century *Sefer ha-Rokeah* for those Jews who have intercourse during menstruation as evidence that not all medieval Jews were as scrupulous as Peter assumes. See *Eros and the Jews*, 82.

151. See Albert Stuten, *Weltchronik des Mönchs Albert 1273/77–1454/56*, ed. Rolf Sprandel, MGH, SS rer. Germ. n.s. 17 (Munich: MGH, 1994), 218.

152. "Et quia Judaei raro coeunt tempore menstrorum, ideo pauci Judaei sunt leprosi." *Die Chirurgie des Heinrich von Mondeville* tr. 3, doctr. 1, cap. 17, in *Leben, Lehre und Leistungen des Heinrich von Mondeville (Hermondavile) nach Berliner, Erfurter und Pariser Codices*, ed. Julius Leopold Pagel (Berlin: August Hirschwald, 1892), 1: 422. See, too, the remarks of the Jewish convert to Christianity, Anton Margaritha in chap. 5, n. 112.

153. For the modern period, see Mitchell B. Hart, *The Healthy Jew: The Symbiosis of Judaism and Modern Medicine* (Cambridge: Cambridge University Press, 2007).

blood itself can communicate leprosy. Michael Scot (d. c. 1235) reflected older traditions when he remarked: "Regarding menses, we say that if a dog eats it, he becomes rabid; if a green plant is sprinkled with it, it dries out." Although it is an aphrodisiac, it also imparts disease: "it infatuates a man ... and renders [him] leprous."[154] In addition, "if a woman is suffering from a flow of [menstrual] blood, and a man has intercourse with her, she will easily injure herself with the penis, as is evident among ignorant adolescents who are injured sometimes by the penis and sometimes with leprosy."[155] Jewish sources also link sex, menstrual blood, and leprosy. Solomon bar Simson's Hebrew Chronicle of the First Crusade does not identify Jesus by name, but rather refers to him as "a bastard and a child of menstruation and lust."[156] The complaint that Jesus was a bastard countered Christian insistence that he had been born of a woman pure and full of grace; instead Mary, the texts imply—as does the Babylonian Talmud—was a licentious, adulterous woman.[157] That Jesus was a *ben niddah* or the offspring of a menstruant also implied a diseased constitution. And, after all, Christians themselves understood the text of Isaiah 53:4 to mean that their messiah was like a leper (*quasi leprosum*). The Jewish polemical assertion that Jesus was a *ben niddah* confirmed his leprous—and perhaps effeminate—nature on generally accepted religious and medical grounds.[158]

154. "De menstruo dicimus quod si a cane comedatur purum fit rabidus; et si aspergatur herba virens siccatur; infatuat hominem ... , et reddit leprosum." Michael Scot, *Liber phisionomiae* cap. 3. For older traditions that describe the poisonous nature of menses, see Rabanus Maurus, *De universo* 6.1 (PL 111: 174B). Cf. Hugh of St. Victor (?), *De bestiis et aliis rebus* 3.60 (PL 177: 131B); and Innocent III, *De contemptu mundi* 1.5 (PL 217: 704C). The source for this notion can be traced back through Isidore of Seville's *Etymologiae* 11.1.141 to Pliny's *Historia Naturalis* 7.15.64–5.

155. "Si vero mulier fluxum patiatur, et vir eam cognoscat, facile sibi virga viciat, ut patet in adolescentulis qui hoc ignorentes viciantur quandoque virga quandoque lepra." Michael Scot, *Liber phisionomiae* cap. 6. I have translated "viciat" here as injure, although it may also have the sense of "infect" or "corrupt."

156. For the entire text, see the translation in the appendix to Chazan's *European Jewry and the First Crusade*, 243–97, citing here 255. Chazan's translation improves upon *The Jews and the Crusaders: The Hebrew Chronicles of the First and Second Crusades*, trans. Shlomo Eidelberg (Madison: University of Wisconsin Press, 1977). For the theme of Jesus as the son of a menstruant, also see Anna Sapir Abulafia, "Invectives against Christianity in the Hebrew Chronicles of the First Crusade," in *Christians and Jews in Dispute* (Ashgate: Variorum, 1998), XVIII, 67.

157. For the Talmudic discussions that suggest that Mary was the adulterous mother of Jesus, see especially Schäfer, *Jesus in the Talmud*, 15–22; 97–102.

158. David Biale argues that this polemical identification of Jesus as a *ben niddah* en-

In the thirteenth century, Joseph ben Nathan Official, author of the *Sefer Yosef ha-Mekane*, suggested more broadly that Gentiles (that is, Christians) generally are careless about sexual relations with menstruants.[159] Therefore, even though the Gentiles are not bound by purity laws, they also may be described as sons of a menstruating woman, allowing the inference that they are subject to that leprosy that Christians increasingly attached to Jews themselves. In contrast, medieval Jews praised God for having protected them from the leprosy that afflicted the Gentiles.[160] At the same time, medieval Jewish rabbinic authorities tended to distinguish between the leprosy that had entered Europe and the biblical *tsara't*, with its implications for moral condemnation. This also may have changed Jewish attitudes toward genuine sufferers of leprosy, allowing for their inclusion in Jewish communities, in contrast to the more common Christian practice of enforced isolation.[161]

But whereas medieval Jews praised God for protection against a disease that had spread widely across Europe, medieval Christians found a different explanation for the Jews' apparent immunity. If the Jews failed to manifest ordinary signs of leprosy, it was because they were protected by the Levitical ordinances that banned sexual intercourse with a menstruating woman. Most indications are that Jews took these ordinances very seriously. Medieval kabbalists, who were especially concerned with laws of ritual purity as a necessary foundation for spiritual contemplation, proposed that the soul of a man who had relations with a menstruant (*niddah*) will transmigrate into a Gentile woman or into the body

---

abled Jews to reflect back upon Christians the charge that Jewish men were effeminate and like women. See Biale, *Blood and Belief: The Circulation of a Symbol between Jews and Christians*, 5.

159. See David Berger, *The Jewish-Christian Debate in the High Middle Ages: A Critical Edition of the Nizzahon Vetus* (Philadelphia: Jewish Publication Society, 1979), 159 and 224. For his polemical work, see also Hanne Trautner-Kromann, *Shield and Sword: Jewish Polemics Against Christianity and the Christians in France and Spain from 1100–1500* (Tübingen: Mohr, 1993), 91ff. Sharon Faye Koren argues that as rabbinic fears of menstrual impurity grew in the Middle Ages, so too did a tendency to vilify Christians as polluted or impure as a *niddah*. See "The Menstruant as 'Other' in Medieval Judaism and Christianity," 35–36.

160. Berger, *The Jewish-Christian Debate in the High Middle Ages*, 210–11, and 330–31 nn. 20–21. See also the work of the fourteenth-century Isaac Polgar, *'Ezer ha-Da'at*, ed. Yaakov Levinger (Tel Aviv: University of Tel Aviv, 1984), 36. My thanks to Alexandra Cuffel for drawing my attention to this passage. On Polgar's work, see Norman Roth, "Isaac Polgar y su libro contra un converso," in *Polémica Judeo-Cristiana Estudios*, ed. Carlos del Valle Rodriguez (Madrid: Aben Ezra Ediciones, 1992), 67–74.

161. Shoham-Steiner, "An Ultimate Pariah?" 6.

of a leper.¹⁶² But to Christian interpreters, it also seemed true that Jews had received these ordinances against sexual relations with a menstruant as a sign of their unnatural proclivities, on the assumption that an act is not banned unless it is frequently performed. One illustration of this popular perception may be evident in an *exemplum* that is found in a collection copied in a late fourteenth-century manuscript in the British Library. After the rubric "God afflicts the good rather than the wicked," the text explains:

There was a dispute between a Christian and a Jew concerning each one's faith. The Jew argued on behalf of his confession [of faith] saying, that you have seen, and it is clear, that a Jew does not suffer leprosy as a divine punishment as other evildoers do, just as we see that many Christians [suffer]. A certain Christian replied: the lightning that has descended from on high has never fallen as a sign upon a dunghill. In the same way, God does not send afflictions upon the worst evildoers in the way that he does upon those he loves.¹⁶³

Lightning will not strike a dunghill. What appears as a sign of divine favor in one context, then, simply points to a foul, impure, and depraved nature—a dunghill—in another.¹⁶⁴ God sends his worst afflictions, in-

---

162. See Sharon Faye Koren, "Kabablistic Physiology: Isaac the Blind, Nahmanides, and Moses de Leon on Menstruation," *AJS Review* 28, no. 2 (2004): 333–35.

163. "Contentio fuit inter Christianum et Judaeum de fide utriusque. Judaeus allegescit pro statu suo confessionis dicens: quod vidisti et liquet non iudeum leprosum ut divinam poenitentiam [?] ut caeteri iniquii pati, sicut videmus multos christianos. Quidam christianus respondit: fulmen quod de alto descendit nusquam incedit super signaculum ut cloacam. Sicut super pessimis iniquiis non mittit deus sicut afflictiones super dilectis." MS British Library Cotton, Cleopatra D. viii fol. 116b. (Again, my thanks to Alexendra Cuffel for bringing this text to my attention.) Another possibility is that the Christian's response alludes to the patient suffering of Job, who was often depicted in medieval art as afflicted with leprosy while sitting upon a dungheap (see Job 2:8, Vulg.). But the Vulgate uses the term *sterquilinium* rather than *cloaca*, as in our text. Nonetheless, it does seem that the Christian is claiming the virtue of Job's patient suffering, and implies that if Christians suffer from leprosy and not Jews, it is because "God does not send afflictions upon the worst evildoers in the way that he does upon those he loves."

164. At Lam. 4:5, the inhabitants of Jerusalem at the time of its destruction "embrace a dunghill," a symbol not only of how they have been brought low but also of their contamination by impurity. In Talmudic literature, dunghills were prohibited in Jerusalem (see B.T. *Baba Kamma* 82b). Similarly, "dunghill" can be found as a term of abuse, or an excremental polemic, in Muslim invectives against Christianity among medieval Arab chroniclers, for example, who referred to the Church of the Holy Sepulcher or Church of the Resurrection, in Arabic *al-Qiyama*, as *al-Qumana*, i.e., a dung heap. See Josef W. Meri, *A Lonely Wayfarer's Guide to Pilgrimage: 'Ali ibn Abi Bakr al-Harawi's Kitab al-Isharat ila ma'rifat al-Ziyarat* (Princeton, N.J.: Darwin press, 2005), 76; Ibn al-Furat, *Ta'rīkh al-duwal wa'l- mulūk*, trans. U. and M. C. Lyons, *Ayyubids, Mamlukes and Crusaders* (Cambridge: Heffer, 1971), 3;

cluding leprosy, only upon those he loves. If Jews rarely suffer leprosy, it is because they have been deprived of God's love, which has been transferred to Christians.

THE LEPERS' PLOT AND THE JEWS

The perception that Jews were almost immune to leprosy because of the purity laws God commanded them to observe, may also have contributed to charges in the first quarter of the fourteenth century that Jews and lepers were co-conspirators in a plot to destroy Christendom. The "Lepers' plot" must be traced back to the Pastoureaux or the Shepherds' Crusade, which began in 1320 with a young boy's vision that encouraged a crusade against the Moors in Grenada but which, instead, turned against the Jews. Ten-thousand "shepherds"—both men and women, including some lesser nobles—gathered in Paris and demanded that the king lead them on such a crusade. When the king refused to meet with them, they moved south and attacked royal castles and officials. The Pastoureaux also attacked Jewish communities in Sainte, Verdun, Cahors, Toulouse, and Albi. (See figure 7.) David Nirenberg has argued that the justification for the attacks on royal officials stems from the shepherds' conviction that the king is a sacred monarch whose task is to defend the faith. The crown's dealings with Jews, from whom it still extracted significant financial gain, polluted both king and kingdom. When the crown imposed heavy fines on those localities in which Jews had been massacred, it merely reinforced the perception that Jews were an extension of the crown's fiscal policy.

It does not seem accidental that it was in these locales that in the following year the Pastoureaux rebelled again by attacking lepers first and then Jews, whom they accused of conspiring together to destroy Christendom by poisoning wells and foodstocks in order to spread leprosy to the larger population. The fear that Jews would injure Christians by selling poisoned foodstuffs in the marketplace expressed itself earlier in statutes in Prague in 1267 that forbade Christians from buying meat from Jews.[165] It is significant that both Jews *and* lepers were thought to

---

Francesco Gabrieli, *Arab Historians of the Crusades* (Berkeley: University of California Press, 1969), 148 n. 1.

165. Gottleib Bondy and Franz Dworsky, *Zur Geschichte der Juden in Böhmen, Mähren und Schlesien von 906 bis 1620* par. 26, 2 vols. (Prague: Bondy, 1906), 1: 31.

harbor malevolent intent toward the larger, Christian community, in order to bring about its destruction. In 1346 (more than half a century after Jews had been expelled from England) a writ from King Edward III warned of lepers that consort with healthy people and seek to spread their disease—either through the infectious poison of their foul breath or by having intercourse with women in public bathhouses or houses of prostitution, who may then transmit the illness to others—in order to increase the number of fellow sufferers.[166] This perceived shared hostility toward the healthy, Christian community had led some communities in France to petition the crown by 1321 both to expel the Jews and to enforce the segregation of lepers.[167] The purity of the land demanded that it be purged of the sources of physical and spiritual danger. Expelling the Jews and enforcing the segregation of lepers appeared to be good medicine for the body politic.

Carlo Ginzburg has examined closely the lepers' plot and the allegations that Jews and lepers were co-conspirators.[168] Ginzburg has demonstrated that the earliest records show that a plot was first ascribed to the lepers alone, during Holy Week 1321. The lepers were also accused, along with other unnamed Christians, of having given the consecrated host to Jews to profane, but the Jews were not accused of participation in a plot to poison the population. Initially, the anger of the populace turned against the lepers alone. In the inquisitorial proceedings immediately after Holy Thursday 1321, lepers were tortured and some confessed to having introduced poison to the wells. Many lepers were burned. As the arrested conspirator Guillaume Agasse was tortured over many months, the plot became more elaborate, involving the King of Granada and the

166. The warning provided the basis for instructions to Londoners to expel lepers from their midst. For the Latin text, see Frank Rexroth, *Deviance and Power in Late Medieval London*, trans. Pamela E. Selwyn (Cambridge: Cambridge University Press, 2007), Appendix 11, 337–39.

167. See David Nirenberg, *Communities of Violence: Persecution of Minorities in the Middle Ages* (Princeton, N.J.: Princeton University Press, 1996), part 1, chaps. 2–4. My discussion here is deeply indebted to Nirenberg.

168. See Carlo Ginzburg, *Ecstasies: Deciphering the Witches Sabbath*, trans. Raymond Rosenthal (New York: Pantheon Books, 1991), 33–62. On elements of the role of the Jews in the lepers' plot, see also Françoise Beriac, "La persécution des lépreux dans la France méridionale en 1321," *Le moyen âge* 93, no. 2 (1987): 203–21; Malcolm Barber, "Lepers, Jews and Moslems: The Plot to Overthrow Christendom in 1321," *History* 66 (1981): 1–17; Touati, *Maladie et société au moyen âge*, 715–35; and Bénédicte Bauchau, "Science et racisme: les Juifs, la lépre et la peste," *Stanford French Review* 13, no. 1 (1989): 21–35.

Sultan of Babylon (the Mamluk Sultan of Cairo). However, as late as June 1321 no evidence had been presented of a Jewish co-conspiracy, despite renewed outbreaks of anti-Jewish violence.

Such evidence appears, however, in a letter sent by Philippe de Valois, the future king Philip VI, to Pope John XXII, which he asked the Pope to read to the cardinals gathered at Avignon. Philippe reports that on June 26, 1321 there had been a solar eclipse in some counties of Anjou and Touraine. Many people thought it was a portent of the end of the world, and on the next day they attacked Jewish homes. In the search of the house of a Jew named Bananias, the letter alleges, they found a casket containing his money and a secret document written in Hebrew characters and sealed with a golden seal. On the seal was carved a crucifix, and a monstrous Jew or Saracen was depicted on a ladder defecating on the face of the Saviour. The document itself was translated from Hebrew to Latin by two baptised Jews, and was said to contain a letter to Amicedich, the king of thirty-one kingdoms in the East (including Jericho, Jerusalem, and Hebron), and to Zabin, the Sultan of Azor, as well as to other powerful rulers. The letter refers to a perpetual pact that had been established between the Jews and these rulers. It alleges that Enoch and Elijah appeared to the Muslim Saracens on Mount Tabor and instructed them in the Jewish law and, after witnessing a number of miracles, the Saracens decided to convert to Judaism and to be circumcised. The Muslim rulers offered to confer Jerusalem, Jericho, and Ay upon the Jews but in return they wanted the Jews to deliver to them the kingdom of France. Hearing of this the Muslim viceroy of Granada, the letter maintains, conceived a plot to use the Jews and lepers to accomplish the goal.

Soon after delivering the letter Philippe left on crusade and, in a sudden about face, Pope John XXII expelled the Jews from papal domains in 1322. Two other forged documents soon appeared. The first was from the king of Granada and was addressed to Samson, son of Helias the Jew; the other was from the king of Tunis. Again, these claim to reveal the Jews' plot, which entailed exchanging the kingdom of France for the Holy Land held by the Muslims. These two letters were translated from a putative Arabic original into French with a Latin appendix. The king was persuaded of Jewish guilt and orders went out to arrest and interrogate Jews, and to confiscate their hidden wealth. A large number of Jews suffered summary judicial punishment: they were imprisoned, tortured, and executed. Allegations of a conspiracy involving the Jews, lepers, and Muslim rulers crossed the border into the kingdom of Aragon, and violence against the Jews spread there as well.

Even though the first stage of this episode attacked lepers alone and allegations of Jewish participation in an elaborate conspiracy appeared only months later, a link between Jews and lepers was, as we have seen, well established. Both were liminal groups at the margins of medieval Christendom, recognized by distinctive clothing, whose dwellings were increasingly separated from the larger community. Both were sources of "pollution" and threat. The allegations of a co-conspiracy, however, may have also rested on the medical assumption already spreading in the Christian world, namely that Jews were practically immune to leprosy. Such immunity rendered their close contact with lepers in a conspiratorial association all the more plausible.

Allegations of an international Jewish conspiracy with the enemies of Latin Christendom had presented themselves centuries earlier as well.[169] On September 29, 1009, Caliph Al Hakim destroyed the church of the Holy Sepulchre in Jerusalem and forced his Christian subjects to convert to Islam. Pilgrims brought the news back to Europe, the pope circulated an encyclical calling for an armed campaign, and rumors spread that European Jews had plotted with the Saracens in Spain to encourage Al Hakim to destroy one of the most important shrines in the Christian world, leading to outbreaks of anti-Jewish violence in Europe.[170] As we

---

169. Similarly, Jews had been accused by eastern Christians of having conspired against them with the Persians, when the latter took Jerusalem in 614 CE and made off with the relic of the True Cross. According to book two of the *Annales* of the Alexandrian patriarch Eutyches (d. c. 939), the emperor Heraclius later took vengeance against the untrustworthy Jews, and slaughtered countless numbers. For this text, see the translation in *Extracts from Aristeas, Hecataeus, Origen and Other Early Christian Writers*, trans. Aubrey Stewart (London: Palestine Pilgrims' Texts Society, 1895), 36, 39–40, 48–49.

170. See Richard Landes, "The Massacres of 1010: On the Origins of Popular Anti-Jewish Violence in Western Europe," in Cohen, *From Witness to Witchcraft: Jews and Judaism in Medieval Christian Thought*, 79–111. (For the dating of Landes's sources see in this same volume, Kenneth R. Stow, "The Avignonese Papacy or, After the Expulsion," 276 n. 5, and 277 n. 6.) For additional discussion, see the following articles that appeared in *Christian Attitudes toward Jews in the Middle Ages: A Casebook*, ed. Michael Frassetto (New York: Routledge, 2007): Daniel Callahan, "The Cross, the Jews, and the Destruction of the Church of the Holy Sepulcher in the Writings of Ademar of Chabannes," 15–24; Phyllis G. Jestice, "A Great Jewish Conspiracy? Worsening Jewish-Christian Relations and the Destruction of the Holy Sepulcher," 25–42; and Michael Frassetto, "Heretics and Jews in the Early Eleventh Century: The Writings of Rodulfus Glaber and Ademar of Chabannes," 43–60.

will see below, in the mid-twelfth century the alleged ritual murder of William of Norwich was likewise attributed to an international Jewish plot. In another example of Jewish-Muslim cooperation against Christian interests, Jews were accused of having conspired to obtain the city of Antioch for sultan Bibars when the city fell in 1268.[171]

JEWISH PHYSICIANS AND A PLOT AGAINST CHRISTENDOM

Jewish physicians were sometimes viewed as likewise organized in an international plot against Christendom. Despite—or perhaps because of—the importance of Jewish physicians in medieval Christendom, Christian authorities warned with increasing frequency that Jewish physicians sought the death of Christian patients. The thirteenth-century Dominican Vincent of Beauvais cautioned that Christians should not call upon Jews to care for them when they are ill, nor accept medicine from them, nor even bathe in the same public baths with them.[172] Several fourteenth-century Spanish church councils—including Zamorra (1313), Valladolid (1322), and Salamanca (1335)—prohibited Christians from seeking medical attention from Jews.[173] During this same period the Jewish convert to Christianity, Abner de Burgos (d. c. 1347), complained not only that Jewish physicians are ignorant of the medicinal qualities of foods forbidden to them by their dietary laws, but even that the Talmud actually commands them to kill Christians and take their property![174] Martin Luther (d. 1546) expressed a common fear that Jewish physicians presented a special danger to the Christian community, using poisons as well as magical formulae to effect its destruction. According to Luther, "if they [the Jews] could kill us all, they would gladly do so, aye,

---

171. *Chronicle of Bury St Edmunds*, 39.

172. Vincent of Beauvais, *Speculum doctrinale*, 9.37, 2: 795.

173. See T. Zvi Langermann, "Science, Jewish" in *Medieval Iberia: An Encyclopedia*, ed. E. Michael Gerli (New York: Routledge, 2003), 745; and especially Joseph Shatzmiller, *Jews, Medicine, and Medieval Society* (Berkeley: University of California Press, 1994), 78–99. See too the prohibitions from session 19 at the Council of Basle (1431–37) against Christians using public baths with Jews (or other unbelievers) or consulting them as physicians. *Conciliorum Oecumenicorum Decreta*, 3rd ed., ed. J. Alberigo, et al., with H. Jedin (Bologna: Istituto per le scienze religiose 1973), 483.

174. See Carlos del Valle, "El libro de las Batallas de Dios, de Abner de Burgos," in *Polémica Judeo-Cristiana Estudios*, ed. Carlos del Valle Rodriguez (Madrid: Aben Ezra Ediciones, 1992), 75–120, but especially appendix 7 (117–18), which contains his polemic against Jewish physicians from cap. 44 of the *Liber bellorum Dei*.

and often do it, especially those who profess to be physicians. They know all that is known about medicine in Germany; they can give poison to a man of which he will die in an hour, or in ten or twenty years; they thoroughly understand this art."[175] Furthermore, "the Jews, who pass themselves off as doctors, kill Christians, who need to be healed by them, for they believe they serve God when they severely injure or secretly kill them." Though they disagreed on so many theological doctrines, nonetheless Luther's Catholic opponent Johannes Eck (d. 1543) confirmed that when Jewish doctors gather at the time of Jewish festivals, "each boasts of the number of Christians he has killed with his medicine; the one who has killed the most is honored."[176]

Such fears had real consequences: Jewish physicians suspected of poisoning were subject to capital punishment, as in the case of the late fourteenth-century Jew Moses Rimos, who was likely executed in 1374 in Orvieto.[177] Nonetheless, according to Trachtenberg, "So strong was the belief that Jewish doctors were poisoners that it easily outweighed the lack of proof."[178] It is clear that practical necessity, however, often outweighed such fears, and the Scholastic John of Naples (fl. 1315) argued that Christians do not sin when they consult "infidel" physicians.[179] Just as Christian physicians might treat Jewish patients, Jewish (and Muslim) physicians treated Christian patients, even those in religious orders, including the mendicant orders, as well as members of royal and papal

175. See *Tischreden*, vol. 4 of *Martin Luthers Werke. Kritische Gesamtausgabe* (Weimar: Hermann Böhlaus, 1916), nr. 4485, 338, cited in John F. Efron, *Medicine and the German Jews: A History* (New Haven: Yale University Press, 2001), 25 and 48; and see also Frank Heynick, *Jews and Medicine: An Epic Saga* (Hoboken, N.J.: KTAV, 2002), 220–21.

176. Johannes Eck, *Ains Jüden büechlins verlegung* (Ingoldstadt: Alexander Weissenhorn, 1542), Fiiij, cited in Efron, *Medicine and the German Jews*, 25. For a good discussion of the views of Eck and Luther concerning Jews, see David Bagchi, "Catholic Anti-Judaism in Reformation Germany: The Case of Johann Eck," in Wood, *Christianity and Judaism*, 253–63.

177. Susan Einbinder, "Moses Rimos: Poetry, Poison, and History," *Italia. Studi e ricerche sulla storia, la cultura e la letteratura degli Ebrei d'Italia* 20 (2010): 67–91.

178. Trachtenberg, *The Devil and the Jews*, 97–98; for broader discussion of the allegation that Jewish physicians were wont to poison their Christian patients, see his chap. 7: "The Poisoners," 97–108.

179. John of Naples, *Quaestiones variae Parisiis disputatae* q. 38, ad 16 (Naples: 1618), 329–30. For John and his career, see Peter Biller, "John of Naples, Quodlibets and Medieval Theological Concern with the Body," *Medieval Theology and the Natural Body*, ed. Peter Biller and A. J. Minnis, York Studies in Medieval Theology 1 (Woodbridge, Suffolk: York Medieval Press, 1997), 3–12.

households.[180] For example, in Avignon in 1374 Abraham of Carcassonne was a medical adviser to the Cordeliers (Franciscans),[181] and in the 1380s the Jewish physician Jacob ben Solomon of Avignon (or b. Solomon ha Tzarfati) served as physician to the brother of Pope Clement VII.[182] Data from Marseilles in the second half of the fourteenth century indicate that Jewish physicians constituted almost 50 percent of the medical practicioners there, and that they continued to serve the Christian community, suggesting that ecclesiastical warnings against Jewish physicians had not gained much traction.[183] Similarly, Jewish physicians in Spain constituted 30 percent, 50 percent, or more of the total number of physicians in urban areas, far exceeding their representation in the general population.[184] Jewish physicians were in demand at least in part because of the perception that they had access to Arab medical texts and to an esoteric tradition not known to their Christian colleagues, despite the fact that by the fourteenth century Jewish physicians were very much dependent on Latin, Scholastic medicine.[185] The presumption, however, that Jewish physicians enjoyed a better knowledge of Arab medical texts also contained an implicit threat. Perhaps to eliminate Jewish physicians as economic rivals to their Muslim counterparts, Arab medical texts themselves sometimes expressed a prejudice that Jewish physicians sought to

180. See Montford, *Health, Sickness, Medicine and the Friars*, 141–44. For a general overview of the medieval Jewish physician, one may consult too Efron, *Medicine and the German Jews: A History*, 13–33. Still useful is Cecil Roth, "Jewish Physicians in Medieval England," in Roth, *Essays and Portraits in Anglo-Jewish History* (Philadelphia: Jewish Publication Society of America, 1962), 46–51. The *Sefer Chasidim* both acknowledges that a Gentile physician may treat Jews and advises Jews always to pay his bill! ([586] 357, p. 331).

181. Montford, *Health, Sickness, Medicine and the Friars*, 141.

182. For Jacob's career, see Susan Einbinder, "Theory and Practice: A Jewish Physician in Paris and Avignon," *AJS Review* 33, no. 1 (2009): 135–53.

183. For the data on Marseilles, see Monica H. Green and Daniel Lord Smail, "The Trial of Floreta d'Ays (1403): Jews, Christians, and Obstetrics in Later Medieval Marseille," *Journal of Medieval History* 34 (2008): 188–90.

184. See especially Michael R. McVaugh, *Medicine before the Plague: Practitioners and Their Patients in the Crown of Aragon 1285–1345* (Cambridge: Cambridge University Press, 2002), 55–67.

185. See Luis García Ballester, "La minoría judía ante la filosofía natural y la medicina escolásticas: problemas sobre la communicación científica en la Europa meridonal de los siglos XIII a XV," in *Proyección histórica de Espana en sus tres culturas: Castille y León, América y el Mediterránneo*, 3 vols., ed. Eufemio Lorenzo Sanz (Valladolid: Junta de Castilla y León, Consejería de Cultura y Turismo, 1993), 1: 101–28; and Luis García Ballester, Lola Ferre, and Eduard Feliu, "Jewish Appreciation of 14th C. Scholastic Medicine," *Osiris* ser 2, no. 6 (1990): 85–117.

poison their patients, or that their sexual lasciviousness represented a special danger to Muslim women.[186]

Similarly, Jewish physicians treating Christian women were especially vulnerable to accusations of sexual misconduct. In 1341 in Manosque (southeast France), the Jewish physician Crescas de Nîmes was convicted of having seduced his female Christian patient, Allaxia Collarda. Moreover, the judicial record notes that he first proposed to have sexual relations in an unnatural position (standing her up against the wall, rather than lying down);[187] when she refused, and after having set up a "sting" to insure that there were witnesses, she allowed him to place her on the bed, where she bound her hips with a night gown so that his Jewish member could not touch her (*strixit cum camisia coxas sic quod membrum judei non possit tangere suum*) while he, inflamed with passion, poured his seed uselessly onto the bed, failing to complete the act of intercourse. Following his conviction, Crescas was condemned to suffer castration (*condempnatus in amissione membri*).[188] Both the presumed lascivious nature of the Jewish physician and his knowledge of Muslim medical science—even though the latter could be viewed positively in some contexts—could bring him under suspicion before Christian authorities.

The perception that Jews enjoyed a special relationship to the Muslim world could equally, then, increase the threat ascribed to them. Precedent already existed for claims of international Jewish conspiracy, even conspiracy involving Muslim rulers. It is also plausible that Latin Christians were aware of Jewish messianic hopes that had revived in the thirteenth century and anticipated the return of a large number of Jews to the Holy Land prior to the appearance of the messiah, to be accompa-

186. See Peter E. Pormann, "The Physician and the Other: Images of the Charlatan in Medieval Islam," *Bulletin of the History of Medicine* 79 (2005): 189–227, but esp. 211–12 and 220–21.

187. According to the late thirteenth or early fourteenth century *De secretis mulierum* attributed to Pseudo-Albert the Great, irregular forms of intercourse can produce monstrous births: "If a man lies in an unusual manner when he is having sex with a woman, he creates a monster in nature." Moreover, according to Commentary A on the text, "Coitus that is performed standing up is irregular in nature (although the unlearned do not care about this) because the seed cannot be received as it ought to be." See *Women's Secrets*, 114.

188. Rodrigue LaVoie, "La Delinquance Sexuelle a Manosque (1240–1430): Schéma générale et singularités juives," *Provence Historique* 37, no. 150 (1987): 571–87, citing 579; the Latin text of the judicial inquiry appears on 583–87. It is perhaps noteworthy not only that the Jew proposed an unnatural posture for intercourse, but also that he experiences premature ejaculation, as Christians might have expected from a circumcised man.

nied by the destruction of the power of Christendom.[189] All of these elements may have contributed to accusations of Jewish conspiracy in 1321. The specific form of the accusation, however, which entailed a plot with lepers—a plot that required special knowledge of poisons—seems also based on the antecedent link between Jews and lepers already examined.

LEPROSY AND DIET

Although it was clearly understood that illicit sexual activity was *one* possible cause of leprosy, it was not the only cause. Some medieval authorities acknowledged that leprosy could be passed on by corrupted semen as an inherited illness. Albert the Great remarks that "one with gout begets one with gout, a leper a leper and sometimes a cancerous person, or one who is melancholic due to corrupt bile [*melancholia*], begets a leper."[190] In the same way, Vincent of Beauvais adds that although leprosy is contagious, it also is received through the semen.[191] Far more attention, however, was given to sources of contagion, including foul air, cohabitation or frequent contact with a leper, or even contact with a leper's food.[192] John Trevisa's (d. 1402) English translation of Bartholomew the Englishman's *On the Properties of Things* (*De propretatibus rerum*), lists among the causes of leprosy: "ta[l]kynge wiþ leprous men" and lying with a woman soon after she has had intercourse with a leper. Also, he repeats that often leprosy occurs when a child is conceived during a woman's period of menstruation, or even when a child is nursed by a wetnurse who has leprosy. Sometimes it is transmitted by corrupt or foul air. Last, leprosy may be caused by a bad diet, as when one has consumed fish or wine and milk at the same time,[193] or melancholy meat that is too cold and dry,

---

189. See Israel Jacob Yuval, "Jewish Messianic Expectations towards 1240 and Christian Reactions," in *Toward the Millennium: Messianic Expectations from the Bible to Waco*, ed. Peter Schäfer and Mark Cohen, Studies in the History of Religions 77 (Leiden: Brill, 1998), 105–21.

190. Albert the Great, *De animalibus* 9.1.6.62, vol. 15, 698 (*SZ* 1: 796–7).

191. "Praeterea quaedam aegritudines contagiosae sunt, quae scilicet de uno ad alium transeunt, ut lepra.... Sunt et quaedam quae in semine hereditantur, ut podagra, phthisis et lepra." Vincent of Beauvais, *Speculum naturale* 31.98, 1: 2370.

192. See *Cyrurgia Guidonis de Cauliaco, et Cyrurgia Bruni, Teodorici, Rolandi, Lanfranci, Rogerii, Bertapalie* tr. 6, doc. 1, pp. 49ff.

193. See the *Secreta secretorum* in Albert of Behaim, *Das Brief- und Memorialbuch* 73, p. 295; Albert the Great, *Topica* 6.7.1, Ed. Borgnet 2, 475B (citing Aristotle). The contention that leprosy is caused by eating (bad) fish appears even in modern texts, e.g., Jonathan Hutchinson, *On Leprosy and Fish-Eating: A Statement of Facts and Explanation* (London: Archibald,

like bear meat or meat from an ass, or from a corrupt meat, like "swynes fleische."[194]

It seems particularly important that "swynes fleische" was perceived to be among the causes contributing to leprosy. As early as the second century the Roman historian Tacitus had argued that Jews abstain from pork because they themselves are afflicted with a disease to which the pig is especially subject, *scabies*, which is an itching, scaly skin disease caused by a parasite (the mite, *Sarcoptes scabiei*), often translated as "leprosy."[195] Plutarch (d. 125) repeats the notion that Jews abominate pork because "barbarians" especially abhor skin diseases like leprosy, and they believe that humans are afflicted with such diseases by contagion from the pig.[196] A thirteenth-century anti-Jewish polemic from England that describes an alleged late twelfth-century ritual murder of a young Christian boy, Adam of Bristol, reiterates a link between leprosy and pigs. A Jewish woman whose true identity is hidden from an itinerant Irish priest refuses to provide him pork for his dinner, lamenting that "pig meat is neither good nor healthy in this city because many are leprous, and they eat human shit in the streets."[197] Similarly, statutes from

---

Constable, 1906). For the perceived relationship between diet and treatments for leprosy, see especially Rawcliffe, *Leprosy in Medieval England*, 213–26.

194. *On the Properties of Things: John Trevisa's translation of Bartholaeus Anglicus De proprietatibus rerum* 7.64, 3 vols. (Oxford: Clarendon Press, 1975), 1: 426.

195. Tacitus, *Histories* 5.2, and 5.4, trans. Clifford H. Moore, Loeb Classical Library (London: Heinemann; New York: Putnam's Son, 1931), 176–77, 180–81. Although this skin ailment afflicted animals, including pigs and horses—Albert the Great provides several remedies for horses suffering from scabies (*De animalibus* 22.2.1.82–83, vol. 16, 1392–93 [SZ 2: 1497–98])—medieval Christians also understood scabies to afflict the Jews as a divine punishment, based on Deut. 28:27; see Ps. Albert the Great, *Commentarii in secundam partem psalmorum* (LI–C), Ed. Borgnet 16, 343. Moreover, although ancient authors identified scabies generally as a reddish, roughening of the skin characterized by severe itching (see Celsus, *De medicina* 5.28.16, ed. C. Daremberg [Leipzig: Teubner, 1891], 291), and although scabies and leprosy may be quite distinct, medieval authors considered scabies to be a common symptom accompanying leprosy, or grouped the two together as related skin afflictions. The ninth-century commentator Christianus Stabulensis remarks that the Greeks identify as leprous one who suffers from scabies that changes color from black to white to red. (*Expositio in evangelium Matthaei*, PL 106: 1325; cf. Cassiodorus, *De orthographia* cap. 4, in *Grammatici Latini*, 8 vols., ed. Heinrich Keil (Leipzig: Teubner, 1880), 7: 166). Also see Bernard of Gordon, *Lilium Medicinae* 1.22, pp. 90–91. For the difficulty in distinguishing clearly scabies and leprosy in medieval texts, see also Grigsby, *Pestilence in Medieval and Early Modern Literature*, 85–86.

196. *Quaestiones convivales* 4.5, available at http://ebooks.adelaide.edu.au/p/plutarch/symposiacs/chapter4.html.

197. The "Passion of Adam of Bristol," fol. 24r. This unusual text is found in British Li-

Avignon in 1243 prohibited the sale of leprous pork.[198] It was not only the flesh of the pig that was linked to leprosy but even its milk which, according to the thirteenth-century rabbi Nachmanides, if fed to infants, caused them to become lepers.[199] Just as Levitical prohibitions against intercourse with a menstruant were thought to "immunize" Jews against leprosy, so too in the sixteenth century Johannes Buxtorf the Elder acknowledged that

> it is true that leprosy is not as frequent among them [Jews] as among Christians. In part this is because Jews are fewer in number and in part it is due to the fact that they refrain from those many foods or other things from which this disease can arise. For they observe the Law of Moses with respect to the foods that can be prepared. They are not more steadfast than with regard to swine flesh.[200]

Similarly, Isaac Cardoso's (1604–83) Christian antagonist, Bustroso, claimed that although because of their odd diet Jews die young and suffer a number of afflictions, like erysipelas (skin lesions and redness), nonetheless leprosy is less frequent among them because they abstain from the flesh of unclean animals and especially from pork, which may communicate leprosy and other disease. In contrast, Cardoso concludes that if there is any illness that may properly be said to be "Jewish" it is melancholy.[201] The perception among Jews that melancholy characterizes the

---

brary, Harleian MS 957, no. 7, a fourteenth-century codex. I am grateful to Robert Stacey for this translation. The Latin text can be found in Christoph Cluse, "'Fabula ineptissima'. Die Ritualmordlegende um Adam von Bristol nach der Handschrift London, British Library 957," *Aschkenas: Zeitschrift für Geschichte und Kulture der Juden* 5, no. 2 (1995): 295–330. For a discussion of the text, see also Robert Stacey, "From Ritual Crucifixion to Host Desecration: Jews and the Body of Christ," *Jewish History* 12, no. 1 (1998): 11–28. For discussion of the Jewish community there, see Michael Adler's still useful essay, "The Jews of Medieval Bristol," in his *Jews of Medieval England* (London: Jewish Historical Society of England, 1893; repr. Amersham, England: 1984).

198. See William C. Jordan, "Problems of the Meat Market of Béziers 1240–1247: A Question of Anti-Semitism," *Revue des Études juives* 135, no. 1–3 (1976): 31–49, citing 36 n. 23.

199. Nachmanides, *Commentary on the Torah: Leviticus,* trans. Charles B. Chavel (New York: Shilo Publishing House, 1974), 136.

200. "Lepra revera non tam frequens est apud eos, atque apud Christianos; partim quia pauci sunt, cum Christianis collati; partim, quia temperant sibi a multis cibis, aliisque rebus, ex quibus morbus hic concipi potest. Cibos enim quod attinet, quam fieri potest, legem Mosis observant. In nullo tamen tam pervicaces sunt, ac in carne suilla." Johannes Buxtorf, *Synagoga Judaica* 45, p. 666.

201. Isaac Cardoso, *Los excelencias y calumnias de los Hebreos* 3 (Amsterdam: En casa de David de Castro Tartas, 1679), 347; cf. Yosef Hayim Yerushalmi, *From Spanish Court to Italian Ghetto: Isaac Cardoso: A Study in Seventeenth-Century Marranism and Jewish Apolo-*

THE JEWS AND LEPROSY 143

Jewish complexion may also help to explain a curious difference between the thirteenth-century Latin translation of the pseudo-Aristotelian *Secret of Secrets* and its roughly contemporary Hebrew version: the latter, perhaps as a form of Jewish self-promotion, recommends that the ideal ruler, Alexander the Great, select a counselor with a "temperament inclined to melancholy." This advice is altogether missing from the Latin.[202]

The Jews therefore seem to enjoy a relative immunity to leprosy because of their laws—those that compel them to avoid sex with a menstruant, but also their dietary laws that prohibit the consumption of pork. But again, quite paradoxically, the suggestion that the dietary laws protect Jews from leprosy does not recommend them to Christians. This stems in part from Christian allegorization of the dietary laws. For Christian theologians, the Old Testament dietary prohibitions merely indicate the Jews' imperfection and their disposition for disease.[203]

---

getics (Seattle: University of Washington Press, 1981), 437. Isaac's brother, Abraham, became a prominent apologist for Sabbatianism. See Bruce Rosenstock, "Messianism, Machismo, and 'Marranism,'" 199–227.

202. Moses Gaster, "The Hebrew Version of the 'Secretum Secretorum,'" 11.106, in *Studies and Texts in Folklore, Magic, Mediaeval Romance, Hebrew Apocrypha and Samaritan Archaeology*, 3 vols. (New York: KTAV, 1971), 2: 803. Gaster examines and translates the text on 742–813. Gaster's edition of the Hebrew text was published previously in the *Journal of the Royal Asiatic Society*, year 1907: 879–912; his translation appeared in the *Journal of the Royal Asiatic Society*, year 1908: 111–62. Cf. Roger Bacon, *Opera hactenus inedita*, fasc. 5: *Secretum secretorum*, 4.17, p. 171.

203. See Claudine Fabre-Vassas, *The Singular Beast: Jews, Christians, and the Pig*, trans. Carol Volk (New York: Columbia University Press, 1997), 104ff. Although Muslims also must abstain from pork, the Qur'an explains the more extensive dietary restrictions imposed by God on the Jews as a "punishment for their rebellion" (Qur'an 6:146). Sander L. Gilman examines nineteenth-century medical debates concerning Jewish dietary laws—and especially the practice of ritual slaughter—that assign to Jews a relative immunity to certain diseases (e.g., tuberculosis), but sometimes recommend such practices for Christians as well as a matter of public hygiene, revealing a very different attitude than the medieval polemics. See his "You Are What You Eat: Fantasies of Jews, Purity, and Slaughter at the Fin de Siècle," in *Zwischen den Kulturen: Theorie und Praxis des interkulturellen Dialogs*, ed. Carola Hilfrich-Kunjappu and Stéphane Mosès (Tübingen: Niemeyer, 1997), 143–54, esp.147–49.

4

THE DIETARY LAWS, FOOD, AND ILLICIT SEXUALITY

It may be worthwhile here to consider the dietary laws and to examine their role in Christian-Jewish polemical encounters. These laws indicate the foods that Jews may or may not eat, according to a basic taxonomy of animals found in the world: that is, animals of the land, animals in the waters, and animals of the air. Among land quadrupeds, the fundamental division between those that are "clean" and "unclean" rests on whether or not such animals ruminate, that is, chew the cud, and whether they have a split or cloven hoof. This basic principle can be found in Leviticus 11:3–7 and Deuteronomy 14:6–8, which insist that only those land animals that both ruminate and have a split hoof are "clean." In both books, the swine, camel, and hare are explicitly identified as "unclean," forbidden foods. For Christians, however, just as the commandment to circumcise male infants in the flesh ceased after the advent of the Christ, so, too, the dietary laws of the Jews ceased once the old Law had been fulfilled by Jesus. In part, this conviction stems from the words attributed to Jesus in the Gospel of Matthew that assert that it is not what goes into a man's mouth that defiles him, but what comes out of it (Matt. 15:11, 18). In part, too, the repudiation of the dietary laws stemmed from the experience of Peter, who was instructed by a heavenly voice to eat *any* manner of four-footed beast (Acts 10:11–15), utterly subverting the dietary regulations.

Later traditions that asserted that in Paradise Adam ate no meat or that Jesus refused to eat meat but only fish and vegetables did not alter the basic premise that Christians are not bound by the dietary laws of the Jews.[1] But it is one thing for foods to be forbidden by divine command, and quite another to elect to avoid certain foods on the path to spiritual perfection or in response to ecclesiastical ordinance, such as the dietary restrictions imposed for Lent. It was in pursuit of a higher calling that Christian monastic communities, which acknowledged a close connection between gluttony and sexual desire or *luxuria*—the last two of the seven capital sins—chose to avoid meat and to engage in frequent fasts, except when discouraged for medical reasons.[2] Peter Damian (d. 1072) states clearly that "the stomach and the sexual organs are closely related, and when the former is intemperately satisfied, the latter is quickly aroused to shameful action."[3] The link between food

---

1. For the claim that Jesus ate only fish and vegetables, see Vincent of Beauvais, *Speculum naturale* 30.77, 1: 2274. The sole exception, Vincent maintains, was the Paschal lamb which Jesus ate because of divine command. For the commonplace that Adam ate no meat in Paradise, see for example Nemesius of Emesa, *Of the Nature of Man* 1.5, ed. William Telfer, in *Cyril of Jerusalem and Nemesius of Emesa*, Library of Christian Classics 4 (Philadelphia: The Westminster Press, 1955), 240. This text was translated into Latin in the eleventh and twelfth centuries. See *Nemesii Episcopii Premnon Physicon a N. Alfano Archiepiscopo Salerni in Latinum translatus*, ed. Carolus Burkhard (Leipzig: Teubner, 1917), and *Némésius D'Émèse, De natura hominis, traduction de Burgundio de Pise*, ed. G. Verbeke and J. R. Moncho, Corpus Latinum Commentariorum in Aristotelem Graecorum Suppl. 1 (Leiden: Brill, 1975); cf. Ps. William of Champeaux, *Dialogus inter christianum et judaeum de fide catholica* (PL 163: 1066C); Alexander Neckam, *De naturis rerum* 2.156, 251; and Albert the Great, *Super Matthaeum* 5.18, ed. Bernhard Schmidt, Ed. Colon. 21.1 (Münster in Westfalorum: Aschendorff, 1987), 126, 11–15. For a recent treatment of diet in Christian tradition, see David Grumett and Rachel Muers, *Theology on the Menu: Asceticism, Meat and Christian Diet* (New York: Routledge, 2010).

2. See Benedict's *Rule* cap. 39 for Benedict's advice that all monks avoid meat, except the weak or the ill. For the importance of restraining the appetite, see Peter Damian, Epist. 132.5–10 and Epist. 142.6, in *Die Briefe des Petrus Damiani*, 3: 440–43 and 3: 505; for translation see *The Letters of Peter Damian, 121–150*, 59–61, 129. Fasting as a penitential exercise also extended to the lay community, and the number of fast days gradually increased in the medieval Church, having a concomitant impact on the medieval diet, for which consult Kathy L. Pearson, "Nutrition and the Early-Medieval Diet," *Speculum* 72 (1997): 1–32. According to Thomas Aquinas, ecclesiastical fast days were instituted as well in order to restrain concupiscence of the flesh (*jejunium ab Ecclesia est institutum ad reprimendas concupiscentias carnis*) by restricting consumption of foods that promote *luxuria* and increase sexual desire. These are especially meat, but sometimes even dairy products from animals whose meat we consume. Thomas Aquinas, *Summa theologica* 2.2, q. 147, art. 8, resp. For discussion, see Michel Dupuis, "Les plaisirs de la chair. Abstinence et analogies (autour de Saint Thomas d'Aquin)," in *Anthropozoologica. Second numéro spécial: bulletin de l'Association l'homme et l'animal, Société de recherche interdisciplinaire* (Liège: Anthropozoologica, 1988), 133–38. St. Antoninus of Florence explicitly identifies gluttony (*ventris ingluvies*) as third on a lengthy list of "occasions" of *luxuria*. See his *Summa theologica* 2, tit. 5, cap. 1, 2: 638C.

3. Damian, Epist. 96.17, in *Die Briefe des Petrus Damiani*, 3: 58; trans. in *The Letters of Peter Damian, 91–120*, 62.

and illicit passion is made clear in a story he relates of a monk whose gluttony led directly to a masturbatory fantasy and seminal emission:

> A certain monk reported to me, that while carrying a dish of fried food into the refectory, a sudden urge to gluttony affected him. Directly, he popped a piece into his mouth and secretly ate it. Suddenly, such a fierce wave of passion assailed him that, acting as he had never done before, he could no longer contain himself until with his own hands he had discharged a defiling flow of semen.[4]

Food and sex could not be separated one from the other.

The monastic dietary regimen was even stricter during the penitential seasons in the Church, while outside monastic communities laypeople too were expected to avoid meat on Fridays during Lent and other days of observance. The Benedictine *Rule,* which provided the primary model for western monasticism for 1,000 years, clearly advocates a monastic vegetarian diet on the pathway to spiritual perfection, even if Benedict was willing to relax this restriction for elderly and infirm monks. The semi-eremitic Carthusian order, however, will make a vegetarian diet an absolute monastic requirement allowing no exception, prompting a medical defense at the beginning of the fourteenth century from no less an authority than Arnau of Villanova.[5] Although the Church expected laypeople also to restrict their diet and to eliminate meat at certain times of the year, monastic or ecclesiastical food ordinances were treated quite differently from the dietary prohibitions in the Old Testament.

Even though New Testament texts like those cited above would seem to free Christians from the dietary laws, still these commandments were understood to have some spiritual meaning, or to prefigure some Christian reality. Bruno of Segni (d. 1123), in a fascinating allegorical exegesis, suggests that in truth the biblical texts defining kosher animals actually describe Christians, who are the clean, ruminant animals because they—and not the Jews—twice "digest" the text of scripture, locating in

---

4. Damian, Epist. 142.26, in *Die Briefe des Petrus Damiani,* 3: 515; trans. in *The Letters of Peter Damian,* 121–50, 138. The Benedictine *Rule* cap. 39, recommends meals of cooked (not fried) vegetables and fruit, which suggests that the fried food in Damian's anecdote was itself a violation of good monastic order.

5. *De esu carnium,* in *Arnaldi de Villanova Opera Medica Omnia* 11, ed. Dianne M. Bazell (Barcelona: Seminarium Historiae Scientiae Cantabricense, 1999). Although an eminent medical authority, Arnau's theological opinions were sometimes suspect, so much so that the Oxford master Henry of Harclay (b. 1270) accused him of being a secret or crypto-Jew. See Henry of Harclay, *Ordinary Questions* 1.35, ed. Mark Henninger, Auctores Britannici Medii Aevi 17–18 (Oxford: Oxford University Press, 2008), 1: 24.

it the spiritual and not merely the literal sense.⁶ This trope finds an echo in Hermann of Cologne's (c. 1107–c. 1181) account of his own conversion from Judaism to Christianity. Since Jews, he laments, have been content with only a literal interpretation of scripture, they are the unclean animals that do not chew the cud, whereas Christians, using reason, twice refresh themselves with its spiritual understanding. After having adopted Christianity Hermann, like a clean animal, "transferred to the stomach of memory for frequent rumination" whatever edifying lessons he learned from the Bishop of Munster.⁷

This trope, reiterated in the thirteenth century by Thomas Aquinas, allowed Christians to identify themselves and their scriptural hermeneutic with the clean animals of scripture, while at the same time it suggested that contact with Jews entails impurity and pollution.⁸ Jews will often be compared to unclean animals—like dogs⁹ and pigs¹⁰—since biblical purity laws amply demonstrate that such animals, whether they are consumed or from contact with their carcasses, are obstacles to holiness.¹¹ Medieval bestiaries, which Debra Higgs Strickland calls "the most popular and widely disseminated of Christian polemical texts directed against

---

6. Bruno of Segni, *Expositio in Leviticum* 11: "Ruminare quid est, nisi sanctam Scripturam diligenter investigare et cordis sensu minutissime frangere, et ad spiritualem intelligentiam diutissime volvendo perducere? Judaei ergo neque ungulam dividunt, neque ruminant, quoniam neque utrumque Testamentum recipiunt, neque quod suscipiant ruminando spiritualiter intelligunt; litteram enim solam et integram deglutientes, nihil aliud quam litteram sapiunt." (PL 164: 414C). See also his *Expositio in Genesim* 24 (PL 164: 201D–202A). This trope that identified unclean animals with those content with a carnal interpretation supported only with the Old Testament, and the clean beasts that accept both the Old and New Testaments in order to digest the spiritual sense, was clearly well established. See the 8th century(?) Ps. Bede, *In Pentateuchum commentarii—Leviticus* cap. 11 (PL 91: 345B–D). Among the unclean men symbolized by unclean animals, Ps. Bede condemns those men that are like fish without fins, that have "light" *mores,* and are effeminate (*hi sunt qui leves mores et effeminatos*). The broader trope can be found even in Aelfric's (d. c. 1020) Anglo-Saxon vernacular exegesis of 1 and 2 Maccabees. See Andrew P. Scheil, "Anti-Judaism in Aelfric's *Lives of the Saints,*" *Anglo Saxon England* 28 (1999): 65–86, citing 74 75.

7. Herman of Cologne, *A Short Account of His Own Conversion,* 79.

8. Thomas Aquinas, *Summa theologica* 1.2, q. 102, art. 6, resp.

9. Otloh of St. Emmeram, *Liber visionum* 13 (PL 146: 368B); Peter the Venerable, *Adversus Judeorum inveteratam duritiem* cap. 3, p. 57; Rudolf of Schlettstadt remarks that "Jews ... are unclean and stinking and more vile than dogs." See his *Historiae Memorabiles,* 101.

10. See Albert the Great, *Super Matthaeum* 7.6, p. 247, 12. Here Albert identifies Jews and heretics both with dogs and pigs. The pig he describes as a monstrous animal because it straddles classifications: it has a split hoof, but does not ruminate.

11. On the relationship between the laws of *kashrut* and the notion of impurity in Judaism, see the helpful study of Hyam Maccoby, *Ritual and Morality,* chap. 6.

Jews," consistently identified Jews with the unclean animals forbidden in Levitical legislation, whose uncleanness they were said to share.[12]

Dogs could sometimes symbolize loyalty and fidelity, as in the case of the Dominican friars, often nicknamed the "watch dogs of the Lord" (*Domini canes*).[13] St. Dominic himself was represented as a dog with a burning torch in his mouth, to shine his light upon the wolves of heresy and ward them off with his barking.[14] Near the beginning of the twelfth century, Theodoric, the Abbot of St. Trond (d. 1107) had composed an elegant lament in praise of his little dog, "Peewee" (*Pitulus*).[15] The Aberdeen bestiary (c. 1200) compares ecclesiastical preachers that chase away the Devil to dogs that chase away intruders, and compares the fruit of confession to the dog's saliva, which it uses to heal its own wounds.[16] By the thirteenth century a cult had even emerged in France to venerate Saint Guinefort, a greyhound, who was held to be a special protector of young children.[17] Nonetheless, it was a Dominican Inquisitor, Stephen of Bourbon, who ridiculed this cult as an insulting superstition.

Despite some positive associations, in most contexts dogs clearly carried a negative valuation. One such context appears in Psalm 21:17, with a description of Christ's tormentors as "many dogs [that] surrounded me" (*circumdederunt me canes multi*)—a text that was too easily transferred to the Jews.[18] Dogs were vilified as symbols of greed or gluttony, who

12. Debra Higgs Strickland, "The Jews, Leviticus, and the Unclean in Medieval English-Bestiaries," in *Beyond the Yellow Badge: Anti-Judaism and Antisemitism in Medieval and Early Modern Visual Culture*, ed. Mitchell B. Merback (Leiden: Brill, 2008), 204.

13. Ambrose, *Hexaemeron* 6.4.17; Jacques de Vitry, *Historia Orientalis* 92, p. 219.

14. *Malleus Malificarum* 1, q. 6, col. 40C, 1: 282–83. In a more mundane context, some medieval texts provided recipes that promised to stop a dog from barking at passersby. See *Picatrix: The Latin Version of the Ghāyat Al-Hakīm* 4.9, p. 225.

15. For the text and translation of this poem, see *The Virgilian Tradition: The First Fifteen Hundred Years*, ed. Jan M. Ziolkowski and Michael C. J. Putnam (New Haven: Yale University Press, 2008), 481–85.

16. *The Aberdeen Bestiary*, fol. 19v, available at http://www.abdn.ac.uk/bestiary/translat/19v.hti.

17. See Jean-Claude Schmitt, *The Holy Greyhound: Guinefort, Healer of Children since the Thirteenth Century*, trans. Martin Thom (Cambridge: Cambridge University Press, 1983). Stephen of Bourbon's tale is available at http://www.fordham.edu/halsall/pgc.asp?page=source/guinefort.html.

18. James H. Marrow, "*Circumdederunt me canes multi*: Christ's Tormentors in Northern European Art of the Late Middle Ages and Early Renaissance," *Art Bulletin* 59, no. 2 (1977): 167–81; Marrow, *Passion Iconography in Northern European Art of the late Middle Ages and Early Renaissance: a Study of the Transformation of Sacred Metaphor into Descriptive Narrative*, Ars Neerlandica 1 (Kortrijk: Van Ghemmert, 1979), 33–43.

returned to consume their own vomit. Pigs too were symbols of gluttony and filth, and it was well known that Jesus had once exorcized demons and cast them into swine (Matt. 8:31–32; Mk. 5:12–13; Lk. 8:32–33). Both dogs and pigs, moreover, are domesticated animals with a "servile" status, in the sense that they are bred to serve human needs and interests, and living in close proximity to humans. In another sense, however, domestic animals are the most nearly human of all the animals, and this may be especially true for dogs and pigs. Indeed, in an era when human dissection was not permitted by the Church, pigs were dissected because their anatomy was judged closest to the human.[19] The pig's anatomy was therefore presented to educated readers in the eleventh- or twelfth-century Latin text, the *Anatomy of the Pig (Anatomia porci)*.[20] Vincent of Beauvais attributes to Avicenna the claim that because pig blood and pig flesh are very similar to human blood and flesh, some vendors in the markets sold human flesh as pig meat, concealing the fact until human fingers were found in it![21]

Precisely because the dog and pig were so nearly human and a part of human experience, they evinced a disturbing ambivalence.[22] According to an oft retold tale from Gilles of Orval's chronicle of the acts of the bishops of Liège, during the reign of Obertus of Liege (d. mid-twelfth century), a sow even gave birth to a piglet with a human face.[23]

---

19. Human bodies were sometimes opened for inspection after death, but true human dissection or autopsy does not appear until the end of the thirteenth century. See Katherine Park, "The Criminal and the Saintly Body: Autopsy and Dissection in Renaissance Italy," *Renaissance Quarterly* 47, no. 1 (1994): 1–33; and Park, "The Life of the Corpse: Division and Dissection in Late Medieval Europe," *Journal of the History of Medicine and Allied Sciences* 50, no. 1 (1994): 111–32. For public dissection and medical instruction, see also Florike Egmond, "Execution, Dissection, Pain and Infamy—a Morphological Investigation," in *Bodily Extremities: Preoccupations with the Human Body in Early Modern European Culture*, ed. Florike Egmond and Robert Zwijenberg (Burlington, Vt.: Ashgate, 2003), 92–128.

20. For the claim that the pig's internal organs are analogous to those of the human, see *Summa theologica* 4.2.2.1.4 (pp. 575–56) attributed to Alexander of Hales. For discussion, see Plinio Prioreschi, *A History of Medicine* (Lewiston, N.Y.: Edwin Mellen Press, 1991), 214–19; and Ynes Viole O'Neill, "Another Look at the *Anatomia Porci*," *Viator* 1 (1970): 115–25, for reexamination of the origins and dating of the text.

21. Vincent of Beauvais, *Speculum naturale* 18.83, 1: 1372.

22. For ambivalent attitudes toward the pig in medieval iconography, see Michael Camille, "At the sign of the 'Spinning Sow': the 'other' Chartres and images of everyday life of the medieval street," in *History and Images: Toward a New Iconology*, ed. Axel Bolvig and Phillip Lindley (Turnholt: Brepols, 2003), 249–76.

23. Aegidius Aureaevallensis [Gilles d'Orval], *Gesta episcoporum Leodiensium*, ed. I. Heller, MGH SS 25 (Hannover, 1880), 14–129, citing 95. See also *Albertus Miliolus notarius*

They are most often invoked in jokes and insults and curses. To be compared to a pig or a dog was clearly an insult that Christians cast upon Jews that Jews occasionally sought to turn back upon Christians themselves. *The Glosses of Solomon of Troyes* (*De glosis Salomonis Trecensis*), a thirteenth-century Latin collection of exegetical texts drawn from the work of the rabbinic commentator Rashi (R. Solomon bar Isaac of Troyes; d. 1105), whose biblical interpretation became *the* authoritative guide to Jewish exegesis for many Christian scholars,[24] explains that for Rashi the dogs mentioned in Exodus 22:31—"the flesh that beasts have tasted before, you shall not eat, but shall cast it to the dogs"—refer to the *goy* or Christian.[25] In early fourteenth-century Marseilles a Jewish woman was fined five sous for having replied to a Christian woman, "You are more of a dog than I am."[26] Similarly, in a seemingly humorous Jewish reply, Isaac Cardoso explains that a Christian mocked a Jew and called him a dog. Suddenly a dog passed, and the Jew lifted its tail to point out that the dog was not circumcised![27] If either party were to be likened to a dog, Cardoso implied, the image seemed more fitting for the Christian.

Despite this, medieval Christian society aggressively linked Jews and dogs, especially in their treatment. Near the end of the eleventh century, the Jewish interlocutor in the *Disputation of a Jew and a Christian concerning the Christian Faith* by Gilbert Crispin (d. c. 1117), Abbot of West-

---

Regini, *Liber de temporibus et aetatibus* (-1286), ed. O. Holder-Egger, MGH SS 31 (Hannover, 1903), 353–572, citing 430.

24. Such was the case for the early fourteenth-century Franciscan Hebraist, Nicholas of Lyra. See Deeana Copeland Klepper, *The Insight of Unbelievers: Nicholas of Lyra and Christian Reading of Jewish Text in the Later Middle Ages* (Philadelphia: University of Pennsylvania Press, 2007), 59. For Christian utilization of Jewish exegesis and exegetes, see also Gilbert Dahan, "La connaissance de l'exegese Juive par les Chretiens du XIIe au XIVe siecle," in *Rashi et la culture juive en France du Nord au moyen âge*, ed. Gilbert Dahan, Gérard Nahon, and Elie Nicholas (Paris: Peeters, 1997), 343–59, and esp. 358 for Nicholas of Lyra's reliance on Rashi.

25. See Gilbert Dahan, "Un dossier latin de textes de Rashi autour de la controverse de 1240," *Revue des Etudes Juives* 151, no. 3–4 (1992): 329. In one sense, this interpretation of Exod. 22:31 merely underscored an empirical fact: although Levitical legistation forbid Jews to eat animals killed by other animals, Christians usually dismissed these restrictions or allegorized them. Nonetheless, as Joyce Salisbury has shown, many Church ordinances sought to prevent Christians from eating the meat of animals killed by other predators, in order to more clearly delineate the behaviors that separated humans and beasts. See Joyce E. Salisbury, *The Beast Within: Animals in the Middle Ages* (New York: Routledge, 1994), 66–69.

26. Archives Départementales des Bouches-du-Rhône, B 1940, fl. 129v, quoted in Green and Smail, "The Trial of Floreta d'Ays," 202.

27. Isaac Cardoso, *Los excelencias y calumnias de los Hebreos* 3, p. 349. Recall that centuries earlier, in some copies, *Pirkê de Rabbi Eliezer* (p. 208) had compared an uncircumcised person to a dog.

minster, objected, "if the Law must be observed, why do you treat its defenders like dogs and pursue them everywhere after having driven them away with cudgels?"[28] Similarly, Herman of Cologne, in his account of a debate with Rupert of Deutz, complained that Christians revile Jews as "dead dogs" (*canes mortuos*).[29] Not only did Jews complain that they were treated like dogs, but from the thirteenth century it was an increasingly common practice to impose a special form of capital punishment upon Jews (or converted Jews): to be hanged, upside down, between two dogs.[30] The practice evidently offered an opportunity for scientific observation to some medieval physicians, since, according to Withington, "[Bernard of] Gordon remarks that when Jews are hung up by their feet, if you give them anything to drink, it will ascend to their stomachs, whence he concludes that that organ possessives a special attractive faculty."[31]

28. "Si autem lex observanda est, cur ejus observatores canibus assimulatis, fustibus extrusos usquequaque insectatis?" *Disputatio Judaei cum Christiano de fide Christiana* 12, in *The Works of Gilbert Crispin Abbot of Westminster*, ed. Anna Sapir Abulafia and G. R. Evans, Auctores Britannici Medii Aevi 8 (London: Oxford University Press, 1986), 10–11. A variant reading—"Si autem lex observanda est, cur eius observatores canibus assimilamur, fustibus extrusi usquequaque insectamur?"—is found in a second group of manuscripts.
29. *Opusculum de conversione sua* 3, p. 77.
30. See Norbert Schnitzler, "Anti-Semitism, Image Desecration, and the Problem of 'Jewish Execution,'" in Bolvig and Lindley, *History and Images: Toward a New Iconology*, 357–78. The practice by which the Jew was hung upside down perhaps responds to the legend of Werner of Oberwesel, who was allegedly murdered by Jews in 1287 and hung in an inverted posture to drain his blood, as one would do to an animal. For an illustration, see Heinz Schreckenberg, *The Jews in Christian Art: An Illustrated History* (New York: Continuum, 1996), 276. This form of execution of Jews continued for centuries. A woodcut from Johannes Stumpf's sixteenth-century *Gemeiner loblicher Eydgnoschafft* depicts the Jew Ansteet hung between two dogs that snap at his face. For the illustration, see Elisheva Carlebach's *Divided Souls: Converts from Judaism in Germany, 1500–1700* (New Haven: Yale University Press, 2001), 41; another illustration from a later edition is found in Schreckenberg, *The Jews in Christian Art*, 360. A similar depiction of a Jew hung upside down, with a dog likewise hung upside down beside him, while a fire burns below, is seen in a woodcut-illustration in Thomas Murner's *Entehrung Mariä*, printed in Strassburg in 1515. See Schreckenberg, *The Jews in Christian Art*, 263.
Esther Cohen notes that although hanging upside down between dogs or even wolves was a form of execution specific to Jews in the later Middle Ages, to be hanged upside down had earlier been applied to vassals guilty of murdering their lord. See her "Animals in Medieval Perceptions: The Image of the Ubiquitous Other," in *Animals and Human Society: Changing Perspectives*, ed. Aubrey Manning and James Serpell (London: Routledge, 1994), 69. Moreover, when Bertulf, provost of Bruges, was hanged in 1127 for the murder of Charles the Good the townspeople also wrapped the viscera of a dog around his neck. See Galbert of Bruges, *The Murder of Charles the Good* 57, trans. James Bruce Ross (New York: Columbia University Press, 2005), 210.
31. Withington, *Medical History from the Earliest Times*, 402.

Yet as Christian theology allegorized biblical dietary or purity laws, uncleanness came to represent moral and spiritual danger. Animal images were useful instruments to illustrate the Jews' intellectual and not merely moral shortcomings. Such animal imagery was easily transferred to medieval art and iconography; perhaps the *Judensau* ("Jew's Sow") motif, found most commonly in Germanic lands, in which Jews are shown suckling the teats of a sow or eating her excrement, is best known.[32] English manuscript illuminations of the fourteenth century also depict the enemies of Christ, particularly in Passion scenes (and, therefore, especially Jews) with a snub-nosed pig snout, reinforcing the identification Jews = enemies of Christ = pigs.[33] This identification may have been influenced too by a variant text of of Psalms 16:14 found in some patristic texts, including the fifth-century *Debate over the Law between a Jew, Simon, and a Christian, Theophilus*, in some medieval Bible manuscripts, and in the Roman Psalter. The variant text of Psalms 16(17):12, in which Christ calls down the Father's judgment upon the Jews because "they have taken me now like a lion prepared for the prey" (*Susceperunt me sicut leo paratus ad praedam*), proclaims that the Jews' bellies are "filled with pork" (*saturati sunt porcina*), rather than "filled with children" (*saturati sunt filiis*) as in the Vulgate.[34]

32. For the *Judensau* and its appearances in medieval iconography, see Isaiah Shachar, *The Judensau: A Medieval Anti-Jewish Motif and its History* (London: Warburg Institute, 1974). See also Claudine Fabre-Vassas's fascinating ethno-anthropological study, *La Bête singulière: les Juifs, les chrétiens, le cochon* (Editions Gallimard, 1994), available in English as *The Singular Beast: Jews, Christians, and the Pig*.
33. Wendelien A. W. van Welie-Vink, "Pig Snouts as Sign of Evil in Manuscripts of the Low Countries," *Quaerendo* 26, no. 3 (1996): 213–28.
34. The variant Latin reading of Ps. 16:14 can be traced back to the early Church and Old Latin versions of the Psalms. St. Augustine is familiar with it and notes it in his Epist. 121.6 in *S. Aureli Augustini Hipponiensis episcopi Epistulae*, ed. A. Goldbacher, CSEL 34.2 (Vienna:Temsky, 1898), 728; Augustine, Epist. 149.1, ed. A. Goldbacher, CSEL 44, 351; it also appears in the fifth-century anti-Jewish polemic of Evagrius, *Altercatio legis inter Simoneum Judaeum et Theophilum Christianum* 7; and *Eadwine's Canterbury Psalter* (from the MS in Trinity College, Cambridge), ed. Fred Harsley, Part 2: Text and Notes (London, Published for the Early English Text Society by N. Trübner, 1889), 21. The twelfth-century text contains the Latin text of the Roman Psalter and an Old English Gloss. For its production, see especially the contributions to *The Eadwine Psalter: Text, Image, and Monastic culture in Twelfth-Century Canterbury*, ed. Margaret Gibson, T. A. Heslop, and Richard W. Pfaff (London: Modern Humanities Research Association; University Park: Pennsylvania State University Press, 1992). This Latin reading will also be found in the eleventh-century (?) Old English Paris Prose Psalter. See *King Alfred's Old English Prose Translation of the First Fifty Psalms*, ed. Patrick P. O'Neill (Cambridge, Mass.: Medieval Academy of America, 2001). For

While the *Debate over the Law between a Jew, Simon, and a Christian, Theophilus* treats the pork in their bellies as a symbol for the sinful inclination that Jews bequeath to their children, and therefore presents the dietary laws as a consequent of the Jews' sin, the Anglo-Saxon gloss of the Paris Prose Psalter regards the pork in their bellies in a more literal fashion as a punishment God visits upon his enemies: to be so tormented by hunger that they will eat of the flesh of swine. The connection between Jews and pigs was extended to include lepers as well, as we will show in more detail below. John Carpenter's 1419 compilation of London town ordinances includes an entry "Of Jews, Lepers and Swine that are to be removed from the City." Since there had been no Jews in England for more than a century, the repetition of ordinances that treated Jews, lepers, and swine under the same rubric seems instructive.[35] At times medieval art also depicted Jews in association with other animals that are both sources of impurity and possess a suspect or threatening nature: for example, cats,[36] owls,[37] hyenas,[38] scorpions,[39] and the monstrous lamia.[40]

the scribal origins of the Paris Psalter, see Richard Emms, "The Scribe of the Paris Psalter," *Anglo Saxon England* 28 (1999): 179–84. My thanks to Professor Vanita Neelakanta for help with the Anglo-Saxon.

35. Rexroth, *Deviance and Power in Late Medieval London*, 1–2. The "swine" are evidently stray pigs that should be removed, much as modern cities seek to round up and remove stray dogs.

36. See Sara Lipton, *Images of Intolerance. The Representation of Jews and Judaism in the* Bible moralisée (Berkeley: University of California Press, 1999), chap. 4. Alain de Lille (d. 1202) remarks that the heretical Cathars derive their name from *cato*; that they obscenely and ritually kiss the cat's hindquarters; and that Lucifer appears to them in the form of a cat. See his *Contra Haereticos* 1.63 (PL 210: 366A). Similarly, *Malleus Maleficarum* 2, q. 1, cap. 9, col. 125A, (1: 445) identifies cats—and not only black cats—as agents of the devil that properly represent those who have abandoned the Christian faith.

37. The *Book of Beasts* reports that "Owls are symbolical to the Jews, who repulse our Saviour when he comes to redeem them [because] . . . They value darkness more than light." See *Book of Beasts being a Translation from a Latin Bestiary of the Twelfth Century*, ed. T. H. White (New York: Dover Publications, 1984), 134. Cf. *Physiologus* 7, trans. Curley, p. 11. See also Mariko Miyazaki, "Misercord Owls and Medieval Anti-semitism," in *The Mark of the Beast: The Medieval Bestiary in Art, Life, and Literature*, ed. Debra Hassig (New York: Garland, 1999), 23–50; and Elaine C. Block, "Judaic Imagery on Medieval Choir Stalls," *International Reynard Society/Annuaire de la la Sociee' internationale renardienne* 8 (1995): 26–47.

38. Debra Hassig, *Medieval Bestiaries: Text, Image, Ideology* (Cambridge: Cambridge University Press, 1995), 145–55. See also chap. 1, n. 139.

39. Shachar, *The Judensau*, 1.

40. See Irven M. Resnick and Kenneth F. Kitchell Jr., "The Sweepings of Lamia: Transformations of the Myths of Lilith and Lamia," in *Religion, Gender, and Culture in the Pre-Modern World*, eds. Alexandra Cuffel and Brian Britt (New York: Palgrave Macmillan, 2007), 77–104.

Allegorical exegesis sought to free Christians from the dietary laws—as Evagrius explained that the Levitical condemnation of pork is meant to instruct the faithful only to avoid *pig-like behavior*.[41] This explanation becomes very common, as seen at the end of the twelfth century in Peter of Blois's claim that it is not swine itself that is unclean but a "swinish" will or appetite: "because it is the swinish will that is designated as unclean by swine flesh, not swine flesh but a [swinish] desire is prohibited as unclean."[42] By contrast, the Jewish disputant in Gilbert Crispin's late eleventh-century *Disputation of a Jew and a Christian concerning the Christian Faith* insists that a figurative or allegorical meaning ascribed to the dietary restrictions does not supplant the literal: "Let us abstain from pork, because the Law commands, and let us abstain from sin if that is what pork signifies."[43]

The question remains, however: for what purpose were these laws given to the Jews? One response suggested that the dietary laws, like circumcision, were given to the Jews to differentiate them from their neighbors.[44] In Peter Abelard's *A Dialogue of a Philosopher with a Jew, and a Christian*, the Jew explains that both circumcision and the dietary laws have this same purpose: circumcision prevents marriage between Jews and non-Jews, and the dietary laws prevent social interaction, seemingly providing Jewish support for the wisdom of the ecclesiastical canons.[45] Another common response, however, holds that the dietary laws were given to the Jews to restrain their inclination to vice. Rabanus Maurus closely linked the Jew and the pig both because of the latter's uncleanness

---

41. Evagrius, *Altercatio legis inter Simoneum Judaeum et Theophilum Christianum* 7. The text is likely from the early fifth century.

42. "sed quia per suillam carnem suilla voluntas significatur immunda, non caro suilla sed voluptas prohibetur immunda." Peter of Blois, *The Later Letters of Peter of Blois* 64.4, p. 285.

43. "Abstineamus a porco, quia lex jubet, abstineamus et ab eo si quod est quod per porcum significatur, peccato." *Disputatio Judaei cum Christiano de fide Christiana* (PL 159: 1011A). The Christian in this dialogue also points out that some of the forbidden foods are not harmful to human nature and are actually good to eat, suggesting to him a deeper "mystery" [*sacramentum*]. (PL 159: 1008B)

44. See Petrus Alfonsi, *Dialogi contra Iudaeos* 12, pp. 138–39, where this view is attributed to the Jewish interlocutor, Moses. Petrus rejects it.

45. Peter Abelard, *A Dialogue of a Philosopher with a Jew, and a Christian*, pp. 34, 47. Ecclesiastical canons often sought to punish Christians—both lay and clerical—for eating or feasting with Jews. For examples, see Amnon Linder, *The Jews in the Legal Sources of the Early Middle Ages*, 445, 466–68, 544, 569, 576–81, 586, 597, 600, 631, 662, 672–73.

and because of the pig's natural attributes, namely, its wantonness and gluttony.[46] These are the qualities that the Jew and the pig share. Similarly, Petrus Comestor (d. 1178) remarked that "In fact, in the text [of scripture] the Lord restricted the foods that were permitted to them [the Jews] owing to their gluttony."[47] Likewise, Vincent of Beauvais insists that the animals that scripture identified as unclean are not unclean per se, but were designated unclean *for the Jews* in order to restrain their gluttony (*ut eorum castrimargiam restringeret*) and wickedness.[48]

This term for gluttony—*gastrimargia*—explains Albert the Great, is illustrated by the insatiable hunger of pigs, grunting clamorously when they see acorns.[49] Similarly, among Thomas Aquinas's several justifications for the dietary restrictions given the Jews, he recognizes that some foods can affect the soul in an accidental fashion (*per accidens*), producing in it lust or sexual desire. For this very reason even some Christians avoid meat and wine.[50] In the same fashion, the fifteenth-century Dominican St. Antoninus of Florence offers not only allegorical interpretations of the dietary restrictions imposed upon the people of Israel in the book of Leviticus, but also a literal interpretation. Certain meats were prohibited to the Jews, he remarks, because they generate superfluous or bad humors in the body. For this reason animals not having a cloven hoof were prohibited, owing to their earthiness and the fact that they generate choleric and adust humors. Citing Maimonides, who was himself a physician, St. Antoninus explains that the Jews are forbidden blood and fat because they do not generate good nutriment, and because fat in

---

46. Rabanus Maurus *De universo* (PL 111: 206D). Isidore of Seville had provided the etymology that understood the name pig, *porcus*, to be derived from *spurcus*, "unclean." He also recorded that the philosopher Epicurus had been known as "the pig" because he asserted that carnal pleasure is the highest good (*The Etymologies of Isidore of Seville* 8.6.15, p. 179; 12.1.25, p. 248), encouraging again a link between the pig and the "carnal" Jew. Finally, the sow is often identified as the most lustful animal because she will allow herself to be covered by the male even when she is already pregnant. See Fabre-Vassas, *The Singular Beast: Jews, Christians, and the Pig*, 105–6.

47. Petrus Comestor, *Eine deutsche Schulbibel des 15. Jahrhunderts: Historia scholastica des Petrus Comestor in deutschen Auszug mit lateinischem Paralleltext* cap. 17, ed. D. Hans Vollmer (Berlin: Weidmannsche Buchhandlung, 1925), 224.

48. Vincent of Beauvais, *Speculum historiale* 2.33, 4: 58; 2.36, 4: 59.

49. *Commentarii in Iob* 330.5, p. 342. Similarly Thomas of Chobham notes that *castrimargia* denotes gluttony and a slothful belly (*ventris pigritia*). See *Summa Confessorum* art. 3, dist. 1, q. 5a, fol. 3va, 24.

50. *Summa theologica* 1.2, q. 102, art. 6, resp. ad 1.

particular brings forth gluttony.[51] But while individual Christians may elect to avoid these foods in order to restrain desire, the food prohibitions in Leviticus were obligatory for *all* Jews, and for that reason they appear to have been intended by God to counteract the Jews' natural inclinations for gluttony, immorality, and illicit sexual activity.

Medieval Christians, especially after the First Crusade, were aware that Saracens also avoided pork and certain other foods, and sought to assign appropriate reasons for this. Petrus Alfonsi, drawing on the text of Qur'an 2:172–73, remarks that "all flesh is permitted to them to eat, moreover, except the flesh and blood of the pig [and] likewise carrion."[52] He attributes the Muslim's dietary rules in part to Jewish influence on the early development of Islam, and in part to Mohammad's desire to differentiate his followers from Christian neighbors. Jacques de Vitry relates that when Mohammad wished to assign a reason *why* his followers should avoid pork, it was because the pig was created after the great flood from camel's dung, and one born from something so unclean ought not to be eaten by a clean people.[53] More polemical traditions indicated that the Muslim's rejection of pork stems from the fact that pigs were responsible for Mohammad's death, a tradition included even in the medieval Jewish collection *Nizzaḥon Vetus* or *Old Book of Polemic*. According to this text Muslims repudiate pork because "their god Mohammad got drunk from wine and was thrown into the garbage, and when the pigs came and passed through the dump, they found him ... [and] killed him, and ate him."[54] Other Christian biographies of Mohammad indicate that Jews murdered and dismembered him, and then fed his body parts to pigs, accounting thereby for the animosity that exists between Jews and Muslims.[55] Felix Fabri remarked that not only do Jews and

---

51. St Antoninus of Florence, *Summa theologica* 1, tit.14, cap. 5, §4, 1: 733A–B.

52. See Petrus Alfonsi, *Dialogi contra Iudaeos* 5, p. 63.

53. Jacques de Vitry, *Historia Orientalis* 6, p. 20. Cf. Job 14:4: "Who can produce something clean out of something unclean? No one."

54. See Berger, *The Jewish-Christian Debate in the High Middle Ages*, 217. For discussion of this tradition, see Norman Daniel, *Islam and the West: The Making of an Image* (Edinburgh: Edinburgh University Press, 1960), 104–5. It was clearly well known, and was reiterated by the fifteenth-century Christian pilgrim Felix Fabri, in his *Evagatorum in Terrae Sanctae, Arabiae et Egyptii peregrinationem*, fol. 260B, 2: 221; see also St. Antoninus of Florence, *Summa theologica* 4, tit. 11, cap. 6, §1, 4: 588.

55. See John Tolan, "Un cadavre mutilé: le déchirement polémique de Mahomet," *Le Moyen Âge* 104 (1998): 53–72, citing 57–58.

Muslims in the East refuse to eat pork, they also abominate the pig itself, a common domestic animal among Christians, and do not permit them in their communities.[56]

Regardless of the origin of the Muslim prohibition, Christians understood Muslims' dietary restrictions to be a *judaizing* tendency and therefore as foolish as the dietary laws of the Jews.[57] Conversely, both Jewish and Muslim anti-Christian polemics sometimes singled out Christian consumption of pork as a sign of the uncleanness and foulness of Christians.[58] The Franciscan Alonso de Espina (c. 1412–c. 1464) complains that Jews regard Christians as unclean (*immundi*) because they eat swine's flesh that is prohibited under the Law of Moses, but the author cites the eleventh-century R. Moses ha-Darshan of Narbonne to demonstrate that Jewish authorities themselves understand that in the time of the messiah this prohibition will be lifted.[59] Therefore, because Christians know the messiah has come, the consumption of pork attests to the truth of their messianic faith. Much the same argument can be found in the anti-Jewish polemic of the twelfth-century Jewish convert to Christianity, Petrus Alfonsi.[60] The conclusion of the seventh-century Byzantine Greek anti-Jewish polemic the *Trophies of Damascus* presents some unconverted and unpersuaded Jews as having risibily remarked that had they understood that Jesus was in truth the Messiah, "How much ham we could have had!"[61] Pork consumption, then, also symbolized profound theological assumptions.

56. "lethalem inimicitiam habent Sarreceni ad porcos et abominantur eos, sicut Judaei, nec quovis modo sustinent secum porcos." Felix Fabri, *Evagatorum in Terrae Sanctae, Arabiae et Egyptii peregrinationem*, fol. 130b, 3: 163.

57. Alain de Lille, *Contra Haereticos* 4.10 (PL 210: 427A).

58. Lindsay, *Daily Life in the Medieval Islamic World*, 119, citing the ninth-century al-Jahiz, author of a *Contra Christianorum*, in which the latter complains that "at heart the Christian is a foul and a dirty creature ... because he is uncircumcised ... and eats pig meat." The Judeo-Arabic *Account of the Disputation of the Priest* also objects that Jesus "ordered you [Christians] to eat pork and to make sacrifice of bread and wine, which becomes smelly dung inside your bodies." *The Polemic of Nestor the Priest*, 1: 77.

59. Al[ph]onso de Espina, *Fortalitium fidei contra Judeos: Sarracenos: aliosq[ue] christiane fidei inimicos*, 3.5.2 (Lyons: Venūdātur a Stephano gueynard: prope sanctū Anthonium, 1512), fol.110v. For Alonso de Espina's life and career, see Ana Echevarria, *The Fortress of Faith: The Attitude toward Muslims in Fifteenth-Century Spain* (Leiden: Brill, 1999), 47–55.

60. See *Dialogus contra Judaeum* 12, in *Der Dialog des Petrus Alfonsi*, pp. 139–40.

61. "De combien de jambons avons-nous été privés!" *Les Trophées de Damas: Controverse Judéo-Chrétienne du VIIe Siècle* 3.7.1, ed. and trans. Gustave Bardy, in *Patrologiae Orientalis* 15, no. 2 (1920): 173–275, citing 275.

In many instances, the dietary laws prevented Jews or Saracens from sharing a Christian's meal. Food had become an obstacle to social interaction. But it was not only the dietary restrictions of Jews or Saracens that prevented interaction. Christians also often instructed their brethren not to eat with Jews, or Saracens. The Carolingian bishop Agobard of Lyon remarks that just as the Jews believe that they should not share a feast with Gentiles, lest they be led into idolatry, so too Christians now are forbidden to share food or drink with Jews for fear of being led into their error.[62] His successor as archbishop, Amolo of Lyon (841–851), laments that by their contact with Jews, "rabid dogs who attack Christ," Christians have too often been led to violate ecclesiastical dietary restrictions imposed for the Lenten season, which may suggest that Christians were eating meat with Jews when they were not supposed to do so.[63] A Cistercian statute from 1232 chastises an abbot for allowing Jews to dine at his table.[64] Thomas of Chobham (d. c. 1236) expresses surprise in his *Summa Confessorum* (composed c. 1215) that canon law allows a Christian to eat with pagans and not with Jews, but explains that it is for the reason that "Jews are very skilled in the literal sense of the Law, whence they could corrupt simple Christians more easily than pagans."[65] Vincent of Beauvais, reflecting increasingly restrictive canon law traditions regarding commensality,[66] adds that Christians should neither eat with

62. Agobard of Lyon, *De cavendo convictu et societate Judaica*, ed. L. Van Acker, in *Opera omnia*, CCCM 52 (Turnholt: Brepols, 1981), ln. 50. This letter was written c. 827. For Agobard's compositions, see J. Allen Cabaniss, "Agobard of Lyons," *Speculum* 26, no. 1 (1951): 50–76, and 62–63, for this letter. For his views on Jews, see Robert Bonfil, "Cultural and Religious Traditions in Ninth-Century French Jewry," in *Jewish Intellectual History in the Middle Ages*, ed. Joseph Dan (Westport, Conn.: Praeger, 1994), 1–17.

63. Amulon, *Epistola seu liber contra Judaeos ad Carolum Regem* 41 (PL 116: 170A) Although this text has sometimes been attributed to Florus of Lyon, for a useful discussion see Alfred Raddatz, "Zur Vorgeschichte der 'Epistula seu liber contra Judaeos' Amulos von Lyon," in *Ecclesia Peregrinans. Josef Lenzenweger zum 70. Geburtstag* (Vienna: Verband der Wissenschaftlichen Gesellschaften Österreichs, 1986), 53–57.

64. *Statuta Capitulorum Generalium Ordinis Cisterciensis ab anno 1116 ad annum 1786*, ed. D. Josephus-Mia Canivez, Bibliothèque de la Revue d'histoire ecclésiastique, fasc. 9–14 (Louvain: Bureaux de la Revue, 1933–41), 10: 1232, 51.

65. "[Unde mirum videtur quare non possumus comedere cum iudeis sed cum paganis. Quod tamen ideo factum est] quia iudei periti sunt in lege secundum literam, unde facilius possent corrumpere simplices christianos quam pagani." Thomas de Chobham, *Summa Confessorum* art. 6, dist. 1, fol. 51ra, p. 252.

66. See David M. Freidenreich, "Sharing Meals with Non-Christians in Canon Law Commentaries, circa 1116–1260: A Case Study in Legal Development," *Medieval Encounters* 14 (2008): 41–77.

Jews because of the contempt the latter show for Christian foods, nor should they eat with Saracens, because Saracens are "Judaizers."[67]

Not only should Christians not eat with Jews but, as Maurice Kriegel has shown, medieval Spanish municipal documents contain numerous laws regulating the behavior of Jews (as well as prostitutes and Muslims) in the marketplace, which forbid Jews even to touch various foods on sale. Should they touch them, either they must buy them or pay a fine. Kriegel has argued that Christians viewed such food items, once they had been touched by Jews, as impure, polluted, or unclean.[68] Similar legislation appeared also in France from the thirteenth century, and often treated Jews, prostitutes, and lepers as a single group forbidden to touch foods sold in the market.[69] It is also possible that, based on a perception that Jews were not only impure but also "sick," their presence in the marketplace had become a source of anxiety, just as lepers in fourteenth-century England were often forbidden to enter urban markets or to touch food for sale out of fear of contagion.[70]

Certainly there was Christian religious resentment too that Jews could sell to them meats that they could not eat themselves (see Deut. 14:21) or because they displayed some blemish or imperfection, rendering them unfit (that is, not kosher), while Jews refused meats and wine produced by Christians.[71] As early as the first half of the ninth century

67. Vincent of Beauvais, *Speculum doctrinale* 9.40, 2: 796. Vincent's complaint that Saracens are "Judaizers" implies that Islamic food prohibitions—like Islam itself—were derived from the dietary laws of Judaism. Perhaps, too, he was aware of debates within Islamic communities in Spain, for example, over contemporary Jewish influence upon Muslim dietary practices. See Camilla Adang, "Ibn Chazm's Criticism of Some 'Judaizing' Tendencies among the Mâlikites," *Medieval and Modern Perspectives on Muslim-Jewish Relations*, ed. Ronald L. Nettler, Studies in Muslim-Jewish Relations 2 (Luxembourg: Harwood Academic Publishers, 1995), 1–15.

68. Maurice Kriegel, "Un trait de psychologie sociale dans les pays méditerranéens du bas moyen age: le juif comme intouchable," *Annales* 31 (1976): 325–30. Cf. Louis Stouff, "Les Juifs et l'alimentation en Provence a la fin de la période medieval," in *Armand Lunel et les juifs du Midi. Actes du colloque international du centre regional d'histoire des mentalities 14–16 juin 1982* (Monpellier: SUP exam, 1986), 141–53; Nirenberg, *Communities of Violence: Persecution of Minorities in the Middle Ages*, 167–70; Kenneth Stow, *Jewish Dogs: An Image and Its Interpreters* (Stanford: Stanford University Press, 2006), 20–22.

69. See Noël Coulet, "'Juif intouchable' et interdits alimentaires," in *Exclus et systems d'exclusion dans la literature et la civilization medievales* (Aix-en-Provence: CUERMA, 1978), 209–21, but esp. 210–11, 214.

70. Carole Rawcliffe, *Leprosy in Medieval England*, 280–81.

71. For the complaint that Jews refuse Christian wine, when more properly Christians should refuse the wine Jews produce because it is a product of their sinful hands, see the

the Frankish Bishop Agobard of Lyon complained to Emperor Louis the Pious that "it is the practice of the Jews that when they slaughter an animal . . . if the liver appears to be damaged once the entrails are opened, or if a lung clings to the side or breath inflates it, or bile is not found, and other things of this sort, it is rejected by the Jews as unclean and sold to the Christians and these are called by the insulting expression 'Christian beasts' [*christiana pecora*]."[72] Similarly, in a letter to the Count of Nevers dated January 17, 1208, Pope Innocent III complains that after Jews have slaughtered an animal according to their rite, they leave the "leftovers" for Christians.[73] Such resentment led to legislation that prohibited Christians from purchasing meat from Jewish butchers, legislation made difficult to enforce since Jews and Christians (or Muslims) were sometimes partners in a joint business venture.[74] As William C. Jordan points out, however, ecclesiastical legislation also sought to prevent Christian butchers from selling meats provided by Jews, and market restrictions on Jewish foodstuffs were especially common in southern France.[75] A London ordinance of 1274 threatened with excommunication any Christian that purchased such meats from Jewish butchers; as a penalty, the meat would be seized and given either to lepers or to the dogs to eat![76] Al-

---

Altercatio legis inter Simoneum Judaeum et Theophilum Christianum 7. Peter Abelard's Jewish interlocutor also notes that "just as we abhor flesh slaughtered by Gentiles, so they abhor flesh prepared by us, and we all likewise abstain from wine prepared by strangers." See *Dialogue of a Philosopher with a Jew and a Christian*, pp. 34 and 66.

72. "Est enim Iudaeorum usus ut, quando quodlibet pecus ad esum mactant . . . si apertis intraneis iecur lesum apparuerit, si pulmo lateri adheserit vel eum insufflatio penetraverit, si fel inventum non fuerit, et alia huiusmodi, hec tanquam immunda a Iudeis repudiata christianis vendantur, et insultario vocabulo christiana pecora appelentur." Agobard of Lyons, *De insolentia Iudaeorum*, in *Opera omnia*, ed. L. Van Acker, CCCM 52 (Turnholt: Brepols, 1981), 193.

73. See Grayzel, *The Church and the Jews*, 127.

74. For market regulations, see Norman Roth, "Food Use by Jews, Laws Relating to," in *Medieval Jewish Civilization: An Encyclopedia*, ed. Norman Roth (New York: Routledge, 2003), 263–64. On interfaith business ventures, including butcher shops, see Chris Lowney, *A Vanished World: Medieval Spain's Golden Age of Enlightenment* (New York: Free Press, 2005), 205–6. Curiously, Felix Fabri notes without criticism that in the city of Modon he saw Turks selling pigs that they had raised to Christians, because Turks, like Jews, are forbidden to eat them. See *Evagatorum in Terrae Sanctae, Arabiae et Egyptii peregrinationem*, fol. 189A, 3: 336. This seems to contradict his claim (see n. 56), that Muslims do not allow pigs in their communities.

75. Jordan, "Problems of the Meat Market of Béziers 1240–1247: A Question of Anti-Semitism," 31–49.

76. "'Notorium est quod Judei omnia animalia et volatilia, quorum carnibus vescuntur, propriis manibus interficiunt . . . de carnibus illorum que sunt de lege commedunt, et non

though a seemingly harsh penalty, in fact the ordinance comments that if this punishment should seem light, it is only because the Jews belong to the King, and the town is unwilling to impose a harsher (and more deserving) penalty without the monarch's consent. In much the same way, the Dominican preacher Vincent Ferrer (d. 1419) not only insisted that Christians should not eat with Jews, but added that if the Jews should send them bread, they should throw it to the dogs.[77] St. Antoninus of Florence also remarks that it is insulting for Christians to eat foods from Jews that the Jews have rejected as unclean.[78] That such prohibitions had to be repeated during the fourteenth and fifteenth centuries would suggest that economic reality often prevailed over fears of impurity engendered by social contact.[79] In addition, we should remind ourselves that, for their part, Jews could not eat the one food that defined substantially the Christian community: the "food" of the sacrament of the Eucharist.

What one eats or refuses to eat does not only erect a social barrier. We must also bear in mind that humoral theory assumed that food digested and decocted in the body is transformed into nutriment for the organs and into bodily humors or fluids. Since the humors affect an individual's complexion and, as a result, also his habits, mental state, and behavior, the foods we eat represent the material causes of a person's characteristics, health, and physical condition. This basic principle also helps explain the important role that physicians played in establishing a healthful dietary regimen for their clients. We see an early example of this in a sixth-century letter from a Greek physician, Anthimus, to the

---

de aliorum carnibus. Quid ergo faciunt Judei de carnibus illorum que non sunt de lege sua? An liceat Christianis illas emere et manducare?' Ad quod responsum per Cives, quod si quis Christianus aliquas tales carnes de Judeo emerit, ipse statim erit excommunicatus; et si super hoc per Vicecomites Civitatis vel per aliquem alium convictus fuerit, amittet carnes illas et dabuntur leprosis vel carnibus manducandum." *Liber de antiquis legibus. Cronica maiorum et vicecomitum Londoniarum,* ed. Thomas Stapleton (London: Camden Society Publications, 1846), 171 72. Noting that the meats were to be distributed to *lepers* (or dogs), Rexroth (*Deviance and Power in Late Medieval London,* 6) speculates that this is because both Jews and lepers were thought to live in sin, and to present bodily infirmities or illness that visibly signified this state of sin.

77. *Sermons* 3.13–14, cited by Nirenberg, "Conversion, Sex, and Segregation: Jews and Christians in Medieval Spain," 1084.

78. St. Antoninus of Florence, *Summa theologica* 2, tit. 14, cap. 2, §3, 2: 1149A–B.

79. See *The Jews of Tortosa 1373–1492. Regesta of Documents from the Archivo Histórico de Protocolos de Tarragona,* Sources for the History of the Jews in Spain 3, compiled by Josefina Cubells i Llorens, ed. Yom Tov Assis (Jerusalem: Henk Schussheim Memorial Series, 1991), v.

Frankish king Theodoric, entitled *On the Rule for Foods* (*De obseruatione ciborum*), which instructs the king on which foods to eat and how to prepare them in order to enjoy a long and healthy life.[80] Such medical advice was frequently collected in guides that fall under the rubric of regimens for health (*regimina sanitatis*), or rules for hygiene and healthy living, and dietary guides were sometimes written for specific groups united by their humoral composition.[81] One example from the later Middle Ages is Gabriele Zerbi's *Gerontocomia*, composed by the Veronese physician in Rome in 1489, that outlines a diet especially appropriate for the elderly, whose complexion will typically be colder and drier than a young person's.[82]

Because of this link, however, between diet and humoral complexion, one can assert that generally for medieval medicine *you are what you eat*. Strangely, as Claudine Fabre-Vassas remarks in her fascinating anthropological study, *Singular Beast: Jews, Christians, and the Pig*, "contrary to the universal rule that associates the other, the foreigner, with what he eats, Jews are associated with the flesh they are forbidden."[83] As pork became a more important part of the European Christian's diet its consumption

---

80. Anthimus, *De obseruatione ciborum epistula ad Theodericum regem Francorum*, ed. and trans. Eduard Liechtenhan, Corpus medicorum Latinorum 8.1 (Berlin: In aedibus Academiae Scientiarum, 1963), 1–33. For a brief discussion of this text, and its place within the collection of texts known as "regimens of health," see Pedro Gil Sortes, "The Regimens of Health," in *Western Medical Thought from Antiquity to the Middle Ages*, 291–318, but esp. 295; and Prioreschi, *A History of Medicine*, 146–49.

81. See *Regimen Sanitatis Salerni: The School of Salernum*, ed. J. Harington (Salerno: Ente Provinciale Per Il Tourismo, 1953); and, *Tacuinum Sanitatis. The Medieval Health Handbook*, ed. Luisa Cogliati Arano, trans. Oscar Ratti and Adele Westbrook (New York: Braziller, 1976). This richly illustrated volume contains five medieval handbooks on health and diet: the *Tacuinum* of Liège; the *Tacuinum* of Paris; the *Tacuinum* of Vienna; the *Theatrum* of the Casanatense library, Rome; and the *Tacuinum* of Rouen. The term *Tacuinum* is derived from the Arabic *taqwīm*, or "tables," and presents its medical doctrines for a broad public in the form of forty tables. The work was written by a Christian physician, Ibn Butlan, who practiced in Damascus in the eleventh century. The *Tacuinum* may have been translated first by Gerard of Cremona in the twelfth century; it was certainly available to Manfred of Sicily by the middle of the thirteenth century. For a general introduction to this medical genre, see Melitta Weiss Adamson, "Regimen sanitatis," in *Medieval Science, Technology, and Medicine: an Encyclopedia*, ed. Thomas F. Glick, Steven J. Livesey, and Faith Wallis (New York: Routledge, 2005), 438–39.

82. Gabriele Zerbi, *Gerontocomia: On the Care of the Aged*, and *Maximianus: Elegies on Old Age and Love*, trans. L. R. Lind (Philadelphia: American Philosophical Society, 1988), 17–308.

83. Fabre-Vassas, *The Singular Beast: Jews, Christians, and the Pig*, 94.

served to proclaim Christian difference and physical, moral, and intellectual superiority, at the same time that in Spain medieval Jewish kabbalists understood their more restricted diet to be connected to their own spiritual attainment.[84] Christians were different because they could eat what had been forbidden to the Jew, and they were superior, as we will see below, because they understood that they could prevail over the filth, gluttony, concupiscence, and sexual excess that the pig represented.[85]

For Christians, then, the ability properly to digest and utilize pork as a meat suggests a superior constitution or bodily complexion. Conversely, the first-century grammarian Erotian associated the Jews abhorrence of pork with disease. Commenting on Hippocrates's discussion of the "sacred disease" (epilepsy), so-called because some insisted that it had a supernatural rather than a natural cause, Erotian remarked that some say that "one should inquire to which type the sick man belongs, in order that if he is a Jew we should refrain from giving him pig's flesh."[86] The Jews' peculiar constitution or complexion demands a special diet, and this must be considered when treating them for illness. Later, when a Jew converted to Christianity, the consumption of pork often became a sign of his transfer from one community as well as a sign of a physical, intellectual, and moral transformation, while his continuing observance of the dietary laws indicated the defective nature of his conversion. An example can be found in Solomon bar Simson's twelfth-century Hebrew chronicle of the First Crusade, which praises those Jews forcibly converted to Christianity who continued to observe the laws of *kashrut*, which served as a sign to the Gentiles that the Jews had only converted out of fear.[87] The dietary laws served then as a clear marker of religious identity, helping to explain why, as early as the seventh-century Visigothic legislation in Spain contained in the Reccesvinth codex, Jewish converts to Christianity were required to take an oath to repudiate the Jewish di-

---

84. Jonathan Brumberg-Kraus, "Meat-Eating and Jewish Identity: Ritualization of the Priestly 'Torah of Beast and Fowl' (Lev. 11: 46) in Rabbinic Judaism and Medieval Kabbalah," *AJS Review* 24, no. 2 (1999): 227–62. For pork as the most commonly consumed meat in medieval England, see F. W. Grube, "Meat Foods of the Anglo-Saxons," *Journal of English and Germanic Philology* 34, no. 4 (1935): 511–29, citing 520–21.

85. Albert the Great, *De animalibus* 22.1.5.9, vol. 16, 1353 (SZ 2: 1445).

86. See Martin Goodman, *Rome and Jerusalem: The Clash of Ancient Civilizations* (New York: Knopf, 2007), 366.

87. See Chazan, *European Jewry and the First Crusade*, Appendix, 294. For the dating of the text, see 42–43.

etary laws. If, because of his former habit the convert could not eat pork itself, he promised at least to eat food cooked with pork without loathing or horror. Similarly, Christians who sought a business relationship with a convert were advised to demand first that the convert recite the Lord's Prayer or the creed and also eat the foods Christians eat as a proof of his religious identity.[88] Consumption of pork was on its way to becoming a litmus test of Christian self-definition.

Not only did Christians see pork as a symbol of Christian identity, but Jews did as well. In the thirteenth-century Jewish collection of polemical anti-Christian arguments, Nizzaḥon Vetus, the text of Isaiah 65:4—"a nation ... that dwells in sepulchers, and sleeps in the temple of idols, that eats swine's flesh"—is identified as a reference to the Christians, "because no nation in the world eats swine except for you."[89] Certainly, Jews and Muslims did not eat pork, at least not under ordinary circumstances. Halachic exceptions to the prohibition were acknowledged by the sages of the Talmud, under the principle of *piqquah nefesh*: that is, in order to save a life. Medical treatment, then, might require relaxation of the laws of *kashrut*. This still left a good bit of room for disagreement, however, concerning the definition of medical necessity under which the dietary laws could be suspended: the *Sefer Hasidim*, for example, prohibits Jews from eating nonkosher foods (in particular, fish) for their aphrodisiac properties to treat sexual dysfunction, but recommends instead kosher alternatives.[90] Nonetheless, Christians of the High Middle Ages were certainly aware of this weakening of what, in their minds, had been an absolute commandment for the Jews. It figures prominently in the Jewish-

---

88. "De suillis veris carnibus id observare promittimus, ut si eas pro consuetudine non minime percipere potuerimus, ea tamen, que cum ipsis decocta sunt, absque fastidio et orrore sumamus." Linder, *The Jews in the Legal Sources of the Early Middle Ages*, 279, 281.

89. Berger, *The Jewish-Christian Debate in the High Middle Ages*, 211. In a note on 270, Berger adds that about the middle of the twelfth century, Jacob ben Reuben expressed this same opinion in one of the first Jewish polemics written in western Europe. See his *Milḥamot ha Shem*, ed. Judah Rosenthal (Jerusalem: Mosad ha-Rav Kuk, 1963), 38–39, 114. See also *Liber duelli Christiani in obsidione Damiatae exacti (1217–1220)*, cap. 19, ed. O. Holder-Egger, MGH SS 31 (Hannover, 1903), 675–705, citing 703. For a discussion of the text see Robert Chazan, "The Christian Position in Jacob ben Reuben's *Milḥamot Ha-Shem*," in *From Ancient Israel to Modern Judaism: Intellect in Quest of Understanding; Essays in Honor of Marvin Fox*, 4 vols., ed. Jacob Neusner, Ernest S. Frerichs, and Nahum M. Sarna (Atlanta: Scholars Press, 1989), 2: 157–70; and Chazan, *Fashioning Jewish Identity in Medieval Western Christendom* (Cambridge: Cambridge University Press, 2004), 98–103.

90. *Sefer Chasidim* 404(390), p. 224.

Christian disputation of Mallorca (1286), where the Christian disputant, the lay merchant Inghetto Contardo, asks: can a sick Jew be given pork or other prohibited foods to eat, if medical treatment demands it? The Jew replies that he can, which allows Contardo to insist, then, that the commandments against forbidden foods can be put aside, just as the Christians have done.[91]

In Spain by the late thirteenth century, pork served not only as a static marker separating Jew and Muslim from Christian, but also as a dynamic marker, illustrating the transformation of conversion. Under the eye of the Inquisition and former co-religionists, Jewish converts ate pork to demonstrate their commitment to their new religion. In a study of the significance of food as a marker among *conversos* in Spain at the end of the fifteenth century, Anna Foa records the words that the converso poet Antón de Montoro addressed to Queen Isabella at her coronation, which express both the signs of his conversion and a despairing sense that he could not eliminate all traces of his earlier Jewish identity: "I said the Credo and I knelt, ate lots of pork and lard, half-roasted bacon; heard masses and prayed hard ... never able to discard this trace of being a *confeso*."[92]

Records show that conversos or *Marranos* (Jews who had become New Christians), as well as *Moriscos* (Muslim converts), were frequently denounced to the Inquisition based on claims that they refused to eat pork and continued to observe religious dietary restrictions. The convert Gonzalo Pérez Jarada was brought before the Inquisition in Toledo in 1489 to 1490, and scruples regarding what he would eat loomed large in the charges brought against him. For example, "he refused to eat suffocated partridges [those killed in violation of Jewish ritual], and ordered that they should be brought to him alive, and he had the throats of the

---

91. *Die Disputationen zu Ceuta (1179) und Mallorca (1286). Zwei antijüdische Schriften aus dem mittelalterlichen Genua*, ed. Ora Limor, MGH, Quellen zur Geistesgeschichte des Mittelalters 15 (Munich: MGH, 1994), 172–73. For the difficulties Jewish physicians faced when adopting medical cures that contravened the laws of kashrut, see also Luis García Ballester, "Dietetic and Pharmacological Therapy: A Dilemma among 14th C. Jewish Practitioners in the Montpelier Area," *Clio medica* 22 (1991): 23–37.

92. Antón de Montoro, *Cancionero*, ed. F. Cantera Burgos y C. Carrete Parrondo (Madrid: 1984), 133, cited in Anna Foa, "The Marrano's Kitchen: External Stimuli, Internal Response, and the Formation of the Marranic Persona," in *The Mediterranean and the Jews: Society, Culture and Economy in Early Modern Times* 2, ed. Elliott Horowitz and Moises Orfali (Ramat Gan: Bar-Ilan University Press, 2002), 13.

meat he intended to eat slit with [Jewish] ceremony." In addition, "he ate meat during Lent, even though he was not ill, and this in the houses of Jews, [the meat] having been killed with [Jewish] ceremony. And he sent the birds he intended to eat to Jews to have their throats slit, and *he did not eat bacon.*"[93] In the same way, Leonor, wife of Diego de Salinas and a New Christian, was brought to trial in 1501 for trying surreptitiously to keep the Jewish dietary laws. Her neighbor had brought her bacon to put in her stock pot, but "when she [Leonor] saw the bacon, she turned the pot over so that the bacon fell on the bench and filled it with water again to carry on with the cooking."[94]

The use of food as a marker of religious identity relied at least in part on 2 Maccabees 7:1, which describes the violent martyrdom of seven Jewish brothers who refused to transgress the Law by eating "swine's flesh" during persecution by the Hellenistic ruler, Antiochus IV Epiphanes. That text demonstrated to Christians that in antiquity the Jews also recognized pork consumption as a marker of religious identity and fidelity. At the same time, it may have underscored a link between leprosy and pork, inasmuch as the name of the martyr Eleazar, who chose death rather than eat swine's flesh (2 Macc. 7:18–28; see figure 8), later reappears in abbreviated form as Lazarus, the patron saint of lepers. Philo Judaeus (d. after 40 CE), who understood Moses to have prohibited swine's

93. Haim Benart, *Trujillo: A Jewish Community in Extremadura on the Eve of the Expulsion from Spain*, Hispanica Judaica 2 (Jerusalem: Magnes Press, 1980), 288–89, cited in Edwards, *The Jews in Western Europe 1400–1600*, 41. My emphasis. Eating meat during Lent was another sign of "otherness," and this accusation was sometimes turned against recent converts. In the twelfth century, it was one of the charges directed against a Muslim convert to Christianity, Philip of Mahdīya (who served King Roger II of Sicily) leading to his execution. See Joshua C. Birk, "From Borderlands to Borderlines: Narrating the Past of Twelfth-Century Sicily," in *Multicultural Europe and Cultural Exchange in the Middle Ages and Renaissance*, ed. James P. Helfers, Arizona Studies in the Middle Ages and Renaissance 12 (Turnholt: Brepols, 2005), 11; the charge is confirmed in the twelfth century account of Ibn al-Athīr, *The Complete Treatment of History*, where Philip was alleged to be a Muslim because he did not fast at the appropriate times on the Church calendar, for which he was burned at the stake. See *Medieval Italy: Texts in Translation*, 123.

94. *El tribunal de la Inquisición en el obispado de Soria (1486–1502)*, ed. Carlos Carrete Paddondo, Fontes Iudaeorum Regni Castellae 2 (Salamanca: Salamanca Universidad Pontificia de Salamanca-Universidad de Granada, 1985), 116, cited in Edwards, *The Jews in Western Europe 1400–1600*, 43. For examples of conversas that admitted to the Inquisition that they had followed the dietary laws and, in particular, had sought to avoid eating pork, see Renée Levine-Melammed, "The Ultimate Challenge: Safeguarding the Crypto-Judaic Heritage," *Proceedings of the American Academy for Jewish Research* 53 (1986), esp. 102–3, and 107.

flesh both because it symbolizes gluttony and gluttony leads to illness, remarks that under the Roman prefect Flaccus (38 CE), who promoted the persecution of Jews in Alexandria, women were often arrested and their identity investigated. "If they were found to be of our nation ... [he] gave orders to fetch swine's flesh and give it to the women. Then the women who in fear of punishment tasted the meat were dismissed.... But the more resolute were delivered to the tormentors to suffer desperate ill-usage."[95] Although the eighth-century pope Zachary reflects ancient traditions when he cautioned Christians to avoid eating the hare because it is a particularly lascivious animal, principally it was pork—and not the camel, another explicitly prohibited food (Deut. 14:7)—that would serve as the quintessential marker of religious difference as the Middle Ages progressed.[96]

In the modern world too it has served as a principal marker of religious difference. Some sixteenth-century Scottish religious thinkers speculated on a shared ethnicity and affinity with the Jews that revealed itself in the Scots' peculiar distaste for pork, which almost amounted to "swinophobia."[97] Conversely and more recently, residents of Munich submitted a petition to the Bavarian parliament to express opposition

95. *Against Flaccus* 11.96-97 in *Philo*, 10 vols., trans. F. H. Colson (Cambridge, Mass.: Harvard University Press, 1985), 9: 355-56. For his interpretation of the dietary laws, see Mary Douglas, *Purity and Danger: Analysis of Concepts of Pollution and Taboo* (New York: Routledge, 2003), 45-46.

96. See his Epist. 13 (to St. Boniface; PL 89: 951A). Both Isidore of Seville and the Venerable Bede had also identified the hare as a symbol for effeminate customs, to explain the Mosaic prohibition: "Et cum leporem accusat, deformatos utique in feminas viros damnat." See Isidore's *Quaestiones in Vetus Testamentum: In Leviticum*, 9.7 (PL 83: 326) and Bede's *In Pentateuchum Commentarii: Leviticus* 11 (PL 91: 345D). For the hare as a lubricious symbol in early medieval food regulations, see Bruno Laurioux, "Le lièvre lubrique et la bête sanglante. Réflexions sur quelques interdits alimentaires du haut moyen âge," in *Anthropozoologica. Second numéro spécial: bulletin de l'Association l'homme et l'animal, Société de recherche interdisciplinaire* (Liège: Anthropozoologica, 1988), 127-32. John Boswell also examines the hare as a symbol for homosexuals in his *Christianity, Social Tolerance, and Homosexuality*, 137, 141-43.

97. See Arthur H. Williamson, "'A Pil for Pork-Eaters': Ethnic Identity, Apocalyptic Promises, and the Strange Creation of the Judeo-Scots," in *The Expulsion of the Jews: 1492 and After*, ed. Raymond B. Waddington and Arthur H. Williamson (New York: Garland, 1994), 237-58. Williamson (245-46) points out that King James VI of Scotland, who ruled England and Ireland as James I (d. 1625), and who was "the most visible Scot in England," fully shared this aversion. Williamson (247) notes that the royalist James Howell, who was both anti-Semitic and Scotophobic, went so far as to suggest that the Jews and Scots had become one people, because when Edward I expelled the Jews from England in 1290, they fled to Scotland!

to plans to build a mosque in the city center. Of special interest is the justification offered for their opposition, which sees Islamic dietary rules as explicitly subverting one of the marks of German Christian culture: "'Bavarian life,' the petition declares, 'is marked by the drinking of beer and the eating of pork. In Muslim faith, both are unclean and forbidden.'"[98]

Food prohibitions, then, were an integral part of medieval religious polemics. Such religious polemics also appealed to shared medical doctrines to stigmatize the food rules of the "Other." The late thirteenth-century Spanish kabbalistic work the *Zohar* contains a story of an encounter between a Gentile and Rabbi Eliezer. The Gentile complains:

"You assert that you abstain from forbidden kinds of food in order that you may be healthy, and that health may be given to your bodies. But in reality it is we, who eat whatever we please, that are healthy and strong, while you are weak and afflicted with illnesses and bodily infirmities more than all other nations." R. Eliezer became angry and stared at the Gentile until he was reduced to a heap of bones. Then R. Eliezer wept, and recalled that he once posed the same question about forbidden foods to the prophet Elijah, who told him "Israelites, unlike the Gentiles, abstain from all unclean food, just as the tender and delicate heart, on which the welfare of the all the limbs depends, only absorbs the purest elements of food, leaving all coarser nutriment for the stronger limbs."[99]

This passage reveals the manner in which food came to determine the health not only of the individual body, but also of an entire nation. The Gentile repudiated the notion that the Jewish dietary laws safeguarded the health of the Jews' body. Instead he insisted that the absence of dietary restrictions for Christians attests to their health and strength. He implies that anyone on a special diet must have a weakened constitution, and thus the dietary laws indicate Jewish weakness. Eliezer's stare, which reduced the Gentile to a "heap of bones," belies any sense of weakness. Nonetheless, Elijah confirmed that the Jewish dietary laws do attest

---

98. Mark Landler, "Munich, Provocation in a Symbol of Foreign Faith," *New York Times*, December 8, 2006 (available at http://www.nytimes.com/2006/12/08/world/europe/08mosque.html. 2/7/2011).

99. *Zohar* 3: 220b–221b, quoted in Barry R. Mark, "Kabbalistic *Tocinofobia*: Américo Castro, *Limpieza de Sangre* and the Inner Meaning of Jewish Dietary Laws," in *Fear and Its Representations in the Middle Ages and Renaissance*, ed. Anne Scott and Cynthia Kosso, Arizona Studies in the Middle Ages and Renaissance 6 (Tempe: Arizona Center for Middle Ages and Renaissance Studies (ACMRS) Publications, 2002), 174–75.

to a kind of weakness in Jews: the weakness of a tender and delicate heart which can absorb only the purest food. As the heart is the source of heat and power for the rest of the body, so the Jews seem to be the 'heart' of the world while the Gentiles, who represent its stronger limbs, can tolerate a coarser nutriment. Similarly for Judah Ha-Levi (d. 1141) Jews are the heart of the world and, like the heart in the center of the body, they require the purest nourishment while at the same time, like the heart, they remain more sensitive to the illness and afflictions of the other parts of the body, illnesses that are contracted especially through frequent contact with their Gentile neighbors.[100] Thus the Gentiles' coarser nutriment befits the strength of their bodies, but also attests to a spiritual or intellectual coarseness. The *Zohar* adds: "the nations of the world who are impure cling to what is impure and are linked with the forces of their impure food."[101] Food had become an ethnographic marker that was at least as important to Jews as to Christians.

While the *Zohar* provides this more "mystical" although still medicalized food assessment, in the twelfth century Maimonides adopts the language of humoral theory to explain the Jews' rejection of pork. In his *Guide of the Perplexed* he explains that among all the forbidden foods, pork may be imagined by physicians not to be harmful.

But this is not so, for pork is more humid than is proper and contains much superfluous matter. The major reason why the Law abhors it is its being very dirty and feeding on dirty things. . . . Now if swine were used for food, marketplaces and even houses would have been dirtier than latrines, as may be seen at present in the country of the Franks [that is, of Western Europeans]. You know the dictum [of the Sages], may their memory be blessed: "The mouth of a swine is like walking excrement." The fat of the intestines, too, makes us too full, spoils the digestion, and produces cold and thick blood.[102]

---

100. Judah Ha-Levi, *Book of Kuzari* 2.36–44, trans. Hartwig Hirschfeld (New York: Pardes, 1946), 95–97.
    101. *Zohar* 308, quoted in Mark, "Kabbalistic *Tocinofobia*," 178.
    102. *Guide of the Perplexed* 3.48, pp. 598–99. For this text, see also Jacob Levinger, "Maimonides' *Guide of the Perplexed* on Forbidden Food in Light of his own Medical Opinion," in *Perspectives on Maimonides: Philosophical and Historical Studies*, ed. Joel L. Kraemer (London: Littman Library of Jewish Civilization), 195. Cf. Hanna Kasher, "Well-being of the Body or Welfare of the Soul: the Maimonidean Explanation of the Dietary Laws," in *Moses Maimonides: Physician, Scientist, and Philosopher*, ed. Fred Rosner and Samuel S. Kottek (Northvale, N.J.: Aronson, 1993), 127–138, 257–58.

For Maimonides, then, pork is prohibited to Jews at least in part because it is a "humid" food that contains superfluous material (presumably, fat), causes repletion, spoils digestion, and produces blood that is cold and thick. Citing the Sages, he adds that the pigs mouth "is like walking excrement," recalling the Jewish woman's complaint in the story of Adam of Bristol that pigs eat human excrement. It is a dirty animal, which, in an attack on European Christian habits, Maimonides insists befouls the towns of the Franks, undermining public hygiene.

In fact, pigs (and dogs) do eat excrement. Albert the Great explains that Frisians often tie a pig to a cow's tail while the cow is feeding. The cow does not break down all the grain fed to it, but passes much of it in its excrement which the pig, placed behind it, will then eat and digest from the bovine excrement.[103] According to Alan Dundes, "[this] explains why *schwein* is such an offensive insult in German folk speech. The implication is that the object of the insult is a shit-eater."[104] Biblical prohibitions against consumption of pork could be understood as well to ensure that Jews *not* become what they are forbidden to eat, or not become what the pig eats, namely, foul excrement. Conversely, scatological medieval insults that identified Jews as pigs, or showed them nursing from a sow or eating its excrement, as in the image of the *Judensau*, likely were intended to produce the opposite result: to construct an image of the dirty Jew, the "excrement of the human race" (*humani generis feces*) as Peter the Venerable says.[105]

Like Maimonides, Latin tradition as well viewed the pig as phlegmatic; its meat, then, will be cold and moist or "humid."[106] But God did not impose upon the Christians dietary laws that prohibit pork, and therefore they must be unnecessary for them. This contention is quite explicit in another text, composed c. 1520, Solomon ibn Verga's *Shevet Judah* (*Staff of Judah*), an imaginary and ironic dialogue between a Jew named Abravanel and a Christian named Tomás. According to Abravanel, the Jews form a category above the rest of humanity, and that is why they observe a special diet. Tomás rebuffs this explanation, and treats the dietary

---

103. Albert the Great, *De animalibus* 7.1.5.53, vol. 15, 518 (SZ 1: 609).

104. Alan Dundes, *Life is Like a Chicken Coop: A Portrait of German Culture through Folklore* (New York: Columbia University Press, 1984), 121.

105. *Adversus Judeorum inveteratam duritiem* 3, p. 56, ln. 526.

106. Cf. William of Conches, *De philosophia mundi* 23 (PL 172: 56B); Albert the Great, *Quaestiones super de animalibus* 7.33–39 (QDA, 265–66).

laws as necessary for Jews because of their natural imperfection, and unnecessary for Christians because of their natural perfection. Thus, he alleges, although typically pork increases sexual desire, "Christians because of their humours and perfection change everything to accord with their humors, just as honey changes the bitterness of the orange's peel into sweetness."[107] Therefore, Christians are permitted pork in their diet because they can withstand its influence on carnal desire. Jews, he adds, had to be restrained from such foods because their natural imperfection makes it impossible for them to withstand a desire for sexual intercourse.

In the same way, Jews *need* the dietary laws in order to avoid that leprosy to which they are by nature subject. For the chronicler Sigismondo de' Conti da Foligno, writing before 1512, clearly these laws were either ineffective or inconsistently observed. In his account, syphilis—sometimes known as the Jews' disease or the Marranos' disease (*pestis judaeorum* or *pestis marrana*)—was introduced to Europe by converted Jews, the *Marrani* driven out of Spain. In fact, he also conflated syphilis and leprosy, presumably because leprosy too was thought to be a sexually transmitted disease. But de' Conti da Foligno also inferred that because of their special dietary regulations, the Jews must be *more* subject to leprosy than other peoples:

In fact, the Jews, because they abstain from pork, are subject to leprosy more than other peoples, and this is the reason why, according to the most authoritative Cornelius Tacitus, they were driven out of Egypt. More significantly, Sacred Scripture, in which one must believe, makes clear that leprosy was a sign that revealed an even more vile incontinence: in fact, it began to manifest itself in the genitals.[108]

For this author, it is the same sexual licentiousness that first necessitated the purity laws for the Jews, regulating both their diet and sexual encounters, that later led to the appearance among them of syphilis, that "began to manifest itself in the genitals," and which they then introduced to an unsuspecting Europe. The assignment of a disease's origin to a par-

107. *Shevet Judah*, 36 and 175 n. 8, quoted in E. Gutwirth, "Gender, History, and the Judeo-Christian Polemic," in *Contra Iudaeos. Ancient and Medieval Polemics between Christians and Jews*, ed. Ora Limor and Guy G. Stroumsa (Tübingen: Mohr, 1996), 272.

108. Sigismondo de' Conti da Foligno, *Le storie dei suoi tempi dal 1475 al 1510*, 2 vols. (Rome: Tip. de G. Barbera, 1883), 2: 271–72, quoted in Anna Foa, "The New and the Old: The Spread of Syphilis (1494–1530)," in *Sex and Gender in Historical Perspective*, ed. Edward Muir and Guido Ruggiero, trans. Margaret Gallucci, Mary M. Gallucci, and Carole C. Galluci (Baltimore: Johns Hopkins University Press, 1990), 36.

ticular people had a polemical purpose, but the success of this claim rested especially on the fact that Jews were assumed to have a particularly corrupt sexual nature.[109] By contrast, for the Jew Isaac Abravanel (d. 1508), syphilis—which he also understood to be a type of leprosy and identified as the Gallic (that is, French) disease—occurs only among Gentiles and not among Jews, because the religious laws of the Jews protect them from the Gallic disease just as they protect them from leprosy.[110]

Nonetheless, for Christian interpreters, the Jews' *dietary* laws certainly are an ineffective prophylactic, and point indirectly to a flaw in their very nature. As Anna Foa remarks, "The Jew abstained from pork, but to no effect because they were *by nature* subject to leprosy. Finding pork repugnant not only did not diminish the impurity of the Jew: it actually accentuated it."[111] In this regard, it is worth remarking that some scholars speculate that the term *Marranos*, attached to converted Jews in Spain, receives a vituperative meaning of "swine" perhaps by the end of the fourteenth century, establishing a link between the Jews themselves, or crypto-Jews, and the pig.[112] Pigs were known to be so gluttonous that they will eat their own progeny, other animals, and even humans.[113] Some early medieval penitential books forbade the consumption of pigs that had fed upon a human corpse.[114] We see in the later Middle Ages—certainly, by the fourteenth century—the appearance of legal proceed-

---

109. The claim that Jews are the principal carriers of sexually transmitted disease persists well into the modern era. See Roderich-Stoltheim [Theodor Fritsch], *The Riddle of the Jew's Success*, 268. For the assignment of an unrestrained sexuality to Jews in the Middle Ages, which represented too an obstacle to genuine conversion, see Steven F. Kruger, "Conversion and Medieval Sexual, Religious, and Racial Categories," in *Constructing Medieval Sexuality*, ed. Karma Lochrie, Peggy McCracken, and James A. Schultz (Minneapolis: University of Minnesota Press, 1997), 158–79.

110. Harry Friedenwald, *The Jews and Medicine: Essays*, 2 vols. (Balitmore: Johns Hopkins University Press, 1944), 2: 529.

111. Foa, "The New and the Old," 37.

112. For the origin of the term, see B. Netanyahu, *The Marranos of Spain: From the Late 14th to the Early 16th Century, according to Contemporary Hebrew Sources*, 3rd ed. (Ithaca, N.Y.: Cornell University Press, 1999), 59 n. 153. There the author conjectures that *marrano* is "a haplogic contraction of the Hebrew *mumar-anus*"; these terms imply conversion under constraint. But cf. Norman Roth, *Conversos, Inquisition, and the Expulsion of the Jews from Spain* (Madison: University of Wisconsin Press, 2002), 3–4. There is no doubt that the term is derogatory, but its origin and meaning remain elusive.

113. Albert the Great, *De animalibus* 7.1.5.52, vol. 15, 517 (SZ 1: 608); Albert the Great, *Quaestiones super de animalibus* 7.8.2, p. 175, 73–75 (QDA, 239).

114. Rob Meens, "Pollution in the early middle ages: the case of the food regulations in the penitentials," *Early Medieval Europe* 4, no. 1 (1995): 3–19, citing 10.

ings against sows accused of having killed (and sometimes eaten) human infants. With persuasive force, Jody Enders argues that prosecutions of "homicidal pigs" in medieval Christian communities "turned with a horrifying fervor against the same human animals whom they accused of thirsting animalistically after the blood of Christian children and whom they explicitly equated with pigs: Jews."[115]

Remarkably, then, Jews were both more and less likely to be leprous: more likely because their dietary laws implied that they had a nature so flawed that it had been necessary to forbid them to eat pork, a meat that was linked to leprosy but which a Christian bodily constitution could somehow tolerate without ill effect. Perhaps in actuality there will be fewer Jewish lepers because they do observe their dietary laws, but, as Sigismondo de' Conti da Foligno reveals, as a consequent they must naturally be more subject to this illness. Similarly, Jews may avoid leprosy because they observe scrupulously the laws of sexual purity and abstain from sex with a menstruant. But once again, this presumed empirical reality conceals a threatening principle: that Jews had to be given these laws to protect them from their naturally unrestrained, wanton, and perverse nature.

The apparent immunity of Jews to leprosy—or at least to its obvious manifestation—tended once more to feminize them. William of Conches had explained how a woman who has had intercourse with a leper will transmit the disease to other sexual partners: "the putrid matter coming from coition with the leper remains in the womb. So when a [second] man enters her, his male member, which consists of nerves, enters the womb and, by virtue of its attractive force, draws the corruption to it."[116] Vincent of Beauvais (d. 1264), citing William of Conches as his authority, notes as a special danger that just as progeny conceived during sex with a menstruant will be born with leprosy, so too women who have sex with a leper seem immune to the disease themselves, but function as "carriers,"

---

115. Jody Enders, "Homicidal Pigs and the Antisemitic Imagination," *Exemplaria* 14, no. 1 (2002): 201–9; on prosecutions of animals generally, see Ervin Bonkalo, "Criminal Proceedings Against Animals in the Middle Ages," *Journal of Unconventional History* 3, no. 2 (1992): 25–31. In an apparent effort to link Jews to the infanticidal behavior of the sow, a late fifteenth-century engraving of the ritual murder of Simon of Trent depicts Jews whose garments display the Jews' badge or *rota*; inside the badge is a picture of a pig. See Schreckenberg, *The Jews in Christian Art*, 280.

116. William of Conches, *A Dialogue on Natural Philosophy* 6.8.13, p. 138.

infecting their male partners in the manner already described.[117] Slightly later Bernard of Gordon provides an expanded but natural explanation for her relative or limited immunity:

> Leprosy also arises ... from coitus with a leprous woman. And also in him who lies with a woman who has lain with a leper whose seed still remains in her womb. For, from coitus with a leper the woman is not infected unless she continues a long time, because of the density of the womb. But if a healthy man lies with a woman with whom a leper has lain, the leper's semen yet remaining in her womb, he will necessarily become leprous because the pores are loose in the male and the infection readily moves to the whole body.[118]

The woman's virtual immunity makes her all the more dangerous, because very often she does not display the symptoms of disease. In the same way, one may conclude that the alleged immunity of Jews to leprosy rendered them all the more dangerous. Their threat remained real, but hidden. Like lepers, they too would have to be identified by special garments and isolated to avoid the spread of their special disease.

---

117. Vincent of Beauvais, *Speculum naturale*, 31.5, 1: 2294–5.
118. Bernard of Gordon, *Lilium medicine,* fol. 13ra–b, quoted in Luke Demaitre, "The Description and Diagnosis of Leprosy," 330.

5

THE JEWS AND MELANCHOLY

Although certain foods, corrupt air, or illicit sexual encounters might introduce leprosy, physicians seeking its natural causes also sought an acceptable explanation in the language of Galenic humoralism. Already we have seen that the four bodily humors are related to the four types of leprosy: *elephantia, leonina, tyria,* and *allopicia.* Of these four types of leprosy or skin disease, *elephantia,* caused by adust (that is, "burned") melancholy, was the most severe, and could be introduced by foods that increase the melancholic humor. Pork was one such food. Indeed, Haymo of Halberstadt (d. 853) complained of certain Christians who, like modern Pharisees, had refused to eat pork or eel because they had diagnosed themselves as melancholics.[1] The monastic reformer Peter Damian (d. 1072) likewise condemns a tendency among hypochondriac monks to self-diagnose various ailments in order to prescribe a relaxed dietary regimen. They submit to frequent phlebotomy or the use of leeches to draw out harmful blood, and "take dainty food for their squeamish stomach," to treat illnesses of their own invention.[2] This complaint was echoed in the twelfth century by Bernard of Clairvaux, who reminded monks that they ought not to spurn the foods of the monastery or its fasts because, like physicians, they had diagnosed themselves as suffering from complexional imbalance.[3] A century later, Jacques de

---

1. "id est secundum traditionem Scribarum et Pharisaeorum, et secundum illos qui causa infirmitatis nolunt ea comedere, dicentes: Nolo comedere carnem suillam quia melancholicus sum, neque anguillam." Haymo of Halberstadt, *Expositio in D. Pauli epistolas* 2 (PL 117: 758D).

2. Peter Damian, Epist. 132.16, in *Die Briefe des Petrus Damiani,* 3: 446; translated in *The Letters of Peter Damian, 121–150,* 65.

3. Bernard of Clairvaux, *Sermo* 30.11, in *Sermones super Cantica Canticorum,*

Vitry complains of a certain Cistercian who, having been a physician before he entered the monastery, condemned the foods enjoined by his order as unhealthful and contrary to his complexion.[4] Such complaints, however, merely reflect the medical judgment of the day, seeking to modify the monastic regimen in order to prevent various illnesses, including leprosy. While pork might dispose certain complexions to melancholy or leprosy, other "cold" foods as well could lead to leprosy. Gilbert the Englishman adds that *elephantia* "is brought on by melancholic foods, such as stale goat's flesh, venison, or beef."[5]

Although imbalances of the humors could be induced by diet or other external factors, heredity was also widely accepted as a cause of leprosy, both by medical practitioners and by educated churchmen. Jacques de Vitry repeated the common wisdom that "From lepers, very often lepers are produced."[6] This view was reiterated by Albert the Great, who remarked that because of a flaw in the sperm "a cripple commonly generates a cripple and a leper generates a leper."[7] In his massive commentary on Aristotle's *On Animals* (*De animalibus*), Albert expands the causes of leprosy to include not only a flaw that stems from the fact that a leper cannot adequately complete the body's fourth digestion that produces sperm, but also the deleterious influence of corrupt, black bile. Thus "it happens very often that flaws [*occasiones*] in the parents are reflected in the offspring, either in the same degree or worse. Thus one with gout begets one with gout, a leper a leper, and sometimes a cancerous person or one who is melancholic due to black bile [*melancholia*] begets a leper."[8] Like Gilbert the Englishman, Albert includes leprosy—and *elephantia* in particular—among illnesses related to melancholy, adding, "When the spleen is weak in drawing in melancholy from the liver, melancholic illnesses befall the body, illnesses such as

---

2 vols., ed. Jean Leclercq, C. H. Talbot, and H. M. Rochais (Rome: Editiones Cistercienses, 1957–58), 1: 217. Bernard's complaint not only highlight's the monks' inclination to self-diagnosis, but also likely implies criticism of the concept of *complexio*, which had recently gained wider currency. Luke Demaitre (*Leprosy in Premodern Medicine*, 114) cites a similar complaint from Guibert of Tournai (c. 1260).

4. Jacques de Vitry, *Historia Occidentalis* 14, p. 303.

5. Gilbert the Englishman, "The Symptoms of Leprosy," in Grant, *A Sourcebook of Medieval Science*, 754.

6. Jacques de Vitry, *Historia Orientalis* 92, p. 217.

7. Albert the Great, *Quaestiones super de animalibus* 15.13(3), p. 267 (QDA, 457).

8. Albert the Great, *De animalibus* 9.1.6.62, vol.15, 698 (SZ 1: 796–7).

black morphew, cancer, varicose veins, *elephantia,* leprosy, and the like."⁹

This relationship between melancholy and leprosy can be found among Arab physicians, whose work entered Latin Christendom in the late eleventh century. Constantine the African, the Benedictine translator of Arabic medical treatises at Monte Cassino at the end of the eleventh century, composed his *Two Books on Melancholy* (*Libri duo de melancholia*), often citing word for word the work of Ishāq ibn 'Imrān Maqāla fī l-Mālīhūliyā. There one finds that among various illnesses, epileptics and lepers often become melancholics and vice versa; moreover, the melancholy humor does nothing to improve the sufferer's condition.¹⁰ Because the most acute form of leprosy is related to the melancholy humor, medieval physicians of the later Middle Ages assumed too that nature's way of removing coarse and superfluous black bile, for example, nosebleeds or bleeding hemorrhoids, or therapeutic interventions like bloodletting, could help restore complexional balance by drawing away the melancholy humor.¹¹ Maimonides (d. 1204) in his *Treatise on Melancholy*, written in Arabic for the eldest son of Saladin (d. 1193), al-Afdal (d. 1225), who suffered both from melancholy and from bleeding hemorrhoids, recommended that the hemorrhoids be allowed to bleed to remove the bad blood and to draw off the melancholy humor.¹² The same approach could also prove an effective prophylactic against leprosy. The fourteenth-century Silesian physician Thomas of Wroclaw (d. c. 1378) concluded that "when the veins flow in due measure, a person is

---

9. Albert the Great, *De animalibus* 1.3.5.608, vol. 15, 217 (*SZ* 1: 278). Black morphew probably indicates a kind of sclerodoma, perhaps even a birthmark.

10. "Multi etiam leprosi facti sunt melancholici, nec tamen melancholia iuvit eos a lepra." Ishāq ibn 'Imrān, *Maqāla fī l-Mālīhūliyā* (*Abhandlung über die Melancholie*) *und Constantini Africani Libri duo de Melancholia*, Critical Arabic-Latin Parallel texts and German trans., ed. and trans. Karl Gabers (Hamburg: Helmut Buske Verlag, 1977), 131, Basle ed., 289.

11. For the causal link between melancholy and hemorrhoids, see the *Flos Medicinae Scholae Salerni* 5.3, art. 30, in vol. 5 of *Collectio Salernitana*, ed. Salvatore de Renzi (Naples: Tipografia del Filiatre-Sebezio, 1859).

12. See discussion in Michael W. Dols, *Majnūn: The Madman in Medieval Islamic Society*, ed. Diana F. Immisch (Oxford: Clarendon Press, 1992), 139. Maimonides himself wrote a treatise on hemorrhoids. See his *Treatise on Hemorrhoids. Medical Answers (Responsa)*, trans. and eds. Fred Rosner and Suessman Munter (Philadelphia: Lippincott, 1969); and, *Treatises on Poisons, Hemorrhoids, Cohabitation: Maimonides' Medical Writings*, trans. Fred Rosner (Haifa, Israel: Maimonides Research Institute, 1984). Pormann and Savage-Smith remark that this affliction was a common subject of monographs in the Mediterranean world. See Peter E. Pormann and Emilie Savage-Smith, *Medieval Islamic Medicine* (Washington, D.C.: Georgetown University Press, 2007), 56.

safeguarded from many illnesses which are caused by such coarse blood, like mania, melancholy, quartan [fever], leprosy, morphew and *malum mortuum* [necrosis?], because blood such as this is burned and corrupted if it remains too long [in the body]."[13] The roughly contemporary Englishman John Ardenne remarked that if blood flows immoderately from piles or hemorrhoids, it is harmful and dangerous, but if it flows in a moderate or temperate fashion, it "preserveth the body from many sekeness, aduste and corrupte, as is mania, malencolia, pleuresis, lepre."[14]

I have drawn attention to this apparent relationship between melancholy and leprosy because other medieval traditions identify Jews in particular as having a melancholy complexion (that is, one dominated by *melancholia* or black bile). As already noted, Isaac Cardoso will identify melancholy especially as the Jews' disease. A melancholic was more likely to suffer certain illnesses, both physical and mental. The thirteenth-century Hebrew translator of an Arthurian romance remarks that he undertook the work of translation "to preserve my bodily health" because "I was afraid lest I fall a prey to melancholy, which is to lose my reason, than which death is better."[15]

In itself natural melancholy, which is generated in the liver and travels to other parts of the body as a sediment (*faex* or *ypostasis*) in the blood, is not necessarily bad. Because of its greater earthiness and density, melancholy is required to thicken the blood and to nourish the melancholy members of the body, like bone and, generally, the skeleton. Superfluous melancholy is supposed to be drawn to the spleen to cleanse the body.[16] As a natural residue, the melancholy humor may account for

---

13. "quando hec vene fluunt debito modo preservatur homo a multis egritudinibus qui ex tali sanguine grossa possunt causari ut mania, melancolia, quartana, lepra, morphea et malum mortuum quia sanguis talis si diu remanet aduritur et corrumpitur." *Thomae de Wratislavia Practica medicinalis: A Critical Edition of the "Practica medicinalis" of Thomas of Wroclaw, Prémontré Bishop of Sarepta (1297–c. 1378)*, 72, ed. Theodore James Antry (Warsaw: Polish Academy of Sciences Press, 1989), 279.

14. John Ardenne, *Treatises of Fistula in Ano, Haemorrhoids, and Clysters*, ed. D'Arcy Power, Early English Text Society 139 (London: Oxford University Press, 1910; repr. 1968), 57.

15. Moses Gaster, "The History of the Destruction of the Round Table as Told in Hebrew in the Year 1279," in *Studies and Texts in Folklore, Magic, Mediaeval Romance, Hebrew Apocrypha and Samaritan Archaeology*, 3 vols. (New York: KTAV, 1971), 2: 942–64, citing 947. Cf. *King Artus: A Hebrew Arthurian Romance of 1279*, ed. and trans. Curt Leviant (Syracuse, N.Y.: Syracuse University Press, 2003); Paul R. Rovang, "Hebraizing Arthurian Romance: The Originality of Melech Artus," *Arthuriana* 19, no. 2 (2009): 3–9.

16. Albert the Great, *De animalibus* 3.2.3.117–18, vol. 15, 328 (SZ 1: 401).

FIGURE 1. A friar preaching a (conversionary) sermon to *Synagoga* and a synagogue elder, from a fourteenth-century French Franciscan missal.

FIGURE 2. The circumcision of Isaac (top) replaced by baptism (below), from the thirteenth-century *Bible moralisée*.

FIGURE 3. Historiated initial depicting a hook-nosed Jew circumcising boys, from "The Bible of Robert De Bello," made for Robert de Bello, abbot of the Benedictine abbey of St. Augustine, Canterbury, 1224–53. This polemical image appears at the beginning of the book of Joshua, which later describes Joshua circumcising the Israelites.

FIGURE 4. Jesus healing a leper (cf. Matt. 8:2), from the *Vita gloriossime virginis Mariae atque venerabilis matris filii dei vivi veri et unici* (fourteenth-century, Venetian).

FIGURE 5. The leprous Constantine comforts the women: scenes from the lives of Emperor Constantine and Pope Sylvester I. Santi Quattro Coronati, Rome, interior: Chapel of Saint Sylvester (ca. 1246).

FIGURE 6. A crippled leper, seated, with a bell. Image taken from Pontifical, ca. 1400.

FIGURE 7. The Third Crusade of the Pastoureaux: Jews throwing their children from a tower, from the *Chroniques de France ou de St. Denis* (late fourteenth century).

FIGURE 8. Initial E(t), depicting a soldier of Antiochus slaying a Jew who refused to eat unclean meat and holds a pig's head on a platter. From a thirteenth-century French Bible, accompanying the text of 1 Maccabees.

FIGURE 9. Saturn eating his children, from a fifteenth-century English manuscript.

FIGURES 10A AND B. Initial showing the Jew Samuel's wife and son, who convert to Christianity (*left*), and the Jew Samuel ritually murdering the child martyr Adam of Bristol (*below*), from the "Passion of Adam of Bristol," likely a late thirteenth-century English text.

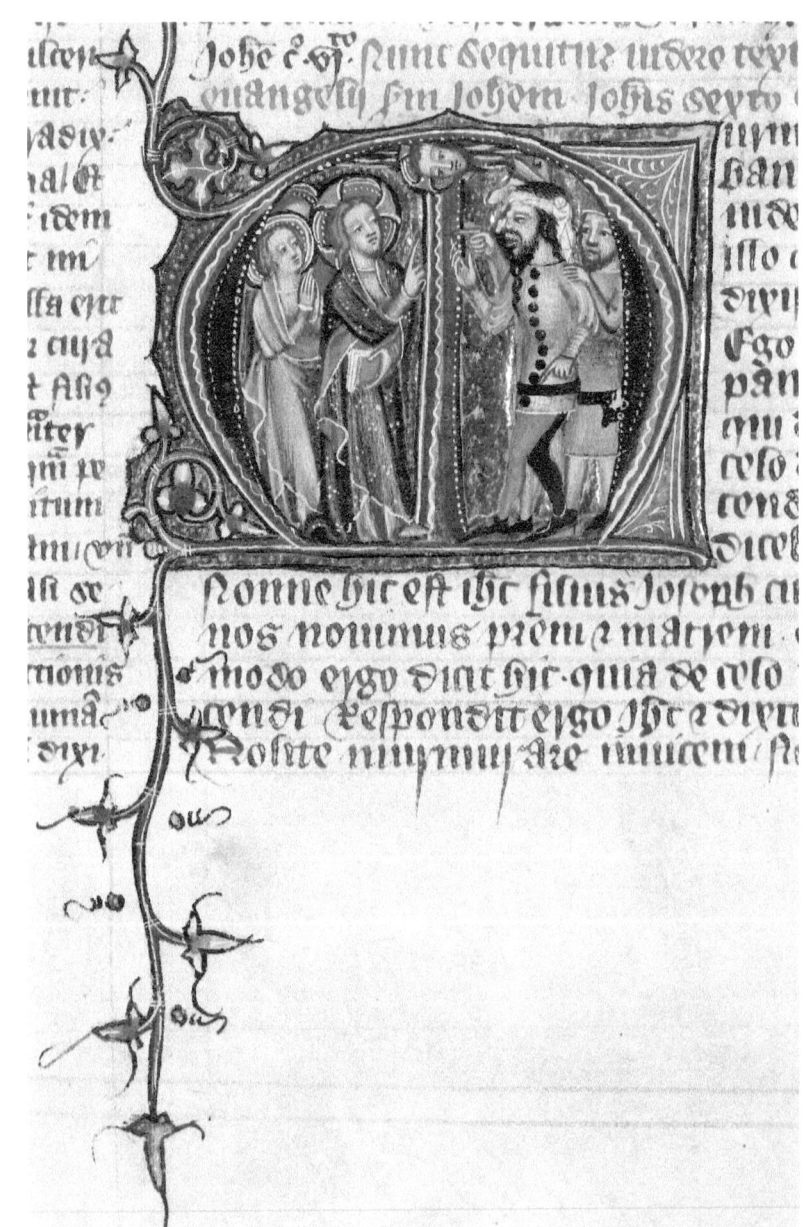

FIGURE 11. A hook-nosed Jew menacing Christ, from William of Nottingham's *Commentary on the Gospels* (fourteenth-century).

certain positive character traits. Albert the Great notes that natural melancholy, when it is not overabundant in the body, accounts for the studious disposition found among the greatest philosophers, and produces the heroic virtues. When there is too much of it, however, and when it passes from the spleen to other organs, it may have a deleterious effect; thus, it is said to oppress the heart, which is the hottest organ and the seat of the emotions, causing one to descend into a sort of depression marked by extreme sadness.[17] This melancholy or black bile, then, introduces a "black" mood, as well as fearfulness and trembling.[18] Although Martin Luther's claim that "all heaviness of mind and melancholy come of the devil," reflects late medieval inquisitorial judgments that emphasized demonic causation in melancholy, most medieval physicians and natural philosophers were far more interested in identifying natural causes for the distribution to other organs of too much natural melancholy, which can be eliminated from the body by a variety of means, including bleeding, sweating, urination, defecation, or vomiting.[19]

But when melancholy is unnatural, when it is drawn off from humors *other* than blood either by the body's excessive cold or heat, then it can introduce a wide variety of ailments.[20] One type of melancholy was known as hypochondriac melancholy because it was occasioned by inflammation of the parts in the hypochondria adjoining the stomach, from which sometimes noxious vapors are transmitted to the brain causing mania, a form of madness or insanity, for which some medieval surgical books recommended trepination as a therapy.[21] *Adust* or burned melancholy was also held responsible for cancer and leprosy, and again certain foods could contribute to these illnesses. One possible therapy for this type of melancholy was sexual intercourse. Ishāq ibn 'Imrān notes that just as brute beasts appear gentle after coition, so too we may overcome

---

17. Albert the Great, *De animalibus* 1.2.2.129, vol. 15, 47 (*SZ* 1: 94); 3.2.3.121, vol. 15, 330 (*SZ* 1: 403–4).

18. For the "blackness" of melancholy, see the useful work of François Azouvi, "The Plague, Melancholy and the Devil," *Diogenes* 108 (1979): 112–30.

19. Martin Luther, *Table Talk or the Familiar Discourse of Martin Luther* 634, trans. William Hazlett (London: David Bogue, 1848), 270. Luther's view that melancholy states were demonically inspired conforms to much later medieval literature, e.g., Henricus Institoris, *Malleus Maleficiarum* 1, q. 5, as well as the work of Reformation physicians, like Johan Weyer. On the latter, see "Melancholy, Witches, and Deceiving Demons," in *The Nature of Melancholy: From Aristotle to Kristeva*, ed. Jennifer Raden (Oxford: Oxford University Press, 2000), 95–106.

20. Albert the Great, *De animalibus* 3.2.3.119–20, vol. 15, 329–30 (*SZ* 1: 402–3).

21. Roger Frugard, *Chiurgia* 1.26, in Hunt, *Anglo-Norman Medicine*, 1: 53.

the frenzy or rage sometimes associated with *adust* melancholy through intercourse.[22] Christian medieval medical authorities, including Constantine the African, author of a text entitled *On Intercourse* (*De coitu*), also remark on the beneficial therapeutic effects of sexual activity for melancholy.[23] Some recommended intercourse as a palliative or even a (homeopathic?) cure for leprosy, while others recommended abstinence as a therapy more in harmony with theological views and caution the leper to avoid intercourse altogether.[24] The tension between these two prescriptions is clearest perhaps in the fourteenth-century surgical text attributed to Johannes Mesuë and said to have been translated from Arabic to Latin by one Ferrarius Judaeus. According to this text, the best remedy for the leper is castration—the very prescription employed by the late eleventh-century bishop of London, Hugh de Orival—followed by monthly purging and phlebotomy. At the very same time (although not for the same patient!) the text recommends sexual intercourse as a possible therapy.[25]

Although some sources recommend sexual intercourse as a therapy for melancholy, the melancholic—like the leper—may sometimes suffer impotence. The lengthy late thirteenth-century Hebrew moralizing fable of Isaac ibn Sahula, the *Meshal Haqadmoni,* proclaims of the individual in whom black bile dominates, "Feeble is his urge to copulate."[26] Similarly, the early fourteenth-century Latin *Book on Complexions* (*Liber de complexionibus*) allows that the melancholic's coldness makes it difficult

22. Isḥāq ibn ʿImrān, *Maqāla fī l-Mālīhūliyā*, 185, Basle ed. 293[393]. As Peter Pormann has pointed out, al-Rāzī shares this view, which is transmitted from Greek medical sources, in his *On Sexual Intercourse, its Harmful and Beneficial Effects*. See "Al-Rāzī (d. 925) on the Benefits of Sex. A Clinician Caught between Philosophy and Medicine," in *O ye gentlemen: Arabic Studies on Science and Literary Culture in Honour of Remke Kruk* (Leiden: Brill, 2007), 115–27.

23. For Constantine the African's *De coitu* in translation, see *Medieval Medicine: A Reader*, ed. Faith Wallis (Toronto: University of Toronto Press, 2010), 511–23, citing cap. 10, p. 518. Also see *Magistri Salernitani nondum editi*, 85; Rufus of Ephesus, *On Melancholy,* trans. Peter E. Pormann (Tübingen: Mohr Siebeck, 2008), 61. For a discussion of conflicting views held by theologians and Constantine the African on therapeutic intercourse (and other topics), see especially Monica H. Green, "Constantinus Africanus and the Conflict between Religion and Science," 47–69; and Danielle Jacquart, "Medical Explanations of Sexual Behavior in the Middle Ages," in *Homo Carnalis: The Carnal Aspects of Medieval Human Life,* ed. Helen Rodnite Lemay (Binghamton: State University of New York at Binghamton, 1990), 1–21, esp. 11–15.

24. For the view that coitus does *not* cure or ameliorate leprosy, see Theodorich Borgognoni, *The Surgery of Theodoric*, 2: 172; and, Bernard of Gordon, *Lilium medicinae* 1.22, p. 108.

25. Johannes Mesuë, the Younger, *Die angebliche Chirurgie des Johannes Mesuë jun.* 3.66, ed. Julius Leopold Pagel (Berlin: August Hirschwald, 1893), 129.

26. Isaac ibn Sahula, *Meshal Haqadmoni: Fables from the Distant Past, A Parallel Hebrew-English Text,* 2 vols., 2, lns. 1097–98, ed. and trans. Raphael Loewe (Oxford: The Littmann Library of Jewish Civilization, 2004), 1: 253 (English) and 254 (Hebrew).

for him to be roused to sexual desire.²⁷ It is not coincidence that canonists regard *frigidity* as a cause of sexual impotence, albeit one difficult to diagnose.²⁸ Moreover, because of his dryness, the melancholic can barely perform the act to ejaculate the moist sperm. Yet he can alter his complexion and increase the natural heat of the body with proper foodstuffs and wine, so much so that in the end he can increase seven-fold the ejaculation of sperm, whereas otherwise he will only be capable of ejaculating once or twice.²⁹ Nevertheless, as Jacquart and Thomasset remark, although the melancholic is often depicted as impotent, "he is also characterized by an unbridled longing, and a twisted judgment which impels him to seek, under the impetus of violent desire, the qualities that he lacks. If he is not impotent, he will be lustful."³⁰ In this way, the qualities of the woman, the leper, and the melancholic are conjoined.

It is this same melancholy complexion found among Jews that, for medieval physicians, explains why nature operates in them specifically to purge this melancholy superfluity through bleeding hemorrhoids. Medieval medicine and culture often seem preoccupied with hemorrhoids, and although they were sometimes viewed as a divine punishment found among Christians of questionable faith or character, they were more frequently identified with Jews.³¹ The link between their melancholy complexion and bleeding hemorrhoids sometimes led to the assertion that bleeding hemorrhoids are, in essence, a Jewish disease, a notion that will be transmitted to early modern culture.³² Not only did learned Jewish physicians like Maimonides give special attention to treatment for hem-

27. Seyfert, "Ein Komplexionentext einer Leipziger Inkunabel ... und seine handschriftliche Herleitung," 290.

28. Thomas of Chobham, *Summa Confessorum* art. 4, dist. 2, q. 7a, cap. 22, fol. 36va, pp. 185–86. Thomas explains that if a woman alleges that her husband is frigid (*frigidum*) and he dissents, they should be put together in the same bed after they have enjoyed food and drink, and "knowledgeable women" (*sagaces mulieres*) should observe them for several nights. If the man's member remains useless and dead, as it were (*si semper fuerit inventum membrum viri inutile et quasi mortuum*), then the marriage can be annulled.

29. Seyfert, "Ein Komplexionentext einer Leipziger Inkunabel ... und seine handschriftliche Herleitung," 290.

30. Jacquart and Thomasset, *Sexuality and Medicine in the Middle Ages,* 143.

31. E.g., the German anti-King Henry (Raspe), who is said to have died from hemorrhoids in Wartburg castle in 1247. See *Annales Erphordenses fratrum Praedicatorum,* 101.

32. The eighteenth-century German physician Johann Adolf Behrends remarked that "nowhere are more inhabitants plagued with hemorrhoids than in the *Judengasse*." Susan Kassouf, "The Shared Pain of the Golden Vein: The Discursive Proximity of Jewish and Scholarly Diseases in the Late Eighteenth Century," *Eighteenth-Century Studies* 32, no. 1 (1998): 101–10, citing 102.

orrhoids, but even a Hebraico-French text from the thirteenth century provides a popular herbal remedy and instructions for treatment of hemorrhoids among Jews.[33]

As early as the late twelfth century the medieval physician Roger de Baron had identified bleeding from hemorrhoids in "some males" according to a monthly pattern as analogous to menstruation.[34] When others drew attention to parallels between bleeding hemorrhoids in Jewish males specifically and menstruation in females, there arose the contention that Jewish men menstruate, both as a natural result of their bodily condition and as a divine punishment for having slain the Christian messiah.[35] While in general medieval culture expressed little squeamishness when blood was shed in battle, an involuntary discharge or flux of blood—such as is found in menstruation or bleeding hemorrhoids—often generated horror and disgust.[36]

A few illustrations here will establish a connection between Jews and melancholy. A late medieval commentary (Commentary B) on Ps. Albert the Great's popular *On the Secrets of Women* (*De secretis mulierum*) notes that

> Melancholic males generate a good deal of black bile which is directed to the spleen, and then to the spine. From there it descends to other veins located around the last intestine which are called hemorrhoids. . . . This is found in Jews more than in others, for their natures are more melancholic.[37]

---

33. For the text from Cod. Paris 2342 (Richler, 1542), fol. 285r, see Kirsten A. Fudeman, *Vernacular Voices: Language and Identity in Medieval French Jewish Communities* (Philadelphia: University of Pennsylvania Press, 2010), 107. It seems suggestive that the text follows immediately after another treating amenorrhea.

34. Roger de Baron, *Practica maior* tr. 1, cap. 42, in *Cyrurgia Guidonis de Cauliaco, et Cyrurgia Bruni, Teodorici, Rolandi, Lanfranci, Rogerii, Bertapalie*, fol. 216va.

35. See especially my "Medieval Roots of the Myth of Jewish Male Menses," *Harvard Theological Review* (2000): 241–63. Also see Willis Johnson, "The Myth of Jewish Male Menses," *Journal of Medieval History* 24, no. 3 (1998): 273–95; David S. Katz, "Shylock's Gender: Jewish Male Menstruation in Early Modern England," *Review of English Studies* ns 50, no. 200 (1999): 440–62; and John L. Beusterien, "Jewish Male Menstruation in Seventeenth-Century Spain," *Bulletin of the History of Medicine* 73, no. 3 (1999): 447–56.

36. For an effort to differentiate the value attached to voluntary versus involuntary bleeding in medieval literature, see Peggy McCracken, *The Curse of Eve, the Wound of the Hero: Blood, Gender, and Medieval Literature* (Philadelphia: University of Pennsylvania Press, 2003). She discusses Jewish male menstruation on 102–4; see also Rachel Elior, "'Present but Absent,' 'Still Life,' and 'A Pretty Maiden who has no Eyes,': On the Presence and Absence of Women in the Hebrew Language, in Jewish Culture, and in Israeli Life," in *Streams into the Sea: Studies in Jewish Culture and Its Context*, ed. Rachel Livneh-Freudenthal and Elchanan Reiner (Tel Aviv: Alma College, 2001), 191–211.

37. Ps. Albert the Great, *Women's Secrets*, 74.

Elsewhere Albert the Great explains the special relationship between Jews and bleeding hemorrhoids with reference to diet:

Hemorrhoids are caused by a superfluity of gross blood, because when such blood is abundant in the body it descends below, namely to the womb, where there are a number of veins, and then often one or two of these veins burst and the blood sometimes flows on account of this opening of their veins. This occurs according to nature especially among people who thrive on gross and salty nourishment, *like the Jews*.[38]

Other foods too were identified as "melancholy," including pears, apples, peaches, milk and cheese, salted meat, venison, rabbit, beef and goat meat.[39] Jews would be more likely to eat quantities of salted meat, since salting meat is a common way to remove the nonvenous blood in order to render the meat kosher. The Jews' observance of the dietary laws, then, likely contributed to the contention that they have a melancholy complexion.

A similar account is present in a quodlibetal disputation from the arts faculty at the University of Paris found in MS Bibl.Nat. lat. 16089 and edited by Peter Biller. One quodlibet (a genre explored only recently for medieval perceptions of Jews)[40] contains the response of either Henry the German or Henry of Brussels to a question posed about Jews, namely "Whether Jews suffer a flux of blood." The response is worth recording here at some length:

It was asked whether Jews suffer a flux of blood.... Jews have a flux of blood of the haemorrhoids, and the first cause of this, is that physicians say that a flux of blood is caused by gross indigested blood which nature purges. This

---

38. "Haemorroidae causantur ex superfluitate sanguinis grossi, quia quando talis sanguis abundat in corporem descendit inferius, ubi est pluralitas venarum, scilicet in matrice, et tunc frequenter rumpitur una vena vel duae, et tunc fluit sanguis propter apertionem earum venarum aliquando. Unde illud maxime accidit viventibus ex nutrimento grosso et salso, sicut Iudeis, per naturam." Albert the Great, *Quaestiones super de animalibus* 9.7, p. 206 (QDA, 310). Elsewhere, at his *De animalibus* 22.2.1.48(33), vol. 16, 1375 [SZ 2: 1474], he identifies meats that are cold and dry as a cause for hemorrhoids. On the prevalence of hemorrhoids among Jews causing in them a menstrual flow, note too that this notion survived among physicians into the modern era, as evidenced by the fact that Abbé Grégoire must refute it at the end of the eighteenth century. See the excerpt from his "An Essay on the Physical, Moral and Political Reformation of the Jews" in *The Jew in the Modern World: A Documentary History*, 2nd ed., ed. Paul Mendes-Flohr and Jehuda Reinharz (New York: Oxford University Press, 1995), 52.

39. Harington, *Regimen Sanitatis Salerni: The School of Salernum*, 25; Bernard of Gordon, *Lilium Medicinae* 1.22, pp. 88–89.

40. See especially Gilbert Dahan, "Juifs et judaïsme dans la littérature quodlibétique," in Cohen, *From Witness to Witchcraft: Jews and Judaism in Medieval Christian Thought*, 221–45.

abounds more in Jews because for the most part they are melancholics. [They are melancholics] because the melancholic shuns dwelling and assembling with others and likes cut off or solitary places. However, Jews naturally withdraw themselves from society and from being connected with others, as is patent, therefore they are melancholics. Item, they are pallid, therefore they are of melancholic complexion. Item, they are naturally timid, and these three are the contingent properties of melancholics, as Hippocrates says. But he who is melancholic has a lot of melancholic blood, and manifestly must have a flux of blood, but Jews are of this sort. I prove this, because they use roast foods and not boiled or cooked [cooked here means in a way other than roasting or frying], and these are difficult to digest, as is said in the fourth book of the *Meteora*. Item, they have roast fat, such as oil, etc., and these are difficult to digest.... Item, they do not have blood-letting, or very little, therefore they emit blood through the outside pores, etc.[41]

This university exercise from c. 1300, then, expands upon the scientific explanation already offered by Albert the Great. The Parisian master who responds during the quodlibetal disputation locates the cause of

41. "Consequenter queritur utrum iudei paciuntur fluxum. Arguitur quod non, quia xpistiani et aliqui iudei sunt eiusdem complexionis, ergo etc. Oppositum patet ex veritate quia illi leccatores paciuntur fluxum ut in pluribus. Ad quaestionem dicendum quod iudei habent fluxum sanguinis hemoreidarum. Et cause est prima quia dicunt medici quod fluxus sanguinis causatur ex sanguine grosso indigesto quem [que MS] natura purgat. Sed isrte [istis MS] magis habundat in iudeis quia ipsi sunt melancolici ut in pluribus. Quia melancolicus fugit cohabitacionem et congregacionem et diligit loca secretaria vel solitaria; sed iudei naturaliter retrahunt se a societate et coniuncti [possibly recte coniungi] cum aliis ut patet, ergo sunt melancolici. Item, pallidi sunt, ergo melancolice complexionis. Item, timidi sunt naturaliter et hec tria sunt [supra? MS] accidencia propria melancolicorum, ut dicit Ipocras. Sed ille qui multum est melancolicus multum habet de sanguine melancolico, et inde debet habere fluxum sanguinis, sed iudei sunt huiusmodi. Probo quia utuntur alimentis assatis et non elixatis non coctis, et hec sunt difficile digestibilia, ut dicitur 4to Me[teorum or -telologicorum]. Item, utuntur assarem [recte assatam] pinguedinem scilicet in oleo etc. et hec sunt difficile indigestibilia [recte digestibilia], ut patet manifestum sens[i; manifestym sensui perhaps recte ubi supra], ideo etc. . . . Item, ipsi non minuunt, vel valde parum, ideo ipsi emittunt sanguinem per poros extrinsecos, ideo etc." This provisional edition of the quodlibet is found in appendix B of Peter Biller's "Views of Jews from Paris around 1300: Christian or 'Scientific'?" in Wood, *Christianity and Judaism*, 205-7. The translation is also Biller's and appears on 192-93. Also see Peter Biller, "A Scientific View of Jews from Paris Around 1300," in *Gli Ebrei e le Scienze/The Jews and the Sciences*, vol. 9 of *Micrologus. Natura, scienze e società medievali* (Florence: SISMEL, 2001), 138-67, but esp. 161-62. The claim that Jews did not often bleed Jewish patients is certainly belied by Jewish sources. The twelfth- to thirteenth-century *Sefer Chasidim* ([461] 1006, pp. 259-60) acknowledges the practice of bloodletting in Jewish communities, and advises Jews to rest after phlebotomy. Over time the practice may have been overused: a popular seventeenth-century medical work, *Be'er Mayim Chaim*, by Issachar Bär Teller, complains that Jews "use bloodletting, without rhyme or reason," i.e., almost indiscriminately. See his *The Wellspring of Living Waters: A Medical Self-Help Book*, trans. Arthur Teller (New York: Tal Or Orth Publishers, 1988), 15.

hemorrhoids in a melancholy complexion found especially among Jews because of the nature of their diet. He expands on Albert's account by adding the psychological and physiological evidence of Jewish *melancholia*: namely, timidity, pallor, and a certain anti-social disposition. In a commonplace of medieval medicine, Constantine the African, citing Hippocrates, had earlier maintained that fear and sadness are twin signifiers of a melancholy disposition.[42] A text from Salerno, citing Galen, notes that "melancholy is an infection of the brain that fear and sadness have generated. Thus it is no surprise that melancholics are fearful, since they carry within themselves the cause of fear."[43]

For medieval theologians, however, such fear and sadness were both indicators of a physical illness, such as melancholy, and a spiritual defect. As a spiritual defect, sadness in particular found expression as the sin of *acedia*, a type of despair or dejection that brought on a culpable spiritual idleness.[44] Raymund Lull (d. 1315) linked both *acedia* and avarice (another vice commonly attributed to Jews) to melancholy.[45] For Thomas Aquinas, such sadness in melancholics can deprive the sufferer of the use of reason.[46] By the later Middle Ages melancholy was widely held responsible for both Judas's avarice and his suicide, and in artistic representation Judas came to stand for melancholic despair.[47]

42. "Haec duo accidentia melancholiae sunt propria. Unde in aphorismis Hippocrates: Timorem et tristitiam diu patiens, melancholiam intelligitur habere passionem." Constantine the African, *Theorices* 9.8 (Basel: Henri cum Petrum, 1536), 3: 250. Albert the Great, in his commentary on Aristotle's *De anima*, also identified baseless fear and timidity as traits of the melancholic. *De anima* 1.1.6, p. 13.

43. "Melencholia est infectio cerebri quam timor et tristitia generaverunt. Unde non mirum si melencholici timent, cum causam timoris secum portent." *Magistri Salernitani nondum editi*, p. 84.

44. See S. W. Jackson, "Acedia the Sin and Its Relationship to Sorrow and Melancholy in Medieval Times," *Bulletin of the History of Medicine* 55 (1981): 172–85; and Christoph Flueler, "Acedia und Melancholie im Spätmittelalter," *Freiburger Zeitschrift für Philosophie und Theologie* 34, no. 3 (1987): 379–98.

45. Raymund Lull, *Liber de uirtutibus et peccatis siue Ars maior praedicationis* dist. 4, sermo 48, ln. 44f., ed. F. Dominguez Reboiras and A. Soria Flores, CCCM 76 (Turnholt: Brepols, 1987). Noel L. Brann, however, shows that by the sixteenth century Battista da Crema had linked acedia not to melancholy but to phlegm. See Noel. L. Brann, "Is Acedia Melancholy? A Re-examination of This Question in the Light of Fra Battista da Crema's *Della cognitione et vittoria di se stesso* (1531)," *Journal of the History of Medicine* 34, no. 2 (1979): 180–99.

46. Thomas Aquinas, *Summa theologica* 1.2, q. 37, resp. obj. 3.

47. See Raymund Klibansky, Erwin Panofsky, and Fritz Saxl, *Saturn and Melancholy: Studies in the History of Natural Philosophy, Religion and Art* (Nendeln, Liechtenstein: Kraus; repr. 1979), 121 and 286; Moshe Barasch, "Despair in the Medieval Imagination," *Social Research* 66, no. 2 (1999): 565–76, but esp. 568–70.

When the melancholy humor is concentrated in the brain, and in particular in its central chamber,[48] it may produce as well mental illness (*alienatio mentis*), delusions, a loss of reason,[49] and misanthropy.[50] While in the seventh century Isidore of Seville confirmed that "those men are called melancholics that flee from human society,"[51] the link to antisocial behavior recalls the ancient canard of the Jews' misanthropy recorded already in Josephus's *Against Apion,* composed in the last decade of the first century, and repeated by Tacitus.[52] When this particularly "smoky" melancholy vapor ascends to the brain, it causes mental confusion, like too much wine.[53] It may lead to nightmares or even waking hallucinations, and a foul odor.[54]

Characteristics of melancholics such as timidity and pallor were also understood by medieval authors to be "womanish." As women may occasionally exhibit masculine traits, however, so men may display the characteristics of women.[55] The psychological traits attached to melan-

48. Bartholomew the Englishman distinguishes between mania, which, following Constantine the African, he views as an infection of the anterior cell of the brain with injury to the imagination, and melancholy, which is an infection of the central cell of the brain with loss of one's reason. See his *De proprietatum rerum* 7.5.

49. Constantine the African, *Theorices* 9.8, 3: 249.

50. The seventh-century Byzantine physician Paul of Aegina, whose work influenced Arab physicians, notes that "fear, despondency, and misanthropy" are common to all types of melancholy. See Francis Adams, *The Seven Books of Paulus Aegineta*, 3 vols. (London: 1844), 1: 383, quoted in Peter E. Pormann, "Theory and Practice in the Early Hospitals in Baghdad—Al-Kaškarī on Rabies and Melancholy," *Zeitschrift für Geschichte der Arabisch-Islamischen Wissenschaften* 15 (2002/2003), 214.

51. "melancholici appellantur homines qui et conuersationem humanam refugiunt." Isidore of Seville, *Etymologies* 10.177 (PL 82: 386A). Melancholy, for Isidore as for most medieval thinkers, is both a bodily humor and an illness. For discussion, see J. Pigeaud, "De la mélancholie et de quelques autres maladies dans les Etymologies IV d'Isidore de Séville," in *Mémoires V Textes médicaux latins antiques*, ed. G. Sabbah (Saint-Etienne: Publication de l'Université de Saint-Etienne, 1984), 87–108.

52. See Josephus, *Contra Apion* 1.34.309; 2.10.121–23 (see Josephus, *The Life Against Apion*, trans. H. St. J. Thackeray, in *Works*, 10 vols. [Cambridge, Mass.: Harvard University Press, 1976], 1: 287, 341); Tacitus, *Histories* 5.5, pp. 180–81. For the charge of misanthropy directed against the Jews in antiquity, see the lengthy account in Feldman, *Jew and Gentile in the Ancient World*, 125–49.

53. "Fumosior est enim nigra colera quolibet alio humore et similes effectus habet vino quod similiter fumosum est." David of Dinant, *Davidis de Dinanto Quaternulorum Fragmenta* 7.17.

54. Albert the Great, *Summa theologiae* tr. 8, q. 30, membrum 2, Ed. Borgnet 32, 328. Albert and others referred these hallucinations to demonic influence.

55. According to the anonymous Latin *Physiognomnia*, the primary distinction in the study of physiognomy is between a masculine type and a feminine type, atlhough these

choly—timidity and an anti-social disposition—tend to intensify and reinforce social and economic roles permitted to Jews, who were increasingly separated from the majority Christian culture by royal or ecclesiastical legislation and required special "protection."

Bernard of Gordon's influential *Lily of Medicine* (*Lilium medicinae*; c. 1303), helps to confirm the depiction of Jews as both melancholy and "womanish." According to Bernard:

> Jews suffer an immoderate flow of blood from hemorrhoids, for three reasons: generally, because they are in idleness, and for that reason the melancholic superfluities are gathered. Second, they are generally in fear and anxiety, and for this reason melancholic blood is increased, according to this [saying] of Hippocrates: "Fear and timidity, if they have a lot of time [to work], generate the melancholic humor." Third, this occurs as a divine punishment, according to [the text], "And he struck them in their posteriors and gave them over to perpetual opprobrium."[56]

The addition of idleness as a quality associated with Jews is significant. As indicated above, their idleness is linked to melancholy. Idleness, however, implied a negative judgment about the Jews' economic activities as well, which depended not on manual labor but often on usury. According to Nicholas of Cusa (d. 1464), "an excess of covetous melancholy ... gives rise to the most varied pestilences in the body—usury, fraud, deceit, theft, pillage, and all the arts by which great riches are won not by work but only by a certain deceitful craftiness."[57]

Similarly, idleness was a characteristic assigned to women's cold, phlegmatic complexion and reinforced their social and economic roles. Women were characterized as both sedentary and harmed by manual labor or excessive exercise. Constantine the African explains that "among

---

need not correspond, the author remarks, to the division between the sexes. Ian Repath, "Anonymous Latinus, *Book of Physiognomy*," 3, in Swain, *Seeing the Face, Seeing the Soul*, 557. For a very useful discussion of masculine and feminine characteristics, see especially Joan Cadden's *Meanings of Sex Difference in the Middle Ages*, 201–9, and 212–15.

56. "Iudei ut plurimum patiuntur fluxum haemorrhoid. propter tria, et quia communiter sunt in ocio, et ideo congregantur superfluitates melancholicae. Secundo, quod communiter sunt in timore et anxietate, ideo multiplicatur sang. melancholicus, iuxta illud Hipp. Timor et pusilanimitas si multum tempus habuerint, melancholicum faciunt hum. Tertio quia hoc ex ultione divina, iuxta illud. Et percussit eos in posteriori dorsi, opprobrium sempiternum dedit illis." *Lilium medicine* 5.21, fol. 77r. Cf. Luke E. Demaitre, *Doctor Bernard de Gordon: Professor and Practicioner*, Studies and Texts 51 (Toronto: Pontifical Institute of Mediaeval Studies, 1980), 9.

57. Nicholas of Cusa, *Opera*, 3 vols. (Paris, 1514; repr. Frankfurt: Minerva, 1962), fol. 75v, cited in Klibansky, *Saturn and Melancholy*, 119–20.

all animals, the males are hotter and dryer [in complexion] than the females. Therefore the females are colder and more moist.... [And] from the fact that their hands are idle, women are shown to be colder."[58] In a circular explanation, then, women were judged to be naturally phlegmatic because they are idle, and their idleness is a sign of a phlegmatic or a melancholy—that is, cold—complexion. The late-medieval *Diverse Anatomical Problems* (*Problemata varia anatomica*) promotes as well the link between melancholy Jews and phlegmatic women, adding that because Jews do not perform (manual) labor and therefore appear idle, like women, they have a cold, melancholic complexion, and menstruate, like women:

Why do Jews indiscriminately [*indifferenter*] suffer this flux [of blood]? One should reply first of all theologically, because at the time of Christ's passion they cried out, "Let his blood." [cf. Matt. 27:25] One should reply in another way, and more according to nature, that Jews eat phlegmatic and cold foods, for many good meats are forbidden to them in their law; [and] from their meats melancholic blood is generated, which is purged through the flux of haemorrhoids. The second natural reason is that Aristotle says in the book *De caelo et mundo* [II.7, 289a20-30] that motion makes heat; and motion is the cause of health, and heat causes digestion, as is evident through Aristotle in the fourth [book] of the *Meteora* [IV.2, 379b18] and the second book of *De anima* [II.4, 416a10]. But because the Jews are not in work or motion nor in converse with men, and also because they are in great fear because we avenge the passion of Christ our redeemer—all these things produce coldness and impede digestion. For this reason much melancholic blood is generated in them, *which is expelled or purged in them at menstrual time.*[59]

58. "In omnibus animalibus calidiores et sicciores sunt masculi quam foeminae. Foeminae ergo frigidiores et humidiores.... Manibus quietae, ex quibus frigidiores probantur esse." Constantine the African, *Theorices* 1.22, 3: 19.
59. "Quare Judei patiuntur indifferenter hunc fluxum? Respondetur primo theologice quia ipsi tempore passionis Christi clamabant: Sanguis eius super nos et super filios nostros! Ideo dicitur in psalmo: Percussit eos in posteriora dorsi. Aliter respondetur et magis naturaliter quia Judei vescuntur cibariis flegmaticis et frigidis quia multe carnes bone in lege eorum sunt prohibite eis ex quibus carnibus generatur sanguis melanconicus qui per fluxum emoroidarum expurgatur. Secunda ratio naturalis est quia dicit Aristoteles in libro de caelo (fol. 17r) et mundo quia motus facit calorem, et motus est causa sanitatis, et calor causat digestionem, ut patet Aristotelem quarto Metheorum et secundo de anima. Sed quia Judei non sunt labore neque in motu neque in conversatione hominum et etiam quia sunt in magno timore quia nos ulciscantur [ulciscamur] passionem Christi redemptoris nostri, hec omnia faciunt frigiditatem et impediunt digestionem. Ideo in eis generatur multus sanguis melanconicus qui in ipsis tempore menstruali expellitur seu expurgatur." Pseudo-Aristotle, *Problemata Varia Anatomica*, pp. 38-9. It may be noted too that although in general medieval medical texts regarded melancholy as occurring less often among women because of

This text establishes then the peculiar diet of Jews, their idleness, and their chronic anxiety from fear of Christian vengeance, as both causes and symptoms of their *melancholia*. Their diet, however, according to their flawed, literal interpretation of the dietary laws, was one that God had required of them under the Law; but it also seems that God required it of them in recognition of the Jews' peculiar nature. It is not at all clear, then, that if one were to change the Jew's diet, or lift him out of his idleness, or eliminate the cause of his anxiety through Christian baptism, that his melancholy complexion would be wholly changed.

By contrast, early modern medical texts sought to establish the social and environmental factors that caused certain illnesses or diseases to be more common in Jews. For example, in his chapter on "The Illnesses of Jews" in the larger *On the Diseases of Craftsmen* (*De Morbis Artificum Diatriba*), the University of Padua professor of medicine Bernardino Ramazzini (d. 1714) acknowledges that there is a hereditary form of leprosy (*Elephanticae labis*) that appears to afflict Jews. Yet he will explain most illnesses among urban Jews as occupational illnesses stemming both from their sedentary labor or their poor living conditions. Not surprisingly, many of the same afflictions attributed to Jews in older medieval texts reappear there: "almost all," he remarked, "are consumptive, melancholics, gloomy, and, for the most part, scabrous." These illnesses, he suggests, can be overcome by better working conditions and communal hygiene.[60] Despite his new optimism, we cannot disregard the fact that the association of Jews with melancholy had became a medical commonplace—so much so that the converso physician Amatus Lusitanus (1511–68), who returned to Judaism at the end of his life, when describing the melancholy condition of the Jewish patient and man of letters Azariah dei Rossi (b. c. 1514), noted that:

---

their moist complexion, nonetheless when it did arise it was more severe. See, for example, Peter E. Pormann, "The Art of Medicine: Female Patients and Practitioners in Medieval Islam," *Lancet* 373 (2009), 1598.

60. "omnes fere cachetici sunt, melancholici, tetrici, ac ut plurimum scabiosi." Bernardino Ramazzini, *De Morbis Artificum Diatriba* cap. 34: *De morbis Judaeorum*, reproduced and trans. in Heinrich Singer, *Allgemeine und spezielle Kranksheitlehre der Juden* (Leipzig: Benno Konegin Verlag, 1904), 134. Singer, himself a physician, notes at the bottom of 135 that it is unclear whether *Elephanticae labis* should refer to leprosy or rather to psoriasis. For Ramazzini's influence on eighteenth-century discussions of Jews and the illnesses caused by their social and economic activities, see also Kassouf, "The Shared Pain of the Golden Vein," 101–2.

Almost all Hebrews are by their nature black-biled [*atrabilis*], which chiefly results, I think, from a number of causes: first because they are in bondage and therefore live in fear and sadness and are consequently black-biled. According to Hippocrates's view (*Aphorisms*): "Those who suffer from fear and sadness for a long time develop black bile." Moreover they are all most studious; and following rigidly their religious laws, the Hebrews are accustomed to eat black-biled food. Especially in Italy they like to eat goose, duck, smoked beef, vegetables and much salted cheese; . . . and many other foods that produce black bile. It is for this reason that it is an acknowledged fact that all Hebrews are black-biled.[61]

The list of foods thought to generate black bile or melancholy is not consistent among medieval authors. In Roger Bacon's Latin edition of the popular *Secret of Secrets* (*Secretum secretorum*), we read that "indeed there are certain foods that generate melancholy, like bison meat (*caro bubali*), beef, mutton, and all those that are coarse (*grosse*) and dry and bitter."[62] Coarse, dry, or "cold" foods are not in themselves necessarily unhealthful. In general, for good health a person should eat the food that is appropriate to his complexional nature: for example, if the body is dense and dry, let him eat light or subtle, moist food. Also, one's diet should be appropriate to the season. Since the summer is hot and dry, foods that are cold and moist will be most appropriate, operating on the principle that contraries are cured by contraries (*contraria contrariis curentur*).[63] For this reason, Thomas of Cantimpré recommends

---

61. Amatus Lusitanus, *Curationum medicinalium centuriae* 42, quoted in Harry Friedenwald, *The Jews and Medicine: Essays*, 2 vols. (Baltimore: Johns Hopkins University Press, 1944), 2: 395. In Amatus Lusitanus's published patient case histories, known as the *Centuriae*, melancholy is a frequent complaint and therefore is addressed often by the author. For discussion, see Eleazar Gutwirth, "Jewish Bodies and Renaissance Melancholy: Culture and the City in Italy and the Ottoman Empire," in *The Jewish Body: Corporeality, Society, and Identity in the Renaissance and Early Modern Period*, ed. Maria Diemling and Giuseppi Veltri (Leiden: Brill, 2009), 57–93. For Amatus Lusitanus's discussion of the influence of diet upon the Jews' melancholy, see esp. 77, 85–89. For a broader discussion of Amatus Lusitanus, see Eleazar Gutwirth, "Amatus Lusitanus and the Location of Sixteenth-Century Cultures," in *Cultural Intermediaries: Jewish Intellectuals in Early Modern Italy*, ed. David B. Ruderman and Giuseppi Veltri (Philadelphia: University of Pennsylvania Press, 2004), 216–38.

62. "Quaedam vero cibaria sunt que generant melancoliam, sicut caro bubali, vaccina, ovina, et omnes que sunt grosse et sicce et aspere." Roger Bacon, *Opera hactenus inedita*, fasc. 5: *Secretum secretorum* 2.21, p. 90, 70b. For the identification of the *bubali* as either a bison or the European wisent, see Albert the Great, *De animalibus* 22.2.1(13), vol. 16, 1355 (SZ 2: 1455–56). For another list of melancholic foods, including pears, apples, cheese, salted meat, beef, and goat, see Harington, *Regimen Sanitatis Salerni. The School of Salernum*, 25.

63. Roger Bacon, *Opera hactenus inedita*, fasc. 5: *Secretum secretorum* 2.11, p. 78, 103a.

lemons to those who have a hot complexion or live in a hot climate, since lemons are cold and dry and produce a tempering, melancholy humor.[64] But such foods will contribute to illness when consumed by individuals who already have a cold complexion, rendering them more imbalanced or distempered. Consequently, one must infer that it is not the Jews' diet per se that causes them to be in some sense diseased, but the fact that this diet has—by divine command—been prescribed for a people that already has a colder, drier, more melancholy complexion than others, forcing them into a diseased condition.

Diverse Anatomical Problems, also known as *Omnes homines,* which identifies the Jewish male's bloody flux with the menstrual cycle, also "en-genders" him in another way: Jews, like women, have a naturally cold complexion because they live in fear and are idle.[65] In fact, it is coldness that the phlegmatic complexion (cold and moist) and the melancholic (cold and dry) have in common. This idleness sometimes appears as a kind of somnolence[66] and, when accompanied by a pallor or whitening of the skin, indicates a number of melancholy illnesses, including leprosy.[67] Certainly a melancholy complexion falls far from the ideal, temperate complexion in one whose humors are properly balanced.

In one sense, all humans in the state of fallen nature fall short of a perfectly balanced complexion; this was one of the consequences of original sin. As William of Conches (d. c. 1150) notes,

the first human being was perfectly temperate, as he had equal shares of the four qualities. But after he had been driven out of the amenity of paradise and began to eat bread by the labor of his hands in the valley of tears and misery, his body began to dry out from this labor of his as well as the deprivations of food and sleep, his natural heat to fade away.... His descendants, therefore,

---

64. Thomas of Cantimpré, *De natura rerum (Lib. IV–XII): Tacuinum Sanitatis,* 318.

65. Interestingly, however, the medieval Jewish author of *The Treatise on Procreation* proclaims that although Jewish women have a complexion that is cold and wet (i.e., phlegmatic), Jewish men are "cold and dry" (i.e., melancholic), confirming thereby the determination of Christian medical texts. See Barkai, *A History of Jewish Gynaecological Texts in the Middle Ages,* 217.

66. The Venerable Bede remarks that the phlegmatic humor produces individuals who are slow, somnolent, and forgetful: "phlegmata tardos, somnolentos, obliviosos generant." Bede, *De temporum ratione liber* 35, p. 393.

67. Constantine the African remarks: "Quae significationes cum appareant morbos melancholicos nunciant sicut lentigines, morpheam nigram, lepram, maniam, mentis perditionem, dura apostema, cancer ... saliva de ore effluente, multis sputis, somno nimio, tumore facie, gravitate capitis, mutatione cutis in albedinem." *Theorices* 10.11, 3: 310.

born as they were from a corrupt ancestor, have all been corrupted, and never afterward has perfect health been found in humans.[68]

The loss of a tempered complexion introduced illness and, ultimately, death. Hildegard of Bingen (1098–1180) adds that Adam's blood was so modified by the fall that he developed superfluous humors. After the fall, the humors became unbalanced, a melancholy temperament dominated, and diseases arose.[69] Similarly, according to the *Sententiae divinae paginae* attributed to the "school" of Anselm of Laon (d. 1117), Adam's sin resulted in a weakening of his complexion, as well as our own, as a punishment for sin.[70] Such changes underscored the importance of medical knowledge in this *fallen* world, whereas some thirteenth-century thinkers concluded that physicians would have been unnecessary had Adam not sinned.[71] Nevertheless, the impact of original sin on our somatic constitution will vary among different groups or populations. As already noted, women, descended from Eve, will naturally have a phlegmatic complexion; Jews a melancholy complexion; whereas Christian males typically display the best, sanguineous (hot and moist) complexion. This seems to be because, as Ps. Albert the Great remarks, "a sanguineous complexion is nobler than a choleric or melancholy one."[72] It is therefore unsurprising

---

68. "Primus enim homo inter quatuor qualitates fuit temperatus. Sed postquam amoenitate paradise expulsus in ualle lacrimarum et miseriae in labore manuum suarum coepit uesci pane, suo labore uigiliis ieiuniis cepit desiccari atque naturalis calor extingui.... Omnes igitur ex eo nati, utpote ex corrupto, sunt corrupti, neque postea perfecta sanitas in homine fuit inuenta." William of Conches, *Dragmaticon*, 6.13.2–3, p. 227 (147, Ronca trans.). The *Dragmaticon Philosophiae* was likely composed between 1147–49, according to the translators (xx).

69. "Cum autem Adam transgressus est ... fel immutatum est in amaritudinem et melancholia in nigredinem impietatis." Hildegard of Bingen, *Causae et Curae*, 38, 18. For a translation of the relevant section from Hildegard's *Causae et curae*, or *Book of Holistic Healing* (c.1151–58), see *The Nature of Melancholy from Aristotle to Kristeva*, ed. Jennifer Raden (Oxford: Oxford University Press, 2000), 81ff. (reprinted from Hildegard of Bingen, *Holistic Healing*, trans. Manfred Pawlik, et al. [Collegeville, Minn.: The Liturgical Press, 1994]). For an insightful discussion of Hildegard's understanding of the introduction of noxious melancholy to the human complexion as a result of the fall, see Peter E. Pormann, "Melancholy in the Medieval World: The Jewish, Christian, and Muslim Traditions," in *Rufus of Ephesus On Melancholy*, ed. Peter E. Pormann (Tubingen: Mohr Siebeck, 2008), 183–86.

70. See Anselm of Laon, *Sententie divine pagine* 4, in *Anselms von Laon systematische Sentenzen*, fol. 91b, p. 25; and see p. 33.

71. See Joseph Ziegler's discussion of a quodlibet of James of Viterbo from the last decade of the thirteenth century in "Medicine and Immortality in Terrestrial Paradise," in *Religion and Medicine in the Middle Ages*, 201–42.

72. Ps. Albert the Great, *Quaestiones super Evangelium* 19.1.1, Ed. Borgnet 37, 42–43.

that an anonymous text found in the British Library's MS Egerton 843, entitled *Legitur in annalibus hebreorum,* identifies Jesus as having had a sanguine, Jovian complexion.[73] By contrast, John Trevisa (d. 1402), in his English translation of Bartholomew the Englishman's *On the Properties of Things* (*De proprietatibus rerum*), placed even phlegm above black bile, remarking that even "fleume is noblere þan colera or melancolia."[74]

In the hierarchy of the humors, then, melancholy appears at the very bottom. It affects the body and the mind. As a cold, dry, and "earthy" complexion, it weighs the mind down and seems to inhibit knowledge of the sciences or of heavenly things.[75] Moreover, melancholy is not infrequently associated with the devil and demonic possession. Albert the Great notes that Avicenna called the melancholy defect a demon, because it is especially through melancholy illnesses that demons disturb the intellect.[76] Moreover, a melancholy complexion enhances the impression made by images from the imagination but weakens the mind's ability to receive external, sensory impressions. For this reason and owing to this bad complexion, melancholics are often disturbed by horrible phantasms, even leading them to think that they see and speak with demons.[77] Raymond de Tarrega, the author of *On the Secrets of Nature, or, On the Fifth Essence* (*De secretis naturae sive quinta essentia*) written c. 1319, remarks that "demons are attached to human bodies because of bad disposition and corrupt humor, or because of melancholic infection which generates evil, black and horrible images in fantasy, and disturbs the intellect, for the demons habitually take on such forms."[78] It does not seem merely accidental that Robert of Soest (d. 1298), a scholar and canon of the church of Soest who converted to Judaism, is said to have abandoned his Christian faith only after succumbing to melancholy:

73. See Ziegler, "Text and Context: On the Rise of Physiognomic Thought," 171 n. 32.

74. Bartholomaeus Anglicus, *On the Properties of Things: John Trevisa's translation of Bartholomaeus Anglicus De proprietates rerum* 4.9, 1: 156, 21.

75. "Unde qui corpus habent terrestre grave et melancholicum scientiis intendere non possunt qui vero corpus habent leve igneum cholericum magis praeferunt." Adalboldus Ultraiectensis, *Ars musica,* cited in J. M. A. F. Smits Van Waesberghe, "Neue Kompositionen des Johannes von Metz (um 975)," in *Speculum musicae artis. Festgabe für Heinrich Husmann zum 60. Geburtstag am 16. Dez 1968,* ed. Heinz Becker and Reinhard Gerlach (Munich: Fink, 1970), 17.

76. Albert the Great, *Summae theologiae* 2, tr. 7, q. 29, pp. 317–18.

77. Albert the Great, *De homine,* p. 373, 65–75.

78. Raymond de Tarrega, *De secretis naturae sive quinta essentia* 2, cap. 6, quoted in Raphael Patai, *The Jewish Alchemists* (Princeton, N.J.: Princeton University Press, 1994), 201.

While [Robert] was still a person of notable authority, after succumbing to *melancholy*, he abandoned the Christian faith, associated with Jews and was circumcised, taken off to Frankfort and there instructed in [its] rituals. There, Judaizing over a period of many years, he was completely befouled. Finally, he died and is entombed in a vile, small vessel.[79]

BLOOD AND RITUAL MURDER

In this report, conversion to Judaism and Judaism itself appear as products of illness, while conversely conversion to Christianity restores health. If their melancholy is one cause for the hemorrhoidal or menstrual bleeding Jewish males were thought to suffer, the ramifications of such bleeding were extensive. As I have argued elsewhere, late medieval Christian culture proposed a link between this bloody flux in Jews and accusations of ritual murder.[80] Ritual murder accusations appear for the first time in the middle of the twelfth century in England, with the charge that Jews murdered young William of Norwich as part of a worldwide Jewish conspiracy against Christians, and in order to display visibly their contempt for the God of the Christians. Such accusations multiplied in England and in Europe thereafter.[81]

According to Thomas of Monmouth's *Life and Passion of St. William the Martyr of Norwich*, completed in 1172 or 1173, the Jews had crucified a young Christian boy, William, for rather vague religious purposes at the time of the Passover.[82] The conspiracy was allegedly revealed to Thomas

---

79. "Cum enim esset auctoritatis magne, tandem in melancoliam incidens fidem reliquit, Iudeis associatur, circumciditur, in Francfort abducitur et ibi cerimonialibus imbuitur. Et annis multis iudayzans sordescebat. Mortuus tandem et in vasculo vili concluditur." Albert Stuten, *Weltchronik des Mönchs Albert 1273/77-1454/56*, 195. Italics are mine.

80. Irven M. Resnick, "Medieval Roots of the Myth of Jewish Male Menses," *Harvard Theological Review* (2000): 241–63.

81. See Jörg R. Müller, "Erez gezerah—'Land of Persecution': Pogroms against the Jews in the *regnum Teutonicum* from c. 1280–1350," in *The Jews of Europe in the Middle Ages (Tenth to Fifteenth Centuries). Proceedings of the International Symposium Held at Speyer, 20–25 October 2002*, ed. Christoph Cluse (Turnholt: Brepols, 2004), 245–60.

82. Begun perhaps between 1150 and 1155, the work was completed in 1172/73. The text is found in Thomas of Monmouth, *The Life and Miracles of St.William of Norwich by Thomas of Monmouth. Now First Edited from the Unique Manuscript, with an Introduction, Translation and Notes* by Augustus Jessopp and M. R. James (Cambridge: Cambridge University Press, 1896). For the Jewish community of Norwich, see especially V. D. Lipman, *The Jews of Medieval Norwich* (London: Jewish Historical Society of England, 1968). For a very good study of the case of William of Norwich and the origins of the blood libel, see Gavin Langmuir, *Toward a Definition of Antisemitism* (Berkeley: University of California Press, 1990),

THE JEWS AND MELANCHOLY   195

by "certain Jews, who were afterwards converted to the Christian faith."[83] One of these may have been the monk Theobald, a convert from Judaism (if he lived at all), who instructed our author, Thomas, that

it was written that the Jews, without the shedding of human blood, could neither obtain their freedom, nor could they ever return to their fatherland. Hence it was laid down by them in ancient times that every year they must sacrifice a Christian in some part of the world to the Most High God in scorn and contempt of Christ, so that they might avenge their sufferings on Him; inasmuch as it was because of Christ's death that they had been shut out from their own country, and were in exile as slaves in a foreign land. Wherefore the chief men and Rabbis of the Jews who dwell in Spain assemble together at Narbonne, where the Royal seed [resides], and where they are held in the highest estimation, and they cast lots for all the countries which the Jews inhabit; and whatever country the lot falls upon, its metropolis has to carry out the same method with the other towns and cities, and the place whose lot is drawn has to fulfill the duty imposed by authority. Now in that year in which we know that William, God's glorious martyr, was slain, it happened that the lot fell upon the Norwich Jews, and all the synagogues in England signified, by letter or by message, their consent that the wickedness should be carried out at Norwich.[84]

---

chap. 9. For a discussion of various approaches to the origins of the blood libel, see David Berger, "From Crusades to Blood Libels to Expulsions: Some New Approaches to Medieval Antisemitism," Second Annual Lecture of the Victor J. Selmanowitz Chair of Jewish History, Touro College Graduate School of Jewish Studies (March 16, 1997). John M. McCulloh provides a detailed and informative discussion of the twelfth-century origins of the ritual murder charge in, "Jewish Ritual Murder: William of Norwich, Thomas of Monmouth, and the Early Dissemination of the Myth," *Speculum* 72 (1997): 698–740. For the date of Thomas of Monmouth's *Life*, see 706-9. McCulloh also argues that an independent source for information regarding the death of William of Norwich is evident in a German martyrology from before 1150, demonstrating that "the earliest extant documentary evidence, regarding not only his [William's] death but also his veneration as a saint, comes not from England but from Bavaria." (728) For the popularity of the Norwich account, see also Friedrich Lotter, "*Innocens virgo et martyr*: Thomas von Monmouth und die Verbreitung der Ritualmordlegende im Hochmittelalter," in *Die Legende vom Ritualmord: zur Geschichte der Blutbeschuldigung gegen Juden*, ed. Rainer Erb (Berlin: Metropol, 1993), 25–72. For the spread and development of the ritual murder charge in England in the second half of the twelfth century, see also Joe Hillaby, "The Ritual-Child-Murder Accusation: Its Dissemination and Harold of Gloucester," *Jewish Historical Studies* 34 for 1994-96 (1997): 69–109; and also Georg R. Schroubek, "Zur Tradierung und Diffusion einer europäischen Aberglaubensvorstellung," in *Die Legende vom Ritualmord*, 239–52. Finally, for discussion of Thomas's *vita* of William of Norwich as a rhetorical template for later ritual murder narratives, see Denise L. Despres, "Adolescence and Sanctity: The Life and Passion of Saint William of Norwich," *Journal of Religion* 90, no. 1 (2010): 33–62.

83. "A iudeis enim quibusdam ad fidem christianam postea conversis." *The Life and Miracles of St.William of Norwich by Thomas of Monmouth* 1.2, p. 15.

84. Thomas of Monmouth, *The Life and Miracles of St.William of Norwich by Thomas of Monmouth* 2.11, p. 94.

Thomas's claim that the conspiracy originated in Narbonne, "where the Royal [seed] resides," is itself interesting.[85] Certainly, it acknowledges the prominence of the Jewish community there, which produced exegetical schools in the eleventh and twelfth centuries so important that it may reasonably be thought to have had authority among the French Jews that settled in England in the twelfth century.[86] More curious, however, is the fact that Thomas seems untroubled that individuals like Theobald may have had a particular interest in uncovering the "wickedness" of the Jews to establish their own *bona fides,* that is, both their own "good faith" and their credentials as trustworthy Christians. To the contrary, Thomas insists that Theobald's evidence is all the more reliable because it has been provided by a "converted enemy" who had once had access to the Jews' secrets.[87] The role of Jewish converts to Christianity as sources for such accounts remains to be studied fully. Nonetheless, in the accusation that Jews of Norwich had slain the boy William, the Jewish community did

---

85. Peter the Venerable alludes to this tradition as well in his *Adversus Judeorum inveteratam duritiem* cap. 4, p. 70, 78, written c. 1144–47. An English source may be William of Malmesbury's *De laudibus et miraculis Sanctae Mariae,* composed before the author's death in 1143. William remarks there that it has been said that the Jews have a "high pope" in Narbonne: "Denique non semel auditum est quod apud Narbonam habent summam papam, ad quam a iudaeis ex toto curritur orbe." See J. M. Canal, *El libro de Laudibus et Miraculis Sanctae Mariae de Guillermo de Malmesbury,* O.S.B. 1.2.14, in *Claretianum* 8 (1968): 71–242, citing 137. For discussion of this tradition of a Jewish ruler at Narbonne, see Aryeh Graboïs, "La dynastie des 'rois juifs' de Narbonne (XIIe–XIIIe siècle)," in *Narbonne. Archéologie et histoire,* vol. 2 of *Narbonne au moyen âge* (Montpelier: Fédération historique du Languedoc méditerranéen et du Roussillon, 1973), 49–54. Graboïs demonstrates that by the middle of the twelfth century both Jewish and Christian sources attest that a Jewish communal leader in Narbonne had assumed the title *Nasi* ("prince") and traced his—and his family's—lineage back to King David; it was commonly accepted that Charlemagne had confirmed the family in this "royal" title. It is not necessary to see in Thomas of Monmouth's remarks support for Zuckerman's more extravagant claims of a Jewish "king" in Narbonne [Arthur J. Zuckerman *A Jewish Princedom in Feudal France 768–900* (New York: Columbia University Press, 1972)]. Cf. Aryeh Graboïs, "Une Principaute Juive dans la France du Midi a l'Époque Carolingienne," in Graboïs, *Civilisation et société dans l'Occident médiévale* (London: Variorum, 1983), XV: 191–202. Although the title "king" of the Jews—attested in diplomatic sources—implied only seigneurial rank, among some non-Jews it became a source of complaint. For further discussion that located a *rex judaeorum* at Rouen, see Norman Golb, *The Jews in Medieval Normandy: A Social and Intellectual History* (Cambridge: Cambridge University Press, 1998), 202–7.

86. For the community of Francophone Jews in England, see R. C. Stacey, "Jews and Christians in Twelfth-Century England: Some Dynamics of a Changing Relationship," in *Jews and Christians in Twelfth-Century Europe,* ed. Michael A. Signer and John Van Engen (Notre Dame, Ind.: University of Notre Dame Press, 2001), 340–54.

87. Thomas of Monmouth, *The Life and Miracles of St.William of Norwich by Thomas of Monmouth* 2.11, p. 94.

have an important defender, namely Sheriff John of Chesney, who found no basis for the allegation. Thomas of Monmouth indicates that the sheriff's support had been "bought" by the Jewish community, thereby implicating the king's officer in the murder. For his role, Thomas insists, he suffered an appropriate divine punishment, which was foretold of the Jews as well, when they cried out "Let the innocent blood be upon us and upon our children." (Matt. 27:25) The sheriff's punishment for having thrown in his lot with the Jews was to suffer a flux of blood that dripped from his posterior (*per posteriora eius sanguis guttatim profluere inchoavit*) for two years, until his death.[88] The particular form of the sheriff's affliction recalls the Jews' propensity to suffer from bleeding hemorrhoids as a divine punishment.

Nearly at the same time that Thomas of Monmouth composed his text, Count Theobald V of Blois burned more than thirty Jews in 1171—both men and women—in response to a Christian accusation that Isaac b. Eleazar of Blois had killed a Christian child around Easter.[89] The Jewish victims include Pucellina, a Jewish woman sometimes alleged in later accounts to have had a romantic relationship with Theobald V.[90] To explain disappearances of Christian children in the years following, allegations of Jewish ritual murder spread. By 1255 this belief had been invoked to explain the death of young Hugh of Lincoln, leading King Henry III to confirm the allegation and to imprison ninety-two Jews in the Tower of London and then to execute nineteen Jews by hanging.[91] Geoffrey Chau-

---

88. Ibid., 2.15, p. 111. Note that Jessop and James translated this passage as "he began to suffer from internal haemorrhage," which obscures the fact that the sheriff's punishment is one that the Jews too were said typically to endure, namely, bleeding from the anus. Willis Johnson also made note of this, but drew, I believe the wrong conclusion, choosing to interpret the blood flow as a reenactment of the death of Judas and Arius. See Johnson, "The Myth of Jewish Male Menses," 280.

89. An account of the event was provided by Jewish leaders in Orleans; about twenty years later it was also recalled in a Hebrew chronicle of Ephraim ben Jacob (1132–96), which appears in Jacob Marcus's *The Jew in the Medieval World: A Source Book 315–1791*, rev. ed. (Cincinnati: Union of American Hebrew Congregations, 1938), 127–30; for discussion, see Israel Jacob Yuval, *Two Nations in Your Womb: Perceptions of Jews and Christians in Late Antiquity and the Middle Ages*, trans. Barbara Harshav and Jonathan Chapman (Berkeley: University of California Press, 2006), 190–95; and, Fudeman, *Vernacular Voices*, 60–88.

90. See, however, Susan L. Einbinder, "Pucellina of Blois: Romantic Myths and Narrative Conventions," *Jewish History* 12, no. 1 (1998): 29–46, where Einbinder argues that there was no romantic relationship between the two, but rather a business relationship stemming from Pucellina's role in money lending.

91. *Liber de antiquis legibus. Cronica maiorum et vicecomitum Londoniarum*, 23. For the

cer recalls the child martyr with the words "O younge Hugh of Lyncoln, slayn also with cursed Jewes."[92]

As such accusations spread, however, they also introduced charges that Jews harvested blood from the murdered, often crucified, Christian children.[93] There were as many motives for ritual murder as there were imagined uses for Christian blood. The blood, it was said, was used to anoint the doorposts of Jewish homes at the time of the Passover, mixed into the wine drunk at the Passover seder,[94] baked into Passover matzot or Purim cakes, given to the Jewish bride and bridegroom in the marriage ritual, or employed to anoint the bodies of Jews in danger of death.

---

death of Hugh of Lincoln, see Gavin Langmuir, "The Knight's Tale of Young Hugh of Lincoln," in Langmuir, *Toward a Definition of Antisemitism*, 237–62. Professor David Carpenter's reexamination of the role of King Henry III in these events is available at http://www.finerollshenry3.org.uk/ content/month/fm-01-2010.html and http://www.finerollshenry3.org.uk/ content/month/fm-02-2010.html.

92. Geoffrey Chaucer, "The Prioress's Tale," lns. 684–5, in *Canterbury Tales*, ed. A. C. Cawley (London: Dent, 1984), 381. Chaucer's Hugh was slain because he annoyed the Jews with his constant repetition of the *Alma redemptoris Mater*, a motif found also in Old French Marian devotional literature. See Peter-Michael Spangenberg, "Judenfeindlichkeit in den altfranzösischen Marienmirakeln," in *Die Legende vom Ritualmord*, 169–70. Consider too Denise Despres's remark that "anti-Judaism is integral to the development of an iconography of late-medieval Marian devotion." See her "Mary of the Eucharist: Cultic Anti-Judaism in Some Fourteenth-Century English Devotional Manuscripts," in Cohen, *From Witness to Witchcraft*, 376. William Jordan has even suggested that it was perceived Jewish affronts to Marian devotion that stimulated the attacks on the Talmud in Paris in the 1240s. See his "Marian Devotion and the Talmud Trial of 1240," in *Religionspräche im Mittelalter*, ed. Bernard Lewis and Friedrich Niewöhner (Wiesbaden: Otto Harrassowitz, 1992), 61–76.

93. Thomas of Cantimpré narrates that an old Christian woman sold a seven-year-old girl to the Jews in Pfortzheim in 1271, who beat her body and expressed her blood onto linen cloths. See Thomas of Cantimpré, *Miraculorum et exemplorum memorabilium sui temporis, libri duo* 2.29.22 (Douai: Bellerus, 1605), 305. Similarly, the *Annales Marbacenses* alleges that Jews murdered Christian children in 1236, near the Monastery of Fulda, and harvested blood from them as a healing remedy for an unnamed illness. See *Annales Marbacenses*, ed. Herman Bloch, MGH, SS rer. Germ. 9 (Hannover: Hahn, 1907), 98. An expanded account is found in the *Annales Erphordenses fratrum Praedicatorum*, 92, which nonetheless omits the detail that the Jews used the blood as a healing remedy. This ritual murder accusation prompted an investigation by the Emperor, Frederick II, to determine whether Jews really murder Christian children at the Passover; the Emperor judged such charges to be specious.

94. David Stern and a team of scholars from Germany and Israel are preparing an edition of a late fifteenth-century illustrated Passover Haggadah with a Latin prologue (forthcoming from Penn State University Press), found in Munich, Bayerische Staatsbibliothek Cod. Heb. 200. According to the Latin prologue, Jews not only use the blood of Christian infants for the preparation of matzot or unleavened bread, but also mix Christian blood into the Passover wine. My thanks to Professor Stern for allowing me to review the translation of the Latin prologue in advance of publication.

The blood had a multitude of useful applications and could serve as an aphrodisiac, as an analgesic to relieve the special pain that Jewish women were thought to experience during childbirth, or even as a perfume to eliminate the particular smell or odor commonly associated with Jews.[95]

Other Christian evidence, however, proposed that Jews *need* the blood of murdered Christian children because Jewish males are cursed with a variety of peculiar physical defects. One of those, as we have seen, entailed a monthly bloody flux. As Leon Poliakov noted, medieval Christian polemicists depicted Jewish men as "suffering from a thousand malignant afflictions that only Christian blood can cure.... They are born misshapen, they are hemorrhoidal and, men as well as women, afflicted with menses. From this point of view, they are women, that is, inframen."[96]

Nowhere is this last defect indicated more explicitly than in an early fourteenth-century astronomical treatise that declares "After the death of Christ all Jewish men, like women, suffer menstruation."[97] The implausible contention that, like women, Jewish males menstruate provided yet another motive for the alleged murders of Christian children: only with an infusion of Christian blood, Christian polemicists argued, did Jews believe they could replace and stem their monthly blood loss, thereby transforming twelfth-century accusations of ritual murder into a charge of ritual cannibalism.[98] As early as the thirteenth century, Thomas of Cantimpré (c. 1201–76), a Dominican friar born in Leeuw-Saint-Pierre near Brussels, explains:

95. For a useful survey of such uses, see Andreas Angerstorfer, "Jüdische Reaktionen auf die mittelalterlichen Blutbeschuldigungen vom 13.bis zum 16. Jahrhundert," in *Die Legende vom Ritualmord*, 134–35. Although Levitical legislation forbade Jews to consume blood, Christians were required to observe a lengthy period for penance after drinking blood or semen. See Robert of Flamborough, *Liber Poenitentialis* 5.6.3.335, p. 264.

96. Léon Poliakov, *The History of Anti-Semitism*, 4 vols., trans. Richard Howard (London: Elek Books, 1965), 1: 143. For the French edition, see *Histoire de l'antisémitisme*, 4 vols. (Paris: Calmann Lévy, 1955), 1: 160.

97. "post mortem Christi omnes homines Iudei ut mulieres menstrua patiuntur." From Cecco d'Ascoli's commentary on Sacrobosco's *De sphaera* (c. 1324). For the text, see Lynn Thorndike, *The Sphere of Sacrobosco and Its Commentators*, cap. 4, 40a (Chicago: University of Chicago Press, 1949), 409.

98. Angerstorfer provides useful evidence that Jews were aware of (and fashioned responses to) Christian accusations of ritual cannibalism. See his "Jüdische Reaktionen auf die mittelalterlichen Blutbeschuldigungen vom 13.bis zum 16. Jahrhundert," 139 and 143–47. For the weakness of the Jewish responses, however, see Israel Jacob Yuval, "'They Tell Lies: You Ate the Man,' Jewish Reactions to Ritual Murder Accusations," in Abulafia, *Religious Violence between Christians and Jews: Medieval Roots, Modern Perspectives*, 86–106.

With this it is seen why the Jews customarily spill Christian blood in every province in which they live. In fact, it has certainly been adequately demonstrated that they cast lots each year in every province for which city or town will deliver Christian blood to the other cities. For it is established by the holy Gospel, that when Pilate washed his hands and said: "I am innocent of the blood of this just man" [Matt. 27:24], the impious Jews cried out: "His blood be upon us and upon our children" [Matt. 27:25]. With respect to this, in a sermon which begins "On the Cross" the blessed Augustine seems to imply that there still runs a vein of evildoing through the children, through a stain of blood, because of the curse of the parents so that the impious progeny is tormented importunately by this [blood] flow without expiation, until, doing penance, he recognizes that he is guilty for the blood of Christ, and is healed. Moreover, I have heard that a certain very learned Jew who converted to the faith in our days said that there was some prophet of theirs, as it were, who prophesied at the end of his life to the Jews, saying: "Most assuredly," he said, "know you that you cannot be healed in any way from that shameful torment with which you are punished, except by Christian blood alone." The blind and impious Jews, always seizing upon this remark, began spilling Christian blood each year in every province, so that they might convalesce with such blood. And he [the convert] added: "they understood the remark badly," he said, "thinking it meant the blood of any Christian at all. But actually as soon as any one of us that is converted to the faith of Christ consumes that blood (as is fitting), which is spilled daily on the altar for the salvation of sinners, he is healed from that paternal curse."[99]

99. "Hinc igitur videndum est, cur Iudaei secundum consuetudinem, in omni provincia quam inhabitant, Christianum sanguinem fundant. Certissime enim compertum est, quod omni anno in qualibet provincia sortes mittunt, que civitas vel oppidum, Christianum sanguinem aliis civitatibus tradat. Constat quidem ex sancto Evangelio, quod Pilato lavante manus, et dicente: Mundus ego sum a sanguine iusti huius: Iudei impiissimi clamaverunt: Sanguis eius super nos et super filios nostros. Super quo beatissimus Augustinus in sermone quodam qui incipit, In cruce, innuere videtur, quod ex maledictione parentum currat adhuc in filios vena facinoris, per macula sanguinis; ut per hanc importune fluidam proles impia inexpiabiliter crucietur, quousque se ream sanguinis Christi recognoscat poenitens, et sanetur. Praeterea audivi quendam litteratissimum Iudeorum nostris temporis conversum ad fidem, dixisse: quendam quasi prophetam eorum in extremo vitae prophetasse Iudeis, dicentem, Certissime vos, inquit, scitote nullo modo sanari vos posse ab illo quo punimini verecundissimo cruciatu, nisi solo sanguine Christiano. Quod verbum caeci semper Iudaei et impii rapientes, induxerunt omni anno in omni provincia fundendum sanguinem Christianum, ut tali sanguine convalescant. Et addidit: Male, inquit, intellexerunt verbum, sanguinem intelligentes Christiani cuilibet; sed prorsus illum sanguinem, qui in salutem peccaminum quotidie funditur in altari, quem, quicunque nostrum conversus ad fidem Christi, sumpserit ut decuerit, mox sanatur ab illa maledictione paterna." Thomas of Cantimpré, *Miraculorum et exemplorum memorabilium sui temporis, libri duo* 2, cap. 29, 23, pp. 305–6. The sermon that Thomas attributes to Augustine is otherwise unknown. Equally unknown is the identity of the Jewish convert who provided this information. One is sorely tempted to think that it may have been the notorious Nicholas Donin.

Thomas of Cantimpré's explanation reflects the worldwide conspiracy theory introduced in Thomas of Monmouth's account approximately a century earlier. It was also transmitted to other Dominicans. In the early fourteenth century the Dominican Rudolph of Schlettstadt reiterates that

I heard from Jews that certain Jews—descended from those who cried out before Pilate at the time of Christ's passion "his blood be upon us and on our children"—flow every month with blood and often suffer dysentery (from which they frequently die). However, they [believe that they] are healed by the blood of a Christian who has been baptized in the name of Christ.[100]

Thomas of Cantimpré and Rudolph of Schlettstadt indicate, then, that Jews mistakenly seek *any* Christian blood rather than the blood of Christ offered in the Eucharist (which Jews neither could nor would consume) as a remedy for their curse. In this way they associated the infamous blood libel, ritual murder, and ritual cannibalism with this Jewish pathology, since Jews were accused of seeking the blood of Christians to replace the blood lost from hemorrhoidal or anal bleeding.[101]

Such charges became a part of official records of ritual murder trials, as in a case at Tyrnau in 1494, which records that "suffering from menstruation, both men and women alike, [the Jews] have noted that the blood of a Christian constitutes an excellent remedy."[102] Similarly at Endingen in 1470, the Jew Mercklin confessed under torture that "Jews need Christian blood because it has great healing power."[103] Not only was it alleged to heal hemorrhoids, but also epilepsy and various other infirmities. As a result, Jews are often depicted in late medieval Christian art harvesting the blood of Christian children.[104] Once again, however,

100. "Audivi a Judeis, quod quidam Judeorum, scilicet qui in passione Cristi clamaverunt coram Pilato: 'sanguis eius super nos et filios nostros,' quod omnes Judei, qui de eorum processerunt, singulis mensibus sanguine fluunt et dissenteriam sepius paciantur et ea ut frequencius moriuntur. Sanantur autem per sanguinem hominis Cristiani, qui nomine Cristi baptisatus est." *Historiae Memorabiles*, p. 65. This tale is retold also by Al[ph]onso de Espina, *Fortalitium fidei* 3.7.5, fol.144v-r.

101. For a brief discussion of the connection between a Jewish requirement for Christian blood and hemorrhoids, see Trachtenberg, *The Devil and the Jews*, 50 and 148.

102. Anton Bonfin, *Rerum Hungaricum Decades* dec. 5.4, cited by Poliakov, *The History of Anti-Semitism*, 1: 143, n. 13.

103. See R. Po-Chia Hsia, *The Myth of Ritual Murder: Jews and Magic in Reformation Germany* (New Haven: Yale University Press, 1988), 21, 138.

104. For several good illustrations from the fourteenth to fifteenth centuries, see Schreckenberg, *The Jews in Christian Art*, 273-5.

Christians insist that it is in fact only the blood of Christ and not any Christian blood whatsoever that can cure bodily afflictions.

A tale or *exemplum* in a late thirteenth-century English collection reports on a Jew in Germany of whom a Christian widow had become quite found. When he became ill and was near death, the widow took him the Eucharist and told him that if he would believe that beneath the qualities of the bread there existed the body of the Lord, he would immediately be cured. The Jew became angry, took a knife and stabbed the Host, whereupon it spurted and sprayed blood on the Jew. Once he was sprayed with the blood, he repented and believed and was cured of his physical illness as well.[105] Christ's blood heals not only a soul wounded by sin, then, but also the body. In the popular medieval hagiographical collection, the *Golden Legend*, Jews frequently are depicted as miraculously healed by blood that pours from the Cross.[106] While William of Malmesbury (d.1143) had narrated an episode in which Jews were alleged to have hidden a wax image of Jesus in their synagogue in Toledo and subjected it to various torments,[107] Nicholas of Ockham (d. c. 1320) transmitted a similar tale: Jews in the East were said to have abused an icon of Christ, piercing his body depicted there with a lance. The site of the wound began to run with water and blood that the Jews harvested and used to anoint those suffering from illness, whereupon they were immediately restored to health.[108]

Such tales helped to explain alleged Jewish host desecration, assaults on sacred images, or upon Christians who were themselves living images of Christ, while Jews sought an effective cure.[109] Trachtenberg reports that in 1401 the City Council of Freiburg in Breisgau petitioned Duke

---

105. *Thesaurus Exemplorum*, fasc. 5: *Le Speculum laicorum* 32.268, ed. J. Th. Welter (Paris: Librarie des Archives Nationales et de la Societé de l'Ecole des Chartes, 1914), 53.

106. Thomas Renna, "The Jews in the Golden Legend," in *Christian Attitudes toward Jews in the Middle Ages: A Casebook*, ed. Michael Frassetto (New York, London: Routledge, 2007), 142–43.

107. William of Malmesbury, *De laudibus et miraculis Sanctae Mariae*; see J. M. Canal, *El libro de Laudibus et Miraculis Sanctae Mariae de Guillermo de Malmesbury*, 138.

108. Nicholas of Ockham, *Quaestiones disputatae de traductione humanae naturae a primo parente* q. 5, resp. 8. Nicholas attributes this tale to Ps. Athanasius, *De passione imaginis Dominicii* cap. 1–3, 7 (PG 28, 814–817). Jacques de Vitry reports that Jews in Beirut had crucified a wooden figure of Jesus, and pierced it with nails. It then poured forth blood, and the miracle caused all the Jews to convert. See his *Historia Orientalis* 26, p. 59.

109. For the development of host desecration accusations, see especially Rubin, *Gentile Tales*; and Rubin, "Desecration of the Host: The Birth of an Accusation."

Leopold to expel the Jews, who represented a special threat because, the Council insisted, they must obtain Christian blood every seven years "particularly from a desire not to stink, for when they lack this blood they stink so foully that no one can remain near them." In the same way, it was alleged, the Jews consumed Christian blood as a prophylactic against leprosy.[110] Moreover, the need for Christian blood to heal Jews of such bodily infirmity was offered as a justification for the accusation of ritual murder. Even Jewish sources attest to this Christian understanding. Thus Isaac Nathan, who lived in Arles in the fifteenth century as a leader of the Jewish community in Provence, in his unpublished ethical work *Me'amets ko'ah (Reinforcing Strength)*, claims that St. Vincent Ferrer (d. 1419) preached to the Jews of the punishment they must endure forever for crucifying Jesus,

upon whose brows there remains a sign and an example of the pointless crime they committed, and that one day of every month of the year worms will be found in their mouths and they will urinate blood in exchange for the blood which they spilled, and while the Jews think that in order to atone for the blood they will steal a small Christian child and slaughter him on Passover and sacrifice his blood to their god and thus think that this will heal their sores.[111]

The Reformation brought about no real change to the anti-Jewish stereotype of the foul-smelling, menstruating Jewish male in need of Christian blood.[112] The seventeenth-century English translator of the medieval polemic *Book on the Already Accomplished Advent of the Messiah* (*Liber de adventu messiae praeterito*) reiterates that "Jews, men, as well as females, are punished *cursu menstruo sanguinis*, with a very frequent bloud-fluxe."[113] He also notes that although only the Eucharistic blood

110. Trachtenberg, *The Devil and the Jews*, 148–49.
111. Cited by Ram Ben-Shalom, "The Social Context of Apostasy among Fifteenth-Century Spanish Jewry," in *Rethinking European Jewish History*, ed. Jeremy Cohen and Moseh Rosman (Oxford: Littman Library of Jewish Civilization, 2009), 173–98, citing 188.
112. The charge reappears in the work of the Jewish convert to Christianity, Anton Margaritha, *Der ganz Jüdisch Glaub mit sampt ainer gründlichen un warhaften Anzaygunge* ... (Augsburg: Heinrich Steiner, 1530), who remarks that Jews suffer "der weiblich flus" (unpaginated; section ki), and who also repeats the contention that Jews are not subject to leprosy (kiiia).
113. Samuel of Morocco, *The Blessed Jew of Morocco or A Blackmoor Made White*, trans. Thomas Calvert (York: Thomas Broad, 1648), 20. See p. 30 for the claim that Jews also require Christian blood to suppress their own fetid odor. The *Liber de adventu messiae praeterito* was allegedly translated into Latin in the fourteenth century from an eleventh-century

of Christ (*sanguine Christi*) will cure Jews of this strange malady, they mistakenly believe that the blood of any Christian (*sanguine Christiano*) will cure them. On account of this error, he repeats, Jews regularly murder Christian children for their blood. On the continent, in the second decade of the seventeenth century Heinrich Kornmann's *Opera curiosa* included a chapter treating Jewish male menses that cites medieval authorities (including Thomas of Cantimpré) to confirm that the blind and ignorant Jews believe they can heal themselves of this curse by harvesting annually the blood of some Christian, when in truth it is only the blood of Christ poured forth on the altar daily that may heal them.[114] Such fantasies of Jewish male menstruation passed into the modern era to create a link between Jewish males, women, and homosexuals.[115]

One would surely like to know why a healthy empiricism was not introduced in order to test these theories, especially when the opportunity was present. For example, when Jews were incarcerated for long periods by secular rulers or by the Inquisition for various crimes, real or supposed, it should have been easy enough to determine whether Jewish males suffered a monthly blood flow. Unfortunately, humoral theory had convincingly identified the Jews as melancholic and therefore subject to hemorrhoidal bleeding, which medieval physicians acknowledged could appear monthly in males, like female menses.[116] In addition, Christian theology identified Jews as cursed by God. Together, these conspired to suppress evidence to the contrary of Jewish male menstruation. But we also must take note of another use for this anti-Jewish fantasy, which may have been of great importance as the rate of Jewish conversions to Christianity increased in the later Middle Ages: namely, as a guide to es-

---

Arabic work attributed to Rabbi Samuel of Morocco, although probably it is a Latin forgery from the hand of the Spanish Dominican, Alphonsus Buenhombre (d. 1353). The text can be found in PL 149: 333–68.

114. Heinrich Kornmann, *Opera curiosa*, 4 vols. (Frankfurt: Gensch, 1694), 1: 128–29.

115. Sander L. Gilman, "The Struggle of Psychiatry with Psychoanalysis: Who Won?" *Critical Inquiry* 13, no. 2 (1987), 304–5.

116. "Now the flow of this sort [bleeding hemorrhoids] is in men: sometimes it is normal, such as the flow of menses in women, whence like a woman they menstruate every month. But some only four times a year, and some once a year." Theodorich Borgognoni, *The Surgery of Theodoric, ca. AD 1267*, 3.41, 2: 111. A similar view is found in the Middle English translation of the *compendium medicinae* of Gilbert the Englishman, whom Theodorich often cites. See *Healing and Society in Medieval England. A Middle English Translation of the Pharmaceutical Writings of Gilbertus Anglicus* cap. 19, ed. Faye Marie Getz (Madison: University of Wisconsin Press, 1991), 279.

tablish whether such conversions were genuine. In the early seventeenth century, an example can be seen in the work of an official at the Spanish court of Philip IV, Juan de Quiñones. De Quiñones insisted that because the Jews crucified Christ, "every month many of them show a flux of blood in the posterior parts as a perpetual sign of ignominy and opprobrium."[117] This assertion adds nothing to what we have already seen above. But more important is the use he makes of this information:

If any are found who have this flux of blood they should be handed over to the Inquisition, since they cannot have ceased to be Jews or apostates. For if they have it they are not baptized, since with baptism it disappears; and if they are baptized and it happens to them each month, they are apostates . . . and thus, being always a manifestation of their sin and guilt . . . it seems to me . . . that an inquisition can be instituted against them, to verify which Law they observe, and which ceremonies they practice.[118]

Juan de Quiñones wrote his medical tract to the Inquisitor Fray Antonio de Sotomayor concerning the case before the Inquisition of Francisco de Andrada. He sought to provide the Inquisition, then, with another tool with which to identify and root out the Jewish or Judaizing heresy—by looking for signs of anal bleeding.[119] This was likely a special concern in late medieval and early modern Spain, where purity of blood (*limpieza de sangre*) assumed great importance for a determination of Christian identity. These laws, which will be discussed in more detail below, sought to establish a clear separation between "Old" and "New" Christians, excluding the latter from religious orders, schools, civic offices, cathedral chapters, universities, and medical faculties because of their "impure" Jewish blood.[120] The difficulty that the conversos presented to

117. Quiñones's untitled work appears in B. N. Lisbon MS 868 (Caleccão Moreira, II) fols. 73r–89r. This passage, which appears at fol. 73r–v, is quoted from Yerusahalmi, *From Spanish Court to Italian Ghetto*, 128.
118. B. N. Lisbon MS 868 (Caleccão Morcira, II) fol. 88v, quoted in Yerusahalmi, *From Spanish Court to Italian Ghetto*, 133.
119. See Beusterien, "Jewish Male Menstruation in Seventeenth-Century Spain," and John L. Beusterien, *An Eye on Race: Perspectives from Theater in Imperial Spain* (Lewisburg, Pa.: Bucknell University Press, 2006), 65–72.
120. Cf. Mercedes Granjel, "Judaísmo y pureza de sangre en la Universidad de Salamanca: La formacíon del médico en el siglo XVI," in *Proyección histórica de Espana en sus tres culturas: Castille y León, América y el Mediterránneo*, 3 vols., ed. Eufemio Lorenzo Sanz (Valladollid: Junta de Castilla y León, Consejería de Cultura y Turismo, 1993), 3: 295–302; and, in the same volume, Luis S. Granjel, "Los médicos Judíos en la Sociedad Castellano-Leonesa," 3: 369–83.

Spanish society was how to uncover crypto-Jews, that is, those who have preserved elements of Jewish ritual or custom. As we saw above, it was not uncommon for New Christians to suffer denunciation to the Inquisition when it was observed that they would not eat pork. Sabbath observance or other festival customs also could tip off the Inquisition. Juan de Quiñones clearly hoped to provide a "scientific" indicator with which to locate and unmask these concealed "Jews." Ironically, according to Isaac Cardoso, de Quiñones himself suffered from the anal hemorrhoidal bleeding he located among the Jews, because he sat so long laboring to complete his treatise![121] Not unlike nineteenth and twentieth century racial "science," which proposed that it could use the tools of science to identify a Jewish race, "science" was invoked in the early modern era for much the same purpose.

MELANCHOLY, FEAR, AND TREMBLING

While melancholy helped explain the Jews' hemorrhoidal bleeding that supported accusations of ritual murder, signs of melancholy include idleness, fear, and trembling. With respect to the Jews, these qualities could be understood to arise either from the nature of their complexion, or as a result of divine providence, or both, since alterations to our original temperate complexion could be viewed as a punishment visited upon us by God as a result of sin. Equally important, for medieval physicians fear and anxiety were also causes and not only symptoms of illness, in a manner analogous to the way in which moderns understand psychological stress to have a deleterious influence on health. Jews will be imagined to live in a state of chronic fear and anxiety, implying, too, a correlative state of chronic illness. For a moment I would like here to consider the confluence of the two in the qualities of fear and trembling associated with the Jews, paying special attention to the biblical exegesis of Bruno (c. 1044–1123), who was Bishop of Segni and, for a brief time, the abbot of Monte Cassino.[122]

Fear and trembling were frequently attached to the Jews as a punishment for the sin of their ancestor, Cain. Most medieval commentators

---

121. Isaac Cardoso, *Los excelencias y calumnias de los Hebreos*, 346–47.

122. For Bruno's life, see P. Godet, "Brunon d'Asti ou de Segni," in *Dictionnaire de Théologie Catholique*, ed. E. Mangenot, vol. 2(1), fasc. 13 (Paris: Letouzey et Ané, 1904), cols. 1150–51.

held Cain to be a representative for the Jewish people: just as Cain slew his brother Abel, so the Jews slew their brother, Jesus; just as Abel's blood called out to the Lord from the ground on which it had been spilled (Gen. 4:10), so, too, the blood of Jesus that they spilled calls out to the Lord;[123] just as Cain was condemned to be a wanderer and vagabond, so the Jews were condemned to live as wanderers, in dispersion or in exile without a proper home or land of their own; just as the Lord had rejected Cain's offering (Gen. 4:4), so, too, now the Lord rejects the Jews' ritual observances as useless; just as the land would yield only thorns and thistles when Cain worked it, so too after having crucified Jesus the Jews' labor will yield only hardship and pain. Finally, just as a mark was placed on Cain as a sign that it was forbidden to slay Cain, so the Jews too were marked and were not to be slain, although their sufferings would be a testament to the triumph of Christianity and the justice of God.[124]

Most of these themes are found in Bruno's explication of the text of Genesis 4.[125] Of particular interest, however, is the sign of Cain by which those who should meet him were instructed not to slay him (Gen. 4:15). This sign was not the artificial *rouelle* or badge that the Church compelled Jews to wear after the Fourth Lateran Council. Rather, it was a natural sign found on Cain's body that befitted a carnal people. According to Bruno,

A trembling in the members is said to have been this sign, moreover, because like one insane, as it were, and like a melancholiac, he provoked men to have compassion for him.... Also the sign of circumcision was given by the Lord to the Jews by which they are differentiated from all the Gentiles, and no one wishes to slay those that have been made subject to all the Gentiles and have been given over to fear and contempt forevermore.[126]

---

123. See Isidore of Seville, *Quaestiones in Vetus Testamentum: In Genesin* 6, 7 (PL 83: 224C).

124. For a lengthy discussion of these images in the Middle Ages, see especially Gilbert Dahan, "L'exégèse de l'histoire de Caïn et Abel du XIIe au XIVe siècle en Occident," *Recherches de théologie ancienne et médiévale* 49 (1982): 21–89; 50 (1983): 5–68. For Cain's "mark," see Ruth Mellinkoff's *The Mark of Cain* (Berkeley: University of California Press, 1981).

125. Bruno of Segni, *Expositio in Genesim* 4 (PL 164: 174f.).

126. "'Posuitque Dominus signum in Cain, ut non eum interficeret omnis qui invenisset eum.' Hoc autem signum membrorum tremor fuisse dicitur, quia quasi insaniens, et melancholico similis, ad miseriam sui homines provocabat.... Judaeis quoque circumcisionis signum a Domino datum est, quo a cunctis gentibus discernuntur, et qui cunctis gentibus subditi sunt, semperque timori et despectui dediti, nemo est qui occidere eos velit." Bruno of Segni, *Expositio in Genesim* 4 (PL 164: 174C).

Above we examined briefly some Christian values assigned to circumcision. Among others, it was an emasculating sign and a punishment instituted to restrain the natural carnality of the Jew. Here we find another interpretation assigned to circumcision: for Bruno of Segni it was a physical sign by which Jews, the descendents of Cain, were marked by the Lord to evade destruction. But of equal interest to us in the passage above are the references to their trembling members, a sign associated with insanity or melancholy. This sign too had been transferred by divine providence from Cain to his descendents, the Jews. In part, this reflects an alternate Scriptural tradition of Genesis 4:14–15, following the text of the Septuagint (LXX) and the *Vetus Latina*,[127] which read "I will be groaning and trembling" (*gemens ero et tremens*) in place of the Vulgate's "I will be a vagrant and a wanderer upon the earth" (*vagus et profugus ero super terram*). For the LXX and the *Vetus Latina*, then, it seems that this tremor serves as a sign not to kill Cain and a reminder of his crime.

The meaning of this sign varied, however. For Bruno, as seen above, the sign evoked compassion, like that extended to a madman or melancholic, whereas for St. Jerome, by contrast, this trembling and groaning revealed Cain's bad conscience and an awareness that he deserved death.[128] For Albert the Great, this "bad conscience" passed from passive awareness to action, for he claims Cain committed suicide, like Judas.[129] Latin exegetes were aware of both the Vulgate and the LXX or *Vetus Latina* traditions, and sometimes combined the two. Thus, Isidore of Seville explains that the Jewish people have become a vagabond and a wanderer across the earth, groaning over the loss of its earthly kingdom and trembling under the yoke of the Christian peoples.[130] The Venerable Bede (d. 735) extends this sign and punishment both to the Jewish people generally and to Judas specifically, adding: "Truly Judas groans and trembles as a vagabond and a wanderer, lest he be slain with a visible death after having lost an earthly kingdom."[131] For Peter the Venerable, God dealt

---

127. See *Vetus Latina*, vol. 2: *Genesis*, ed. Bonifatius Fischer (Freiburg: Herder, 1951), 87.
128. St. Jerome, Epist. 36 [to Pope Damasus] (PL 22: 454).
129. Albert the Great, *Commentarii in Iob* 15.22, p. 197.
130. Isidore of Seville, *Quaestiones in Vetus Testamentum: In Genesin* 6, 13 (PL 83: 225C); cf. Rabanus Maurus, *Commentaria in Genesim* 2, 1 (PL 107: 505B).
131. "Vere Judas vagus et profugus gemit et tremit, ne regno etiam terreno perdito, ista visibili morte occidatur." Bede, *In Pentateuchum Commentarii—Genesis* 4 (PL 91: 218A).

justly with Cain and like Cain, all Jews from the time of the Crucifixion until the end of time, will be "enslaved, wretched, fearful, groaning and wanderers over the face of the earth."[132]

Most Jewish commentators viewed Cain as a repentant sinner, which explains why his punishment—to become a wanderer—was comparatively so light. But there were many variant traditions concerning the sign that marked Cain. *Pirkê de Rabbi Eliezer* and, later, Rashi understood the sign of Cain placed on Cain's forehead to be one of the letters of the divine name.[133] Other commentators—both Jewish and Christian—speculated that the sign was a horn on Cain's forehead.[134] Rupert of Deutz (d. 1129) insisted that in Scripture the sign placed on Cain was *not* a tremor in his body, or a horn on his forehead, or some other such thing. These are merely fables found among the Jews.[135] But Andrew of Saint Victor (d. 1175) noted that Cain was a vagabond, a wanderer, fearful, and that he sustained a "trembling in the members" (*tremor membrorum*) as a sign.[136] Even more explicitly Hugh of St. Victor (d. 1141) avers that the sign of Cain is "a trembling of the members like one who is mad or insane."[137] Petrus Comestor (d. c. 1178) identifies this sign, similarly, as a tremor or shaking of the head,[138] and Peter the Chanter (d. 1197) combines this tremor about the head with a mind seized by fear.[139] Pope Innocent III (d. 1216) explains that God gave this head tremor as a sign to

---

132. "servi, miseri, timidi, gementes, ac profugi sunt super terram." Peter the Venerable, *Letter* 130.2. Ephes. 6:5–6, also identifies fear and trembling as the appropriate attitude of a servant before his master.

133. See *Pirkê de Rabbi Eliezer* 21, p. 156; Rashi, *Commentary to the Pentateuch*, Genesis 4:15.

134. *Midrash Tanhuma-Yelamadenu*, trans. Samuel A. Berman (Hoboken, N.J.: KTAV, 1996), 32; see Mellinkoff, *The Mark of Cain*, 60–63.

135. Rupert of Deutz, *De sancta Trinitate, In Genesin* 4.9, p. 293 (=PL 167: 335C). For medieval illustrations showing a horned Cain, see also Ruth Mellinkoff, *Outcasts: Signs of Otherness in Northern European Art of the Late Middle Ages*, 2 vols. (Berkeley: University of California Press, 1993), 1: 140f.

136. Andrew of Saint Victor, *Expositio super heptateuchum—In Genesim*, eds. C. Lohr and R. Berndt, CCCM 53 (Turnholt: Brepols: 1986).

137. "Cain signum, id est tremorem membrorum quasi fanatici, id est furibundi." Hugh of St. Victor, *Adnotationes in Penteuchon* 7 (PL 175: 44D).

138. "Et posuit Deus signum in Cain, tremorem capitis." Petrus Comestor, *Historia Scholastica—Genesis* 27 (PL 198:1078B).

139. "Cain magis invidens fratri, eum occidit, signumque invidiae suae et sceleris accepit a Domino, timorem scilicet mentis, et tremorem capitis." Petrus Cantor, *Verbum abbreviatum* 11 (PL 205:53A).

Cain so that he would not be slain, and so that like Cain the faces of the Jews, who had been made fugitives or wanderers across the earth, would be filled with ignominy.[140] Finally, Jacques de Vitry (d. 1240) relates this head tremor found among the Jews to other features of the Jews' somatic condition. In the first book of his *History of Jerusalem* Jacques reports that the Jews,

> have become unwarlike and weak even as women, and it is said that they have a flux of blood every month. God has smitten them in their hinder parts, and put them to perpetual opprobrium (Ps. 78:67). After they slew their true brother, Abel [that is, Christ], they were made wanderers and fugitives over the earth, cursed like Cain, with a trembling head, that is, a quaking heart, fearing both day and night, not believing in his life.[141]

This assessment was an important aspect of medieval theological culture. About the same time Thomas of Chobham (d. c. 1236) remarked in a sermon that, "just as Chaim [Cain] thereafter always had a trembling head and was made a vagabond and wanderer across the earth, so too after Christ's death the Jews are always in a trembling and quaking [state] and are dispersed around the world."[142]

The typology that had Cain represent the Jews was not only a literary creation. From medieval illustrations showing Cain wearing the *Judenhut* or Jew's hat Ruth Melinkoff concludes that all Jews—and others who wear the *Judenhut* in negative contexts—are portrayed as evil, like Cain.[143]

The purpose of this digression has been to show that the Jews' fear and trembling could have a supernatural cause, as a sign imposed by

---

140. Innocent III, *Regesta sive epistolae* 190 (PL 215: 1291C).

141. "Alij autem Iudaei de quibus patres eorum clamaverunt: Sanguis eius super nos et super filios nostros . . . Imbelles enim et imbecilles facti sunt quasi mulieres. Unde singulis lunationibus, ut dicitur, fluxum sanguinis patiuntur. Percusit enim eos Deus in posteriora et opprobrium sempiternum dedit illis. Postquam enim fratrem suum verum Abel occiderunt, facti sunt vagi et profugi super terram, sicut maledictus Cain, habentes caput tremulum, id est, cor pavidum, vite sue non credentes." Jacques de Vitry, *Historia Orientalis* 82, pp. 159–60.

142. "Et sicut Chaim semper postea habuit tremulum capud et factus est uagus et profugus super terram, ita Iudei post mortem Christi semper sunt in tremore et pauore et dispersi sunt per orbem terrarum." Thomas of Chobham, Sermon 6, in *Thomas de Chobham Sermones*, ed. Franco Morenzoni, CCCM 82A (Turnholt: Brepols, 1993), ln. 155.

143. Ruth Mellinkoff, *Outcasts: Signs of Otherness in Northern European Art of the Late Middle Ages*, 1: 62. The "Jews' hat" could also be used to designate heretics in medieval art. See Elizabeth Pastan, "Tam Haereticos Quam Judaeos: Shifting Symbols in the Glazing of Troyes Cathedral," *Word and Image* 10 (1994): 66–83.

God upon all Jews as descendants of Cain. Yet this fear and trembling could equally have a natural explanation, resulting from a melancholy complexion. For Albert the Great, melancholy causes gluttony,[144] which Thomas Aquinas identifies as the material cause of *luxuria,* because of the added difficulty the cold melancholic complexion has in digesting food. But melancholy can also be a dangerous humor that "squeezes" the heart until it suffocates the vital spirit, causing the heart to contract so from fear that one may drop dead merely from seeing an enemy.[145] Melancholics, because they have little heat in the heart, are especially subject to fear, even where there is no external cause.[146]

In fact, one should not be surprised to find that the supernatural and the natural causes support one another. Above, Bruno of Segni had remarked that the trembling in Cain's members resembles that of a melancholic, namely, one with an excess of black bile. Augustine had long ago complained in his treatise *Against the Jews* that the Jews have inherited the "biliousness" (*ipsi enim fellei . . . facti sunt*) of their ancestors who crucified Jesus, offering to him on the Cross bitter gall (*fel*) to drink.[147] Medieval Romance authors found ample opportunity to play with the Latin *fellei* (bilious), to describe the Jews as *felluns,* that is, felons, or betrayers of Christ.[148] The double entendre seems to lie behind an episode in the twelfth-century *Jeu d'Adam,* when the prophet Isaiah confronts a contemporary Jew to encourage his conversion. The Jew offers him his hand, and asks the prophet to determine whether he is sick or hale. Isaiah responds, "You have the felon's disease, from which you will never be cured."[149] The Jews' melancholy complexion, then, not only underscores their treacherous disposition, but actually constitutes a source of illness or disease, the "felon's disease." It seems that this disease already had manifested itself in Cain's physical constitution. Perhaps the clearest testimony to the confluence of natural and supernatural explanations will

---

144. Albert the Great, *De homine,* p. 347, 64–74; also see Albert the Great, *De somno et vigilia* 1.2.8, Ed. Borgnet 9, 151B.
145. Albert the Great, *Quaestiones super de animalibus* 4.23, p. 153 (QDA, 184).
146. Albert the Great, *De anima* 1.1.6, p. 13, 47–51.
147. Augustine, *Adversus Iudaeos* 5 (PL 42: 54D).
148. On the connection between *fel* and *fellun* (cf. mod. French *félon*) see also William Chester Jordan, "The Last Tormentor of Christ," *Jewish Quarterly Review* 78 (1987): 21–47, especially 29–30.
149. "Tu as le mal de felonie, dont ne garras ja en ta vie." *Le Jeu d'Adam,* 2nd ed., ed. Wolfgang van Emden (Edinburgh: Société Rencesvals British Branch, 1999), 62, lns. 901–2.

be found in the treatment of Cain's tremor by Bartholomew the Englishman. Although he acknowledges that Cain's tremor is a sign imposed by God, Bartholomew explains nonetheless that

> Two contrary motions are involved in a head tremor: an upward motion of the head, and a downward motion. Upward motion is caused by nature herself; a downward motion is caused by illness. According to Constantine the African, the [natural] cause of this motion [down] is a defect in the power moving the muscles. This power fails either from a bad complexion or from certain accidents of the soul, like fear, which results in the spirits rushing to the heart, which is why the members tend downward, pulled by their weight.[150]

Because the animal spirits rush to the heart, there is not enough of these spirits left in the members of the body to govern or regulate the members' motion. Although Bartholomew certainly understood that the mark of Cain is a divine punishment, he takes some care to establish that the downward motion in Cain's head tremor, which is a sign passed on to the Jews, is "caused by illness." It reflects a defect in a natural power that moves the muscles of the head. This defect stems from a bad and presumably melancholy complexion or from an affect or passion of the soul, namely fear, or more likely from both.

While Christian interpreters, then, understood this trembling of the members to be a divine sign imposed upon the Jews, it is also one that is imprinted on their somatic nature. Their melancholy or diseased nature, compounded by the fear or anxiety in which they must live in Christendom, reinforce the supernatural explanation. By the later Middle Ages, Jewish authors had assimilated some of these features assigned to a Jewish complexion, although necessarily assigning to them a very different value. For example, the Toledan physician R. Shem Tov ben Isaac ben Shaprut (ibn Shaprut) remarked in his polemical *Even Bohan* (*Touchstone*; composed c. 1385 in Tarazona) that the Gentiles treat the people Israel as despised and afflicted by God, bearing disease and infirmities (cf. Isa. 52:14, 53:4), and even assert that the Jews are especially liable to suffer from hemorrhoids,[151] as has been explained above. Unlike Christian interpreters that understood Ps. 78:66 [Ps. 77:66 Vulg.] as the basis for the theological claim that Jews commonly suffer from bleeding hem-

---

150. Bartholomaeus Anglicus, *De rerum proprietatibus* 7.11, p. 289.
151. AD[olf] Neubauer, compiler, *Fifty-Third Chapter of Isaiah according to the Jewish Interpreters*, 2 vols., trans. S. R. Driver (New York: KTAV, 1969), 1:95 (Hebrew), 2: 95.

orrhoids, Shem Tov ibn Shaprut offered instead the explanation that that there are two *natural* causes that render the Jews peculiarly liable to this complaint: namely, the melancholy produced by the constant depression and anxiety of exile, and by their sedentary habits.[152] Rather than a divine punishment, however, such affliction attests to their election as the suffering servant of the Lord identified by Isaiah whereas Christian exegesis, relating these attributes to Jesus, founder on inconsistency. In fact, ibn Shaprut remarks, nowhere in Christian literature is there any evidence that Jesus ever suffered a single illness.[153]

Toward the end of the twelfth century, Jacob ben Reuben had expressed a similar view in his *Wars of the Lord*:

I know, in fact, that you will not find either in your own New Testament, or in the words of the wise men of your own religion who tell you about the Messiah and his deeds ... that he ever had a pain—even a headache—up to the day of his death when he was delivered into the hands of those who smote him: we see then that the very terms themselves which are here employed, "pain" and "sickness," were not realized in his person, and consequently cannot apply to him.[154]

Therefore, one cannot describe Jesus as "despised and forlorn," a "man of pains" that is "known to sickness" (Isa. 53:3–4) and infirmities, and at the same time, as Christians are wont to do, as "fairer than the children of men" (Ps. 45:3), enjoying a perfectly balanced complexion. Later, Moses of Tordesillas (R. Mosheh Kohen ibn Crispin) composed his *Aid to the Faith* (c. 1375). In this text he refers Isaiah 53 not to Jesus but to the future messiah that will bear the pain, suffering, grief and affliction of the Jews. But great grief produces melancholy, he adds, as physicians know, and subjects a man to many diseases and illnesses.[155] This medicalized polemic continues in the work of Don Isaac Abravenel (1437–1508), who attests that the description of the prophet Isaiah suggests a "melancholy ... weak constitution" that is not at all consistent with accounts of Jesus as young and handsome, and, according to Christian theologians, as one having a normal (and even the best possible) complexion.[156] Medieval Jewish exegetes, then, attempt to turn the alleged melancholy and infirmities of the Jews to advantage: for them these become a sign of election

152. Ibid., 2: 95, n. a.   153. Ibid., 2: 93.
154. Ibid., 2: 59.   155. Ibid., 2: 103–4.
156. Ibid., 2: 159–60. A standard work on Abravenel remains B. Netanyahu, *Don Isaac Abravanel: Statesman and Philosopher*, 5th ed. (Ithaca, N.Y.: Cornell University Press, 1998).

and not rejection while at the same time undermining Christian messianic exegesis of an important Old Testament text, explicating Isaiah 53 instead as a reference either to the Jews as a whole living in exile or to the Jewish messiah yet to come.[157]

Both parties to this polemical debate, then, will appeal to explanations drawn from natural science and theology. Exegesis of scripture is no longer sufficient unto itself, for the decrees of heaven are written not only on the soul but upon the body as well. But the heavens act upon bodies below through specific instruments, including the stars and the planets, as medieval astrologizing natural scientists understood perfectly well. For this reason, we shall turn now to a brief discussion of celestial influences upon the Jews and the Jews' body.

---

157. See especially Joel E. Rembaum, "The Development of a Jewish Exegetical Tradition Regarding Isaiah 53," *Harvard Theological Review* 75, no. 3 (1982): 289–311.

6

PLANETARY INFLUENCES; OR, THE JEWS AND SATURN

Even for the Roman historians Tacitus (d. 117) and Dio Cassius (d. 235) a link was presumed to exist between the Jews and Saturn. According to the Roman author Frontinus (d. 103) in a report repeated by Dio Cassius, it was on the day most sacred to the Jews, namely, Saturn's Day, that the emperor Vespasian destroyed Herod's Temple in Jerusalem.[1] Tacitus claimed that according to some authorities the Jews have a special tie to the god Saturn, as evidenced by their practice of having set aside the Sabbath on Saturday, that is, "Saturn's day." as a venerated holy day and a day of sacrifice. Such a connection may have rested on the fact that in Hebrew *Sabbatai* denotes the planet, Saturn. Interestingly, in his *Histories* Tacitus explains the Jews' special attachment to Saturn at the same time as he records that their repugnance for pork stems from the memory that they were once infected with a disease commonly associated with the pig, namely *scabies*, usually translated as "leprosy."[2] Recalling the older calumnies of Manetho and Lysimachus, Tacitus explains that most authorities suppose that it was because they were infected with some plague that the Jews were expelled from Egypt at the time of Moses.[3] Their more remote origin, however, remains for him a matter of uncertainty. One possibility is that

---

1. Sextus Julius Frontinus, *Strategemata* 2.1.17, ed. R. I. Ireland (Leipzig: Teubner, 1990), 33; Cassius Dio Cocceianus, *Epitome* 65.7.2, in *Dio's Roman History*, 9 vols., trans. Earnest Cary, Loeb Classical Library (London: Heinemann; New York: Putnam's Sons, 1925), 8: 270–71.
2. Tacitus, *Histories* 5.4, pp. 180–81.
3. Ibid., 5.3, p. 179.

in the very distant past the Jews were originally refugees from the island of Crete that were expelled to Libya in the company of Saturn, at the time that Saturn was driven from his throne by Jupiter. In a fanciful etymology, Tacitus derives the name *Judaei* from *Idaei*, a people that dwelled around Crete's Mount Ida.[4] Certainly, later readers of the New Testament understood that "Cretans are always liars, evil beasts, slothful bellies." (Tit. 1:12) Therefore, a link between Jews and Crete carried no favor. Moreover, Louis Feldman speculates that older traditions that Cretans eschewed pork only supported this presumed link between the Jews and Crete.[5]

Evidently, the erroneous claim that Jews worshipped or venerated Saturn with their Sabbath observance was so widely known that it could be transferred as well to early Christians. St. Augustine felt compelled to refute it in his *Against Faustus the Manichaean* (*Contra Faustum Manichaeum*), remarking that "the fathers observed the rest of the Sabbath, not because they worshipped Saturn, but because it was incumbent at that time, for it was a shadow of things to come."[6] Although Christians employ the common name Saturn's Day or Saturday to designate the seventh day of the week, Augustine notes, they no more worship Saturn then does Faustus worship Mars when he refers to the month of March, whose name is derived from the god Mars.

Although Augustine repudiated the notion that Christians worship Saturn because their "fathers" observed the Sabbath, the tradition that Jews in some way worshipped Saturn retained a foothold among medieval Christian authors. Isidore of Seville understood Saturn to have originally been a Babylonian god, Bel, later called Saturn, and implied that the Jews conceived an attachment to "Saturn" during their Babylonian captivity.[7] William of Auvergne, the bishop of Paris, attributes to unnamed sages (*sapientes in mundo*) the view that religious diversity is derived from the influence of the stars, and adds that the religion or

---

4. Ibid., 5.2, pp. 176–77. For Tacitus's diverse accounts of the Jews' origins in this text, see especially Feldman, *Jew and Gentile in the Ancient World*, 184–96; and Menahem Stern, "Antisemitism in Rome," in *Antisemitism through the Ages*, ed. Shmuel Almog, trans. Nathan H. Reisner (Oxford/New York: Pergamon Press, 1988), 23–25.

5. Feldman, *Jew and Gentile in the Ancient World*, 225.

6. Augustine, *Contra Faustum Manichaeum* 18.5, ed. J. Zycha, CSEL 25 (Vienna: F. Tempsky, 1891), 494. Cf. *Contra Faustum Manichaeum* 20.13, p. 553; Augustine, *De consensu evangelistarum* 1.22.30, ed. F. Weihrich, CSEL 43 (Vienna: F. Tempsky, 1904), 29.

7. See Isidore of Seville, *The Etymologies of Isidore of Seville* 8.11.23, p. 185; Albert the Great, *Postilla super Isaiam*, ed. Ferdinand Siepmann, Ed. Colon. 19.2 (Münster in Westfalorum: Aschendorff, 1952), 468, 45–58.

"law" of the Hebrews takes it origin from Saturn: "And, on this account, they consider Saturn's day, that is the Sabbath, to be the more renowned, and for the same reason on that same day they are particularly idle, for reading that law, namely for teaching and fulfilling it."[8] Although earlier we saw that the Jews' idleness was attributed to their melancholy complexion, William of Auvergne reminds us now that idleness was also a product of their religious custom, at least one day each week, just as St. Augustine recalls that in Roman antiquity Seneca (d. 65) chided that by observing the Sabbath Jews spend one-seventh of their lives in idleness.[9]

Yet Saturn appeared to the Middle Ages in more than one guise.[10] On the one hand, Saturn was a planet that, like any material body, had certain qualities associated with it. On the other hand, Saturn was an ancient Roman god of obscure origin to whom, once he had become identified with the Greek Kronos, a colorful history was assigned. Many fables arose concerning Saturn in antiquity, and not all were consistent with one another. Often in classical mythology Saturn is depicted as the son of the sky-god Caelus, whom he emasculated with a scythe, for which reason that agricultural instrument was subsequently specially associated with Saturn.[11] In turn, Saturn feared a prophecy that he would be overthrown by his sons, and therefore set about devouring his children. (See figure 9.) When a beautiful male child was born, Saturn's wife, Rhea (or Ops), tricked him: she substituted a stone for the infant Jupiter, and Saturn swallowed it instead. Jupiter survived, emasculated and overthrew his father, and drove

---

8. "Alij vero diversitatem legum attribuunt coelis et stellis, sicut et alias diversificationes, et conditiones hominum, et dixerunt, quia lex Hebraeorum ortum habet a Saturno et caelo ipso. Et propter hoc celebriorem habent diem Saturni, quae est dies Sabbati, et eadem die propter eandem causam maxime vacant legi ill legendae, scilicet docendae, et implendae." William of Auvergne, *De legibus* 20, transcribed from appendix A in Peter Biller's "A 'Scientific' View of Jews from Paris around 1300," 157. For William of Auvergne's view of the Jews, see Lesley Smith, "William of Auvergne and the Jews," in Wood, *Christianity and Judaism*, 107–17.

9. Augustine, *De civitate Dei* 6.11.

10. For diverse treatments of Saturn in medieval literature, see Theresa Tinkle, "Saturn of the Several Faces," *Viator* 18 (1987): 289–307. The twelfth-century Alexander Neckham remarked that the name Saturn refers to the king of the gods, to the planet, and metaphorically to time itself (which, like Saturn, devours its "children," or ages future). See his *De naturis rerum* 1.4, p. 33.

11. Cf. Isidore of Seville, *The Etymologies of Isidore of Seville* 8.8.11.30–33, p. 185; Geoffrey of Monmouth, *Gottfried's von Monmouth* Historia regum Britanniae, *mit literarhistorischer Einleitung und ausführlichen Anmerkungen, und Brut Tysylio, altwälsche Chronik in deutscher Übersetzung* 7.4, ed. San-Marte (Halle: Edouard Anton, 1854), 101; Albert the Great, *De Mineralibus* 2.3.5, Ed. Borgnet 5, 54B; Albert of Behaim, *Das Brief-und Memorialbuch* 174, p. 600.

him away. In one classical tradition, Jupiter was fabled to have been born or raised in Crete, and Saturn is identified as a king of Crete until Jupiter expelled him.[12] As noted above, Tacitus reports that some trace the Jews' origin to Crete's Mount Ida and aver that the Jews' special association with Saturn stems from the period of his expulsion, when the Jews went into exile in Libya together with the god.

The mythic features of Saturn's history were well known in the Middle Ages and were handed down in several sources, including the work of the Vatican Mythographer (after 636). Certain disagreements are to be expected as these tales traveled across time and space. For example, the Vatican Mythographer does not record that Saturn fled to Libya but to Latium, later to become king of Italy, to which he introduced agriculture and a golden age, while still other sources identify Saturn as having first introduced money (*pecunia*) to Italy.[13] Nonetheless, this work retains many of the other important features already noted. In particular, it records that because of an oracle he received from Themis, the goddess of justice and prophecy, Saturn was especially fearful that his children would overthrow him, and therefore he sought to safeguard his reign by devouring them. Rhea, who took special delight in Jupiter, commended the child to the nymphs on a mountain in Crete, where bees nourished him on honey. There Jupiter survived until he rose up against his father Saturn, emasculated and expelled him.[14]

Because of Saturn's monstrous attempt to preserve his reign by eating his own children, medieval authors tended to treat Saturn harshly while often overlooking Jupiter's own crimes. One notable exception appears in the thirteenth-century vernacular allegorical poem, the *Romance of the Rose* (*Roman de la Rose*), in which Lady Reason describes in shocking language that Jupiter cut off Saturn's testicles "as though they were

---

12. In his *De natura deorum* 3.53f., Cicero identifies three distinct Jupiters in theological tradition. One was the child of Aether; another was the child of Caelus and the father of Minerva; a third was born in Crete and was the son of Saturn.

13. *Mythographi Uaticani i et ii* 1.104, ed. Péter Kulcsár, CCSL 91C (Turnholt: Brepols, 1987). Cf. Martianus Capella's *The Marriage of Philology and Mercury* 6.642, in *Martianus Capella and the Seven Liberal Arts*, vol. 2: *The Marriage of Philology and Mercury*, trans. William Harris Stahl and E. L. Burge (New York: Columbia University Press, 1977), 237; Vergil's *Aeneid* 8.319-23; Ovid, *Fasti* 1.235-38; Honorius of Autun, *De imagine mundi* 1.28 (PL 172: 129C); Albert the Great, *Politica* 1.6, Ed Borgnet 8, 43B. For the claim that Saturn introduced money to Italy, see Felix Fabri, *Evagatorum in Terrae Sanctae, Arabiae et Egyptii peregrinationem*, fol. 168b, 3: 277.

14. See *Mythographi Uaticani i et ii* 1.101-4; 2.3, 5, 26, 40, 54, and 80.

sausages" and threw them into the sea.¹⁵ Most other medieval authors, however, recall only Saturn's failings. Thus, in the late eleventh century, Peter Damian compared the anti-pope Honorius II (d. 1072) unfavorably to Saturn and accused him of "devouring" his children, the people of Rome, just as Saturn had devoured his own.¹⁶ Political theology aside, in the *Cosmographia*, a hallmark expression of twelfth-century humanism, Bernardus Silvestris both condemns Saturn for his depravity and treats Saturn as a symbol for decay, death, and disharmony—the very antitheses of the creative forces of Nature:

> Saturn, [is] an old man everywhere condemned, savagely inclined to harsh and bloody acts of unfeeling and detestable malice. Whenever his most fertile wife had borne him sons, he had cut them off at the first budding of life, devouring them newly born. Ceaselessly on guard against childbirth, he neither paused for deliberation nor succumbed to pity.... Nature was horrified by the old man's cruelty, and lest she should profane her divine gaze with so foul a sight, turned away her face in virginal alarm... whenever there was no one whom he [Saturn] might devour, he would mow down with a blow of his sickle whatever was beautiful, whatever was flourishing. Just as he would not accept childbirth, so he forebade roses, lilies, and the other kinds of sweet-scented flowers to flourish. By the spectacle he presented he prefigured the hostility with which he was to menace the race of men to come by the poisonous and deadly propensities of the planet.¹⁷

The suggestion that Saturn is Nature's antithesis is significant, for the propensities of the god will commonly be transferred to the celestial body, so that Saturn emerges as a baleful planet that has a poisonous, mortifying effect on living things.¹⁸ In addition, the identification of Saturn as an "old man" was already a commonplace, derived both from his relation-

---

15. *Roman de la Rose*, lns. 5507–10, cited in Alastair Minnis, "From *Coilles* to *Bel Chose*: Discourses of Obscenity in Jean de Meun and Chaucer," in *Medieval Obscenities*, ed. Nicola McDonald (York: York Medieval Press, 2006), 156–78, cited on 157. Saturn's emasculation made him "another famous castrato," according to Rawcliffe, *Leprosy in Medieval England*, 239 n. 172. Since circumcision and castration might be viewed as analogous (distinguished only in degree), this is one more characteristic that Jews and Saturn shared.

16. See Peter Damian, Epist. 89.17, in *Die Briefe des Petrus Damiani* 2: 537, translated in *The Letters of Peter Damian, 61–90*, trans. Owen J. Blum, The Fathers of the Church, Mediaeval Continuation 3 (Washington, D.C.: The Catholic University of America Press, 1992), 333.

17. *The Cosmographia of Bernardus Silvestris*, trans. Winthrope Weatherbee (New York: Columbia University Press, 1973), 99–100. The depiction of Saturn as a symbol of old age will even be found in the seven-part orchestral suite "The Planets," by the twentieth-century composer Gustov Holst.

18. See Roger Bacon's introduction to the *Secreta Secretorum*, entitled *tractatus brevis et utilis*, in *Opera hactenus inedita*, fasc. 5: *Secretum secretorum*, p. 17.

ship to his young son, Jupiter,[19] and by his position in the heavens. In addition to his status as a pagan god, then, Saturn is also a planetary body and, among the seven planets (the Moon, Mercury, Venus, Sun, Mars, Jupiter, and Saturn), Saturn was understood to be most distant from earth, requiring the longest period in which to complete its movement.

In the thirteenth century, Thomas of Cantimpré presented a typical portrait of Saturn *qua* astronomical body. Saturn is the last and most distant of the seven planets whose slow course across the heavens requires thirty years—far longer than the twelve years for the next most distant planet, Jupiter. In fables and stories, he adds, Saturn is depicted as an old man, because of the slowness of the planet's movement. In itself, Saturn's depiction as an old man was not necessarily a negative one. Alexander Neckam (1157–1217) associates the seven planets with the seven gifts of the Holy Spirit. Saturn, he notes, completes its orbit or passage in thirty solar years, while Jupiter requires twelve, and Mars two, whereas the Sun, Mercury, and Venus complete their course in 365¼ days, and the moon in only one month. But just as wisdom has a superior place among the seven gifts of the Spirit, so too does Saturn among the planets. This is why, he concludes, Saturn is often depicted as old or mature by philosophers.[20] Age could suggest either wisdom and maturity, or decrepitude. More commonly, however, decay or corruption will become the salient characteristics associated with Saturn.

Tied to Saturn's depiction as an old man, however, were certain assumptions concerning this planetary body's humoral complexion. According to Pseudo-Bede's *De mundi celestis terrestrisque constitutione*,

Among all the planets Saturn is the coldest; for this, many reasons are given: the mythical reason is that it was once an old man; for old men are of a cold nature, hence phlegm, which increases in winter, also abounds in them. Or it is said to be cold because it is most distant from the Sun. . . . But when Saturn is in its own houses with the Sun, it causes the most serious blight of coldness. But it is not cold except in its effect; for in its evil constellation it kills men, and dead men are cold.[21]

---

19. Albert the Great remarks that one reason that ancient poets called Saturn an old man was because he was the father of the god of gods, namely, Jupiter. See his *Postilla super Isaiam*, p. 468.

20. Alexander Neckam, *De naturis rerum libri duo* 1.7, p. 41.

21. "Est autem inter omnes planetas Saturnus frigidissimus, cuius plures cause reddun-

Its complexion is said to be both dry and cold, according to Thomas of Cantimpré, because ancient astronomers knew that when the sun is in Cancer it burns the earth, drying it out, but it does so far less in those years when the sun is conjoined with Saturn, whose cold tempers the sun's heat. In general, however, Saturn is noxious or injurious, exercising a baleful influence on all things subject to its power.[22]

Indeed each of the planets, like inferior terrestrial bodies, will be composed of the primary elements—earth, air, fire, and water—and will display the elements' corresponding qualities. It is thus possible to speak of a planet's complexion, just as a human being has a proper humoral complexion. Moreover, the planetary bodies may affect the complexion of living beings. One source for these notions was the wildly popular pseudo-Aristotelian *Secret of Secrets*, first translated from Arabic into Latin in a short form c. 1120 by John of Seville, translated into Hebrew,[23] and translated again in a longer Latin form by Philip of Tripoli in the thirteenth century, and appearing not long after in a number of vernacular translations.[24] Among the works of Roger Bacon (d. 1292) there is preserved his annotated copy of the *Secret of Secrets*, with a lengthy introduction by Bacon himself, in which he sought to defend the work against detractors who found in it a dangerous example of astrological fatalism. With respect to Saturn and the other planets, the *Secret of Secrets* proclaims that each of the planets disposes and assimilates other bodies to

---

tur. Fabulose, quia senex fuit quidem vir; senes autem sunt frigide nature, unde et flegma in eis abundat quod in hieme crescit. Vel ideo frigidus perhibetur, quia remotissimus sit a Sole.... Cum vero in suis domiciliis Saturnus cum Sole positus fuerit, gravissimam facit frigoris uredinem. Nec aliter est frigidus nisi per effectum; mala constellatione sua enecat homines; enacati vero sunt frigidi." Pseudo-Bede, *De mundi celestis terrestrisque constitutione: A Treatise on the Universe and the Soul*, ed. and trans. Charles Burnett (London: Warburg Institute, 1985), 42–44. The date for this work remains difficult to establish. According to the editor, its *terminus post quem* is early ninth century; the oldest manuscripts extant, however, come from the late twelfth century.

22. Thomas Cantimpratensis, *Liber de natura rerum* 20.7, ed. H. Boese (Berlin: de Gruyter, 1973), 418.

23. For the Hebrew see Gaster, "The Hebrew Version of the 'Secretum Secretorum,'" 2: 742–813.

24. For the origins and history of this text and its first Latin translation, see especially chaps. 1–2 in Steven J. Williams, *The Secret of Secrets: The Scholarly Career of a Pseudo-Aristotelian Text in the Latin Middle Ages* (Ann Arbor: University of Michigan Press, 2003). For medieval English prose versions, see *Three Prose Versions of the* Secreta Secretorum, ed. Robert Steele and T. Henderson, Early English Text Society, extra series 74 (London: Kegan Paul, Trench, Trübner, 1898).

the element that predominates in its own nature. "For example, Saturn has in its power earth, Mercury water, Jupiter air, and the Sun fire."[25] Corresponding to these elements are the primary qualities, namely the dry, the cold, the moist, and the hot, respectively. Because the planets are linked to the elements, however, one expects them to communicate in some manner the qualities associated with these elements to those born under their influence. For example, the moon is intemperately cold and moist; Saturn is intemperately cold and dry; Mars is intemperately hot and dry; Venus is temperately cold and moist; and Jupiter is temperately hot and moist.[26] The sun also is hot and temperate in its moisture. In general heat and moisture are understood to be life giving, since all creatures require heat and moisture to flourish (and those that live in a temperately warm and moist region tend to be longer lived).[27] Thus, because Mars has a superfluity of heat and dryness, it is quite noxious, unless it is tempered by conjunction with good planets. By contrast, Jupiter is warm and moist, and next to the sun is most beneficial for the world.

Precisely because the planets and stars influence bodies in the sublunar world, it is essential that the physician take note of their positions before prescribing a regimen to counteract illness. The translation of the *Secret of Secrets* included among the works of Albert of Behaim cautions that before giving a patient medicine, one must look to see in which zodiacal sign the sun is found: if in a choleric sign, it will be necessary to sharpen or intensify the medicine; if it is in a melancholic sign, to prescribe a larger dose and, if in a phlegmatic sign, to prescribe an amount as dictated by the quality and nature of that sign. When Jupiter is in conjunction with the moon, Roger Bacon explains, and one receives a laxative, the effect of the medicine is counteracted. This is because every medicinal laxative except rhubarb is poisonous, and for this reason Jupiter's goodness counteracts the poison's effect when it is in conjunction with the moon. Saturn is the worst and most poisonous celestial body,

---

25. "Verbi gracia, Saturnus tenet terram, Mercurius aquam, Jupiter aerem, sol ignem." Roger Bacon, *Opera hactenus inedita*, fasc. 5: *Secretum secretorum* 3.3, p. 119, fol. 90b.

26. See Albert the Great, *De generatione et corruptione* 2.3.5, p. 206, 38ff.; Albert the Great, *De causis proprietatum elementorum*, 1.2.9, p. 78.

27. Averroes, *Libri Aristotelis de causis longitudinis et brevitatis vite*, in *Averrois Cordubensis Compendia Librorum Aristotelis qui Parva Naturalia Vocantur*, ed. Emilia Ledyard Shields and Henry Blumberg, Corpus Commentariorum Averrois in Aristotelem 7 (Cambridge, Mass.: Mediaeval Academy of America, 1949), 130, 64–131, 7.

because it is cold and dry and a cause of death, and yet it can be beneficial in the same way that a poison may prove medicinally useful as a purgative used to achieve a properly balanced complexion.[28]

The other planetary bodies possess their own complexions and they combine to achieve a temperate balance or harmony in the upper regions; but, they also influence the balance of humors found in an animal body.[29] Evidence that planetary bodies' complexions affect the humoral balance in animal bodies was especially clear in the perceived influence of the moon on a female's menstrual cycle, for example, since in general the watery humors in the body increase and move to the body's surface when the moon waxes.[30] This influence indicates again why the medieval physician must understand astronomy as well as anatomy and the other medical disciplines. Only when the physician understands the influence of the planets on our bodies can he possibly prescribe the proper cure for a particular illness or the appropriate time for its administration. It is astronomy (or medical astrology) that enables the physician to determine the proper times for bloodletting, cauterizing, incisions, and so on.[31]

Once the planets are assigned humoral complexions, however, then it becomes possible to refer to them, as we do to humans or animals, as melancholy, choleric, sanguineous, or phlegmatic in nature. The moon and Venus, which are cold and moist, are phlegmatic; Jupiter, warm and moist, is sanguineous; Mars, hot and dry, is choleric; and Saturn, cold and dry, is melancholy. Moreover, because warmth and moisture are life-giving properties, coldness and dryness signified morbidity and decay. The *Tetrabiblos* of Ptolemy (d. c. 168 CE), translated into Latin c. 1138 by Plato of Tivoli and circulating under the title *Quadripartitum*, remarks,

now two [of the four humors], namely the hot and the moist, are fertile and active, for nothing experiences growth apart from them. But two, namely the

---

28. Albert of Behaim, *Das Brief- und Memorialbuch* 73, p. 309; Roger Bacon, *Opera hactenus inedita*, fasc. 5: *Secretum secretorum*, p. 17.

29. Albert the Great, *De animalibus* 12.2.4.122, vol. 16, 846 (SZ 2: 939–40).

30. See Albert the Great, *De causis proprietatum elementorum* 1.2.7, pp. 73–74.

31. See Joëlle Fuhrman, "L'influence de l'astrologie dans les écrits médicaux allemands du Moyen Age," in *Observer, Lire, Écrire le Ciel au Moyen Age. Actes du Colloque d'Orleans 22–23 Avril 1989* (Paris: Klincksieck, 1991), 101–13; also Hilary M. Carey, "Medieval Latin Astrology and the Cycles of Life: William English and English Medicine in Cambridge, Trinity College MS 0.5.26," in *Astro-Medicine: Astrology and Medicine East and West*, ed. Anna Akasoy, Charles Burnett, and Ronit Yoeli-Tlalim, Micrologus' Library 25 (Florence: SISMEL, 2008), 33–74.

dry and the cold, are destructive, through which things are diminished and destroyed. The ancients said that two of the wandering stars [that is, planets], Jupiter and Venus, together with the moon, are beneficent because of their tempered nature and because they abound in the hot and the moist. But the effects of the aforementioned stars Saturn and Mars naturally will have resisted effects of the opposite nature, one because of its excessive cold and the other for its excessive dryness.[32]

As a result, a child born in the seventh month of pregnancy will be healthy, but according to a common judgment reflected in the *Prose Salernitan Questions* (c. 1200), because cold and dry Saturn is dominant in the first and eighth months, a fetus born in the eighth month often dies from the influence of Saturn's mortificatory qualities.[33] This is because in the eighth month Saturn affects the womb by cooling the embryo, and Saturn's dryness also has a deleterious effect on the embryo's nutriment, namely, the menstrual blood.

In sum, for the medieval world the humoral complexion assigned to Saturn established a link between Saturn and the Jews even more clearly than did Tacitus's fables concerning the Jews' origin on Crete and their expulsion with Saturn. Both Saturn and Jews were distinguished by a cold and dry, melancholy complexion. Similarly, both were assumed to have a malign, baleful, or destructive power.

Yet Saturn's influence in the sublunar sphere will vary not only through its conjunction with other celestial bodies, but also because of its shifting celestial position. As the sun's influence varies from one place to another because of the angle of incidence of its rays, which depends on their zenith distance, so too will the influence of Saturn. As we will see below, certain terrestrial regions will be dominated by the influence of one or another of the celestial bodies, and the peoples or ethnic groups

---

32. "Duae videlicet, calor & humor, procreantes & efficientes, nil etenim nisi per illa, crementum suscepit. Duae vero scilicet frigiditas atque siccitas, destruentes, per eas nanque res minuunt esse quae desistunt. Duas stellarum erraticatunt, Iovem scilicet ac Venerem, Lunam etiam secundum priscae viros auctoritatis, fortunas esse dixere, eo quod earum est complexio temperata, & quod eis multum caloris ac humoris inest. Opera quidem Saturni, ac Martis operibus praedictarum, stellarum naturaliter contraria fore restati sunt, eo quod horum alter per frigiditatem intensam, & alter per siccitatum intensam operatur." Ptolemy, *Quadripartitum* 1.5 (Basel: Johannes Hervagius, 1533), 7.

33. "In octavo, quia Saturnus iterum dominatur, tunc puer moritur si exeat quoniam Saturnas mortificatorias habet qualitates." *The Prose Salernitan Questions. Edited from a Bodleian Manuscript (Auct. F. 3. 10)*, B.194b and P. 144, ed. Brian Lawn (London: Oxford University Press, 1979), 104, 259.

dwelling in these regions will display the influence of the dominating planet. According to the *Malleus Maleficarum* (*Hammer of Sorceresses*), printed in 1486, the stars actually have a greater influence upon whole peoples and provinces than upon individuals, because although an individual's free will may resist astrological influence, that influence will be more evident—or, we might say today, statistically significant—when considering a larger population.[34] Thus, although an individual Jew might escape Saturn's melancholy influence, Jews as a whole came to be viewed as "children" of Saturn, and were particularly subject to its influence.

Raymond Klibanksy, in his classic study of Saturn and melancholy, asserts that the mythic characteristics of Saturn's "children" came to Europe by the tenth century through an astrological work, the *Liber Alchandri philosophi*, for which Saturn's children "were dark, broad-shouldered, round-headed, and sparsely bearded. They were thieves; they were loquacious; they were persons who said one thing with their mouth but thought another ... they nourished resentment, they were sons of the devil."[35] By casting a horoscope, an individual could be identified as a "child" of Saturn; in addition, however, an entire people and religious community could fall under Saturn's influence. Just as the medical doctrine of the humors established a link between Saturn and the Jews' melancholy, Arab astronomical texts popular in Latin Christendom confirmed that not only the fortune of individuals, but also of whole peoples, kingdoms, and religions was subject to the influence of the conjunctions of the superior planets.

Among the most influential texts was Abū Ma'šar's/Albumasar's (787–886 CE) *Introduction to Astronomy* (c. 848), which was translated into Latin in the twelfth century by both John of Seville and Hermann of Carinthia, and his very popular work *The Great Conjunctions* (*De magnis conjunctionibus*), translated by John of Seville. For Albumasar, the rarer the planetary conjunction, the more potent was its influence upon historical events.[36] At the time of a great conjunction, prodigious events occur. Christian astrologers attempted to "predict" retrospectively the

---

34. Henricus Institoris and Jacobus Sprenger, *Malleus Maleficiarum* 1, q. 5, col. 33A, 1: 267.

35. Klibansky, Panofsky, and Saxl, *Saturn and Melancholy: Studies in the History of Natural Philosophy, Religion and Art*, 185. For a discussion of the *Liber Alchandri* (composed before 1000) see also Lynn Thorndike, *History of Magic and Experimental Science*, 8 vols. (New York: Columbia University Press, 1923–58), 4: 716–17.

36. J. D. North, "Astrology and the Fortunes of Churches," *Centaurus* 24 (1980), 185.

flood, the appearance of the biblical prophets, or the birth of Jesus in accord with this notion of the great conjunction, just as the Magi knew of Jesus' birth from the appearance of a star in the heavens. Jewish astrologers like Abraham bar Hiyya attempted to forecast the appearance of the messiah that the Jews still awaited in the same way.[37] In principle, the expert astrologer should also be able to predict events of greatest import, for example, the birth of Antichrist or the arrival of the End of Days.

Similarly, planetary conjunctions helped define world epochs. Roger Bacon was convinced that the conjunction of Jupiter with each of the six other planets signified the six principal religions of the world and defined the historical epoch for each. Jupiter's conjunction with Saturn signified Judaism and its divine law because, like Saturn (the planet most distant from the earth) the origin of Judaism is most remote in time. Michael Scot's commentary on the *Sphere of Sacrobosco* notes that just as the distant Saturn is cold and slow in its motion, so Saturn is the planet that governs the Jews and pagans who are slow to come to the [Christian] faith.[38] Not surprisingly, cold Saturn also has dominion over various diseases already tied to the Jews, for example, melancholy and leprosy.[39]

Islam or the law of the Saracens is identified with the conjunction of Jupiter and Venus. Albumasar had explained in his *On the Great Conjunctions* that at the time of Mohammad's accession (that is, the date of the Hejirah), "Venus was in the sign of its exaltation in the ninth place, signifying religion and, being the indicator of the Arabs by nature, it gave the rulership to them."[40] The link between Islam and Venus provided for the thirteenth-century Bishop Jacques de Vitry an explanation for Muslims' observance of their "Sabbath" on Friday, the "Day of Venus" (*dies Veneris*).[41] Similarly, because Venus was especially linked to

---

37. For other medieval Jewish examples, see Moshe Idel, "Saturn and Sabbatai Tzevi: A New Approach to Sabbateanism," in *Toward the Millenium: Messianic Expectations from the Bible to Waco*, ed. Peter Schäfer and Mark Cohen (Leiden: Brill, 1998), 180–81.

38. "septem sunt planete, Saturnus, Iupiter, Mars, Sol, Venus, Mercurius et Luna, de quibus dicunt theologi quod Saturnus est signator paganorum, Iudaeorum et omnium legi adversantium, qui tardi sunt ad fidem sicut Saturnus tardus est motu et frigidus effectu." See Lynn Thorndike, *The Sphere of Sacrobosco and Its Commentators*, lectio 9, p. 311.

39. See Robertus Anglicus's commentary in Thorndike, *The Sphere of Sacrobosco*, lectio 4, p. 161.

40. See Abū Ma'shar, *On Historical Astrology* 2.8, 2 vols., ed. Charles Burnett and Keiji Yamamoto (Leiden: Brill, 2000), 1: 127.

41. Jacques de Vitry, *Historia Orientalis* 6, p. 29.

lovemaking and desire—our term "venereal" is derived from the name of the goddess—Christian polemicists were accustomed to attribute to Mohammad and to Muslims (just as to Jews) excessive libidinal desire.[42]

While the rise of Islam was consistently assigned to the conjunction of Jupiter and Venus, the association of Saturn and Judaism was also a commonplace for the medieval world. For the tenth-century *Introduction to the Art of the Stars (Introductorium maius)* of Al-Qabīsī, known to the Latin world as Alcabitius:

Among the religions it [Saturn] indicates monotheism, if it is a happy [omen]. If it is an unhappy [omen] it indicates doubts accompanying the reliance on monotheism. Māšā'allāh said: "It indicates Judaism and the wearing of black clothes." Other people say: "Saturn indicates the inner ear, the spleen and the buttocks." Among the colours it has [the colour] black, among the days Saturday, and among the nights Wednesday night [. . .] Māšā'allāh said: "Among the appearances it indicates a man (*ādam*) whose glance, when he walks, is broken; whose complexion is red; who walks heavily . . . [who is] slender and lean; whose eyes are small and whose skin is dry . . . and [who is] of [great] cunning and deception.[43]

A Latin version was produced by John of Seville, and augmented with a fourteenth-century commentary by John of Saxony.[44]

These associations were advanced too by the Latin *Picatrix*, for which "among the languages it [Saturn] has Hebrew and Chaldean [Aramaic]; and among the external members, the right ear, and among the internal ones the spleen, which is a mineral (*minera*) of melancholy. . . . Among the religions it has Judaism, among clothes it has all black clothes." The *Picatrix* also advises anyone that wishes to harness the power of the planets with astrological talismans to adopt a garment appropriate to each planet. For those invoking Saturn, "The color of the garments [belonging to] Saturn is completely black and best among all is wool [fabric]."[45]

42. Cf. Paul Alvarus, *Indiculus Luminosus* 23 (PL 121: 538B-C); Petrus Alfonsi, *Dialogus contra Judaeos* 5, p. 67; and see Jeffrey Jerome Cohen, "On Saracen Enjoyment: Some Fantasies of Race in Late Medieval France and England," *Journal of Medieval and Early Modern Studies* 31, no. 1 (2001): 113-46.

43. Bodleian MS, Cod. Marsh 663, fol. 17 (a thirteenth-century Arabic manuscript). My thanks to Dr. Peter Pormann for this translation.

44. 'Abd al-'Aziz ibn 'Uthman al-Kabīsī/Alcabitius, *Alcabitii ad magisterium iudiciorum astrorum Isagoge: Commentario Joannis Saxonii declarata* (Paris: Vaenundatur a Simone Colinaeo apud scholas decretorum, 1521). My thanks to the Balliol College Library for providing access to this work.

45. "ex idiomatibus habet Hebraicum et Caldeum; et ex membris extrinsecis aurem

Alcabitius's *Introduction to the Art of the Stars* makes reference, above, to the Jewish astrologer Māshā'allāh (c. 740–c. 815), known in the Latin world as Messahala, a fragment of whose work *On Conjunctions, Religions, and Peoples* has survived in a later paraphrase or summary.[46] Māshā'allāh's treatise too affirms that historical cycles or world epochs arise from planetary conjunctions, and especially those of Jupiter and Saturn. These occur at approximately twenty year intervals. Since one divides the heavens into twelve zodiacal signs, with each sign represented by thirty degrees around a circle, the three signs in which three successive conjunctions occur are likely to be evenly spaced, comprising in sixty years a *triplicity*. The same triplicity will recur after roughly 240 years, after which the conjunction will shift to the next triplicity. This shift from one triplicity to the next is a *mutation (coniunctio maior)*. After four such mutations, roughly 960 years, the original triplicity recurs. This latter shift is called a *grand mutation* or *(coniunctio maxima)*. These periods—20, 240, or 960 years—offered interpreters several opportunities to explain world events and their historical frame. Other astronomical events would also be scrutinized for their significance, giving rise to historical astronomy which, as Charles Burnett remarks, "predicts various conditions of changes concerning kings and caliphs, dynasties and religions, wars and conquests, by means of eclipses, conjunctions, periods, revolutions of the years, and other astronomical factors."[47]

Both specific events—for example, the birth of the messiah—might be known in this way, as well historical epochs. Like Alcabitius's *Introduction to the Art of the Stars,* Albumasar's *On the Great Conjunctions* asserts a link between a conjunction of Saturn and Jupiter, and the Jews. According to Albumasar, "If it (Jupiter) is mixed with Saturn, it indicates the faith of the people of that religion is Judaism which is similar to the essence of Saturn, since the 'other' planets apply to it, and it does not apply to any planet among them. Similarly, the people of all other faiths confess Judaism, but it does not confess them (their faiths)."[48] While the

---

dextram, et ex intrinsecis splenem, que est minera melancholie . . . ; et ex legibus Iudaicam habet; et ex pannis omnes pannos nigros." *Picatrix: The Latin Version of the Ghāyat Al-Hakīm* 3.1.3, p. 91, lns. 27–30; and "Color vestimentorum Saturni: est omne nigrum, et melius omnibus laneum." *Picatrix* 3.3.11, p. 98, lns. 17–18.

46. E. S. Kennedy and David Pingree, *The Astrological History of Mâshâ' allâh* (Cambridge, Mass.: Harvard University Press, 1971).

47. Abū Ma'shar, *On Historical Astrology: The Book of Religions and Dynasties,* 1: xi.

48. Ibid., 1.4.4. John of Seville's Latin translation, on 1: 28, reads, "Si enim complexus

conjunction of Saturn and Jupiter was identified with the "reign" or age of Judaism, and the conjunction of Venus and Mars was linked with Islam, the conjunction of the Sun and Jupiter was tied to the rise of the [Christianized] Roman empire. The twelfth-century Hermann of Carinthia remarks that "[astronomers] write that the rule of the Jews is under Saturn, the dominion of the Arabs under Venus and Mars, and the Roman Empire under the Sun and Jupiter. They placed under the rule of the Arabs all the people of Mohammad, and under the Roman Empire, for the most part, all those subject to the Christian faith."[49]

Not only could important historical events be linked to the great conjunctions, but the influence of the seven planets was divided too among the seven *climata*, that is, the seven parallel bands that divided the earth according to differences in latitude and longitude.[50] It was empirically evident that the sun's influence varied according to latitude and longitude, as well as according to the season. It seemed a reasonable inference that just as the sun's influence varied from one place to another, so the influence of the other stars too varied from place to place, especially since the angle of incidence of their radiation, which depends on their zenith distance, would depend on terrestrial coordinates. Cecco d'Ascoli (d. 1327) makes this inference explicit in his commentary on *The Sphere of Sacrobosco*, noting,

---

Saturno, significabit quod fides civium eiusdem secte sit iudaismus qui congruit substantie Saturni, eo quod omnes planete iunguntur ei et ipse nemini eorum iungitur. Et similiter iudiaca fides: omnes cives ceterarum sectarum confitentur ei et ipsa nulli confitetur."

49. "Sic enim regnum Iudeorum sub Saturno scribunt, Arabum dominium sub Venere et Marte, Romanum imperium sub sole et Iove sub Arabum regnno statuentes omnem Machumate gentem, sub Romano imperio plerumque omnes Christianae fidei subiectos." Hermann of Carinthia, *De essentiis*, ed. and trans. Charles Burnett (Leiden: Brill, 1982), 166. For Hermann's career, see also Charles Burnett, "Hermann of Carinthia," in *A History of Twelfth Century Western Philosophy*, ed. Peter Dronke (Cambridge: Cambridge University Press, 1992), 386–406.

50. *Climata*: These are the bands into which ancient and medieval geographers had divided the known world. For early medieval authors, most popular was the Macrobian map showing five *climata*, based on the zones described in his *Commentary on the Dream of Scipio*. Of these five, three were uninhabitable. Later authors often expanded the number of *climata* to seven or eight (see Pseudo-Bede, *De mundi celestis terrestrisque constitutione*, p. 21). The number seven appears clearly in the work of Petrus Alfonsi, *Dialogi contra Judaeos* 1, p. 9, 23; it was adopted by Albert the Great, for example, for the division of the northern hemisphere. For a good discussion of medieval geography and cosmography as revealed in different types of maps, and their placement of the "monstrous races," see John Block Friedman, *The Monstrous Races in Medieval Art and Thought* (Syracuse, N.Y.: Syracuse University Press, 1999), 37–58.

For there are seven climates (*climata*) just as you know, and there are the seven planets which have dominion in them. Now Saturn has dominion in the first climate, Jupiter in the second, Mars in the third, the Sun in the fourth, and Venus in the fifth ... Mercury has dominion in the sixth. This is why the Lombards are such men of science, as you see that they are good in every type of faculty. But because Mercury is their signifier in terms of climate, they are all gluttonous, because Saturn adds uncleanness.... The moon has dominion over the seventh [climate]. The inhabitants of the climate in which a planet has dominion incline toward the nature of its dominant planet.[51]

Jews had been dispersed across the world after the destruction of the Second Temple, and the eleventh-century Muslim scholar Sā'id al-Andalusī remarks that, with the exception of the Arabian peninsula (from which they had been expelled), "there is no kingdom on earth, whether to the east or the west, to the north or the south, that has no Jews living in it."[52] Consequently, Jews might be found in any of the climes. As a result and because of their dispersion, Alonso de Cartagena remarks, they are no longer called Jews because of their geographical origin in Judea, but because of the name of their sect.[53] Nonetheless, it was widely acknowledged that Judaea or Roman Palestine had once been their "home," and despite the length of their exile, Jews continued to possess the humoral complexion dictated by their origin. Although they were permanently in diaspora and therefore, according to the climate theory to be discussed below, their bodies might be expected gradually to adapt to their environment, other factors—including the Jews' distinctive diet—brought about a different outcome. As Suzanne Conklin Akbari has remarked, "Jews take their climate with them."[54] Conse-

51. "Nam septem sunt climata sic ut scitis et septem sunt planete qui dominantur in eis. Nam Saturnus dominatur in primo climata, Iuppiter in secondo, Mars in tertio, sol in quarto, Venus in quinto ... Mercurius dominatur in sexto.... Idcirco Lombardi sunt ita homines scientifici ut videtis eos bonos in omni genere facultatum. Sed quia Mercurius est eorum significator ratione climatis, idcirco omnes sunt gulosi, quia Saturnus addit immunditiam.... Luna dominatur in septimo. Habitantes in climate in quo dominatur planeta inclinantur ad naturam illius planete dominantis." Thorndike, *The Sphere of Sacrobosco*, 374–75.

52. Sā'id al-Andalusī, *Science in the Medieval World: 'Book of the Categories of Nations'* 14, ed. and trans. Sema'an I. Salem and Alok Kumar (Austin: University of Texas Press, 1991), 79–80.

53. Alonso of Cartagena, *Defensorium unitatis Christianae* (*Tratado en favor de los judíos conversos*) 2.4.27, ed. Manuel Alonso (Madrid: Consejo Superior de Investigaciones Científicas, 1943), 238.

54. Suzanne Conklin Akbari, *Idols in the East: European Representations of Islam and the Orient, 1100–1450* (Ithaca, N.Y.: Cornell University Press, 2009), 150.

quently, Jewish as well as Muslim and Christian astrologers, including the Jew Māshā'allāh to whom we referred above, associated Jews with Saturn rather than with the far more benevolent Sun or Jupiter.

As complexion and celestial influences affect human physiology, however, they also influence human psychology and behavior. By the late Middle Ages, then, the myth that Saturn had devoured his children was invoked to substantiate claims that Jews "devoured" Christian infants, consuming their blood. Like the god Saturn, Jews were said to have sought to devour their spiritual progeny, Christians, in an effort to avert their religious rule. Again, like the god Saturn, they would fail and suffer expulsion. Christians, associated by medieval astrologers with Saturn's son, Jupiter, assumed hegemony and the Jews, like Saturn, were consigned to the most distant circle in the religious universe.

Late medieval artists were wont to depict the Jews in woodcuts and illustrations with filicidal Saturn; that association gave additional support to the calumny that Jews ritually murdered Christian children.[55] In a woodcut from an almanac of 1492 issued in German and Latin by the Nuremberg publisher Peter Wagner, Saturn appears as the ancient deity Kronos-Saturn that devoured his children. But Saturn is also depicted there with the hat and badge of the Jew, suggesting a link to a shared behavior.[56] Such images seem often to enjoy a life of their own that far outlasts the life of their component elements. This historical link between the Jews and Saturn may have been intended by a political cartoon published in the British *Independent* in 2003 that depicted Ariel Sharon devouring Palestinian babies.[57] The cartoon bears a striking resemblance to a painting by Francisco Jose de Goya (1746–1828), entitled "Saturn Devouring His Children." The cartoon was subsequently adopted and distributed by a number of radical Islamic groups. Israel unsuccessfully sued the *Independent*.

55. In his *The Jews in Christian Art*, 330–31, Heinz Schreckenberg includes an early sixteenth-century woodcut that depicts the Jews as one of the "children of Saturn" beneath an image of Saturn devouring his children, and a late fifteenth-century woodcut that depicts Saturn wearing the Jews' hat and *rota*, while eating a child.

56. See Eric Zafran, "Saturn and the Jews," *Journal of the Warburg and Courtauld Institutes* 42 (1979), 23.

57. Although as Anthony Bale reminds us when discussing the political cartoon, Saturn devours his *own* children, and not those of his enemies. See *The Jew in the Medieval Book: English Antisemitisms 1350–1500* (Cambridge: Cambridge University Press, 2006), 7–8. The award-winning cartoon is available at http://www.againstnazi.com/british_cartoons.htm.

THE ODOR OF CORRUPTION AND
THE *FOETOR JUDAICUS*

As a benefactor of agriculture, the Romans also sometimes treated Saturn as the god of dung or manure (*Saturnus Sterculius*) who prepared the fields for planting.[58] But this positive feature also lent to Saturn a repulsive odor. According to the popular Latin *Picatrix*, Saturn is the "source of an evil odor and stench" (*auctor mali odoris et fetidi*).[59] This stench could be transferred to those whose humoral complexion is dominated by Saturn's influence, to include the Jews, the "children of Saturn." In John of Spain's Latin translation of Alcabitius's tenth-century *Isagoge*, the "child" of Saturn will also have a stinking odor (*foetidi est odoris*).[60] Moreover, astrological texts often made a connection between Saturn, a melancholy complexion, and an evil smell.[61]

From late antiquity and into the medieval and early modern worlds, Jews were often said to suffer from a distinctive body odor, the *foetor judaicus* (Jewish stench), not unlike Saturn himself.[62] The fourth-century Roman historian Ammianus Marcellinus attributes to the emperor Marcus Aurelius the complaint that, while travelling in Palestine, he had become exceedingly wearied by the rebellious spirit and the foul odor of the Jews.[63] One should recall too that a particularly foul odor and bad breath

58. Macrobius, *Saturnalia* 1.7.25.
59. *Picatrix: The Latin Version of the Ghāyat Al-Hakīm* 3.7, p. 114, ln. 4.
60. 'Abd al-'Aziz ibn 'Uthman al-Kabīsī/Alcabitius, *Alcabitii ad magisterium iudiciorum astrorum Isagoge: Commentario Joannis Saxonii declarata*, 12.
61. Al-Qabīsī (Alcabitius), *The Introduction to Astrology* 2.2, 6, ed. and trans. Charles Burnett, Keiji Yamamoto, and Michio Yano (London: The Warburg Institute, 2004), 63.
62. The first-century author Martial (*Epigrams* 4.4) seems to attribute to Jewish women an especially foul odor that results from their practice of fasting. For text and discussion, see Heather A. McKay, *Sabbath and Synagogue: The Question of Sabbath Worship in Ancient Judaism* (Leiden: Brill. 1994), 110–11. In the nineteenth century, recalling the medieval canard of the *foetor Judaicus*, Hartwig von Hundt-Radowsky remarked that just as white parents may infrequently give birth to a black child, so now and then a Jew may be born, *per accidens*, "lacking the Jewish facial characteristics, *odor* and haggler's disposition." (Italics mine.) See the selection from his *The Jewish Mirror* excerpted and translated in Mendes-Flohr and Reinharz, *The Jew in the Modern World: A Documentary History*, 312.
63. "ille [Marcus Aurelius] enim cum Palaestinam transiret Aegyptum petens, Iudaeorum faetentium et tumultuantium saepe taedio percitus." Ammianus Marcellinus, *Rerum gestarum libri qui supersunt* 22.5.5, ed. Wolfgang Seyfarth, et al. (Leipzig: Teubner, 1978), 257. Martin Goodman (*Rome and Jerusalem*, 296 and n. 28) speculates that this may in fact reflect empirical reality, stemming from differences in climate and sartorial custom as the emperor moved from Rome to Palestine. Nonetheless, I would argue that once transferred

are characteristics assigned to lepers, with whom Jews were associated. Medieval physicians and natural scientists certainly understood that bad breath may simply result from poor oral hygiene or from stomach distress, but often it had a more profound cause.[64] Bartholomew the Englishman remarks that bad breath (*foetor oris*) results "sometimes from a universal infection of the body, as occurs in lepers whose breath is fetid and infectious."[65] Bad breath and body odor were not merely unpleasant realities of daily life; they could also be physiognomic indicators or signs of the corruption of the members.[66] Thus in Herman de Valenciennes's twelfth-century biblical epic, the *Romanz de Dieu et de sa mère*, Jesus is said to have "cured the stinking lepers."[67] Jacques de Vitry commented upon the intolerably foul odor of lepers, but insisted that if they will bear their torment with equanimity, then in the life to come God will transform their stench into a sweet smell (*erit eis pro fetore odor suavis*).[68] Francis of Assisi bathed a leper in fragrant herbs because, the leper remarked, "I stink so bad I cannot stand myself."[69] Thomas Aquinas notes that, in the Old Testament, lepers cleansed of their contagion had to offer a sacrifice of two sparrows, cedar, scarlet, and hyssop (Lev. 14:4). Interpreted on a literal level, Thomas remarks, these four kinds represent the four principal defects of leprosy: putrefaction (cedar), the repulsive skin

---

to Jews in Europe—who shared the same climate and dress as their medieval Christian neighbors, but washed and bathed more frequently—the claim that Jews suffered a peculiar stench became merely a form of abuse.

64. See *The Trotula: A Medieval Compendium of Women's Medicine* 178, 237 and 304–5, ed. and trans. Monica H. Green (Philadelphia: University of Pennsylvania Press, 2001), 140, 163, 186, 188.

65. Foetor oris quandoque causatur . . . ex universali corporis infectione, ut in leprosies, quorum anhelitus est foetidus et infectivus." Bartholomaeus Anglicus, *De rerum proprietatibus* 7.23, 304. See also Jacobus de Voragine, *The Golden Legend* 12, 1:70, where St. Silvester assists two magicians overcome by the foul breath of a dragon.

66. Martin Porter remarks that one of the original aspects of Michael Scot's work on physiognomy "lay in the fact that he seems to have been the first to include the sense of smell in the phenomenon of physiognomical perception." *Windows of the Soul: Physiognomy in European Culture 1470–1780* (Oxford: Clarendon Press, 2005), 70.

67. "Lieprex sana assez qui estoient puanz"; ln. 5332, quoted in Maureen Boulton, "Anti-Jewish Attitudes in Anglo-Norman Religious Texts: Twelfth and Thirteenth Centuries," in *Christian Attitudes toward Jews in the Middle Ages: A Casebook*, ed. Michael Frassetto (New York: Routledge, 2007), 157. For the text, see *Li Romanz de Dieu et de sa mère*, ed. Ina Spiele (Leiden: Presse universitaire de Leiden, 1975).

68. *Statuts d'hôtels-Dieu et de léproseries; recueil de textes du XIIe au XIVe siècle*, 3.

69. Francis of Assisi, *The Little Flowers of St. Francis* 25, in *Francis of Assisi, Early Documents*, 3: 608.

color of the leper (scarlet), numbness in the limbs (the living sparrows), and the leper's offensive stench (hyssop). On the eighth day following his purification the leper was readmitted to the community, but only after having shaved the hair of his body and having washed his clothes, because leprosy rots the hair, soils the clothes, and gives off an evil smell. Once these things had been done, then a sacrifice was offered for sin, since, Thomas reminds us, leprosy frequently results from sin.[70]

Even though in some cases foul odors may have medical benefits—for example, in certain very foul smelling medications—in most cases a terrible odor portends or causes illness or death. Bartholomew the Englishman explains,

There is a stench that is capable of infecting the spirits and nerves and capable of changing a natural consistency into something unnatural, as is evident in lepers, whose fetid breath infects and corrupts healthy people. There is even a stench that is capable of killing an animal fetus in the womb (as Aristotle says), as when a mare smells the stench of a candle that has been extinguished it will cause her to abort her fetus. There is also a stench that will be capable of causing sudden death, for there is a certain species of serpent whose stench can cause sudden death to one smelling it, just as the basilisk kills whoever looks upon it, as Avicenna says.[71]

Similarly, Albert the Great reports a tale of the philosopher Socrates who solved a case of airborne infection for the ruler Philip of Macedon (sic). According to Albert, Socrates used an ingenious device to discover two dragons occupying opposite sides of a mountain pass, whose fetid, stinking and poisonous breath caused travelers to fall down dead,[72] very much like the serpents that Bartholomew mentions above.

As we saw earlier, the sin of *luxuria* can sometimes be perceived by its foul odor. Albert the Great opines too that when individuals have sexual intercourse too frequently it causes their semen to become infected or corrupt. A woman that has too frequent intercourse will cause a cheese

---

70. Thomas Aquinas, Summa theologica 1.2, q. 102, art. 5, resp. 7

71. "Est etiam foetor spirituum & nervorum infectivus et a naturali consistentia in innaturalem alterativus. ut patet in leprosis, quorum anhelitus foetidus sanos inficit & corrupit. Est etiam fetor fetus animalium in utero extinctivus (unde dicit Arist.), quod equa si sentit fetorem candele extincte faciet abbortivum. Potest etiam foetor sic intendi quod erit mortis subitae causativus, nam quaedam est species serpentis cuius foetor subito interfecit rem se odorantem, sicut basiliscus visu interfecit se videntem, ut dicit Avicen." Bartholomaeus Anglicus, *De rerum proprietatibus* 19.39, p. 1168.

72. Albert the Great, *Liber de causis proprietatum elementorum* 2.2.1, p. 95.

to putrefy quickly, and a man of this sort will cause a sword to rust. Such people, he adds, emit an odor as foul and corrupt as a dead body, which is why dogs follow them, sniffing at their heels.[73] By contrast, the bodies of the saints typically exude a very sweet smell, as in the case of young William of Norwich. Although his body had been exposed to the elements for days, when it was discovered, "there was absolutely no bad smell perceptible."[74] In a similar way, the saints in heaven will exude a sweet odor or smell, although perhaps odor should be said equivocally in this instance because their bodies will have become incorruptible, while those condemned to hell will be easily known from their foul stink.[75] The stench of hell became a polemical device in the Paris disputation of 1240, when Nicholas Donin charged the Talmud with blasphemy for placing Jesus in hell in boiling, stinking excrement.[76] While certainly this would have made Jesus stink, Donin also alleges that the Talmud established this punishment for Jesus "in order to make us Christians stink," that is, in order to transfer the stench of Hell to all of Jesus' followers.[77]

---

73. Albert the Great, *Quaestiones super de animalibus* 5.11-14 (QDA, 202).

74. Thomas of Monmouth, *The Life and Miracles of St.William of Norwich by Thomas of Monmouth* 1.13, p. 39.

75. See Albert the Great, *Quaestiones,* ed. Albert Fries, Wilhelm Kübel, and Henryk Anzulewicz, Ed. Colon. 25.2 (Münster in Westfalorum: Aschendorff, 1993): *Quaestio de sensibus corporis gloriosi* art. 2, 1: *De odoratu,* 121-22. Although Albert explains that the Church accepts that the bodies of the saints in heaven will have the sweetest odor (121, 7-9), while in the bodies of the damned there will be stench (*fetor*), he is compelled to investigate how the saints in heaven can have an odor at all, since odors seem to stem from some form of bodily corruption. For a discussion of the stench of fallen humanity and the sweet fragrance of the saints and paradise in patristic texts, see Susan Ashbrook Harvey, *Scenting Salvation: Ancient Christianity and the Olfactory Imagination* (Berkeley: University of California, 2006).

76. Cf. B. T. *Gittin,* 56b-57a, and Peter Schäfer, *Jesus in the Talmud,* 82-94. For the sulfurous stench of Hell, see also Honorius of Autun, *De imagine mundi* 1.37 (PL 172: 133B). For Donin and his career, see Kurt Schubert, "Apostasie aus Identitätskrise—Nicholas Donin," *Kairos: Zeitschrift für Judaistik und Religionswissenschaft* n.s. 30-31 (1988-89): 1-10. For useful discussion of his role in events leading to the burning of the Talmud in Paris in 1242, see André Tuilier, "La condamnation du Talmud par les maîtres universitaires Parisiens, ses causes et sese conséquences politiques et idéologiques," in *Le brûlement du Talmud à Paris 1242-1244,* ed. Gilbert Dahan (Paris: Les Éditions du Cerf, 1999), 59-78; and, in the same volume, Yvonne Friedman, "Anti-Talmudic Invective from Peter the Venerable to Nicolas Donin (1144-1244)," 171-90. According to the *Annales Erphordenses fratrum Praedicatorum,* 98, the King of France (St. Louis), consigned twenty-four cartloads of Jewish books to the flames.

77. Donin claims he explained this to the Queen in the vernacular. See the Hebrew account of R. Yehiel of Paris in Hyam Maccoby's *Judaism on Trial,* 156. This represents a literal translation of an idiom that could also mean "to make us look bad," suggesting a play on words. My thanks to Daniel Lasker for drawing my attention to this.

Both sweet and foul odors, then, became medical and theological signifiers. In contrast to the saints, the bodies of the damned will produce a terrible stench.[78] So too will the devil. Rudolf of Schlettstadt describes a noble woman in Zurich engaged in an adulterous affair at the end of the thirteenth century. She went to meet her lover secretly, but the devil came in his place, disguised as the man she expected. The devil penetrated her painfully, whereupon she made the sign of the Cross, causing the devil to flee, but not before leaving behind an especially foul stench.[79] A foul odor, then, was a product of sin and corruption, as well as a result of illness or disease. Perhaps the clearest indication that an offensive odor is at least indirectly a punishment for sin appears in Vincent of Beauvais's claim that even though in Paradise Adam and Eve would have defecated, this natural function would have occurred without "inconvenience" and without a foul smell because they would have continued to sustain themselves only with pure foods. But once deprived of these foods as punishment and as a result of the fall, a bad odor followed.[80]

A bad odor or stench, then, was associated with Saturn, corruption, sin, and the devil. It was also produced by a variety of illnesses that arose from corruption and signified sin—including leprosy and melancholy. And, finally, it was produced by avarice, by frequent sexual intercourse, and lust or *luxuria*. In medieval art, *luxuria*, one of the seven deadly sins, is sometimes shown riding on a goat, an animal often described as filthy, oversexed, and having a foul odor.[81] Its sexual potency could be transferred to humans, inasmuch as a man that eats the testicles of a goat before sexual intercourse will typically generate a son, provided the woman's complexion does not present some impediment.[82] Not accidentally, the goat was associated with the Jew as well. In the Tucher window of the Freiburg Cathedral, *Synagoga* carries a goat's head, "her most distinctive emblem" and also "the emblem for lust" or *luxuria*.[83]

---

78. See Albert the Great, *Quaestio de sensibus corporis gloriosi* art. 2, 1: *De odoratu*, in *Quaestiones*, 121.

79. Rudolf of Schlettstadt, *Historiae Memorabiles* 43, p. 105.

80. Vincent of Beauvais, *Speculum naturale* 31.16, 1: 2305. Cf. Albert the Great, *Commentarii in II Sententiarum* dist. 20, art. 5, Ed. Borgnet 2, 345.

81. *The Book of Beasts* (p. 74) describes the he-goat (*hrycus*) as "a lascivious and butting animal who is always burning for coition. His eyes are transverse slits because he is so randy."

82. Albert the Great, *De animalibus* 22.2.1.38, vol. 16, 1369 (SZ 2: 1466–67).

83. Seiferth, *Synagogue and Church in the Middle Ages*, 103, 121, 146; see also figs. 28 and 40–42.

Moreover, the goat was the devil's chosen animal, and just as witches will be shown riding a goat[84] Jews, as servants or spiritual sons of the devil,[85] were often depicted riding goats, or wearing a goatlike beard, that is, a goatee.[86] The foul-smelling goat and the Jew were linked, then, in the medieval imagination and, as already mentioned, by the thirteenth century the notion of a specifically Jewish stench or *foetor iudaicus* had also appeared.[87] The *Dialogue on Miracles* (*Dialogus miraculorum*; c. 1220) of the Cistercian Caesarius of Heisterbach contains several *exempla* that describe Jews and Christian encounters with Jews. In one of his tales, he describes a Jewish girl who converted to Christianity and entered a convent, against the wishes of her family. Her father sought to obtain her return from the duke and he visited the convent with members of his family with the hope of bringing her home again. Caesarius reports:

When the Jew came to the aforementioned convent with his friends and relatives, the virgin who was confined inside, although she knew nothing of their coming, actually began to perceive a great smell, such that she said quite plainly, "I do not know where it is coming from, [but] a Jewish stench (*foetor Judaicus*) oppresses me." Meanwhile, while the Jews were knocking on the window, when the abbess said to the girl, as I believe: "daughter Catherine," for thus was she named at her baptism, "your parents want to see you"; she replied: "See, that is the stench I sensed. I will not see them."[88]

84. See Dorinda Neave, "The Witch in Sixteenth-Century German Art," *Woman's Art Journal* 9, no. 1 (1988), 4.

85. St. Vincent Ferrer, *Tractatus contra Judeorum detestabilem horrendam veteremque perfidiam*, in *Oeuvres de Saint Vincent Ferrer*, 2 vols., ed. Pierre Henri Fages (Paris: A. Picard et fils, 1909), 1: 31. For Vincent Ferrer and the Jews, see Manuel Ambrosio Sánchez Sánchez, "Predicación y antisemitismo: El caso de san Vicente Ferrer," in *Proyección histórica de España en sus tres culturas: Castilla y León, América y el Mediterráneo* (Valladolid: Junta de Castilla y León, 1993), 195–203. On the development of medieval traditions identifying Jews with the devil, see Robert Bonfil, "The Devil and the Jews in the Christian Consciousness of the Middle Ages," in Almog, *Antisemitism through the Ages*, 91–98.

86. See Ruth Mazo Karras, "Separating the Men from the Goats: Masculinity, Civilization and Identity Formation in the Medieval University," in *Conflicted Identities and Multiple Masculinities: Men in the Medieval West*, ed. Jacqueline Murray (New York: Garland, 1999), 202. Sara Lipton also remarks upon an illustration in the thirteenth-century *Bible moralisée* in which the devil is portrayed as a horned goat upon an altar, reverenced by a bearded Jew wearing a pointed cap and holding out a moneybag—a symbol of the Jew's avarice—toward the goat. See her *Images of Intolerance*, 42–43. For a fifteenth-century carving from the Church of Notre Dame in Aerschot (Belgium) showing a Jew riding upon a goat, see also Trachtenberg, *The Devil and the Jews*, 45.

87. For a discussion of the earliest medieval appearance of this charge in the work of Venantius Fortunatus (d. 609), see Israel Lévi, "L'odeur des juifs," a subsection in his larger work, "Le Juif de la légende," *Revue des études juives* 20 (1890): 249–52.

88. "Veniente vero Judaeo ad iam fatum coenobium cum amicis et cognatis suis, virgo

The Jewish stench becomes so commonplace that Claudine Fabre-Vassas describes it as "the first and most constant feature of anti-Judaism, and the most universal as well."[89] Additional examples abound. The popular thirteenth-century Franciscan preacher Berthold of Regensburg (d. 1272) also identifies the Jews with a stinking odor, even though he acknowledges that they observe their holy days better than Christians do. In a colorful vernacular sermon, he chides his audience:

> Now you see very well that a stinking goatish Jew, whose odor is offensive to all, honors his holy days better than you. Bah! As a Christian you should be ashamed of yourself that you do not trust in God as much as the stinking Jew, by thinking that if you spent the holy day in His praise as He commanded you, He would certainly reward you.[90]

Similarly, Berthold chastises his audience because Christian spouses fail to observe the periods when sexual intercourse is prohibited to them, for example, during Lent, when a woman is pregnant, or when a woman is "sick" with her menstrual flow. Once more Berthold attempts to shame his Christian audience by comparing it unfavorably to the "stinking Jew" who scrupulously observes the times of separation. If married couples conceive during these prohibited times, he warns, the children born to

---

infra constituta, cum de illorum adventu prorsus nil sciret, sentire coepit foetorem magnum, ita ut palam diceret: Nescio unde sit, foetor Judaicus me gravat. Interim Judaeis pulsantibus ad fenestram, cum puellae diceret Abbatissa, ut puto: Filia Katharina, sic enim vocata fuit in baptismo, parentes tui volunt te videre; respondit illa: Ecce iste est foetor quam sensi. Non videbo illos," Caesarius of Heisterbach, *Dialogus Miraculorum*, 2 vols., ed. Joseph Strange (Cologne: Sumptibus J. M. Heberle, 1851), 1: 96. For Caesarius's anti-Jewish exempla, see also Ivan Marcus, "Images of the Jews in the *Exempla* of Caesarius of Heisterbach," in Cohen, *From Witness to Witchcraft: Jews and Judaism in Medieval Christian Thought*, 247–56.

89. Fabre-Vassas, *The Singular Beast: Jews, Christians, and the Pig*, 103.

90. For this translation (which I have slightly amended), see Marc Saperstein's "Christians and Jews—Some Positive Images," *Harvard Theological Review* 79, no. 1–3 (1986), 238. The German text reads: "'Sê! nû sihst dû wol, daz ein stinkender jüde, der die liute an bokezet, sînen vîgertac baz êret danne dû. Pfi! des möhtest dû kristener dich wol schamen, daz dû got niht alse wol getrûwest als der stinkende jüde, ob dû den vîgertac in sînen lobe vertribest, als er dir geboten hât, daz er dich des ergetzete." Berthold von Regensburg, *Völlstandige Ausgabe seiner Predigten*, 2 vols., notes by Franz Pfeiffer (Vienna: Wilhelm Braumüller, 1862), 1: 270, 24–29. Trachtenberg, correctly it seems, translated the passage to indicate the stinking "goatish" nature of the Jews. See Trachtenberg, *The Devil and the Jews*, 227–28 n. 18. Vernacular sermons very often emphasized the alien character of Jews even more than Latin texts. See Winfried Frey, "Gottesmörder und Menschenfeinde. Zum Judenbild in der deutschen Literatur des Mittelalters," in *Die Juden in ihrer mittelalterlichen Umwelt*, ed. Alfred Ebenbauer and Klaus Zatloukal (Cologne: Böhlau, 1991), 35–51.

them will be leprous or epileptic, or suffer some other infirmity.[91] Similarly, Rudolf of Schlettstadt describes "the Jews [as] unclean and stinking and viler than dogs."[92]

The Jews' stench was more than an offensive odor. It also signified a source of illness and contagion. Michael Gerli notes that the Spanish chronicler Andrés Bernáldez (d. 1516) depicts the "Jews as foul smelling, [and] he virtually faults them for the epidemics of plague in Andalusia since this disease was widely reputed to be spread principally by means of rank odors and corrupted scents."[93] Bernáldez remarks often on the "stinking synagogue" and the "stinking Jews," whose foul odor stemmed from their peculiar diet and from the fact that they remained unbaptized; since the Spanish conversos allegedly shared Jewish dietary practices, they too emitted a terrible smell.[94] Thus, the *foetor Judaicus* was thought to be one of the special punishments imposed upon the Jews by God, and confirmed by nature. Even though Christians also assigned a

---

91. Berthold von Regensburg, *Völlstandige Ausgabe seiner Predigte*, 1: 323, 12–18. Cf. Remo Joseph Iannucci, *The Treatment of the Capital Sins and the Decalogue in the German Sermons of Berthold von Regensburg*, The Catholic University of America, Studies in German 17 (New York: AMS Press, 1942), 29–30.

92. "Judei vero, qui immundi ac fetidi sunt ac viliores canibus." Rudolf of Schlettstadt, O.P., *Historiae Memorabiles* 39, p. 101. For Rudolf's anti-Jewish polemic, see Miri Rubin, "Rudolph of Schlettstadt, O.P.: Reporter of Violence, Writer on Jews," in *Christ among the Medieval Dominicans: Representations of Christ in the Texts and Images of the Order of Preachers*, ed. Kent Emery and Joseph Wawrykow (Notre Dame, Ind.: University of Notre Dame Press, 1998), 283–92; Johannes Grabmayer, "Rudolf von Schlettstadt und das aschkenasische Judentum um 1300," *Aschkenas: Zietschrift für Geschichte und Kultur der Juden* 4, no. 2 (1994): 301–36; and Friedrich Lotter, "Die Judenverfolgung des 'Koenig Rintfleisch' in Franken um 1298," *Zeitschrift für Historische Forschung* 15, no. 4 (1988): 385–423.

93. Michael Gerli, "Social Crisis and Conversion: Apostasy and Inquisition in the Chronicles of Fernando del Pulgar and Andrés Bernáldez," *Hispanic Review* 70, no. 2 (2002), 152.

94. See Andrés Bernáldez, *Memorias del reinado de los Reyes Católicos, que escribá el bachiller Andrés Bernáldez*, chaps. 43–44, ed. Manuel Gómez-Moreno y Juan de M. Carriazo (Madrid: Real Academia de la Historia, 1962). These texts are translated in *The Spanish Inquisition, 1478–1614: An Anthology of Sources*, ed. and trans. Lu Ann Homza (Indianapolis: Hackett, 2006), 1–8. Roth, too, explains this as an allusion to an ancient prejudice (the *foetor judaicus*) but also allows that it may have had some empirical basis. See Norman Roth, *Conversos, Inquisition, and the Expulsion of the Jews from Spain*, 81. An empirical basis does not, however, explain the determination of what constitutes an offensive odor since this is itself a cultural response. For an effort to link the eating of garlic to the Jews' stench, see Maria Diemling, "'As the Jews Like to Eat Garlick': Garlic in Christian-Jewish Polemical Discourse in Early Modern Germany," in *Food and Judaism*, ed. Leonard J. Greenspoon, Ronald A. Simkins, and Gerald Shapiro (Omaha: Creighton University Press, 2004), 215–34.

bad odor to Muslims, their odor was thought less offensive than that of the Jews. Felix Fabri, the Swiss-born Dominican who travelled to Jerusalem from 1480 to 1483, noted this following his visit to the medicinal hot baths at Gazara. Seeking to explain why the Saracens permit Christian pilgrims access to their baths but deny access to Jews, he remarked that

Saracens are befouled with an especially loathsome odor, which explains why they practice frequent and varied ablutions (*baptisimatibus*). Because we do not have an odor, they do not care if we bathe with them. They do not permit this to the Jews, who give off a worse odor. They are happy to see us in the baths, even as a leper rejoices when a healthy person spends time with him, since he is not despised and in this way he hopes to be made healthier himself, so too the stinking Saracen rejoices to be near one who does not smell.[95]

This text illustrates an interesting cultural prejudice, namely, that Christians are without a bad odor, and the absence of body odor signifies that Christians are healthy and not a source of illness. In another passage, the author relates that Christian defenders at a castle near Rhodes have bred "sniffer" guard dogs that can distinguish Christians from Turks by their odor.[96] Muslims have a bad odor, but the worst stench of all is found among the Jews, resulting in their exclusion from public baths. While the ritual ablutions associated with Muslim prayer are interpreted as a way to eliminate their odor, the author fails to credit Jewish ablutions or ritual baths with the same effect. In part this may be because a bad odor or stench is not only an indicator of illness, but also an external sign of moral turpitude. St. Antoninus of Florence outlines the many punishments or afflictions that befall those who are guilty of one of the sins against nature, namely, masturbation, sodomy, bestiality, and homosexuality, which are subspecies of *luxuria*, and notes that "Fifth [among the afflictions] is the bad odor of the flesh, for every [form of] *luxuria*, and especially this one [that is, homosexuality], is a cause of stench."[97] Not

---

95. "Sarraceni quodam teterrimo foetore sordescant; propter quem, creberrimis baptisimatibus et variis utuntur, now vero, quia foetore illo caremus, non curant, quod cum eis balneemur. Quod Judaeis non indulgent, qui pejore foetore squalent; libenter in balneis vident: sicut enim leprosus gaudet, dum sanus communicat ei, ex eo, quod non spernitur, et quod sperat, se propter sanum melius habiturum; sic foetidus Sarracenus gaudet communicare cum non foetente." Felix Fabri, *Evagatorum in Terrae Sanctae, Arabiae et Egyptii peregrinationem*, fol. 15B, 2: 370.

96. Ibid., fol. 164a, 3: 261.

97. "Quintum est foetor carnis, omnis enim luxuria, & illa maxime, est caussa foetoris." St. Antoninus of Florence, *Summa theologica* 2, tit. 5, cap. 4, §3, 2: 672E.

unlike the Saracens in the account of Felix Fabri cited above, St. Antoninus insists that "[A Christian] is prohibited from dwelling with or bathing with Jews." He even adds a canonical penalty for those who violate this rule: "if a cleric, let him be deposed; if a layman, let him be excommunicated."[98] Admittedly, St. Antoninus recognizes that Christians are often guilty of *luxuria* and sexual crimes against nature as well; worse, these sins act like a contagion, entrapping others in their turpitude. For this reason, they are symbolized by leprosy, just as leprosy infects others that interact with lepers. Therefore, just as under law lepers are sequestered to prevent infection, so one ought to avoid any interaction with Jews, or with those guilty of a sin against nature. Both the one and the other may cause an offensive stench; the latter even seems responsible for the plague that has befallen Christendom. St. Antoninus adds that "perhaps this is why plagues often befall many cities in Italy, because this vice abounds in them more than in others."[99] If plague is a result of infection (whether moral or physical) the solution, however, is clear: isolate and protect Christian society from its source.

Just as Juan de Quiñones will invoke the myth of Jewish male menses to help the Inquisition to identify crypto-Jews, so the *foetor Judaicus* will be invoked to achieve the same end. In the Spanish anti-converso polemics of the fifteenth and sixteenth centuries a repulsive body odor was attributed to the Jewish converts that even the waters of baptism could not fully eradicate.[100] Conversely, in a fourteenth-century Old French text, a pilgrim to the Holy Land, Bertrandon de la Broquière, remarked that his local guide was "the son of a Christian woman who had him baptized . . . in order to remove the odor and stench that those who have not been baptized have."[101] The stench or odor that generally afflicts the unbap-

---

98. "Prohibetur habitatio cum Judaeis & balneatio . . . . 'si clericus est, deponatur, si laicus, excommunicetur.'" St. Antoninus of Florence, *Summa theologica* 2, tit. 12, cap. 3, 2: 1151B.

99. "Et forte ista est caussa, quare in multis civitatibus Italiae frequenter superveniunt pestes; quia magis abundat tale vitium, quam in aliis aliquibus." St. Antoninus of Florence, *Summa theologica* 2, tit. 5, cap. 4, §2, 2: 671B.

100. See Moises Orfali, "Jews and Conversos in Fifteenth-Century Spain: Christian Apologia and Polemic," in Cohen, *From Witness to Witchcraft: Jews and Judaism in Medieval Christian Thought*, 346.

101. Bertrandon de la Broquière, *Le Voyage d'outremer de Bertrandon de la Broquière*, ed. Charles Schefer (Paris: Ernest Leroux, 1892; repr. Farnborough: Gregg, 1972), 90. My thanks to Alexandra Cuffel for drawing my attention to this text.

tised evidently is removed by the waters of baptism—except, some imply, among the Jews. Moreover, it seems that Jews in particular were despised for this repulsive odor, and a foul odor or foul breath was a characteristic displayed as well by the servants of Satan.[102] Just like male menstruation, the alleged foul odor of the Jews could be utilized by the Inquisition and secular authorities to "sniff out" crypto-Jews in Spain. While Jews were said to murder and to harvest the blood of Christians to stem the loss of blood they experienced because of male menstruation, Martin Luther (d. 1546) also reminds us of the link between the *foetor Judaicus* and murder. In a remark that is reminiscent of the charge brought to the attention of the City Council of Freiburg in 1401, some Christians, Luther maintains, say that "they [Jews] need the blood of Christians to get rid of their stench."[103] This link between the Jews' odor and Christian blood reappears in the sixteenth-century *Wendunmuth*, which records that "Jews cannot live and exist without Christian blood, and—I beg your pardon— they stink like goats."[104] But once again we may infer that because Jews were thought mistakenly to seek the blood of any Christian rather than the blood of Christ to heal them of their affliction, so long as they remain Jews, unbaptized and separated from the eucharistic body and blood, they can never be cleansed of this foul odor. The attribution of a particularly offensive odor to Jews had become so common that in the early sixteenth century it is invoked to lampoon the Jewish convert Johannes Pfefferkorn in the *Letters of Obscure Men*, in order to reveal him to be a false Christian. The fictional letterwriter, Adolph Klingesor, reports that some say that because "it is commonly said that when Jews are baptized they cease to stink" (*dicunt communiter, quod quando Iudaei baptizan-*

---

102. Ernaldus, Abbot of Bonnevalle, reports that a horrible countenance and fetid breath (or perhaps flatulence) attest to Satanic possession: "vultus terribilis, flatus fetidus, inhabitoris Satanae colluvia testabantur." *Sancti Bernardi Abbatis Clarae-Vallensis Vita et Res Gestae Libris Septem Comprehensae*, 3.13 (PL 185: 276B). Demons often are designated by a terrible stench. See Archanaldus Andegavensis, *Vita Maurilii ep. Andegavensis* 7.29, ed. Bruno Krusch, MGH, SS, Auctores antiquissimi 4, 2 (Berlin: Weidmann, 1885), 88.

103. Martin Luther, *That Jesus Christ Was Born a Jew*, in *Luther's Works*, trans. W. I. Brandt (Philadelphia: Fortress Press, 1971), 45: 195–229, 195, quoted in Stow, *Jewish Dogs*, 9. For the reference to the City Council of Freiburg, see chap. 5, p. 202.

104. "die Jüden vermögen ohne Christen blut nich sein oder leben, und stinken (mit züchten zu reden) wie die böcke." Hans Wilhelm Kirchhof, *Wendunmuth* 5 (Tübingen: Litterarischer Verein in Stuttgart, 1869), 132, quoted in Winfried Frey, "Jews and Christians at the Lord's Table," in *Food in the Middle Ages: A Book of Essays*, ed. Melitta Weiss Adamson (New York: Garland, 1995), 134.

tur, non amplius foetent), Pfefferkorn is not *really* a Christian, since "he still stank like any other Jew" (*adhuc foetebat sicut alius Iudaeus*).[105] In the seventeenth century, Isaac Cardoso devoted an entire chapter to refute this calumny in his *Los excelencias y calumnias de los Hebreos*, arguing that because dry geographical regions are aromatic, and humid ones are malodorous, *science* must conclude that since Jews are natives of hot and dry regions, they do not exude a foul smell.[106] His appeal to climate science, however, could not overthrow older traditions.

JEWISH PHYSIOGNOMY AND RACE

In the late medieval world, enduring physical characteristics associated with Jews were presumed useful for identifying converts to Christianity still stained by Jewish corruption. Male menses, a foul odor, and certain illnesses could provide a guide to those Inquisitors charged with ensuring the purity of the Christian body. So too could the observance of Jewish rituals or customs: for example, an unwillingness to eat pork, or Sabbath or festival observances. The invocation of a quasiracial principle—that is, that such characteristics could not be eliminated or cleansed through baptism—seems to mark a new stage in the development of Christian anti-Jewish sentiment. Modern historians have argued passionately over the origin of this new principle. Some have insisted that the notion of a superior, "pure race" originated with the Jews themselves and was then appropriated by the Old Christians in Spain in order to prevent new converts from displacing them in social, economic, and political life. Others have insisted that the conversos or New Christians invoked the racial heritage of the Jews only in response to acts of discrimination initiated by the Old Christians.[107] Regardless of the source of this new conception, from the point of view of many Old Christians intermarriage with converso families would infect the purity of Spanish blood, corrupt the Spanish character, and eventually cause its demise. The struggle against the conversos was even more bitter than the struggle against unbaptized Jews: Jews were condemned for what they were; conversos were condemned for what they strove to become, namely, Christian Spaniards.

105. *Epistolae obscurorum virorum* 2.25, vol. 2, 185.
106. Isaac Cardoso, *Los excelencias y calumnias de los Hebreos*, 339–45; cf. Yosef Hayim Yerushalmi, *From Spanish Court to Italian Ghetto*, 434.
107. For discussion of the arguments, see B. Netanyahu, *The Origins of the Inquisition in Fifteenth Century Spain* (New York: Random House, 1995), 976–91.

What are some of the causes of this conflict? Fourteenth-century Spain had been faced with the daunting task of assimilating large numbers of Jewish converts to Christianity. Many of these may have been Jews that entered Aragon and Catalonia following their expulsion from France in 1306. Some were also likely recent Jewish converts to Christianity that had fled France but reverted to Judaism in Spain. It was common for converts to relocate to avoid the resentment of former co-religionists; similarly, it was prudent for converts that sought to return to Judaism to move to an area in which they were unknown to avoid the condemnation of the Christian community that had received them. Such conversions followed by a return to Judaism, however, only raised doubts about the loyalty of Jewish converts in general. Likewise, during the anti-Jewish violence of the Pastoureaux in 1320, many Jews converted to Christianity, but after such mass conversions a large number sought to return to Jewish communities.[108] Later events in the fourteenth century also brought about mass conversion, especially following a series of violent attacks upon Jewish communities in Spain in 1391. At that time, all but one Valencian Jewish community was exterminated. The Jews of Mallorca were attacked and, in general, Jews were offered the choice of baptism or death. The fate of Catalan communities was little better.[109] This unprecedented level of violence led to mass conversions, but the king of Aragon lamented that the mass conversions made it nearly impossible to tell who was a Jew and who a Christian, and such potential confusion will renew demands not only that the Jews be marked with a badge but that they be segregated in separate communities or urban quarters as well.[110] Moreover, it seems that the pressure of assimilating large numbers of Jewish

108. Yom Tov Assis, "Juifs de France réfugiés en Aragon (XIII–XIV siècles)," *Revue des Etudes Juives* 142 (1983): 299–302. For a discussion of the effects of mass conversion and reversion on papal and royal policies, see also Yom Tov Assis, "The Papal Inquisition and Aragonese Jewry in the Early Fourteenth Century," *Mediaeval Studies* 49 (1987): 391–410.

109. See the useful introduction by Yom Tov Assis in *The Jews in the Crown of Aragon. Regesta of the* Cartas Reales *in the Archivo de la Corona de Aragón, Part II: 1328–1493*, compiled by Gemma Escribà, ed. Yom Tov Assis, Sources for the History of the Jews in Spain 5 (Jerusalem: Henk Schussheim Memorial Series, 1995).

110. For a more general study of Jewish conversion to Christianity in the medieval world, although with some attention given to the mass conversions in Spain, see Joseph Shatzmiller, "Jewish Converts to Christianity in Medieval Europe 1200–1500," in *Cross Cultural Convergences in the Crusader Period. Essays Presented to Aryeh Grabois on His Sixty-Fifth Birthday*, ed. Michael Goodich, Sophia Menache, and Sylvia Schein (New York: Peter Lang, 1995), 297–318.

converts after 1391 led to the emergence of a late medieval racialism, culminating in the purity of blood laws already mentioned. By 1492 the expulsion of the Jews from Spain (and Portugal in 1497) eliminated their immediate threat. The conversos, however, remained.

During the fifteenth century, purity of blood statutes were promulgated in diverse Spanish institutions and municipalities. It became clear, however, that a law that excluded everyone from public office who had any Jewish blood would be unworkable in a land in which Jews and Christians had lived side by side for centuries. Nonetheless, specific guidelines were provided by the cathedral chapter of Cordoba in 1530, where a candidate for any office in the cathedral chapter was to swear that he was not descended from a Jew or Moor. In addition, he had to provide genealogical details to be investigated by the chapter. Similar rules were applied in the cathedral chapter in Toledo. In Barcelona in 1557 the statutes of the surgeons' guild rejected all persons "infected" with the blood of Jews or Moors or conversos. Nevertheless, once purity of blood was established by investigation to show an absence of Jewish blood going back four generations, it never had to be reestablished, and thus paradoxically the purity of blood laws could work as an instrument of assimilation as well as segregation—when compelling reasons existed to "forget" a person's lineage, and to corroborate claims about his racial origin, he could be grafted onto the old trunk.[111]

Regardless of the source of this concept that treated Christian identity as a quasiracial category, it violently destabilized traditional categories of religious identity in Spain, as David Nirenberg has argued. Old Christians, threatened by the rapid advancement of recent converts after 1391, focused on mapping Jewish cultural or racial characteristics of the sort we have already identified, in order to disenfranchise conversos as "Judaizing" Christians.[112] Despite Paul's claim that in Christ there is no distinction between Jew and Greek (Gal. 3:28; Rom. 10:12), assumptions

---

111. See John Edwards, "Race and Religion in 15th and 16th C. Spain: The 'Purity of Blood' Laws Revisited," *Proceedings of the Tenth World Congress of Jewish Studies, Jerusalem, August 16–24, 1989*, 7 vols., ed. David Assaf (Jerusalem: World Union of Jewish Studies, 1990), BII: 159–66.

112. See David Nirenberg, "Mass Conversion and Genealogical Mentalities: Jews and Christians in Fifteenth-Century Spain," *Past and Present* 174 (2002): 3–41; cf. Nirenberg, "Spanish 'Judaism' and 'Christianity' in an Age of Mass Conversion," in *Rethinking European Jewish History*, ed. Jeremy Cohen and Moshe Rosman (Oxford: Littman Library of Jewish Civilization, 2009), 149–72.

spread that "nature would win out" and, in the end, racial origin would become apparent, manifesting itself in "Jewish" characteristics like greed and viciousness, odor and illness. Some Old Christians went so far as to argue a theory of polygenesis and to claim that Jews were not descendants of Adam and Eve, as were Christians, but rather that they were the progeny of Adam and Lilith. (In earlier Talmudic literature, Jewish traditions had identified Lilith as Adam's first wife who, subsequently, was transformed into a demon that threatened men and newborns.)[113] Now, the polygenetic assumption of a separate origin for Jews as descendants of Adam and Lilith, who had not been created like Eve from Adam's rib, served to corroborate theories of racial difference.[114] Jews and conversos responded with countergeneologies; one traced the origin of some Sephardic Jews to the ancient Jerusalemite nobility. In the fifteenth century, a letter allegedly written by Toledan Jews during the ministry of Jesus—a letter which, it was claimed, had been translated from Aramaic at the command of King Alfonso X—sought to show that Toledan Jews had settled in Spain even before the Christian era, and that their ancestors had been opposed to the Crucifixion, freeing these Sephardim both from the charge of deicide and claims of a corrupt lineage. Precisely because they have not intermarried—in part, because Roman and ecclesiastical legislation criminalized intermarriage—it was the Jews, or the once Jewish conversos, rather than Old Christians, who possessed the purer and more distinguished lineage.[115]

Nonetheless, some converso defenses continued to perpetuate the notion of Jewish traits, at the same time that they insisted that such traits disappeared with baptism. An example can be found in Alonso (or Alphonso) de Cartagena's *Defender of Christian Unity* (*Defensorium unitatis Christianae*). The author's father, Solomon (Shlomo) Halevi (c. 1350–1435), was a prominent rabbi in the Jewish community of Burgos before he converted to Christianity in 1390 or 1391, taking the name Pablo de

113. See Walter Krebs, "Lilith—Adams erste Frau," *Zeitschrift für Religions-und Geistesgeschichte* 27, no. 2 (1975): 141–52. For further discussion of the demonic Lilith and for bibliography, see Resnick and Kitchell, "The Sweepings of Lamia: Transformations of the Myths of Lilith and Lamia," 77–104.

114. Albert the Great, *De homine*, p. 559, 49–50.

115. See Nirenberg, "Mass Conversion and Genealogical Mentalities," 25–32. For ecclesiastical legislation prohibiting intermarriage between Christians and Jews, still helpful is James A. Brundage, "Intermarriage between Christians and Jews in Medieval Canon Law," *Jewish History* 3, no. 1 (1988): 25–40.

Santa Maria. After his conversion, he earned a doctorate in theology from the University of Paris and served at the court of Pope Benedict XIII in Avignon, before returning to Spain to become royal chancellor of Castile. His son Alonso (1384–1456) and his siblings received baptism with the father. Like his father, Alonso became bishop of Cartagena and later archbishop of Burgos (1435). His *Defensorium* was written in 1450 to defend conversos against severe legal restrictions imposed upon them after the Toledan persecutions.[116] In the *Defensorium,* Alonso rejects the premise of blood purity and remarks that nobility can be acquired or lost, just as some peasants have risen to become nobles by feats of arms. Such transformations across class lines are analogous to the transformation wrought by religious conversion. Baptism, then, enables Jewish converts to acquire the nobility of spirit and character that otherwise would be denied to them. Alonso remarks,

Among those who descend from the Israelites, nonetheless, once the impediment that they possessed from the rust of faithlessness was removed by the laver of regeneration, we see that many of them, relative to their small number, freely, with no one compelling them, ceaselessly take up arms, and strive with appropriate boldness in warlike acts, which is all the more unusual inasmuch as prior to the removal of the impediment, they were thought to be, and they were, the most timid men. So great and so notorious is the Israelites' timidity that, when we want to indicate excessive timidity, we call it "Jewness," and we are accustomed to call someone a Jew who is exceedingly timid.[117]

Although Bruce Rosenstock has argued persuasively that Alonso sought to transform the cowardly, timid Jew—"the feminine antitype of virile Christian masculinity"[118] in late medieval Castilian society—into a positive force that was intended to temper the wild masculine ferocity of the Gentiles in the divine economy, this attempted revaluation of Jewish identity was both novel and widely rejected in late fifteenth-century

---

116. P. Sicart, "Alphonse de Cartagéne" in *Dictionnaire d'histoire et de géographie ecclésiastiques,* ed. Alfred Baudrillart, et al. (Paris: Letouzey et Ané, 1914), 2: 702–7.

117. "Ex illis tamen que ex israelitis descendunt impedimento quod ex rubrigine infidelitatis habebant, per lavacrum regenerationis sublato, plures numero respective ad paucitatem eorum, sponte, nemine compellente, armorum usum agredi continue videmus, et in actibus bellicis competenti audacia militare, quod tanto singularius est, quanto ante sublationem impedimenti timidiores putabantur et erant. Tanta namque et tam notoria infidelium israelitarum timiditas est, ut cum excessivam timiditatem exprimere volumus, iudeitatem vocemus et excessive timentem iudeum solemus vocare." Alonso de Cartagena, *Defensorium unitatis Christianae* 2.20, p. 215.

118. Rosenstock, "Messianism, Machismo, and 'Marranism,'" 207.

Spain.[119] Already fear and trembling had been received in Christian culture as characteristics associated with Cain and his alleged descendants, the Jews. Jewish melancholy could account for their "timidity," but it also seemed to be a divine punishment imposed upon the Jews, derived not only from a reading of Genesis 4:14–15 but also from Leviticus 26:36— "I will cast faintness into their hearts in the land of their enemies. The sound of a driven leaf shall put them to flight." Rabanus Maurus explains that the "sound" of the driven leaf is the collapse of their literal interpretation, which has been conquered by Christian allegorical reading.[120] As a result, Jews treat Christians as the enemies indicated in Leviticus 26:36 and flee them as if fleeing from the sword. Additionally, timidity or fearfulness, as we have seen, are characteristics of a melancholic complexion. Whether a divine punishment or the result of their humoral complexion, excessive timidity or fearfulness, which as Elliott Horowitz has shown were traits assigned to Jews and effeminate or homosexual males in early modern texts, were clearly seen as persistent Jewish characteristics and a distinguishing mark.[121] For Alonso de Cartagena, Jewish timidity is so well known that it defines the people of Israel until, transformed by baptism, they take up the sword with a boldness hitherto absent from them. Although the author of the *Defensorium* sought to defend the converts' ability to become like other Christians, he did so by first corroborating the persistent Jewish stereotypes that defined Jews as fearful and unwarlike. His contemporaries too often inferred, however, that such "Jewness" could never be removed, not even by the waters of baptism.

To this point, we have examined a number of Jewish traits or characteristics that, especially from the thirteenth century on, seem to identify Jews in a particular way. Jewish illnesses, stench, timidity, the Jews' particular diet, humoral complexion, as well as circumcision and other rituals, distinguished Jews from their neighbors in Christian perception. Equally important, the imposition of a special garment or badge, as well as canonical legislation intended to keep Jews separated from Christians, established Jewish difference. What we have not determined, however, is whether Christians of the High Middle Ages assigned to Jews other

119. See Bruce Rosenstock, "Alonso de Cartagena: Nation, Miscegenation, and the Jew in Late-Medieval Castile," *Exemplaria* 12, no. 1 (2000): 185–204, and esp. 200–201.
120. Rabanus Maurus, *Expositiones in Leviticum* 7.13 (PL 108: 565C).
121. Elliott Horowitz, "A 'Dangerous Encounter': Thomas Coryate and the Swaggering Jews of Venice," *Journal of Jewish Studies* 52, no. 2 (2001): 341–53.

marks that clearly distinguished their physical appearance. Were Jews really thought to *look* different from their Christian neighbors? Especially as we consider the emergence of racialist language in the later Middle Ages, it seems important to consider additional evidence for a specific Jewish physiognomy.

IS THERE A DISTINCTIVE MEDIEVAL JEWISH PHYSIOGNOMY?

One reason we have left this discussion near to the end of our investigation is simply that the evidence is so contradictory. On the one hand, it seems quite certain that if Jews were clearly perceived to have differentiating physical features or skin color, canon sixty-eight from the fourth Lateran council (1215), which required Jews to wear a distinguishing badge, would have been entirely unnecessary. It seems reasonable to assume that the badge was imposed as an artificial sign only because Christians were unable to distinguish Jews according to any natural signifier. Some modern scholars have argued that for the medieval world the only *physical* difference that separated Jews and Christians was the concealed sign of circumcision; therefore, it is anachronistic to project back onto the medieval world modern racial anxieties about Jews that have often assigned to them distinctive facial features (for example, the "Jewish nose")[122] and treated them as dark-complexioned or black, or, in the fantasies of the far right, as the progenitors of dark "mud people."[123] The medieval evidence, however, although often contradictory, sometimes suggests that Jews had become "visible" in Christendom not only through the Jews' badge, but also by the imposition of physical differ-

---

122. See especially Sander L. Gilman, "The Jewish Nose: Are the Jews White? Or, the History of the Nose Job," in Gilman, *The Jew's Body*, 169–93.

123. José Pardo Tomás, "Physicians' and Inquisitors' Stories?" 171. For the notion of a Jewish race as a modern social construction, see also Matthew Frye Jacobson's *Whiteness of a Different Color: European Immigrants and the Alchemy of Race*, chap. 5: "Looking Jewish, Seeing Jews," (Cambridge, Mass.: Harvard University Press, 1998), 171–200. However, the concept of "mud people" may have a medieval parallel, insofar as those with a melancholy complexion (like Jews), were sometimes said in texts on humoral complexion to be timid and to have skin the "color of mud" (*Melancolicus . . . timidus luteique coloris*). An example will be found in the *Liber de complexionibus* sometimes attributed to the thirteenth-century John of Paris. See Werner Seyfert, "Ein Komplexionentext einer Leipziger Inkunabel (angeblich eines Johann von Neuhaus) und seine handschriftliche Herleitung aus der Zeit nach 1300," 291; Lynn Thorndike, "De complexionibus," *Isis* 49, no. 4 (1958): 398–408, esp. 398 n. 3, and 404.

ences intended to reveal what was concealed by the hidden sign of circumcision.

The instability of the physical depiction of medieval Jews—treating them at one moment as indistinguishable and at another as clearly marked by difference—can be supported from medieval written sources. One example appears from the life of St. Hugh of Avalon (d. 1200). Hugh, who had been a Carthusian monk, was consecrated Bishop of Lincoln in 1186 during the reign of Henry II and was canonized in 1220 by Pope Honorius III.[124] Hugh's episcopacy was evidently marked by good relations with the local Jewish community, if only because during his reign the Jewish community in Lincoln was largely spared the anti-Jewish violence that had spread at the time of the coronation of Richard I in September 1189, and reappeared across England as the King prepared to depart on the Third Crusade in the Spring of 1190, leaving the Jews largely unprotected. The anti-Jewish violence began in London in September 1189, although the cause behind the violence remains obscure.[125] Ralph of Diceto (d. 1202), the dean of St. Paul's church in London, attributes the outbreak of violence to the presence of unindentified "foreigners."[126] The late twelfth-century Richard of Devizes, a monk at the Priory of St. Swithun in Winchester, provides a nearly contemporaneous report in a chronicle composed before 1199:

Thus in the year 1189 after the Incarnation of the Lord, Richard, the son of King Henry II [and] Eleanor [of Aquitaine], and the brother of King Henry III, was consecrated king of the English at Westminster by Baldwin, the Archbishop of Canterbury, on the day [before] the nones of September [3 September, 1189]. On the same day as the coronation, about the solemn hour when the Son was sacrificed to the Father, the Jews in the city of London began to sacrifice to their father, the devil. The duration of this famous mystery was so long that the sacrificial offering [*holocaustum*] could hardly be completed

124. For a consideration of Hugh's monastic piety, see Jacqueline Murray, "Mystical Castration: Some Reflections on Peter Abelard, Hugh of Lincoln and Sexual Control," in *Conflicted Identities and Multiple Masculinities: Men in the Medieval West*, ed. Jacqueline Murray (New York: Garland, 1999), 73–92.

125. For an effort to explain the violence as a response to Jewish money lending, see R. C. Stacey, "Crusades, Martyrdoms, and the Jews of Norman England, 1096–1190," in *Juden und Christen zur Zeit der Kreuzzüge*, ed. Alfred Haverkamp (Sigmaringen: Jan Thorbecke Verlag, 1999), 233–51.

126. "pax Judaeorum, quam ab antiquis temporibus semper obtinuerant, ab alienigenis interrumpitur." Ralph of Diceto, *Ymagines Historiarum*, in *Opera historica*, 2 vols., ed. William Stubbs (London: Longman, 1876), 2: 69.

by the next day. The other cities and towns of the region imitated the faith of the Londoners and, with like devotion, sent their bloodsuckers with blood to hell. Everywhere throughout the kingdom something was readied against the damned [*perditos*] during that period, although unequally, for Winchester alone, a prudent and provident population and a town that always behaved in a civil manner, spared its [Jewish] vermin. It never did anything hastily, [for] it considered the outcomes rather than the beginnings of things, fearing nothing more than having cause to repent. It did not want while still unprepared to vomit forth in partial fashion the undigested mass, violently and at its peril, even though pressed to do so, but it hid it in its bowels, modestly concealing its disgust meanwhile, until at an opportune time for remedies it might cast out all the diseased matter at one and the same time.[127]

Richard of Devizes's satirical medicalized account, which describes Winchester's Jews as a diseased matter hidden in the city's bowels, is frustratingly cryptic and elusive. What does emerge, however, is a sense that anti-Jewish violence spread across much of England (excepting Winchester) in response to an alleged diabolical Jewish rite. Nowhere does Richard identify that rite with more precision; he only indicates that it began at about the same time of day as Jesus' Crucifixion. What this "sacrifice" might be is unclear, although the reference to the "bloodsuckers" sent with blood to the devil might recall Christian condemnation of the circumcision ritual of *metzizah b'peh*, or perhaps anticipate the accusation that Winchester's Jews had ritually crucified a Christian youth about the time of the Passover in 1190, a charge that Richard describes

127. "Anno igitur ab incarnatione Domini millesimo centesimo octogesimo nono, Ricardus ex Alienor filius regis Henrici secundi, frater regis Henrici tertii, consecratus est in regem Anglorum a Baldewino archepiscopo Cantuariae, apud Westmonasterium, tertio nonas Septembris. [3 Sept.] Eodem coronationis die, circa illam sollemnnitatis horam qua Filius immolabatur Patri, incoeptum est in civitate Londoniae immolare Judaeos patri suo diabolo; tantaque fuit hujus celebris mora mysterii, ut vix altera die compleri potuerit holocaustum. Aemulatae sunt aliae civitates regionis et urbes fidem Londoniensium, et pari devotione suos sanguisugas cum sanguine transmiserunt ad infernos. Aliquid, sed inaequaliter, ea tempestate contra perditos paratum est ubique per regnum, sola tantum suis vermibus pepercit Wintonia, populus prudens et providus ac civitas semper civiliter agens. Nihil umquam egit praepropere, nihil plus metuens quam poenitere, rerum exitus aestimat ante principia. Noluit indigeriem qua premebatur imparata, periculo sui, per partes violenter evomere, cavitque visceribus, dissimulans interim modeste molestiam, donec opportuno medendi tempore totam liceat sibi morbi materiam simul et semel egere." Richard of Devizes, *Chronicon Richardi Divisiensis de rebus gestis Ricardi primi regis Angliae* 3, ed. Joseph Stevenson (London: Sumptibus Societatis, 1838), 5–6. For Richard's satirical treatment of Winchester's Jews, see Robert Levine, "Why Praise Jews: History and Satire in the Middle Ages," *Journal of Medieval History* 12 (1986): 291–96.

later in this same work. Although the accusation did not result in a conviction, Richard does not attribute the acquittal to the provident and prudent character of the people of Winchester, but rather to the weight that Jewish gold carried with English judges, leading his Jewish narrator of the tale to describe Winchester as the Jews' "Jerusalem."[128] Nonetheless, in both 1225 and 1232 Jews were accused again of ritual murder in Winchester, and their situation there would continue to deteriorate.[129]

The thirteenth-century chronicler, Roger of Wendover, offers a somewhat different account of events, emphasizing that the anti-Jewish violence was a result of the Jews' unwanted presence at the coronation ceremony itself:

> Many Jews were present at this coronation [in September 1189], contrary to the king's command; for he had caused proclamation to be made the day before, that no Jews or women should attend, on account of the magical incantations which take place sometimes at royal coronations. But the courtiers laid hands on them, although they came in secret, and when they had robbed and scourged them dreadfully, they cast them out of the church; some of them died, and others could hardly be said to have life left in them. The populace of the city hearing of the attack of the courtiers on the Jews, made a similar assault on those who remained in the city.[130]

According to this account, "no Jews or women" were to attend the coronation because of a fear of "magical incantations." The author does not explain what outcome these incantations might have attempted to produce. It seems that they are unrelated to the allegation that Jewish physicians advised Richard I to bathe in the blood of newborns as a cure for leprosy, since this condition was thought to have arisen only *after* his participation in the Third Crusade. It seems noteworthy that Jews and women were treated as a single group in the account above. Nevertheless, when several prominent Jews sought to attend the coronation, as

---

128. See Richard of Devizes, *Chronicon* 79–83, pp. 59–64, and esp. 82, p. 62 (for Jerusalem). The tale can be read in translation in a slightly abridged version in Chazan, *Church, State, and Jew in the Middle Ages*, 146–48.

129. For these later ritual murder charges, see Anthony Bale, "Fictions of Judaism in England before 1290," in *Jews in Medieval Britain: Historical, Literary, and Archaeological Perspectives*, ed. Patricia Skinner (Rochester, N.Y.: Boydell & Brewer, 2003), 129–45, esp. 134–45, and Nicholas C. Vincent, "Jews, Poitevins, and the Bishop of Winchester, 1231–1234," in Wood, *Christianity and Judaism*, 119–32.

130. Roger of Wendover, *Flowers of History*, 2 vols., trans. J. A. Giles (Felinbach: Llanerch, 1994), 2.1: 81.

had been customary, they were treated badly. Among those ejected from the hall were Joce and Benedict of York. Joce escaped, but Benedict was caught and forced to accept baptism, whereupon he adopted the name "William" because he was baptized by Prior William of the Church of St. Mary of York. "William" later reverted to Judaism, although according to Ralph of Hoveden (d. c. 1201) upon William's death neither Jews nor Christians would accept his body for burial![131] Other Jews, when they could, took refuge in the Tower of London while the violence spread across the city, even to Christian households. Christians in other cities repeated the assault and plunder of the Jews. On the day after his coronation, however, once he had received homage from his nobles, Richard ordered that the Jews should be left in peace throughout the kingdom. Nevertheless, as the king and a number of nobles prepared to depart for the Crusade in the spring of 1190, anti-Jewish violence erupted once again, in Norwich, Stamford, York, and Bury St. Edmunds. At York, says Ralph of Diceto, the Jews slew one another, because "they preferred to be struck down by their own people than to perish at the hands of the uncircumcised."[132] Bishop Hugh of Lincoln had prevented violent attacks on his Jewish community, however, whose wealthiest member, Aaron of Lincoln (d. 1186), had loaned money for the construction of Lincoln Minster. For this reason, according to Adam of Eynsham, author of a life of St. Hugh, following Hugh's death, "Even the Jews came out, weeping to render him what homage they could, mourning and lamenting him aloud as the faithful servant of the one God. Their behavior towards the man of God made us realise that the prophecy 'The Lord has caused all

---

131. According to William of Newburgh's *Historia rerum Anglicarum*, "William" returned to Judaism, and died soon after at Northampton. According to Roger of Hovedon (d. 1201?), Jews would not allow him to be buried with Jews because he had apostatized, and Christians would not allow him to be buried with Christians because he had abandoned the faith. See *Chronica magistri Rogeri de Houedene*, 4 vols., ed. William Stubbs, Rerum Brittanicarum Medii Aevi Scriptores 51 (London: Longman, 1868–71), 3: 13; see also *The Jews of Angevin England*, ed. and trans. Joseph Jacobs (London: David Nutt, 1893), 104–6. For the growth of anti-Jewish sentiment at the end of the reign of Henry II, leading to the violence at York in 1190, see John D. Hosler, "Henry II, William of Newburgh, and the Development of English Anti-Judaism," in *Christian Attitudes toward Jews in the Middle Ages: A Casebook*, ed. Michael Frassetto (New York: Routledge, 2007), 167–82.

132. "[Judaei] Malebant enim a propria gente percuti, quam manibus incircumcisorum perire." Ralph of Diceto, *Ymagines Historiarum* 2: 75. For the violence at York, see especially R. Barrie Dobson, *The Jews of Medieval York and the Massacre of March, 1190* (York: St. Anthony's Press, 1974).

the nations to bless him' (Wisd. 44:25) had in his case been fulfilled."[133]

Previously, on September 5, 1189 Hugh had been called to Westminster, with the other notables of the realm, to pledge loyalty to King Richard I, two days after the anti-Jewish violence had begun in London. The destruction was everywhere still evident. According to Gerald of Wales,

> When he [Hugh] had gone a little way, an unburied human body was found in the street. He inquired immediately whether the dead man was a Jew or a Christian, because of the massacre of the Jews the day before. When he heard it was a Christian, he dismounted at once with his men and had the corpse sewn up in a new cloth that he ordered to be purchased.[134]

What interests us is that Hugh was unable to determine on his own whether the body was that of a Jew or a Christian. He had to obtain that information from someone else: perhaps either from someone who knew the deceased, or from someone who could inspect the body, if it was the body of a male, to determine whether it had been circumcised. Although other interpretations are possible, still this episode suggests that Jewish identity was not immediately apparent from outward appearances—neither from skin coloring nor other distinctive features.

Another text from England leads to the same conclusion. In the already mentioned ritual crucifixion tale now known as the "Passion of Adam of Bristol," the alleged Jewish ritual murderers, namely Samuel and his wife and son, are recognized as Jews neither by the victim, Adam, nor by the itinerant Irish priest and his companions who are persuaded to carry Adam's body to Ireland.[135] Indeed, it is only by the miracu-

---

133. Adam of Eynsham, *Magna vita sancti Hugonis*, 2 vols., ed. Decima Doule and Hugh Farmer (London: Nelson, 1961–62), 2: 229. On the Jewish community of Lincoln, see Cecil Roth, "Medieval Lincoln Jewry and its Synagogue," in Roth, *Essays and Portraits in Anglo-Jewish History*, 50–62.

134. Gerald of Wales, *The Life of St. Hugh of Avalon, Bishop of Lincoln (1186–1200)*, ed. and trans. Richard M. Loomis, Garland Library of Medieval Literature 31, series A (New York: Garland, 1985), 25. This text was probably written in 1214, i.e., twenty-five years after the event described.

135. This anonymous text is found in a single manuscript in the British Library (Harleian MS. 957, no. 7), but the manuscript does not itself include a descriptive title. The eighteenth-century editor of the catalogue of Harleian manuscripts had entitled the work, *Fabula ineptissima de filio Willelmi Wallensis civis Bristolliae*. This title obscures the central concern of the work, namely, the alleged ritual crucifixion of a young boy, Adam of Bristol, son of William of Wales. Although the account attempts to locate the ritual murder at the end of the twelfth century, the date of the composition remains uncertain. Robert Stacey, who has worked extensively with the text, suggests in private communication that the work

lous intervention of an angel that Samuel is revealed to this priest to be a Jew.[136] The Jews' clothes, their lodging, and their physical appearance fail to reveal their religious identity. Indeed, this seems to be essential to the text's message: namely, that precisely because Jewish identity is easily hidden and concealed, Jews are all the more dangerous to a Christian society. They may appear, outwardly, to be like their Christian neighbors but in reality they are treacherous, duplicitous, and blaspheming murderers. Moreover, the text differs from other ritual murder tales, inasmuch as despite Marian intervention and despite hearing the voice of God Himself, the alleged perpetrator, Samuel, neither converts to Christianity nor suffers punishment: his crime remains unknown to the community around him, and Samuel survives to kill again. Although his wife and son repented of their involvement in the murder of young Adam and express a desire to embrace Christianity, Samuel murders them as well. Such a message of Jewish threat—which extends even to members of the Jew's own family—and the apparent conclusion that Jews cannot or will not successfully be converted, may have helped establish the context for the expulsion of England's Jews in 1290.[137]

The text's warnings of concealed Jewish danger, however, are balanced by a remarkable pair of illustrations that accompany it. (See figures 10a and 10b.) At the top of fol. 22r there are two illuminated initials. The illuminated initial at the top left corner depicts Samuel's wife and son as they are about to accept baptism. Although Samuel's son wears a conical cap that identifies him as a Jew, there is nothing about his appearance, or that of his mother, that is particularly threatening. To the contrary, one may infer that their appearance has been normalized by their repentance. By contrast, in a much larger illustration on the right side of this folio, Samuel is depicted in profile, wearing a Jews' cap and with a large and very prominent hooked nose. His body is turned away from a cross standing behind him, on which is suspended the martyr, Adam. The cross itself is shown placed over a privy, and thus the illustration is faithful to the text. Although Samuel's body is turned away from

---

may have been composed sometime after 1260 but, presumably, before the expulsion of England's Jews in 1290.

136. Ibid., fol. 26v.

137. See Harvey J. Hames, "The Limits of Conversion: Ritual Murder and the Virgin Mary in the Account of Adam of Bristol," *Journal of Medieval History* 33 (2007): 43–59.

the cross, suggesting that he has rejected the crucified Christian God-Man whom Adam represents, his upper torso is violently twisted backwards to reveal in his left (or *sinister*) hand the knife Samuel had used to mutilate the young innocent and to pierce his side. His malicious expression, his prominent nose, and his cap all mark him iconographically as a Jew. In sum, then, there is a significant disconnect between the text, which cautions that Jews are hidden, concealed, and not readily recognized, and the illustration that depicts Samuel according to various Jewish stereotypes. It seems that the illustrator would have the reader understand that although Jews may look much like anyone else, when viewed *with the eyes of faith* their true nature and reality becomes evident. The illustrator gives us some insight, then, into what one *should* see when one looks upon a Jew, despite the testimony of the senses.

Another episode from late medieval England may lead to the same conclusion. Long after Jews had been expelled from England in 1290, the female mystic Margery Kempe (d. 1438) found herself suspected of heresy and under investigation by the archbishop of York and other ecclesiastics. Although the archbishop would later attest to her orthodoxy, "Sum of the pepil askyd whedyr sche wer a Cristen woman er a Jewe; sum seyd sche was a good woman, and sum seyd nay."[138] The people inquired, then, whether she was a Christian or a Jew. Clearly, her beliefs or teachings may have occasioned the question, but it seems equally significant that the question could not be answered simply by virtue of her physical appearance.

Let one more example suffice, drawn from the work of the thirteenth-century Dominican Thomas of Cantimpré. Thomas composed a collection of tales or *exempla* with the title *[A Book] of Miracles or Memorable Tales of his Age* (*Miraculorum et exemplorum memorabilium sui temporis*), sometimes known under the title *The Common Good* (*expounded*) *in Relation to Bees* (*Bonum universale de apibus*). The latter title is a bit misleading, since the work has nothing to do with beekeeping, but rather reflects the fact that bees and their hives were viewed as models of social organization.[139] In his work, he describes the conversion of a young

---

138. Margery Kempe, *The Book of Margery Kempe* 1.2, lns. 2933–34, ed. Lynn Staley (Kalamazoo, Mich.: Medieval Institute Publications, 1996), 52.

139. Guy Guldentops examines this Aristotelian topos in the work of Thomas of Cantimpré and other thirteenth-century thinkers in "The Sagacity of the Bees," in *Aristotle's*

Jewish girl, Rachel, to the Christian faith. Her introduction to Christianity was managed in secret by a priest in Louvain, Reinerius, who instructed her for six months from age six. Once her parents discovered what had happened, they sought to send her across the Rhine and away from Louvain and to betroth her to a young Jewish man. That night, the Virgin appeared in a dream to Rachel, addressed her as Catherine, and consoled her. The next morning, Rachel fled to the priest, received baptism, and was placed in a convent. In a clear retelling of the *exemplum* of Caesarius of Heisterbach, discussed above, the girl's parents sought to have her returned to them, appealing to the bishop of Liège and even to Pope Honorius [III?] with money payments. The young girl was brought before a tribunal of clerics and magistrates to determine whether she had sought baptism of her own free will and, inspired by the Virgin, she expressed her desire to remain a Christian. The girl's parents were not so easily persuaded, however. Two years after this case had been decided in court, a handsome Jewish youth came to her convent and falsely received baptism, presented himself as the girl's relative, and asked to speak to her. She, however, perceived his deception and refused to meet him. After this, the Jews left her alone, and the mendacious youth "returned to his vomit."[140]

Our text begins its tale even earlier with a description of Rachel as a precocious four-year-old. Despite her young age, the child inquired of her parents: "why should Jews and Christians have different names when the people of each race have one countenance and one language?"[141] Once again, we have evidence that although Jews and Christians differed—they bear different names—nonetheless they "have one countenance and one language." One point of the *exemplum* is no doubt to reinforce certain stereotypes: the Jews are shown to be capable of the worst kind of deception, even feigning Christian identity through false baptism. As we have seen, this will become a serious concern in Spain later, when large

---

Animals in the Middle Ages and Renaissance, ed. Carlos Steel, Guy Guldentops, and Pieter Beullens (Leuven: Leuven University Press, 1999), 275–96.

140. Cf. 2 Peter 2:22.

141. "cur distinctio nominum fieret Iudaeorum pariter et Chrstianorum, cum unius vultus atque loquelae homines essent utriusque gentis?" Thomas of Cantimpré, *Miraculorum et exemplorum memorabilium sui temporis, libri duo* 2.29.20, p. 297. Note too that the term *vultus,* which we translate as "countenance," may also be translated as "complexion." although not in a technical, medical sense.

numbers of Jews will convert to Christianity to escape persecution and Christian authorities will investigate whether they are *really* Christian. But the concern surely can be traced back to the anti-Jewish violence of the First and Second Crusades as well, when some members of the Jewish communities attacked by Crusaders submitted to forced baptism but, after the danger had passed, resumed their Jewish identities. Crusade chroniclers like Albert of Aachen recognized that during the violence of the First Crusade "a few [Jews] had been baptized through fear of death rather than for love of the Christian religion."[142] feigning a loyalty to their new faith that only resulted in broad suspicion of Jewish conversions. Similarly, the *Annales Hildesheimenses* complained that after more than one thousand Jews had been slain at Mainz in 1096, Jews in many provinces converted to Christianity, but then abandoned their new faith.[143] From the twelfth century, Christians increasingly demanded confirmation of the genuineness of Jewish conversions by the appearance of concomitant miracles.[144] In the absence of the evidence of miracles, converts were often viewed with suspicion by their Christian neighbors, and equally they were viewed with suspicion when they attempted to return to the Jewish communities they had abandoned—communities that increasingly demanded of returning apostates some form of ritual immersion as a sort of "debaptism" intended to wash the converted Jew clean of the defiling effects of the Christian ritual.[145]

142. "paucis timore pocius mortis quam amore Christiane professionis baptizatis." Albert of Aachen, *Historia Ierosolimitana* 1.28, p. 52. This seems to suggest that Jews were given a *choice* of baptism or death at the time of the first Crusade. David Malkiel has argued, however, that that assumption of choice is misguided, and that the primary goal of those who attacked the Rhineland Jewish communities was the destruction (not conversion) of the Jews, demanding a reevaluation of the phenomenon of Jewish self-martyrdom. See his "Destruction or Conversion: Intention and Reaction, Crusaders and Jews, in 1096," *Jewish History* 15 (2001): 257–80 (and 264–65 for discussion of Albert of Aachen's chronicle); see also Malkiel, *Reconstructing Ashkenaz*, 74–94.

143. "Apud Mogontiam Iudei numero virorum ac mulierum et infantum mille et 14 interfecti sunt, et maxima pars civitatis exusta est. Iudei per diversas provincias christiani facti sunt, et iterum a christianitate recesserunt." *Annales Hildesheimenses*, ed. George Waitz, MGH, SS rer. Germ. 8 (Hannover: Hahn, 1878), Ind. 3.

144. See Jonathan M. Elukin, *Living Together, Living Apart: Re-thinking Jewish Christian Relations in the Middle Ages* (Princeton, N.J.: Princeton University Press, 2007), esp. 70–74. Peter the Venerable, having rejected the possibility of converting Jews by reason or by an appeal to scripture, concluded that only the persuasive power of miracles remains to bring them to the true faith. Peter the Venerable, *Adversus Iudaeorum*, 4, p. 114.

145. Ephraim Kanarfogel, "Returning to the Jewish Community in Medieval Ashkenaz:

Christian sources both reflect and distort this Jewish ritual purification. According to the sixteenth-century chronicler Andrés Bernáldez, as a result of new pressures on Jews at the beginning of the reign of Ferdinand and Isabella, "Those [Jews] who could avoid baptizing their children, did so; and those who did baptize them, washed them in their houses as soon as they brought them home."[146] This washing was evidently intended to reverse the effects of baptism. With much greater precision, the Dominican Inquisitor Bernard Gui (d. 1331) describes a Jewish process to "re-judaize" lapsed Jewish converts to Christianity. According to Gui, the lapsed Jew must take a ritual bath; his nails are clipped, his head is shaved, and the Jews "assign him a [new] name, usually that which he had prior to baptism." In addition, "the Jews vigorously scour his entire body with sand, but especially . . . on the very places that were anointed with holy chrism in baptism."[147] In a more fantastic account, the thirteenth-century Cistercian Caesarius of Heisterbach records the story of a Jewish mother who volunteers to undo her daughter's baptism: "The girl, wishing to find out what her mother meant by this, asked how she would do it. 'I would draw you,' said the Jewess, 'three times through the opening of the latrine, and thus the virtue of your baptism would be left behind.' When the daughter heard this, she cursed her mother and, fleeing from her, she spat on her."[148]

Just as Jewish communities, then, understood that converts were befouled by the "stinking waters" of baptism, so too some Christian au-

---

History and Halakhah," in vol. 1 of *Turim: Studies in Jewish History and Literature Presented to Dr. Bernard Lander*, ed. Michael A. Schmidman (New York: Touro College Press, 2007), 69–97.

146. Andrés Bernáldez, *Memorias del reinado de los Reyes Católicos*, chap. 43, trans. in Homza, *The Spanish Inquisition, 1478–1614*, 4.

147. [The Jews] "imponunt sibi nomen, communiter illud quod prius habuerat in baptismo . . ." . . . "tunc Judei confricant eum fortiter cum arena per totum corpus, sed maxime . . . in illis videlicet locis in quibus in baptismo fuit positum Sanctum Crisma"; Bernard Gui, *Practica inquisitionis heretice pravitatis* 5.5.2, ed. C. Douai (Paris: Alphonse Picard, 1886), 288–89.

148. "Volens puella probare quid mater dicere vellet, respondet: Quomodo hoc faceres? Ego, inquit Judaea, tribus vicibus te sursum traham per foramen latrinae, sicque remanebit ibi virtus baptismi tui. Quod verbum puella audiens et execrans, contra matrem spuit, fugiens ab illa." Caesarius of Heisterbach, *Dialogus Miraculorum* 2.26, 1: 98. The *exemplum* is surely meant to evoke disgust for Jewish practices, not to mention Jews themselves. For an analogous polemic against pagan practices, see Carolyne Larrington, "Diet, Defecation and the Devil: Disgust and the Pagan Past," in *Medieval Obscenities*, ed. Nicola McDonald (York: York Medieval Press, 2006), 138–55.

thorities suggested that Jews sought to reverse the purifying effects of the waters of the sacrament.[149] Although a caricature of ritual "debaptism," nonetheless Caesarius of Heisterbach's tale draws attention to the problem Jewish communities faced in accepting lapsed members, whose steadfastness had already been tested and found wanting. As Kanarfogel has observed, medieval rabbinic authorities suspected that some Jewish penitents seeking to re-enter the Jewish world sought to have things both ways: to be accepted by the Jewish community when some advantage was to be gained, but to present themselves as Christians to the larger world when it served their purposes.[150] These individuals may represent serial converts: that is, individuals known from medieval texts who converted, reverted, and converted again, sometimes many times, moving back and forth between Jewish and Christian communities. While they may have had their own legitimate reasons for doing so, to the observer they appeared to be naught but deceivers.[151] In addition to their penchant for deception, in Thomas of Cantimpré's *exemplum* describing Rachel/Catherine, the Jews are also shown attempting to bribe ecclesiastical authorities, subverting justice. But there is no attempt to establish that they in any way *look* different or speak a different language.[152] Instead the text draws our attention to a quite different distinguishing feature: they have different names.

JEWISH NAMES AND JEWISH DIFFERENCE

In the *exemplum* cited, Rachel may only intend to inquire why Jews are called Jews, and Christians, Christians—why do they have different

---

149. For the "stinking waters" of baptism, see the *Book of Nestor the Priest* 127, in *The Polemic of Nestor the Priest*, p. 123; also see the Hebrew Crusade chronicle, the Mainz Anonymous, in Chazan, *European Jewry and the First Crusade*, Appendix, 231, 242.

150. Kanarfogel, "Returning to the Jewish Community in Medieval Ashkenaz: History and Halakhah," 90.

151. For a discussion of serial converts and the historiographical problem of Jewish apostasy, see the very interesting work of David Malkiel, "Jews and Apostates in Medieval Europe—Boundaries Real and Imagined," *Past and Present* 194, no. 1 (2007): 3-34, and especially 12-13; Malkiel, *Reconstructing Ashkenaz*, 137-39.

152. In medieval Spain as well, it has been argued, it would have been extremely difficult (if not impossible) to distinguish Jews from Christians based solely on linguistic differences of Judeo-Spanish. See Elaine R. Miller, "Linguistic Identity in the Middle Ages: The Case of the Spanish Jews," in *Crossing Boundaries: Issues of Cultural and Individual Identity in the Middle Ages and the Renaissance,* ed. Sally McKee (Turnholt: Brepols, 1999), 57-77. Nonetheless, although Jews might not be distinguishable in their use of the vernacular tongue,

names when they otherwise look the same and speak the same language? But she may equally have meant to inquire why Jews and Christians are distinguished by different personal names. This should remind us that names are cultural documents and that they are important in order to establish religious identity.[153] As already indicated, a parallel exists between baptism and circumcision, insofar as infants receive their names at the time of each rite. To the extent that each rite is also viewed as a ritual of initiation, the names they receive identify them to the community about to receive them.

Names are not static identifiers, however. Just as a name introduces one into an existing religious community, should one choose religious conversion a *new* name will signify the transition from the old to the new. As we saw above, Rachel will receive the name Catherine, a name revealed to her by the Virgin in a dream. In another *exemplum* Thomas of Cantimpré recalls the conversion of a Jewish woman, Sara, who after her baptism in Cologne became known as Gertrude.[154] Conversely, as Bernard Gui remarks, converted Jews who reverted to Judaism took a new name, or received again the name that they had had before their baptism while, according to the *Sefer Hasidim*, Jews who had converted to Christianity often were "renamed" in the Jewish community with a derogatory nickname.[155]

In many cases, Jews who converted to Christianity would simply adopt the name of their sponsor. For example, Benedict of York adopted

---

their use of Hebrew was certainly distinctive, even if not, in most instances, public. In fact it was especially the concealed or private nature of the Jews' use of Hebrew that sometimes led medieval Christian texts and iconography to treat Hebrew as demonic, or as the language of sorcery and necromancy. For discussion, see Ruth Mellinkoff, *Outcasts: Signs of Otherness in Northern European Art of the Late Middle Ages*, vol. 1, chap. 4. Cf. Sander Gilman, *The Jew's Body*, 10–37; and Sander L. Gilman, *Jewish Self-Hatred: Anti-Semitism and the Hidden Language of the Jews* (Baltimore: Johns Hopkins University Press, 1986), 23–41.

153. Samuel Cooper, "Names and Cultural Documents," in *These Are the Names: Studies in Jewish Onomastics*, 2 vols., ed. Aaron Demsky (Ramat Gan: Bar-Ilan University Press, 1999), 2: 13–23.

154. Thomas of Cantimpré, *Miraculorum et exemplorum memorabilium* 2.29.21, p. 304. For an excellent study of the conversion of Jewish women in Germany, see Alfred Haverkammp, "Baptised Jews in German Lands during the Twelfth Century," in *Jews and Christians in Twelfth-Century Europe*, ed. Michael A. Signer and John Van Engen, Notre Dame Conferences in Medieval Studies 10 (Notre Dame, Ind.: University of Notre Dame Press, 2001), 255–310.

155. For example, a Jew known as Avraham before his conversion might be "renamed" Afar (from *afar*, dust or ashes). See Yehudah HeChasid, *Sefer Chasidim* 138(191), p. 85.

the name William, after his sponsor, the prior of the church of St. Mary of York. In the first decade of the twelfth century, the well-known convert Petrus Alfonsi, who earlier had been known as Moses, assumed the name *Petrus* or Peter because he was baptized on the feast day of Sts. Peter and Paul, and the name Alfonsi because his godfather was the emperor Alfonso I. During the reign of Philip Augustus in France (1180–1223), a Jewish convert adopted the king's name at his own baptism.[156] Early in the twelfth century, Guibert of Nogent recounts the story of a Jewish child rescued by Christians from anti-Jewish violence in Rouen, who at his baptism took the name of his Christian patron, William, and later became a monk at Fly.[157] One Jewish convert in England, who found residence in the *domus conversorum* (Converts' Residence) in London in the middle of the thirteenth century, adopted the name Robert Grosseteste, in honor of the famous bishop of Lincoln of that name.[158] Another convert, the powerful Henry of Winchester, took his name in honor of his patron, King Henry III (d. 1272).[159] In early fifteenth-century Spain, Bonafós de la Caballería of Saragossa converted in 1414 and took the name Fernando, after his patron King Fernando I (r. 1412–16).[160]

In other cases, the reason behind the selection of a new name is hidden from us. But a new identity was clearly appropriated with the adoption of a new name. Herman of Cologne was formerly Judas (or Judah)

156. Stow, *Jewish Dogs*, 106.
157. Guibert of Nogent, *De vita sua* 2.5 (PL 156: 904A).
158. See Michael Adler, *Jews of Medieval England*, 290. Adler studies the *Domus conversorum* on 281–339; also see Adler, *The History of the Domus Conversorum 1290–1891* (London[?]: Ballantyne Press, n.d.); cf. Rotha Mary Clay, *The Mediaeval Hospitals of England* (London: Methuen, 1909), 19–23, 99–100, which also mentions a *domus conversorum* at Oxford, although mistakenly. For this institution of the *domus*, created by Henry III, see also Robert. C. Stacey, "The Conversion of Jews to Christianity in Thirteenth-Century England," *Speculum* 67, no. 2 (1992): 263–83. Fogle speculates that Henry, who endowed the *domus* with 700 marks, paying each resident a stipend, may have been inspired by a house that had been created for converts in Bristol by the Kalendar's Guild. See Lauren Fogle, "The *Domus Conversorum*: The Personal Interest of Henry III," *Jewish Historical Studies* 41 (2007): 1–7, and esp. 6. The existence of a *domus* in Bristol remains conjectural, however.
159. Adler, *Jews of Medieval England*, 285.
160. *The Tortosa Disputation. Regesta of Documents from the Archivo de la Corona de Aragón Fernando I 1412–1416*, compiled by Gemma Escribà, ed. Yom Tov Assis, Sources for the History of the Jews in Spain 6 (Jerusalem: Henk Schussheim Memorial Series, 1998), xx-viii. On Bonafós and one of his sons—by his second (Christian) wife, Leonor de la Cabria—Pedro de la Cavelleria/Caballería, who was the author of an anti-Jewish/anti-Muslim polemic entitled *Tractatus Zelus Christi contra Iudæos, Sarracenos, & infideles*, see Echevarria, *The Fortress of Faith*, 29–32.

ben David ha-Levi.[161] Although one expects that no Christian convert would wish to be known as Judas, Herman does not tell us how he chose his new name, but only that as he had changed the order of his former life in the laver of baptism, so too he changed his name and adopted the name Herman.[162] Perhaps Herman simply chose a name that was well known in Cologne. Indeed, many of its archbishops bore the name Herman, most recently Herman III of Cologne (d. 1099). In another instance, at the beginning of the thirteenth century the Oxford Jew Joscepin assumed the name Alberic after his conversion; it is unclear why he chose that name, but perhaps it is because at the beginning of the thirteenth century the Earl of Oxford was Alberic II (or Aubrey) de Vere.[163] In late fourteenth-century Spain, Solomon ha-Levi became Pablo de Santa Maria, a change that likely recalls the transformation of the apostle Paul, who had been Saul of Tarsus prior to his conversion experience (Acts 13:9). Regardless of the reasons that led to choosing a specific name, conversion signified a transformation that demanded a new name to signify a new religious identity.

The same phenomenon can be observed in the other direction. That is, Christians who converted to Judaism also changed their names. In one celebrated instance in 838, the royal deacon Bodo took the name Eliezar after his conversion to Judaism, scandalizing the Carolingian church before removing himself to Muslim Spain.[164] Bodo not only changed his

161. Herman of Cologne identifies himself as "Herman, formerly known as Judas, of the Israelite race, from the Levitical tribe, from [his] father David and mother Sephora" (*Hermannus quondam Iudas dictus, genere Israelita, tribu Levita, ex patre David et matre Sephora*). See his *Opusculum de conversione sua* 1, p. 70; for a comprehensive review of recent scholarship concerning this text and its author, see Jean-Claude Schmitt, *The Conversion of Herman the Jew: Autobiography, History and Fiction in the Twelfth Century*, trans. Alex J. Novikoff (Philadelphia: University of Pennsylvania Press, 2010), esp.12–32.

162. Herman of Cologne, *Opusculum de conversione sua* 19, p. 120.

163. Cecil Roth, *The Jews of Medieval Oxford* (Oxford: Clarendon Press, 1951), 11.

164. See Amulon, *Epistola seu liber contra Judaeos ad Carolum Regem* 42 (PL 116: 171C); and Prudentius of Troyes, *Annales Bertiniani* 2, ed. G. Waitz, MGH, SS rer. Germ. 5 (Hannover: Hahn, 1883), 17, which provides a putative motive for his conversion: to marry a Jewish woman. On the question of assigning a motive for conversion, see Heinz Löwe, "Die Apostasie des Pfalzdiakons Bodo (838) und das Judentum der Chasaren," in *Person und Gemeinschaft im Mittelalter: Karl Schmid zum fünfundsechzigsten Geburtstag*, ed. Gerd Althoff (Sigmaringen: Thorbecke, 1988), 157–69. Upon his arrival in Spain, Bodo-Eleazar engaged in debate with Paul Álvaro of Cordoba (see *Epistulae*, PL 121: 475–514). For discussion, see Alan Cabaniss, "Bodo-Eleazar: A Famous Jewish Convert," *Jewish Quarterly Review* 43, no. 4 (1953): 313–28; and Frank Riess, "From Aachen to al-Andalus: The Journey of Deacon

name: he also was circumcised and, according to Prudentius of Troyes, he let grow his hair and beard, suggesting that his new religious identity also demanded a change in his physical appearance. Another example may be that of the clerk Wecelin, who converted to Judaism in 1006, leading to an exchange of letters with an enraged King Henry II of Germany.[165] Typically conversion was a transformation, however, symbolized by a change of name to signify a change in religious identity.

Nonetheless, although young Rachel inquired why Jews and Christians should have different names, when in language and countenance or appearance (*vultus*) they are otherwise the same, the situation remains a bit more complicated. For us the question is not simply whether converts adopted different names—we know that they did—but did the customary names that Jews and Christians had identify them to one another as different according to religion? The answer will vary across medieval Europe by region and, to some extent, by gender as well. For medieval England, Jacobs provides a lengthy list of Jewish names drawn from the Pipe Rolls in the Records Office. Most of the names of males are clearly biblical, although sometimes the biblical names are given a vernacular equivalent: for example, Chaim may be rendered as Vives or Vivard, or Joseph becomes Josce or Joce. The most popular Jewish names were Isaac (59); Josce (55); Abraham (49); Benedict (49); Jacob (40); Moses (38); Samuel (37), Vives or Vivard (23); Elias (19); Aaron (18); Samson (16); and Solomon (15). The numbers in parentheses indicate how often these names appear to designate discrete individuals. In England Jews also adopted surnames that typically identify them by place of dwelling or origin—for example, Aaron of York—or sometimes by a descriptive feature ("the Fat," "the Tall," "the Younger," and so on). Jewish women tended far less often to adopt biblical names.[166] Adler notes that "the large majority of English Jewesses were given purely Norman-French names. This cus-

---

Bodo (823–76)," *Early Medieval Europe* 13, no. 2 (2005): 131–57. For Bodo and other examples of Christian converts to Judaism before 1100, see Bernhard Blumenkranz, "Jüdische und christliche Konvertiten im jüdische-christlichen Religionsgespräch des Mittelalters," in *Judentum im Mittelalter. Beiträge zum christlich-jüdischen Gespräch*, ed. Paul Wilpert, Miscellanea Mediaevalia 4 (Berlin: de Gruyter, 1966), 264–82; Raphael Patai and Jennifer Patai Wing, *The Myth of the Jewish Race* (New York: Scribner's, 1975), 73–90.

165. See Anna Sapir Abulafia, "An Eleventh-Century Exchange of Letters between a Christian and a Jew," *Journal of Medieval History* 7 (1981): 153–74. For the documentary evidence, see the appendix, 165–71.

166. See Jacobs, *The Jews of Angevin England*, 345–70.

tom was more prevalent in England than in any other country, the men usually being satisfied with Biblical names."¹⁶⁷ A similar phenomenon may be discovered in France, although not consistently across every region.¹⁶⁸ Simon Seror has compiled an impressive onomastic list for the Jews of medieval France, and attempts to identify those names as Jewish that have a Hebrew or Aramaic root, while identifying all others—for example, those with a Greek or vernacular root—as "non-Jewish." Once again, biblical names predominate for men, but "non-Jewish" names seem more common among the Jews of d'Oc than d'Oïl, whereas almost all the women bear "non-Jewish" names.¹⁶⁹

For us, however, the important question remains: would those outside the Jewish community have been able to identify a Jew simply by his or her name? According to Bernhard Blumenkranz, in medieval France and England this would have been quite difficult, because while Jews—especially Jewish males—bore biblical names, so too did a number of prominent Christian clerics.¹⁷⁰ New Testament names would have been a good indicator of Christian faith, but Old Testament names remained at best an ambiguous marker. Moreover, because Jewish females tended more often to adopt Norman-French names, their religious identity would have been even more difficult to establish by virtue of their names

167. Michael Adler, *Jews of Medieval England*, 20; Roth, *The Jews of Medieval Oxford*, 169–72; cf. Simon Seror, "Les noms des femmes juives en Angleterre au Moyen Age," *Revue des études juives* 154 (1995): 295–325. For a good illustration, consider the influential thirteenth-century Anglo-Jewish lender, David of Oxford, whose name had good biblical roots. His first wife, however, whom he divorced because she left him childless, was Muriel, while his second wife was named Licoricia. For Muriel's "story," see Charlotte Newman Goldy, "A Thirteenth-Century Anglo-Jewish Woman Crossing Boundaries: Visible and Invisible," *Journal of Medieval History* 34 (2008): 130–45. Licoricia had a successful career, possibly enjoying the patronage of King Henry III. See Barrie Dobson, "The Role of Jewish Women in Medieval England," in Wood, *Christianity and Judaism. Papers*, 145–68, and esp. 163; and Reva Berman Brown and Sean McCartney, "The Business Activities of Jewish Women Entrepreneurs in Medieval England," *Management Decision* 39, no. 9 (2001): 699–709, esp. 705–7. Her name, however, reflects the popularity of upper-class French names among both Jewish and Christian women in England. See Suzanne Bartlet, "Women in the Medieval Anglo-Jewish Community," in Skinner, *Jews in Medieval Britain: Historical, Literary, and Archaeological Perspectives*, 113–28, esp. 118–19.

168. See Richard W. Emery, *The Jews of Perpignan in the Thirteenth Century* (New York: Columbia University Press, 1959), 12–14, 200–2.

169. Simon Seror, *Les noms des Juifs de France au Moyen Âge* (Paris: Editions du centre national de la recherche scientifique, 1989), xiii–xiv.

170. Bernhard Blumenkranz, *Juifs et chrétiens dans le monde occidental, 430–1096* (Paris: Mouton, 1960), esp. 6–10.

alone. Of more importance for England, as Robert Stacey has shown, is the fact that because Jews employed Norman-French and identified with its culture, they would have been more easily identified as "foreigners" (although not necessarily as Jewish foreigners) and associated with a sometimes despised ruling class.[171]

The situation seems to have been quite different in Spain, however. There Jewish identity was more clearly identifiable through one's name, even if not through linguistic dialect and the use of Judeo-Spanish, although once more differences appear between Aragon and Castille.[172] Nina Melechen notes that "Identifying Jews—specifically, Jewish men— in Christian documents from Toledo and its diocese between the twelfth and fourteenth centuries is strikingly easy. . . . The Jew's given name and surname also identified him as a Jew, since Toledan Jews shared a pool of mostly biblical names that was not used by Christians. Finally, in case this indirect information was not enough, a Jew was explicitly described as a 'judio.'"[173] This appears to be quite different from the situation, generally, in France and England, where often Christians and Jews shared the same names. Moreover, legislation in Spain in 1313 *required* Jewish men to employ a restricted pool of names, while Jewish women, by contrast, rarely used biblical names and shared many names with Muslim and Christian women.[174] The developing trend to require that the names

171. Stacey remarks that "French was the language of the Jewish hearth and home in postconquest England and seems to have remained so right up until the expulsion in 1290." See his "Jews and Christians in Twelfth-Century England: Some Dynamics of a Changing Relationship," 341. Kirsten A. Fudeman argues that on the Continent at *some* times the Jews' French was recognizably distinctive because of the use of Hebrew loan words. See *Vernacular Voices*, 3 and chap. 1.

172. On the difficulties attached to establishing the origins and distinctiveness of Judeo-Spanish, see Elaine R. Miller, "Linguistic Identity in the Middle Ages: The Case of the Spanish Jews," 57–77. Although it is true that the use of Hebrew in sacred texts and religious ceremonies distinguished medieval Jews from Christians, these ceremonies were typically private affairs, which may justify Gilman's description of Hebrew as a "secret language" (see Gilman, *Jewish Self-Hatred, Anti-Semitism and the Hidden Language of the Jews*, esp. chap. 2). In their social or economic interactions, however, Jews would have used the vernacular. Curiously, in the preface to R. Samuel of Morocco's *Liber de adventu messiae praeterito* by the Dominican Alfonso Buenhombre, Alfonso remarks that because some Jews know Arabic, which is unknown to most Christians, Jews (like R. Samuel) compose their "secrets" in Arabic—and not Hebrew—to hide them from Christians.

173. Nina Melechen, "Calling Names: The Identification of Jews in Christian Documents from Medieval Toledo," in Kagay and Vann, *On the Social Origins of Medieval Institutions*, 21–22.

174. Ibid., 32.

of Jewish men be easily identifiable seems consistent with concerns in Spain clearly to differentiate Jews, Muslims, and Christians.

To return to our text, young Rachel asked her parents: "why should Jews and Christians have different names when the people of each race have one countenance and one language?"[175] As we have seen, in France and England their personal names were not so different after all, at least not so different that one's religious identity could be securely established simply from one's name. Their "names" were different only in the sense that one could be called a Jew, and another a Christian, and no doubt this is what Rachel meant.

---

175. Thomas of Cantimpré, *Miraculorum et exemplorum memorabilium sui temporis, libri duo* 2.29.20, p. 297.

7

CASE STUDIES REVEALING A JEWISH PHYSIOGNOMY

APPEARANCES CAN BE DECEIVING?

If personal names alone were not often sufficiently distinct to separate Jew and Christian, what about physical appearance and, in particular, skin coloring or what today we would call "complexion"? Here again, as already indicated, some of our evidence suggests that Jews and Christians were, outwardly, physically indistinguishable. The badge on the outer clothing was intended to remedy this. That Jewish converts to Christianity in England were sometimes explicitly identified by appending to their new names the appellation "the Convert/le Convers"— for example, Roger le Convers, John le Convers, and Nicholas le Convers—seems to suggest, too, that otherwise their previous Jewish identity could have gone unnoticed. Nonetheless, we do have some evidence from the twelfth and thirteenth centuries that suggests that Jews *were* seen as having a different skin color. Although such evidence is clear in medieval iconography and manuscript illuminations from the thirteenth century, in which Jews increasingly will be depicted with dark skin tones, bulbous eyes, hooked noses, and a malevolent countenance, it appears that such depictions construct a reality shaped by theological expectations rather than empirical observations, as already observed for the Jew Samuel in the "Passion of Adam of Bristol." Another good illustration comes from a tale contained in the late thirteenth-century collection of Marian songs, the *Cantigas de Santa Maria*. Pamela Patton has studied the visual images that accompanied many of these songs and draws attention to cantiga four, a retelling of the popular tale of the Jew of Bourges.¹ In this cantiga a Jewish boy who takes communion with Christian friends is depicted with an oversized, beaky nose, a miniature of the one worn by his father. The "Jewish nose," according to Robert Bartlett, is one of the most important physiological markers used to designate ethnicity in medieval illustations.² (See figure 11.) The "Jewish nose," usually depicted as large and beaked or crooked, was judged a deformity: in the Old Testament priests with a large or crooked nose were ineligible for Temple service (Lev. 21:18). For Thomas of Chobham, this text also applied to Christians seeking to serve at the altar, since when the nose is especially large and crooked, he remarks, it makes the face appear more beast-like than human.³ After the boy in cantiga four takes communion, however, he undergoes a "miraculous rhinoplasty" and "the boy's Jewish nose becomes instantly smaller and straighter, as if reflecting his purified condition."⁴ Such physical transformations, then, tell us something both about how Christians perceived a Jewish physignomy and how that physiognomy was expected to change as a result of conversion. This miraculous rhinoplasty brought the convert closer to the ideal physiognomy of Jesus himself, which the *vita* of Thomas of Cantimpré described. According to the *Gesta venerabilis Thomae de Cantiprato,* when gazing upon the consecrated host in a church in Douai, Thomas saw the face of Jesus. He saw "the face of the man honored above every image [*effigiem*], turned to the right [in profile].... His nose was rather long and very straight; his

---

1. The tale of the Jew of Bourges can be found (in translation) in Joan Young Gregg, *Devils, Women, and Jews,* 232–33. It was often illustrated in medieval manuscripts. See Denise L. Despres, "Immaculate Flesh and the Social Body: Mary and the Jews," *Jewish History* 12, no. 1 (1998), 58–60.

2. Robert Bartlett, "Illustrating Ethnicity in the Middle Ages," in *The Origins of Racism in the West,* ed. Miriam Eliav Feldon, Benjamin Isaac, and Joseph Ziegler (Cambridge: Cambridge University Press, 2009), 132–56, citing 133–34.

3. "hoc sciendum est quod sit tanta fuerit deformitas quod facies potius videatur esse bellvina quam humana, irregularis est qui tale vitium corporis habet ... et si homo potius videatur habere nasum simie quam hominis, irregularis est." Thomas of Chobham, *Summa Confessorum* art. 3, dist. 2, q. 5a, p. 71.

4. Pamela A. Patton, "Constructing the Inimical Jew in the *Cantigas de Santa Maria*: Theophilus's Magician in Text and Image," in *Beyond the Yellow Badge: Anti-Judaism and Antisemitism in Medieval and Early Modern Visual Culture,* ed. Mitchell B. Merback (Leiden: Brill, 2008), 239. This sequence in the cantigas is available at http://www.youtube.com/watch?v =IRMU5G1Z-CM&feature=related. For a general discussion of the image of the Jew in the cantigas, see also Dwayne E. Carpenter, "The Portrayal of the Jew in Alfonso the Learned's *Cantigas de Santa Maria,*" in *In Iberia & Beyond: Hispanic Jews between Cultures,* ed. Bernard Dov Cooperman (Cranbury, N.J.: Associated University Presses, 1998), 15–42.

eyebrows were arched [and] he had the most guileless and unassuming eyes, with long hair flowing down over his shoulders."[5] This description continues at some length, to include even details of his dimpled cheeks. Clearly, however, a straight and not a crooked nose characterized this ideal profile. From such texts we can discover something about how Christians perceived the Jewish body.

CASE 1: ANACLET II, THE "JEWISH POPE"

The most intriguing evidence stems from the contested papal election in 1130 following the death of Pope Honorius II. Following the pope's death, two candidates were elected to the papal throne. One was the Roman Gregory, cardinal deacon of St. Angelo, who took the name Innocent II. The other was Petrus Pierleoni, cardinal priest of St. Calixtus, who took the name Anaclet II. These two should also serve as a sufficient reminder that just as converts indicated a change of religious identity with a change of name, so too kings and popes typically indicated a change of status, signified by ritual anointing, by assuming a new name.[6] Petrus Pierleoni had the support of a large number of the clergy and people. He had been educated in Paris when the controversial philosopher and theologian Peter Abelard was teaching there, and he became a close friend of the French king Louis VI (d. 1137). Pierleoni had taken the vows of a Benedictine monk at Cluny before returning to Rome to become cardinal deacon of SS. Cosma and Damiano and before he was elevated to become cardinal priest of St. Calixtus.

This was neither the first nor the last disputed papal election to involve imperial and ecclesiastical politics as well as Roman family rivalries. Neither had the earlier election of Honorius II in 1124 been untroubled, since Honorius was able to obtain the papal throne only after the newly elected

---

5. "[vidit] faciem hominis super omnem effigiem honoratam, conversam ad dextram... Nasus erat admodum longus, directus valde, supercilia arcuata, oculos simplicissimos atque demissos habebat, caesariem longum super humeros descendentem." *Gesta venerabilis Thomae de Cantiprato*, in Thomas of Cantimpré, *Miraculorum et exemplorum memorabilium sui temporis, libri duo*, p. 13.

6. In the case of kings, their new name might simply entail adding a Roman numeral: thus Henry, son of King Henry, would become Henry II upon his accession, etc. These were not the only instances when individuals changed their names. Name changing also had its purposes for medieval magic. Trachtenberg records instances when individual Jews might change their names to escape an illness thought to have been brought upon them by angelic intervention. See Trachtenberg, *Jewish Magic and Superstition*, 204–6.

Celestine II had stepped down, following a campaign of intimidation. The disputed election of 1130, however, introduced a new element. In a model of "negative campaigning," several of Innocent II's supporters attacked Petrus Pierleoni as a "Jewish" pope, and whipped up popular animosity.[7]

Pierleoni's alleged Jewishness was based on the fact that the members of his family were relatively "new" Christians. His Jewish great-grandfather, Baruch (d. 1051), who had married a Christian woman of the house of Frangipani, converted to Christianity c. 1030 and Latinized his name as Benedict.[8] His son was named in honor of his baptismal patron, Pope Leo IX (r. 1049–54). By 1059 Benedict's son Leo had become one of the most distinguished men of Rome, and in 1061 he was a leading supporter of Pope Alexander II against the anti-Pope Cadalous.[9]

Although his father had converted to Christianity, there is some evidence to suggest that Leo had been circumcised as an infant. In a letter to Emperor Henry IV (r. 1084–1105) from the partisan Bishop Benzo of Alba (d. 1085), Benzo refers dismissively to Leo as *Leo Judaeus*. Benzo, a supporter of the imperial party and of the anti-Pope Cadalous, attacked the enemies of the Church and empire by invoking Proverbs 30:21–22: "By three things the earth is disturbed, and the fourth it cannot bear." The "fourth it cannot bear" he referred to the Normans; the three by which the earth is disturbed he identified as Leo the Jew, Alexander II ("Anselm [of Lucca] the Pharisee"), and the "cuckoo" Dohech the Idumean.[10] Zema identifies the "cuckoo" Dohech as Hildebrand, who was later elevated to the papacy as Gregory VII (r. 1073–85).[11] Benzo condemns Hildebrand as a "new little Antichrist" (*novus antichristellus*) who took counsel with Leo, "who had arisen originally from the Jewish community" (*originaliter procedenti de Iudaica congregatione*).[12]

---

7. The most accessible study of the contested election is by Mary Stroll, *The Jewish Pope: Ideology and Politics in the Papal Schism of 1130* (Leiden: Brill, 1987).

8. See H. Dittmann, "Anaklet II, Papst," in *Lexikon des Mittelalters*, 10 vols (Stuttgart: Metzler, [1977]–99), 1: 568.

9. Cadalous (d. 1072) assumed the name Honorius II, challenged Pope Alexander II, and was excommunicated in 1063.

10. Benzo of Alba, *Ad Heinricum IV* 2.4, MGH, SS rer. Germ. 65 (Hannover: Hahn, 1996), 208.

11. Demetrius B. Zema, "The Houses of Tuscany and of Pierleone in the Crisis of Rome in the Eleventh Century," *Traditio* 2 (1944), 172. See also H. E. J. Cowdrey, *Pope Gregory VII, 1073–1085* (Oxford: Oxford University Press, 1998), 51–52.

12. Benzo of Alba, *Ad Heinricum* 2.4, p. 204.

One possible interpretation is that Leo, a Christian, is simply tainted by his father's Jewish origins. For several reasons, I think this interpretation fails to reconcile adequately the discordant information. We do not know the date of Leo's birth and although it seems unlikely that Leo could have lived as a Jew with his convert father until Leo was baptized, nonetheless, if Leo received baptism only between 1049 and 1054 during the papacy of Leo IX, and yet Leo was already an important man in Rome in 1059, the conclusion seems inescapable that Leo must have passed his early years as a Jew before his baptism. One problem with this inference is that we know that his father, Baruch (Latinized as Benedict), married a Christian woman, which was perhaps a motive for his conversion. If this Christian woman were Leo's mother, it is inconceivable that Leo could have been circumcised as an infant. But if this marriage was a second marriage for Baruch, then we can perhaps make some sense of the situation. Leo could have been circumcised as an infant and then gone to live with his convert-father and Christian stepmother. Assuming the existence of a Jewish mother, he would still have been regarded by rabbinic and Church authorities as a member of the Jewish community until his own conversion. In this reconstruction, Leo is in reality one "who had arisen originally from the Jewish community" and not merely a Christian son tainted by his father's former Jewish identity. According to this interpretation, we can view Leo quite literally as having once been a Jew, *Leo Judaeus,* while Benzo satisfies his polemical purpose too by refusing him the title adopted by Herman of Cologne in the next century that identified Herman as *formerly* (*quondam*) a Jew. If this interpretation is correct, then Leo's grandson, the future Anaclet II, is drawn one generation closer to his Jewish background.

Leo died sometime before 1072, and his position in the family was taken up by his son Peter I, from whom the family derived the name Pierleoni (*Petrus Leonis*—Peter, [son] of Leo).[13] Peter I (d. c. 1124–30) had no fewer than nine sons, led the family for another sixty years, and became a powerful supporter of Pope Gregory VII and the Gregorian

---

13. M. Thumser, "Pierleoni," in *Lexikon des Mittelalters,* 6: 2136. 1063 is accepted as the year of Leo's death by both Demetrius B. Zema, "The Houses of Tuscany and of Pierleone in the Crisis of Rome in the Eleventh Century," 170, and Herbert Bloch, "The Schism of Anacletus II and the Glanfeuil Forgeries of Peter the Deacon of Monte Cassino," *Traditio* 8 (1952), 163.

Reform movement.[14] William of Malmesbury identified Peter I disparagingly as the "chief of the Roman princes," and indeed the Pierleoni family remained the chief support in Rome of the Reform party well into the twelfth century.[15] Peter I Pierleoni's entombment in a rich marble sarcophogus in the cloisters of St. Paul-Outside-the Walls is an indication of the family's importance.

The Frangipani family had helped to orchestrate the election of Pope Honorius II in 1124 as well as the election of Innocent II in 1130, at which time Peter I Pierleoni's son and also Leo's grandson, Peter II, struggled to secure the papal throne as Anaclet II. Precisely because the election of Anaclet II was more regular than that of Innocent II, Innocent's supporters, who were especially numerous in France and included such luminaries as St. Bernard of Clairvaux and the Cluniac abbot Peter the Venerable, were driven to wage a "dirty tricks" campaign to discredit his person and character.[16] Petrus Pierleoni's most vicious enemy, however, was Manfred, Bishop of Mantua, who attacked the anti-pope's "Jewishness":

Now then how much more do Jewish perfidy and Leonine rabies[17] and Peter's heresy rage against the Church and against an innocent, just, chaste, civi-

---

14. Mary Stoll's *The Jewish Pope* has convincingly overturned the thesis that it was because Anaclet was a representative of the older Gregorian ideology that the cardinals divided their support between him and Innocent II, with the latter viewed as a putative representative of a new religiosity promoted by St. Bernard of Clairvaux. The explanation that relies on opposition between a Gregorian ideology and a new religiosity can be found in Stanley Chodorow's "Ecclesiastical Politics and the Ending of the Investiture Contest: The Papal Election of 1119 and the Negotiations of Mouzon," *Speculum* 46, no. 4 (1971): 613–40; Hayden White, "Pontius of Cluny, the *Curia Romana* and the End of Gregorianism in Rome," *Church History* 27, no. 3 (1958): 195–219; and, Bloch, "The Schism of Anacletus II and the Glanfeuil Forgeries of Peter the Deacon of Monte Cassino," 159–259.

15. William of Malmesbury, *De gestis pontificum Anglorum* 1.68, p. 128.

16. Gillian Knight ["Politics and Pastoral Care: Papal Schism in some Letters of Peter the Venerable," *Revue Bénédictine* 109, no. 3–4 (1999), 366–67] has pointed out that Peter tended to avoid the personal invective that characterized Innocent's supporters' attacks on Anaclet—at least until Anaclet was dead. In *De Miraculis* (composed between 1135–42) Peter refers to the schism retrospectively and describes Anaclet, with a pun on his name, as that lion's whelp that raged against the church, the Antichrist and chief of all schismatics; see Peter the Venerable, *De Miraculis* 16, ed. D. Bouthillier, CCCM 83 (Turnholt: Brepols, 1988), 127, 19–23.

17. "Leonine rabies": Perhaps a pun, recalling his descent through his grandfather, Leo, but also a reference to a form of mental disturbance or madness resulting when natural melancholy dominates the brain. According to Ishāq ibn 'Imrān, an important source for Constantine the African, it is called Leonine because those suffering it rise up like lions and are bold and strong. See Ishāq ibn 'Imrān, *Maqāla fī l-Mālīhūliyā* (*Abhandlung über die Melancholie*) *und Constantini Africani Libri duo de Melancholia*, p. 107, Basle ed., 284.

lized man, elected and consecrated according to the Catholic rite, Innocent by name, when they struggle with their [supporters] to destroy and to pervert all goods ... and let him, that iniquitous Peter, the son of perdition,[18] with his [supporters], either repent through you [that is, the Church] or perish through you ... Who, although he may be a monk, a priest, and a cardinal, does not cease to couple with whores, married women, nuns, his own sister, even those related to him by blood, just like a dog, in every way he could have them."[19]

As a result, from alleged incestuous relations with his own sister, Anaclet II was said to have become "a father to his nephews, an uncle to his sons—he so confused the laws of nature that his brothers were also his kinsmen. No longer merely a Jew, he was even worse than a Jew."[20]

Arnulf (d. 1184), archdeacon of Séez and later Bishop of Lisieux was a second powerful enemy. In an invective written to one of Anaclet's chief supporters, Gerard, Bishop of Angoulême, whom Anaclet II had appointed a papal legate, Arnulf ties Anaclet's perfidy and error to his family's

---

18. For the Son of Perdition, see 2 Thess. 2:3. The Son of Perdition was sometimes imagined to be a forerunner to the anti-Christ, and often identified with Mohammad or Muslims generally. Kenneth Baxter Wolf, "Muhammad as Antichrist in Ninth-Century Córdoba," in *Christians, Muslims, and Jews in Medieval and Early Modern Spain: Interaction and Cultural Change,* ed. Mark D. Meyerson and Edward D. English, Notre Dame Conferences in Medieval Studies 8 (Notre Dame, Ind.: University of Notre Dame Press, 2000), 3–19. See Robert the Monk, *Historia Iherosolomitana,* and Ralph of Caen's *Gesta Tancredi,* in *Recueil des historiens des croisades. Historiens Occidentaux,* 5 vols. (Paris: Academie des Inscriptions et Belles-Lettres, 1844–95), 3: 695, and 828; Jacques de Vitry, *Historia Orientalis* 4, p. 9; and *Lettres de Jacques de Vitry* 6, p. 152; Felix Fabri, *Evagatorum in Terrae Sanctae, Arabiae et Egyptii peregrinationem,* fol. 91a, 3: 48. See also Iogna-Prat, *Order and Exclusion: Cluny and Christendom Face Heresy, Judaism, and Islam (1000–1150),* chap. 11: "Islam and Antichrist"; and David Burr, "Antichrist and Islam in Medieval Franciscan Exegesis," in *Medieval Christian Perceptions of Islam: A Book of Essays,* ed. John Victor Tolan (New York: Garland, 1996), 131–52.

19. "Nunc igitur quanto magis iudaica perfidia et Leonina rabies et Petri haeresis in ecclesiam furiunt et virum innocentem, iustum, castum, bene morigeratum, catholice electum et consecratum, Innocentium nomine, cum suis perdere et omnia bona moliuntur subvertere ... et ille iniquus Petrus, perditionis filius, cum suis aut per vos paeniteat aut per vos pereat. ... Qui licet monacus, presbyter, cardinalis esset, scorta, coniugatas, monachas, sororem propriam, etiam consanguineas ad instar canis, quomodo habere potuit, non deficit." *Pontificum Romanorum qui fuerunt inde ab exeunte saeculo IX usque ad finem saeculi XIII vitae ab aequalibus conscriptae, quas ex Archivi pontifici, bibliothecae Vaticanae aliarumque codicibus adiectis suis cuique et annalibus et documentis gravioribus,* ed. Johann Matthias Watterich; vol. 2: *Paschalis II-Coelestinus III (1099–1198)* (Lepizig: sumptibus Guilhelmi Engelmanni, 1862), n. 1, 275–76.

20. "Nepotum pater, filiorum factus avunculus—sic natura iura confudit, ut eosdem sibi invicem fratres et cognatos. Iam nec Iudaeus quidem, sed Iudaeo etiam deterior." Watterich, *Pontificum Romanorum,* 260 n. 3.

avarice and struggle to achieve wealth and standing in Rome, which he treats as quasi-racial characteristics that can hardly be expunged. Somewhat disingenuously, he wrote:

And so it is pleasing to pass over the ancient origin of [his] birth and [his] similarly ignoble race, and I do not think that the Jewish name from which he himself drew not only the material for his flesh but even certain first fruits of native error ought to be set before us.... Although his grandfather [that is, Leo] collected inestimable wealth from multiple usurious transactions, he condemned the circumcision that he had received with the water of baptism. He was ashamed of his powerlessness rather than of his error, lest perpetual darkness condemn his race [that is] confounded by the opprobrium of infidelity. Therefore, once he had received the sacraments of the faith, he was made a Roman in dignity when he was grafted on as a new citizen. And since a series of good issues bestowed upon him numerous progeny, while the queen bestows race and form for money, he tied to himself all the nobles of the city by marriage, one after another, already conspiring with the enemy of the human race, so that as if by an old yeast the entire dough of Roman purity would be corrupted. [cf. Gal. 5:9] From this mixture of various races, then, Gerard, this Peter of yours arose, who displays a Jewish image on [his] face and repays perfidy for a sacred promise and goodwill.[21]

Later, Arnulf depicts Gerard, Bishop of Angoulême, as an owl (*bubo*) that is blinded by the light of day, whose obstinate heart will not permit him to hear the truth, namely, that "that faithless company you follow is the Pierleoni family that is not yet cleansed inwardly of the yeast of Jewish corruption."[22] Arnulf's metaphor is well chosen. According to

21. "Libet igitur praeterire antiquam nativitatis originem et ignobilem similem prosapiam nec iudaicum nomen arbitror opponendum, de quibus ipse non solum materiam carnis, sed etiam quasdam primitias ingeniti contraxit erroris. Ipse enim sufficiens est et copiosa materia neque quidquam domui eius ipso turpius vel esse vel fuisse coniecto. Cuius avus cum inestimabilem pecuniam multiplici corrogasset usura, susceptam circumcisionem baptismatis unda damnavit. Pudebat eum impotentiae suae potius, quam erroris, ne genus eius, infidelitatis opprobrio confusum, perpetua damnaret obscuritas: susceptis itaque fidei sacramentis, ubi novus civis insitus, est factus dignitate Romanus. Cumque ipsi numerosam progeniem series successionis afferet, dum genus et formam regina pecunia donat, alternis matrimoniis omnes sibi nobiles civitatis adscivit, machinante iam humani generis hoste, ut quasi quodam veteri fermento tota Romanae sinceritatis conspersio corrumperetur. Ex hac itaque diversorum generum mixtura, Girarde, Petrus iste tuus exortus est, qui et judaicam facie repraesentet imaginem et perfidiam voto referat et affectu." Arnulf of Séez, *In Girardum Engolismensem invectiva de schismate Petri Leonis* 3, in Watterich, *Pontificum Romanorum*, 2: 259–60.

22. "Infidelis universitas illa, quam sequeris, familia Petri Leonis est, nondum fermento iudaicae corruptionis penitus expiata." Arnulf of Séez, *Invectiva in Girardum Engolismensem episcopum* 8, p. 107.

the twelfth-century *Book of Beasts*, "Owls are symbolical to the Jews, who repulse our Saviour when he comes to redeem them.... [because] They value darkness more than light."[23] In medieval ecclesiastical art and ornaments too, the owl—identified as unclean at Leviticus 11:16f.—often symbolized the Jews.[24] In the same way, Jews were frequently condemned for a benighted, stubborn or obstinate heart that would not permit them to acknowledge Jesus as the Christ. The implication seems to be that simply by following one "not yet cleansed inwardly of the yeast of Jewish corruption" Gerard has been infected by the Jews' blindness and obduracy. Later authors add that the owl (*bubo*) as well as the pig also represent *luxuria* and its subordinate vices so frequently associated with the Jews.[25]

Arnulf casts doubt as well upon the sincerity of Leo's Christian faith, Anaclet's grandfather, and suggests that Leo converted from Judaism to obtain worldly standing, because "he was ashamed of his powerlessness rather than of his error." His grandson Peter, now Anaclet II, is the product of a marriage arranged with the old Roman nobility, but rather than "naturalizing" Peter as a Christian, instead he is a product of a mixture of races, and "by an old yeast the entire dough of Roman purity" is corrupted. Arnulf warns Gerard that "That unfaithful company that you follow is the Pierleoni family, which has still not been completely cleansed of the Jewish yeast of corruption."[26] And, lest anyone miss the point, in a letter to King Lothair of Germany (d. 1137), later the Holy Roman Emperor, the cardinal bishops who supported Innocent II and opposed Anaclet II pointed out that Anaclet had assumed the papal insignia at that very sixth hour when the Jews had crucified Christ.[27]

His behavior, moreover, linked Anaclet II to Antichrist. A medieval consensus had coalesced to affirm that the Antichrist would be born of

---

23. *The Book of Beasts*, 134; See also *Physiologus* 7, trans. Curley, 10–12.
24. See Miyazaki, "Misercord Owls and Medieval Anti-semitism," 23–50.
25. St. Antoninus of Florence, *Summa theologica* 1, tit. 14, cap. 5, §4, 1: 734D.
26. "Infidelis universitas illa, quam sequeris, familia Petri Leonis est, nondum fermento iudaica corruptionis penitus expiata." Arnulf of Séez, *In Girardum Engolismensem invectiva de schismate Petri Leonis* 8, in Watterich, *Pontificum Romanorum*, 2: 274
27. "Petrus Leonis hora sexta, qua Judaea Christum crucifixit et tenebrarum caligo mundum involvit, cum suis conspiratoribus atque consanguineis aliisque manifesto pretio conductis ecclesiam sancti Martii (l. Marci), turribus fratrum propinquam, festinanter adiit, cappam rubeam indecenter induit fictitiaque Pontificatus insignia arripuit." Watterich, *Pontificum Romanorum*, 2: 182.

the Jews, from the tribe of Dan.[28] In the middle of the thirteenth century Vincent of Beauvais adds, however, that Antichrist will first be circumcised—indeed, he will circumcise himself—only when he arrives in Jerusalem to persuade the Jews that he is the messiah promised to them.[29] This suggests that Antichrist will be first a hidden or concealed Jew, a crypto-Jew, one who lacks the concealed physical mark by which Jews are differentiated. So too Anaclet is an uncircumcised Christian but, drawing upon the perfidy of his Jewish origins, conspires with the aid of his grandfather's wealth first to obtain the Roman See and then to rule the entire world.[30] It is almost certainly Arnulf's description of Peter as one corrupted by the yeast of his Jewish origin, as one who displays a Jewish image on his face, that led the late nineteenth-century Church historian, Philip Schaff, to remark that "Anacletus betrayed his Semitic origin in his physiognomy, and was inferior to Innocent in moral character."[31]

Even St. Bernard of Clairvaux became involved in the campaign against Anaclet II. In a letter to King Lothair, who supported Anaclet II, Bernard also insisted that "it is an insult to Christ that the offspring of a Jew has occupied the chair of Peter."[32] It is remarkable that Anaclet's Jewish origins—indeed, not his own, but his grandfather's—aroused no antipathy while he was still a cardinal, but when he was elevated to the papacy it became the basis for a series of attacks. Of interest to us, however, is Arnulf's claim that Anaclet II "displays a Jewish image on [his] face." This suggests that already during the first half of the twelfth century the notion that Jews had distinctive features or complexion could be invoked without requiring further explanation.

28. This can be traced back in the early Church to Irenaeus, *Adversus Haereses* 5.25–30, and Cyril of Jerusalem, *Catechetical Lectures* in *Cyril of Jerusalem and Nemesius of Emesa*, ed. William Teller, Library of Christian Classics 4 (Philadelphia: Westminster Press, 1955), 158–60. For discussion, see C. E. Hill, "Antichrist from the Tribe of Dan," *Journal of Theological Studies* 46, no. 1 (1995): 99–117. For the Middle Ages, this tradition can be found in Adso of Montier-en-Der, *De ortu et tempore Antichristi*, ed. D. Verhelst, CCCM 45 (Turnholt: Brepols, 1976), ln. 19.

29. Vincent of Beauvais, *Speculum naturale* 32.113, 1: 2476.

30. Arnulf of Séez, *In Girardum Engolismensem invectiva de schismate Petri Leonis* 3, in Watterich, *Pontificum Romanorum*, 2: 260.

31. Philip Schaff, *History of the Christian Church*, 8 vols. (Oak Harbor, Wash.: Logos Research Systems, 1997), 4: 217.

32. "constat Judaicam sobolem sedem Petri in Christi occupasse injuriam." Bernard of Clairvaux, *Sancti Bernardi Opera genuina*, 8 vols., Epist. 139.1, ed. Monks of St. Benedict (Lyons: Perisse Frères, 1854), 1:125.

We have one other piece of evidence that this so is from this same controversy. Anaclet II had a brother, Gratian. At the Council of Rheims in 1119, during which Pope Callixtus II excommunicated Emperor Henry V, Gratian, who had been a hostage during negotiations, was released to Calixtus II. According to the contemporary historian Oderic Vitalis (d. 1142), at the Council

The Archbishop of Cologne ... also freely surrendered a son of Peter [I] Leonis, whom he held as a hostage. Announcing this as if it were a great triumph and exceptional pleasure, the envoy pointed out with his finger a dark-haired, pale youth, more like a Jew or a Saracen than a Christian, dressed in splendid garments, but physically deformed. At the sight of him seated beside the Pope the French and many others laughed scornfully, and called down shame and swift destruction on his head, out of hatred for his father whom they knew as an infamous usurer.[33]

Marjorie Chibnall's elegant translation obscures one point: the Latin text does not describe Gratian as "a dark-haired, pale youth" but rather simply as a dark—or even black—and pallid youth (*nigrum et pallidum adolescentem*). Chibnall's translation fits better a passage from a late thirteenth-century text falsely attributed to Albert the Great, which remarks that "with respect to their innate complexion, offspring are accustomed to be like their parents, and vice versa. But we see that in many cases the race of Jews has black hair."[34] While a pale complexion may often produce dark or black hair, the passage in the history of Oderic Vi-

33. "Coloniensis archiepiscopus ... filium quoque Petri Leonis, quem obsidem habebat ob amoris specimen gratis reddidit. Haec dicens, quasi ob insigne tripudium laetiamque mirabilem, digito monstravit nigrum et pallidum adolescentem, magis Judaeo vel Agareno quam christiano similem, vestibus quidem optimis indutum, sed corpore deformen. Quem Franci, aliique plures papae adsistentem intuentes, deriserunt, eique dedecus perniciemque citam imprecati sunt, propter odium patris ipsius quem nequissimum foeneratorem nouerunt." Oderic Vitalis, *The Ecclesiastical History of Oderic Vitalis* 12.21, 6 vols., ed. and trans. Marjorie Chibnall (Oxford: The Clarendon Press, 1978), 6: 266–68. The twelfth-century *Deeds of Albero of Trier* indicates that Gratian had been offered as a hostage by his father during negotiations between Pope Paschal II (d. 1118) and Henry V. See Balderich [of Florennes], *A Warrior Bishop of the Twelfth Century: The Deeds of Albero of Trier, by Balderich* 5, p. 32.

34. "Secundum complexionem innatam soboles solent assimilari parentibus, et e contra; sed videmus, quod genus Judaeorum ut in pluribus habet nigros capillos." [Ps.] Albert the Great, *Quaestiones super Evangelium* 19.2.5, p. 44. For a discussion of this text and its treatment of physiognomy, see my "Ps. Albert the Great on the Physiognomy of Jesus and Mary," *Medieval Studies* 64 (2002): 217–40. William of Conches explains that black hair is itself a sign of a melancholy complexion, whereas red hair indicates a choleric one, and fair or blond hair a phlegmatic one. See his *Dragmaticon* 6.17.4, p. 236.

talis seems more likely to refer to a dark-complexioned yet pallid youth, "more like a Jew or a Saracen than a Christian." A century later, Matthew Paris evoked as well a contrast between the dark-skinned Saracens and the French.[35] Although in medieval literature some Saracens may be depicted as fair-skinned and handsome, anticipating the possibility of Christian baptism and assimilation, it seems fair to say that these remain exceptions. Thus, in illuminations accompanying William of Tyre's famous Crusader chronicle, the *History of Deeds Done Beyond the Sea*, "Muslims are most frequently represented with black skin and black faces."[36] I suspect that Chibnall supplied *dark-haired* in order to avoid the seeming contradiction between dark and pallid, although no such contradiction existed for medieval humoral theory.[37]

In sum, in this highly charged polemical atmosphere, Anaclet II was charged with displaying "a Jewish image on [his] face"; Gratian was derided for having a dark complexion, "more like a Jew or a Saracen than a Christian"; and the entire Pierleoni family was denigrated (lit., "blackened") for not having been completely cleansed of the Jewish yeast of corruption. In part, the traits that marked these "new" Christians as "Jews" were universal vices: avarice, ambition, and a lust for power. But in part they were also identified by physical characteristics: an unspecified but "Jewish" facial appearance, and a dark but pallid complexion. Evidently these "Jewish" moral and physical characteristics could not be completely washed away even by Christian baptism. It may not be solely coincidence that the Jewish exegete Abraham ibn Ezra, who arrived in Rome in 1140 only two years after the death of Anaclet II, anticipates Shylock's famous speech in the *Merchant of Venice* and remarks in his commentary on Isaiah, "how many nations are there in the world who

---

35. See Matthew Paris, *The Illustrated Chronicles of Matthew Paris: Observations of Thirteenth-Century Life*, ed. and trans. Richard Vaughn (Phoenix Mill, U.K.: Sutton, 1993), 176. Muslim chroniclers, similarly, remarked upon the pale-skinned Franks that shaved their beards. See the account of al-Qazwini (d. 1283) in Carole Hillenbrand, *The Crusades: Islamic Perspectives* (New York: Routledge, 1999), 272.

36. Svetlana Luchitskaya, "Muslims in Christian Imagery of the Thirteenth-Century: The Visual Code of Otherness," *Al-Masāq* 12 (2000), 46.

37. That is, pallor indicated a lack of natural heat in complexion, whereas blackness could stem from a predominance of melancholy or black bile, caused either by an internal condition or from the external power of the melancholy planet, Saturn. In fact a melancholy complexion is itself a cold and dry complexion, and one frequently finds both black (or dark or dusky) and pallor together in descriptions of such a complexion.

think that the features of the Jew are disfigured and unlike those of other men, and ask whether a Jew has a mouth or an eye! This is done, for example, in the countries of Ishma'el and Edom."[38]

In his defense of Innocent II, Arnulf appeals not only to Innocent's moral character, which he regards as clearly superior to that of his rival, but also to his physical appearance which, in many respects, displays the virtues of the Aristotelian mean. He exhorts Gerard to compare the features of Innocent II and Anaclet II and remarks:

> If his [Innocent's] race is investigated, reckoned from his birth, he will be observed to be a faithful Christian born from faithful Christians; if [one investigates] the counsel of his parents in his education and instruction, [he will be observed to be] one that dwells in the house of the Lord all the days of his life (cf. Ps. 22:5; 26:6) and that perceives the will of the Lord; if [one investigates] the quality of his person, to describe first his physical appearance, he is a man of modest stature, and neither does a rather short stature render [him] abject nor does enormous size render [him] monstrous. A robust simplicity appears in his eyes and his countenance, and a shyness, which indicates the chastity of his soul, appears on his face. That face is so resplendent with dignity that it imparts a certain reverence to anyone gazing upon him. Also, among the other gifts of its munificence, divine power has bestowed upon him a special grace so that all those that see him he reconciles with a gentle kindness and love for him that is borne from his appearance alone. Moreover, supernal bounty has inspired his eyes with something divine, that is, that is full of grace, worthy of veneration, that in general is considered congruent with honor. [His] voice is smooth, but not so much so that it is rendered too weak, and not so that it lacks an inclination to sweetness and the authority of strength. [He has] a constant liveliness upon his face, a frequent laugh during a discussion's digression, yet nonetheless an appearance so pleasing that it can only increase not lessen the dignity of [his] face and words. This attracts those gazing upon him all the more, since in him it seems to be the beginning of his eternal joy, whose first fruits I think that he received in his body.[39]

---

38. AD[olf] Neubauer, compiler, *Fifty-Third Chapter of Isaiah According to the Jewish Interpreters*, 1: 45 (Hebrew), 2: 45. Edom refers to Rome and Christendom. For the dating of his commentary see especially Shlomo Sela and Gad Freudenthal, "Abraham Ibn Ezra's Scholarly Writings: A Chronological Listing," *Aleph* 6 (2006): 13–55. My reference to Shylock is, of course, to his impassioned query, "Hath not a Jew eyes?" *The Merchant of Venice* 3.1.58.

39. "Si genus eius, recensita nativitate, disquiritur, fidelis natus ex fidelibus advertetur; si parentum in ipsius educatione vel doctrina consilium, ut habitaret in domo Domini omnibus diebus vitae suae et videret voluntatem Domini; si personae qualitas, ut prius habitudo corporea describatur, vir staturae mediocris, quae nec abiectum brevitas nec immanem reddat immensae quantitatis excessus. Apparet in oculis eius et vultu robusta simplicitas, et quae castitatem animi probet, verecundia faciei. Quae profecto facies tanta dignitate resplendet,

In contrast to Anaclet, in whose flesh the first fruits of native error appeared, in Innocent's body, born from faithful Christian parents, there appear the first fruits of eternal joy. He is neither too short nor too tall. His eyes are portals to a chaste soul. His voice is pleasing but not lacking authority. His face is lively and given to laughter or humor, yet at the same time his is a dignified appearance. He is not physically deformed, like Gratian, Anaclet's brother, nor dark like a Jew or a Saracen. It may not be mere coincidence that Albero of Trier, whom Balderich described as "exceedingly skilled in physiognomy, to such a degree that he would discern the secrets of character and behavior from different facial appearances," was himself an advocate for Innocent II. Physiognomy seems to have been important to the defense of Innocent's claim on the papal throne.

Anaclet II died in Rome in 1138, bringing this schism to an end. According to Oderic Vitalis, his body was hidden in Rome by his brothers, so that no one knows where he is buried.[40] Later orthodox traditions supply details of the unseemly nature of his death. One is found in the *exempla* of the thirteenth-century Dominican, Stephen of Bourbon (d. 1261). Stephen composed his book of *exempla* to benefit preachers like himself, drawing upon older writers—classical authors and the Church Fathers—as well as upon contemporary events. His *Treatise on Various Materials for Preaching* (*Tractatus de diversis materiis praedicabilibus*) is arranged in seven parts, according to the Seven Gifts of the Holy Spirit. According to Stephen's narrative, at the time of the schism Bernard of Clairvaux went to Italy to try to restore unity to the Church. A certain holy man, who was ill and near death, begged Bernard to visit him so that he could leave this world strengthened by Bernard's prayers. Since Bernard could not come to him, due to the urgent negotiations, he told

---

ut et ipsi quandam reverentiam ingerat intuenti. Ei quoque hanc inter cetera munificentiae suae dona specialem gratiam vis divina largita est, ut omnes se videntes mansueta sibi benignitate conciliet et dilectionem solo nanciscatur aspectu. Ipsius etenim oculis divinum quiddam superna bonitas inspiravit, quod plenum gratiae, quod reverentia dignum, quod honori congruum generaliter arbitretur. Vox blanda, sed non in nimiam tamen resoluta molliciem, ut et suavitatis favor et magnitudinis non desit auctoritas. Continua vultus alacritas, risus in sermonis excursu sepissimus, tanta tamen habitus honestate, ut verborum vultusque possit augere, non minuere dignitatem. Quod quidem eo magis allicit intuentes, quoniam id in ipso quoddam illius eternae iocunditatis videtur initium, cuius eum in ipso corpore quasdam existimo primitias accepisse." Arnulf of Séez, *Invectiva in Girardum Engolismensem episcopum* 4, p. 96.

40. Oderic Vitalis, *The Ecclesiastical History of Oderic Vitalis* 13.35, 6: 508.

the holy man that if he wanted to leave this world with more confidence, he should pray and petition the Blessed Virgin to bring an end to the schism.

Once he had done this, it seemed to the other holy man [to whom Bernard wrote] that a council was gathered in a great church, and there placed in the middle was a high throne. Seated on thrones too were abbots, cardinals, archbishops, bishops, and many other magnates, and on the high throne was Petrus Leonis, called Pope Anaclet. A certain very beautiful lady appeared there, before whom there appeared an elderly man, cloaked from behind with a sack, and he leaned his staff on one of the columns of the church. The aforementioned lady said to him: "Why have you come so late, elder lord?" And, descending from the altar, she took the staff of the elder man and, spinning it around, she struck the throat of Petrus Leonis with its point, saying, "Why have you presumed to sit on the chair [or: in the See] that my son granted to the apostle Peter and to his canonically elected successors?" Having said this, the vision disappeared. Peter Leonis, however, died from a swollen throat, and peace was restored to the church that was united once again.[41]

The tale is clearly meant to demonstrate that divine judgment took Anaclet's life, using the Virgin as its instrument. Although one cannot determine from the text the nature of the sudden swelling that resulted in Anaclet's death, it is possible that the reader is meant to infer that he succumbed to scrofula, a disfiguring illness that results from swollen lymph nodes of the neck and throat, and an illness which, for the Middle Ages, could easily be identified with one of the more benign forms of leprosy.[42] Scrofula also was commonly linked to pigs, from which animals it was thought to take its origin, and whose humoral complexion was thought

---

41. "Quo de facto, cuidam alteri visum est sancto quod in quadam magna ecclesia congregabatur concilium, et in medio collocabatur cathedra excelsa, et in sedilibus sedebant cardinales, abbates, archepiscopi, episcopi et multitudo aliorum magnorum, et in magna cathedra Petrus Leonis, papa Anacletus dictus. Venit ibi quedam domina speciosissima, ante quam venit quidam senior indutus sacco postremus, et cambuscam [reading cambuca for cambusca] suam ad columpnam ecclesie appodiavit. Cui dixit dicta domina: 'Cur ita tarde venisti, domine senior?' Et de altari descendens, accepit cambuscam dicti senioris; et girans eam, percussit cuspide ejus guttur dicti Petri Leonis, dicens: 'Cur sedere presumpsisti in sede quam filius meus concessit Petro apostolo et successoribus electis canonice?' Et hoc dicto, visio disparuit. Petrus autem Leonis. gutture inflato, mortuus est, et Ecclesia in unum redacta, pace sibi reddita." Stephen of Bourbon/Etienne de Bourbon, *Anecdotes Historiques, Légendes et Apologues tirés du recueil inédit d'Étienne de Bourbon* 2.6, no. 138, ed. A. Lecoy de la Marche (Paris: Librairie Renouard, 1877), 118–19.

42. In his *Vita* of Clare of Assisi (d. 1253), Thomas of Celano (?) indicates that tumors of the throat are commonly called, in the vernacular (*vulgari sermone*), scrofula. See *Legenda sanctae Clarae Virginis* 58, ed. Francesco Pannecchi (Assisi: Tip. Metastasio, 1910).

to produce swellings in the pigs themselves.[43] Finally, as already noted, scrofula was sometimes specially identified with the Jews as an affliction appropriate to them, sometimes under the rubric of the "king's evil" or the royal disease (*morbus regius*).[44] It would be altogether fitting, then, for the "Jewish" pope to have met his end suffering a "Jewish" illness. An additional mystery here is: who is the elderly man carrying a staff and a sack? It is very tempting to see in this pilgrim the already well-known figure of the wandering Jew.[45] If this is the case, then Mary uses the staff of a Jew who, according to legend, had struck and mocked Jesus before the crucifixion, for which he is punished to wander the earth ceaselessly until the Second Coming. Perhaps the staff pointing at Anaclet's throat is intended, then, to identify him as a Jew (just as the nature of his sudden illness may have been meant to do) who has mocked or insulted Jesus by occupying the See of Peter.

One wonders just how long the Pierleonis could be expected to display these allegedly Jewish traits. Were they perceived truly as racial characteristics that would endure forever because they somehow expressed an essential nature? Or, were they perceived to be a divine punishment, to endure "unto the third and fourth generation of them that hate me,"[46] much as conversos in Spain would have to demonstrate an absence of Jewish blood going back four generations? Twelfth-century theologians acknowledged that certain inherited psychological dispositions persist only until the third or fourth generation.[47] In the early fourteenth century, Duns Scotus argued that although forced baptism of Jewish adults may not produce positive results, nonetheless among the children of such converts the Christian faith may take root by the third or fourth generation.[48] Alonso de Espina adopts a similar position in the second half of the fifteenth century in his *Fortalitium Fidei* (*Fortress of Faith*), where he both defends the practice of compulsory baptism for Jewish children—the adults likely being too hardhearted to benefit

---

43. Albert the Great, *Quaestiones super de animalibus* 7.33–39, pp. 186–88 (QDA, 265).

44. See chap. 3, n. 21.

45. The story of the wandering Jew can be found under the year 1228 CE in Roger of Wendover, *Flowers of History* 2.2, p. 513.

46. Ex. 20:5; Ex. 34:7; Num. 14:18; Deut. 5:9.

47. Anselm of Laon, *Sententie Anselmi* [of Laon], in *Anselms von Laon systematische Sentenzen*, pp. 75–76.

48. Turner, "Jewish Witness, Forced Conversion, and Island Living: John Duns Scotus on Jews and Judaism," 197.

from Christian baptism—and acknowledges nonetheless that baptism's positive effect may not be seen in the present generation.[49] The fifteenth-century *Hammer of Sorceresses* attempts to reconcile Ezekiel 19:20 ("The son shall not bear the iniquity of the father") and Exodus 20:5 ("I am the Lord your God . . . visiting the iniquity of the fathers upon the children, unto the third and fourth generation") by arguing that although God does not impose a spiritual penalty on the son for the father's iniquity, temporal or corporeal punishments for sin may be transferred to the third and fourth generations.[50] In the thirteenth and fourteenth centuries, it was not only scripture that might be invoked to support the claim that physical traits or psychological characteristics were passed down so far as the fourth generation; Aristotle, or Pseudo-Aristotle, was also cited as an authority who taught that although grandchildren may look like their grandparents, or even their great-grandparents, this resemblance does not extend more than four generations.[51]

Moreover, why did these physical characteristics become problematic "Jewish" traits only when Anaclet II ascended the throne of St. Peter? We have examples of other Jewish converts in high episcopal office. Both Pablo de Santa Maria and his son, Alonso, became Archbishop of Burgos, and they are not isolated examples. Other converts occupied high positions in the papal court. One example from early fifteenth-century Spain is Pablo de Santa Maria's friend Joshua Halorque (or ha-Lorki), the pope's physician, who as a Christian took the name Jerónimo de Santa Fe and became one of the chief architects of the Tortosa disputation (1413–

---

49. Al[ph]onso de Espina, *Fortalitium fidei* 3.12.2, fol.181r; see Steven J. McMichael, "The End of the World, Antichrist, and the Final Conversion of the Jews in the *Fortalitium fidei* of Friar Alonso de Espina (d. 1464)," *Medieval Encounters* 12, no. 2 (2006): 224–73, but esp. 247. For a helpful summary of the contents and structure of the *Fortalitium fidei*, see Alisa Meyuhas Ginio, "The Fortress of Faith—at the End of the West: Alonso de Espina and his *Fortalitium fidei*," in *Contra Iudaeos. Ancient and Medieval Polemics between Christians and Jews*, ed. Ora Limor and Guy G. Stroumsa (Tübingen: Mohr, 1996), 215–38.

50. Henricus Institoris and Jacobus Sprenger, *Malleus Maleficarum* 2, q.1, ca 13, col. 14A, 1: 469.

51. Pseudo-Aristotle, *Problemata varia anatomica*, p. 69.

52. For a general discussion, see Hyam Maccoby, "The Tortosa Disputation, 1413–1414, and its Effects," in *The Expulsion of the Jews and Their Emigration to the Southern Low Countries (15th–16th C.)*, ed. Luc Dequeker and Werner Verbeke, Mediaevalia Lovaniensia, ser. 1, studia 26 (Leuven: Leuven University Press, 1998), 23–34. For Hebrew and Latin accounts of Tortosa (in translation), see also Maccoby, *Judaism on Trial*, 168–215, and 82–94, for a historical introduction.

14).⁵² Was it somehow a reflection of developments in the political theology of the papacy in the twelfth century that, as Bernard of Clairvaux insisted, "it is an insult to Christ that the offspring of a Jew has occupied the chair of Peter"?

We cannot answer all of these questions. Certainly the myth that a convert to Christianity, but in reality a crypto-Jew, would obtain the papal throne expressed potent, quasi-messianic longings in a medieval Jewish world yearning for deliverance. This myth may have arisen from the Talmudic tradition that the messiah is already waiting and sitting hidden or concealed *among the lepers* by the gates of Rome, but ready to appear if only Israel would hearken to the voice of the Lord (cf. Ps. 95:7).⁵³ This tradition was a central element in the anti-Jewish polemic documented in both the Hebrew and Latin accounts of the Barcelona Disputation (1263), during which Pablo Christiani, a convert from Judaism, attempted to force the rabbi Nachmanides to acknowledge that, based on this tradition, Jews must accept that the messiah has already come.⁵⁴ Nonetheless, the fears expressed at Anaclet's elevation of a Jewish conspiracy to steal the papacy seem to precede, not to follow, Christian awareness of this Talmudic tradition.

---

53. B.T. *Sanhedrin* 98a. For the development of the tradition that the messiah is at the gates of Rome, see Abraham Berger, "Captive at the Gate of Rome: The Story of a Messianic Motif," *Proceedings of the American Academy for Jewish Research* 44 (1977): 1–17. For the early modern workings of the myth of the "Jewish" pope, see Joseph Sherman, *The Jewish Pope: Myth, Diaspora and Yiddish Literature*, Studies in Yiddish 4 (Oxford: European Humanities Center, 2003). As Sherman notes, however, the seventeenth-century Yiddish versions that form his subject are based on medieval Hebrew materials. Most prominent is the Ashkenazic legend of Elhanan, son of the tenth-century rabbi Simon "the Great" of Mainz (for whom, see Lucia Raspe, "Payyetanim as Heroes of Medieval Folk Narrative: The Case of R. Shim'on B. Yishaq of Mainz," in *Jewish Studies between the Disciplines/Judaistik zwischen den Disziplinen* [Leiden: Brill, 2003], 354–72), although a Sephardic legend relates a similar tale concerning the son of R. Shlomo ibn Aderet of Barcelona (d. 1310). Elhanan is said to have been forcibly baptized as a child, given an ecclesiastical education, and then elected pope. Once he discovered his Jewish origins, sources contend, he either committed suicide or repented and sought to return to Judaism. For discussion, see David Levine Lerner, "The Enduring Legend of the Jewish Pope," *Judaism* 40 (1981): 148–70. Several scholars have assumed a link between Elhanan's legend and the history of Anacletus II. See Salo Wittmeyer Baron, *A Social and Religious History of the Jews*, 2nd ed., 11 vols. (New York: Columbia University Press, 1960), 7: 304 n. 56; Kenneth Stow, "The '1007 Anonymous' and Papal Sovereignty: Jewish Peceptions of the Papacy and Papal Policy in the High Middle Ages," in Stow, *Popes, Church, and Jews in the Middle Ages* (Burlington, Vt.: Ashgate, 2007), IV: 14.

54. These texts have been translated by Hyam Maccoby, *Judaism on Trial*, 113, 117, 148.

CASE 2: HENRY OF WINCHESTER AND ST. THOMAS CANTILUPE

Although many questions must remain unanswered, we can assert confidently that the entire Anacletan controversy seems predicated on the assumption that there are enduring Jewish moral and physical traits that may not be erased by baptism. Nor can we dismiss this as a wholly isolated episode. In the late thirteenth century we encounter an analogous situation, although at the royal rather than papal court. This involves Sir Henry of Winchester, a favorite and a godson of the English king Henry III and a recent convert to Christianity. Henry was not the only convert to rise to some prominence in Henry's administration. Two more, namely Roger le Convers and John le Convers, became the king's sergeant at arms, a post of great honor and dignity (essentially, part of the king's household guard). Another wealthy convert to serve Henry was Nicholas le Convers, who became Keeper of the Forest in the Peak in Derbyshire.[55] Under Henry's son, King Edward I (r. 1272–1307), Henry of Winchester served the crown by orchestrating a "sting" to prove allegations that Jews, and some Christians, were guilty of coin clipping.

Charges that Jews were engaged in coin clipping—the practice of "shaving" a bit of the precious metal from a coin—were certainly not new. Matthew Paris observed the increasingly heavy taxes or exactions imposed on the Jews of England during the reign of Henry III, but he insists that the Jews deserve no sympathy because they are all forgers and coin clippers, and he likens coin clipping to circumcision.[56] Under Edward I, the government adopted an increasingly hostile attitude toward its Jews, who were, nonetheless, servants of the crown. As a result of Henry of Winchester's efforts, 600 Jews were imprisoned in the Tower of London in 1278, and more were held at the Guildhall. By May 1279, 269 Jews and 29 Christians had been hanged on coin-clipping charges.[57] These events certainly contributed to the atmosphere that enabled the

---

55. Adler, *Jews of Medieval England*, 296–97.

56. Matthew Paris, *The Illustrated Chronicles of Matthew Paris: Observations of Thirteenth-Century Life*, 159. For the repeated accusations of coin clipping directed against Jews in English sources, accusations that also concerned rabbinic authorities, see especially Willis Johnson, "Textual Sources for the Study of Jewish Currency Crimes in Thirteenth-Century England," *British Numismatic Journal* 66 (1997): 21–32. For the equation of coin clipping and circumcision, see 28–29.

57. The Latin Peterborough Chronicle, treating English history from 1122 CE, goes so

king to resolve the "Jewish problem": first by expelling Jews in 1287 from Gascony and then from all his French possessions, and next from England by a mass expulsion in 1290.[58]

More interesting for our study, however, is the special objection raised against Henry of Winchester by St. Thomas Cantilupe (d. 1282), Bishop of Hereford, the last medieval English Catholic to be canonized (1320). There is some disagreement among historians concerning the role that Henry of Winchester played in the judicial proceedings following the arrest of those accused of coin clipping, although there seems to be no disagreement over Henry's role in the "sting" operation, a role which, because of Henry's earlier ties to the Jewish community, Paul Brand describes as that of an *agent provocateur*. In addition, however, Brand remarks that in the canonization dossier of Bishop Thomas Cantilupe of Hereford, Chief Justice Hengham recalls a proposal made by Edward I to give Henry of Winchester

power that he should have testimony or record (*testimonium sive recordum*), that is to say, that he should have authority and power such that by his word and testimony or record (*ad ejus dictum et testimonium sive recordum*) other men could lose life and limb, over Christians who had clipped or forged the king's money.[59]

This extraordinary power would have made it impossible for the accused to dispute the evidence already gathered by Henry of Winchester in his "sting"; the evidence he provided the court would be unassailable.

---

far as to assert that the King had "all the Jews of England seized for coin clipping in a single day and night" (*omnes Judei Anglie capti sunt simul infra unum diem et noctem, propter tonsuram monete*); only a few of those convicted on the charge, it adds, were converted to Christianity from fear. *Chronicon Petroburgense*, ed. Thomas Stapleton (London: Camden Society, 1849), 26, 29. Similarly the *Chronicle of Bury St Edmunds* (p. 66) remarks that once the Jews had been imprisoned, their homes were searched and the instruments necessary for coin clipping were found. For useful discussions of these events and growing anti-Semitism in England, see R. C. Stacey, "The English Jews under Henry III," in Skinner, *The Jews in Medieval Britain. Historical, Literary and Archaeological Perspectives*, 41–54; R. C. Stacey, "Antisemitism and the Medieval English State," in *The Medieval English State: Essays Presented to James Campbell*, ed. J. R. Maddicott and D. M. Palliser (Hambledon Press, 2000), 163–77; Robin Mundill, "Edward I and the Final Phase of Anglo-Jewry," in Skinner, *Jews in Medieval Britain, Historical, Literary and Archaeological Perspectives*, 55–70; R. C. Stacey, "Parliamentary Negotiation and the Expulsion of the Jews from England," in *Thirteenth Century England VI*, ed. R. H. Britnell, R. Frame, and M. Prestwich (Woodbridge: Boydell, 1997), 77–101.

58. Thomas Walsingham, *Historia anglicana*, 1: 30–31.

59. Paul Brand, "Jews and the Law in England, 1275–90," *English Historical Review* 115 (2000), 1152.

Thomas of Cantilupe opposed this extraordinary power, and threatened to step down as a king's councilor. Thomas was an important figure in England who had twice been chancellor of the University of Oxford, and had once been Lord High Chancellor of the realm.[60] His opposition, according to the acts of his canonization proceedings, stemmed from the fact that "it was not fitting that the aforementioned convert and Jew should have such power over Christians."[61] When these remarks were entered into the canonization proceedings conducted in 1307, the editor explained the saint's justification: "Namely he judged that it was unworthy and not at all pleasing to God to subject Christ's faithful, born from Christian parents, to a man who had only recently converted from Judaism to Christ . . . whose conversion and conduct he held perhaps suspect from the longstanding Jewish perfidy and hatred of this people toward Christians."[62] Although it is of course possible that Thomas's opposition to Henry's role in the judicial proceedings expressed merely a personal dislike, Robert Bartlett has remarked that "Thomas opposed the promotion of Jewish converts to positions of authority, [and] he had argued that the remaining Jews ('enemies of God and rebels against the faith') should either convert or be expelled from the kingdom."[63]

Despite the efforts of Jewish converts to assimilate or integrate into the majority culture in England in the second half of the thirteenth century, there is evidence that they faced a growing number of impediments. Some, who enjoyed sponsorship from King Henry III, were sent to monastic houses that received them with evident reluctance.[64] Oth-

60. For Thomas's career, see D. S. Martin, "The Life of Saint Thomas of Hereford," in *St. Thomas Cantilupe, Bishop of Hereford: Essays in his Honor*, ed. Meryl Jancey (Hereford: Friends of Hereford Cathedral, 1982), 15–19, and in the same volume, Jeremy Catto, "The Academic Career of Thomas Cantilupe," 45–56, and David Carpenter, "St. Thomas Cantilupe: His Political Career," 57–72.

61. "quod non erat conveniens ut praedictus conversus et Judaeus haberet tantam potestatem super Christianos." *Acta Sanctorum, Octobris* (Paris: Apud Victorem Palme, 1866), 1: 548.

62. "Scilicet quia indignum Deoque minime gratum judicabat, Christi fideles ex Christianis natos parentibus homini a Judaismo ad Christum nuper converso subjacere . . . cujus conversionem aequitatemque forsitan suspecta habebat ex Judaica perfidia veterique gentis in Christianos odio." *Acta Sanctorum, Octobris*, 1: 547–48.

63. Robert Bartlett, *The Hanged Man: A Story of Miracle, Memory, and Colonialism in the Middle Ages* (Princeton N.J.: Princeton University Press, 2004), 24. Bartlett seems to reiterate the opinion of Thomas's early modern biographer. See Richard Strange, *The Life of St. Thomas of Hereford* (London: Burns and Oates, 1879), 207–8.

64. See Joan Greatrex, "Monastic Charity for Jewish Converts: The Requisition of Corrodies by Henry III," in Wood, *Christianity and Judaism*, 133–43.

ers—perhaps hundreds—entered the *Domus conversorum* in London, which King Henry III had created as a half-way house to ease the entry of Jewish converts into English life. There too, however, they confronted the passive indifference or active hostility of the Christian population at large, which did little or nothing to address their poverty and isolation.[65] Robert Stacey has shown just how infrequently converts succeeded in leaving the *domus* and in establishing themselves on the outside. The evidence justifies the conclusion, Stacey remarks,

By the middle of the thirteenth century in England there was clearly an irreducible element to Jewish identity in the eyes of many Christians, which no amount of baptismal water could entirely eradicate, at least from a layman. Through baptism, converts from Judaism became Christians, but this did not mean that they had entirely ceased to be Jews in the eyes of their brothers and sisters in Christ.[66]

Perhaps the difficulty of finding acceptance in the larger Christian community lies behind the case of the "London Thirteen": thirteen Jewish converts to Christianity—almost all of them women that had married Christian men—who were ineffectively prosecuted by the secular arm in the early 1280s for having reverted to Judaism, and who found refuge in the London Jewry.[67] Although Henry of Winchester did succeed "on the outside," Thomas of Cantilupe's attack upon him supports Stacey's more general conclusion. Ironically, it may even have been the growing Christian emphasis upon missionizing among the Jews that brought about this attitude. In the thirteenth through fifteenth centuries, Jews converted to Christianity in larger numbers, sometimes under threat of violence, and sometimes as a result of material incentives offered, but rarely delivered, and sometimes from a genuine change of heart. When the conditions that led to conversion had changed, or after they encountered resistance to their assimilation, they sometimes returned to their Jewish communities and sought to take up again their Jewish identity.

Reversion had long been a concern to the Church, as evidenced by ecclesiastical documents following the forced conversion of Jews during

---

65. Lauren Fogle, "Between Christianity and Judaism: The Identity of Converted Jews in Medieval London," *Essays in Medieval Studies* 22 (2005): 107–16, and esp. 110–11.

66; Stacey, "The Conversion of Jews to Christianity in Thirteenth-Century England," 278.

67. For this episode, see especially F. D. Logan, "Thirteen London Jews and Conversion to Christianity: Problems of Apostasy in the 1280s," *Bulletin of the Institute of Historical Research* 45 (1972): 214–29.

the violence accompanying the First Crusade. In a letter from 1097 or 1098, Pope Clement III chastised Bishop Rupert of Bamberg for failing to correct a situation in which such Jewish converts had been permitted to return to Judaism.[68] But such relapses from Christian faith reinforced the stereotype of Jewish obduracy, and "raised anew questions about the extent to which Jewish character could be transformed by baptism."[69] Even entry to a religious order, ordinarily a sign of greater devotion to Christian perfection, could not protect the Jewish convert, as the Dominican Raymond de Tarrega (d. 1371) discovered when he was imprisoned by the Inquisition late in life.[70]

This Winchester affair recalls the opposition that surrounded Petrus Pierleoni's elevation to the papacy. Although Henry of Winchester had been baptized and enjoyed the king's favor, Thomas described him as a "convert and Jew" and apparently suspected that the "longstanding Jewish perfidy and hatred of this people toward Christians" persisted. Baptism might cleanse the soul of original sin, but not of this hatred. Therefore, Thomas insisted that it was inappropriate for a convert to exercise such power and judicial authority over Christians.

Certainly, canon law had consistently forbidden Jews (or Muslims) to exercise legal authority over Christians.[71] In the early fourteenth century, this issue was revisited in university circles. John of Naples (fl. 1315) inquired whether it is permissible for a Christian king to use Muslim mercenaries in defense of the kingdom. One of the problems he anticipated was simply that the use of mercenaries might give these unbelievers an improper authority over Christians under their command.[72] But canon

---

68. Simonsohn, *The Apostolic See and the Jews. Documents: 492–1404*, 42. Note, however, Kenneth Stow's argument that Christians were as much concerned with the canonical legitimacy of forced conversions as they were with the problem of the apostasy of those who reverted to Judaism. See Kenneth Stow, "Conversion, Apostasy, and Apprehensiveness: Emicho of Flonheim and the Fear of the Jews in the Twelfth Century," *Speculum* 76 (2001): 911–33.

69. Carlebach, *Divided Souls*, 43.

70. On Raymond de Tarrega, see Raphael Patai, *The Jewish Alchemists*, chap. 13.

71. Gregory IX, in a letter to the Archbishop of Gran (March 3, 1231), complains that he has heard that in Hungary Jews and Saracens are in positions of public office that grant them authority over Christians, in violation of conciliar decrees. See Grayzel, *The Church and the Jews*, 186–87.

72. See John of Naples, *Quaestiones variae Parisiis disputatae* q. 38 (Naples: 1618), 323–30. In an interesting digression, John inquires, too, whether even following the orders of a Jewish physician places a Christian under the authority of an infidel.

law had never stipulated that *converts* to Christianity should likewise be kept from positions of power. Nonetheless, some members of the Church surely held this view, as evidenced by the complaint raised by Alonso de Cartagena, Bishop of Burgos, that converted Jews cannot enter all the orders or receive the dignities awarded other Christians.[73] Once more, it seems that the perception that certain Jewish traits persisted beyond baptism provided the theoretical justification for their exclusion.[74]

Although Thomas of Cantilupe's attack focused attention once again on the perceived persistence of anti-Christian hatred and other vices among Jewish converts to Christianity, he did not, however, identify Henry of Winchester according to any physical marker. Petrus Pierleoni and his brother Gratian were denigrated for their "Jewish" appearance and Gratian, in particular, was mocked for having a dark complexion, "more like a Jew or a Saracen." This type of anti-Jewish invective is absent from what we know about the episode involving Thomas of Cantilupe and Henry of Winchester. Was there, however, a growing perception that Jews, if not converts from Judaism, were "dark" or distinct in their physical appearance?

CASE 3: *NIZZAḤON VETUS*

Curiously, perhaps the most persuasive evidence to confirm that in the thirteenth-century Christians had begun to identify Jews in this way will be found in Jewish sources. Our first source is the *Nizzaḥon Vetus* or *Old Book of Polemic,* an encyclopedic collection of anti-Christian arguments employed by late thirteenth-century Franco-German Jews. In this collection one encounters the following argument that reflects upon our inquiry into perceptions of a Jewish complexion:

The heretics ask: Why are most Gentiles fair-skinned and handsome while most Jews are dark and ugly? Answer them that this is similar to a fruit: when it begins to grow it is white but when it ripens it becomes black, as is the case with sloes and plums. On the other hand, any fruit which is red at the beginning becomes lighter as it ripens, as is the case with apples and apricots. This, then, is testimony that Jews are pure of menstrual blood so that there is no

---

73. Alonso de Cartagena, *Defensorium unitatis Christianae* 2.4.17, p. 207.

74. In the modern era, Richard Wagner reflects a similar view, condemning the "cultured Jew" who has sought, albeit unsuccessfully, "to make a Christian baptism wash away the traces of his origin." See the excerpt from his "Das Judenthum in Musik," in Mendes-Flohr and Reinharz, *The Jew in the Modern World: A Documentary History,* 329.

initial redness. Gentiles, however, are not careful about menstruant women and have sexual relations during menstruation; thus, there is redness at the outset, and so the fruit that comes out, that is, the children, are light. One can respond further by noting that Gentiles are incontinent and have sexual relations during the day, at a time when they see the faces on attractive pictures; therefore, they give birth to children who look like those pictures, as it is written, "And the sheep conceived when they came to drink before the rods." [Gen. 30:38–39][75]

This rich narrative responds to a question posed by a "heretic," that is, an apostate Jew, concerning the skin color of Jews and Gentiles. "Gentiles," he alleges, are "fair-skinned and handsome while most Jews are dark and ugly." Why should this be the case? Although it is possible to understand this as merely a metaphor—that Jews, as enemies of the faith, were made dark and ugly by sin—the reality seems much more complex. Note that the Jewish respondent does not challenge the premise, but only tries to interpret the allegation in a way that is favorable to Jews. In this respect, he may simply echo the view of the commentator, Rashi, who understood the image of the suffering servant in Isaiah 53 to refer to the Jews who suffer debasement in exile for the sins of the other nations. One sign of this debasement is a claim that Rashi willingly embraces, namely, that the "[Jews'] form is darker than that of other men, as we see with our own eyes."[76] The Jew's reply in the *Nizzaḥon Vetus* expands upon this and provides an explanation drawn from nature, to avow that there are certain fruits whose flesh is white when they are immature, but which darkens as they ripen. These fruits represent the Jews, who, mature in their faith and religious customs, were "white" in some sense at the outset but gradually became darker, like ripe fruit. In contrast, Gentiles are compared to those fruits whose flesh is reddish when still immature, and which grows whiter as they ripen. Their subsequent whiteness is interpreted as a pejorative sign that reveals a deeper truth about sexual misconduct. Because Jews avoid sexual relations with a menstruant, in them "there is no initial redness" whereas Gentiles "are not careful about menstruant women and have sexual relations." Just as sex with a menstruant could afflict the fetus's body with leprosy, so too since their children

---

75. Berger, *The Jewish-Christian Debate in the High Middle Ages* cap. 238, p. 224.
76. AD[olf] Neubauer, compiler, *Fifty-Third Chapter of Isaiah according to the Jewish Interpreters*, 1:37 (Hebrew), 2:37 (English); cited by Alexandra Cuffel, *Gendering Disgust in Medieval Religious Polemic* (Notre Dame, Ind.: University of Notre Dame Press, 2007), 189.

take their origin from impure blood, they are tainted with a redness that gradually whitens, leaving them "fair-skinned." Moreover, Gentiles have sexual intercourse in the daylight, and "when they see the faces on attractive pictures . . . they give birth to children who look like those pictures." Once more this is a comment intended to disclose their sexual misconduct, since rabbinic tradition generally condemned intercourse during daylight hours or even by the light of a candle.[77] Consequently, Gentiles may *appear* fair-skinned and handsome, while Jews appear "dark and ugly," but their appearances mask a deeper truth: that Jews are faithful to God's law, and Gentiles are not, because Jews avoid intercourse with a menstruant while Christians do not.

In the same tradition, in another Jewish polemical text entitled *Sefer ha-Nizzaḥon*, likely written in Prague about 1400 by Rabbi Yom Tov Lipmann Mühlhausen, the author responds to Christian claims that Jews are dark and ugly in appearance because they have rejected God. Once again, Mühlhausen does not deny that Jews may be dark complexioned and ugly, but instead he insists that Jews will experience an extreme makeover when "in the messianic age we will all be better looking than anybody else."[78] This transformation, postponed to the messianic age, presupposes that a change in external appearance will faithfully reflect a change in an internal, moral state as well, since Jewish interpreters were also inclined, in other contexts, to understand dark or black skin as a punishment for transgression or sexual deviation.[79]

In a Christian, Latin epitome of arguments drawn from Yom-Tov Lipmann Mühlhausen's polemics, the author links this change to an important Bible verse: "If the Ethiopian can change his skin, or the leopard his spots, you may also do well, when you have learned evil." (Jer. 13:23) This passage could be employed by both Jews and Christian exegetes to show that if God can cause the Ethiopian to change his skin color or the

77. See Berger, *The Jewish-Christian Debate in the High Middle Ages*, 340 n. 29, citing B. T. *Niddah*, 16b; Trachtenberg, *Jewish Magic and Superstition*, 186.
78. *Sefer ha-Nizzaḥon*, 239, quoted by Ora Limor and Israel Jacob Yuval, in "Skepticism and Conversion: Jews, Christians, and Doubters in *Sefer ha-Nizzaḥon*," in *Hebraica Veritas: Christian Hebraists and the Study of Judaism in Early Modern Europe*, ed. Allison P. Coudert and Jeffrey S. Shoulson (Philadelphia: University of Pennsylvania Press, 2004), 169.
79. See Paul H. D. Kaplan, "Jewish Artists and Images of Black Africans in Renaissance Venice," in *Multicultural Europe and Cultural Exchange in the Middle Ages and Renaissance*, ed. James P. Helfers, Arizona Studies in the Middle Ages and Renaissance 12 (Turnholt: Brepols, 2005), 67–90.

leopard to change his spots, then *a fortiori* moral conversion or transformation is possible to all those who believe in Him. For example, the Venerable Bede (d. 735) remarked that by putting aside sin, the Ethiopian changes his skin and is "whitened" (*dealbatus*) in the laver of baptism.[80] Similarly Rabanus Maurus notes that the whitened "Ethiopian" symbolizes the Gentile Church, because "the Gentile people freed itself from the blackness of sins."[81]

Contrariwise, other Christian interpreters were keen to identify the as yet unredeemed black-skinned Ethiopian with the Jews since, as Ambrose of Milan insists, Jeremiah 13:23 does not refer merely to external appearances, but to internal transformation as well, of which the Jews, wild beasts that have been rejected by God, are incapable.[82] Isidore of Seville, in his anti-Jewish polemic, *On the Catholc Faith*, maintains that just as in nature the Ethiopian's skin color does *not* change, nor does the leopard change his spots, so too the hardheartedness (*duritia*) of Jews remains unaltered.[83] In the same way the Irish exegete and grammarian, Sedulius Scotus (fl. 840–60), insisted that the black Ethiopian symbolizes the Jews, who are discolored by sin.[84]

Yom-Tov Lipmann Mühlhausen also employs an allegorical reading of the text of Jeremiah 13:23, but with a result opposite to that obtained by Isidore of Seville or Sedulius Scotus. For him, just as it seems impossible in nature for an Ethiopian to change his skin color or a leopard his spots, so it seems impossible for a man to abandon evil and turn to good. But, as the Holy One commands in the Law, so is it possible to prevail over that "nature" that has been established by customary practice and to turn away from evil.[85] In the messianic age, as we saw, Jews will be utterly transformed. No longer dark and ugly, they will be handsome and appealing to look upon.

It is tempting, then, to dismiss all references to dark-complexioned Jews (or dark-complexioned Saracens) as a reference to their spiritual

---

80. Bede, *Expositio super acta apostolorum* 7 (PL 92: 962B). Cf. Jerome, *Commentarium in Jeremiam prophetam liber sex* (PL 24: 768B).

81. Rabanus Maurus, *Commentaria in libros IV Regum* 17 (PL 109: 108A).

82. Ambrose of Milan, *Hexaemeron* 6.3.15.

83. Isidore of Seville, *De fide catholica . . . contra Judaeos* 1.18.4 (PL 83: 477B).

84. Sedulius Scotus, *Collectaneum miscellaneum* 67, ed. D. Simpson, CCCM 67 (Turnholt: Brepols, 1988–90).

85. R. YomTov Lippmann Mühlhausen, *Disputatio adversus Christianos ad Jeremie, Ezechielis, Psalmorum et Danielis libros institute*, 1253.

condition, and not their physical appearance at all. Once they find the Christian faith, they will put aside the "blackness" of sin and be "whitened" by the waters of baptism. But such transformations cannot be dismissed as mere metaphors when they are illustrated by somatic change. An example of this latter type of change may be located in the fourteenth-century English poem, the *King of Tars*, in which for the sake of her people a young Christian princess marries a Saracen king, after feigning conversion to Islam. She bears a child that is horribly deformed as a lump of flesh. Upon his baptism, however, he is transformed into a beautiful, healthy baby and when the boy's father also converts his black skin bleaches white.[86] A similar type of transformation may be implied by the early modern English translation of R. Samuel of Morocco's *Book on the Already Accomplished Advent of the Messiah* (*Liber de adventu messiae praeterito*), subtitled *The Blessed Jew of Morocco: or, A Blackamoor Made White*.[87] These appear as cases, then, in which biology is influenced by theology: the whitening of the body manifestly expresses the purification of the soul. The reverse seems also true—whiteness may turn to blackness to indicate the soul's corruption. Thus, Johannes Burchard recorded that the body of the hated Borgia pope Alexander VI (d. 1503), when it was exhibited following his death, so quickly putrified that "corruption advanced apace, and the face became black, so that on the thirty-third hour, when I saw it, it was reduced to a black mask, or rather seemed that of a Negro."[88]

In a similar fashion, by the twelfth century not only theology but also medicine and natural science conspired to treat the Jews' black or dark complexion not only as an image of the soul but also as an empirical fact supported by scientific explanation. Science did not erase the negative valuation assigned to blackness in theological tradition, however; it merely established a separate justification for it. Observations that belong to a primitive cultural anthropology also confirmed the negative

86. For discussion of this theme, see Lisa Lampert, "Race, Periodicity, and the (Neo-) Middle Ages," *Modern Language Quarterly* 65, no. 3 (2004), 405. For the text, see *The King of Tars*, from the Auchinleck MS, Advocates 19.2.1, ed. Judith Perry (Heidelberg: Winter, 1980).

87. Samuel of Morocco, *The Blessed Jew of Morocco: or, A Blackamoor Made White*.

88. "et continuo crevit turpitudo et nigredo facie; adeo quod hora vigesima tertia, qua eum vidi, factus est sicut pannus vel morus nigerrimus." Johannes Burchard, *Diarium: sive rerum urbanarum commentarii*, 3 vols. (Paris: E. Leroux, 1883–85), 3: 243, in Sergio Bertelli, *The King's Body*, trans. R. Burr Litchfield (University Park: Pennsylvania State University Press, 2001), 40.

valuation among Europeans. For example, Jacques de Vitry, who had accompanied the Fifth Crusade to the East, remarked that Latin Christians consider black Ethiopians to be unattractive.[89] This negative valuation seems consistent too with medieval recommendations for women's cosmetics, which include numerous recipes for whitening the skin that not only Christian but Saracen women as well used.[90]

The effort to find an explanation based in nature for the dark-complexioned Jew is already evident in the passage cited above from the *Nizzaḥon Vetus*. The text accepts that Jews "are dark and ugly" and seeks to relate this to other natural phenomenon: in this case, the maturation or ripening of fruit. It also explains the rosy, fair complexion of the Gentiles in terms of sexual misconduct, but a form of sexual misconduct involving a menstruant that, as we have already shown, communicates illness and especially leprosy.[91] Finally, it invokes a third explanation also related to sexual behavior: that Gentile couples have sex during the daytime, when the women may gaze upon attractive pictures that cause them to produce handsome children.

Moderns will likely view this last argument as the most perplexing.[92] What do pretty pictures have to do with handsome children? To appreciate the argument, one must first understand that the imagination is an important mental faculty for medieval psychology. Images are imprinted upon the interior imagination through sense experience, as one might make an imprint upon wax with a stylus or seal, bringing the outside world in. But as sense experience of the external world imprints itself on

89. "Nos autem nigros Aethiopes turpes reputamus." Jacques de Vitry, *Historia Orientalis* 92, p. 216.

90. *The Trotula*, 174, 236, 278, 280, 284, 296 (with reference to Saracen women whitening their faces), 138, 162, 178, 180, 184. Using rouge to redden the skin or other products to whiten it was condemned too by the canonist Gratian, attesting to the practice among women. See *Decreta* pars 3, dist. 5, cap. 38, 12, in *Corpus iuris canonici* 1:1422.

91. It is of some interest that the eighth-century Muslim author Ibn Ishaq attributes physiognomic properties or characteristics to the great prophets: Mohammad, Abraham (who is said to resemble Mohammad), Moses, and Jesus. In particular, he remarks that "Moses was a ruddy faced man, tall, thinly fleshed, curly haired with a hooked nose ... Jesus, son of Mary, was a *reddish* man of medium height with lank hair with many freckles on his face as though he had just come from a bath." [my italics] Ibn Ishaq, *The Life of Muhammad*, trans. A. Guillaume (Lahore: Oxford University Press, 1967), 184.

92. Despite the persistence of similar beliefs into the early modern era. See Paul-Gabriel Bouce, "Imagination, Pregnant Women and Monsters in Eighteenth-Century England and France," in *Sexual Underworlds of the Enlightment*, ed. G. S. Rousseau and Roy Porter (Chapel Hill: University of North Carolina, 1988), 86–100.

the imagination, so too the imagination can "imprint" on the body. This is especially apparent in human sexual behavior. The mental image of a lover who is absent, explains Albert the Great, is enough to cause sexual stimulation, like an erection or nocturnal emission.[93] Similarly, "the recollection of intercourse arouses desire for it, for an accidental trait of the soul changes the body greatly."[94] Not only does the imagination, as a faculty of the mind or soul, have the power to influence one's own body, it may also pass on its "power" to a fetus by influencing the power of the sperm. In his massive commentary on Aristotle's work *On Animals*, Albert the Great records the power of imagination over fetal development and explains that "a certain king once imagined a black monstrosity during intercourse and made mention of this to the queen while he was having intercourse with her. The fetation, when born, was monstrous and black."[95] In another text, he explains that this is because,

the entire body is altered by various imaginings.... Thus various types of imagining cause a change in every part of the body and this is why that royal woman, whom Avicenna described,[96] imagining the shape of a demon or a dwarf (or, according to others, an Ethiopian) bore children resembling them, because her own power succumbed at the moment of conception[97] owing to the violent imagination, and the natural power was altered according to the kind of thing she was imagining. And it was the same for the animals looking upon things of various colors, because a different impression on the soul results in a change in the entire body.[98]

The "animals looking upon things of various colors" are no doubt the "sheep conceived when they came to drink before the rods" (Gen. 30:30–43) alluded to above in the *Nizzaḥon Vetus*. In the description in Genesis, Jacob, who had served his father-in-law Laban for many years, wanted to take his wives and children and return to his own land. Laban was reluctant to let him go, and proposed instead to pay him a handsome wage for tending his flock. Jacob proposes to take as his payment all the animals of the flock that are spotted or multicolored, while Laban and his sons would retain all those sheep or goats that were either all white,

---

93. Albert the Great, *De animalibus* 22.1.3, vol. 16, 1350 (SZ 2: 1441).
94. Ibid., 9.1.1, vol. 15, 678 (SZ 1: 778).
95. Ibid., 22.3.7, vol. 16, 1352 (SZ 2: 1443–44).
96. See Albert the Great, *Quaestiones super de animalibus* 7.3, p. 172, 31 (QDA, 230).
97. Or: "in the fetus."
98. Albert the Great, *Quaestiones super de animalibus* 18.3, 2, p. 298, 4–9 (QDA, 536).

or all black. The offer evidently appealed to Laban because spotted or mottled sheep are quite rare. But when Jacob took the flock to water, he partially stripped the bark off the rods of poplar, exposing the whiteness below, while other trees he left untouched so that the green of the bark was visible. As a result, "in the very heat of coition, the sheep beheld the rods, and brought forth spotted, and of divers colours, and speckled." (Gen. 30:38) With this device, the sheep conceived spotted lambs and Jacob's flock expanded dramatically, making him a wealthy man.

One could simply regard this as a miraculous event, but the tendency of Scholastic theologians was to struggle to find a natural explanation and natural purpose. In this instance, it was the power of the imagination that produced the sheep of different colors, a power that Jacob clearly understood and used to breed sheep that would increase his flock. Isidore of Seville appeals to the same principle when he explains that breeders present thoroughbred stallions to the mare's view when she conceives from inferior males, in order to produce offspring resembling the stallions. In the same way,

> Dove fanciers also place pictures of the most beautiful doves in those places where the doves are mated, so that, catching sight of the picture, they may produce offspring similar in appearance. Whence also people advise pregnant women not to gaze at repulsive animal faces, such as *cynocephali* or apes, lest they should bear offspring resembling what they have seen. Indeed, the nature of women is such that whatever sort of thing they look at or imagine in the extreme heat of desire, while they are conceiving is the sort of progeny they will bear.[99]

Similarly, Thomas of Cantimpré explains that,

> some [doctors] will not allow pregnant women to look on the faces of disgusting animals such as the baboon (*sic*) and the ape lest they give birth to children having the same appearance. For they say that the nature of women is such, that whatever they look upon or think about at the moment of conception will affect the appearance of the child. For an animal, while mating, transmits inwardly the forms of things seen outside and, when filled with images, takes their forms into their own substance. Hence Aristotle says: A woman had intercourse with an Ethiopian and gave birth to a daughter who was white. This

---

99. Isidore of Seville, *The Etymologies of Isidore of Seville* 12.1.59–60, pp. 250–51. The *cynocephali* are dog-headed men or creatures, sometimes identified in medieval bestiaries as a type of monkey (see *The Book of Beasts*, 35), although the epithet was often used to identify Saracens (or infidels in general) as a race of dogs. See especially John Block Friedman, *The Monstrous Races in Medieval Art and Thought*, 66–72 and 186–90.

daughter afterward gave birth to a dark Ethiopian daughter, even though the father was not Ethiopian.[100]

The first-century rhetor Quintillian had defended a white woman accused of giving birth to a black Ethiopian, arguing that this resulted not from an instance of miscegenation but from looking upon an image of an Ethiopian she saw from her bed.[101] The ancient physician Hippocrates reports as well on a woman who was punished for adultery because she gave birth to a very beautiful child, completely unlike either the mother or her husband, although Hippocrates wondered whether this was not because she had gazed upon a picture of rare beauty in the bedroom.[102] This interpretation is confirmed in the fourteenth-century pseudo-Aristotelian medical text, *Diverse Anatomical Problems*:

by virtue of the mother's strong imagining of something colored at the time of conception, a child will particularly receive the disposition or the color of the thing imagined, and this was made clear above concerning the queen who imagined a black and distorted image and gave birth to a black son. And this is clear once more from a certain queen of Ethiopia, who imagined at the time of conception a very white image and then generated a very white and beautiful son, and this same thing is held [to have happened] by Jacob's artifice, because he sent discolored rods into the water at the time of the entry of the sheep and the sheep saw the rods while drinking, for which reason they gave birth to bi-colored and discolored lambs.[103]

In a prelapsarian human condition, according to the theological *Summa* attributed to the Franciscan Alexander of Hales (d. 1245), the power of imagination to "imprint" on the fetus worked to the good. At that time, when will and desire were properly subject to reason's power, had man intended and willed to generate a male, from the fact that a male was imagined, the natural power would be invigorated and the masculine sex generated. Had he imagined and willed to generate a female, then the female

---

100. Thomas of Cantimpré, *De natura rerum* (Lib. IV–XII), 253, fol. 4r.

101. See Jerome, *Liber quaestionum Hebraicarum in Genesim* cap. 30.32–33, CCSL 72 (Turnholt: Brepols, 1959), 48.

102. Vincent of Beauvais, *Speculum naturale* 31.40, 1: 2322.

103. Pseudo-Aristotle, *Problemata varia anatomica*, p. 69. Michael Scot introduces another possible explanation. Articulating a Galenic doctrine of two sperms—that is, both male and female—Michael Scot suggests that when a white woman had intercourse with an Ethiopian, she gave birth to a white daughter because her seed or sperm dominated the male sperm at conception. Similarly, a black woman had intercourse with a white man and gave birth to a black son, for the same reason. See his *Liber phisionomiae* cap. 1.

sex would be generated. Consequently, so long as procreation was in this way subject to imagination and reason and not the lust of the flesh, male and female progeny would be produced in equal number, insuring that each human would have a partner of the opposite sex, and none would be superfluous.[104] But in our postlapsarian condition, the appeal to the power of imagination in procreation clearly sought to explain away cases of adultery and miscegenation. We have labored over them simply to show that when the text of *Nizzaḥon Vetus* explains that Gentiles are handsome because during sex "they see the faces on attractive pictures" and consequently produce "children who look like those pictures," our text is giving expression to the most current scientific theory. It appeals to a natural rather than a supernatural explanation, while at the same time imposing a negative moral valuation on the sexual habits of Gentiles. If Jews are dark and ugly, it is in part because of their fidelity to religious law. Ultimately, their dark ugliness will be replaced by a surpassing beauty, as R. Yom-Tov Lipmann Mühlhausen insists. Neither text repudiates the premise that is treated as an empirical or scientific statement, namely that Jews *are* dark complexioned.

BLACK OR DARK JEWS

Some of our texts, then, propose as an empirical and scientific truth that Jews are dark complexioned. This conviction is present too in the work of the early Reformation Christian Hebraist Sebastian Münster (d. 1552), who composed a brief bilingual (Hebrew-Latin) conversionary dialogue entitled *The Messiah of Christians and Jews* (*Messias Christianorum et Iudaeorum*). In the dialogue, a Christian meets a Jew on the road and greets him in Hebrew. When the Jew asked how he knew him to be a Jew, the Christian replied "I knew that you are a Jew from the form of your face. So indeed you Jews have a certain peculiar facial appearance, different in form and shape from the rest of mortals, which fact has often led me to wonder. In fact you are black and ugly, and barely white at all

---

104. Alexander of Hales, *Summa theologica* 2.1, Inq. 4, tr. 3, q. 2, resp. a, 725–26. A number of thirteenth-century theologians defended the principle that, had Adam not fallen, men and women would have been generated in equal number. For discussion see Peter Biller, "Applying Number to Men and Women in the Thirteenth and Fourteenth Centuries: An Enquiry into the Origins of the Idea of 'Sex-Ratio,'" in *The Work of Jacques Le Goff and the Challenges of Medieval History*, ed. Miri Rubin (Woodbridge: Boydell Press, 1997), 27–51.

in the manner of other men."[105] The Jewish interlocutor invokes another Christian anti-Jewish stereotype when he remarks: "It is surprising, if we are ugly, why do you Christians desire our women so much; they must appear to be more beautiful than yours." To this the Christian answers: "Your women are more beautiful than the men, and you seduce them incorrigibly."[106] In a short passage, this dialogue not only confirms the contention that Jewish men are dark and ugly, but also contrasts them to the beautiful and exotic Jewess who is sexually exploited by the Jewish male's lust, but who appears to be more beautiful than Christian women and is a subject of the Christian's latent desire.[107]

Regardless of whether only Jewish men—or both men and women—were understood to be dark-complexioned in medieval Christian perception, it remains to determine why a dark skin color should be assigned to Jews at all. For theologians, the link between dark or black skin and the blackness of sin seemed assured. Medieval Scholastic natural philosophers, however, sought causes rooted in nature. An investigation into these causes could be divided according to the medical theory of the natural, nonnatural, and contranatural influences on the body. For our purposes, however, it will be simpler to divide our discussion into two: external or internal influences upon skin color.

Of the external causes, the more important are the environmental influences of climate and geography, and astrological virtues, that is, the influence of the planets at one's birth. Scholastics derived their knowledge of world geography primarily from the works of classical authors

---

105. "Christianus [. . .] ex forma autem facie tue cognovi te esse Iudeum. Si quidem est vobis Iudeis peculiaris quaedam faciei imago diversa a reliquorum mortalium forma a figura, quae res saepe in admirationem me duxit. Estis enim vos nigri et deformes, et minime albicantes more reliquorum hominum." *Messias Christianorum et Iudaeorum. Hebraice et Latine* sig. A5v (Basel: Heinrich Petrus, 1539), quoted by Ronnie Po-chia Hsia, "Witchcraft, Magic, and the Jews in Germany," in *From Witness to Witchcraft: Jews and Judaism in Medieval Christian Thought*, ed. Jeremy Cohen, Wolfenbütteler Mittelalter-Studien 11 (Wiesbaden: Harrassowitz Verlag, 1996), 428 n. 32.

106. "Mirum est, si deformes sumus, cur vos Christiani adeo amatis mulieres nostras, illaque pulchriores vobis vestris appareant." *Messias* sig. A5v; "Mulieres quidem vestrae pulchriores sunt viris, at vos perditissime seducitis eas." *Messias* sig. A6r. These passages are cited in Hsia, "Witchcraft, Magic, and the Jews in Germany," 428 nn. 33–34.

107. For the beautiful Jewess in medieval Christian sexual fantasy, see Anthony Bale, "The Female 'Jewish' Libido in Medieval Culture," in *A Search for the Erotic in Medieval Britain*, ed. Amanda Hopkins and Cory Rushton (Cambridge: Brewer, 2007), 94–104. My thanks to Dr. Bale for a prepublication copy of his manuscript.

like Aristotle and Pliny the Elder, and from later Arab scientific texts, in which skin color will be referred to four principal internal and external causes. Climate, as the primary external cause, refers to temperature and humidity, but temperature and humidity were clearly determined by geographical location. Northern climes tend to be colder and moister; the more southern climes will be hot and drier, parched by the sun. These conditions will affect skin color in the populations that dwell in these *climata,* that is, the bands that divide the earth into regions. Similarly, astrological influence will have an effect on the body's internal complexion, and will as a consequent manifest itself indirectly in skin coloring.

In addition to the external causes that affect the skin color and complexion of entire populations, there are also two internal causes. The more important for our purposes will be the influence of the body's humoral composition. Just as the sun "burns" the earth and turns vegetation black, so too an excessive internal heat stemming from one's complexion can "burn" the blood beneath the skin, causing discoloration. In addition to the influence of humoral composition on skin color, we must consider the influence of one last internal cause: transient affections or passions of the soul. These give us some insight into medieval psychology, which clearly understood that changes to the soul (or, to use a more modern term, mental states) make themselves visible in the body, just as the power of imagination, a mental faculty, could affect the fetus. For example, embarrassment or shame will cause one to "blush" or redden, while excessive anger will cause one to turn pale. Thus the twelfth-century Petrus Alfonsi invokes the language of humoral theory to explain that "Anger [occurs] ... when red bile [*cholera rubea*], that is bile [*fel*], boils over and is diffused over the liver and mixes with blood. From this a man heats up and becomes pale in the face."[108] While anger can

---

108. "Ira ... colera rubea, id est fel, fervet et super epatem diffunditur et sanguini commiscetur. Inde siquidem homo calescit et in facie pallescit." Petrus Alfonsi, *Dialogi contra Judaeos* 1, p. 14, 33–36. A person with a complexion dominated by red bile typically is understood to be prone to anger. See Bede, *De temporum ratione liber* 35, p. 392. Yet I have not found a source for this description of anger as the boiling over of red bile and its diffusion over the liver. Alfonsi's older contemporary, the Cassinese monk and physician Constantine the African, defines anger or wrath as a "bubbling" of the blood that is within the heart, and the sudden exit of natural heat: "Ira est ebullitio sanguinis in corde existentis, et motus caloris naturalis subito extra corpus vindicandum exeuntis." *Theorices* 5, 37. For Alfonsi's contributions to medical discussion, see my "Humoralism and Adam's Body: Twelfth-Century Debates and Petrus Alfonsi's *Dialogus contra Judaeos*," *Viator* 36 (2005): 181–95.

cause a temporary pallor, the Scholastic philosopher Albert the Great also draws attention to a relationship between facial coloring and shame or embarrassment. Thus, "When the entire face gets red, and if there is a greater redness on the forehead along with downcast eyes, it signifies shame."[109] Although skin coloration stemming from humoral composition may be long lasting, changes to skin coloration stemming from internal, affective states tend to be transient and not to last very long.

In sum, then, skin color may depend on any or all of these internal and external factors. Almost absent from medieval discussion is any sense that human beings were *created* with different colors or complexions. One exception appears in a Jewish legend transmitted to the Latin world in a work entitled *Fabulae Saracenorum* (*Fables of the Saracens*), translated by Robert of Ketton in Spain just before the middle of the twelfth century. The *Fabulae Saracenorum* forms part of the Toledan Collection, a group of Arabic texts translated into Latin at the request of the Cluniac abbot Peter the Venerable and intended to educate European Christians on Islamic doctrines and traditions. This account contends that at the creation of Adam or humankind from the dust of the earth (Gen. 2:7), God gathered "multicolored dust" in his fist, and this is why some men are white, some are black, and some are in between.[110] But for whatever reasons, this explanation held little appeal. More influential will be those explanations that appeal to natural, external causes that remain visible throughout an entire population, unless other, internal causes interfere. The internal causes, by contrast, will affect skin color in individuals but may be more temporary: once a temperate humoral balance is restored, once illness is cured, or once the passions of the soul change, the skin should also reveal a change in coloration.

A discussion of medieval conceptions of skin color and physical markers can hardly avoid the debate over whether or not medieval authors had a conception of true racial difference. Although medieval texts do not rest on racial principles first expounded in the modern era as a result of stud-

---

109. Albert the Great, *De animalibus* 1.3.7.624, vol. 15, 223 (SZ 1: 285).

110. *Fabulae Saracenorum*, fol. 5vs, cited in Kritzeck, *Peter the Venerable and Islam*, 77, and n. 17. Kritzeck identifies this as a Jewish legend found in Ginzberg's *Legends of the Jews*, 1: 55. One source may certainly be *Pirkê de Rabbi Eliezer* 11, pp. 76–77. That text remarks, "The Holy One ... began to collect the dust of the first man from the four corners of the world; red, black, white, and 'pale green,' (which) refers to the body." In n. 2, 77, the translator inquires: "Might the four colours indicate the different colours of the skin of men?"

ies in physical anthropology, nonetheless they do reveal an interest in the questions raised by contemporary discussions of race.[111] Are there immutable, persistent features that distinguish one population from another? Medieval authors certainly were aware of differences in physiognomy—differences in skin color, facial features, and other physical and concomitant psychological characteristics. They were equally aware of religious, cultural, and linguistic differences that clearly were subject to change: one could change religion, learn a new language, and adopt different customs. What about differences in physiognomy and skin coloration? Were these too subject to change? As we will see, they were often thought to be subject to change over time. For this reason, they may not constitute a true theoretical racism. Nonetheless, for practical purposes, changes to skin coloration across larger populations would require generations, leading to a result not so different from racist ideologies in the modern world.

External Causes: Climate

Among the principal external influences upon skin color, physiognomy, and physical or psychological qualities or characteristics one must begin with a theory of the climates or *climata*. Scholastic thinkers tended to prefer a scheme that divided the world into seven climes, corresponding to the seven planets.[112] Regardless of their number, the more northern climes were understood to be colder and more humid because the sun's most intense rays did not reach them, while the more southern climes were hotter and drier, baked by the sun's most intense light and heat. In the middle one finds the more temperate climes or zones. Human beings living in their climes have, over time, become adapted to atmospheric conditions—to temperature and humidity, winds and location—so much so that, as Albert the Great remarks, "a Dacian [that is, one from Romania] whose complexion is nearly balanced for his habita-

---

111. See Joseph Ziegler, "Physiognomy, Science, and Proto-racism 1200–1500," in *The Origins of Racism in the West*, ed. M. Eliav-Feldon, B. Isaac, J. Ziegler (Cambridge: Cambridge University Press, 2009), 181–99. My thanks to Professor Ziegler for sending me a prepublication copy of his work.

112. For the division of seven *climata* according to the seven planets, see Māshā'allāh, *De revolutione annorum mundi* cap. 3, ed. Joachim Heller (Nuremberg: Johannes Montanus & Ulricus Neuberus, 1549), n.p. This work was available in Latin translation by the twelfth century. Also see Cecco d'Ascoli's remarks in Thorndike, *The Sphere of Sacrobosco and Its Commentators*, p. 374.

tion would quickly die in India or Ethiopia, and it is the same for other differences in *clima*."¹¹³ Even though humans have adapted to the different climes, they fail to do so with equal success. The more temperate climes are more favorable for human habitation, and its inhabitants will typically enjoy a longer life span.¹¹⁴ These more temperate climes most nearly imitate the climate that existed in Paradise, which was neither too hot nor too cold but well balanced, where the air was pure and clear, the trees never lost their foliage, and the flowers never withered or died.¹¹⁵ Had Adam not been expelled from Paradise, he could have lived forever, never discomforted by excessive cold or heat.

The climes at the extremes are more severe. Humans and animals have adapted there with more difficulty, introducing imbalances to their complexion, and typically they do not live as long. This is because as a rule, "those animals with a more balanced and temperate complexion live longer and those that stray from this balance have a shorter lifespan."¹¹⁶ Although humans and other animals do adapt to their environment, nonetheless in the more extreme climes their complexions are forced to depart more and more from the temperate, balanced mean. Where one lives, then, has a dramatic impact on life's quality and longevity. According to Albert the Great, those who live in the hottest and driest clime age very quickly because the desiccating heat dries out their bodies. As a result, they rarely live more than thirty years.¹¹⁷

In addition, because the environment of the clime in which one dwells influences humoral complexion, geographical location helps to determine skin color, physical attributes, and national character. The *Tetrabiblos* or *Quadripartitum* of Ptolemy (translated in the twelfth century), one of the more influential discussions of astrology and Aristotelian natural philosophy, reveals the relationship between climate and skin color and physiognomy:

for those people who live in areas under the more southern parallels, that is, those from the equator to the summer tropic, since the sun travels directly over their heads, it burns them, and this is why they have black bodies and

---

113. Albert the Great, *De animalibus* 12.1.4.59, vol. 16, 820 (SZ 2: 915).
114. Cf. Albert the Great, *De natura loci* 2.3, ed. Paul Hossfeld, Ed. Colon. 5.2 (Münster: Aschendorff, 1980), 103.
115. Bartholomaeus Anglicus, *De rerum proprietatibus* 15.92, p. 682.
116. Albert the Great, *Quaestiones super de animalibus* 8.11–14, p. 193, 56–58 (QDA, 281).
117. Albert the Great, *De natura loci* 2.3, p. 103.

black, rough and curly hair, and their faces are dried out and their bodies are shrunken in stature, and their natures are hot, and their habits are for the most part savage owing to the Sun's long and unremitting station over the regions [in which they dwell]; these are those that we call by the general name, Ethiopians.[118]

Those living in the more southern clime, nearer the equator, are oppressed by the sun's constant, burning heat—so much so, that it turns their skin black, curls their hair, dries out their complexion, and produces a savage or uncivilized disposition. These people are the Ethiopians. "Ethiopian," however, does not designate merely those who live in the modern country of that name, but all those who are subject to the same conditions of the first clime. Consequently, Albert the Great remarks that

> the inhabitants of the first clime—that is, the one nearest the equator [*circulus aequinoctialis*], which is called the equator [*linea aequalitatis*] because, when the sun touches it, night is equal to day—acquire a superabundant heat and superabundant dryness owing to the constant fixed presence of the solar rays over their heads, and this is why cold and moisture are reduced in them.[119]

Because of this hot, dry climate "all the Ethiopians are black and curly haired and dry. In all of them there appears a black color, and there is curliness to their hair."[120] The Ethiopians' bodies are so hot that at conception the semen in the womb is scorched, and the women conceive infants that are dark from scorching. Nevertheless their *internal* members, like bones or teeth, are very white, suggesting to Albert the Great that if one could temper the external heat and sun, Ethiopians would be white on the outside as well.

Nonetheless, because the Ethiopians' bodies are surrounded by intensely hot air, the skin's pores open and dry out their internal moisture, making their bodies light and agile. Paradoxically, the external heat of the scorching sun, which has opened the pores, also allows their internal heat and moisture to escape, rendering their hearts cold in an acci-

---

118. "his qui in ea morantur, sub lineis parallelis meridiei proximioribus, & sunt linea quae protenduntur inter punctum solstitialem aestivalem, & punctum aequinoctialem, Sol per zenith suorum capitum currit eosque comburit, ideoque nigra sunt eorum corpora, nigrique crines ac crispi cum asperitate, facies eorum sicca, & corpora macilenta, naturae quoque eorum sunt calidae, & animae qualitates in maiori parte sunt crudeles, propter longam & assiduam Solis moram in eorum regionibus, & hi sunt qui generaliter Aethiopes ab eis vocantur." Ptolemy, *Quadrapartitum* 2.2, p. 22.

119. Albert the Great, *Liber de causis proprietatum elementorum* 1.1.5.

120. Ibid., 1.1.5.

dental fashion (*per accidens*). This internal cooling is sometimes treated as analogous to another observed natural phenomenon: namely, that in winter the water in springs and streams appears warmer than the air, but colder than the air in summer. This is because the cold air of winter closes up or contains the heat in the earth, causing the waters on its surface to be warmed, whereas in summer the air's heat turns the earth's coldness back upon itself, causing the water of streams to cool.[121] Similarly, in human bodies an excessive external heat produces a cold and dry internal state, contrary to our expectations. But a cold and dry internal state constitutes a melancholy complexion. It is not only the influence of an external heat and dryness, then, that causes the bodies of those in the first clime to be black or dark-skinned. This same external heat contributes to a melancholy humoral complexion that is dominated by black bile, with attendant theological implications. Not coincidentally, Satan will be depicted as black, and the Prince of Darkness is cold, without vital warmth, and melancholy in complexion,[122] infusing the poison of melancholy into others.[123]

Those whose hearts are thus "cooled" and dried out by extreme environmental heat will be very timid since, generally, boldness originates from the internal heat and motion of the blood. By contrast, "fear stems from coldness and the congealing of the spirits"[124] and "melancholy animals," like the hare—an animal prohibited to the Jews by their dietary laws—which are cold and dry by complexion, "are naturally timid owing to their weak heat and shortage of spirits."[125] Similarly, black Ethiopians, Albert remarks, have a frivolous character and they are weak and timid because of the evaporation of spirit.

Whereas commonly the savage and uncivilized people of hot regions are naturally timid and unwarlike, by contrast those in cold climes are bolder and naturally larger in stature. In a cold region, the cold causes the pores to close and therefore intensifies the internal heat, which can-

---

121. Honorius of Autun, *De imagine mundi* 1.47 (PL 172: 135C).

122. In the second or third-century *Epistle of Barnabas* 4.9, and 20.1, the Devil is designated "the Black One [ὁ μέλας]." See also Azouvi, "The Plague, Melancholy and the Devil," and Strickland, *Saracens, Demons, and Jews*, chap. 3.

123. See Caesarius of Heisterbach, *Dialogus Miraculorum* 4.39.

124. Albert the Great, *Quaestiones super de animalibus* 1.13, p. 89, 56–57 (QDA, 37).

125. Albert the Great, *Quaestiones super de animalibus* 1.34–37, p. 101, 40–41 (QDA, 61); *De animalibus* 12.2.1.103, vol. 15, 838 (SZ 2: 932); 22.2.1.110, vol. 16, 1408 (SZ 2: 1515).

not escape the body. As a result, the increased internal heat of those living in colder climes makes them bolder, stronger, and more warlike. In people in a hotter region the internal heat is typically dispersed through the opened pores, but if it is intensified, it is intensified only by some temporary cause, like illness, or by a brief, cooling change in their weather. As a result, if they are bold, their boldness will not last, and in war they will soon retreat. Albert the Great apparently sees evidence of this fleeting boldness even among those living in warmer parts of southern Europe, and remarks that such are "the French, who want to do wondrous things at the beginning and in the end accomplish nothing, and people like this are called *hardi* [bold] in French."[126] Perhaps Albert is venting frustration at the utter failure a few years earlier of the seventh Crusade (1248–54), led by the French king Louis IX.

The contrast between North and South, cold and hot climes, was basic to medieval European ethnography. Ptolemy states a commonplace when he remarks that "Those who live under the more northern parallels, however ... since they are far removed from the zodiac and the cold overcomes the heat of the sun there, and because they have a greater share of moisture, which is most nourishing, and because there is no heat among them to dry it out, are white in complexion [*color*], straight-haired, with large, fleshy bodies, and their natures are cold."[127] Albert the Great confirms that

> in those who dwell in the seventh clime, which is nearest the North Pole and furthest from the equator [*linea aequalitatis*] and from the path of the sun and of the other planets, opposite qualities occur in them for the opposite reason. In fact, these are all cold and their places of habitation are quickly cooled, and this is why the women's wombs are cold and moist, and for this reason a whiteness and intense paleness [*subalbedo*] occurs in them, just as it occurs among the Slavs [*Sklavi*] and the Parthians and those of Dacia [Romania] and the Teutons [Germans] and Angles [English] and such nations of this sort, which dwell around the shore of the northern ocean.[128]

---

126. Albert the Great, *Quaestiones super de animalibus* 7.28, p. 184, 2–4 (QDA, 258).
127. "In illis autem qui sub lineis parallelis propioribus septentrioni morantur ... qua magna est eorum remotio a circulo signotum, & solis calorem vincit frigiditas, quapropter quia est magna eorum humiditas multaeque vegetationis, nec est apud eos calor, qui eam desiccat, sunt eorum colores albi, & crines plani, corpora magna atque carnosa, frigidae sunt etiam eorum naturae." Ptolemy, *Quadrapartitum* 2.2, p. 22.
128. Albert the Great, *Liber de causis proprietatum elementorum* 1.1.5.

Germans, Dacians, the English, and Slavs are white because of the cold and because their bodies' pores are nearly closed, thereby preserving their internal moisture and heat. The same may be said of the French (despite Albert's disparagement noted above) or those living in Gaul. Because cold constricts the body's pores, causing the moisture to remain inside, northerners' bodies will also tend to be fleshy and phlegmatic, since the internal moisture cannot escape and the external cold converts their moisture to water, like steam when it is cooled. Their women conceive and give birth with difficulty because of their cold complexion. Albert adds that German women are an exception (perhaps reflecting his own German background) because they conceive easily, although they too give birth with difficulty. Whereas Bartholomew the Englishman also agrees that German women conceive more readily than others in the northern clime, he explains this solely by appealing to an etymology. Germany (*Germania*), he claims, is so called from the fecund ability (*germinando*) of its people to procreate.[129] Albert the Great attempts a more scientific explanation, and insists that German women conceive more readily because of the coldness in their region, which causes the pores to constrict, impeding the evaporation of fluids and spirits. Just as the opening of the pores for those who dwell in hot, southern climes paradoxically cools their heart and internal organs as their internal heat escapes, so too in cold climes, because the pores constrict, the internal heat turns inward and intensifies.[130] As a result, their bodies become quite hot, and the heat facilitates conception, just as heat and moisture cause a seed to germinate. For the same reasons, these hot-blooded men are naturally bold and can expect to live longer. They have an abundance of blood, and a thick head of hair that is straight and not curly. However, they are also dull-witted and stupid and not inclined to study. "The proof of this," Albert remarks, drawing a contrast between northern and southern Europeans, "is that the people of Milan always study law, liberal studies, and the arts, about which the Dacians and the Slavs care little."[131] But when those in northern climes do study, they persevere and are improved by it.

As has been shown above, medieval ethnography rested on a deter-

---

129. "a foecunditate gignendorum populorum, a germinando Germania est vocata." Bartholomaeus Anglicus, *De rerum proprietatibus* 15.13, p. 630.

130. Vincent of Beauvais, *Speculum naturale* 31.40, 1: 2344.

131. Albert the Great, *De natura loci* 2.3, p. 103.

mination of environmental factors: temperature, humidity, and even the cooling effects of wind or large bodies of water. As a general rule those in the northern, colder climes will have fair, straight hair and white skin. To European physiognomers, they will typically be more handsome or beautiful, bolder and more belligerent. Those in hotter, southern climes will have black skin that has been burned by the sun, curly or frizzy hair, and dessicated bodies that rarely allow them to survive past age thirty. They are timid, weak, and unwarlike.

These basic principles of humoral complexion were accepted not only in Europe, but also among intellectuals in lands to the East, although with sometimes different valuative outcomes. For example, the 'Abbasid writer al-Mas'udi (d. 956) attributes the excessive whiteness of the Franks (or northern Europeans in general), the blue of their eyes and red of their hair, to the weakness of the sun's heat and the cold and dampness of their environment. These environmental factors, he infers, cause them to be especially dull-witted, although also particularly belligerent and even savage in warfare.[132] In a similar way, Sā'id al-Andalusī's eleventh-century *Categories of the Nations* describes the men to the far north as barbarians with frigid temperaments, raw humors, of pale color, without keen understanding, more like animals than human, overcome by ignorance and apathy.[133] Conversely, in his *Introduction to Astronomy* Albumasar agrees that the burning heat of the sun turns Ethiopians black, kinks their hair, and deprives them of intelligence.[134]

Essential to this environmental ethnography, however, is the possibility of change, since skin color is treated as an accident of body.[135] In other words, if external, environmental causes are held responsible for skin color and national character, than a change of environment should, in principle, produce a change in the body. In fact, this is precisely what one finds. Again, Bartholomew the Englishman remarks:

132. See Hillenbrand, *The Crusades: Islamic Perspectives*, 270.
133. Sā'id al-Andalusī, *Science in the Medieval World: 'Book of the Categories of Nations'* 3, p. 7. The author was a Muslim jurist in Toledo.
134. Albumasar, *Liber Introductorii maioris ad scientiam judiciorum astrorum*, tr. 3.3, ed. Richard Lemay, vol. 5[2] (Naples: Istituto Universitario Orientale, 1996), 98.
135. Thus Gilbert Crispin compares the change whereby a black man becomes white, or the other way around, to a change of accidents in which the one completely replaces the other: "In accidentium enim quorumdam alteratione, cum homo niger fit albus, seu albus niger, superveniente altero, perit omnino alterum." *Disputatio Judaei cum Christiano de fide Christiana* 92, p. 31.

For Mauritania is a very hot region in Ethiopia, in which, owing to the continuous heat, the subcutaneous blood is burned, and is blackened and becomes adust, and from the diffusion of this blackened blood between the skin and the flesh all the members in general are blackened. In this way the first person inhabiting Ethiopia was blackened, but later, from the continuing cooperative heat of the sun, the defect of this first inhabitant was transmitted to later generations, so that from a black father and from a similarly black mother a black infant is born, generally. But this only happens in a place where the burning of the sun continuously afflicts those generating [children]. And for this reason, in regions that are more temperate and tending toward cold, Ethiopians generate children that are temperate in color. . . . Contrariwise, the Scots and the Germans inhabit cold regions, and for this reason with the cold constricting the exterior pores the heat is recalled to the interior, and this is why the surface of the exterior part of the body is whitened.[136]

In the same way, Robert the Englishman (*Robertus Anglicus*) remarks in his commentary on the *Sphaera* of Sacrobosco that Ethiopians are black because they dwell in a very hot clime. Yet, "if it were the case that they dwelt in a temperate habitation this side of the Tropic of Cancer, they would not be as dark-skinned as they are, since the blackness in them is not caused except by too much burning and heat of the sun."[137] This is imagined to be a natural process, justified by scientific principles, that holds true not only for human beings but for animals as well. Albert the Great asserts that just as one finds that people in cold and moist, northern climes are white, so too are the animals: there one finds white bears (polar bears) and white hares, whereas these same animals in more southern climes are black or brown.[138] Should you remove a black bear to

---

136. "Nam Mauritania est regio in Aethiopia calidissima, in qua propter calorem continuum sanguis aduiritur intercutaneus, et denigrator et fit adustus, a cuius denigrati sanguinis diffusione inter cutem et carnem, omnia membra generaliter denigrantur. Unde primus Aethiopiam inhabitans denigratus sic est, sed postea cooperante calore Solis continuitate primi illius habitatoris vitium in posteris propagavit, quod ex nigro patre et consimili matre nigri foetus generaliter nascerentur. Sed hoc solum habet locum, ubi Solis adustio continue afficit generantes. Et ideo in regionibus temperatis et ad frigiditatem declinantibus Aethiopes generant in colore filios temperatos. . . . E contrario vero Scoti et Alemanni frigidas inhabitant regions, et ideo frigiditate poros exterius constringente calor ad interiora revocatur, et ideo exterioris parties corporum superficies dealbatur." Bartholomaeus Anglicus, *De rerum proprietatibus* 19.8, pp. 1147–48.

137. "Si ita esset quod habitarent in habitatione temperata citra tropicum Cancri, non essent ita denigrati sicut sunt, cum nigredo in eis non causetur nisi ex nimia adustione et calore solis." See Thorndike, *The Sphere of Sacrobosco and Its Commentators*, 235. The Latin text appears in *lectio* 12, p. 185.

138. Albert the Great, *De natura loci* 2.4.

a northern clime, one expects that over time the black bear will become white in response to a change in environment. Vincent of Beauvais also plants this type of color change firmly within the orbit of nature, just as over time a person's black hair turns white with age.[139]

Nonetheless, Albert the Great does display some discomfort at the notion that a black Ethiopian will turn white should his habitation be moved to a northern clime. Although he never repudiates this notion—perhaps because of the influence of contemporaries like Thomas of Cantimpré and Vincent of Beauvais, who regarded white skin as more "natural"[140]—he does qualify it, since experience would suggest that black people may be born even in the fourth and fifth, that is, more northern, climes. Perhaps a color change requires several—perhaps four?—generations. Therefore, he remarks, "they take their blackness from their first ancestors who are complexioned in the first and second climes, and a little at a time, they are altered to whiteness when they are transferred to other climes."[141] It is not clear how long this will take. Nonetheless, over successive generations, then, blacks will naturally become white. Although there were few blacks living in medieval Europe, still it is not inconceivable that Albert the Great and his contemporaries might have known of mixed race marriages or alliances that produced children of lighter skin, supporting the notion of a gradual lightening of skin color.[142] Nonetheless, empirical evidence drawn from over successive generations would have created a tension for a theory that attributed skin color to climate and, by the Renaissance, this tension promoted instead a notion that skin color is hereditary, although the older climate-based model does not disappear.[143] Evidence of its persistence can be found even among some early twentieth-century Ethiopian Jews, who adhered to this environmental doctrine in order to assert that their own black-

---

139. Vincent of Beauvais, *Speculum naturale* 2.69, 1: 124.

140. See Thomas of Cantimpré, *Liber de natura rerum* 1.42, p. 47; and Vincent of Beauvais, *Speculum naturale*, 28.30, 1: 2012. For some discussion, see Biller, "Black Women in Medieval Scientific Thought," 477–80.

141. Albert the Great, *De natura loci* 2.3, p. 102.

142. See Maaike van der Lugt, "La Peau noire dans la science médiévale," in *La pelle umana; The Human Skin*, vol. 13 of *Micrologus. Natura, scienze e società medievali* (Florence: SISMEL, 2005), 461.

143. See, for example, Anu Korhonen, "Conceptualising Black Skin in Renaissance England," in *Black Africans in Renaissance Europe*, ed. T. F. Earle and K. J. P. Lowe (Cambridge: Cambridge University Press, 2005), 94–112.

ness was dictated by climate and geography and, when transplanted to cooler and more northern regions, they would gradually whiten.[144]

Helinand de Froidment (d. between 1223-37), in his polemical *Disputation against Astrologers* (*Disputatio contra mathematicos*), an attack upon Odo of Champagne's *Little Book on the Efficacy of the Art of Astrology* (*Libellus de efficatia artis astrologice*; c. 1192-97), is one of the few to challenge this position.[145] He too acknowledges that the sun affects the color of the skin, as is seen among black Ethiopians and, conversely, the white-skinned natives in Gaul, but he rejects the claim that Ethiopians are black or that Gauls are white solely from the effects of climate and the sun. The fact is, he says, that an Ethiopian in Gaul will produce a black Ethiopian and a Gaul in Ethiopia will produce a white Gaul. Clearly the sun's rays alter skin color, but Gallic peasants working naked in the fields of Gaul will have their skin darkened or tanned by the sun's rays far more readily than the Ethiopian will change his color. Consequently, one must say more truthfully that Ethiopians do not derive their black color from the sun, but only the *intensity* of their blackness, whereas they receive their color at conception, just as Jacob demonstrated by the sheep he bred.[146] Helinand voices a tension, then, already seen above perhaps in the remarks of Bartholomew the Englishman. While the sun's intensity does contribute to skin coloration, still Ethiopians "receive their color at conception" and the sun only makes them more or less black. Albert the Great too had suggested that in Ethiopians the semen in the womb is heated and dried out, blackening the body of the fetus at conception. Along the same lines, Michael Scot indicates that in hot climes, the children will typically have a brown skin coloration, but when the

144. See Steven Kaplan, "Can the Ethiopian Change His Skin? The Beta Israel (Ethiopian Jews) and Racial Discourse,"*African Affairs* 98, no. 393 (1999), 546.
145. This constitutes book 6, chap. 5 of Helinand's imperfect *Chronicorum*.
146. "Versimilius est ergo Ethyopes non a Sole trahere nigredinem, sed nigredinis intensionem. Nam principium trahunt a conceptu, sicut iam ostensum est. Similiter a conceptu fiunt colores animalium, ut ex commento Iacob monastratum est. Nam cum in eadem climate et in eadem etiam civitate solaris radius equaliter afflet cignum et corvum et picam et pavonem, quomodo una et eadem operatoine in uno et eodem subiecto, idest in plumarum substantia, facere colorem credendus est in cigno candidum, in corvo nigrum, in pica medium, in pavone gemmeum et stellatum? Magis ergo credendum est huiusmodi colores nativos ex affectibus et aspectibus concipientium in pecoribus et volatilibus variari." Eudes de Champagne [Odo of Champagne], "Eudes de Champagne, *Libellus de efficatia artis astrologice*. *Traité astrologique* d'Eudes de Champagne, XIIe siècle," cap. 28, ed. Malgorzata Hanna Malewicz, *Medievalia Philosophica Polonorum* 20 (1974), 59.

mother's womb is also hot, its heat multiplies the environmental heat, so that the child will be born—and will remain—black.[147] These comments cast some doubt on the assumption that a change in environment alone will result in a change in skin coloration, or they postpone such a change for at least several generations.

External Causes: Celestial Bodies

Although environment helps to establish skin color and the body's complexion, in addition the humoral complexion of planets or celestial bodies will affect living beings. Saturn and Jupiter are principal celestial causes; consequently, Albert the Great remarks, "the first [planets] moreover that introduce complexion are Saturn and Jupiter, because the one moves the cold and dry and the other the hot and moist."[148] Since the cold and dry are mortifying properties, Bartholomew the Englishman expresses the common wisdom that "because [Saturn] has these two deadly qualities—cold and dryness—an infant born or conceived under its influence either dies or follows after these very bad qualities."[149] Cold and dry are also the qualities associated with the melancholy humor, however, that is, with black bile. Bartholomew adds, then, that according to Ptolemy "[Saturn] causes men to be dark [in appearance], base, doing wicked things, slothful, severe, sad, and not inclined to laughter."[150] Those subject to Saturn are not repulsed by foul and smelly clothes, and they like stinking and unclean animals, because the melancholy humor is dominant in them.[151] Robert the Englishman confirms that Saturn has dominion over cold or phlegmatic and melancholic diseases like leprosy, cancer, morphew, and gout.[152] Saturn also influences one's character and

---

147. Michael Scot, *Liber phisionomiae*, cap. 44.

148. "Prima autem ad complexionem ducentia sunt Saturnus et Iuppiter, eo quod unus movet frigidum et siccum et alter calidum et umidum." Albert the Great, *Liber de causis proprietatum elementorum* 1.2.9, p. 78.

149. "[Saturn] quia duas habet qualitates mortiferas, scilicet frigiditatem et siccitatem, et ideo foetus sub ipsius dominio natus et conceptus, vel moritur vel pessimas consequitur qualitates." Bartholomaeus Anglicus, *De proprietatibus rerum* 8.23, p. 400.

150. "[Saturn] dat hominem esse fuscum, turpem, iniqua operantem, pigrum, gravem, tristem, raro hilarem seu ridentem." Bartholomaeus Anglicus, *De proprietatibus rerum* 8.23, 401.

151. Ibid., p. 401.

152. See Thorndike, *The Sphere of Sacrobosco and Its Commentators*, lectio 4, p. 161. A similar list linking Saturn and leprosy can be found in the Middle English vernacular translation of William the Englishman's *De urina non visa*, suggesting that a connection between

religion. As Chaucer's Saturn proclaims, "myne be the maladyes colde, the derke tresons and the castes olde."¹⁵³

For our discussion of the external causes of skin coloration, however, it is relevant that "[Saturn] causes men to be dark [in appearance]." Pseudo-Albert the Great adds too that Saturn causes the fetus conceived under its influence to be dark in color, because Saturn is itself cold, dry, and earthy.¹⁵⁴ Saturn also inclines one's character toward melancholia, and melancholics are typically sad, anti-social, envious and perfidious. By contrast, Jupiter is a benevolent planet that expels Saturn's influence. According to the astronomers, Jupiter causes the face of one born under its sanguineous influence to be rosy white, which is the most beautiful color.¹⁵⁵ According to Ptolemy's *Quadripartitum*, Saturn makes his subjects dark-skinned in appearance and melancholy in complexion, although Jupiter makes his subjects light skinned and confers a warm and moist complexion.¹⁵⁶ For Bartholomew the Englishman also Jupiter is a hot and moist, benevolent planet with masculine qualities, whereas typically Saturn—both the planet and the emasculated god—is treated as feminine.¹⁵⁷ Some medieval authors asserted that Saturn's influence generally will produce female offspring, while male planets help produce males.¹⁵⁸

Just as the poets sing that Jupiter expelled his father Saturn from his realm, so too Jupiter restrains and expels the influence of Saturn here

---

Saturn and leprosy was widespread. For the text, see Hilary M. Carey, "Medieval Latin Astrology and the Cycles of Life: William English and English Medicine in Cambridge, Trinity College MS 0.5.26," 57–74, but esp. 61.

153. Chaucer, "The Knight's Tale," vv. 1608–10 in *The Canterbury Tales*. For a discussion of the "children of Saturn" in Chaucer, see Anna Czarnowus, "'My cours, that hath so wyde for to turne, / hath moore power than wood any man': The Children of Saturn in Chaucer's Monk's Tale," *Studia Anglica Posnaniensia* 40 (2004): 299–310.

154. "Saturnus facit natum suum fuscum in colore. Ratio est, quia Saturnus est similis terrae quia est frigidus et siccus, obscurus niger, et virtualiter facit natum obscurum." Pseudo-Albert the Great, *De secretis mulierum* cap. 3 (Amsterdam: 1643), 57. This is echoed in Albert the Great, *De mineralibus* 2.3.5, p. 54B.

155. "secundum astonomos qui nascitur sub Iove perveniet ad multos honores; facit faciem pulchram, et facies est nobilior pars corporis . . . et facit hominem album rubedine permixtum; quia ille color est pulchrior inter alios, quia est sanguineus." Ps. Albert the Great, *De secretis mulierum* cap. 3, p. 59.

156. Ptolemy, *Quadrapartitum* 3.11, p. 50.

157. Roger Bacon, *tractatus brevis et utilis* to the *Secreta Secretorum* 7, p. 22.

158. See Helen Lemay, "The Stars and Human Sexuality," *Isis* 71, no. 256 (1980): 127–37, citing 129.

below and produces a healthy, sanguineous complexion.[159] The contrast between these two planets and their effects is consistent. Albert the Great remarks upon their influence upon the birth process too, noting that

> Saturn is the first among the planets in superior realms, and next is Jupiter, and then Mars, and so on for the others. But Saturn is cold and dry, and it is a malevolent planet. Thus, one born under Saturn is given to evil. Jupiter is warm and moist and it is a benevolent planet, for it makes a person lovable, and so on for the others. Therefore if the child that is born should come forth in the seventh month, and is then born under the moon, the birth will be for the good. If however the fetus has not been adequately arranged for its exit in the seventh month and its exit is delayed until the eighth month, it is a sign of weakness in the fetus and in the same way its birth will depend on Saturn, and under this planet the birth is bad or leads to something bad. And if it should come forth in the ninth month it is born under Jupiter, which is warm and moist, and the birth will be for the good. Thus the Philosopher [Aristotle] says that according to the opinion of the astrologers if a woman should give birth in the eighth month the fetus will die or, if it lives, it will languish.[160]

The text of the *Prose Salernitan Questions,* composed about 1200 CE, also explains that when the infant is born in the eighth month, which is subject to Saturn's cooling and drying influence, Saturn has a deleterious effect on the womb, the fetus, and its nutriment, often resulting in its death.[161] These notions of astrological influence on fetal development can be found as well in the work of Constantine the African at the end of the eleventh century.[162] Saturn's influence, then, helps to account not only for birth defects, illness, and disease, but also for psychological characteristics and skin color.

The link between planetary influence and skin color is again not only a western European conviction. In fact, the notion enters medieval culture in part through Arab texts on astronomy and astrology. Alcabitius (Abd al-Aziz ibn Uthman al-Qabīsī; fl. 960) tied Saturn to dark-skinned people,[163] and the eleventh-century ethnographic work by Sā'id al-Andalusī,

---

159. Bartholomaeus Anglicus, *De proprietatibus rerum* 8.24, p. 401.

160. Albert the Great, *Quaestiones super de animalibus* 9.19–23, p. 212 (QDA, 322–32); cf. Aristotle, *Historia Animalium* 7.4 (584b1–3).

161. Lawn, *The Prose Salernitan Questions. Edited from a Bodleian Manuscript* (Auct. F. 3. 10), 54–55, 104, 259.

162. See C. S. F. Burnett, "The Planets and the Development of the Embryo," in *The Human Embryo. Aristotle and the Arabic and European Traditions,* ed. G. R. Dunstan (Exeter: University of Exeter Press, 1990), 95–112.

163. Abd al-Aziz ibn Uthman al-Qabīsī /Alcabitius, *The Introduction to Astrology* 2.6, p. 65.

the *Categories of Nations,* explains that Saturn's influence accounts for the fact that Indians are a dark-skinned people, "which puts them in the same category as the blacks, [although] Allah, in His glory, did not give them the low characteristics associated with this group," because of the countervailing influence of Mercury.[164] Similarly, in later medieval Islamic iconography, "Saturn is depicted as an old, bearded, dark-skinned Indian."[165]

Both external causes, then—namely, the scorching temperatures of an arid land, and celestial influence—could be responsible for the claim that Jews were "dark" complexioned. Even though some small number of Jews still was to be found in and around Jerusalem, the duration of the Jews' exile, conceived by Christians as a divine punishment for their responsibility for the Crucifixion, should have undermined once more the "environmental thesis." Why had the dark-complexioned Jews in Europe not "whitened," just as the Ethiopian was supposed gradually to change his color? Although Scholastics might find refuge in the argument that "Ethiopians" had not been in Europe long enough to display this color change, certainly the Jews had. Nonetheless, doubts over the real capacity for change support a notion that Jews inherit their color from birth and not merely from their geographical origins just as, for Helinand of Froidment, Ethiopians derive their color at conception and the influence of the Sun only determines the intensity of their blackness. Equally important, however, astrological doctrines associated the Jews and Saturn. Even though their environment may have changed, Saturn made them dark complexioned and ugly, and continues to have an influence over them and their complexion.

Internal Causes

Of the internal causes of skin color, we can treat most easily the influence of mental states, or what medieval Scholastic authors called passions or affections of the soul. As already indicated, then, a temporary change in skin coloration can result from shame, anger, sadness, fear, pain, and so on.[166] One who is ashamed or embarrassed will blush and

164. Sa'id al-Andalusi, *Science in the Medieval World: "Book of the Categories of Nations,"* pp. 11–12.

165. Eva Baer, "Representations of 'Planet Children' in Turkish Manuscripts," *Bulletin of the School of Oriental and African Studies, University of London* 31, no. 3 (1968): 526–33, citing 527.

166. Vincent of Beauvais, *Speculum naturale* 31.109, 1: 2382; Bartholomaeus Anglicus, *De proprietatibus rerum* 19.8, p. 1147.

redden, while someone who is overcome by anger will turn pale. Similarly, illness—for example, fever—can bring about a change in coloring. Normally, these accidental changes will be temporary; once the illness or mental state passes, then the skin will again assume its original color. But as a group, the Jews were said to live in a state of constant fear and anxiety as a result of their exile and insecurity in Christendom. As a result, their affective state seems to be more lasting or chronic, contributing to a certain fear-induced pallor that was said to be displayed on their faces—as in the case of Gratian, Anaclet's brother, who was described as a dark-complexioned yet pallid youth, "more like a Jew or a Saracen than a Christian."

More difficult to summarize are the discussions that attribute skin color to complexion or the state of the humors in the body. Complexion depends, as we have seen, on the mix or proportion of the four humors in the body. All living things require heat and moisture in order to live, thereby establishing as a rule that the sanguineous nature, which is hot and moist, constitutes the best or most noble complexion, with which God endowed human beings. Other species of living creatures, however, will have their own normative complexion as, for example, the ass or lion is hot and dry, or a dog is melancholic, that is, cold and dry.[167] Finally, within the species, one will find variation and diversity, most easily illustrated by differences between the sexes. Women, consequently, will be naturally phlegmatic (cold and moist), although among women some may be relatively hotter or drier; a man, by contrast, generally has a hotter complexion, although castration or genital injury may cause a man to assume a female's complexion.[168] Consequently, "a male can be rendered effeminate because once the members in which heat and power flourish have been cut off, he returns to the female's complexion, and from that point he is cold and moist in the manner of a female."[169] Some ancient physicians maintained that because both eunuchs and women are cold and moist, neither the one group nor the other are subject to elephantiasis (that is, leprosy), gout, or arthritis, and as a result some even pre-

---

167. Albert the Great, *Quaestiones super de animalibus* 7.33–39, p. 187, 34–35 (QDA, 266). Albert adds that the dog is also especially given to sexual intercourse.

168. Ibid., 5.10, p. 159, 75–77 (QDA, 200); Cf. *De animalibus* 12.1.2.32, 12.1.7.85, vol. 15, 810, 831 (SZ 2: 906, 926).

169. Albert the Great, *Quaestiones super de animalibus* 15.4–5, p. 262, 67–70 (QDA, 446).

scribed medical castration to address such illnesses.[170] While a castrated man may receive a female's complexion, contrariwise, if a woman has a complexion that is somewhat hotter when compared to other women, she may display certain characteristics associated with men—for example, facial hair—but she never properly becomes "virile," says Albert the Great, because a woman is a defective or flawed male: while the male can lose that which defines him as a male, the woman can never acquire what she never had.[171] And, finally, the individual may have a complexion in an absolute sense—he may be not merely hotter and drier in comparison with another individual, as one woman may be hotter than another, but when compared to the species as a whole. As a result, an individual human may be choleric, phlegmatic, or melancholic even though as a species we were endowed with a tempered, balanced hot and moist complexion. And even though as a species we once enjoyed a balanced and tempered complexion in our prelapsarian state, all humanity became distempered after the fall. Although both the spiritual medicine of baptism and the physician's cures that seek to heal the body may restore relative balance to humankind, nonetheless women as a group continue to display a phlegmatic complexion and Jews as a group, as we have seen, display a melancholy humoral complexion. According to the Salerno *Regimen sanitatis*, or handbook on health, bodies in which phlegm predominates will typically be white in color; those in which choler is dominant will be rosy or ruddy; while those in whom black bile or melancholy dominates will be dark-complexioned or black.[172] The dominant influence of melancholy upon their complexion, as well as planetary influences and geographical origins, help form an increasingly common assumption that Jews will be dark-complexioned.

170. See H. F. J. Horstmanshoff, "La castration dans les texts latins médicaux," 90–91.
171. Albert the Great, *Quaestiones super de animalibus* 15.4–5, p. 262, 64–66 (QDA, 446).
172. "Hi sunt humores qui praestant cuique colores. Omnibus in rebus ex phlegmate fit color albus. Sanguine fit rubens: cholera rubea quoque rufus. Corporibus fuscum bilis dat nigra colorem; Esse solent fusci quos bilis possidet atra." Harington, *Regimen Sanitatis Salerni. The School of Salernum*, p. 78.

CONCLUSION

The Jews' saturnine, melancholy nature is not to be explained simply by exterior influences attached to a particular clime, that is, by the "environmental thesis." Rather, it seems that their complexional nature is also determined, for many Christian thinkers, by the natural power of the stars. One advantage of the astrological explanation is simply that it can support contradictory conclusions: it is consistent that an *individual* Jew might escape the influence of Saturn, while Jews *as a group* cannot. This makes the "astrological thesis" extraordinarily adaptable and resistant to empirical falsification. Consequently, although the "environmental thesis" alone may fail to explain why Jews should be perceived as "dark" in complexion when as a group they had been in exile in northern Europe for centuries, the "astrological thesis" can supply all that is required: Jews are, on the whole, melancholy; their melancholy complexion derives from their attachment to Saturn; and, the melancholy humor not only accounts for their psychological shortcomings and inclination to disease or illness, but also for the growing perception in late medieval Christian Europe that Jews were dark-skinned.

Whether they could be transformed through conversion and baptism depended on a variety of factors: economics, politics, and religion. It seems that as the pressure increased on Jewish communities to convert, and as the number of Jewish converts grew dramatically, at precisely that moment the power of baptism to change the Jews' appearance became subject to growing doubts. Although in some instances somatic change followed baptism—as in the case of the Jewish boy in the *Cantigas de Santa Maria* who undergoes a "miraculous rhinoplasty" after receiving communion, or the change suggested by the English subtitle to R. Samuel of Morocco's *Book on the Already Accom-*

plished *Advent of the Messiah*, namely, *A Blackamoor Made White*—there are other cases surely when it is seems that after baptism Jewish converts remained distinguished still by a Jewish odor, appearance, or by an unnatural bloody flux akin to menstruation. After baptism Jewish males remained indelibly marked by their circumcision, both as a physical sign and as a symbol of their inclination to error and vice. The presence of this sign undermined confidence in the authenticity of their religious transformation, as evidenced in the report in the *Letters of Obscure Men* (*Epistolae obscurorum virorum*) of a quodlibetal disputation in which theologians argued that when a Jew becomes a Christian his foreskin will be restored to him, just as some theologians had argued that at his resurrection Jesus' foreskin had been restored to his body. The continued absence of the foreskin in Jewish converts to Christianity, then, could be seen as a sign of continuing infidelity.

Similarly, we have seen the assumption that Jews reveal a bloody flux akin to menstruation that can only be healed by conversion to Christianity. Indeed, *The Book of Peter Madsen, Curate at St. Peter's Church in Ribe* (Denmark), a handbook for preachers from the second half of the fifteenth century, states explicitly that this bloody flux in Jews will cease if they are converted and baptized.[1] Nonetheless, claims that this bodily condition persists among Spanish conversos will not only point to the imperfect character of their baptism or faith, but it also could be invoked as a scientific test of their Christian conversion. As a result, just as Juan de Quiñones will invoke the myth of Jewish male menses to help the Inquisition to identify crypto-Jews, the *foetor Judaicus* will be invoked to achieve the same end, and in Spanish anti-converso polemics a repulsive body odor was attributed to Jewish converts that even the waters of baptism could not fully eradicate. That this conviction also had travelled to Germany and central Europe is evident in the *Letters of Obscure Men*, which would reveal the Jewish convert Johannes Pfefferkorn to be a false Christian because although "it is commonly said that when Jews are baptized they cease to stink," "[Pfefferkorn] still stank like any other Jew."

Not only were Jewish converts still differentiated by the absence of

1. See *Liber Petri Mathie curati ecclesie sancti petri Ripis*, transcribed by Anne Riising from Msc. Ny kgl. Samling 123 4°, The Royal Library, Copenhagen, fol. 347r, p. 674 (available at http://static.sdu.dk/mediafiles//Files/Om_SDU/Institutter/Ihks/Projekter/Middelalderstudier/Ny_Peder_Madsen.pdf).

the foreskin, by allegations of menstrual bleeding, and by a distinctive and offensive odor, but they were also sometimes perceived to have a darker skin color or complexion. The "yeast" of Jewish corruption continued to affect Anaclet II and the members of his family, even two generations after his grandfather's baptism, and his brother Gratian was derisorily dismissed as dark and pallid, "more like a Jew or a Saracen than a Christian."

Among Christian theologians, these persistent physical signs raised doubts that Jews could truly benefit from the cleansing waters of baptism, at least in the near term. For Duns Scotus the positive effects of baptism among Jewish converts may not become visible until the third or fourth generation; similarly, Alonso de Espina avers that Jewish adults are likely too hardhearted to benefit from Christian baptism, and that baptism's positive effect may only become apparent after several generations among the progeny of Jewish converts.

Such doubts tended to reinforce social reality. As already discussed, evidence suggests that converted Jews that found refuge in King Henry III's London *Domus conversorum* generally failed to assimilate into the larger Christian population. They remained separate and apart from their Christian neighbors, as a sort of *tertium quid*. During the fifteenth century, purity of blood statutes promulgated in diverse Spanish institutions and municipalities prevented converted Jews from entering some religious orders, excluded them from university posts or cathedral chapters, and refused to them some of the dignities awarded other Christians, based on the contention that, despite the sacrament of baptism, they remained polluted or defiled by Jewish blood.

Attempts to explain by natural causation the alleged somatic differences that separated medieval Jews and Christians are never wholly isolated from theology. The Jews' complexional nature was dictated in part by the condition of the soul, and the soul's differences could be deciphered through the science of physiognomy. In some instances Jewish difference stems from divine punishment: Jews will bear *on their bodies* the mark of Cain, regardless of how that mark is identified. Jews will provide a visible canvas on which were depicted the passions and desires that Christians most earnestly sought to erase in themselves: lust, sensuality, avarice, irrationality, and stubborn pride. The danger that they represented had to be neutralized, and thus they were seen as cursed or afflicted with a diseased or flawed nature as a punishment for infidelity, in the same way that women are cursed with a flawed or defective nature and fall short of masculine perfection because they have inherited the weakness of Eve. A flawed complexion is responsible for the claim that Jewish males menstruate; it is their flawed complexion that demanded ritual circumcision under the Old Law, to temper their lust and sensuality. It is their complexion as well that helps account for the special dietary restrictions imposed upon them as a curb upon their wickedness, and it is their melancholy complexion that makes them especially inclined to various illnesses but especially leprosy, despite the perception that Jews were relatively immune to leprosy because of the prophylactic influence of the Levitical laws of ritual purity.

Were these physiognomic properties truly visible? Did they mark out Jews for their neighbors in a way that the invisible sign of circumcision could not? In a sense, they did. They were consistent with and derived from accepted scientific principles, and they were compatible with theological assumptions. Given their lack of faith and persistent sinfulness, Jews *ought* to appear dark-complexioned, melancholy in complexion, fearful, timid, lustful, avaricious, and so on—and therefore they *did* assume this appearance, regardless of the empirical reality. They bore on their bodies marks of distinction, and were separated from their Christian neighbors not only by their religious practices, customs, and beliefs, but equally by a physical reality that could be viewed as ineradicable.

BIBLIOGRAPHY

PRIMARY SOURCES

'Abd al-'Aziz ibn 'Uthman al-Kabīsī/Alcabitius. *Alcabitii ad magisterium iudiciorum astrorum Isagoge: Commentario Joannis Saxonii declarata*. Paris: Vaenundatur a Simone Colinaeo apud scholas decretorum, 1521.

———. *The Introduction to Astrology*. Edited and translated by Charles Burnett, Keiji Yamamoto, and Michio Yano. London: The Warburg Institute, 2004.

The Aberdeen Bestiary. Aberdeen University Library MS 24. Available at http://www.abdn.ac.uk/bestiary/bestiary.hti. 2/7/2011.

Abū Ma'shar. *Liber Introductorii maioris ad scientiam judiciorum astrorum*. Edited by Richard Lemay. Vol. 5[2]. Naples: Istituto Universitario Orientale, 1996.

———. *On Historical Astrology*. 2 vols. Edited by Charles Burnett and Keiji Yamamoto. Leiden: Brill, 2000.

Account of the Disputation of the Priest. In *The Polemic of Nestor the Priest*. 2 vols. Edited and translated by Daniel J. Lasker and Sarah Stroumsa. Jerusalem: Ben-Zvi Institute for the Study of Jewish Communities in the East, 1996.

Acta Sanctorum, Octobris. Paris: Apud Victorem Palme, 1866.

Adam of Eynsham. *Magna vita sancti Hugonis/The Life of St Hugh of Lincoln*. 2 vols. Edited and translated by Decima Doule and Hugh Farmer. London: Nelson, 1961–62.

Adso of Montier-en-Der. *De ortu et tempore Antichristi*. Edited by D. Verhelst. CCCM 45. Turnholt: Brepols, 1976.

Agobard of Lyons. *De cavendo convictu et societate Judaica*. Edited by L. Van Acker. In *Opera omnia*. CCCM 52. Turnholt: Brepols, 1981.

———. *De insolentia Iudaeorum*. Edited by L. Van Acker. In *Opera omnia*. CCCM 52. Turnholt: Brepols, 1981.

———. *De judaicis superstitionibus*. Edited by L. Van Acker. In *Opera omnia*. CCCM 52. Turnholt: Brepols, 1981.

Alain de Lille. *Liber poenitentialis*. 2 vols. Edited by Jean Longère. Analecta mediaevalia Namurcensia 18. Louvain: Éditions Nauwelaerts, 1965.

———. *Contra Haereticos*. PL 210: 305–428.

Albert of Aachen. *Historia Ierosolimitana*. Edited and translated by Susan B. Edgington. Oxford: Clarendon Press, 2007.

Albert of Behaim. *Das Brief-und Memorialbuch*. Edited by Thomas Frenz and Peter Herde. MGH. Briefe des späteren Mittelalters 1. Munich: MGH, 2000.

Albert the Great. *De vegetabilibus libri VII*. Edited by Ernst Meyer and Charles Jessen. Berlin: Georgius Reimeris, 1867.

———. *De somno et vigilia*. Ed. Borgnet, 9. Paris: L. Vivès, 1890, 121–212.
———. *De causis et processu universitatis a prima causa*. Ed. Borgnet, 10. Paris: L. Vivès, 1891, 361–628.
———. *Politica*. Ed. Borgnet, 8. Paris: L. Vivès, 1891.
———. *Commentarii in II Sententiarum*. Ed. Borgnet, 27. Paris: L. Vivès, 1894.
———. *In Evang. Lucae*. Ed. Borgnet, 22. Paris: L. Vivés, 1894.
———. *Super IV Sententiarum*. Ed. Borgnet, 29. Paris: L. Vivès, 1894.
———. *De Mineralibus*. Ed. Borgnet, 5. Paris: L. Vivés, 1895, 1–116.
———. *Summa theologiae*. Ed. Borgnet, 32. Paris: L. Vivés, 1895.
———. *Quaestiones super Evangelium*. Ed. Borgnet, 37. Paris: L. Vivès, 1899, 1–362.
———. *Commentarii in Iob*. Edited by Melchior Weiss. Freiburg: Herder, 1904.
———. *De animalibus*. Beiträge zur Geschichte der Philosophie des Mittelalters 15–16. Edited by Hermann Stadler. Münster: Aschendorff, 1916–20.
———. *Postilla super Isaiam*. Edited by Ferdinand Siepmann. Ed. Colon. 19.2. Münster in Westfalorum: Aschendorff, 1952, 1–632.
———. *Quaestiones super de animalibus*. Edited by Ephrem Filthaut. Ed. Colon. 12. Monasterii Westfalorum: Aschendorff, 1955, 77–361.
———. *De incarnatione*. Edited by Ignatius Backes. Ed. Colon. 26. Monasterii Westfalorum: Aschendorff, 1958, 171–235.
———. *De sacramentis*. Edited by Albert Ohlmeyer. Ed. Colon. 26. Monasterii Westfalorum: Aschendorff, 1958, 1–170.
———. *De anima*. Edited by Clemens Stroick. Ed. Colon. 7.1. Monasterii Westfalorum: Aschendorff, 1968, 1–284.
———. *De causis proprietatum elementorum*. Edited by Paul Hossfeld. Ed. Colon. 5.2. Münster: Aschendorff, 1980, 49–106.
———. *De generatione et corruption*. Edited by Paul Hossfeld. Ed. Colon. 5.2. Münster: Aschendorff, 1980, 109–219.
———. *De natura loci*. Edited by Paul Hossfeld. Ed. Colon. 5.2. Münster: Aschendorff, 1980, 1–46.
———. *Super Matthaeum*. Edited by Bernhard Schmidt. Ed. Colon. 21.1. Monasterii Westfalorum: Aschendorff, 1987.
———. *Quaestiones*. Edited by Albert Fries, Wilhelm Kübel, and Henryk Anzulewicz. Ed. Colon. 25.2. Münster in Westfalorum: Aschendorff, 1993, 1–364.
———. *On Animals: A Medieval Summa Zoologica*. 2 vols. Translated by Kenneth J. Kitchell Jr. and Irven Michael Resnick. Baltimore: Johns Hopkins University Press, 1999.
———. *Super Dionysium de ecclesiastica hierarchia*. Edited by Maria Burger. Ed. Colon. 36.2. Monasterii Westfalorum: Aschendorff, 1999, 1–232.
———. *Albert the Great's Questions Concerning Aristotle's On Animals*. Translated by Irven M. Resnick and Kenneth F. Kitchell Jr. Fathers of the Church, Medieval Continuation 9. Washington, D.C.: The Catholic University of America Press, 2008.
———. *De homine*. Edited by Henryk Anzulewicz and Joachim R. Söder. Ed. Colon. 27.2. Monasterii Westfalorum: Aschendorff, 2008.
———. *On the Causes of the Properties of the Elements*. Translated by Irven M.

Resnick. Mediaeval Philosophical Texts in Translation 46. Milwaukee, Wisc.: Marquette University Press, 2010.

Albert the Great [pseud.]. *De secretis mulierum*. Amsterdam: 1643

———. *Philosophia Pauperum*. Ed. Borgnet, 5. Paris: L. Vivès, 1895, 445–536.

———.*Commentarii in secundam partem psalmorum (LI–C)*. Ed. Borgnet, 16. Paris: L. Vivès, 1892.

Al[ph]onso de Espina. *Fortalitium fidei contra Judeos: Sarracenos: aliosq[ue] christiane fidei inimicos*. Lyons: Venūdātur a Stephano gueynard: prope sanctū Anthonium, 1512.

Alexander Neckam. *De naturis rerum libri duo*. Edited by Thomas Wright. London: Longman, Green, Longman, Roberts, and Green, 1863.

Alexander of Hales. *Summa theologica*. Quaracchi: Collegii S. Bonaventurae, 1930.

Alonso of Cartagena. *Defensorium unitatis Christianae (Tratado en favor de los judíos conversos)*. Edited by Manuel Alonso. Madrid: Consejo Superior de Investigaciones Científicas, 1943.

Altercatio Ecclesiae et Synagogae. Edited by J. N. Hillgarth. CCSL 69A. Turnholt: Brepols, 1999.

Ambroise. *The History of the Holy War: Ambroise's Estoire de la Guerre Sainte*. 2 vols. Edited and translated by Marianne Ailes and Malcolm Barber. Woodbridge, Suffolk, 2003.

Ambrose of Milan. *De Cain et Abel* and *De Noe*. In *Sancti Ambrosii opera*. Edited by C. Schenkl. CSEL 32.1. Vienna: Temsky, 1897.

———. *Explanatio psalmorum xii*. In *Sancti Ambrosii opera*. Edited by M. Petschenig. CSEL 64. Vienna: Temsky, 1919.

Amédée de Lausanne. *Huit Homélies Mariales*. Edited by Jean Deshusses. Translated by Antoine Dumas. SC 72. Série des Textes Monastiques d'Occident 5. Paris: Les Éditions du Cerf, 1960.

Ammianus Marcellinus. *Rerum gestarum libri qui supersunt*. Edited by Wolfgang Seyfarth, et al. Leipzig: Teubner, 1978.

Amulon. *Epistola seu liber contra Judaeos ad Carolum Regem*. PL 116:141–84.

al-Andalusī, Sā'id. *Science in the Medieval World: "Book of the Categories of Nations."* Edited and translated by Sema'an I. Salem and Alok Kumar. Austin: University of Texas Press, 1991.

Andrew of St. Victor. *Expositio super heptateuchum—In Genesim*. Edited by C. Lohr and R. Berndt. CCCM 53. Turnholt: Brepols, 1986.

Annales Erphordenses fratrum Praedicatorum. Edited by Oswald Holder-Egger. MGH, SS rer. Germ. 42. Hannover: Hahn, 1899.

Annales Hildesheimenses. Edited by George Waitz. MGH, SS rer. Germ. 8. Hannover: Hahn, 1878.

Annales Marbacenses. Edited by Herman Bloch. MGH, SS rer. Germ. 9. Hannover: Hahn, 1907.

Anonyme Latin Traité de physiognomie. Translated by Jacques André. Paris: Les Belles Lettres, 1981.

Anselm of Canterbury. *Cur Deus homo*. Edited by F. S. Schmitt. In vol. 2 of

S. Anselmi cantuariensis archiepiscopi opera omnia. 6 vols. Rome: Thomas Nelson and Sons, 1938–61, 37–133.

———. *Epistola de incarnatione Verbi*. Edited by F. S. Schmitt. In vol. 2 of *S. Anselmi cantuariensis archiepiscopi opera omnia*. 6 vols. Rome: Thomas Nelson and Sons, 1938–61, 1–36.

———. *Monologion*. Edited by F. S. Schmitt. In vol. 1 of *S. Anselmi cantuariensis archiepiscopi opera omnia*. 6 vols. Rome: Thomas Nelson and Sons, 1938–61, 7–87.

———. *Pourquoi Dieu s'est fait homme*. Edited and translated by René Roques. SC 91. Paris: Les Éditions du Cerf, 1963.

Anselm of Laon. *Anselms von Laon systematische Sentenzen*. Edited by Franz Pl. Bliemetzrieder. Beiträge zur Geschichte der Philosophie des Mittelalters 18. Münster in Westfalorum: Aschendorff, 1919, 2–3.

Anthimus. *De obseruatione ciborum epistula ad Theodericum regem Francorum*. Edited and translated by Eduard Liechtenhan. Corpus medicorum Latinorum 8.1. Berlin: In aedibus Academiae Scientiarum, 1963, 1–33.

Antoninus of Florence. *Summa theologica*. 4 vols. Verona: 1740. Reprint, Graz: Akademische Druck-u. Verlagsanstalt, 1959.

The Apostolic See and the Jews. Documents: 492–1404. 8 vols. Edited by Shlomo Simonsohn. Toronto: Pontifical Institute of Mediaeval Studies, 1988–90.

Archanaldus Andegavensis. *Vita Maurilii ep. Andegavensis*. Edited by Bruno Krusch. MGH, SS Auctores antiquissimi 4, 2. Berlin: Weidmann, 1885.

Aretaeus the Cappadocian. *The Extant Works of Aretaeus the Cappadocian*. Edited and translated by F. Adams. London: Sydenham Society, 1856.

Aristotle. *Generation of Animals*. Translated by A. L. Peck. Loeb Classical Library. Cambridge, Mass.: Harvard University Press, 1953.

———. *De animalibus: Michael Scot's Arabic-Latin Translation; Part Three: Books XV–XIX: Generation of Animals*. Edited by Aafke M. I. Van Oppenraaij. Leiden: Brill, 1992.

Aristotle [pseud.]. *Problemata varia anatomica, after University of Bologna MS 1165*. Edited by L. R. Lind. University of Kansas Publications Humanistic Studies 38. Lawrence: University of Kansas Publications, 1968.

———. *Physiognomonics*. In vol. 1 of *The Complete Works of Aristotle: The Revised Oxford Translation*. 2 vols. Edited by Jonathan Barnes. Princeton, N.J.: Princeton University Press, 1984, 1237–50.

Arnold of Villanova. *De esu carnium*. In *Arnaldi de Villanova Opera Medica Omnia* 11, edited by Dianne M. Bazell. Barcelona: Seminarium Historiae Scientiae Cantabricense, 1999.

Arnulf of Séez. *In Girardum Engolismensem invectiva de schismate Petri Leonis*. In *Pontificum Romanorum qui fuerunt inde ab exeunte saeculo IX usque ad finem saeculi XIII vitae ab aequalibus conscriptae, quas ex Archivi pontifici, bibliothecae Vaticanae aliarumque codicibus adiectis suis cuique et annalibus et documentis gravioribus*. Vol. 2 of *Paschalis II-Coelestinus III (1099–1198)*, edited by Johann Matthias Watterich. Lepizig: sumptibus Guilhelmi Engelmanni, 1862.

BIBLIOGRAPHY 329

Augustine. *De civitate Dei*. 2 vols. Edited by B. Dombart. Leipzig: Teubner, 1877.
———. *Adversus Iudaeos*. PL 42: 51–63.
———. *Contra Faustum Manichaeum*. Edited by J. Zycha. CSEL 25. Vienna: F. Tempsky, 1891.
———. *De consensu evangelistarum*. Edited by F. Weihrich. CSEL 43. Vienna: F. Tempsky, 1904.
———. *De civitate Dei*. CCSL 47.1. Turnholt: Brepols, 1955.
Averroes. *Libri Aristotelis de causis longitudinis et brevitatis vite*. In *Averrois Cordubensis Compendia Librorum Aristotelis qui Parva Naturalia Vocantur*, edited by Emilia Ledyard Shields and Henry Blumberg. Corpus Commentariorum Averrois in Aristotelem 7. Cambridge, Mass.: Mediaeval Academy of America, 1949.
Avicenna. *Liber canonis medicine*. Venice: 1527. Reprint, Brussels, 1971.
Balderich [of Florennes]. *A Warrior Bishop of the Twelfth Century: The Deeds of Albero of Trier*. Translated by Brian A. Pavlac. Toronto: Pontifical Institute of Mediaeval Studies, 2008.
Baldericus Scholasticus. *Gesta Alberonis archiepisopi*. Edited by G. Waitz. MGH SS 8. Hannover: Hahn, 1847.
Bär Teller, Issachar. *The Wellspring of Living Waters: A Medical Self-Help Book*. Translated by Arthur Teller. New York: Tal Or Orth Publishers, 1988.
Bartholomaeus Anglicus. *De rerum proprietatibus*. Frankfurt, 1601. Reprint, Frankfurt on Main: Minerva, 1964.
———. *On the Properties of Things: John Trevisa's Translation of Bartholaeus Anglicus De proprietates rerum*. 3 vols. Oxford: Clarendon Press, 1975–88.
Bede. *De temporum ratione liber* 35. Edited by Ch. W. Jones and Th. Mommsen. CCSL 123B. Turnholt: Brepols, 1977.
———. *In Pentateuchum commentarii*. PL 91: 189–392.
———. *Expositio super acta apostolorum*. PL 92: 937–95.
Bede [pseud.]. *De mundi celestis terrestrisque constitutione: A Treatise on the Universe and the Soul*. Edited and translated by Charles Burnett. London: Warburg Institute, 1985.
Benedict of Nursia. *Regula*. Edited by Rudolph Hanslik. CSEL 75. Vienna: Hoelder-Pichler-Tempsky, 1960.
Benedict of Peterborough. *Miracula sancti Thomas Cantuarensis*. In vol. 2 of *Materials for the History of Thomas Becket*, edited by James Craigie Robertson. 7 vols. Rolls Series. London: Longman, 1875–85.
Benzo of Alba. *Ad Heinricum IV*. MGH, SS rer. Germ., 65. Hannover: Hahn, 1996.
Bernáldez, Andrés. *Memorias del reinado de los Reyes Católicos, que escribá el bachiller Andrés Bernáldez*. Edited by Manuel Gómez-Moreno and Juan de M. Carriazo. Madrid: Real Academia de la Historia, 1962.
Bernard Gui. *Practica inquisitionis heretice pravitatis*. Edited by C. Douai. Paris: Alphonse Picard, 1886.
Bernard of Clairvaux. *Sancti Bernardi opera genuina*. 8 vols. Edited by the Monks of St. Benedict. Lyons: Perisse Frères, 1854.
———. *Sermones super Cantica Canticorum*. 2 vols. Edited by Jean Leclercq, C. H.

Talbot, and H. M. Rochais. Rome: Editiones Cistercienses, 1957–58.
Bernard of Gordon. *Lilium medicinae.* Lyon: Gulielmus Rouillius, 1551.
Bernardus Silvestris. *The Cosmographia of Bernardus Silvestris.* Translated by Winthrope Weatherbee. New York: Columbia University Press, 1973.
Berthold von Regensburg. *Völlstandige Ausgabe seiner Predigten.* 2 vols. Notes by Franz Pfeiffer. Vienna: Braumüller, 1862.
Bertrandon de la Broquière. *Le Voyage d'outremer de Bertrandon de la Broquière.* Edited by Charles Schefer. Paris: Ernest Leroux, 1892. Reprint, Farnborough: Gregg, 1972.
Boethius, Anicius Manlius Severinus. *Interpretatio priorum analyticorum Aristotelis.* PL 64: 639–712.
Bonaventure. *Commentaria in Quatuor Libros Sententiarum.* In vols. 1–4 of *Petri Lombardi Doctoris seraphici S.Bonaventurae opera omnia.* Quaracchi: Collegii Sancti Bonaventurae, 1885.
———. *Sermones dominicales.* Edited by J. G. Bougerol. Grottaferrata: Collegio S. Bonaventura, Padri Editori di Quaracchi, 1977.
The Book of Beasts being a Translation from a Latin Bestiary of the Twelfth Century. Edited by T. H. White. New York: Dover, 1984.
Bruno of Segni. *Expositio in Pentateuchum.* PL 164: 147–551.
———. *Libellus de symoniacis.* Edited by E. Sackur. MGH, Ldl, 2. Hannover: Hahn, 1892.
Burchard, Johannes. *Diarium: sive rerum urbanarum commentarii.* 3 vols. Paris: E. Leroux, 1883–85.
Buxtorf, Johannes. *Synagoga Judaica.* Hildesheim: G. Olms, 1989.
Caesarius of Arles. *Sermones.* Edited by Gervais Morin. CCSL 103. Turnholt: Brepols, 1953.
Caesarius of Heisterbach. *Dialogus Miraculorum.* 2 vols. Edited by Joseph Strange. Cologne: Sumptibus J. M. Heberle, 1851.
———. *The Dialogue of Miracles.* 2 vols. Edited and translated by H. von E. Schott and C. C. Swinton Bland. London: George Routledge and Sons, 1929.
Callixtus II, Pope. *Sermo 3, De S. Jacobo.* PL 163: 1397–1404.
Capitularia regum Francorum. 2 vols. Edited by Alfred Boretius. MGH, LL. Hannover: Hahn, 1883–97.
Cardoso, Isaac. *Los excelencias y calumnias de los Hebreos.* Amsterdam: En casa de David de Castro Tartas, 1679.
Cassiodorus. *De orthographia.* In vol. 7 of *Grammatici Latini.* 8 vols. Edited by Heinrich Keil. Leipzig: Teubner, 1880.
Cassius Dio Cocceianus. *Dio's Roman History.* 9 vols. Translated by Earnest Cary. Loeb Classical Library. London: Heinemann, 1914–27.
Celsus. *De medicina.* Edited by C. Daremberg. Leipzig: Teubner, 1891.
Chaucer, Geoffrey. *Canterbury Tales.* Edited by A. C. Cawley. London: Dent, 1984.
Chromatius of Aquileia. *Tractatus in Matthaeum.* Edited by R. Étaix and J. Lemarié. CCSL 9A. Turnholt: Brepols, 1974.
The Chronicle of Bury St Edmunds 1212–1301. Edited and translated by Antonia Gransden. London: Thomas Nelson and Sons, 1964.

Chronicon Petroburgense. Edited by Thomas Stapleton. London: Camden Society, 1849.
Concilia aevi Karolini. 2 vols. Edited by Albertus Werminghoff. MGH, LL 3, Concilia. Hannover: Hahn, 1906–8.
Conciliorum Oecumenicorum Decreta. 3rd ed. Edited by J. Alberigo, et al. with H. Jedin. Bologna: Istituto per le scienze religiose, 1973.
Constantine the African. *Theorices.* Basel: Henri cum Petrum, 1536.
———. *L'Arte universale della medicina (Pantegni), Part 1—Book 1.* Translated by Marco T. Malato and Umberto de Martini. Rome: Istituto di storia della medicina dell'università di Roma, 1961.
———.*Tratado médico de Constantino el Africano. Constantini Liber de elephancia.* Edited by Ana Isabel Martín Ferreira. Valladolid: Universidad de Valladolid, 1996.
———. *De coitu.* In *Medieval Medicine: A Reader,* edited and translated by Faith Wallis. Toronto: University of Toronto Press, 2010, 511–23.
Crescas, Hasdai. *The Refutation of the Christian Principles.* Translated by Daniel J. Lasker. Albany: State University of New York, 1992.
Cronica minor Minoritae Erphordensis. Edited by Oswald Holder-Egger. MGH, SS rer. Germ. 42. Hannover: Hahn, 1899.
Cyril of Jerusalem. *Catechetical Lectures.* In *Cyril of Jerusalem and Nemesius of Emesa,* edited by William Teller. Library of Christian Classics 4. Philadelphia: Westminster Press, 1955.
Cyrurgia Guidonis de Cauliaco, et Cyrurgia Bruni, Teodorici, Rolandi, Lanfranci, Rogerii, Bertapalie. Verona: 1530.
David of Dinant. *Davidis de Dinanto Quaternulorum Fragmenta.* Edited by Marianus Kurdzialek. Studia Mediewistyczne 3. Warsaw: Panstwowe Wydawnictwo Naukowe, 1963.
Decrees of the Ecumenical Councils. 2 vols. Edited by Norman P. Tanner. Washington, D.C.: Georgetown University Press, 1990.
Le dictionionnaire des inquisiteurs (Valence, 1494). Edited by L. Sala-Molins. Paris: Galilée, 1981.
Die Disputationen zu Ceuta (1179) und Mallorca (1286). Zwei antijüdische Schriften aus dem mittelalterlichen Genua. Edited by Ora Limor. MGH, QQ Geistesgesch., 15. Munich: Monumenta Germaniae Historica, 1994.
Documents of the Christian Church. 3rd ed. Edited by Henry Bettenson and Chris Maunder. Oxford: Oxford University Press, 1999.
Eccumenical [sic] Council of Florence (1438–1445). Available at http://www.Ewtn.Com/Library/COUNCILS/FLORENCE.HTM. 2/7/2011.
Écrits théologiques de l'école d'Abélard. Textes inédits. Edited by Artur Landgraf. Spicilegium sacrum Lovaniense, études et documents fasc. 14. Louvain: 1934.
Egbert of York. *Poenitentiale.* PL 89: 401–35.
Epiphanius. *Sancti Epiphanii episcopi Interpretatio Evangeliorum.* Edited by Alvar Erikson. Lund: Harrassowitz, 1939.
Epistolae obscurorum virorum. 2 vols. Edited and translated by Francis Griffin Stokes. London: Chattowindus, 1909.

Ernaldus, Abbot of Bonnevalle. *Sancti Bernardi Abbatis Clarae-Vallensis Vita et Res Gestae Libris Septem Comprehensae.* PL 185: 267-302.
Eudes de Champagne [Odo of Champagne]. "Eudes de Champagne, *Libellus de efficatia artis astrologice. Traité astrologique* d'Eudes de Champagne, XIIe siècle." Edited by Malgorzata Hanna Malewicz. *Medievalia Philosophica Polonorum* 20 (1974): 3-95.
Evagrius. *Altercatio legis inter Simoneum Judaeum et Theophilum Christianum.* Edited by R. Demeulenaere. CCSL 64. Turnholt: Brepols, 1985.
L'Évangile de Nicodème: Les versions courtes en ancien francais et en prose. Edited by Alvin E. Ford. Geneva: Librarie Droz, 1973.
Extracts from Aristeas, Hecataeus, Origen and Other Early Christian Writers. Translated by Aubrey Stewart. London: Palestine Pilgrims' Texts Society, 1895.
Fabliaux et contes des poètes Francois des XI, XII, XIII, XIV et XVe siècle . . . publiés par Barbazon. 4 vols. Edited by Dominique Martin Méon. Paris: B. Warée, 1808.
Felix Fabri. *Evagatorum in Terrae Sanctae, Arabiae et Egyptii peregrinationem.* 3 vols. Edited by Konrad Dietrich Hassler. Stuttgart: Stuttgart Literary Society, 1843-49.
Flores historiarum. 3 vols. Edited by Henry Richard Luard. Rerum britannicarum medii aevi scriptores 95. London: H. M. Stat. Off., 1890. Reprint, Kraus, 1965.
Flos Medicinae Scholae Salerni. In vol. 5 of *Collectio Salernitana,* edited by Salvatore de Renzi. Naples: Tipografia del Filiatre-Sebezio, 1859.
Francis of Assisi. *Francis of Assisi: Early Documents.* 3 vols. Edited by Regis J. Armstrong, J. A. Wayne Hellmann, and William J. Short. New York: New City Press, 1999-2002.
Frontinus, Sextus Julius. *Strategemata.* Edited by R. I. Ireland. Leipzig: Teubner, 1990.
Galbert of Bruges. *The Murder of Charles the Good.* Translated by James Bruce Ross. New York: Columbia University Press, 2005.
Geoffroy de Courlon. *Chronique de l'Abbaye de Saint-Pierre-le-Vif de Sens, rédigée vers la fin du XIIIe siècle par Geoffroy de Courlon.* Sens: C. Duchemin, 1876.
Geoffrey of Monmouth. *Gottfried's von Monmouth* Historia regum Britanniae, *mit literar-historischer Einleitung und ausführlichen Anmerkungen, und* Brut Tysylio, *altwälsche Chronik in deutscher Übersetzung.* Edited by San-Marte. Halle: Edouard Anton, 1854.
Gerald of Wales. *The Life of St. Hugh of Avalon, Bishop of Lincoln (1186-1200).* Edited and translated by Richard M. Loomis. Garland Library of Medieval Literature 31. Series A. New York: Garland, 1985.
Gerhoh of Reichenberg. *De quarta vigilia noctis.* Edited by E. Sackur. MGH, Ldl, 3. Hannover: Hahn, 1897.
Gilbert Crispin. *Disputatio Judaei cum Christiano de fide Christiana.* In *The Works of Gilbert Crispin Abbot of Westminster,* edited by Anna Sapir Abulafia and G. R. Evans. Auctores Britannici Medii Aevi 8. London: Oxford University Press, 1986.
Gilbert the Englishman. *Compendium medicine Gilberti Anglici.* Lyons: Impressum per Jacobum Sacconum, expensis Vincentii de Portonariis, 1510.

———. "The Symptoms of Leprosy." [From the *Compendium medicine Gilberti Anglici.*] Translated by Michael McVaugh. In *A Sourcebook of Medieval Science*, edited by Edward Grant. Cambridge, Mass.: Harvard University Press, 1974, 752–54.

———. *Healing and Society in Medieval England: A Middle English Translation of the Pharmaceutical Writings of Gilbertus Anglicus*. Edited by Faye Marie Getz. Madison: University of Wisconsin Press, 1991.

Gilo. *Vita Sancti Hugonis abbatis*. Edited by Herbert E. J. Cowdrey. In "Two Studies on Cluniac History, 1049–1109." *Studi Gregoriani* 11 (1978): 45–109.

Gratian. *Decretum magistri Gratiani*. In *Corpus iuris canonici*, edited by A. Friedberg. 2nd ed. Leipzig: Tauchnitz, 1879–81.

Gregory of Tours. *Glory of the Martyrs*. Translated by Raymond Van Dam. Liverpool: Liverpool University Press, 1988.

Guerric of Saint-Quentin. *Quaestiones de quolibet*. Edited by Walter H. Principe, revised by Jonathan Black. Studies and Texts 143.Toronto: Pontifical Institute of Mediaeval Studies, 2002.

Guibert of Nogent. *De vita sua*. PL 156: 837–962.

Guillaume le Clerc. *Le Bestiaire*. Introduction and glossary by Robert Reinsch. Altfranzösische Bibliothek 14. Leipzig: O. R. Reisland, 1892.

Haymo of Halberstadt. *Expositio in D. Pauli epistolas*. PL 117: 361–938.

"The Hebrew Version of the 'Secretum Secretorum.'" Translated by Moses Gaster. In *Studies and Texts in Folklore, Magic, Mediaeval Romance, Hebrew Apocrypha and Samaritan Archaeology*. 3 vols. New York: KTAV, 1971, 2: 742–813.

Helgaud of Fleury. *A Brief Life of King Robert the Pious*. Translated by Phillipe Buc (2003). Available at www.stanford.edu/dept/history/people/buc/HELG-W.DOC. 5/15/2009.

Helinand of Froidment. *De cognitione sui*. PL 212: 721–46.

Henricus Institoris, and Jacobus Sprenger. *Malleus Maleficiarum*. 2 vols. Translated by Christopher S. Mackay. Cambridge: Cambridge University Press, 2004.

Henry of Harclay. *Ordinary Questions*. Edited by Mark Henninger. Auctores Britannici Medii Aevi 17–18. Oxford: Oxford University Press, 2008.

Henry of Mondeville. *Die Chirurgie des Heinrich von Mondeville*. In vol. 1 of *Leben, Lehre und Leistungen des Heinrich von Mondeville (Hermondavile) nach Berliner, Erfurter und Pariser Codices*, edited by Julius Leopold Pagel. Berlin: August Hirschwald, 1892.

Herard, Archbishop of Tours. *Capitula*. Edited by Rudolf Pokorny and Martina Stratmann. MGH, Capitula Episcoporum 2. Hannover: Hahnsche Buchhandlung, 1995.

Herman of Cologne. *Opusculum de conversione sua*. Edited by Gerlinde Niemeyer. MGH, QQ Geistesgesch., 4. Weimar: Böhlaus, 1963.

———. *A Short Account of His Own Conversion*. In *Conversion and Text: The Cases of Augustine of Hippo, Herman-Judah, and Constantine Tsatsos*. Translated by Karl F. Morrison. Charlottesville: University of Virginia Press, 1992, 39–113.

Hermann of Carinthia. *De essentiis*. Edited and translated by Charles Burnett. Leiden: Brill, 1982.

Hermannus de Runa. *Sermones festiuales*. Edited by E. Mikkers, I. Theuws, and R. Demeulenaere. CCCM 64. Turnholt: Brepols, 1986.
Hildegard of Bingen. *Causae et Curae*. Edited by Paul Kaiser. Leipzig: Teubner, 1903.
Hincmar of Reims. *Vita Remigii episcopi*. Edited by Bruno Krusch. MGH SS rer. Merov., 3. Hannover, 1896.
Homiliarium Ueronense. Edited by Lawrence T. Martin. CCCM 186. Turnholt: Brepols, 2000.
Honorius of Autun. *De offendiculo*. Edited by J. Dietrich. MGH, Ldl, 3. Hannover: Hahn, 1897.
———. *De imagine mundi*. PL 172: 115–88.
Hugh of St. Victor. *Adnotationes in Penteuchon*. PL 175: 29–86.
Humbertus a Silva Candida. *Adversus simoniacos*. Edited by F. Thaner. MGH, Ldl, 1. Hannover: Hahn, 1891.
Ibn Ezra, Abraham [?]. *Sefer Hanisyonot: The Book of Medical Experiences Attributed to Abraham Ibn Ezra*. Edited and translated by J. O. Leibowitz and S. Marcus. Jerusalem: Magnes Press, 1984.
Ibn 'Imrān, Isḥāq. *Maqāla fī l-Mālīhūliyā (Abhandlung über die Melancholie) und Constantini Africani Libri duo de Melancholia*. Critical Arabic-Latin Parallel texts and German translation. Edited and Translated by Karl Gabers. Hamburg: Helmut Buske Verlag, 1977.
Ibn Ishaq. *The Life of Muhammad*. Translated by A. Guillaume. Lahore: Oxford University Press, 1967.
Ibn Matut, Samuel. *The Mašōbēb Natībōt of Samuel Ibn Matut ("Motot"): Introductory Excursus, Critical Edition, and Annotated Translation*. 2 vols. Edited and translated by Israel Moshe Sandman. Ph.D. diss., University of Chicago, 2006.
Ibn Sahula, Isaac. *Meshal Haqadmoni: Fables from the Distant Past, A Parallel Hebrew-English Text*. 2 vols. Edited and translated by Raphael Loewe. Oxford: Littmann Library of Jewish Civilization, 2004.
Innocent III, Pope. *Regesta sive epistolae*. PL 215.
Iohannes de Fonte. *Auctoritates Aristotelis, Senecae, Boethii, Platonis, Apulei, Porphyrii, Gilberti*. Speyer: Johann and Konrad Hist, c. 1490.
Isidore of Seville. *Etymologiae*. PL 82: 73–729.
———. *De fide catholica . . . contra Judaeos*. PL 83: 449–537.
———. *Mysticorum expositiones sacramentorum seu Quaestiones in Uetus Testamentum*. PL 83: 207–425.
———. *De ecclesiasticis officiis*. Edited by Christopher M. Lawson. CCSL 113. Turnholt: Brepols, 1989.
———. *The Etymologies of Isidore of Seville*. Edited and translated by Stephen A. Barney, W. J. Lewis, J. A. Beach, and Oliver Berghof. Cambridge: Cambridge University Press, 2006.
Ivo of Chartres. *Decretum*. PL 161: 47–1021.
Jacobus de Voragine. *The Golden Legend*. 2 vols. Translated by William Granger Ryan. Princeton, N.J.: Princeton University Press, 1993.
Jacques de Vitry. *Libri dvo, quorum prior Orientalis, siue hierosolymitanæ: Alter,*

Occidentalis Historiae nomine inscribitur. Edited by F. Moschus. Douai: Belleri, 1597.

———. *Lettres de Jacques de Vitry.* Edited by R. B. C. Huygens. Leiden: Brill, 1960.

Jean Bodel. "Les Adieux du Lépreux." In *Anthologie poétique francaise: Moyen Âge,* edited by André Mary. 2 vols. Paris: Garnier Frères, 1967, 1: 302–13

Jerome. *Commentariorum in Epistolam ad Ephesios.* PL 26: 439–555.

———. *Commentarium in Jeremiam prophetam liber sex.* PL 24: 679–899.

———. *Liber quaestionum Hebraicarum in Genesim.* Edited by P. de Lagarde. CCSL 72. Turnholt: Brepols, 1959.

Jerusalem Pilgrims before the Crusades. Translated by John Wilkinson. Warminster, England: Aris and Phillips, 2002.

Le Jeu d'Adam. Edited by Wolfgang van Emden. 2nd ed. Edinburgh: Société Rencesvals British Branch, 1999.

The Jew in the Modern World: A Documentary History. Edited by Paul Mendes-Flohr and Jehuda Reinharz. 2nd ed. New York: Oxford University Press, 1995.

The Jews in the Legal Sources of the Early Middle Ages. Edited by Amnon Linder. Detroit: Wayne State University Press, 1997.

The Jews of Tortosa 1373–1492. Regesta of Documents from the Archivo Histórico de Protocolos de Tarragona. Sources for the History of the Jews in Spain 3. Compiled by Josefina Cubells i Llorens. Edited by Yom Tov Assis. Jerusalem: Henk Schussheim Memorial Series, 1991.

John Ardenne. *Treatises of Fistula in Ano, Haemorrhoids, and Clysters.* Edited by D'Arcy Power. Early English Text Society 139. London: Oxford University Press, 1910. Reprint, 1968.

John of Naples, O.P. *Quaestiones variae Parisiis disputatae.* Naples: 1618.

John of Salisbury. *Policraticus.* Edited by K. S. B. Keats-Rohan. CCCM 118. Turnholt: Brepols, 1993.

———. *Policraticus.* Translated by Cary J. Nederman. Cambridge: Cambridge University Press, 1996.

Johannes Mesuë, the Younger. *Die angebliche Chirurgie des Johannes Mesuë jun.* Edited by Julius Leopold Pagel. Berlin: August Hirschwald, 1893.

Josephus, Flavius. *The Life Against Apion.* In vol. 1 of *Works.* Translated by H. St. J. Thackeray. Cambridge, Mass.: Harvard University Press, 1976.

Judah Ha-Levi. *Book of Kuzari.* Translated by Hartwig Hirschfeld. New York: Pardes, 1946.

Kempe, Margery. *The Book of Margery Kempe.* Edited by Lynn Staley. Kalamazoo, Mich.: Medieval Institute Publications, 1996.

Liber de antiquis legibus. Cronica maiorum et vicecomitum Londoniarum. Edited by Thomas Stapleton. London: Camden Society Publications, 1846.

Liber Pontificalis, Epitome Feliciana. Edited by Theodor Mommsen. MGH, SS Gesta Pontif. Rom., 1. Berlin: Weidmann, 1898.

Lothar of Segni [Pope Innocent III]. *De contemptu mundi sive de miseria conditionis humanae.* PL 217: 701–45.

Luther, Martin. *Table Talk or the Familiar Discourse of Martin Luther.* Translated by William Hazlett. London: David Bogue, 1848.

———. *Tischreden*. In vol. 4 of *Martin Luthers Werke. Kritische Gesamtausgabe*. Weimar: Hermann Böhlaus, 1916.
———. *That Jesus Christ Was Born a Jew*. In vol. 45 of *Luther's Works*. Translated by W. I. Brandt. Philadelphia: Fortress Press, 1971, 195–229.
Magistri Salernitani nondum editi. Edited by Piero Giacosa. Torino: Fratelli Bocca, 1901.
Maimonides. *The Guide of the Perplexed*. Translated by Shlomo Pines. Chicago: University of Chicago Press, 1963.
———. *Treatise on Hemorrhoids: Medical Answers (Responsa)*. Edited and translated by Fred Rosner and Suessman Munter. Philadelphia: Lippincott, 1969.
———. *Epistle to Yemen*. In *A Maimonides Reader*, edited by Isidore Twersky. New York: Behrman House, 1972, 437–62.
———. *Treatises on Poisons, Hemorrhoids, Cohabitation: Maimonides' Medical Writings*. Translated by Fred Rosner. Haifa, Israel: Maimonides Research Institute, 1984.
Majrīṭī, Maslamah ibn Aḥmad. *Picatrix: The Latin Version of the Ghāyat Al-Hakīm*. Edited by David Pingree. London: Warburg Institute, 1986.
Mandeville, John. *The Book of John Mandeville: An Edition of the Pynson Text with Commentary on the Defective Version*. Edited by Tamarah Kohanski. Medieval and Renaissance Texts and Studies 231. Tempe: Arizona Center for Medieval and Renaissance Studies, 2001.
Manegold of Lautenbach. *Ad Gebehardum*. Edited by Kuno Francke. MGH, Ldl 1. Hannover: Hahn, 1891.
Margaritha, Anton. *Der ganz Jüdisch Glaub mit sampt ainer gründlichen un warhaften Anzaygunge* . . . . Augsburg: Heinrich Steiner, 1530.
Martianus Capella. *Martianus Capella and the Seven Liberal Arts*. In vol. 2 of *The Marriage of Philology and Mercury*. Translated by William Harris Stahl and E. L. Burge. New York: Columbia University Press, 1977.
Māshā'allāh. *De revolutione annorum mundi*. Edited by Joachim Heller. Nuremberg: Johannes Montanus & Ulricus Neuberus, 1549.
Michael Scot. *Liber phisionomiae*. Venice, 1477.
Midrash Tanhuma-Yelamadenu. Translated by Samuel A. Berman. Hoboken, N.J.: KTAV, 1996.
Mühlhausen, R. Yom Tov Lippmann. *Disputatio adversus Christianos ad Jeremie, Ezechielis, Psalmorum et Danielis libros institute*. Translated by M. Sebaldus Snellius. Altdorf: Typis Viduae Balthasaris Scherffi, 1645.
Mythographi Uaticani i et ii. Edited by Péter Kulcsár. CCSL 91C. Turnholt: Brepols, 1987.
Nachmanides. *Commentary on the Torah: Leviticus*. Translated by Charles B. Chavel. New York: Shilo Publishing House, 1974.
Nemesius of Emesa. *Of the Nature of Man*. Translated by William Telfer. In *Cyril of Jerusalem and Nemesius of Emesa*. Library of Christian Classics 4. Philadelphia: Westminster Press, 1955, 203–453.
Niccolò da Poggibonsi. *A Voyage Beyond the Seas (1346–1350)*. Translated by T. Bellorini and E. Hoade. Jerusalem: Franciscan Press, 1945.

Nicholas of Cusa. *Nicholas of Cusa's* De Pace fidei *and* Cribratio Alkorani: *Translation and Analysis*. 2nd ed. Translated by Jasper Hopkins. Minneapolis: A. J. Banning Press, 1994.

Nicholas of Ockham. *Quaestiones disputatae de traductione humanae naturae a primo parente*. Edited by Caesaris Saco Alarcón. Spicilegium Bonaventurianum 27. Grottaferrata: Editiones Collegii S. Bonaventurae ad Claras Aquas, 1993.

Obadiah the Convert. *Epistle*. In *Other Middle Ages: Witnesses at the Margins of Medieval Society,* edited by Michael Goodich. Philadelphia: University of Pennsylvania Press, 1998, 68–74.

Oderic Vitalis. *The Ecclesiastical History of Oderic Vitalis*. 6 vols. Edited and translated by Marjorie Chibnall. Oxford: Clarendon Press, 1978.

Origen. *Homilies on Joshua*. Edited by Cynthia White. Translated by Barbara J. Bruce. The Fathers of the Church 105. Washington, D.C.: The Catholic University of America Press, 2002.

Otloh of St. Emmeram. *Liber visionum*. PL 146: 341–87.

Paris, Matthew. *The Illustrated Chronicles of Matthew Paris: Observations of Thirteenth-Century Life*. Edited and translated by Richard Vaughn. Phoenix Mill, UK: Sutton, 1993.

The Passion of Adam of Bristol. In Christoph Cluse, "'Fabula ineptissima.' Die Ritualmordlegende um Adam von Bristol nach der Handschrift London, British Library 957." *Aschkenas: Zeitschrift für Geschichte und Kultur der Juden* 5, no. 2 (1995): 295–330.

Paul Alvarus. *Indiculus Luminosus*. PL 121: 513–55.

Peter Abelard. *Dialogus inter philosophum, Judaeum et Christianum*. PL 178: 1609–85.

———. *Collationes*. Edited and translated by John Marenbon and Giovanni Orlandi. Oxford: Clarendon Press, 2001.

———. *A Dialogue of a Philosopher with a Jew, and a Christian*. Translated by Pierre J. Payer. Toronto: Pontifical Institute of Mediaeval Studies, 1979.

Peter Damian. *Die Briefe des Petrus Damiani*. 4 vols. Edited by Kurt Reindel. MGH, Epp. Kaiserzeit. Munich: MGH, 1983–93.

———. *The Letters of Peter Damian, 31–60*. Translated by Owen J. Blum. The Fathers of the Church, Mediaeval Continuation Continuation 2. Washington, D.C.: The Catholic University of America Press, 1990.

———. *The Letters of Peter Damian, 61–90*. Translated by Owen J. Blum. The Fathers of the Church, Medieval Continuation 3. Washington, D.C.: The Catholic University of America Press, 1992.

———. *The Letters of Peter Damian, 91–120*. Translated by Owen J. Blum. The Fathers of the Church, Mediaeval Continuation 5. Washington, D.C.: The Catholic University of America Press, 1998.

———. *The Letters of Peter Damian, 121–150*. Translated by Owen Blum and Irven M. Resnick. The Fathers of the Church, Mediaeval Continuation 6. Washington, D.C.: The Catholic University of America Press, 2004.

Peter Lombard. *Sententiarum libri IV*. 4 vols. Translated by Giulio Silano. Toronto: Pontifical Institute of Mediaeval Studies, 2007–10.

Peter Madsen. *Liber Petri Mathie curati ecclesie sancti petri Ripis*. Transcribed by Anne Riising from Msc. Ny kgl. Samling 123 4°, The Royal Library, Copenhagen. Available at http://static.sdu.dk/mediafiles//Files/Om_SDU/Institutter/Ihks/Projekter/Middelalderstudier/Ny_Peder_Madsen.pdf.

Peter of Blois. *Contra perfidiam Judaeorum*. PL 207: 825–71.

———. *The Later Letters of Peter of Blois*. Edited by Elizabeth Revell. Auctores Britannici Medii Aevi 13. Oxford: Oxford University Press, 1993.

Peter of Poitiers. *Summa de confessione: compiliatio praesens*. Edited by Jean Longère. CCCM 51. Turnholt: Brepols, 1980.

Peter the Venerable. *The Letters of Peter the Venerable*. 2 vols. Edited by Giles Constable. Cambridge, Mass.: Harvard University Press, 1967.

———. *Adversus Judeorum inveteratam duritiem*. Edited by Yvonne Friedman. CCCM 58. Turnholt: Brepols, 1985.

———. *De Miraculis*. Edited by D. Bouthillier. CCCM 83. Turnholt: Brepols, 1988.

Petrus Alfonsi. *Der Dialog des Petrus Alfonsi: seine Überlieferung im Druck und in den Handschriften Textedition*. Edited by Klaus Peter-Mieth. Inaug. diss., Freien Universität Berlin, 1982.

———. *Petrus Alfonsi's Dialogue Against the Jews*. Translated by Irven M. Resnick. The Fathers of the Church, Medieval Continuation 8. Washington, D.C.: The Catholic University of America Press, 2006.

Petrus Cantor. *Verbum abbreviatum*. PL 205: 21–555.

Petrus Comestor. *Eine deutsche Schulbibel des 15. Jahrhunderts: Historia scholastica des Petrus Comestor in deutschen Auszug mit lateinischem Paralleltext*. 2 vols. in 1. Edited by D. Hans Vollmer. Berlin: Weidmannsche Buchhandlung, 1925.

———. *Historia Scholastica* PL 198: 1049–1721.

Petrus de Abano. *Conciliator seu enucleatus differentiarum philosophicarum et medicarum*. Edited by G. Horst. Giessae: 1621.

Philo of Alexandria. *Against Flaccus*. In vol. 9 of *Philo*. 10 vols. Translated by F. H. Colson. Cambridge, Mass.: Harvard University Press, 1985.

Physiologus. Translated by Michael J. Curley. Austin: University of Texas Press, 1979.

Pirkê de Rabbi Eliezer. Translated by Gerald Friedlander. New York: Hermon Press, 1916. Reprint, 1970.

Pliny the Elder. *Natural History*. 10 vols. Translated by Harris Rackham. Cambridge, Mass.: Harvard University Press, 1967–75.

Plutarch. *Quaestiones convivales*. eBooks-Adelaide2009. Available at http://ebooks.adelaide.edu.au/p/plutarch/symposiacs/chapter4.html. 2/7/2011.

Pontificum Romanorum qui fuerunt inde ab exeunte saeculo IX usque ad finem saeculi XIII vitae ab aequalibus conscriptae, quas ex Archivi pontifici, bibliothecae Vaticanae aliarumque codicibus adiectis suis cuique et annalibus et documentis gravioribus. Edited by Johann Matthias Watterich. Vol. 2 of *Paschalis II–Coelestinus III (1099–1198)*. 2 vols. Lepizig: sumptibus Guilhelmi Engelmanni, 1862.

The Prose Salernitan Questions. Edited from a Bodleian Manuscript (Auct. F. 3. 10).

Edited by Brian Lawn. London: Oxford University Press, 1979.
Prudentius of Troyes. *Annales Bertiniani*. Edited by G. Waitz. MGH, SS rer. Germ. 5. Hannover: Hahn, 1883.
Ptolemy. *Cl. Ptolomaei Pheludiensis Alexandrini Quadripartitum*. Basel: Johannes Hervagius, 1533.
Rabanus Maurus. *De universo*. PL 111: 9–613.
———. *Commentaria in libros IV Regum*. PL 109: 9–279.
Ralph of Caen. *Gesta Tancredi*. In *Recueil des historiens des croisades. Historiens Occidentaux*. 5 vols. Paris: Academie des Inscriptions et Belles-Lettres, 1844–95.
Ralph of Diceto. *Ymagines Historiarum*. In vol. 2 of *Opera historica*, edited by William Stubbs. 2 vols. London: Longman, 1876.
Ramazzini, Bernardino. *De Morbis Artificum Diatriba*. Translated by Heinrich Singer. In *Allgemeine und spezielle Kranksheitlehre der Juden*. Leipzig: Benno Konegin Verlag, 1904.
Raymund Lull. *Liber de uirtutibus et peccatis siue Ars maior praedicationis*. Edited by F. Dominguez Reboiras and A. Soria Flores. CCCM 76. Turnholt: Brepols, 1987.
Raymund Martini. *Pugio Fidei adversus Mauros et Judaeos*. Leipzig: Sumptibus haeredum Friderici Lanckisi, 1687.
Regimen Sanitatis Salerni: The School of Salernum. Edited by J. Harington. Salerno: Ente Provinciale Per Il Tourismo, 1953.
Richard of Devizes. *Chronicon Richardi Divisiensis de rebus gestis Ricardi primi regis Angliae*. Edited by Joseph Stevenson. London: Sumptibus Societatis, 1838.
Richard of St. Victor. *Adnotationes mysticae in Psalmos*. PL 196: 265–405.
Robert Grosseteste. *Templum Dei*. Edited by Joseph Goering and F. A. C. Mantello. Toronto: Pontifical Institute of Mediaeval Studies, 1984.
———. *De cessatione legalium*. Edited by Richard C. Dales and Edward B. King. London: Oxford University Press, 1986.
———. *Expositio in epistulam sancti Pauli ad Galatas*. Edited by J. McEvoy and L. Rizzerio. CCCM 130. Turnholt: Brepols, 1995.
Robert of Flamborough. *Liber Poenitentialis*. Edited by J. J. F. Firth. Toronto: Pontifical Institute of Mediaeval Studies, 1971.
Robert the Monk. *Historia Iherosolomitana*. In *Recueil des historiens des croisades. Historiens Occidentaux*. 5 vols. Paris: Academie des Inscriptions et Belles-Lettres, 1844–95.
Roger Bacon. *Secretum secretorum*. Edited by Robert Steele. In *Opera hactenus inedita Rogeri Baconi*, fasc. 5. Oxford: Clarendon Press, 1920.
Roger Frugard. *Chiurgia*. In vol. 1 of *Anglo-Norman Medicine*, edited by Tony Hunt. 2 vols. Cambridge: Brewer, 1994.
Roger of Hovedon. *Chronica magistri Rogeri de Houedene*. 4 vols. Edited by William Stubbs. Rerum Brittanicarum Medii Aevi Scriptores 51. London: Longman, 1868–71.
Roger of Wendover. *Flowers of History*. 2 vols. Translated by J. A. Giles. Felinbach: Llanerch, 1994.

Li Romanz de Dieu et de sa mere. Edited by Ina Spiele. Leiden: Presse universitaire de Leiden, 1975.

Rudolf von Schlettstadt. *Historiae Memorabiles zur Dominikanerliteratur und Kulturgeschichte des 13. Jahrhunderts*. Edited by Erich Kleinschmidt. Cologne: Böhlau, 1974.

Rufus of Ephesus. *On Melancholy*. Translated by Peter E. Pormann. Tübingen: Mohr Siebeck, 2008.

Rupert of Deutz. *De sancta Trinitate*. Edited by R. Haacke. CCCM 22. Turnholt: Brepols, 1971–72.

———. *Anulus seu Dialogus inter Christianum et Judaeum*. In *Ruperto di Deutz e la controversia tra Cristiani ed Ebrei nel secolo XII*, by M. L. Arduini. Rome: Istituto storico italiano per il Medio Evo, 1979, 183–242.

Samuel of Morocco. *Liber de adventu messiae praeterito*. PL 149: 333–68.

———. *The Blessed Jew of Morocco or A Blackmoor Made White*. Translated by Thomas Calvert. York: Thomas Broad, 1648.

Scriptores physiognomonici Graeci et Latini. 2 vols. Edited by Richard Foerster. Leipzig: 1893. Reprint, Stuttgart: Teubner, 1994.

Sedulius Scotus. *Collectaneum miscellaneum*. Edited by D. Simpson. CCCM 67. Turnholt: Brepols, 1988–90.

Sefer nitsaḥon yashan. The Jewish-Christian Debate in the High Middle Ages: A Critical Edition of the Nizzaḥon Vetus. Translated by David Berger. Philadelphia: Jewish Publication Society, 1979.

Statuta Capitulorum Generalium Ordinis Cisterciensis ab anno 1116 ad annum 1786. Edited by D. Josephus-Mia Canivez. Bibliothèque de la Revue d'histoire ecclésiastique, fasc. 9–14. Louvain: Bureaux de la Revue, 1933–41.

Statuts d'hôtels-Dieu et de léproseries; recueil de textes du XIIe au XIVe siècle. Edited by Léon Le Grand. Paris: A. Picard, 1901.

Stephen of Bourbon [Etienne de Bourbon]. *Anecdotes Historiques, Légendes et Apologues tirés du recueil inédit d'Étienne de Bourbon*. Edited by A. Lecoy de la Marche. Paris: Librairie Renouard, 1877.

Stuten, Albert. *Weltchronik des Mönchs Albert 1273/77–1454/56*. Edited by Rolf Sprandel. MGH, SS rer. Germ. n.s. 17. Munich: MGH, 1994.

[Conrad of Höxter?] *Summula magistri Conradi*. In *Trois sommes de pénitence de la première moitié du XIIIe siècle: la "Summula Magistri Conradi", les sommes "Quia non pigris" et "Decime dande sunt,"* edited by Jean-Pierre Renard. 2 vols. Louvain-la-Neuve: Diffusion, Centre Cerfaux-Lefort, 1989.

Tacitus. *Histories: Books 4–5*. Translated by Clifford H. Moore. Loeb Classical Library. London: Heinemann, 1931.

Tacuinum Sanitatis. The Medieval Health Handbook. Edited by Luisa Cogliati Arano. Translated by Oscar Ratti and Adele Westbrook. New York: Braziller: 1976.

Theodoric, Abbot of St. Trond. *Pitulus*. In *The Virgilian Tradition: The First Fifteen Hundred Years*, edited by Jan M. Ziolkowski and Michael C. J. Putnam. New Haven: Yale University Press, 2008, 481–85.

Theodorich Borgognoni. *The Surgery of Theodoric, ca. AD 1267*. 2 vols. Edited by

B. Locatellus. Translated by Eldridge Campbell and James Colton. New York: Appleton-Century-Crofts, 1955-60.
Thesaurus Exemplorum. Edited by J. Th. Welter. Fasc. 5: *Le Speculum laicorum*. Paris: Libraire des Archives Nationales et de la Societé de l'Ecole des Chartes, 1914.
Thomas Aquinas. *Summa theologica*. 6 vols. Rome: Ex typographia Forzani, 1927-28.
———. *Scriptum super libros Sententiarum*. 4 vols. Edited by P. Mandonnet and M. F. Moos. Paris: Lethielleux, 1929-47.
Thomas Ebendorfer. *Chronica regum Romanorum*. Edited by Harald Zimmermann. MGH, SS rer. Germ. n.s. 18. Hannover: Hahn, 2003.
Thomas of Cantimpré. *Miraculorum et exemplorum memorabilium sui temporis, libri duo*. Douai: Bellerus, 1605.
———. *Liber de natura rerum*. Edited by H. Boese. Berlin: de Gruyter, 1973.
———. *De natura rerum (Lib. IV-XII): Tacuinum Sanitatis*. 2 vols. Codice C-67 (fols. 2v-116r) de la Biblioteca Universitaria de Granada, commentarios a la edición facsimile. Edited by Luis García Ballester. Granada: Universidad de Granada, 1974.
Thomas of Celano [?]. *Legenda sanctae Clarae Virginis*. Edited by Francesco Pannecchi. Assisi: Tip. Metastasio, 1910.
Thomas of Chobham. *Summa Confessorum*. Edited by F. Broomfield. Analecta mediaevalia Namurcensia 25. Louvain: Éditions Nauwelaerts, 1968.
———. *Thomas de Chobham Sermones*. Edited by Franco Morenzoni. CCCM 82A. Turnholt: Brepols, 1993.
Thomas of Monmouth. *The Life and Miracles of St.William of Norwich by Thomas of Monmouth. Now First Edited from the Unique Manuscript, with an Introduction, Translation and Notes*. Edited and translated by Augustus Jessopp and M. R. James. Cambridge: University Press, 1896.
Thomas of Wroclaw. *Thomae de Wratislavia Practica medicinalis: A Critical Edition of the "Practica medicinalis" of Thomas of Wroclaw, Prémontré Bishop of Sarepta (1297-c. 1378)*. Edited by Theodore James Antry. Warsaw: Polish Academy of Sciences Press, 1989.
Thomas Walsingham. *Historia anglicana*. 2 vols. Edited by Henry Thomas Riley. London: Longman, 1863-64.
Three Prose Versions of the Secreta Secretorum. Edited by Robert Steele and T. Henderson. Early English Text Society, extra series 74. London: Kegan Paul, Trench, Trübner, 1898.
The Treasurie of Health Containing Many Profitable Medicines, Gathered Out of Hipocrates, Galen and Avicenna by One Petrus Hyspanus. Translated by Humphry Lloyd. London: Thomas Hacker, 1585.
El tribunal de la Inquisición en el obispado de Soria (1486-1502). Edited by Carlos Carrete Paddondo. Fontes Iudaeorum Regni Castellae 2. Salamanca: Salamanca Universidad Pontificia de Salamanca- Universidad de Granada, 1985.
Les Trophées de Damas: Controverse Judéo-Chrétienne du VIIe Siècle. Edited and translated by Gustave Bardy. In *Patrologiae Orientalis* 15, no. 2 (1920): 173-275.

The Trotula: A Medieval Compendium of Women's Medicine. Edited and translated by Monica H. Green. Philadelphia: University of Pennsylvania Press, 2001.

Vallo, Lorenzo. *De falso credita et ementita Constantini donatione.* Edited by Wolfram Setz. MGH, QQ Geistesgesch, 10. Weimar: Böhlau, 1976.

La Vengeance de Nostre-Seigneur. The Old and Middle French Prose Versions: The Version of Japheth. Edited by Alvin E. Ford. Studies and Texts 63. Toronto: Pontifical Institute of Mediaeval Studies, 1984.

Vetus Latina. Vol. 2: *Genesis.* Edited by Bonifatius Fischer. Freiburg: Herder, 1951.

Vincent of Beauvais. *Speculum quadruplex, sive, Speculum maius: naturale, doctrinale, morale, historiale.* Graz, Austria: Duaci: Akademische Druck-u. Verlagsanstalt; ex officina typographica Baltazaris Belleri, 1964–65.

Vincent Ferrer. *Tractatus contra Judeorum detestabilem horrendam veteremque perfidiam.* In vol. 1 of *Oeuvres de Saint Vincent Ferrer,* edited by Pierre Henri Fages. 2 vols. Paris: A. Picard et fils, 1909.

Werner of St. Blaise. *Libri deflorationum.* PL 157: 721–1255.

William of Auvergne. *De legibus.* In *Opera omnia.* 2 vols. in 1. Venice: Ex officina Damiani Zenari, 1591.

William of Auxerre. *Summa Aurea in quattuor libros Sententiarum.* 6 vols. Edited by Jean Ribailler. Spicilegium Bonaventurianum 16–20. Grottaferrata and Paris: Collegii S. Bonaventurae ad Claras Aquas, 1980–87.

William of Canterbury. *Vita et Passio S. Thomas.* In vol. 1 of *Materials for the History of Thomas Becket,* edited by James Craigie Robertson. 7 vols. Rolls Series. London: Longman, 1875–85.

William of Champeaux. *Dialogus inter christianum et judaeum de fide catholica.* PL 163: 1045–73.

William of Conches. *De philosophia mundi.* PL 172: 39–101.

———. *Glosae super Platonem.* Edited by Édouard Jeauneau. Paris: Librairie Philosophique J. Vrin, 1965.

———. *A Dialogue on Natural Philosophy (Dragmaticon Philosophiae).* Translated by Italo Ronca and Matthew Curr. Notre Dame, Ind.: University of Notre Dame Press, 1997.

———. *Dragmaticon.* Edited by Italo Ronca. CCCM 152. Turnholt: Brepols, 1997.

William of Malmesbury. *Gesta regum Anglorum atque Historia Novella.* 2 vols. Edited by Thomas Duffus Hardy. London: 1840.

———. *De gestis pontificum Anglorum.* Edited by N. E. S. A. Hamilton. London: Longman, 1870.

———. *El libro de Laudibus et Miraculis Sanctae Mariae de Guillermo de Malmesbury, O.S.B.,* Edited by J. M. Canal. *Claretianum* 8 (1968): 71–242.

William of St. Thierry. *The Nature of the Body and Soul.* Translated by Benjamin Clark. In *Three Treatises on Man. A Cistercian Anthropology,* edited by Bernard McGinn. Kalamazoo, Mich.: Cistercian Publications, 1977.

———. *Liber de natura corporis et animae.* Edited by Stanislas Ceglar and Paul Verdeyen. CCCM 86–88, part 3. Turnholt: Brepols, 1988.

Yehudah HeChasid. *Sefer Chasidim: The Book of the Pious.* Translated by Avraham Yaakov Finkel. Northvale, N.J.: Jason Aronson, 1997.

Zachary, Pope. *Epistola* 13 [to St. Boniface]. PL 89: 950–53.
Zerbi, Gabriele. *Gerontocomia: On the Care of the Aged, and Maximianus: Elegies on Old Age and Love.* Translated by L. R. Lind. Philadelphia: American Philosophical Society, 1988.

Manuscripts
Bodleian MS Cod. Marsh 663.
British Library Cotton, Cleopatra D.

SECONDARY SOURCES

Abramson, Henry, and Carrie Hanson. "Depicting the Ambiguous Wound: Circumcision in Medieval Art." In *The Covenant of Circumcision: New Perspectives on an Ancient Rite,* edited by Elizabeth Wyner Mark. Lebanon, N.H.: University Press of New England, 2003, 98–113.
Abulafia, Anna Sapir. "An Eleventh-Century Exchange of Letters between a Christian and a Jew." *Journal of Medieval History* 7 (1981): 153–74.
———. "Christian Imagery of Jews in the Twelfth Century: A Look at Odo of Cambrai and Guibert of Nogent." *Theoretische Geschiedenis* (= *Historiography and Theory*) 16, no. 4 (1989): 383–91.
———. *Christians and Jews in the Twelfth-Century Renaissance.* London: Routledge, 1995.
———. "Twelfth-Century Renaissance Theology and the Jews." In *From Witness to Witchcraft: Jews and Judaism in Medieval Christian Thought,* edited by Jeremy Cohen. Wolfenbütteler Mittelalter-Studien 11. Wiesbaden: Harrassowitz Verlag, 1996, 125–39.
———. "Invectives against Christianity in the Hebrew Chronicles of the First Crusade." In Abulafia, *Christians and Jews in Dispute.* Ashgate: Variorum, 1998, XVIII: 66–72.
———. "The Intellectual and Spiritual Quest for Christ and Central Medieval Persecution of Jews." In *Religious Violence between Christians and Jews: Medieval Roots, Modern Perspectives,* edited by Anna Sapir Abulafia. New York: Palgrave, 2002, 61–85.
Adang, Camilla. "Ibn Chazm's Criticism of Some 'Judaizing' Tendencies among the Mâlikites." *Medieval and Modern Perspectives on Muslim-Jewish Relations,* edited by Ronald L. Nettler. Studies in Muslim-Jewish Relations 2. Luxembourg: Harwood Academic Publishers, 1995, 1–15.
Adler, Michael. *Jews of Medieval England.* London: Jewish Historical Society of England, 1893. Reprint, Amersham, England, 1984.
———. *The History of the Domus Conversorum 1290–1891.* London[?]: Ballantyne Press, n.d.
Ages, Arnold. "Tainted Greatness: The Case of Voltaire's Anti-Semitism." *Neohelicon* 21, no. 2 (1994): 357–67.
Agrimi, Jole. "Fisiognomica e 'Scolastica.'" In *I Discorsi dei corpi.* Vol. 1 of *Micrologus: natura, scienze e società medievali.* Turnholt: Brepols, 1993, 235–71.

---. "Fisiognomica: nature allo specchio ovvero luce e ombre." In *Il Teatro della natura*. Vol. 4 of *Micrologus, natura, scienze e società medievali medievali. Nature, Sciences, and Medieval Societies*. Turnholt: Brepols, 1996, 129-78.

Agrimi, Jole, and Chiara Crisciani. "Charity and Aid in Medieval Christian Civilization." In *Western Medical Thought from Antiquity to the Middle Ages*, edited by Mirko D. Grmek and translated by Antony Shugaar. Cambridge, Mass.: Harvard University Press, 1998, 170-96.

Akasoy, Anna. "Arabic Physiognomy as a Link between Astrology and Medicine." In *Astro-Medicine: Astrology and Medicine East and West*, edited by Anna Akasoy, Charles Burnett, and Ronit Yoeli-Tlalim. Micrologus Library 25. Florence: SISMEL, 2008, 119-41.

Akbari, Suzanne Conklin. *Idols in the East: European Representations of Islam and the Orient, 1100-1450*. Ithaca, N.Y.: Cornell University Press, 2009.

Aldeeb Abu-Sahlieh, S. A. "Jehovah, His Cousin Allah, and Sexual Mutilations." In *Sexual Mutilations: A Human Tragedy*, edited by George Denniston and Marilyn Fayre Milos. New York: Plenum Press, 1997, 41-63.

Allen, Peter Lewis. *The Wages of Sin: Sex and Disease, Past and Present*. Chicago: University of Chicago Press, 2000.

Angerstorfer, Andreas. "Jüdische Reaktionen auf die mittelalterlichen Blutbeschuldigungen vom 13.bis zum 16. Jahrhundert." In *Die Legende vom Ritualmord: zur Geschichte der Blutbeschuldigung gegen Juden*, edited by Rainer Erb. Berlin: Metropol, 1993, 133-77.

Arad, Yitzhak, Yisrael Gutman, and Abraham Margaliot, eds. *Documents on the Holocaust*. 4th ed. Jerusalem: Yad Vashem, 1990.

Assis, Yom Tov. "Juifs de France réfugiés en Aragon (XIII-XIV siècles)." *Revue des Etudes Juives* 142 (1983): 299-302.

---. "The Papal Inquisition and Aragonese Jewry in the Early Fourteenth Century." *Mediaeval Studies* 49 (1987): 391-410.

---, ed. *The Jews in the Crown of Aragon. Regesta of the* Cartas Reales *in the Archivo de la Corona de Aragón, Part II: 1328-1493*. Sources for the History of the Jews in Spain 5. Compiled by Gemma Escribà. Jerusalem: Henk Schussheim Memorial Series, 1995.

---, ed. *The Tortosa Disputation. Regesta of Documents from the Archivo de la Corona de Aragón, Fernando I 1412-1416*. Sources for the History of the Jews in Spain 6. Compiled by Gemma Escribà. Jerusalem: Henk Schussheim Memorial Series, 1998.

Avril, J. "Le IIIe Concile de Latran et les communautés de lépreux." *Revue Mabillon. Archives de la France monastiques* 60, no. 284 (1981): 21-32; 60, no. 285 (1981): 33-64; 60, no. 286 (1981): 65-76.

Azouvi, François. "The Plague, Melancholy and the Devil." *Diogenes* 108 (1979): 112-30.

Baer, Eva. "Representations of 'Planet Children' in Turkish Manuscripts." *Bulletin of the School of Oriental and African Studies, University of London* 31, no. 3 (1968): 526-33.

Bagchi, David. "Catholic Anti-Judaism in Reformation Germany: The Case of Johann Eck." In *Christianity and Judaism. Papers Read at the 1991 Summer*

Meeting and the 1992 Winter Meeting of the Ecclesiastical History Society, edited by Diana Wood. Cambridge, Mass.: Ecclesiastical History Society, 1992, 253–63.
Bale, Anthony. "Fictions of Judaism in England before 1290." In *Jews in Medieval Britain: Historical, Literary, and Archaeological Perspectives,* edited by Patricia Skinner. Rochester, N.Y.: Boydell & Brewer, 2003, 129–45.
———. *The Jew in the Medieval Book: English Antisemitisms 1350–1500.* Cambridge: Cambridge University Press, 2006.
———. "The Female 'Jewish' Libido in Medieval Culture." In *A Search for the Erotic in Medieval Britain,* edited by Amanda Hopkins and Cory Rushton. Cambridge: Brewer, 2007, 94–104.
Barasch, Moshe. "Despair in the Medieval Imagination." *Social Research* 66, no. 2 (1999): 565–76.
Barbado, F. M. "La physionomie, le tempérament et le caractère, d'après Albert le Grand et la science modern." *Revue Thomiste* 36 (1931): 314–51.
Barber, Malcolm. "Lepers, Jews and Moslems: The Plot to Overthrow Christendom in 1321." *History* 66 (1981): 1–17.
Barlow, Frank. "The King's Evil." In Barlow, *The Norman Conquest and Beyond.* London: Hambledon Press, 1983, 23–47.
Baron, Salo Wittmeyer. *A Social and Religious History of the Jews.* 2nd ed. 11 vols. New York: Columbia University Press, 1960.
Bartlet, Suzanne. "Women in the Medieval Anglo-Jewish Community." In *Jews in Medieval Britain: Historical, Literary, and Archaeological Perspectives,* edited by Patricia Skinner. Rochester, N.Y.: Boydell & Brewer, 2003, 113–28.
Bartlett, Robert. *The Hanged Man: A Story of Miracle, Memory, and Colonialism in the Middle Ages.* Princeton N.J.: Princeton University Press, 2004.
———. "Illustrating Ethnicity in the Middle Ages." In *The Origins of Racism in the West,* edited by Miriam Eliav Feldon, Benjamin Isaac, and Joseph Ziegler. Cambridge: Cambridge University Press, 2009, 132–56.
Bauchau, Bénédicte. "Science et racisme: les Juifs, la lépre et la peste." *Stanford French Review* 13, no. 1 (1989): 21–35.
Baumgarten, Elisheva. "Marking the Flesh: Circumcision, Blood, and Inscribing Identity on the Body in Medieval Jewish Culture." In *La pelle umana; The Human Skin.* Vol. 13 of *Micrologus: Natura, scienze e società medievali. Nature, Sciences and Medieval Societies.* Florence: SISMEL, 2005, 313–30.
Bédier, Joseph. "The Legend of Tristan and Isolt." *International Quarterly* 9, no. 1 (1904): 103–28.
Benart, Haim. *Trujillo: A Jewish Community in Extremadura on the Eve of the Expulsion from Spain.* Hispanica Judaica 2. Jerusalem: Magnes Press, 1980.
Bennett, Wendy Ayres. *A History of the French Language through Texts.* New York: Routledge, 1996.
Ben-Shalom, Ram. "The Social Context of Apostasy among Fifteenth-Century Spanish Jewry." In *Rethinking European Jewish History,* edited by Jeremy Cohen and Moshe Rosman. Oxford: Littman Library of Jewish Civilization, 2009, 173–98.
Berger, Abraham. "Captive at the Gate of Rome: The Story of a Messianic Motif." *Proceedings of the American Academy for Jewish Research* 44 (1977): 1–17.

Berger, David. "St. Peter Damian. His Attitudes toward the Jews and the Old Testament." *Yavneh* 4 (1965): 80–112.
Bériac, Francoise. "La persécution des lépreux dans la France méridionale en 1321." *Le moyen âge* 93, no. 2 (1987): 203–21.
———. "Connaisances médicales sur la lèpre et protection contre cette maladie au Moyen Age." In *Maladies et société (XIIe–XVIIIe siècles). Actes du Colloque de Bielfeld, novembre 1986*, edited by Neithard Bulst and Robert Delort. Paris: Editions du C.N.R.S., 1989, 145–63.
———. "À propos de la fin de la lèpre: XIIIe–XVe siècles." In *The Regulation of Evil. Social and Cultural Attitudes to Epidemics in the Late Middle Ages*, edited by Agostino Paravicini Bagliani and Francesco Santi. Florence: SISMEL, 1998, 159–173.
Beriou, Nicole. "L'image de l'autre: Le lepreux sous le regard des predicateurs au moyen age." *L'histoire aujourd'hui*, section d'histoire. Liège: Université de Liège, 1988, 1–12.
———, and François-Olivier Touati. *Voluntate Dei Leprosus: Les Lépreux entre conversion et exclusion aux XIIème et XIIIème siècles*. Spoleto: Centro italiano di studi sull'alto medioevo, 1991.
Berkey, Jonathan. "Women in Medieval Islamic Society." In *Women in Medieval Western European Culture*, edited by Linda E. Mitchell. New York: Garland, 1999, 95–116.
Bertelli, Sergio. *The King's Body*. Translated by R. Burr Litchfield. University Park: Pennsylvania State University Press, 2001.
Beusterien, John L. "Jewish Male Menstruation in Seventeenth-Century Spain." *Bulletin of the History of Medicine* 73, no. 3 (1999): 447–56.
———. *An Eye on Race: Perspectives from Theater in Imperial Spain*. Lewisburg, Pa.: Bucknell University Press, 2006.
Biale, David. *Eros and the Jews: From Biblical Israel to Contemporary America*. New York: Basic Books, 1992.
———. *Blood and Belief: The Circulation of a Symbol between Jews and Christians*. Berkeley: University of California Press, 2007.
Biller, Peter. "Views of Jews from Paris around 1300: Christian or 'Scientific'?" In *Christianity and Judaism. Papers Read at the 1991 Summer Meeting and the 1992 Winter Meeting of the Ecclesiastical History Society*, edited by Diana Wood. Cambridge, Mass.: Ecclesiastical History Society, 1992, 187–207.
———. "Applying Number to Men and Women in the Thirteenth and Fourteenth Centuries: An Enquiry into the Origins of the Idea of 'Sex-Ratio.'" In *The Work of Jacques Le Goff and the Challenges of Medieval History*, edited by Miri Rubin. Woodbridge, Suffolk: Boydell Press, 1997, 27–51.
———. "John of Naples, Quodlibets and Medieval Theological Concern with the Body." *Medieval Theology and the Natural Body*, edited by Peter Biller and A. J. Minnis. York Studies in Medieval Theology 1. Woodbridge, Suffolk: York Medieval Press, 1997, 3–12.
———. "A 'Scientific' View of Jews from Paris around 1300." In *Gli Ebrei e le Scienze; The Jews and the Sciences*. Vol. 9 of *Micrologus. Natura, scienze e società*

medievali. Nature, Sciences, and Medieval Societies. Florence: SISMEL, 2001, 138–67.

———. "Black Women in Medieval Scientific Thought." In *La pelle umana; The Human Skin.* Vol. 13 of *Micrologus: Natura, scienze e società medievali. Nature, Sciences and Medieval Societies.* Florence: SISMEL, 2005, 477–92.

Biller, Peter, and Joseph Ziegler, eds. *Religion and Medicine in the Middle Ages.* York: York Medieval Press, 2001.

Biraben, Jean Noël. "Diseases in Europe: Equilibrium and Breakdown of the Pathocenosis." In *Western Medical Thought from Antiquity to the Middle Ages,* edited by Mirko D. Grmek. Translated by Antony Shugaar. Cambridge, Mass.: Harvard University Press, 1998, 319–54.

Bloch, Herbert. "The Schism of Anacletus II and the Glanfeuil Forgeries of Peter the Deacon of Monte Cassino." *Traditio* 8 (1952): 159–259.

Bloch, Marc. *Les rois thaumaturges: étude sur le caractére surnaturel attribué à la puissance royale particuliérement en France et en Angleterre.* Paris: Gallimard, 1983.

———. *The Royal Touch.* Translated by J. E. Anderson. New York: Dorset Press, 1989.

Blumenkranz, Bernhard. *Juifs et chrétiens dans le monde occidental, 430–1096.* Paris: Mouton, 1960.

———. "Jüdische und christliche Konvertiten im jüdische-christlichen Religionsgespräch des Mittelalters." In *Judentum im Mittelalter. Beiträge zum christlich-jüdischen Gespräch,* edited by Paul Wilpert. Miscellanea Mediaevalia 4. Berlin: de Gruyter, 1966, 264–82.

Bondy, Gottlieb, and Franz Dworsky. *Zur Geschichte der Juden in Böhmen, Mähren und Schlesien von 906 bis 1620.* Prague: Bondy, 1906.

Bonfil, Robert. "The Devil and the Jews in the Christian Consciousness of the Middle Ages." In *Antisemitism through the Ages,* edited by Shmuel Almog. Oxford: Pergamon Press, 1988, 91–98.

———. "Cultural and Religious Traditions in Ninth-Century French Jewry." In *Jewish Intellectual History in the Middle Ages,* edited by Joseph Dan. Westport, Conn.: Praeger, 1994, 1–17.

Bonkalo, Ervin. "Criminal Proceedings against Animals in the Middle Ages." *Journal of Unconventional History* 3, no. 2 (1992): 25–31.

Boswell, John. *Christianity, Social Tolerance, and Homosexuality: Gay People in Western Europe from the Beginning of the Christian era to the Fourteenth Century.* Chicago: University of Chicago Press, 1980.

Bouce, Paul-Gabriel. "Imagination, Pregnant Women and Monsters in Eighteenth-Century England and France." In *Sexual Underworlds of the Enlightment,* edited by G. S. Rousseau and Roy Porter. Chapel Hill: University of North Carolina, 1988, 86–100.

Boulton, Maureen. "Anti-Jewish Attitudes in Anglo-Norman Religious Texts: Twelfth and Thirteenth Centuries." In *Christian Attitudes toward Jews in the Middle Ages: A Casebook,* edited by Michael Frassetto. New York: Routledge, 2007, 151–65.

Brand, Paul. "Jews and the Law in England, 1275–90." *English Historical Review* 115 (2000): 1138–58.
Brenner, Elma. "Recent Perspectives on Leprosy in Medieval Western Europe." *History Compass* 8, no. 5 (2010): 388–406.
Brodman, James W. "Shelter and Segregation: Lepers in Medieval Catalonia." In *On the Social Origins of Medieval Institutions: Essays in Honor of Joseph F. O'Callaghan,* edited by Donald J. Kagay and Theresa M. Vann. Leiden: Brill, 1998, 35–45.
Brody, Saul N. *The Disease of the Soul: Leprosy in Medieval Literature*. Ithaca, N.Y.: Cornell University Press, 1974.
Brown, Reva Berman, and Sean McCartney. "The Business Activities of Jewish Women Entrepeneurs in Medieval England." *Management Decision* 39, no. 9 (2001): 699–709.
Brumberg-Kraus, Jonathan. "Meat-Eating and Jewish Identity: Ritualization of the Priestly 'Torah of Beast and Fowl' (Lev. 11:46) in Rabbinic Judaism and Medieval Kabbalah." *AJS Review* 24, no. 2 (1999): 227–62.
Brundage, James A. "Prostitution, Miscegenation and Sexual Purity in the First Crusade." In *Crusade and Settlement,* edited by Peter W. Edbury. Cardiff, UK: University College Cardiff Press, 1985, 57–65.
———. "Intermarriage between Christians and Jews in Medieval Canon Law." *Jewish History* 3, no. 1 (1988): 25–40
Buc, Phillipe. "David's Adultery with Bathsheba and the Healing Power of Capetian Kings." *Viator* 24 (1993): 101–20.
Bullough, Vern L., and Gwen Whitehead Brewer. "Medieval Masculinities and Modern Interpretations: The Problem of the Pardoner." In *Conflicted Identities and Multiple Masculinities: Men in the Medieval West,* edited by Jacqueline Murray. New York: Garland, 1999, 93–110.
Burnett, Charles. "The Planets and the Development of the Embryo." In *The Human Embryo: Aristotle and the Arabic and European Traditions,* edited by G. R. Dunstan. Exeter: University of Exeter Press, 1990, 95–112.
———. "Hermann of Carinthia." In *A History of Twelfth Century Western Philosophy,* edited by Peter Dronke. Cambridge: Cambridge University Press, 1992, 386–406.
———. "Michael Scot and the Transmission of Scientific Culture from Toledo to Bologna via the Court of Frederick II Hohenstaufen." In *Le scienze alla corte di Federico II*. Vol. 2 of *Micrologus: Natura, scienze e società medievali*. Turnholt: Brepols, 1994, 101–26.
Burr, David. "Antichrist and Islam in Medieval Franciscan Exegesis." In *Medieval Christian Perceptions of Islam: A Book of Essays,* edited by John Victor Tolan. New York: Garland, 1996, 131–52.
Cabaniss, Alan. "Bodo-Eleazar: A Famous Jewish Convert." *Jewish Quarterly Review* 43, no. 4 (1953): 313–28.
Callahan, Daniel "The Cross, the Jews, and the Destruction of the Church of the Holy Sepulcher in the Writings of Ademar of Chabannes." In *Christian Attitudes toward Jews in the Middle Ages: A Casebook,* edited by Michael Frassetto. New York: Routledge, 2007, 15–24.

Carey, Hilary M. "Medieval Latin Astrology and the Cycles of Life: William English and English Medicine in Cambridge, Trinity College MS 0.5.26." In *Astro-Medicine: Astrology and Medicine East and West*, edited by Anna Akasoy, Charles Burnett, and Ronit Yoeli-Tlalim. Micrologus' Library 25. Florence: SISMEL, 2008, 33–74.

Carlebach, Elisheva. *Divided Souls: Converts from Judaism in Germany, 1500–1700*. New Haven: Yale University Press, 2001.

Carpenter, David. "St. Thomas Cantilupe: His Political Career." In *St Thomas Cantilupe, Bishop of Hereford: Essays in His Honor*, edited by Meryl Jancey. Hereford: Friends of Hereford Cathedral, 1982, 57–72.

Carpenter, Dwayne E. "The Portrayal of the Jew in Alfonso the Learned's *Cantigas de Santa Maria*." In *In Iberia and Beyond: Hispanic Jews between Cultures*, edited by Bernard Dov Cooperman. Cranbury, N.J.: Associated University Presses, 1998, 15–42.

Castro, Américo. "Disputa entre un cristiano y un judío." *Revista der filología española* 1 (1914): 173–80.

Catalini, Claire. "*Luxuria* and Its Branches." In *Sex, Love and Marriage in Medieval Literature and Reality: thematische Beiträge im Rahmen des 31th International Congress on Medieval Studies an der Western Michigan University* (Kalamazoo, USA) 8.–12. Mai 1996. Kalamazoo, Mich.: International Congress on Medieval Studies, 1996, 13–20.

Catane, Moché. "Le vetement en France au XIe siecle d'apres les ecrits de Rashi." In *Rashi et la culture juive en France du Nord au moyen âge*, edited by Gilbert Dahan, Gérard Nahon, and Elie Nicholas. Paris: Peeters, 1997, 123–33.

Cattin, Yves. "Proslogion et De Veritate, 'Ratio, Fides, Veritas.'" In *Les mutations socio-culturelles au tournant des XIe–XIIe siècles*. Actes du Colloque international du CNRS, Études Anselmiennes (IVe session). Paris: Editions du Centre national de la recherche scientifique, 1984, 595–610.

Catto, Jeremy. "The Academic Career of Thomas Cantilupe." In *St Thomas Cantilupe, Bishop of Hereford: Essays in His Honor*, edited by Meryl Jancey. Hereford: Friends of Hereford Cathedral, 1982, 45–56.

Chazan, Robert. *Barcelona and Beyond: The Disputation of 1263 and Its Aftermath*. Berkeley: University of California Press, 1992.

———. *European Jewry and the First Crusade*. Berkeley: University of California Press, 1996.

———. "Twelfth-Century Perceptions of the Jews: A Case Study of Bernard of Clairvaux and Peter the Venerable." In *From Witness to Witchcraft: Jews and Judaism in Medieval Christian Thought*, edited by Jeremy Cohen. Wolfenbütteler Mittelalter-Studien 11. Wiesbaden: Harrassowitz Verlag, 1996, 187–201.

———. *Medieval Stereotypes and Modern Antisemitism*. Berkeley: University of California Press, 1997.

———. *Fashioning Jewish Identity in Medieval Western Christendom*. Cambridge: Cambridge University Press, 2004.

———. "'Let Not a Remnant or a Residue Escape': Millenarian Enthusiasm in the First Crusade." *Speculum* 84, no. 2 (2009): 289–313.

———, ed. *Church, State, and Jew in the Middle Ages.* West Orange, N.J.: Behrman House, 1980.
Chodorow, Stanley. "Ecclesiastical Politics and the Ending of the Investiture Contest: The Papal Election of 1119 and the Negotiations of Mouzon." *Speculum* 46, no. 4 (1971): 613–40.
Clark, Elizabeth A. "The Place of Jerome's Commentary on Ephesians in the Origenist Controversy: The Apokatastasis and Ascetic Ideals." *Vigiliae Christianae* 41, no. 2 (1987): 154–71.
Clay, Rotha Mary. *The Mediaeval Hospitals of England.* London: Methuen, 1909.
Cohen, Esther. "Animals in Medieval Perceptions: The Image of the Ubiquitous Other." In *Animals and Human Society: Changing Perspectives,* edited by Aubrey Manning and James Serpell. London: Routledge, 1994, 59–80.
Cohen, Jeffrey Jerome. "On Saracen Enjoyment: Some Fantasies of Race in Late Medieval France and England." *Journal of Medieval and Early Modern Studies* 31, no.1 (2001): 113–46.
Cohen, Jeremy. *Living Letters of the Law: Ideas of the Jew in Medieval Christianity.* Berkeley: University of California Press, 1999.
———. *Christ Killers: The Jews and the Passion from the Bible to the Big Screen.* New York: Oxford University Press, 2007.
Cohen, Shaye J. D. "A Brief History of Jewish Circumcision Blood." In *The Covenant of Circumcision: New Perspectives on an Ancient Jewish Rite,* edited by Elizabeth Wyner Mark. Hanover, N.H.: University Press of New England, 2003, 30–42.
———. *Why Aren't Jewish Women Circumcised? Gender and Covenant in Judaism.* Berkeley: University of California Press, 2005.
Cooper, Samuel. "Names and Cultural Documents." In *These Are the Names: Studies in Jewish Onomastics,* edited by Aaron Demsky. 2 vols. Ramat Gan: Bar-Ilan University Press, 1999, 13–23.
Courtenay, William. "Curers of Body and Soul: Medical Doctors as Theologians." In *Religion and Medicine in the Middle Ages,* edited by Peter Biller and Joseph Ziegler. York: York Medieval Press, 2001, 69–75.
Cowdrey, H. E. J. *Pope Gregory VII, 1073–1085.* Oxford: Oxford University Press, 1998.
Cristiani, Riccardo. "Integration and Maginalization: Dealing with the Sick in Eleventh-Century Cluny." In *From Dead of Night to End of Day: The Medieval Customs of Cluny,* edited by Susan Boynton and Isabelle Cochelin. Turnholt: Brepols, 2005, 287–95.
Cuffel, Alexandra. *Gendering Disgust in Medieval Religious Polemic.* Notre Dame, Ind.: University of Notre Dame Press, 2007.
Cule, Johon. "The Stigma of Leprosy: Its historical origins and consequences with particular reference to the laws of Wales." In *The Past and Present of Leprosy. Archaeological, historical, palaeopathological and clinical approaches: Proceedings of the International Congress on the Evolution and Palaeoepidemiology of the Infectious Diseases 3 (ICEPID), University of Bradford, 26th–31st July 1999,* edited by C. A. Robertson, et al. Oxford: Archaeopress, 2002, 149–54.

Curry, Walter Clyde. *Chaucer and the Medieval Sciences.* New York: Barnes and Noble, 1960.

Cutler, Allan. "Peter the Venerable and Islam." *Journal of the American Oriental Society* 86 (1966): 184–98.

Czarnowus, Anna. "'My cours, that hath so wyde for to turne, / hath moore power than woot any man': The Children of Saturn in Chaucer's Monk's Tale." *Studia Anglica Posnaniensia* 40 (2004): 299–310.

Dahan, Gilbert. "L'exégèse de l'histoire de Caïn et Abel du XIIe au XIVe siècle en Occident." *Recherches de théologie ancienne et médiévale* 49 (1982): 21–89; 50 (1983): 5–68.

———. "Un dossier latin de textes de Rashi autour de la controverse de 1240." *Revue des Etudes Juives* 151, no. 3–4 (1992): 321–36.

———. "L'usage de la *ratio* dans la polémique contres les juifs, XIIe–XIVe siècles." In *Diálogo Filosófico-Religioso Entre Christianismo, Judaísmo e Islamismo Durante La Edad Media En La Península Iberica,* edited by Horacio Santiago-Otero. S.I.E.P.M. 3. Turnout: Brepols, 1994, 289–307.

———. "Juifs et judaïsme dans la littérature quodlibétique." In *From Witness to Witchcraft: Jews and Judaism in Medieval Christian Thought,* edited by Jeremy Cohen. Wolfenbütteler Mittelalter-Studien 11. Wiesbaden: Harrassowitz Verlag, 1996, 221–45.

D'Arcy, Anne Marie. "Li anemis meismes: Satan and Synagogue in La Queste del Saint Graal." *Medium Aevum* 66, no. 2 (1997): 207–35.

Demaitre, Luke. *Doctor Bernard de Gordon: Professor and Practicioner.* Studies and Texts 51. Toronto: Pontifical Institute of Mediaeval Studies, 1980.

———. "The Description and Diagnosis of Leprosy by Fourteenth-Century Physicians." *Bulletin of the History of Medicine* 59 (1985): 327–44.

———. "The Relevance of Futility: Jordanus de Turre (fl. 1313–1335) on the Treatment of Leprosy." *Bulletin of the History of Medicine* 70 (1996): 25–61.

———. *Leprosy in Premodern Medicine: A Malady of the Whole Body.* Baltimore: Johns Hopkins University Press, 2007.

Despres, Denise L. "Mary of the Eucharist: Cultic Anti-Judaism in Some Fourteenth-Century English Devotional Manuscripts." In *From Witness to Witchcraft: Jews and Judaism in Medieval Christian Thought,* edited by Jeremy Cohen. Wolfenbütteler Mittelalter-Studien 11. Wiesbaden: Harrassowitz Verlag, 1996, 375–401.

———. "Immaculate Flesh and the Social Body: Mary and the Jews." *Jewish History* 12, no. 1 (1998): 47–69.

———. "Adolescence and Sanctity: The Life and Passion of Saint William of Norwich." *Journal of Religion* 90, no. 1 (2010): 33–62.

DeWhurst, Kenneth. *John Locke (1632–1704): Physician and Philosopher.* London: Wellcome Historical Medical Library, 1963.

Diemling, Maria. "'As the Jews like to Eat Garlick': Garlic in Christian-Jewish Polemical Discourse in Early Modern Germany." In *Food and Judaism,* edited by Leonard J. Greenspoon, Ronald A. Simkins, and Gerald Shapiro. Omaha: Creighton University Press, 2004, 215–34.

Dobson, R. Barrie. *The Jews of Medieval York and the Massacre of March, 1190.* York: St. Anthony's Press, 1974.

———. "The Role of Jewish Women in Medieval England." In *Christianity and Judaism. Papers Read at the 1991 Summer Meeting and the 1992 Winter Meeting of the Ecclesiastical History Society,* edited by Diana Wood. Cambridge, Mass.: Ecclesiastical History Society, 1992, 145–68.

Dols, Michael W. "Leprosy in Medieval Arabic Medicine." *Journal of the History of Medicine* 34, no. 3 (1979): 314–33.

———. "The Leper in Medieval Islamic Society." *Speculum* 58, no. 4 (1983): 891–916.

———. *Majnūn: The Madman in Medieval Islamic Society.* Edited by Diana F. Immisch. Oxford: Clarendon Press, 1992.

Dundes, Alan. *Life Is Like a Chicken Coop: A Portrait of German Culture through Folklore.* New York: Columbia University Press, 1984.

Eamon, William. *Science and the Secrets of Nature: Books of Secrets in Medieval and Early Modern Culture.* Princeton, N.J.: Princeton University Press, 1994.

Echevarria, Ana. *The Fortress of Faith: The Attitude toward Muslims in Fifteenth-Century Spain.* Leiden: Brill, 1999.

Edwards, John. "Race and Religion in 15th and 16th C. Spain: The 'Purity of Blood' Laws Revisited." In *Proceedings of the Tenth World Congress of Jewish Studies, Jerusalem, August 16–24, 1989,* edited by David Assaf. 7 vols. Jerusalem: World Union of Jewish Studies, 1990, B II: 159–66.

———, ed. and trans. *The Jews in Western Europe 1400–1600.* Manchester: Manchester University Press, 1994.

Efron, John F. *Medicine and the German Jews: A History.* New Haven: Yale University Press, 2001.

Egmond, Florike. "Execution, Dissection, Pain and Infamy—a Morphological Investigation." In *Bodily Extremities: Preoccupations with the Human Body in Early Modern European Culture,* edited by Florike Egmond and Robert Zwijenberg. Burlington, Vt.: Ashgate, 2003, 92–128.

Einbinder, Susan L. "Pucellina of Blois: Romantic Myths and Narrative Conventions." *Jewish History* 12, no. 1 (1998): 29–46.

———. "Theory and Practice: A Jewish Physician in Paris and Avignon." *AJS Review* 33, no. 1 (2009): 135–53.

———. "Moses Rimos: Poetry, Poison, and History." *Italia. Studi e ricerche sulla storia, la cultura e la letteratura degli Ebrei d'Italia* 20 (2010): 67–91.

Ell, Stephen R. "Blood and Sexuality in Medieval Leprosy." *Janus: Revue internationale de l'histoire des sciences, de la médecine de la pharmacie et de la technique* 71, no. 1–4 (1984): 153–64.

Elliott, Dyan. "The Physiology of Rapture and Female Spirituality." In *Medieval Theology and the Natural Body,* edited by Peter Biller and A. J. Minnis. York Studies in Medieval Theology 1. Woodbridge, Suffolk: York Medieval Press, 1997, 141–73.

Elukin, Jonathan M. "From Jew to Christian? Conversion and Immutability in Medieval Europe." In *Varieties of Religious Conversion in the Middle Ages,* edited by James Muldoon. Gainesville: University Press of Florida, 1997, 171–89.

———. *Living Together, Living Apart: Re-thinking Jewish-Christian Relations in the Middle Ages.* Princeton, N.J.: Princeton University Press, 2007.

Emery, Richard W. *The Jews of Perpignan in the Thirteenth Century.* New York: Columbia University Press, 1959.

Enders, Jody. "Homicidal Pigs and the Antisemitic Imagination." *Exemplaria* 14, no. 1 (2002): 201–9.

Engbring, Gertrude. "Saint Hildegard, Twelfth-Century Physician." *Bulletin of the History of Medicine* 8 (1940): 770–84.

Evans, Elizabeth C. "The Study of Physiognomy in the Second Century A.D." *Transactions and Proceedings of the American Philological Association* 72 (1941): 96–108.

Evans, Gillian R. "The *Cur Deus Homo*: The Nature of St. Anselm's Appeal to Reason." *Studia Theologica* 31, no. 1 (1977): 33–50.

Everest, Carol A. "Pears and Pregnancy in Chaucer's 'Merchant's Tale.'" In *Food in the Middle Ages: A Book of Essays,* edited by Melitta Weiss Adamson. New York: Garland, 1995, 161–75.

Fabre-Vassas, Claudine. *The Singular Beast: Jews, Christians, and the Pig.* Translated by Carol Volk. New York: Columbia University Press, 1997.

Feldman, Louis H. *Jew and Gentile in the Ancient World: Attitudes and Interactions from Alexander to Justinian.* Princeton, N.J.: Princeton University Press, 1993.

Fernández Tijero, Carmen. "Ego Peripateticus Sum: Los textos de clase para la enseñanza de la medicina en Montpellier." *Eä* 2, no. 1 (2010): 1–16. Available at http://www.ea-journal.com/en/archive/61-vol-2-no-1-agosto-2010/231-ego-peripateticus-sum-los-textos-de-clase-para-la-ensenanza-de-la-medicina-en-montpellier.

Filotas, Bernadette. *Pagan Survivals, Superstitions and Popular Cultures.* Toronto: Pontifical Institute of Mediaeval Studies, 2005.

Fischell, Jack R., and Susan M. Ortmann. *The Holocaust and Its Religious Impact: A Critical Assessment and Annotated Bibliography.* Westport, Conn.: Praeger, 2004.

Flores, Nona C. "'Effigies amicitiae . . . veritas inimicitae': Antifeminism in the Iconography of the Woman-Headed Serpent in Medieval and Renaissance Art and Literature." In *Animals in the Middle Ages: A Book of Essays,* edited by Nona C. Flores. New York: Garland, 1996, 167–95.

Flueler, Christoph. "Acedia und Melancholie im Spätmittelalter." *Freiburger Zeitschrift für Philosophie und Theologie* 34, no. 3 (1987): 379–98.

Foa, Anna. "The New and the Old: The Spread of Syphilis (1494–1530)." In *Sex and Gender in Historical Perspective,* edited by Edward Muir and Guido Ruggiero. Translated by Margaret Gallucci, Mary M. Gallucci, and Carole C. Gallucci. Baltimore: Johns Hopkins University Press, 1990, 26–45. ["Il nuovo e il vecchio: L'insorge della sifilide (1494–1530)." *Quaderni Storici* 55 (1984): 11–34.]

———. "The Marrano's Kitchen: External Stimuli, Internal Response, and the Formation of the Marranic Persona." In *The Mediterranean and the Jews: Society, Culture and Economy in Early Modern Times,* edited by Elliott Horowitz and Moises Orfali. Ramat Gan: Bar-Ilan University Press, 2002, 13–25.

Fogle, Lauren. "Between Christianity and Judaism: The Identity of Converted Jews in Medieval London." *Essays in Medieval Studies* 22 (2005): 107–16.

———. "The *Domus Conversorum*: The Personal Interest of Henry III." *Jewish Historical Studies* 41 (2007): 1–7.

Frassetto, Michael. "Heretics and Jews in the Early Eleventh Century: The Writings of Rodulfus Glaber and Ademar of Chabannes." In *Christian Attitudes toward Jews in the Middle Ages: A Casebook,* edited by Michael Frassetto. New York: Routledge, 2007, 43–60.

Frey, Winfried. "Gottesmörder und Menschenfeinde. Zum Judenbild in der deutschen Literatur des Mittelalters." In *Die Juden in ihrer mittelalterlichen Umwelt,* edited by Alfred Ebenbauer and Klaus Zatloukal. Cologne: Böhlau, 1991, 35–51.

———. "Jews and Christians at the Lord's Table." In *Food in the Middle Ages: A Book of Essays,* edited by Melitta Weiss Adamson. New York: Garland, 1995, 113–44.

Friedenwald, Harry. *The Jews and Medicine: Essays.* 2 vols. Baltimore: Johns Hopkins University Press, 1944.

Friedman, John Block. *The Monstrous Races in Medieval Art and Thought.* Syracuse, N.Y.: Syracuse University Press, 1999.

Friedman, R. Avraham Peretz. *Marital Intimacy: A Traditional Jewish Approach.* Linden, N.J.: Compass Books, 2005.

Friedman, Yvonne. "An Anatomy of Anti-Semitism: Peter the Venerable's Letter to Louis VII, King of France (1146)." *Bar-Ilan Studies in History* 1 (Ramat-Gan, 1978): 87–102.

———. "Anti-Talmudic Invective from Peter the Venerable to Nicolas Donin (1144–1244)." In *Le brûlement du Talmud à Paris 1242–1244,* edited by Gilbert Dahan. Paris: Les Éditions du Cerf, 1999, 171–90.

Fritsch, Theodor. *Handbuch der Judenfrage: Die wichtigsten Tatsachen zur Beurteilung des jüdischen Volkes.* 40th ed. Leipzig: Hammer Verlag, 1937.

Fritz, Jean-Marie. "La théorie humorale comme moyen de penser le monde. Limites et contradictions du système." In *Ecriture et modes de pensée au Moyen Age (VIIIe–XVe siècles),* edited by Dominique Boutet and Laurence Harf-Lancner. Paris: Presses de l'ecole normale superieure, 1993, 13–26.

Frojmovic, Eva. "Christian Travelers to the Circumcision: Early Modern Representations." In *The Covenant of Circumcision: New Perspectives on an Ancient Jewish Rite,* edited by Elizabeth Wyner Mark. Hanover, N.H.: University Press of New England, 2003, 128–37.

———. "Reframing Gender in Medieval Jewish Images of Circumcision." In *Framing the Family: Narrative and Representation in the Medieval and Early Modern Periods,* edited by Rosalynn Voaden and Diane Wolfthal. MRTS 280. Tempe: Arizona Center for Medieval and Renaissance Studies, 2005, 221–43.

Fudeman, Kirsten A. *Vernacular Voices: Language and Identity in Medieval French Jewish Communities.* Philadelphia: University of Pennsylvania Press, 2010.

Fuhrman, Joëlle. "L'influence de l'astrologie dans les écrits médicaux allemands du Moyen Age." In *Observer, Lire, Écrire le Ciel au Moyen Age. Actes du Colloque d'Orleans 22–23 Avril 1989.* Paris: Klincksieck, 1991, 101–13.

Gabriele, Matthew. "Against the Enemies of Christ: The Role of Count Emicho in the Anti-Jewish Violence of the First Crusade." In *Christian Attitudes toward Jews in the Middle Ages: A Casebook,* edited by Michael Frassetto. New York: Routledge, 2007, 61–82.
Gabrieli, Francesco. *Arab Historians of the Crusades.* Berkeley: University of California Press, 1969.
Gaignebet, Claude, and Jean-Dominique Lajoux. *Art profane et religion populaire au Moyen Age.* Paris: Presses universitaires de France, 1985.
García Ballester, Luis. "La minoria judía ante la filosofía natural y la medicina escolásticas: problemas sobre la communicación científica en la Europa meridonal de los siglos XIII a XV." In *Proyección histórica de Espana en sus tres culturas: Castille y León, América y el Mediterránneo,* edited by Eufemio Lorenzo Sanz. 3 vols. Valladollid: Junta de Castilla y León, Consejería de Cultura y Turismo, 1993. 1: 101–28.
García Ballester, Luis, Lola Ferre, and Eduard Feliu. "Jewish Appreciation of 14th C. Scholastic Medicine." *Osiris,* ser. 2, no. 6 (1990): 85–117.
Gaster, Moses. "The History of the Destruction of the Round Table as Told in Hebrew in the Year 1279." In *Studies and Texts in Folklore, Magic, Mediaeval Romance, Hebrew Apocrypha and Samaritan Archaeology.* 3 vols. New York: KTAV, 1971, 2: 942–64.
Gerli, Michael. "Social Crisis and Conversion: Apostasy and Inquisition in the Chronicles of Fernando del Pulgar and Andrés Bernáldez." *Hispanic Review* 70, no. 2 (2002): 147–67.
Gilman, Sander L. *Jewish Self-Hatred: Anti-Semitism and the Hidden Language of the Jews.* Baltimore: Johns Hopkins University Press, 1986.
———. "The Struggle of Psychiatry with Psychoanalysis: Who Won?" *Critical Inquiry* 13, no. 2 (1987): 293–313.
———. *The Jew's Body.* London: Routledge, 1991.
———. "Decircumcision: The First Aesthetic Surgery." *Modern Judaism* 17, no. 3 (1997): 201–10.
Ginio, Alisa Meyuhas. "The Fortress of Faith—at the End of the West: Alonso de Espina and His *Fortalitium fidei.*" In *Contra Iudaeos. Ancient and Medieval Polemics Between Christians and Jews,* edited by Ora Limor and Guy G. Stroumsa. Tübingen: Mohr, 1996, 215–38.
Ginzberg, Louis. *The Legends of the Jews.* 7 vols. Translated by Henrietta Szold. Philadelphia: 1909–28. Reprint, Hildesheim: Georg Olms Verlag, 2000.
Ginzburg, Carlo. *Ecstasies: Deciphering the Witches Sabbath.* Translated by Raymond Rosenthal. New York: Pantheon Books, 1991.
Godet, P. "Brunon d'Asti ou de Segni." In *Dictionnaire de Théologie Catholique,* edited by E. Mangenot. Vol. 2(1), fasc. 13. Paris: Letouzey et Ané, 1904, cols. 1150–51.
Golb, Norman. "The Music of Obadiah the Proselyte and His Conversion." *Journal of Jewish Studies* 18 (1967): 43–63.
———. *Jewish Proselytism—a Phenomenon in the Religious History of Early Medieval Europe.* Tenth Annual Rabbi Louis Feinberg Memorial Lecture. Cincinnati: University of Cincinnati, 1988.

———. *The Jews in Medieval Normandy: A Social and Intellectual History.* Cambridge: Cambridge University Press, 1998.
Goldberg, Harriet. "Two Parallel Medieval Commonplaces: Antifeminism and antisemitism in the *Hispanic Literary Tradition.*" In *Aspects of Jewish Culture in the Middle Ages,* edited by Paul E. Szarmach. Albany: SUNY Press Albany, 1979, 85–120.
Goldy, Charlotte Newman. "A Thirteenth-Century Anglo-Jewish Woman Crossing Boundaries: Visible and Invisible." *Journal of Medieval History* 34 (2008): 130–45.
Goodman, Martin. *Rome and Jerusalem: The Clash of Ancient Civilizations.* New York: Knopf, 2007.
Graboïs, Aryeh. "La dynastie des 'rois juifs' de Narbonne (XIIe–XIIIe siècle)." In *Narbonne: Archéologie et histoire.* Vol. 2 of *Narbonne au moyen âge.* Montpelier: Fédération historique du Languedoc méditerranéen et du Roussillon, 1973, 49–54.
———. "Une Principaute Juive dans la France du Midi a l'Époque Carolingienne." In *Civilisation et société dans l'Occident medieval,* by Aryeh Gaboïs. London: Variorum, 1983, XV: 191–202.
Grabmayer, Johannes. "Rudolf von Schlettstadt und das aschkenasische Judentum um 1300." *Aschkenas: Zietschrift für Geschichte und Kultur der Juden* 4, no. 2 (1994): 301–36.
Granjel, Luis S. "Los médicos Judíos en la Sociedad Castellano-Leonesa." In *Proyección histórica de Espana en sus tres culturas: Castille y León, América y el Mediterránneo,* edited by Eufemio Lorenzo Sanz. 3 vols. Valladollid: Junta de Castilla y León, Consejería de Cultura y Turismo, 1993, 3: 369–83.
Granjel, Mercedes. "Judaísmo y pureza de sangre en la Universidad de Salamanca: La formacíon del médico en el siglo XVI." In *Proyección histórica de Espana en sus tres culturas: Castille y León, América y el Mediterránneo,* edited by Eufemio Lorenzo Sanz. 3 vols. Valladollid: Junta de Castilla y León, Consejería de Cultura y Turismo, 1993, 3: 295–302.
Grant, Edward, ed. *A Source Book in Medieval Science.* Cambridge, Mass.: Harvard University Press, 1974.
Grayzel, Solomon. *The Church and the Jews in the XIIIth Century.* New York: Hermon Press, 1966.
Greatrex, Joan. "Monastic Charity for Jewish Converts: The Requisition of Corrodies by Henry III." In *Christianity and Judaism. Papers Read at the 1991 Summer Meeting and the 1992 Winter Meeting of the Ecclesiastical History Society,* edited by Diana Wood. Cambridge, Mass.: Ecclesiastical History Society, 1992, 133–43.
Green, Monica H. "Constantinus Africanus and the Conflict between Religion and Science." In *The Human Embryo. Aristotle and the Arabic and European Traditions,* edited by G. R. Dunstan. Exeter: University of Exeter Press, 1990, 47–69.
Green, Monica H., and Daniel Lord Smail. "The Trial of Floreta d'Ays (1403): Jews, Christians, and Obstetrics in Later Medieval Marseille." *Journal of Medieval History* 34 (2008): 185–211.

Gregg, Joan Young. *Devils, Women, and Jews: Reflections of the Other in Medieval Sermon Stories.* Albany, N.Y.: SUNY Press, 1997.
Grigsby, Bryon Lee. *Pestilence in Medieval and Early Modern Literature.* New York: Routledge, 2004.
Groebner, Valentin. "*Complexio*/Complexion: Categorizing Individual Natures, 1250–1600." In *The Moral Authority of Nature*, edited by Lorraine Daston and Fernando Vidal. Chicago: University of Chicago Press, 2004, 361–83.
Gross, Abraham. "The Blood Libel and the Blood of Circumcision: An Ashkenazic Custom that Disappeared in the Middle Ages." *Jewish Quarterly Review* 86 (1995): 171–74.
Grumett, David and Rachel Muers. *Theology on the Menu: Asceticism, Meat and Christian Diet.* New York: Routledge, 2010.
Gryting, Loyal A. T. "The Venjance Nostre Seigneur as a Mediaeval Composite." *Modern Language Journal* 38, no. 1 (1954): 15–17.
Guldentops, Guy. "The Sagacity of the Bees." In *Aristotle's Animals in the Middle Ages and Renaissance*, edited by Carlos Steel, Guy Guldentops, and Pieter Beullens. Leuven: Leuven University Press, 1999, 275–96.
Gutwirth, E. "Gender, History, and the Judeo-Christian Polemic." In *Contra Iudaeos. Ancient and Medieval Polemics between Christians and Jews*, edited by Ora Limor and Guy G. Stroumsa. Tübingen: Mohr, 1996, 257–79.
Haastrup, Ulla. "Representations of Jews in Danish Medieval Art—Can Images Be Used as Source Material on Their Own?" In *History and Images: Toward a New Iconology*, edited by Axel Bolvig and Phillip Lindley. Turnholt: Brepols, 2003, 341–56.
Haberman, Bonna Devorah. "Foreskin Sacrifice: Zipporah's Ritual and the Bloody Bridegroom." In *The Covenant of Circumcision: New Perspectives on an Ancient Jewish Rite*, edited by Elizabeth Wyner Mark. Hanover, N.H.: University Press of New England, 2003, 18–29.
Hames, Harvey J. "The Limits of Conversion: Ritual Murder and the Virgin Mary in the Account of Adam of Bristol." *Journal of Medieval History* 33 (2007): 43–59.
Hamesse, Jacqueline. "Johannes de Fonte, compilateur des *Parvi flores*. Le témoignage de plusieurs manuscrits de la Bibliothèque Vaticane." *Archivum franciscanum historicum* 88 (1995): 515–31.
Handerson, Henry A. *Gilbertus Anglicus: Medicine of the Thirteenth Century.* Cleveland, Ohio: Cleveland Medical Library Association, 1918.
Hart, Mitchell B. *The Healthy Jew: The Symbiosis of Judaism and Modern Medicine.* Cambridge: Cambridge University Press, 2007.
Harvey, Susan Ashbrook. *Scenting Salvation: Ancient Christianity and the Olfactory Imagination.* Berkeley: University of California Press, 2006.
Hassig, Debra. *Medieval Bestiaries: Text, Image, Ideology.* Cambridge: Cambridge University Press, 1995.
Haverkammp, Alfred. "Baptised Jews in German Lands during the Twelfth Century." In *Jews and Christians in Twelfth-Century Europe*, edited by Michael A. Signer and John Van Engen. Notre Dame Conferences in Medieval Studies 10. Notre Dame, Ind.: University of Notre Dame Press, 2001, 255–310.

Heffernan, Thomas J. *Sacred Biography: Saints and Their Biographers in the Middle Ages.* Oxford: Oxford University Press, 1992.

Heschel, Susannah. *The Aryan Jesus: Christian Theologians and the Bible in Nazi Germany.* Princeton, N.J.: Princeton University Press, 2008.

Hill, C. E. "Antichrist from the Tribe of Dan." *Journal of Theological Studies* 46, no. 1 (1995): 99–117.

Hillaby, Joe. "The Ritual-Child-Murder Accusation: Its Dissemination and Harold of Gloucester." *Jewish Historical Studies* 34 for 1994–96 (1997): 69–109.

Hillenbrand, Carole. *The Crusades: Islamic Perspectives.* New York: Routledge, 1999.

Hodges, Frederick M. "The Ideal Prepuce in Ancient Greece and Rome: Male Genital Aesthetics and Their Relation to *Lipodermos,* Circumcision, Foreskin Restoration, and the *Kynodesme.*" *Bulletin of the History of Medicine* 75 (2001): 375–405.

Hollengreen, Laura. "The Politics and Poetics of Possession: Saint Louis, the Jews, and Old Testament Violence." In *Between the Picture and the Word: Manuscript Studies from the Index of Christian Art,* edited by Colum Hourihane. Princeton, N.J.: Index of Christian Art, Department of Art and Archaeology, Princeton University, in association with Penn State University Press, 2005, 51–71; 90–115.

Homza, Lu Ann, ed. and trans. *The Spanish Inquisition, 1478–1614: An Anthology of Sources.* Indianapolis: Hackett, 2006.

Horowitz, Elliott. "A 'Dangerous Encounter': Thomas Coryate and the Swaggering Jews of Venice." *Journal of Jewish Studies* 52, no. 2 (2001): 341–53.

———. "Le Peuple de l'image: les juifs et l'art." *Annales: Histoire, Sciences Sociales* 3 (2001): 665–84.

———. "The Jews and the Cross in the Middle Ages." In *Philosemitism, Antisemitism and 'the Jews': Perspectives from the Middle Ages to the Twentieth Century,* edited by Tony Kushner and Nadia Valman. Aldershot: Ashgate, 2004, 114–31.

———. *Reckless Rites: Amalek, Purim, and the Legacy of Jewish Violence.* Princeton, N.J.: Princeton University Press, 2006.

Horowitz, Maryanne Cline. "Aristotle and Women." *Journal of the History of Biology* 9 (1976): 183–213.

Horstmanshoff, H. F. J. "La castration dans les texts latins médicaux." In *Maladie et maladies dans les texts latins antiques et médiévaux,* edited by Carl Deroux. Collection Latomus 242. Brussels: Latomus, 1998, 85–94.

Hosler, John D. "Henry II, William of Newburgh, and the Development of English Anti-Judaism." In *Christian Attitudes toward Jews in the Middle Ages: A Casebook,* edited by Michael Frassetto. New York: Routledge, 2007, 167–82.

Hossfeld, Paul. *Albertus Magnus über die Frau.* Bad Honnef: s.p. 1982.

Hsia, R. Po-Chia. *The Myth of Ritual Murder: Jews and Magic in Reformation Germany.* New Haven: Yale University Press, 1988.

———. "Witchcraft, Magic, and the Jews in Germany." In *From Witness to Witchcraft: Jews and Judaism in Medieval Christian Thought,* edited by Jeremy Cohen. Wolfenbütteler Mittelalter-Studien 11. Wiesbaden: Harrassowitz Verlag, 1996, 419–33.

Hughes, Diane. "Distinguishing Sign: Ear-rings, Jews, and Franciscan Rhetoric in the Italian Renaissance City." *Past and Present* 112 (1986): 3–59.
Hunt, Richard William. "The Disputation of Peter of Cornwall against Symon the Jew." In *Studies in Medieval History Presented to Frederick Maurice Powicke*, edited by R.W. Hunt, et al. Oxford: Clarendon Press, 1948, 143–56.
Hutchinson, Jonathan. *On Leprosy and Fish-Eating: A Statement of Facts and Explanation*. London: Archibald, Constable, 1906.
Iannucci, Remo Joseph. *The Treatment of the Capital Sins and the Decalogue in the German Sermons of Berthold von Regensburg*. The Catholic University of America Studies in German 17. New York: AMS Press, 1942.
Ibàñez, Josep Hernando I Angels. "El procés contra el convers Nicolau Sanxo, ciutadà de Barcelona acusat d'haver circumcidat el seu fill (1437–1438): Processus inquisitionis facte contra Sanxo, conversum, civem Barchinone, A.D.B. Processos n.762." *Acta historica et archaeologica mediaevalia* 13 (1992): 75–100.
Idel, Moshe. "Saturn and Sabbatai Tzevi: A New Approach to Sabbateanism." In *Toward the Millenium: Messianic Expectations from the Bible to Waco*, edited by Peter Schäfer and Mark Cohen. Leiden: Brill, 1998, 173–202.
Iogna-Prat, Dominique. *Order and Exclusion: Cluny and Christendom Face Heresy, Judaism, and Islam (1000–1500)*. Translated by Graham Robert Edwards. Ithaca, N.Y.: Cornell University Press, 2002.
Jackson, S. W. "Acedia the Sin and Its Relationship to Sorrow and Melancholy in Medieval Times." *Bulletin of the History of Medicine* 55 (1981): 172–85.
Jacobs, Joseph, ed. and trans. *The Jews of Angevin England*. London: David Nutt, 1893.
Jacobson, Matthew Frye. *Whiteness of a Different Color: European Immigrants and the Alchemy of Race*. Cambridge, Mass.: Harvard University Press, 1998.
Jacquart, Danielle. "Medical Explanations of Sexual Behavior in the Middle Ages." In *Homo Carnalis. The Carnal Aspects of Medieval Human Life*, edited by Helen Rodnite Lemay. Binghamton: State University of New York at Binghamton, 1990, 1–21.
———. "La Physiognomonie à l'époque de Frédéric II: Le traité de Michel Scot." In *Le scienze alla corte di Federico II*. Vol. 2 of *Micrologus: Natura, scienze e società medievali*. Turnholt: Brepols, 1994, 19–38.
Jacquart, Danielle, and Claude Thomasset. *Sexuality and Medicine in the Middle Ages*. Translated by Matthew Adamson. Oxford: Polity Press, 1988.
Jansen, Katherine L., Joanna Drell, and Frances Andrews, eds. *Medieval Italy: Texts in Translation*. Philadelphia: University of Pennsylvania Press, 2009.
Jestice, Phyllis G. "A Great Jewish Conspiracy? Worsening Jewish-Christian Relations and the Destruction of the Holy Sepulcher." In *Christian Attitudes toward Jews in the Middle Ages: A Casebook*, edited by Michael Frassetto. New York: Routledge, 2007, 25–42.
Johnson, Willis. "Textual Sources for the Study of Jewish Currency Crimes in Thirteenth-Century England." *British Numismatic Journal* 66 (1997): 21–32.
———. "The Myth of Jewish Male Menses." *Journal of Medieval History* 24, no. 3 (1998): 273–95.

Jordan, Mark D. "Homosexuality, *Luxuria*, and Textual Abuse." In *Constructing Medieval Sexuality*, edited by Karma Lochrie, Peggy McCracken, and James A. Schultz. Minneapolis: University of Minnesota Press, 1997, 24–39.

Jordan, William C. "Problems of the Meat Market of Béziers 1240–1247: A Question of Anti-Semitism." *Revue des Études juives* 135, no. 1–3 (1976): 31–49.

———. "The Last Tormentor of Christ." *Jewish Quarterly Review* 78 (1987): 21–47.

———. "Marian Devotion and the Talmud Trial of 1240." In *Religionspräche im Mittelalter*, edited by Bernard Lewis and Friedrich Niewöhner. Wiesbaden: Otto Harrassowitz, 1992, 61–76.

Kanarfogel, Ephraim. "Returning to the Jewish Community in Medieval Ashkenaz: History and Halakhah." In *Turim: Studies in Jewish History and Literature Presented to Dr. Bernard Lander*, edited by Michael A. Schmidman. New York: Touro College Press, 2007, 1: 69–97.

Kaplan, Paul H. D. "Jewish Artists and Images of Black Africans in Renaissance Venice." In *Multicultural Europe and Cultural Exchange in the Middle Ages and Renaissance*, edited by James P. Helfers. Arizona Studies in the Middle Ages and Renaissance 12. Turnholt: Brepols, 2005, 67–90.

Kaplan, Steven. "Can the Ethiopian Change His Skin? The Beta Israel (Ethiopian Jews) and Racial Discourse." *African Affairs* 98, no. 393 (1999): 535–50.

Karras, Ruth Mazo. *Common Women: Prostitution and Sexuality in Medieval England*. New York: Oxford University Press, 1996.

———. "Separating the Men from the Goats: Masculinity, Civilization and Identity Formation in the Medieval University." In *Conflicted Identities and Multiple Masculinities: Men in the Medieval West*, edited by Jacqueline Murray. New York: Garland, 1999, 189–213.

———. *Sexuality in Medieval Europe: Doing Unto Others*. New York: Routledge, 2005.

Kasher, Hanna. "Maimonides' View of Circumcision as a Factor Uniting the Jewish and Muslim Communities." In *Medieval and Modern Perspectives on Muslim-Jewish Relations*, edited by Ronald L. Nettler. Studies in Muslim-Jewish Relations 2. Luxembourg: Harwood Academic Publishers, 1995, 103–8.

Kassouf, Susan. "The Shared Pain of the Golden Vein: The Discursive Proximity of Jewish and Scholarly Diseases in the Late Eighteenth Century." *Eighteenth-Century Studies* 32, no. 1 (1998): 101–10.

Katz, David S. "Shylock's Gender: Jewish Male Menstruation in Early Modern England." *Review of English Studies* n.s. 50, no. 200 (1999): 440–62.

Kedar, B. Z. "The Subjected Muslims of the Frankish Levant." In *Muslims under Latin Rule*, edited by J. M. Powell. Princeton, N.J.: Princeton University Press, 1990, 135–74.

———. "*De Iudeis et Sarracenis*: On the categorization of Muslims in medieval canon law." In Kedar, *The Franks in the Levant, 11th to 14th centuries*. Brookfield, Vt.: Variorum, 1993, 207–13.

———. "Multidirectional Conversion in the Frankish Levant." In *Varieties of Religious Conversion in the Middle Ages*, edited by James Muldoon. Gainesville, Fla.: University Press of Florida, 1997, 190–99.

———. "Convergences of Oriental Christian, Muslim, and Frankish Worshippers:

The Case of Saydnaya." In *De Sion exibit lex et verbum domini de Hierusalem: Essays on Medieval Law, Liturgy and Literature in Honour of Amnon Linder,* edited by Yitzhak Hen. Turnholt: Brepols, 2001, 59–69.
Kennedy, E. S., and David Pingree. *The Astrological History of Mâshâ' allâh.* Cambridge, Mass.: Harvard University Press, 1971.
Klepper, Deeana Copeland. *The Insight of Unbelievers: Nicholas of Lyra and Christian Reading of Jewish Text in the Later Middle Ages.* Philadelphia: University of Pennsylvania Press, 2007.
Klibansky, Raymund, Erwin Panofsky, and Fritz Saxl. *Saturn and Melancholy: Studies in the History of Natural Philosophy, Religion and Art.* Nendeln, Liechtenstein: Kraus. Reprint, 1979.
Knight, Gillian. "Politics and Pastoral Care: Papal Schism in some Letters of Peter the Venerable." *Revue Bénédictine* 109, no. 3–4 (1999): 359–90.
Kogman-Appel, Katrin. *Illuminated Haggadot from Medieval Spain: Biblical Imagery and the Passover Holiday.* University Park: Pennsylvania State University Press, 2006.
Koren, Sharon Faye. "Mystical Rationales for the Laws of *Niddah*." In *Women and Water: Menstruation in Jewish Life and Law,* edited by Rahel R. Wasserfall. Hanover, N.H.: University Press of New England, 1999, 101–21.
———. "Kabbalistic Physiology: Isaac the Blind, Nahmanides, and Moses de Leon on Menstruation." *AJS Review* 28, no. 2 (2004): 317–40.
———. "The Menstruant as 'Other' in Medieval Judaism and Christianity." *Nashim: A Journal of Jewish Women's Studies & Gender Issues* 17 (2009): 33–59.
Korhonen, Anu. "Conceptualising Black Skin in Renaissance England." In *Black Africans in Renaissance Europe,* edited by T. F. Earle and K. J. P. Lowe. Cambridge: Cambridge University Press, 2005, 94–112.
Kornmann, Heinrich. *Opera curiosa.* 4 vols. Frankfurt: Gensch, 1694.
Krebs, Walter. "Lilith—Adams erste Frau." *Zeitschrift für Religions-und Geistesgeschichte* 27, no. 2 (1975): 141–52.
Kriegel, Maurice. "Un trait de psychologie sociale dans les pays méditerranéens du bas moyen age: le juif comme intouchable." *Annales* 31 (1976): 325–30.
Kritzeck, James. *Peter the Venerable and Islam.* Princeton, N.J.: Princeton University Press, 1964.
Kruger, Steven F. "Conversion and Medieval Sexual, Religious, and Racial Categories." In *Constructing Medieval Sexuality,* edited by Karma Lochrie, Peggy McCracken, and James A. Schultz. Minneapolis: University of Minnesota Press, 1997, 158–79.
Kuryluk, Ewa. *Veronica and Her Cloth: History, Symbolism and Structure of a 'True' Image.* Oxford: Blackwell, 1991.
Lampert, Lisa. *Gender and Jewish Difference from Paul to Shakespeare.* Philadelphia: University of Pennsylvania Press, 2004.
———. "Race, Periodicity, and the (Neo-) Middle Ages." *Modern Language Quarterly* 65, no. 3 (2004): 391–421.
Landes, Richard. "The Massacres of 1010: On the Origins of Popular Anti-Jewish Violence in Western Europe." In *From Witness to Witchcraft: Jews and Judaism in Medieval Christian Thought,* edited by Jeremy Cohen. Wolfenbütteler

Mittelalter-Studien 11. Wiesbaden: Harrassowitz Verlag, 1996, 79–111.
Langermann, T. Zvi. "Science, Jewish." In *Medieval Iberia: An Encyclopedia.* Edited by E. Michael Gerli. New York: Routledge, 2003, 743–45.
Langmuir, Gavin I. *Toward a Definition of Anti-Semitism.* Berkeley: University of California Press, 1990.
Laqueur, Thomas W. "Amor Veneris vel Dulcedo Appeletur." In *Fragments for a History of the Human Body,* edited by Michel Feher, with Ramona Naddaff and Nadia Tazi. 3 vols. New York: Zone Books, 1989, 3: 91–131.
Larrington, Carolyne. "Diet, Defecation and the Devil: Disgust and the Pagan Past." In *Medieval Obscenities,* edited by Nicola McDonald. York: York Medieval Press, 2006, 138–55.
Lasker, Daniel. "Transubstantiation, Elijah's Chair, Plato, and the Jewish-Christian Debate." *Revue des etudes juives* 143, no. 1–2 (1984): 31–58.
——. "Jewish-Christian Polemics at the Turning Point: Jewish Evidence from the Twelfth Century." *Harvard Theological Review* 89, no. 2 (1996): 161–73.
——. "Jewish Philosophical Polemics in Ashkenaz." In *Contra Iudaeos. Ancient and Medieval Polemics between Christians and Jews,* edited by Ora Limor and Guy G. Stroumsa. Tübingen: Mohr, 1996, 195–213.
LaVoie, Rodrigue. "La Delinquance Sexuelle a Manosque (1240–1430): Schéma générale et singularités juives." *Provence Historique* 37, no. 150 (1987): 571–87.
Le Goff, Jacques. "Le mal royal ay moyen âge: du roi malade au roi guerisseur." *Mediaevistik* 1 (1988): 101–9.
Lemay, Helen. "The Stars and Human Sexuality." *Isis* 71, no. 256 (1980): 127–37.
Lerner, David Levine. "The Enduring Legend of the Jewish Pope." *Judaism* 40 (1981): 148–70.
Lévi, Israel. "'L'odeur des juifs,' in 'Le Juif de la legend.'" *Revue des études juives* 20 (1890): 249–52.
Levine, Robert. "Why Praise Jews: History and Satire in the Middle Ages." *Journal of Medieval History* 12 (1986): 291–96.
Levine-Melammed, Renée. "The Ultimate Challenge: Safeguarding the Crypto-Judaic Heritage." *Proceedings of the American Academy for Jewish Research* 53 (1986): 91–109.
Lichtenstadter, Ilse. "The Distinctive Dress of Non-Muslims in Islamic Countries." *Historia Judaica* 5 (1943): 35–52.
Lidaka, Juris G. "Bartholomaeus Anglicus in the Thirteenth Century." In *Pre-Modern Encyclopaedic Texts. Proceedings of the Second COMERS Congress, Groningen, 1–4 July 1996,* edited by Peter Binkley. Leiden: Brill, 1997, 393–406.
Lie, Orlanda S. H. "Women's Medicine in Middle Dutch." In *Science Translated: Latin and Vernacular Translations of Scientific Treatises in Medieval Europe,* edited by Michèle Goyens, Pieter de Leemans, and An Smets. Leuven: Leuven University Press, 2008, 449–66.
Limor, Ora. "The Epistle of Rabbi Samuel of Morocco: A Best-Seller in the World of Polemics." In *Contra Iudaeos. Ancient and Medieval Polemics between Christians and Jews,* edited by Ora Limor and Guy G. Stroumsa. Tübingen: Mohr, 1996, 177–94.
Limor, Ora, and Israel Jacob Yuval. "Skepticism and Conversion: Jews, Christians,

and Doubters in *Sefer ha-Nizzaḥon*." In *Hebraica Veritas: Christian Hebraists and the Study of Judaism in Early Modern Europe*, edited by Allison P. Coudert and Jeffrey S. Shoulson. Philadelphia: University of Pennsylvania Press, 2004, 159–80.

Lindsay, James. E. *Daily Life in the Medieval Islamic World*. Westport, Conn.: Greenwood Press, 2005.

Lipman, V. D. *The Jews of Medieval Norwich*. London: Jewish Historical Society of England, 1968.

Lipton, Sara. *Images of Intolerance: The Representation of Jews and Judaism in the Bible moralisée*. Berkeley: University of California Press, 1999.

———. "The Temple Is My Body: Gender, Carnality, and Synagoga in the Bible moralisée." In *Imagining the Self, Imagining the Other*, edited by Eva Frojmovic. Leiden: Brill, 2002, 129–63.

Logan, F. D. "Thirteen London Jews and Conversion to Christianity: Problems of Apostasy in the 1280s." *Bulletin of the Institute of Historical Research* 45 (1972): 214–29.

Lotter, Friedrich. "Die Judenverfolgung des 'Koenig Rintfleisch' in Franken um 1298." *Zeitschrift für Historische Forschung* 15, no. 4 (1988): 385–423.

———. "*Innocens virgo et martyr*: Thomas von Monmouth und die Verbreitung der Ritualmordlegende im Hochmittelalter." In *Die Legende vom Ritualmord: zur Geschichte der Blutbeschuldigung gegen Juden*, edited by Rainer Erb. Berlin: Metropol, 1993, 25–72.

Löwe, Heinz. "Die Apostasie des Pfalzdiakons Bodo (838) und das Judentum der Chasaren." In *Person und Gemeinschaft im Mittelalter: Karl Schmid zum fünfundsechzigsten Geburtstag*, edited by Gerd Althoff. Sigmaringen: Thorbecke, 1988, 157–69.

Luchitskaya, Svetlana. "Muslims in Christian Imagery of the Thitreenth-Century: The Visual Code of Otherness." *Al-Masāq* 12 (2000): 37–67.

Maccoby, Hyam. *Judaism on Trial: Jewish-Christian Disputations in the Middle Ages*. London: Littman Library of Jewish Civilization, 1993.

———. "The Tortosa Disputation, 1413–1414, and Its Effects." In *The Expulsion of the Jews and Their Emigration to the Southern Low Countries (15th–16th C.)*, edited by Luc Dequeker and Werner Verbeke. Mediaevalia Lovaniensia, ser. 1, studia 26. Leuven: Leuven University Press, 1998, 23–34.

———. *Ritual and Morality: The Ritual Purity System and Its Place in Judaism*. Cambridge: Cambridge University Press, 1999.

Maclehose, William F. "Nurturing Danger: High Medieval Medicine and the Problem(s) of the Child." In *Medieval Mothering*, edited by John Carmi Parsons and Bonnie Wheeler. New York: Garland, 1996, 3–24.

Maitland, Frederic William. "The Deacon and the Jewess." In *Roman Canon Law in the Church of England: Six Essays*. London: Methuen, 1898, 158–79.

Makowski, Elizabeth M. "The Conjugal Debt and Medieval Canon Law." *Journal of Medieval History* 3 (1977): 99–114.

Malkiel, David. "Infanticide in Passover Iconography." *Journal of the Warburg and Courtauld Institutes* 56 (1993): 85–99.

———. "Destruction or Conversion: Intention and Reaction, Crusaders and Jews, in 1096." *Jewish History* 15 (2001): 257–80.

———. "Jews and Apostates in Medieval Europe—Boundaries Real and Imagined." *Past and Present* 194, no. 1 (2007): 3–34.

———. *Reconstructing Ashkenaz: The Human Face of Franco-German Jewry, 1000–1250.* Stanford Studies in Jewish History and Culture. Stanford: Stanford University Press, 2009.

Manchester, Keith. "Leprosy: The Origins and Development of the Disease in Antiquity." In *Maladie et Maladies: histoire de conceptualisation. Mélanges en l'honneur de Mirko Grmek,* edited by Danielle Gourevitch. Geneva: Librarie Droz, 1992, 31–49.

Marcus, Ivan. "Images of the Jews in the *Exempla* of Caesarius of Heisterbach." In *From Witness to Witchcraft: Jews and Judaism in Medieval Christian Thought,* edited by Jeremy Cohen. Wolfenbütteler Mittelalter-Studien 11. Wiesbaden: Harrassowitz Verlag, 1996, 247–56.

Marcus, Jacob Rader. *The Jew in the Medieval World: A Sourcebook, 315–1791.* Revised ed. Introduction by Marc Saperstein. Cincinnati: Hebrew Union College Press, 1999.

Marienberg, Evyatar. "Baraita de-Niddah." *Jewish Women: A Comprehensive Historical Encyclopedia.* March 1, 2009. Jewish Women's Archive. Available at http://jwa.org/encyclopedia/article/baraita-de-niddah. 2/7/2011. Accessed June 9, 2009.

Mark, Barry R. "Kabbalistic *Tocinofobia*: Américo Castro, *Limpieza de Sangre* and the Inner Meaning of Jewish Dietary Laws." In *Fear and Its Representations in the Middle Ages and Renaissance,* edited by Anne Scott and Cynthia Kosso. Arizona Studies in the Middle Ages and Renaissance 6. Tempe: Arizona Center for Middle Ages and Renaissance Studies (ACMRS) Publications, 2002, 152–88.

Marr, Wilhelm. *Der Sieg des Judenthums über das Germanenthum vom nicht confessionellen Standpunkt aus betrachtet.* Bern: Rudolph Costenoble, 1879.

Marrow, James H. "*Circumdederunt me canes multi*: Christ's Tormentors in Northern European Art of the Late Middle Ages and Early Renaissance." *Art Bulletin* 59, no. 2 (1977): 167–81.

Martin, D. S. "The Life of Saint Thomas of Hereford." In *St. Thomas Cantilupe, Bishop of Hereford: Essays in His Honor,* edited by Meryl Jancey. Hereford: Friends of Hereford Cathedral, 1982, 15–19.

Mattelaer, Johan J., Robert A. Schipper, and Sakti Das. "The Circumcision of Jesus." *Journal of Urology* 178, no. 31–34 (2007): 31–34.

McCracken, Peggy. *The Curse of Eve, the Wound of the Hero: Blood, Gender, and Medieval Literature.* Philadelphia: University of Pennsylvania Press, 2003.

McCulloh, John M. "Jewish Ritual Murder: William of Norwich, Thomas of Monmouth, and the Early Dissemination of the Myth." *Speculum* 72 (1997): 698–740.

McInerny, Maud Burnett, ed. *Hildegard of Bingen: A Book of Essays.* New York: Garland, 1998.

McVaugh, Michael R. "Moments of Inflection: The Careers of Arnau of Villanova." In *Religion and Medicine in the Middle Ages,* edited by Peter Biller and Joseph Ziegler. York: York Medieval Press, 2001, 47–67.

―――. *Medicine before the Plague: Practitioners and Their Patients in the Crown of Aragon 1285-1345*. Cambridge: Cambridge University Press, 2002.

―――. "Who Was Gilbert the Englishman?" In *The Study of Medieval Manuscripts of England: Festschrift in Honor of Richard W. Pfaff*, edited by G. H. Brown, L. E. Voigts. Turnholt: Brepols, 2010, 295-324.

McKay, Heather A. *Sabbath and Synagogue: The Question of Sabbath Worship in Ancient Judaism*. Leiden: Brill. 1994.

McMichael, Steven J. "The End of the World, Antichrist, and the Final Conversion of the Jews in the *Fortalitium fidei* of Friar Alonso de Espina (d. 1464)." *Medieval Encounters* 12, no. 2 (2006): 224-73.

Meens, Rob. "Pollution in the Early Middle Ages: The Case of the Food Regulations in the Penitentials." *Early Medieval Europe* 4, no. 1 (1995): 3-19.

Meersseman, P. G. *Introductio in opera omnia B. Alberti Magni O.P.* Bruges: Beyaert, 1931.

Mehl, James V. "Language, Class, and Mimic Satire in the Characterization of Correspondents in the *Epistolae obscurorum virorum*." *Sixteenth Century Journal* 25, no. 2 (1994): 289-305.

Melechen, Nina. "Calling Names: The Identification of Jews in Christian Documents from Medieval Toledo." In *On the Social Origins of Medieval Institutions: Essays in Honor of Joseph F. O'Callaghan*, edited by Donald J. Kagay and Theresa M. Vann. Leiden: Brill, 1998, 21-34.

Mellinkoff, Ruth. *The Mark of Cain*. Berkeley: University of California Press, 1981.

―――. *Outcasts: Signs of Otherness in Northern European Art of the Late Middle Ages*. 2 vols. Berkeley: University of California Press, 1993.

Meri, Josef W. *A Lonely Wayfarer's Guide to Pilgrimage: 'Ali ibn Abi Bakr al-Harawi's Kitab al-Isharat ila ma'rifat al-Ziyarat*. Princeton, N.J.: Darwin Press, 2005.

Mews, Constant J. "Abelard and Heloise on Jews and *Hebraica Veritas*." in *Christian Attitudes toward Jews in the Middle Ages: A Casebook*. Edited by Michael Frassetto. New York: Routledge, 2007, 83-108.

Michel, Francisque. *Histoire des Races maudites de la France et de l'Espagne*. 2 vols. Paris: A. Franck, 1847.

Miklautsch, Lydia. "Der Antijudaismus in den mittelalterlichen Legendem am Beispiel der Silvesterlegende in der Fassung des Konrad v. Würzburg." In *Die Juden in ihrer mittelalterlichen Umwelt*, edited by Alfred Ebenbauer and Klaus Zatloukal. Cologne: Böhlau, 1991, 173-82.

Miller, Elaine R. "Linguistic Identity in the Middle Ages: The Case of the Spanish Jews." In *Crossing Boundaries: Issues of Cultural and Individual Identity in the Middle Ages and the Renaissance*, edited by Sally McKee. Turnholt: Brepols, 1999, 57-77.

Minnis, Alastair. "*De impedimento sexus*: Women's Bodies and Medieval Impediments to Female Ordination." In *Medieval Theology and the Natural Body*, edited by Peter Biller and A. J. Minnis. York Studies in Medieval Theology 1. Woodbridge, Suffolk: York Medieval Press, 1997, 109-39.

―――. "From *Coilles* to *Bel Chose*: Discourses of Obscenity in Jean de Meun and

Chaucer." In *Medieval Obscenities,* edited by Nicola McDonald. York: York Medieval Press, 2006, 156–78.

Mitchell, Piers D. "Leprosy and the Case of King Baldwin IV of Jerusalem: Mycobacterial Disease in the Crusader States of the 12th and 13th Centuries." *International Journal of Leprosy* 61, no. 2 (1993): 283–91.

———. "The Myth of the Spread of Leprosy with the Crusades." In *The Past and Present of Leprosy. Archaeological, historical, palaeopathological and clinical approaches: Proceedings of the International Congress on the Evolution and Palaeoepidemiology of the Infectious Diseases 3 (ICEPID), University of Bradford, 26th–31st July 1999,* edited by C. A. Robertson, et al. Oxford: Archaeopress, 2002, 171–77.

———. *Medicine in the Crusades.* Cambridge: Cambridge University Press, 2005.

Mitterer, Albert. "Mas occasionatus: oder zwei Methoden der Thomasdeutung." *Zeitschrift für katholische Theologie* 72 (1950): 80–103

Miyazaki, Mariko. "Misercord Owls and Medieval Anti-semitism." In *The Mark of the Beast: The Medieval Bestiary in Art, Life, and Literature,* edited by Debra Hassig. New York: Garland, 1999, 23–50.

Monroe, Elizabeth. "'Fair and Friendly, Sweet and Beautiful': Hopes for Jewish Conversion in Synagoga's Song of Songs Imagery." In *Multicultural Europe and Cultural Exchange in the Middle Ages and Renaissance,* edited by James P. Helfers. Arizona Studies in the Middle Ages and Renaissance 12. Turnholt: Brepols, 2005, 33–61.

Montford, Angela. *Health, Sickness, Medicine and the Friars in the Thirteenth and Fourteenth Centuries.* Burlington, Vt.: Ashgate, 2004.

Moore, R. I. "Heresy as Disease." In *The Concept of Heresy in the Middle Ages (11th–13th C.),* edited by W. Lourdaux and D. Verhelst. Louvain: Louvain University Press, 1976, 1–11.

———. "Anti-Semitism and the Birth of Modern Europe." In *Christianity and Judaism. Papers Read at the 1991 Summer Meeting and the 1992 Winter Meeting of the Ecclesiastical History Society,* edited by Diana Wood. Cambridge, Mass.: Ecclesiastical History Society, 1992, 33–58.

Moos, Peter von. "Le vêtement identificateur: L'habit fait-il ou ne fait-il pas le moine?" In *Le corps et sa parure; The Body and Its Adornment.* Micrologus Library 15. Florence: SISMEL, 2007, 41–60.

Moss, Leonard W., and Stephen C. Cappannari. "*Mal'occhio, Ayin ha ra, Oculus fascinus, Judenblick*: The Evil Eye Hovers Above." In *The Evil Eye,* edited by Clarence Maloney. New York: Columbia University Press, 1976, 1–15.

Moulinier, Laurence. "Une encyclopédiste sans précédent? Le cas de Hildegarde de Bingen." In *L'enciclopedismo medievale: Atti del convegno 'L'enciclopedismo medievale', San Gimignano 8–10 Ottobre 1992,* edited by Michelangelo Picone. Ravenna: Longo, 1994, 119–34.

Müller, Jörg R. "Erez gezerah—'Land of Persecution': Pogroms against the Jews in the *regnum Teutonicum* from c. 1280–1350." In *The Jews of Europe in the Middle Ages (Tenth to Fifteenth Centuries). Proceedings of the International Symposium Held at Speyer, 20–25 October 2002,* edited by Christoph Cluse. Turnholt: Brepols, 2004, 245–60.

Mundill, Robin. *England's Jewish Solution: Experiment and Expulsion 1262–1290.* Cambridge: Cambridge University Press, 1998.

———. "Edward I and the Final Phase of Anglo-Jewry." In *Jews in Medieval Britain, Historical, Literary and Archaeological Perspectives,* edited by Patricia Skinner. Rochester, N.Y.: Boydell & Brewer, 2003, 55–70.

Murray, Jacqueline. "Gendered Souls in Sexed Bodies: The Male Construction of Female Sexuality in Some Medieval Confessors' Manuals." In *Handling Sin: Confession in the Middle Ages,* edited by Peter Biller and A. J. Minnis. Woodbridge, Suffolk: York Medieval Press, 1998, 79–93.

———. "Mystical Castration: Some Reflections on Peter Abelard, Hugh of Lincoln and Sexual Control." In *Conflicted Identities and Multiple Masculinities: Men in the Medieval West,* edited by Jacqueline Murray. New York: Garland, 1999, 73–92.

Nahon, Gérard. "Didascali, Rabbins et Écoles du Paris Médiéval 1130–71." In *Rashi et la culture juive en France du Nord au moyen âge,* edited by Gilbert Dahan, Gérard Nahon, and Elie Nicholas. Paris: Peeters, 1997, 15–31.

———. "From the *Rue aux Juifs* to the *Chemin du Roy*: The Classical Age of French Jewry, 1108–1223." In *Jews and Christians in Twelfth-Century Europe,* edited by Michael A. Signer and John Van Engen. Notre Dame Conferences in Medieval Studies, 10. Notre Dame, Ind.: University of Notre Dame Press, 2001, 311–39.

Neave, Dorinda. "The Witch in Sixteenth-Century German Art." *Woman's Art Journal* 9, no. 1 (1988): 3–9.

Netanyahu, B. *The Origins of the Inquisition in Fifteenth Century Spain.* New York: Random House, 1995.

———. *Don Isaac Abravanel: Statesman and Philosopher.* 5th ed. Ithaca, N.Y.: Cornell University Press, 1998.

———. *The Marranos of Spain: From the Late 14th to the Early 16th Century,* according to Contemporary Hebrew Sources. 3rd ed. Ithaca, N.Y.: Cornell University Press, 1999.

Neubauer, AD[olf], compiler. *Fifty-Third Chapter of Isaiah according to the Jewish Interpreters.* 2 vols. Translated by S. R. Driver. New York: KTAV, 1969.

Niccoli, Ottavia. "*Menstruum quasi monstrum*: Monstrous Births and Menstrual Taboo in the Sixteenth Century." In *Sex and Gender in Historical Perspective,* edited by Edward Muir and Guido Ruggiero. Translated by Margaret Gallucci, Mary M. Galluci, and Carole C. Galluci. Baltimore: Johns Hopkins University Press, 1990, 1–25.

Nirenberg, David. "Muslim-Jewish Relations in the Fourteenth-Century Crown of Aragon." *Viator* 24, no. 4 (1993): 249–68.

———. *Communities of Violence: Persecution of Minorities in the Middle Ages.* Princeton, N.J.: Princeton University Press, 1996.

———. "Conversion, Sex, and Segregation: Jews and Christians in Medieval Spain." *American Historical Review* 107, no. 4 (2002): 1065–93.

———. "Mass Conversion and Genealogical Mentalities: Jews and Christians in Fifteenth-Century Spain." *Past and Present* 174 (2002): 3–41.

———. "Spanish 'Judaism' and 'Christianity' in an Age of Mass Conversion." In

Rethinking European Jewish History, edited by Jeremy Cohen and Moshe Rosman. Oxford: Littman Library of Jewish Civilization, 2009, 149–72.

Nolan, Michael. "The Defective Male: What Aquinas Really Said." *New Blackfriars* 75 (1994): 156–65.

North, J. D. "Astrology and the Fortunes of Churches." *Centaurus* 24 (1980): 181–211.

Ober, William B. "Can the Leper Change His Spots? Part I." *American Journal of Dermatopathology* 5, no. 1 (1983): 43–58.

———. "Can the Leper Change His Spots? Part II." *American Journal of Dermatopathology* 5, no. 2 (1983): 173–86.

O'Neill, Ynes Viole. "Another Look at the *Anatomia Porci*." *Viator* 1 (1970): 115–25.

Orfali, Moises. "Jews and Conversos in Fifteenth-Century Spain: Christian Apologia and Polemic." In *From Witness to Witchcraft: Jews and Judaism in Medieval Christian Thought,* edited by Jeremy Cohen. Wolfenbütteler Mittelalter-Studien 11. Wiesbaden: Harrassowitz Verlag, 1996, 337–60.

Ostrer, Boris S. "Leprosy: Medical Views of Leviticus Rabba." *Early Science and Medicine* 7, no. 2 (2002): 138–54.

Palazzo, Robert P. "The Veneration of the Sacred Foreskin(s) of Baby Jesus—A Documented Analysis." In *Multicultural Europe and Cultural Exchange in the Middle Ages and Renaissance,* edited by James P. Helfers. Arizona Studies in the Middle Ages and Renaissance 12. Turnholt: Brepols, 2005, 155–76.

Pardo Tomás, José. "Physicians' and Inquisitors' Stories? Circumcision and Crypto-Judaism in Sixteenth-Eighteenth-Century Spain." In *Bodily Extremities: Preoccupations with the Human Body in Early Modern European Culture,* edited by Florike Egmond and Robert Zwijenberg. Burlington, Vt.: Ashgate, 2003, 168–94.

Park, Katherine. "Medicine and Society in Medieval Europe, 500–1500." In *Medicine and Society: Historical Essays,* edited by Andrew Wear. Cambridge: Cambridge University Press, 1992, 59–90.

———. "The Criminal and the Saintly Body: Autopsy and Dissection in Renaissance Italy." *Renaissance Quarterly* 47, no. 1 (1994): 1–33.

———. "The Life of the Corpse: Division and Dissection in Late Medieval Europe." *Journal of the History of Medicine and Allied Sciences* 50, no. 1 (1994): 111–32.

Pastan, Elizabeth. "Tam Haereticos Quam Judaeos: Shifting Symbols in the Glazing of Troyes Cathedral." *Word and Image* 10 (1994): 66–83.

Patai, Raphael. *The Jewish Alchemists.* Princeton. N.J.: Princeton University Press, 1994.

Patai, Raphael, and Jennifer Patai Wing. *The Myth of the Jewish Race.* New York: Scribner's, 1975.

Patton, Pamela A. "Constructing the Inimical Jew in the *Cantigas de Santa Maria*: Theophilus's Magician in Text and Image." In *Beyond the Yellow Badge: Anti-Judaism and Antisemitism in Medieval and Early Modern Visual Culture,* edited by Mitchell B. Merback. Leiden: Brill, 2008, 233–56.

Paulmier-Foucart, Monique, and Marie-Christine Duchenne. *Vincent de Beauvais et le Grand miroir du monde.* Turnholt: Brepols, 2004.

Pendergraft, Mary. "'Thou Shalt Not Eat the Hyena': A Note on 'Barnabas' Epistle 10.7." *Vigiliae Christianae* 46 (1992): 75–79.

Pichon, Genevièvie. "Essai sur la lèpre du haut moyen age." *Le moyen âge* 90, no. 3–4 (1984): 331–56.
Poliakov, Léon. *The History of Anti-Semitism*. 4 vols. Translated by Richard Howard. London: Elek Books, 1965.
———. *Histoire de l'antisémitisme*. 4 vols. Paris: Calmann Lévy, 1955–77.
Pormann, Peter E. "Theory and Practice in the Early Hospitals in Baghdad—Al-Kaškarī on Rabies and Melancholy." *Zeitschrift für Geschichte der Arabisch-Islamischen Wissenschaften* 15 (2002/2003): 197–248.
———. "The Art of Medicine: Female Patients and Practitioners in Medieval Islam." *The Lancet* 373 (2009): 1598–99.
Porter, Martin. *Windows of the Soul: Physiognomy in European Culture 1470–1780*. Oxford: Clarendon Press, 2005.
Prawer, Joshua. "The Autobiography of Obadyah the Norman, a Convert to Judaism at the Time of the First Crusade." In *Studies in Medieval Jewish History and Literature*, edited by Isadore Twersky. 2 vols. Cambridge, Mass.: Harvard University Press, 1979, 1:110–34.
Prioreschi, Plinio. *A History of Medicine*. Lewiston, N.Y.: Edwin Mellen Press, 1991.
Purday, K. M. "Berengar and the Use of the Word *Substantia*." *Downside Review* 91 (1973): 101–10.
Raban, Sandra. *England under Edward I and Edward II 1259–1327*. Oxford: Blackwell, 2000.
Raddatz, Alfred. "Zur Vorgeschichte der 'Epistula seu liber contra Judaeos' Amulos von Lyon." In *Ecclesia Peregrinans. Josef Lenzenweger zum 70. Geburtstag*. Vienna: Verband der Wissenschaftlichen Gesellschaften Österreichs, 1986, 53–57.
Raden, Jennifer, ed. *The Nature of Melancholy from Aristotle to Kristeva*. Oxford: Oxford University Press, 2000.
Raspe, Lucia. "Payyetanim as Heroes of Medieval Folk Narrative: The Case of R. Shim'on B. Yishaq of Mainz." In *Jewish Studies between the Disciplines/Judaistik zwischen den Disziplinen*. Leiden: Brill, 2003, 354–72.
Rawcliffe, Carole. *Leprosy in Medieval England*. Rochester, N.Y.: Boydell Press, 2006.
Rembaum, Joel E. "The Development of a Jewish Exegetical Tradition regarding Isaiah 53." *Harvard Theological Review* 75, no. 3 (1982): 289–311.
Renna, Thomas. "The Jews in the Golden Legend." In *Christian Attitudes toward Jews in the Middle Ages: A Casebook*, edited by Michael Frassetto. New York: Routledge, 2007, 137–50.
Repath, Ian. "Anonymous Latinus, *Book of Physiognomy*." In *Seeing the Face, Seeing the Soul: Polemon's Physiognomy from Classical Antiquity to Medieval Islam*, edited by Simon Swain. Oxford: Oxford University Press, 2007, 549–636.
Resnick, Irven M. "*Scientia liberalis*, Dialectics, and Otloh of St. Emmeram." *Revue Bénédictine* 97, no. 3–4 (1987): 241–52.
———. "Attitudes toward Philosophy and Dialectic during the Gregorian Reform." *Journal of Religious History* 16, no. 2 (1990): 115–25.
———. "Medieval Roots of the Myth of Jewish Male Menses." *Harvard Theological Review* (2000): 241–63.

———. "Ps. Albert the Great on the Physiognomy of Jesus and Mary." *Medieval Studies* 64 (2002): 217–40.

———. "Humoralism and Adam's Body: Twelfth-Century Debates and Petrus Alfonsi's *Dialogus contra Judaeos*." *Viator* 36 (2005): 181–95.

———. "Odo of Tournai and the Dehumanization of Medieval Jews: A Reexamination." *Jewish Quarterly Review* 98, no. 4 (2008): 471–84.

Resnick, Irven, M., and Kenneth F. Kitchell Jr. "The Sweepings of Lamia: Transformations of the Myths of Lilith and Lamia." In *Religion, Gender, and Culture in the Pre-Modern World*, edited by Alexandra Cuffel and Brian Britt. New York: Palgrave Macmillan, 2007, 77–104.

Rexroth, Frank. *Deviance and Power in Late Medieval London*. Translated by Pamela E. Selwyn. Cambridge: Cambridge University Press, 2007.

Reynolds, Philip Lyndon. "Scholastic Theology and the Case against Women's Ordination." *Heythrop Journal* 36, no. 3 (1995): 249–85.

Richards, Jeffrey. *Sex, Dissidence and Damnation: Minority Groups in the Middle Ages*. New York: Barnes and Noble, 1990.

Riess, Frank. "From Aachen to al-Andalus: The Journey of Deacon Bodo (823–76)." *Early Medieval Europe* 13, no. 2 (2005): 131–57.

Robert, Ulysse. *Les signes d'infamie au moyen age. Juifs, Sarrasins, hérétiques, lépreux, cagots et filles publiques*. Paris: Honoré Champion, 1891.

Roberts, Victor W. "The Relation of Faith and Reason in St. Anselm of Canterbury." *American Benedictine Review* 25 (1974): 494–512.

Roderich-Stoltheim, F. [Theodor Fritsch]. *The Riddle of the Jew's Success*. Translated by Capel Pownall. Leipzig: Hammer-Verlag, 1927.

Röhrkasten, Jens. *The Mendicant Houses of Medieval London 1221–1539*. Münster: Lit Verlag, 2004.

Romano, David. "Conversion de Judios al Islam (Corona de Aragon 1280 y 1284)." *Sefarad* 36, no. 2 (1976): 333–37.

Roques, René. "La méthode de Saint Anselme dans le 'Cur Deus Homo.'" *Aquinas. Ephemerides Thomisticae* 5 (1962): 3–57.

Rosenstock, Bruce. "Alonso de Cartagena: Nation, Miscegenation, and the Jew in Late-Medieval Castile." *Exemplaria* 12, no. 1 (2000): 185–204.

———. "Messianism, Machismo, and 'Marranism': The Case of Abraham Miguel Cardoso." In *Queer Theory and the Jewish Question*, edited by Daniel Boyarin, Daniel Itzkovitz, and Ann Pellegrini. New York: Columbia University Press, 2003, 199–227.

Rosenwein, Barbara H. "Feudal War and Monastic Peace: Cluniac Liturgy as Ritual Aggression." *Viator* 2 (1972): 129–57.

Roth, Cecil. *The Jews of Medieval Oxford*. Oxford: Clarendon Press, 1951.

———. *Essays and Portraits in Anglo-Jewish History*. Philadelphia: Jewish Publication Society of America, 1962.

Roth, Norman. "Isaac Polgar y su libro contra un converse." In *Polémica Judeo-Cristiana Estudios,* edited by Carlos del Valle Rodriguez. Madrid: Aben Ezra Ediciones, 1992, 67–74.

———. *Conversos, Inquisition, and the Expulsion of the Jews from Spain*. Madison: University of Wisconsin Press, 2002.

Rovang, Paul R. "Hebraizing Arthurian Romance: The Originality of Melech Artus." *Arthuriana* 19, no. 2 (2009): 3-9.

Rowe, Nina. "Idealization and Subjection at the South Façade of the Strasbourg Cathedral." In *Multicultural Europe and Cultural Exchange in the Middle Ages and Renaissance,* edited by James P. Helfers. Arizona Studies in the Middle Ages and Renaissance 12. Turnholt: Brepols, 2005, 179-201.

Roy, Bruno. "Un inédit d'Albert le Grand dans *l'Unguentarius* de Guillaume de Werda." In *Comprendre et Maîtriser la Nature au Moyen Ages, Mélanges d'histoire des Sciences offerts à Guy Beujouan*. Geneva: Libr. Droz, 1994, 171-80.

Rubin, Miri. "Desecration of the Host: The Birth of an Accusation." In *Christianity and Judaism. Papers Read at the 1991 Summer Meeting and the 1992 Winter Meeting of the Ecclesiastical History Society,* edited by Diana Wood. Cambridge, Mass.: Ecclesiastical History Society, 1992, 169-85.

———. "Rudolph of Schlettstadt, O.P.: Reporter of Violence, Writer on Jews." In *Christ among the Medieval Dominicans: Representations of Christ in the Texts and Images of the Order of Preachers,* edited by Kent Emery and Joseph Wawrykow. Notre Dame, Ind.: University of Notre Dame Press, 1998, 283-92.

———. *Gentile Tales: The Narrative Assault on late Medieval Jews.* New Haven: Yale University Press, 1999.

———. *Mother of God: A History of the Virgin Mary.* New Haven: Yale University Press, 2009.

Salvadori , Patrizia. "La Peste e la Lebbra in 'medioevo Latino'. Un prospetto biblio—geografico." In *Maladies et société (XIIe-XVIIIe siècles). Actes du Colloque de Bielfeld, novembre 1986,* edited by Neithard Bulst and Robert Delort. Paris: Editions du C.N.R.S., 1989, 177-93.

Salvat, Michel. "Le ciel des vulgarisateurs: note sur les traductions de *De proprietatibus rerum.*" In *Observer, Lire, Écrire le Ciel au Moyen Age. Actes du Colloque d'Orleans 22-23 Avril 1989*. Paris: Klincksieck, 1991, 301-13.

Sánchez Sánchez, Manuel Ambrosio. "Predicación y antisemitismo: El caso de san Vicente Ferrer." In *Proyección histórica de España en sus tres culturas: Castilla y León, América y el Mediterráneo*. Valladolid: Junta de Castilla y León, 1993, 195-203.

Sansy, Danièle. "Marquer la Différence: L'imposition de la rouelle aux XIIe et XIVe siècles." *Médiévales* 41 (2001): 15-36.

———. "Signe distinctif et Judéité dans l'image." In *Le corps et sa parure; The Body and Its Adornment,* Micrologus Library 15. Florence: SISMEL, 2007, 87-106.

Saperstein, Marc. *Decoding the Rabbis: A Thirteenth-Century Commentary on the Aggadah.* Cambridge, Mass.: Harvard University Press, 1980.

———. "Christians and Jews—Some Positive Images." *Harvard Theological Review* 79, no. 1-3 (1986): 236-46.

Schäfer, Peter. *Jesus in the Talmud.* Princeton, N.J.: Princeton University Press, 2007.

Schaff, Philip. *History of the Christian Church.* 8 vols. Oak Harbor, Wash.: Logos Research Systems, 1997.

Scharold, Hans. "Die Physiognomie des Albertus Magnus und die moderne Wissenschaft." *Bayerische Blätter fur das Gymnasial—Schulwesen* 68, no. 5 (1932): 289–301.

Schenk, Richard. "Convenant Initiation: Thomas Aquinas and Robert Kilwardby on the Sacrament of Circumcision." In *Ordo sapientiae et amoris: Image et message de saint Thomas d'Aquin à travers les récentes études historiques, hérméneutiques et doctrinales. Hommage au Professeur Jean-Pierre Torell OP à l'occasion de son 65e anniversaire,* edited by Carlos-Josaphat Pinto de Oliveira. Studia Friburgensia, n.s. 78. Fribourg: Editions Universitaires, 1993, 555–93.

Schmitt, Charles. "Pseudo-Aristotle in the Latin Middle Ages." In *Pseudo-Aristotle in the Middle Ages,* edited by Jill Kraye, W. F. Ryan, and C. B. Schmitt. London: Warburg Institute, 1986, 3–15.

Schmitt, Jean-Claude. *The Holy Greyhound: Guinefort, Healer of Children since the Thirteenth Century.* Translated by Martin Thom. Cambridge: Cambridge University Press, 1983.

———. *The Conversion of Herman the Jew: Autobiography, History and Fiction in the Twelfth Century.* Translated by Alex J. Novikoff. Philadelphia: University of Pennsylvania Press, 2010.

Schmitz, Rolf. "Jacob ben Rubén y su obra Milḥamot ha-Šem." In *Polémica Judeo-Cristiana Estudios,* edited by Carlos del Valle Rodriguez. Madrid: Aben Ezra Ediciones, 1992, 45–58.

Schnitzler, Norbert. "Anti-Semitism, Image Desecration, and the Problem of 'Jewish Execution.'" In *History and Images: Toward a New Iconology,* edited by Axel Bolvig and Phillip Lindley. Turnholt: Brepols, 2003, 357–78.

Schreckenberg, Heinz. *The Jews in Christian Art: An Illustrated History.* New York: Continuum, 1996.

Schubert, Kurt. "Apostasie aus Identitätskrise—Nicholas Donin." *Kairos: Zeitschrift für Judaistik und Religionswissenschaft* n.s. 30–31 (1988–89): 1–10.

Scior, Volker. "The Mediterranean in the High Middle Ages: Area of Unity or Diversity? Arnold of Lübeck's *Chronica Slavorum.*" In *Mobility and Travel in the Mediterranean from Antiquity to the Middle Ages,* edited by Renate Schlesier and Ulriche Zellmann. Münster: LIT, 2004, 99–116.

Seiferth, Wolfgang S. *Synagogue and Church in the Middle Ages: Two Symbols in Art and Literature.* Translated by Lee Chadeayne and Paul Gottwald. New York: Ungar, 1970.

Sela, Shlomo, and Gad Freudenthal. "Abraham Ibn Ezra's Scholarly Writings: A Chronological Listing." *Aleph* 6 (2006): 13–55.

Seror, Simon. *Les noms des Juifs de France au Moyen Âge.* Paris: Editions du centre national de la recherche scientifique, 1989.

———. "Les noms des femmes juives en Angleterre au Moyen Âge." *Revue des études juives* 154 (1995): 295–325.

Seyfert, Werner. "Ein Komplexionentext einer Leipziger Inkunabel (angeblich eines Johann von Neuhaus) und seine handschriftliche Herleitung aus der Zeit nach 1300." *Archiv für Geschichte der Medizin* 20 (1928): 272–99; 372–89.

Seymour, M. C. *Bartholomaeus Anglicus and His Encyclopedia.* Aldershot, U.K.: Ashgate, 1992.

Shachar, Isaiah. *The Judensau: A Medieval Anti-Jewish Motif and Its History.* London: Warburg Institute, 1974.
Shatzmiller, Joseph. *La deuxième controverse de Paris. Un chapitre dans la polémique entre chrétiens et juifs au Moyen Age.* Paris: Peeters, 1994.
———. *Jews, Medicine, and Medieval Society.* Berkeley: University of California Press, 1994.
———. "Jewish Converts to Christianity in Medieval Europe 1200–1500." In *Cross Cultural Convergences in the Crusader Period. Essays Presented to Aryeh Grabois on His Sixty-Fifth Birthday,* edited by Michael Goodich, Sophia Menache, and Sylvia Schein. New York: Peter Lang, 1995, 297–318.
Sherman, Joseph. *The Jewish Pope: Myth, Diaspora and Yiddish Literature.* Studies in Yiddish, 4. Oxford: European Humanities Center, 2003.
Shoham-Steiner, Ephraim. "An Ultimate Pariah? Jewish Social Attitudes toward Jewish Lepers in Medieval Western Europe." *Social Research* 70, no. 1 (2003): 237–68.
———. "Pharoah's Bloodbath: Medieval European Jewish Thoughts about Leprosy, Disease, and Blood Therapy." In *Jewish Blood: Reality and Metaphor in History, Religion and Culture,* edited by Mitchell Hart. New York: Routledge, 2009, 99–115.
Sicart, P. "Alphonse de Cartagéne." In *Dictionnaire d'histoire et de géographie ecclésiastiques,* edited by Alfred Baudrillart, et al. Paris: Letouzey et Ané, 1914, 2: 702–7.
Singer, Charles. "The Scientific Views and Visions of Saint Hildegard of Bingen." In *Studies on the History and Method of Science.* 2nd ed. London: William Dawson and Sons, 1955, 1–55.
Smith, Katherine Allen. "Saints in Shining Armor: Martial Asceticism and Masculine Models of Sanctity, ca. 1050–1250." *Speculum* 83, no. 3 (2008): 572–602.
Smith, Lesley. "William of Auvergne and the Jews." In *Christianity and Judaism. Papers Read at the 1991 Summer Meeting and the 1992 Winter Meeting of the Ecclesiastical History Society,* edited by Diana Wood. Cambridge, Mass.: Ecclesiastical History Society, 1992, 107–17.
———. "William of Auvergne and the Law of the Jews and the Muslims." In *Scripture and Pluralism: Reading the Bible in the Religiously Plural Worlds of the Middle Ages and Renaissance,* edited by Thomas Heffernan and Thomas Burman. Leiden: Brill, 2005, 95–122.
Smits, E. R. "Vincent of Beauvais: A Note on the Background of the *Speculum*." In *Vincent of Beauvais and Alexander the Great,* edited by W. J. Aerts, E. R. Smits, and J. B. Voorbij. Groningen: Egbert Forsten, 1986, 1–9.
Smits Van Waesberghe, J. M. A. F. "Neue Kompositionen des Johannes von Metz (um 975)." In *Speculum musicae artis. Festgabe für Heinrich Husmann zum 60. Geburtstag am 16. Dez 1968,* edited by Heinz Becker and Reinhard Gerlach. Munich: Fink, 1970, 285–303.
Smoller, Laura Ackerman. *History, Prophecy, and the Stars: The Christian Astrology of Pierre d'Ailly 1350–1420.* Princeton, N.J.: Princeton University Press, 1994.
Sobol, Peter G. "The Shadow of Reason: Explanations of Intelligent Animal Be-

havior in the Thirteenth Century." In *The Medieval World of Nature: A Book of Essays,* edited by Joyce E. Salisbury. New York: Garland, 1993, 109-28.

Southern, R. W. *Scholastic Humanism and the Unification of Europe.* 2 vols. Oxford: Blackwell, 1995-2001.

Spangenberg, Peter-Michael. "Judenfeindlichkeit in den altfranzösischen Marienmirakeln." In *Die Legende vom Ritualmord: zur Geschichte der Blutbeschuldigung gegen Juden.* Edited by Rainer Erb. Berlin: Metropol, 1993, 157-77.

Stacey, Robert. "The Conversion of Jews to Christianity in Thirteenth-Century England." *Speculum* 67, no. 2 (1992): 263-83.

———. "History, Religion, and Medieval Antisemitism: A Response to Gavin Langmuir." *Religious Studies Review* 20, no. 2 (1994): 95-101.

———. "Parliamentary Negotiation and the Expulsion of the Jews from England." In *Thirteenth Century England VI,* edited by R. H. Britnell, R. Frame, and M. Prestwich. Woodbridge, Suffolk: Boydell, 1997, 77-101.

———. "Crusades, Martyrdoms, and the Jews of Norman England, 1096-1190." In *Juden und Christen zur Zeit der Kreuzzüge,* edited by Alfred Haverkamp. Sigmaringen: Jan Thorbecke Verlag, 1999, 233-51.

———. "Antisemitism and the Medieval English State." In *The Medieval English State: Essays Presented to James Campbell,* edited by J. R. Maddicott and D. M. Palliser. London: Hambledon Press, 2000, 163-77.

———. "Jews and Christians in Twelfth-Century England: Some Dynamics of a Changing Relationship." In *Jews and Christians in Twelfth-Century Europe,* edited by Michael A. Signer and John Van Engen. Notre Dame Conferences in Medieval Studies 10. Notre Dame, Ind.: University of Notre Dame Press, 2001, 340-54.

———. "The English Jews under Henry III." In *The Jews in Medieval Britain: Historical, Literary and Archaeological Perspectives,* edited by Patricia Skinner. Rochester, N.Y.: Boydell, 2003, 41-54

———. "'Adam of Bristol' and Tales of Ritual Crucifixion in Medieval England." In *Thirteenth-Century England XI, Proceedings of the Gregynog Conference 2005,* edited by Björn Weiler, Janet Burton, Phillipp Schofield, and Karen Stöber. Woodbridge, Suffolk: Boydell Press, 2007.

Steenberghen, Fernand van. "Travaux récents sur la pensée du XIIIe siècle." *Revue néo-scolastique de philosophie* 42 (1939): 469-85.

Stern, Josef. "Maimonides on the Covenant of Circumcision and the Unity of God." In *The Midrashic Imagination: Jewish Exegesis, Thought, and History,* edited by Michael Fishbane. Albany: SUNY Press, 1993, 131-54.

Stern, Menahem. "Antisemitism in Rome." In *Antisemitism through the Ages,* edited by Shmuel Almog. Oxford: Pergamon Press, 1988, 16-25.

Stow, Kenneth. "The Avignonese Papacy or, After the Expulsion." In *From Witness to Witchcraft: Jews and Judaism in Medieval Christian Thought,* edited by Jeremy Cohen. Wolfenbütteler Mittelalter-Studien 11. Wiesbaden: Harrassowitz Verlag, 1996, 275-97.

———. "Conversion, Apostasy, and Apprehensiveness: Emicho of Flonheim and the Fear of the Jews in the Twelfth Century." *Speculum* 76 (2001): 911-33.

———. *Jewish Dogs: An Image and Its Interpreters.* Stanford: Stanford University Press, 2006.

———. "The '1007 Anonymous' and Papal Sovereignty: Jewish Peceptions of the Papacy and Papal Policy in the High Middle Ages." In *Popes, Church, and Jews in the Middle Ages,* by Kenneth Stow. Burlington, Vt.: Ashgate, 2007, IV: 1–81.

Strange, Richard. *The Life of St. Thomas of Hereford.* London: Burns and Oates, 1879.

Strickland, Debra Higgs. "The Jews, Leviticus, and the Unclean in Medieval English Bestiaries." In *Beyond the Yellow Badge: Anti-Judaism and Antisemitism in Medieval and Early Modern Visual Culture,* edited by Mitchell B. Merback. Leiden: Brill, 2008, 203–32.

Stroll, Mary. *The Jewish Pope: Ideology and Politics in the Papal Schism of 1130.* Leiden: Brill, 1987.

Thorndike, Lynn. "Buridan's Questions on the Physiognomy Ascribed to Aristotle." *Speculum* 18, no. 1 (1943): 99–103.

———. *The Sphere of Sacrobosco and Its Commentators.* Chicago: University of Chicago Press, 1949.

———. "De complexionibus." *Isis* 49, no. 4 (1958): 398–408.

———. *History of Magic and Experimental Science.* 8 vols. New York: Columbia University Press, 1923–58.

Tinkle, Theresa. "Saturn of the Several Faces." *Viator* 18 (1987): 289–307.

Toaff, Ariel. *Pasque di sangue, Ebrei d'Europa e omicidi rituali.* Bologna: Il Mulino, 2008.

Tolan, John. "Peter the Venerable on the 'Diabolical Heresy of the Saracens.'" In *The Devil, Heresy and Witchcraft in the Middle Ages: Essays in Honor of Jeffrey B. Russell,* edited by Alberto Ferreiro. Leiden: Brill, 1998, 345–67.

———. "Un cadavre mutilé: le déchirement polémique de Mahomet." *Le Moyen Âge* 104 (1998): 53–72.

Torrell, Jean-Pierre "La notion de prophètie et la méthode apologétique dans le *Contra Saracenos* de Pierre le Vénérable." *Studia Monastica* 17 (1975): 257–82.

Touati, Francois-Olivier. *Maladie et société au moyen âge: La lèpre, les lépreux et les léproseries dans la province ecclésiastique de Sens jusqu'au milieu du XIVe siècle.* Paris: De Boeck, 1998.

Trachtenberg, Joshua. *The Devil and the Jews: The Medieval Conception of the Jew and Its Relation to Modern Antisemitism.* New Haven: Yale University Press, 1943.

———. *Jewish Magic and Superstition: A Study in Folk Religion.* Cleveland: World Publishing, 1961.

Trautner-Kromann, Hanne. *Shield and Sword: Jewish Polemics against Christianity and the Christians in France and Spain from 1100–1500.* Tübingen: Mohr, 1993.

Tuilier, André. "La condamnation du Talmud par les maîtres universitaires Parisiens, ses causes et sese conséquences politiques et idéologiques." In *Le brûlement du Talmud à Paris 1242–1244,* edited by Gilbert Dahan. Paris: Les Éditions du Cerf, 1999, 59–78.

Turner, Nancy. "Jewish Witness, Forced Conversion, and Island Living: John Duns Scotus on Jews and Judaism." In *Christian Attitudes toward Jews in the*

Middle Ages: A Casebook, edited by Michael Frassetto. New York: Routledge, 2007, 183–209.

Valle, Carlos del. "El libro de las Batallas de Dios, de Abner de Burgos." In *Polémica Judeo-Cristiana Estudios,* edited by Carlos del Valle Rodriguez. Madrid: Aben Ezra Ediciones, 1992, 75–120.

Van der Lugt, Maaike. *Le Ver, le Démon et la Vierge: Les théories médiévales de la génération extraordinaire.* Paris: Les Belles Lettres, 2004.

———. "La Peau noire dans la science medieval." In *La pelle umana; The Human Skin.* Vol. 13 of *Micrologus: Natura, scienze e società medievali. Nature, Sciences and Medieval Societies.* Florence: SISMEL, 2005, 439–75.

———. "Les maladies héréditaires dans la pensée scolastique (XIIe–XVIe siècle)." In *L'hérédité entre Moyen Âge et Époque modern. Perspectives historiques.* Edited by Maaike van der Lugt and Charles de Miramon. Florence: SISMEL, 2008, 273–320.

Vincent, Nicholas C. "Jews, Poitevins, and the Bishop of Winchester, 1231–1234." In *Christianity and Judaism. Papers Read at the 1991 Summer Meeting and the 1992 Winter Meeting of the Ecclesiastical History Society,* edited by Diana Wood. Cambridge, Mass.: Ecclesiastical History Society, 1992, 119–32.

———. "Two Papal Letters on the Wearing of the Jewish Badge, 1221 and 1229." *Jewish Historical Studies: Transactions of the Jewish Historical Society of England* 34 (1997): 209–24.

Voorbij, J. B. "The *Speculum Historiale*: Some Aspects of Its Genesis and Manuscript Tradition." In *Vincent of Beauvais and Alexander the Great,* edited by W. J. Aerts, E. R. Smits, and J. B. Voorbij. Groningen: Egbert Forsten, 1986, 11–55.

Wack, Mary Frances. "The Measure of Pleasure: Peter of Spain on Men, Women, and Lovesickness." *Viator* 17 (1986): 173–96.

Welie-Vink, Wendelien A. W. van. "Pig Snouts as Sign of Evil in Manuscripts of the Low Countries." *Quaerendo* 26, no. 3 (1996): 213–28.

White, Hayden. "Pontius of Cluny, the *Curia Romana* and the End of Gregorianism in Rome." *Church History* 27, no. 3 (1958): 195–219.

Wickersheimer, Ernest. "Lèpre et Juifs au Moyen Âge." *Janus* 36 (1932): 43–48.

Wilkinson, John, ed. *Jerusalem Pilgrims before the Crusades.* Warminster, England: Aris and Phillips, 2002.

Williams, Steven J. "The Early Circulation of the Pseudo-Aristotelian *Secret of Secrets* in the West: The Papal and Imperial Courts." In *Le scienze alla corte di Federico II.* Vol. 2 of *Micrologus: Natura, scienze e società medievali.* Turnholt: Brepols, 1994, 127–44.

———. *The Secret of Secrets: The Scholarly Career of a Pseudo-Aristotelian Text in the Latin Middle Ages.* Ann Arbor: University of Michigan Press, 2003.

Williamson, Arthur H. "'A Pil for Pork-Eaters': Ethnic Identity, Apocalyptic Promises, and the Strange Creation of the Judeo-Scots." In *The Expulsion of the Jews: 1492 and After,* edited by Raymond B. Waddington and Arthur H. Williamson. New York: Garland, 1994, 237–58.

Wilson, Erasmus. *Diseases of the Skin.* 6th ed. Philadelphia: Lea and Blanchard, 1865.

Withington, E. T. *Medical History from the Earliest Times: A Popular History of the Healing Art.* London: Scientific Press, 1894.

Wolf, Kenneth Baxter. "Muhammad as Antichrist in Ninth-Century Córdoba." In *Christians, Muslims, and Jews in Medieval and Early Modern Spain: Interaction and Cultural Change,* edited by Mark D. Meyerson and Edward D. English. Notre Dame Conferences in Medieval Studies 8. Notre Dame, Ind.: University of Notre Dame Press, 2000, 3–19.

Wolfson, Elliot R. "Circumcision and the Divine Name: A Study in the Transmission of Esoteric Doctrine." *Jewish Quarterly Review* 78, no. 1–2 (1987): 77–111.

———. "Martyrdom, Eroticism, and Asceticism in Twelfth-Century Ashkenazi Piety." In *Jews and Christians in Twelfth-Century Europe,* edited by Michael A. Signer and John Van Engen. Notre Dame Conferences in Medieval Studies 10. Notre Dame, Ind.: University of Notre Dame Press, 2001, 171–220.

———. "Circumcision, Secrecy, and the Veiling of the Veil: Phallomorphic Exposure and Kabbalistic Esotericism." In *The Covenant of Circumcision: New Perspectives on an Ancient Jewish Rite,* edited by Elizabeth Wyner Mark. Lebanon, N.H.: University Press of New England, 2003, 58–70.

Wood, Charles T. "The Doctors' Dilemma: Sin, Salvation, and the Menstrual Cycle in Medieval Thought." *Speculum* 56, no. 4 (1981): 710–27.

Yerushalmi, Yosef Hayim. *From Spanish Court to Italian Ghetto: Isaac Cardoso: A Study in Seventeenth-Century Marranism and Jewish Apologetics.* Seattle: University of Washington Press, 1981.

Yuval, Israel Jacob. "Jewish Messianic Expectations towards 1240 and Christian Reactions." In *Toward the Millennium: Messianic Expectations from the Bible to Waco,* edited by Peter Schäfer and Mark Cohen. Leiden: Brill, 1998, 105–21.

———. "'They Tell Lies: You Ate the Man,' Jewish Reactions to Ritual Murder Accusations." In *Religious Violence between Christians and Jews: Medieval Roots, Modern Perspective,* edited by Anna Sapir Abulafia. New York: Palgrave, 2002, 86–106.

———. *Two Nations in Your Womb: Perceptions of Jews and Christians in Late Antiquity and the Middle Ages.* Translated by Barbara Harshav and Jonathan Chapman. Berkeley: University of California Press, 2006.

Zacour, Norman. *Jews and Saracens in the Consilia of Oldradus de Ponte.* Toronto: Pontifical Institute for Mediaeval Studies, 1990.

Zafran, Eric. "Saturn and the Jews." *Journal of the Warburg and Courtauld Institutes* 42 (1979): 16–27.

Zema, Demetrius B. "The Houses of Tuscany and of Pierleone in the Crisis of Rome in the Eleventh Century." *Traditio* 2 (1944): 155–75.

Zias, Joseph. "Lust and Leprosy: Confusion or Correlation?" *Bulletin of the American schools of Oriental Research* 275 (1989): 27–31.

Ziegler, Joseph. "Reflections on the Jewry Oath in the Middle Ages." In *Christianity and Judaism. Papers Read at the 1991 Summer Meeting and the 1992 Winter Meeting of the Ecclesiastical History Society,* edited by Diana Wood. Cambridge, Mass.: Ecclesiastical History Society, 1992, 209–20.

———. "Medicine and Immortality in Terrestrial Paradise." In *Religion and Medi-*

cine in the Middle Ages, edited by Peter Biller and Joseph Ziegler. York: York Medieval Press, 2001, 201–42.

———. "Text and Context: On the Rise of Physiognomic Thought." In *De Sion exibit lex et verbum domini de Hierusalem: Essays on medieval law, liturgy, and literature in honour of Amnon Linder,* edited by Yitzhak Hen. Turnholt: Brepols, 2001, 159–82.

———. "Hérédité et physiognomonie." In *L'hérédité entre Moyen Âge et Époque modern. Perspectives historiques,* edited by Maaike van der Lugt and Charles de Miramon. Florence: SISMEL, 2008, 245–71.

———. "Physiognomy, Science, and Proto-Racism 1200–1500." In *The Origins of Racism in the West,* edited by M. Eliav-Feldon, B. Isaac, and J. Ziegler. Cambridge: Cambridge University Press, 2009, 181–99.

Zimmermann, Moshe. *Wilhelm Marr, the Patriarch of Antisemitism.* Oxford: Oxford University Press, 1986.

INDEX

Aaron of York, 264
Abd al-Aziz ibn Uthman al-Qabīsī. *See* Alcabitius
Abel, 207, 210
Abgar of Edessa, King, 94
Abner de Burgos, 136
Abraham, biblical patriarch, 53, 56–57, 59, 61, 72
Abraham of Carcassonne, 138
Abraham bar Hiyya, 226
Abramson, Henry, 70
Abulafia, Anna Sapir, ix, 5, 40
Abū Ma'šar'. *See* Albumasar
Adam, 22, 30-31, 45, 51, 144, 192, 236, 246, 303, 305
Adam of Bristol, 141, 170, 254–55, 268
Adam of Eynsham, 253
Adler, Michael, 264
Adolf of Nassau, 11
Agobard of Lyon, 158, 160
Akbari, Suzanne Conklin, 230
Alain de Lille, 100
al-Andalusī, Sā'id, 230, 310, 316
Alberic II, Earl of Oxford, 263
Albero of Trier. *See* Aldabero of Trier
Albert of Aachen, 48–49, 258
Albert of Behaim, 16, 222
Albert the Great, 16–17, 21, 25, 27–28, 31–32, 45, 55–57, 71, 79, 90, 109, 112, 118, 140, 155, 170, 176, 179, 183–84, 192–93, 208, 211, 234, 278, 297, 303 6, 308 9, 311 14, 316, 319
Albumasar, 225, 228, 310
Alcabitius, 227–28, 232, 316
Aldabero of Trier, 13, 281
Alexander II, Pope, 39, 74, 271
Alexander VI, Pope, 295
Alexander the Great, 143
Alexander of Hales, 299
Alexander Neckam, 30, 220
Alfonso X, King, 246

Al Hakim, Caliph, 135
Alonso de Cartagena, 230, 247, 248, 291
Alonso de Espina, 157, 283, 322
Al-Qabīsī. *See* Alcabitius
Ambrose of Milan, 71
Amédée of Lausanne, 36
Ammianus Marcellinus, 232
Amolo of Lyon, 74, 158
Anaclet II, anti-Pope, 270, 272–74, 276–82, 284, 322
Andrew of Saint Victor, 209
Angles. *See* English people
Anselm of Canterbury, 35, 106
Anselm of Laon, 54, 70, 192
Anselm of Lucca. *See* Alexander II
Anthimus, 161
Antichrist, 226, 271, 276–77
Antiochus IV Epiphanes, 166
Anti-Semitism, 1–5, 8, 12, 39
Antoninus of Florence, 68, 155, 161, 240–41
Apion, 125
Aretaeus of Cappadocia, 116
Aristotle, 25, 176, 188, 234, 284, 297–98, 302, 316
Arnau of Villanova, 146
Arnaud of Verniolle, 121
Arnulf of Séez, 274–77, 280
Assumption, Feast of the, 75
Astral bodies: Jupiter, 220, 222–24, 228–31, 314–16; Mars, 23, 222–24, 229–30; Mercury, 23, 222, 230; Moon, 22–23, 222; Saturn, 22, 215, 217, 219, 220–32, 314–17, 320; Sun, 23, 221–22, 229–31; Venus, 23, 222, 224, 229–30
Astrologer, 226, 228
Astrology, 223, 305, 316
Astronomy, 23, 223, 228, 316
Atonement, Day of, 61
Augustine of Hippo, 44, 200, 211, 216–17
Avicenna, 19, 111, 118, 149, 193, 234, 297

379

Badge, Jews', 80–83, 86–88, 207, 231, 244, 248–49, 268
Balderich of Florennes, 13, 281
Baldwin, Archbishop of Canterbury, 250
Bale, Anthony, ix
Baptism, 33, 54–55, 57, 59, 66, 79, 92, 97, 122–24, 189, 205, 237, 242–44, 246–48, 253, 255–59, 261–63, 272, 275, 279, 283–84, 286, 289–91, 294–95, 320–22
Barcelona, Disputation of, 285
Bartholomaeus Anglicus. *See* Bartholomew the Englishman
Bartholomew the Englishman, 109, 111, 117, 140, 193, 212, 233–34, 309–10, 313–15
Bartholomew of Exeter, 41
Bartholomew of Messina, 15
Bartlett, Robert, 269, 288
Baude Fastoul d'Aras, 125
Baumgarten, Elisheva, 58
Bede, the Venerable, 20, 208, 294
Benedict XIII, Pope, 247
Benedict, Abbot of Peterborough, 106
Benedict of York, 253, 261
Benzo of Alba, 271–72
Berengar of Tours, 7
Bernáldez, Andrés, 239
Bernard of Clairvaux, 175, 273, 277, 281, 285
Bernard of Gordon, 107, 111, 113, 151, 174, 187
Bernard Gui, 259, 261
Bernardus Silvestris, 219
Berthold of Regensburg, 238
Bertrandon de la Broquière, 241
Biller, Peter, 47, 183
Biraben, Jean Noël, 107
Blood libel. *See* Murder, ritual
Blumenkranz, Bernhard, 265
Bodo Eleazar, 263
Bonafós de la Caballería, 262
Bonaventure, St., 68, 99, 117
Brand, Paul, 287
Bruno of Segni, 101, 146, 206, 208, 211
Burchard of Strasburg, 74
Burnett, Charles, 228

Cadalous, anti-Pope, 271
Caesarius of Arles, 122
Caesarius of Heisterbach, 52, 237, 257, 259, 260
Cain, 206–12, 248, 322
Callixtus II, Pope, 105, 278

Cancer, 177, 179, 314
Cancer, Tropic of, 311
Cardoso, Isaac, 142, 150, 178, 206, 243
Carpenter, John, 153
Castration, 318-19
Cecco d'Ascoli, 229
Celestine II, Pope, 271
Cervantes, Miguel de, 49
Chaeremon, 125
Chaucer, Geoffrey, 18, 126, 197, 315
Chazan, Robert, ix, 5
Chibnall, Marjorie, 278–79
Chromatius of Aquileia, 98
Circumcision: blood of, 61–64; Feast of the, 65; of Jesus, 62–63, 66; ritual, 52, 54–60, 64–65, 67, 69, 72–73, 251, 323; and sexuality, 69–70, 77–79, 88–89, 91–92; spiritual, 53–54, 65; surgical, 78; theological symbol, 207–8, 248–49, 261, 275, 321
Citizenship: of Jews in Nazi Germany, 2
Clement III, Pope, 290
Clement VII, Pope, 138
Clement of Bohemia, 90–91
Climata, 229, 230, 302, 304–9, 311–12, 320
Clime. *See Climata*
Clovis, King, 97
Cluny, monastery of, 39, 43, 270
Cohen, Jeremy, ix, 33, 40
Cohen, Shaye, 61, 90–92
Coin-clipping, 286–87
Cologne, 26–27, 261, 263, 278
Complexion, humoral, 11, 17–19, 21–23, 26–34, 45, 52, 110, 113, 115, 143, 161–63, 176, 178, 181, 185, 187–88, 189, 191–93, 206, 211–13, 220–24, 227, 230–32, 236, 248, 268, 277–79, 282, 291, 295–96, 304–10, 314–20, 323
Constantine, Emperor, 95-97
Constantine the African, 22, 108, 117, 177, 180, 185, 187, 316
Conversos, 165, 205, 243, 245–47, 283, 321
Coryat, Thomas, 65
Councils, Church: First Nicaea, 119; Florence, 55; Fourth Lateran, 4, 9, 80, 100, 107, 207, 249; Nablus, 83; Paris, 94; Rheims, 278; Salamanca, 136; Third Lateran, 103; Valladolid, 136; Zamorra, 136
Crescas de Nîmes, 139
Crete, 216, 218, 224
Crotus Rubeanus, 67
Crusades: First, 4, 48, 58, 76, 82, 129, 156,

163, 258, 290; Second, 4, 38; Third, 73, 96, 250, 252, 253; Fifth, 296; Seventh, 308; Shepherds', 132

Dacians, 309
David ha-Levi, 263
de' Conti da Foligno, Sigismondo, 171
Despres, Denise, ix
Diego de Salinas, 166
Dio Cassius, 215
Domus conversorum, 262, 289, 322
Dundes, Alan, 170
Duns Scotus, 54, 283, 322

Eck, Johannes, 137
Eden, Garden of, 30, 59
Edward I, King, 286–87
Edward III, King, 133
Egypt, 48, 61, 63, 75, 96, 171, 215
Elements, four primary, 221–22
Elukin, Jonathan M., 77
Emicho, Count, 48
Enders, Jody, 173
England, 133, 141, 153, 159, 194–96, 250–51, 254, 256, 262, 264–68, 286, 288–89
English people, 309
Epilepsy, 163, 201
Epiphanius, Bishop, 97
Erotian, 163
Ethiopia, 299, 305, 311, 313
Ethiopians, 68, 293–94, 296–99, 306–7, 310–13, 317
Eucharist, 7–9, 25, 60, 62, 108, 161, 201–2
Eve, 28, 30, 44–45, 51, 70, 116, 192, 236, 246, 323
Evil eye, 23

Fabre-Vassas, Claudine, 162, 238
Feldman, Louis, 216
Felix Fabri, 19, 86, 156, 240–41
Ferdinand and Isabella, Spanish monarchs, 85, 259
Fernando I, King, 262
Flaccus, Roman prefect, 167
Foa, Anna, 165, 172
Foetor judaicus, 232, 237, 239, 242, 321
Foetor luxuriae, 68
Foetor oris, 233
France, 38, 49, 89, 126, 133–34, 139, 148, 159–60, 244, 265–67, 273

Francis of Assisi, 102, 233
Francisco de Andrada, 205
Frederick I, Emperor, 74
Frederick II, Emperor, 6, 8, 15–16
Fritsch, Theodor, 88
Frontinus, Sextus Julius, 215

Galen, 19, 106, 185
Gehazi, 122, 124
Gerald of Wales, 254
Gerli, Michael, 239
Germans, 308–9, 311
Germany, 41, 88, 137, 202, 309, 321; Nazi, 2
Gilbert the Englishman, 117, 176
Gilbert Crispin, 150, 154
Gilbertus Anglicus. *See* Gilbert the Englishman
Gilles of Orval, 149
Ginzburg, Carlo, 133
Gonzalo Pérez Jarada, 165
Gout, 140, 176, 314, 318
Goya, Francisco Jose de, 231
Grabmayer, Johannes, 10
Gratian (Pierleoni), 278–79, 281, 291, 318, 322
Gregg, Joan Young, 79
Gregory VII, Pope, 271–72
Gregory IX, Pope, 80–81
Guerric of Saint-Quentin, 42
Guibert of Nogent, 262
Guillaume Agasse, 133
Guillaume le Clerc, 50
Guinefort, St., 148
Guy de Chauliac, 78

Hames, Chaim, ix
Hanson, Carrie, 70
Hasdai Crescas, 62
Haymo of Halberstadt, 175
Helinand de Froidment, 313, 317
Heloise, Abbess, 51
Henri de Mondeville, 128
Henry II, King of England, 250
Henry II, King of Germany, 264
Henry III, King of England, 197, 250, 262, 286, 288–89, 322
Henry IV, Emperor, 271
Henry V, Emperor, 278
Henry of Brussels, 183
Henry the German, 183
Henry of Winchester, 262, 286–87, 289–91

Henry Sully, Archbishop of Bourges, 100
Herman III, Archbishop of Cologne, 263
Herman of Cologne, 123, 147, 151, 262, 272
Herman de Valenciennes, 233
Hermann of Carinthia, 225, 229
Herod, King, 215
Hildebrand. *See* Gregory VII
Hildegard of Bingen, 30, 51, 192
Hincmar of Reims, 97
Hippocrates, 163, 299
Holocaust, the, 3
Holy Sepulcher, Church of the, 75, 135
Honorius II, anti-Pope, 219
Honorius II, Pope, 270, 273
Honorius III, Pope, 250
Horowitz, Elliott, 9, 248
Host, desecration of the, 4, 7–9, 10–11, 133, 202
Hugh of Avalon, St., 250, 253–54
Hugh of Cluny, 102
Hugh of Lincoln, 6, 197–98
Hugh of Lincoln, Bishop. *See* Hugh of Avalon
Hugh of St. Victor, 209
Hugh de Orival, 78, 180
Humbert of Romans, 116
Humors, bodily, 20, 22–23, 32, 110–11, 117–18, 155, 161, 171, 175–76, 191–93, 223, 310, 318. *See also* Complexion
Hungary, 80
Hutten, Ulrich von, 67

ibn Crispin, Mosheh Kohen, 213
ibn Ezra, Abraham, 279
ibn 'Imrān, Ishāq, 177, 179
ibn Matut, Samuel, 60
ibn Sahula, Isaac, 180
ibn Shaprut, Shem Tov ibn Isaac, 212–13
ibn Verga, Solomon, 170
India, 305
Inghetto Contardo, 165
Innocent II, Pope, 270–71, 273, 276–77, 280–81
Innocent III, Pope, 100, 121, 160, 209
Innocent IV, Pope, 6, 81
Inquisition, 165, 204–6, 241, 290
Iogna-Prat, Dominique, 39
Ireland, 254
Isaac, 62, 72–73
Isaac Abravanel, 172, 213

Isaac ben Eleazar of Blois, 197
Isaac ben Yedaiah, 89–91
Isaac Nathan, 203
Isidore of Seville, 20, 37, 56, 98, 101, 186, 208, 216, 294, 298
Ivo of Chartres, 48, 120

Jacob ben Solomon, 138
Jacob ben Reuben, 213
Jacobs, Joseph, 264
Jacquart, Danielle, 181
Jacques de Vitry, 47, 156, 176, 210, 233, 296
Jean Bodel, 103
Jerome, St., 46, 98, 114, 120, 123, 208
Jerónimo de Santa Fe, 284
Jesus of Nazareth, 8, 31–34, 40, 56–57, 62–63, 65–66, 74–77, 93–101, 122–24, 129, 144, 149, 157, 193, 202–3, 207, 211, 213, 226, 233, 235, 246, 251, 269, 276, 283, 321
Johannes Buxtorf the Elder, 60, 142
Johannes de Fonte, 25
Johannes Mesuë, 180
John XXII, Pope, 134
John of Chesney, 197
John of Damascus, 57
John of Gaddesden, 114
John of Naples, 137, 290
John of Salisbury, 14
John of Spain, 232
John Ardenne, 178
John de Joinville, 42
John le Convers, 268, 286
John Pecham, 33
Jordan, William C., 160
Joseph of Hamadan, 59
Joseph ben Nathan Official, 130
Josephus, Flavius, 186
Juan de Quiñones, 205–6, 241, 321
Judah Ha-Levi, 169

Kalonymous of Mainz, 48
Kanarfogel, Ephraim, 260
Kedar, Benjamin Z., 83
Kempe, Margery, 256
King's evil. *See Morbus regius*
Klibanksy, Raymond, 225
Kogman-Appel, Katrin, 64
Kornmann, Heinrich, 204
Kriegel, Maurice, 159

Langmuir, Gavin, 3–5, 7–9
Lasker, Daniel, ix
Lazarus, Order of St., 104
Leo IX, Pope, 271, 272
Lepers, 93–95, 101–8, 110–11, 113–14, 116–18, 122–23, 125–29, 131–35, 140, 142, 153, 159–60, 166, 173–74, 176–77, 180–81, 233–34, 240–41, 285
Leprosaria, 103–4, 111, 121, 127–28
Leprosy: Allopicia, 175; Elephantia, 110, 175–77; Elephantiasis, 96, 119; Leonina, 110, 175; Tyria, 110, 175
Libya, 216, 218
Lipton, Sara, ix
Lilith, 246
Locke, John, 126
London, 160
Lothair, King of Germany, 276–77
Lothar of Segni. *See* Innocent III
Louis VI, King of France, 270
Louis VII, King of France, 38
Louis VIII, King of France, 104
Louis IX, King of France, St., 42, 308
Louis the Pious, Emperor, 160
Lusitanus, Amatus, 189
Luther, Martin, 136–37, 179, 242
Lysimachus, 125, 215

Madsen, Peter, 321
Maimonides, 57, 73, 78, 88, 93, 155, 170, 177, 181
Manetho, 125, 215
Manfred, Bishop of Mantua, 273
Marcus Aurelius, Emperor, 232
Marr, Wilhelm, 1
Marranos, 165, 171–72
Māshā'allāh, 228, 231
Matthew Paris, 286
Mauritania, 311
Melechen, Nina, 266
Melinkoff, Ruth, 210
Menstruation, 23, 30, 116; conception during, 119–21, 128, 140, 173; intercourse during, 114–15, 118–19, 129, 142, 173, 238; male, 70, 182, 188, 191, 199, 201, 203–5, 242, 321
Messahala. *See* Māshā'allāh
Michael Scot, 15, 226, 313
Mohammad, 156, 226-27, 229
Montaigne, Michel de, 65
Monte Cassino, monastery of, 108, 177, 206

Montoro, Antón de, 165
Moos, Peter von, 81
Morbus regius, 97, 283
Moriscos, 165
Moses, 101, 124, 142, 157, 166, 215
Moses ben Maimon. *See* Maimonides
Moses ben Nachman. *See* Nachmanides
Moses ha-Darshan of Narbonne, 157
Moses Rimos, 137
Mühlhausen, Yom Tov Lipmann, 293–94
Münster, Sebastian, 300
Murder, ritual, 4–7, 11, 136, 141, 194, 197–99, 201, 203, 206, 242, 252, 255

Naaman, 122–24
Nachmanides, 142, 285
Narbonne, 195-96
Nativity, Feast of the, 75
Neumann, Dale and Leilani, 99
Nicholas of Cusa, 76, 187
Nicholas of Ockham, 202
Nicholas Donin, 235
Nicholas le Convers, 268
Nirenberg, David, 87, 132, 245

Obadiah the Convert, 82
Obertus of Liege, 149
Oderic Vitalis, 278, 281
Odo of Beumont-sur-Sarthe, 113
Odo of Champagne, 313
Odo of Tournai, 36, 40-41
Origen, 46, 125
Oxford, University of, 288

Pablo Christiani, 285
Pablo de Santa Maria, 247, 263, 284
Pachomius, 68
Padua, University of, 189
Palestine, 230
Paradise, 20, 30, 144, 191, 236, 305
Paris, 38, 52, 132, 270; Disputation of 1240, 235; Second Disputation of, 58; University of, 183, 247
Passover, 96, 194, 198, 203, 251
Pastoureaux, 132, 244
Patton, Pamela, 268
Peter I, King of Spain, 86
Peter of Blois, 41–42, 45, 154
Peter of Bruis, 38
Peter the Chanter, 209

Peter of Poitiers, 121, 128
Peter the Venerable, 37, 39, 43, 72, 75, 170, 208, 273, 303
Peter Abelard, 45, 51, 70, 72, 77, 154, 270
Peter D'Ailly, 32
Peter Damian, 28, 46, 68, 71, 86–87, 123, 145, 175, 219
Peter Lombard, 44, 46
Petrus Alfonsi, 55–56, 63, 72, 94, 156–57, 262, 302
Petrus Comestor, 155
Petrus Pierleoni, 270–73, 290–91
Pfefferkorn, Johannes, 91, 242, 243, 321
Philip IV, King, 205
Philip V, King, 87
Philip VI, King, 134
Philip the Fair, King, 128
Philip of Macedon, 234
Philip of Tripoli, 15-16, 221
Philip Augustus, King, 262
Philo Judaeus, of Alexandria, 166
Physicians, 98–99, 100, 102, 106–7, 114, 117, 138–39, 155, 161–62, 176–77, 182, 189, 212, 222–23, 284, 299, 319
Physiognomy, science of, 13–19, 29–31, 33–34, 81, 281, 322
Pigs: dietary rules and, 155, 157, 163, 172; diseases and, 141–42, 215, 282–83; symbolism of, 147, 149–50, 152–56, 162–63, 170, 172–73, 276
Planets. *See* Astral bodies
Plato, 14, 31
Plato of Tivoli, 223
Pliny the Elder, 96, 302
Plutarch, 141
Poliakov, Leon, 199
Portugal, 245
Prudentius of Troyes, 264
Pseudo-Albert the Great, 115, 182, 315
Pseudo-Aristotle, 71, 284
Pseudo-Bede, 220
Ptolemy, 223, 305, 308, 314, 315
Pucellina, 197

Quintillian, Marcus Fabius, 299

Rabanus Maurus, 120, 154, 248
Rachel of Mainz, 58
Ralph of Diceto, 250, 253
Ralph of Hoveden, 253

Ramazzini, Bernadino, 189
Rashi, 150, 209, 292
Raymond de Tarrega, 193, 290
Raymund Lull, 185
Raymund Martini, 54, 64, 72, 116
Remigius of Reims, St., 97
Richard I, King of England, 96, 250, 252, 254
Richard of Devizes, 250–51
Richard of St. Victor, 29
Richards, Jeffrey, 87
Robert the Englishman, 311, 314
Robert of Flamborough, 68, 103
Robert of Ketton, 303
Robert of Reading, 84–85
Robert of Soest, 193
Robert Grosseteste, 30, 54, 85, 262
Roderich-Stoltheim, F. *See* Fritsch, Theodor
Roger of Wendover, 252
Roger Bacon, 85, 190, 221–22, 226
Roger de Baron, 182
Roger le Convers, 268, 286
Rosenstock, Bruce, 247
Rossi, Azariah dei, 189
Rouelle. See Badge, Jews'
Rubin, Miri, ix
Rudolph of Schlettstadt, 10, 201, 236, 239
Rupert of Bamberg, 290
Rupert of Deutz, 151, 209

Saladin, Sultan, 73, 177
Samuel of Morocco, 75, 295, 320
Saperstein, Marc, 89
Saracens, 38–39, 73–76, 78, 80–83, 134–35, 156, 158–59, 226, 240–41, 279, 281, 291, 296, 303
Saturn, god, 215–19, 231, 236. *For the planet, see* Astral bodies
Scabies, 98, 118, 141, 215
Schaff, Philip, 277
Scots, 167, 311
Scrofula, 98, 282-83
Sedulius Scotus, 294
Seror, Simon, 265
Shoham-Steiner, Ephraim, 127
Simon of Trent, 65
Sin, original, 30–31, 33, 53, 70, 79, 97, 123, 191–92, 290
Slavs, 308–9
Solomon bar Isaac of Troyes. *See* Rashi
Solomon bar Simson, 76, 163

Solomon ha-Levi, 263
Spain, 39, 59, 64, 74, 81, 86, 104, 109, 135, 138, 163, 165, 171–72, 195, 205, 242, 243–46, 248, 257, 262–63, 266–67, 283–84, 303
Stacey, Robert, ix, 5–7, 266, 289
Stephen of Bourbon, 148, 281
Stephen Langton, Archbishop of Canterbury, 84
Strickland, Debra Higgs, 147
Sylvester I, Pope, 95
Synagoga, 37, 47, 125, 236
Synagogue, 37, 42, 64, 195, 202, 239
Syphilis, 127, 171–72
Syria, 75

Tacitus, 141, 171, 186, 215–16, 218, 224
Talmud, 6, 63, 88, 129, 136, 164, 235
Teutons. See Germans
Theobald, convert to Christianity, 195-96
Theobald V of Blois, 197
Theodoric, Abbot of St. Trond, 148
Theodoric, King, 162
Theodorich Borgognoni, 113
Theriac, 106
Thomas of Cantilupe, 287–89, 291
Thomas of Cantimpré, 190, 199, 201, 204, 220–21, 256, 260–61, 269, 298, 312
Thomas of Chobham, 100, 158, 210, 269
Thomas of Monmouth, 194, 197, 201
Thomas of Wroclaw, 177
Thomas Aquinas, 25, 31, 54, 62, 68, 78, 107, 125, 147, 155, 185, 211, 233
Thomas Becket, St., 106
Thomasset, Claude, 181
Tiberius, Emperor, 94
Titus, Emperor, 95

Toaff, Ariel, 9
Tortosa, Disputation of, 284
Trachtenberg, Joshua, 137, 202

Uzziah, King, 124

Vatican Mythographer, 218
Vespasian, Emperor, 94–95, 215
Vincent of Beauvais, 56, 68, 96, 109–15, 140, 149, 155, 158, 173, 236, 277, 312
Vincent Ferrer, 161
Virgin Mary, 28, 31, 40, 74–75, 129, 257, 261, 282–83
Voltaire, 126

Werner of St. Blaise, 100–101, 102
William, Archbishop of Bourges, 63
William, Prior of St. Mary of York, 253
William of Auvergne, 69, 108, 119, 216–17
William of Auxerre, 55, 69
William of Bourges, 63
William of Canterbury, 105–6, 113
William of Conches, 27, 30, 173, 191
William of Malmesbury, 47, 202, 273
William of Norwich, 136, 194, 196, 235
William of St. Thierry, 21, 45
William of Tyre, 279
William Rufus, King of England, 41, 47
Withington, E. T., 151
Wolfson, Elliot R., 60, 88

Zachary, Pope, 167
Zema, Demetrius B., 271
Zerbi, Gabriele, 162
Ziegler, Joseph, 33
Zodiac, signs of the, 228

Marks of Distinction: Christian Perceptions of Jews in the High Middle Ages
was designed in Minion and typeset by Kachergis Book Design of Pittsboro,
North Carolina. It was printed on 60-pound House Natural Smooth and
bound by Sheridan Books of Ann Arbor, Michigan.

www.ingramcontent.com/pod-product-compliance
Lightning Source LLC
Chambersburg PA
CBHW020856020526
44107CB00076B/1825